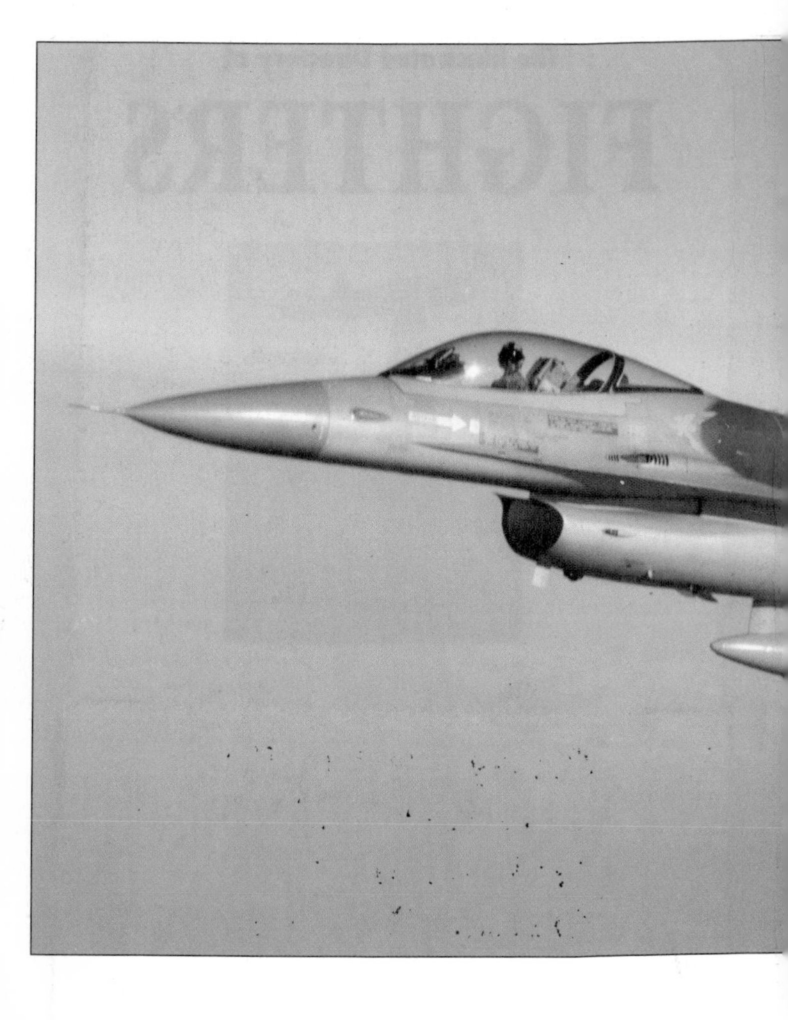

The Illustrated Directory of

FIGHTERS

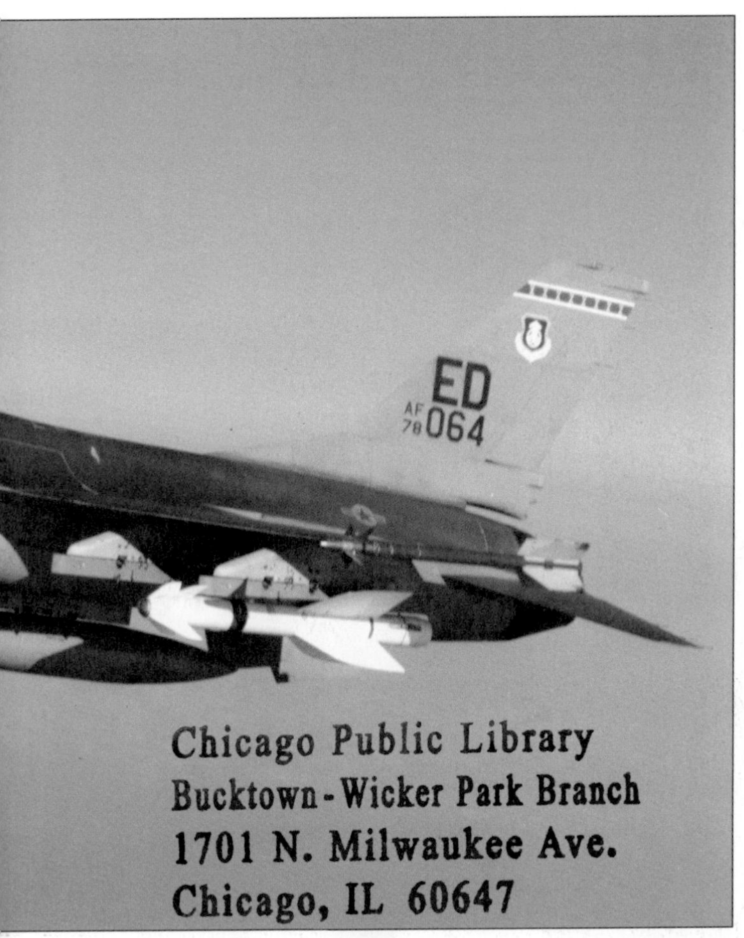

Mike Spick

MBI Publishing Company

A Salamander Book

This edition first published in 2002 by MBI Publishing Company,
Galtier Plaza, Suite 200, 380 Jackson Street, St. Paul, MN 55101-3885 USA

A member of Chrysalis Books plc

MBI Publishing Company books are also available at discounts in bulk quantity for industrial or sales-promotional use. For details write to Special Sales Manager at Motorbooks International Wholesalers & Distributors,
Galtier Plaza, Suite 200, 380 Jackson Street, St. Paul, MN 55101-3885 USA

Library of Congress Cataloging-in-Publication Data Available

ISBN 0-7603-1343-1

The Author

Mike Spick is a leading commentator on military aviation, with more than 30 books to his credit. He maintains close ties with former and current serving fighter pilots and aircraft design personnel, and several distinguished test pilots. For many years a consultant to the Swiss-based helicopter programme Project Atlas, he has also been Consultant Editor to *AirForces Monthly* journal, and contributor to *Air International*, *Air Enthusiast*, and the Malaysian-based *Asia Pacific Defense Review*.

Acknowledgments

The publishers thank the many manufacturers, international armed forces, and private individuals who have provided illustrations for this book, in particular Philip Jarrett, who made very many available from his collection.

Credits

Project Manager: Ray Bonds
Designers: Interprep Ltd
Reproduction: Anorax Imaging Ltd
Printed and bound in: Slovenia

Contents

SD T

Introduction

The definition of what constitutes a fighter has become blurred. Among the many fighter types that have attained widespread service, there are few that have not, at one time or another, had air-to-surface ordnance or cameras hung on them. Other types, designed specifically for the attack or reconnaissance missions, have been given a secondary air combat capability for self-defence. Matters have not been helped by the use of fighter designations like F-105 and F-117 for aircraft intended to deliver ordnance to ground targets. The definition adopted for this directory is that a fighter is an aircraft designed to destroy other aircraft in air combat. This must have been its primary mission at the design stage, even though it may subsequently have gone on to achieve success in other fields.

Other points require clarification. Many World War II night fighters were modified from bombers but, since the modifications turned them into dedicated aircraft destroyers, they qualify for inclusion here. The same applies to the interceptor variant of the Tornado. Finally, although the modern trend is for multi-rôle aircraft, such as the Joint Strike Fighter, these tend to be fighters first and attack aircraft second. It would therefore be unreasonable to omit them.

The choice of entries for this directory has not been easy. Many fighters were self-selecting, among them the Fokker Eindecker, the Spitfire and Mustang, the F-4 Phantom II and the F-16 Fighting Falcon. For the rest, the following criteria were used. They had to be (a) numerically significant, (b) technically innovative, (c) historically significant, or (d) interestingly odd, with the proviso that they actually flew at least once. To avoid confusion often caused by mergers and takeovers, they are listed in alphabetical order by manufacturer or designer; the names are those current at the time of first flight. For example, the F-16 is listed under General Dynamics, not Lockheed Martin.

The fighter was born out of necessity. First, this was the need to deny information to enemy reconnaissance aircraft and artillery spotters. Then, as air arms grew and developed, it became essential to dominate the air space over the battlefield. Other threats emerged: bombers and airships had to be countered. World War I was a steep learning curve for all concerned. By 1918, the most usual fighter configuration was a single-engined tractor, single-seat biplane, armed with one or two fixed rifle-calibre machine guns which were aimed by pointing the whole aircraft. There were of course a few exceptions.

The 1930s saw the perceived threat change. Advances in all branches of aeronautics produced a revolution. Bigger and more efficient engines, with supercharging to increase power at high altitudes; more streamlined shapes; retractable undercarriages; monoplanes rather than biplanes; monocoque metal stressed skin construction; all combined to increase performance. And initially the main beneficiary was the bomber! A new breed of bomber emerged, too fast to be intercepted by the biplane fighters of the time.

Fighter aircraft designers of the day would not let this go unchallenged. The result was the fast, rapid-climbing, multi-gunned monoplane, with an enclosed cockpit, retractable undercarriage and, most importantly, radio. Most of the important fighter types of World War II had prewar origins. One other fighter trend, which was largely unsuccessful, was the twin-engined, long-range strategic fighter.

World War II saw the widespread use of self-sealing fuel tanks and armour protection, ever heavier gun armament, the introduction of radar in night fighters, and a constant quest for greater performance. By the end of the conflict, the piston engine was nearing the limits of what was possible, but already the turbojet, and to a lesser degree the rocket motor, had started to enter service.

The Korean War, 1950-1953, saw the ever faster, ever higher fighter combat reach its zenith. But more serious threats were already emerging. The first was the fast, high-flying nuclear bomber; the second was the possibility of an all-out war in Europe between NATO and the Warsaw Pact. The situation prompted what amounted to a technological explosion. Fighter speeds increased, firstly to supersonic, then bisonic, with Mach 3 on the horizon. Batteries of unguided rockets were supplanted by homing missiles, while interceptors carried radar and automated fire control systems. The weapons system was born.

The confrontation in Europe was another matter. The debate here was quantity versus quality. The Warsaw Pact had quantity in abundance, hordes of inexpensive fighters and tactical aircraft. The best Western fighter was the ubiquitous Phantom, although its performance against Russian fighters in Vietnam was uninspiring. While this was shortly to be backed up by the superb F-14 and F-15, the newcomers were proving unaffordable in the quantities needed. The U.S. solution adopted was the hi-lo mix, lots of austere dogfighters, backed up by fewer hi-tech birds. Thus was born the F-16, the fighter that set new standards for close air combat.

Since then, the existing fighters have held the ring. The next generation will use stealth, supercruise, advanced electronics, and vectored thrust for supermanoeuvrability. But these are yet to enter service.

Fighter aircraft have been with us for less than nine decades, but in that time their performance, weaponry and systems have progressed from barely adequate to almost incredible. But what of the future? As at 2002, predictions are focused around the Unmanned Combat Air Vehicle, or UCAV. This has long been forecast, but only now does the technology appear to be reaching maturity. Also, public opinion in the Western world seems to require that wars, if they have to be fought, are without casualties. This is another factor pushing us towards the UCAV.

It is therefore possible that we are now seeing the final generation of manned fighters. If this seems like heresy, consider the fate of the armoured knight, the archer, the musket, and the battleship. All fell to the onward march of technology. Will the fighter pilot go the same way?

AIDC A-1 Ching Kuo

Origin: AIDC, Taiwan.
Type: Single-seat, twin-engined interceptor and air defence fighter with a secondary ground attack and anti-shipping function. The two-seater conversion trainer is fully combat capable, albeit with reduced internal fuel.
Engines: Two ITEC TFE1042-70 afterburning turbofans rated at 9,250lb (4,196kg) thrust maximum and 6,300lb (2,858kg) thrust military.
Dimensions: Span 30ft 10.25in (9.42m); length 46ft 7.75in (14.20m); height 15ft 6in (4.72m); wing area 260sq.ft (24.20m^2).
Weights: Empty 14,300lb (6,486kg); normal takeoff 21,000lb (9,526kg); maximum takeoff 27,000lb (12,247kg).
Loadings (at normal takeoff weight)**:** Wing 81lb/sq.ft (394kg/m^2); thrust 0.90.
Performance: Maximum speed (altitude) Mach 1.65; maximum speed (sea level) Mach 1.05; operational ceiling 50,000ft (15,239m); initial climb rate 50,000ft/min (254m/sec).
Armament: One 20mm M61A1 cannon with 511 rounds in the port wing root; four Sky Sword I heat-homing AAMs plus two Sky Sword II SARH AAMs; two AGM-65 Maverick or three Hsiung Feng II ASMs; or a variety of conventional air-to-surface weaponry. Maximum weight of stores 8,600lb (3,901kg).
History: First flight prototype 28 May 1989; production delivery 10 January 1994 to 2000.
User: Republic of China Air Force (Taiwan).

By 1982, Taiwan was no longer able to obtain fighters from the USA. Faced with an aging fleet, AIDC commenced the development of an indigenous defence fighter with technical aid from General Dynamics. The design, with F-16 influence clearly visible, was finalised in 1985. The wing planform was similar, although the trailing edge featured a shallow reverse sweep. The tail surfaces varied mainly in having raked-back tips.

As no suitable large powerplant was available, two small ITEC TFE1042-70 afterburning turbofans were adopted, developed from Garrett engines. These provided an adequate, if not exceptional, thrust to weight ratio, and were fed by fixed geometry oval side intakes located under the wing root extensions.

Construction is mainly of aluminium alloy, but with some composites in the tail

Below: The Ching-Kuo is the only indigenous Taiwanese fighter in service.

***Above:* From this angle the design influence of General Dynamics is obvious.**

and speed brakes, and titanium engine nozzles. The flight control system is triplex digital fly-by-wire, with many similarities to that used in the JAS 39 Gripen.

Unlike the F-16, the canopy is orthodox, with a wrap-around windshield, but the cockpit layout clearly shows Fort Worth influence. Two multi-function displays dominate the dash, a sidestick controller replaces a central control column, and the ejection seat is a steeply raked Martin Baker Mk 12.

Radar is the indigenous Golden Dragon 53, developed from the Westinghouse APG-67(V) multi-mode pulse-Doppler set. This has a maximum search range of about 35 miles (56km) and can provide guidance for semi-active homing missiles. A 20mm M61 Vulcan cannon is housed in the left wing root. There are six weapons stations for missiles: two wingtip rails; two underwing pylons, and two underfuselage hardpoints in tandem.

The second seat displaces a fuel tank in the conversion trainer but, as three hardpoints are plumbed for external tanks, this makes little difference. Surprisingly, the vertical tail remains the same size.

The prototype Ching Kuo first flew on 28 May 1989, piloted by Wu Kang Ming. There were however anomalies in the FCS, which caused a spectacular landing accident five months later. These were cleared up, and deliveries started to reach the squadrons in January 1994. Initial Operational Capability was reached a year later.

Originally 250 aircraft had been ordered, but by now US restrictions had been lifted. With F-16s now available, Ching Kuo production was curtailed. The last of 130 aircraft, 28 of them two-seaters, was delivered in 2000. No Ching Kuos have been exported.

AIRCO DH 2

Origin: Aircraft Manufacturing Company (Airco), Hendon, England.
Type: Single-seat, pusher type biplane fighter.
Engine: One 100hp Gnome Monosoupape rotary (most); a few were built with Le Rhone rotaries of similar power.
Dimensions: Span 28ft 3in (8.61m); length 25ft 2.5in (7.68m); height 9ft 6.5in (2.91m); wing area 249sq.ft (23.13m²).
Weights: Empty 943lb (428kg); normal takeoff 1,441lb (654kg).
Loadings (at takeoff weight): Wing 5.79lb/sq.ft (28kg/m²); power 14.41lb (6.64kg) per hp.
Performance: Maximum speed 93mph (150kph) at sea level, 77mph (124kph); sustained climb 12 min to 6,500ft (1,981m); service ceiling 14,500ft (4,419m); endurance 2hr 45min.
Armament: One .303in drum-fed Lewis machine gun.
History: First flight 1 June 1915. Entered service late that year. To the Western Front February 1916. Served also in Macedonia and Palestine. Withdrawn from front line service mid-1917.
User: Britain (Royal Flying Corps).

The DH 2 was designed by Geoffrey de Havilland at a time when machine guns could not be reliably synchronized to fire through the propeller without damaging it. This problem was avoided by using a pusher configuration. This had both engine and pilot housed in a short nacelle, with the pilot in front, giving him a clear field of fire in the front hemisphere.

While this was an obvious advantage, there was a price to be paid. With the propeller rotating just behind the trailing edges of the wings, the tail surfaces had to be carried on four braced tubular steel booms from the upper and lower wings, respectively, starting outboard of the propeller disc. Tapering steeply in to where the tail surfaces were mounted, this was a drag-inducing, aerodynamically inefficient layout, which reduced performance.

There were other drawbacks. Largely exposed to the elements, and with no heat available from the rear-mounted engine, the DH 2 was a very cold aeroplane in which to fly, which affected pilot efficiency. In addition, rearward view, from which direction most attacks could be expected to come, was poor.

Below: Mainly used on the Western Front, the DH 2 also served in Palestine.

Above: Western Front 1916; the frail booms of the DH 2 are evident here.

Finally, in the event of a heavy crash landing, if the engine broke free the pilot might be crushed under it.

Armament was a single rifle calibre Lewis gun, and initially this was given a mounting that enabled it to be aimed over much of the front hemisphere. The problem here was that the pilot was expected to aim the gun accurately while continuing to fly the aeroplane! This was quickly exposed as impracticable, and a new mounting, allowing the gun to move only in the vertical plane, was devised.

In the second half of 1915, the German Fokker Eindecker was rampant on the front, its successes giving rise to the legend of the "Fokker Scourge". To counter it, the Royal Flying Corps started to form squadrons of dedicated fighters late in 1915. One of these was the DH 2-equipped No 24 Squadron, which arrived in France in February 1916.

The DH 2 could handily outfly the Eindecker. Its small size and low wing loading made it agile, but also rather tricky to fly. The rotary engine produced a lot of torque, tending to accelerate any rolling motion in the same direction, making it easy to get into a spin. In the days before spin recovery was put on a sound footing and taught, many pilots were lost as a result.

Like all rotary engines of the period, the Gnome Monosoupape ran at just two speeds: full throttle and off. For power control in the air, a "blip" switch was used, which cut the ignition when pressed. But the main problem was that the Gnome was chronically unreliable. Pistons would seize solid, bearings would break, but worst of all, occasionally the Gnome would shed a cylinder in flight. When this happened, it would whirl off, wrecking everything in its path.

In combat, pilots preferred to use a rigid gun mounting and aim the weapon by aiming the whole aircraft. The Lewis was drum-fed, and changing a drum in the heat of battle while continuing to fly the aeroplane was not easy.

The DH 2, in conjunction with the FE 2 and Nieuport 11 (which see), put an end to the Fokker Scourge by mid-1916, but was outclassed by the new breed of German biplanes which entered service later that year.

Of the 400 DH 2s built, 266 reached the Western Front, where they remained in service until mid-1917.

Albatros D II

Origin: Albatros Werke, Germany.
Type: Single-seat, single-engined tractor biplane fighter.
Engine: One 160hp Benz D.III inline.
Dimensions: Span 27ft 10.67in (8.50m); length 24ft 3.33in (7.40m); height 8ft 6in (2.59m); wing area 263.72sq.ft (24.50m²).
Weights: Empty 1,404lb (637kg); normal takeoff 1,958lb (888kg).
Loadings (at takeoff weight): Wing 7.42lb/sq.ft (36.24kg/m²); power 12.24lb (5.55kg) per hp.
Performance: Maximum speed 109mph (175kph) at sea level; sustained climb 5min 30sec to 3,281ft (1,000m); service ceiling 17,061ft (5,200m); endurance 1hr 30min.
Armament: Two fixed belt-fed 7.92mm Spandau machine guns firing through the propeller disc.
History: In service from September 1916, numbers peaked at approx. 250 in January 1917 but were being rapidly phased out by the end of that year. Flown by Boelcke and Richthofen, among others.
Users: Austria-Hungary, Germany.

Developed from the Albatros D I, which was designed to wrest control of the air from the DH 2 and Nieuport 11, the D II differed from it only in having the upper wing lowered in height and the cabane in front of the cockpit modified. These improvements corrected the worst fault of the earlier fighter, the poor view forwards and upwards from the cockpit.

A biplane with the lower wing having slightly less span than the upper, the early

Albatros D III

Origin: Albatros Werke, Germany.
Type: Single-seat, single-engined tractor biplane fighter.
Engine: One 180hp Mercedes D IIIa inline engine.
Dimensions: Span 29ft 8in (9.04m); length 24ft 0.05in (7.62m); height 9ft 9.25in (2.98m); wing area 220.66sq.ft (20.50m²).
Weights: Empty 1,457lb (661kg); normal takeoff 1,953lb (886kg).
Loadings (at normal takeoff weight): Wing 8.85lb/sq.ft (43.22kg/m²); power 10.85lb (4.92kg) per hp.
Performance: Maximum speed 108mph (165kph); sustained climb 3min 45sec to 3,281ft (1,000m); service ceiling 18,046ft (5,500m); endurance 2hr.
Armament: Two fixed belt-fed 7.92mm Spandau machine guns firing through the propeller disc.
History: A direct development of the Albatros D II, the D III prototype first flew in August 1916, and entered service early in the following year. In the summer of 1917, outclassed by the Allied SE 5a, Camel and Spad, it began to be superseded by the Albatros D V. Numbers peaked in November of that year at 446, and a few remained in service until the end of the war.
Users: Austria-Hungary, Germany, post-war, Poland.

Albatros designer Robert Thelen did not rest on his laurels. With the

Right: The V-struts of the AlbatroS D III distinguished it from the D II.

Above: This Austrian AlbatroS D II served with Flik 21 as late as June 1917.

Albatros series was innovative in having a sleek semi-monocoque wooden fuselage instead of the braced box frame widely used at that time. In 1916 it was also unusual in having synchronized twin machine guns firing through the propeller disc, but the large and powerful inline engine easily coped with the increased weight and drag of the second gun without significant loss of performance.

The Albatros D I/D II series was effectively the first of the performance fighters, its superiority over the DH 2 and Nieuport 11 demonstrated by a higher top speed, rate of climb, ceiling, and dive. While it could not match either of the Allied scouts in rate of turn or rate of roll, it could force battle on them, or if need be, disengage at will. And with double their firepower it was far more deadly in the attack.

D II in production, he immediately set about improving it. The result was the D III, with which he adopted some of the features of the French Nieuport series. The semi-monocoque fuselage and tail surfaces were retained, but the wings were very different. The lower wing was made narrower, which improved pilot vision. It contained a single spar, connected to the upper wing outboard by a V-strut. In fact, this type became known to its opponents as a V-strutter. Span was increased, and both upper and lower wings featured raked tips, rather than the square ends of the D II.

A feature that was not appreciated at the time was that the lower wing was far too flexible. This eventually manifested itself when D IIIs started to shed their wings during combat, which did nothing for pilot morale. From April 1917, reinforced wings were introduced. Another wing feature that needed attention was the radiator, which was of aerofoil section, located in the mid-section of the top wing. If it was hit by a single bullet, the pilot received a stream of scalding water. To avoid this the radiator was relocated to the starboard side of the centre section.

Albatros D V/Va

Origin: Albatros Werke, Germany.
Type: Single-seat, single-engined tractor biplane fighter.
Engine: One 180hp Mercedes inline.
Dimensions: Span 28ft 8in (9.04m); length 24ft 0.05ft (7.62m); height 8ft 10.25in (2.70m); wing area 228.19sq.ft (21.20m^2).
Weights: Empty 1,515lb (687kg); normal takeoff 2,066lb (937kg).
Loadings (normal takeoff weight): Wing 9.05lb/sq.ft (44.20kg/m^2); power 11.48lb (5.21kg) per hp.

A high proportion of the German aces flew the Albatros D III, including Manfred von Richthofen, whose mount was painted all-red, and Werner Voss, who sported a white swastika on his fuselage, although this was at that time regarded merely as a good luck charm.

The Albatros D III was also built under licence in Austria, and was fitted with Daimler engines of 185, 200 and 225hp, which boosted maximum speed to about 115mph (185kph). About 220 examples were supplied. In Germany, an increase in compression ratio boosted the output of the standard engine.

The baseline Albatros D III offered nothing in terms of maximum speed over its predecessor; if anything it was marginally slower, but rate of climb was greatly improved, mainly by the better power loading, as was duration. In terms of manoeuvre, the D III was faster in rate of roll than its predecessor, but with a higher wing loading it did not turn as well.

Post-war, Poland acquired 60 Austrian-built Albatros D IIIs, powered by the 200hp engine, and operated them on the Eastern Front between August 1920 and May 1921. They were flown by American volunteer pilots.

Performance: Maximum speed 115mph (185kph) at 3,281ft (1,000m); sustained climb 4min to 3,281ft (1,000m); service ceiling 20,506ft (6,250m); endurance 2hr.
Armament: Two fixed belt-fed 7.92mm Spandau machine guns firing through the propeller disc.
History: The Albatros D V started to enter service in the summer of 1917, and remained in widespread use until the end of the war, on the Western Front, in Italy, and Palestine. Production ceased in February 1918 in favour of the far superior Fokker D VII.
Users: Germany.

The apparent superiority of the D II and D III over their British and French opponents in late 1916 and early 1917 seemed to have lulled the Albatros Werke into a false sense of security. Whereas the Allies strove to improve performance and manoeuvrability in their next generation of fighters, the German constructor made no such effort. In consequence, the Albatros D V and D Va, which entered service in May of 1917, offered few performance advantages over the D III, and found themselves generally out-performed by SE 5as and Camels, and the latest SPADs and Nieuports.

The D V used basically the same engine as the D III, and performance improvements were main-ly linked to drag reduction measures. The fuselage was redesigned to have a more oval section. This involved widening it slightly, and incorporating a new longeron on each side. A

Left: Forced down and captured, this Albatros D V was flown by RFC pilots.

headrest was introduced behind the cockpit, although since this interfered with rearward vision it was not popular with the pilots, and in service was often removed. Streamlining was further improved by the introduction of a large spinner, and the rudder was given a more rounded shape.

The wings were identical to those of the D III, but the gap between them was reduced by about 4in (100mm), in the interests of better pilot vision.

Another modification was to the aileron control cables. Where these had previously run through the bottom wing, they were now moved to the upper wing, then angled back to pulleys on the aileron leading edge. Small shrouds covered these last pieces of cable, which would otherwise have been exposed.

That this last proved less than satisfactory was shown by the fact that the almost identical D Va reverted to the lower wing location for aileron control cables.

Strengthening of the lower planes had not really cured the tendency of

the D III to shed its wings in a prolonged dive, and the same fault manifested itself in the D V shortly after it entered service. The reasons for this were for long unknown, and static tests seemed to indicate that strength was adequate. But it was later discovered that the single main spar was set too far aft. As speed built up in a long dive, vibration set in and the lower wing eventually twisted and failed. A short strut from the leading edge to the front of the V-strut proved a partial solution, while pilots were advised to limit their dives. This cannot have made them very happy; it restricted them in both attack and evasion. Not that the wing failure was alway fatal; von Hippel once lost a lower wing at high altitude, but succeeded in crash-landing.

More than 1,600 Albatros D Vs and Vas were ordered and in May 1918 no fewer than 1,059 were in service, although by the end of the war, fewer

Below: The swastika on this Albatros D V of Jasta 12 was just a lucky charm.

Above: The brightly painted Albatros D Va of Lt von Hippel of Jasta 5.

Ansaldo AC 3

Origin: Aeronautico Ansaldo, Italy.
Type: Single-seat, single-engined parasol-winged monoplane fighter
Engine: One 420hp Gnome-Rhône Jupiter IV nine cylinder radial.
Dimensions: Span 41ft 11.88in (12.80m); length 23ft 10.67in (7.28m); height 9ft 7.33in (2.93m); wing area 269.1sq.ft (25.00m²).
Weights: Empty 2,114lb (959kg); normal takeoff 2,981lb (1,352kg).
Loadings (normal takeoff weight): Wing 11.08lb/sq.ft (54.08kg/m²), power 7.10lb (3.22kg) per hp.
Performance: Maximum speed 153mph (247kph) at sea level; sustained climb 6min 12sec to 9,843ft (3,000m); service ceiling n/a; endurance 2hr 50min.
Armament: Typically four 7.62mm Darne machine guns, two mounted in the fuselage and two in the wing.
History: First flight of prototype early 1926; production of 150 aircraft between September 1926 and April 1927. Withdrawn from service summer 1938.
User: Italy (*Regia Aeronautica*).

From 1916, designer Celestino Rosatelli of Ansaldo had designed a series of only moderately successful fighters and other aircraft, the main fault being a lack of agility. Then in 1924 the company acquired manufacturing rights from Dewoitine and modified the designs for home consumption.

The AC 3 was based on the Dewoitine D 9. Dimensionally it was large, with a huge wing area for a monoplane of this period. Reasonably fast for its time, it had an excellent rate of climb, and could reach 3,281ft (1,000m)

Above: The broad-chord parasol wing was a feature of the Ansaldo AC 3.

in just 102 seconds. On some models, the wing-mounted guns were replaced by a single, obliquely mounted gun above the centre section.

With the availability of higher performance fighters, the AC 3 was relegated to close air support in the 1930s and retired in summer 1938.

Arado Ar 68E

Origin: Arado Flugzeugwerke, Germany.
Type: Single-seat, single-engined biplane fighter.
Engine: One 690hp supercharged Junkers Jumo 210 Da liquid-cooled inverted V.
Dimensions: Span 36ft 1in (11.00m); length 31ft 2in (9.50m); height 10ft 9in (3.28m); wing area 293.85sq.ft (27.3m²).
Weights: Empty 3,527lb (1,600kg); normal takeoff 4,453lb (2,020kg).
Loadings (at normal takeoff weight): Wing 15.15lb/sq.ft (74kg/m²); power 6.45lb (2.93kg) per hp.
Performance: Maximum speed 190mph (306kph) at sea level; 208mph (335kph) at 8,695ft (2,650m); initial climb rate 2,477ft/min (12.58m/sec); service ceiling 26,576ft (8,100m); range 310 miles (500km).
Armament: Two 7.92mm MG 17 machine guns with 500 rounds each, located in the upper engine cowling.
History: Prototype first flight in summer 1934. Various engines were tried in the development phase before the Jumo 210 became standard. Service entry late summer 1936. Trials as night interceptor in Spain in 1938, and some served briefly in this role in the first weeks of World War II. Then relegated as advanced trainers and nuisance bombers on the Eastern Front.
User: Germany.

Ordered as a replacement for the Heinkel He 51 (which see), which had entered service only in 1935, the Ar 68 was destined to be the last biplane fighter in *Luftwaffe* service. The upper and lower wings had unequal span and unequal

Armstrong Whitworth Siskin IIIA

Above: The Arado 68E was obsolescent even at the time of its first flight.

chord, with N-shaped interplane struts. Most of the fuselage was of fabric-covered welded steel tube; otherwise construction was orthodox. With generously sized dynamically balanced control surfaces, the Ar 68 was extremely agile, and during trials comprehensively outflew the He 51. An exotic variant was the Ar 197 carrier fighter which mounted a BMW radial engine, 20mm cannon, and an enclosed cockpit, but this failed to enter production.

Origin: Sir W. G. Armstrong Whitworth Aircraft, Coventry, England.
Type: Single-seat, single-engined biplane fighter.
Engine: One 450hp supercharged Armstrong Siddeley Jaguar IV radial.
Dimensions: Span 33ft 2in (10.10m); length 25ft 4in (7.72m); height 10ft 2in (3.10m); wing area 293sq.ft (27.22m^2).
Weights: Empty 2,061lb (935kg); normal takeoff weight 3,012lb (1,366kg).
Loadings (at normal takeoff weight): Wing 10.28lb/sq.ft (50kg/m^2); power 6.69lb (3.03kg) per hp.
Performance: Maximum speed 156mph (251kph) at sea level; 142mph (228kph) at 15,000ft (4,572m); sustained climb 10min 30sec to 15,000ft (4,572m); service ceiling 27,000ft (8,229m).
Armament: Twin synchronized .303in (7.7mm) Vickers machine guns.
History: First flight on 20 October 1925; service entry March 1927; withdrawn from service October 1932.
Users: Britain (RAF), Canada, Estonia.

Left: The uncowled radial engine was a feature of the superb Siskin IIIA.

The Siskin IIIA was ultimately descended from the Siddeley SR 2 Siskin of 1918 vintage, powered by the ABC Dragonfly, one of the first radials. Armstrong Whitworth having bought the company, the next step was the extensively redesigned Siskin II. This failed to enter production, and the design was once again rehashed to become the Siskin III. This attracted a small RAF order.

The IIIA differed considerably from its predecessor. Length increased by 2ft 10in (0.87m), with raised decking, and a much more powerful Jaguar radial engine was installed. The formerly slab-sided fuselage was rounded, and the

Avia B 534.III and .IV

Origin: Avia (Skoda), Czechoslovakia.
Type: Single-seat, single-engined biplane with enclosed cockpit.
Engine: One 860hp supercharged Avia-built Hispano-Suiza HS 12 Ydrs liquid-cooled.
Dimensions: Span 30ft 10in (9.40m); length 26ft 10.9in (8.20m); height n/a; wing area 253.60sq.ft (23.56m^2).
Weights: Empty 3,219lb (1,460kg); normal takeoff 4,376lb (1,985kg).
Loadings (at normal takeoff weight): Wing 17.26lb/sq.ft (84kg/m^2); power 5.09lb (2.31kg) per hp.
Performance: Maximum speed 252mph (405kph) at 14,436ft (4,400m); initial climb rate 2,953ft/min (15m/sec); service ceiling n/a; range 360 miles (580km).
Armament: Four 7.7mm Model 30 machine guns.

distance between the wings was increased. Dihedral on the top plane was reduced, and finally the tail surfaces were redesigned.

The result was a superbly responsive aerobatic machine, which thrilled the crowds at the annual Hendon Air Pageant with displays of tied-together aerobatics. The Siskin IIIA proved a great success. In all, 365 single-seat Siskin IIIAs were built, plus 47 dual control trainers. These equipped no fewer than 11 RAF squadrons, and the Siskin IIIA was for several years the main RAF fighter type. An experimental IIIB, with an uprated cowled engine, was built, but as this showed no advantages it was rejected.

History: Production ordered 17 July 1933 for B 534.I and that for .II, .III and .IV substantially complete before the outbreak of World War II.
Users: Bulgaria, Czechoslovakia, Germany, Greece, Slovak Air Force, Yugoslavia.

In many ways the Avia B 534.III and .IV series was an anachronism. In appearance it was a sleek modern fighter, complete with enclosed cabin faired into the rear fuselage, but with biplane wings complete with N-shaped interplane struts and a fixed spatted undercarriage.

Design accent was clearly on performance, but this was bought at the expense of the pilot's field of view. The closely faired cockpit made his seating position low. This resulted in a poor view over the long nose and not

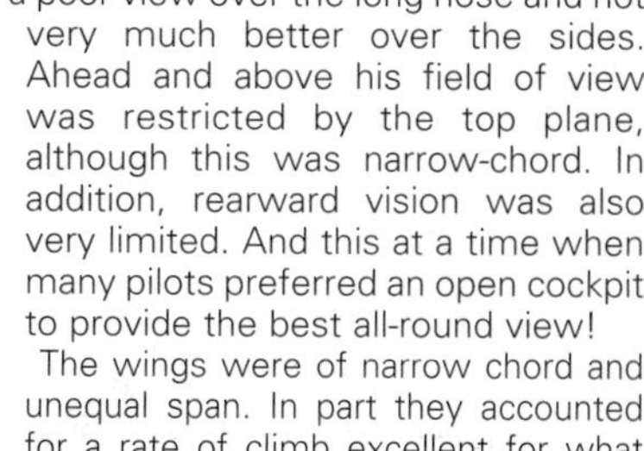

very much better over the sides. Ahead and above his field of view was restricted by the top plane, although this was narrow-chord. In addition, rearward vision was also very limited. And this at a time when many pilots preferred an open cockpit to provide the best all-round view!

The wings were of narrow chord and unequal span. In part they accounted for a rate of climb excellent for what was essentially a fighter of the mid-1930s, and can be assumed to have allowed a fast rate of roll. The four machine gun armament was par for the course in the mid-thirties, but plans were made to introduce an engine-mounted 20mm Oerlikon MGFF cannon. This failed due to difficulties with the ammunition feed.

In all, some 450 B 534s were in the inventory of the Czech Air Force in March 1939, of which more than half were the latest .IVs. It is known that the type saw action on the Eastern Front later in the war, notably with the Slovak Air Force, but little is known about it.

Left: The Avia B 534.IV was one of the finest biplane fighters ever built.

Avro Canada CF-100 Mk5 Canuck

Origin: Avro Aircraft, Canada.
Type: Two-seat, twin-engined transonic night and all-weather long range interceptor.
Engines: Two Orenda 11 or 14 single stage axial flow turbojets rated at 7,275lb (3,300kg) thrust.
Dimensions: Span 58ft 0in (17.68m); length 54ft 1in (16.48m); height 15ft 6.5in (4.73m); wing area 591sq.ft ($54.90m^2$).
Weights: Empty 23,100lb (10,478kg); normal takeoff 37,000lb (16,783kg); maximum 45,500lb (20,639kg).
Loadings (at normal takeoff weight): Wing 63lb/sq.ft ($306kg/m^2$); thrust 0.39.
Performance: Maximum speed 650mph at 10,000ft (3,048m); initial climb rate 8,380ft/min (43m/sec); service ceiling 54,000ft (16,458m); endurance up to 12 hr.

Armament: 104 2.75in (70mm) folding fin aircraft rockets in two wingtip pods.
History: Design commenced October 1946. First flight 19 January 1950. Developed through several models; service entry summer 1953 (Mk 3). Production ended in 1957, after a total build of 692 CF-100s of all marks.
Users: Belgium, Canada.

Canada is a vast and sparsely populated country, with airfields far apart. The weather is often appalling, and the terrain generally inhospitable. Much of the country lies above the Arctic Circle, where daylight hours in winter are few or non-existent. The perceived threat that the CF-100 was designed to counter

Below: The CF-100 Mk 5 was the final variant of the all weather Canuck.

was Soviet bombers coming in over the North Pole.

Given this, the two essentials were all-weather capability, which in turn required radar and a two-man crew, and extended endurance, which demanded a large fuel capacity. A large aircraft was thus inevitable, at the expense of manoeuvrability. But since unescorted bombers were the target, this consideration was secondary.

The Canuck (the name is unofficial) was simple in concept. A radar nose was followed by a two-man tandem cockpit, behind which were large fuel tanks. Two engine nacelles flanked the fuselage without ever encroaching into it. The wings, which were low-set, were straight, with ailerons and double-slotted flaps on the trailing edge. They also contained large fuel tanks. The horizontal tail surfaces were set high on the plain fin. The one unusual feature was de-icing to all leading edges on wings, tail and fin, and also the engine intakes.

The first prototype was flown on 19 January 1950, powered by two Rolls-Royce Avon engines, since Orendas were not yet ready. Results were

Avro Canada CF-105 Arrow

Origin: Avro Aircraft, Canada.
Type: Two-seat, twin-engined bisonic night and all-weather long range interceptor.
Engines: Two Orenda PS-13 Iroquois two-spool afterburning turbojets rated at 26,000lb (11,794kg) thrust maximum and 19,250lb (8,732kg) military.
Dimensions: Span 50ft 0in (15.24m); length 83ft 0in (25.30m); height 20ft 6in (6.25m); wing area 1,225sq.ft (113.81m^2).
Weights: Empty 49,040lb (22,244kg); maximum takeoff 68,602lb (31,118kg).
Loadings (at maximum takeoff weight): Wing 56lb/sq.ft (273kg/m^2).
Performance: Maximum speed Mach 1.98 at 50,000ft (15,239m) with J75 engines); rate of climb n/a; service ceiling (projected) 65,000ft (19,811m); interception radius 410 miles (660km).
Armament: Typically three AIM-7 Sparrow 2 and eight AIM-4 Falcon homing missiles in an internal weapons bay. The Sparrows and four Falcons would use SARH; the remaining Falcons would be IR homers.
History: Designed to an "impossible" RCAF requirement in 1953, the Arrow first flew on 25 March 1958. With five aircraft complete, the programme was cancelled on 20 February 1959.
User: Failed to enter RCAF service.

Despite its incredibly advanced specification, no prototypes of the Arrow were ordered. Instead, production went straight to development aircraft, the first five of which had to be powered by the Pratt & Whitney J75-P-3, since the Iroquois was not yet ready. Chief test pilot Jan Zurakowski took the first CF-105 aloft on 25 March 1958, for a trouble-free first flight. Four more Arrows followed in the space of seven months.

To say that the CF-105 was huge is an understatement. It started at the nose with a 40in (1.01m) diameter radar scanner. This determined fuselage size, as did the need for a weapons bay that could hold 11 AAMs. Empty, it weighed almost as much as a normally laden Lancaster

promising, and 10 pre-production aircraft followed. The first production machine was the Mk 3, powered by Orenda 8s rated at 6,000lb (2,722kg). Radar was APG-33, and armament consisted of eight 0.50in Browning heavy machine guns in a ventral pack.

By this time, the American collision-course interception method looked promising, and this was adopted for the Mk 4, which was extensively redesigned. A bluff nose housed the APG-40 radar, linked to the Hughes MG-2 fire control system. Armament now consisted of 58 rockets in two wingtip pods, and another 48 unguided rockets in the ventral pack, which was interchangeable with the gun pack. A significant weight increase was mainly offset by the more powerful Orenda 9 on the Mk 4A and Orenda 11 on the Mk 4B.

The final model was the Mk 5. To increase the operational ceiling, various weight-saving measures were employed. Wing span was increased by 6ft (1.83m) and area by 51sq.ft (4.74m2). The ventral weapons pack was deleted, and larger wingtip rocket pods were used. From 1961, surviving Canucks were converted, mainly for electronic warfare.

---

bomber. To meet the range and endurance demands at supersonic speed, internal fuel capacity was of the order of 3,000 US gallons (11,305 litres). To achieve the high altitude performance and manoeuvrability required, a modest wing loading was needed, and an enormous delta wing was used. This carried leading edge notches to arrest spanwise flow at high speeds.

The Arrow did however feature one sign of its times. The pilot's cockpit canopy, which had a V-shaped windshield, had a very restricted view sideways and aft, while the radar operator was almost entirely enclosed, with only small side vision panels.

The Arrow fell victim to the thinking of the times, that surface-to-air missiles could do a better job more cheaply. Yet with hindsight, and the examples of the F-14 and F-15 of a decade or so later, it seems probable that the CF-105 would have proved unaffordable.

Below: The CF-105 Arrow was huge. This is the second development aircraft.

Bachem Ba 349 Natter

Origin: Bachem-Werke, Germany.
Type: Single-seat, vertical takeoff, rocket-propelled point defence interceptor.
Engines: One Walther HWK 509A-2 liquid-fuel rocket rated at 3,748lb (1,700kg) thrust, supplemented by two or four Schmidding 109-533 solid fuel booster rockets for takeoff.
Dimensions: Span 13ft 1.5in (4.00m); length 19ft 9in (6.02m); height 7ft 4.5in (2.25m); wing area 50.59sq.ft (4.70m²).
Weights: Empty 2,414lb (1,095kg); launch (minus booster rockets) 4,432lb (2,010kg).
Loadings (at launch weight above): Wing 88lb/sq.ft (428kg/m²); thrust/weight ratio 0.85.
Performance: Maximum speed 621mph (1,000kph) at 16,405ft (5,000m); rate of climb 42,522ft/min (216m/sec); service ceiling 45,934ft (14,000m); range 25-36 miles (40-58km) depending on altitude.
Armament: 24 73mm Hs 217 Föhn or 33 55mm R4M unguided rockets in nose tubes.
History: First flight, unpowered, towed launch, 14 December 1944; first unmanned powered vertical launch, 22 December 1944; first (and only) manned powered vertical launch, 23 February 1945.
Users: Intended primarily for Germany's SS, but failed to enter service.

The Natter was a desperate attempt to counter the USAAF daylight bomber fleets. Construction was mainly of wood, and the shape was basic, with squared off wings and tail surfaces. Unusually, no ailerons were fitted; lateral control was by

---

Bell FM-1 Airacuda

Origin: Bell Aircraft Corporation, USA.
Type: Five-seat, twin-engined long range bomber destroyer.
Engines: Two 1,150hp Allison V-1710-23 pusher-mounted liquid cooled V-12s.
Dimensions: Span 70ft 0in (21.33m); length 45ft 11.46in (14.00m); height 12ft 5in (3.78m); wing area 600sq.ft (55.74m²).
Weights: Empty 13,674lb (6,203kg); normal takeoff 19,000lb (8,618kg).
Loadings (at normal takeoff weight): Wing 32lb/sq.ft (155kg/m²); power 8.26lb/hp (3.75kg/hp).
Performance: Maximum speed 268mph (431kph) at 12,600ft (3,840m); initial climb rate 1,520ft/min (7.72m/sec); service ceiling n/a; range 1,670 miles (2,687km).
Armament: Two traversing 37mm T-9 cannon with 110 rounds, one in each forward engine nacelle; four traversing 0.30in (7.62mm) M-2 machine guns with 500 rounds each, one in a retractable dorsal turret; one in a ventral tunnel, and one in each beam position. 20 small bombs could also be carried internally.
History: The 1930s saw a fashion for heavy fighters, of which the Airacuda is one of the most extreme. The prototype first flew on 1 September 1937, and a dozen evaluation models were delivered to the USAAC in 1940.
User: USA (USAAC service test only).

The Airacuda appears to owe something to the battleplane concept postulated by Italian General Guilio Douhet, whereby heavy all-round armament was to compensate for lack of performance. Having said that, it had many ingenious features, not the least of which was installing enclosed gun positions ahead of the engine nacelles, each with a 37mm cannon. In an emergency, such as an

---

Right: The Bachem Ba 349 Natter on its tower ready for vertical launching.

differentially moving elevators. Rapid takeoff was achieved by launching from a vertical ramp, assisted by solid fuel booster rockets. A high rate of climb was sustained by a Walther liquid-fuelled rocket, with an endurance of between 70 and 120 seconds. Punch was provided by a battery of unguided rockets in the nose.

The high-g climbout was controlled by a preset autopilot. Once above the bombers, the pilot was to select a target, attack, then break away downwards. The Natter was semi-disposable. Once clear, the pilot was to reduce speed and jettison the nose section, which even included the instrument panel. A parachute would then stream from the rear. This had two purposes. First, it would lower the rear end, complete with rocket motor, safely to the ground for re-use. Second, the deceleration would pitch the pilot out of his seat; once clear of the aircraft he would use his own 'chute.

On the only manned powered flight, the cockpit canopy flew off shortly after launch; the Natter turned on its back while climbing, then dived into the ground, killing test pilot Lothar Siebert.

Above: The Airacuda was designed as a long range bomber destroyer.

engine fire, the gunners could regain the fuselage via crawlways in the wings.

The cannon constituted the main armament. The other, rifle calibre weapons, provided an all-round defensive field of fire, possibly enough to deter enemy fighters if they were around.

The prototype XFM-1 first flew on 1 September 1937. Initial results were sufficiently promising for 12 YFM-1 evaluation aircraft to be ordered, nine of which were orthodox tail-draggers, and three had tricycle undercarriages. The first of these was delivered in February 1940, the last in October of that year. But by this time the war in Europe was raging, and experience showed that there was little use for a heavy fighter in daylight. The Airacuda programme quietly lapsed.

Bell P-39D Airacobra

Origin: Bell Aircraft Corporation, USA.
Type: Single-seat, single-engined fighter.
Engine: One 1,150hp supercharged Allison V-1710 liquid cooled V-12.
Dimensions: Span 34ft 0in (10.36m); length 30ft 2in (9.19m); height 11ft 10in (3.60m); wing area 213sq.ft (19.79m^2).
Weights: Empty 5,462lb (2,477kg); normal takeoff 7,650lb (3,470kg); maximum 8,850lb (4,014kg).
Loadings (at normal takeoff weight): Wing 36lb/sq.ft (175kg/m^2); power 6.65lb (3.02kg) per hp.
Performance: Maximum speed 360mph (579kph) at 15,000ft (4,572m); sustained climb 4min 30sec to 15,000ft (4,572m); service ceiling 35,000ft (10,667m); range 450 miles (724km).
Armament: One 37mm T-9 nose-mounted cannon with 15 rounds (on later aircraft one 20mm cannon with 60 rounds); plus two .50in (12.7mm) machine guns in the nose and four .30in (7.62mm) machine guns in the wings.
History: Prototype XP-39 first flown on 6 April 1938. Production commenced August 1939 and continued until July 1944, by which time 9,584 had been built in nine main variants.
Users: Britain (RAF), France (Free French), Soviet Union, USA (USAAF).

Like many unorthodox fighters, the Airacobra was a good idea in theory, intended primarily as an interceptor. Bell Aircraft appreciated the value of a heavy weight of fire against bombers. The chosen weapon was the huge 37mm T-9 cannon produced by the American Armament Corporation, mounted on the aircraft centreline and firing through the propellor hub. This virtually ruled out having the engine in the traditional nose position. The answer was simple: locate the engine on the centre of gravity. This had four potential advantages. First, it ought to improve manoeuvrability. Second, the cockpit could be sited forward, giving the pilot a better forward and downward view than would otherwise have been the case. Third, it made a

Below: Many high-scoring soviet aces flew the Bell P-39 Airacobra.

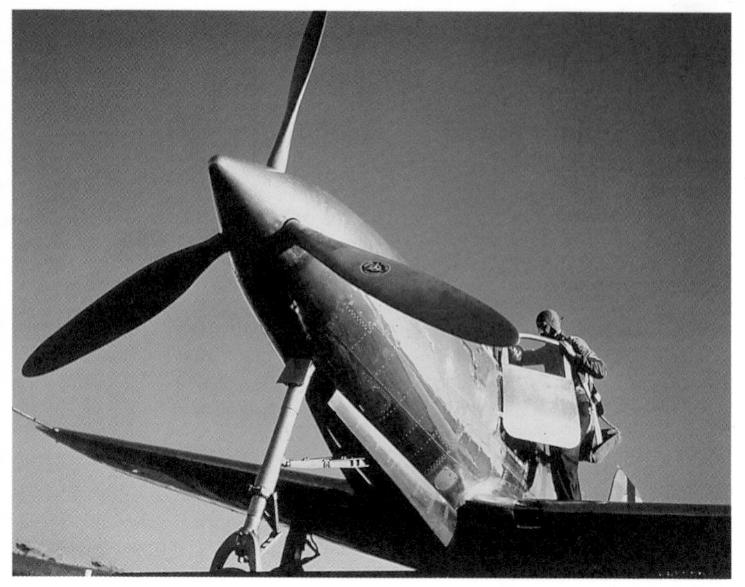

Above: The mid-engine and "car-door" cockpit access made the P-39D unusual.

battery of nose guns possible. Finally, it allowed space for a nosewheel, a tricycle landing gear having better handling on unprepared fields. The Airacobra was the first single-engined fighter to enter service with a retractable tricycle gear.

Unfortunately things did not work out as planned. The P-39 layout needed a 2.5in (64mm) diameter transmission shaft 8ft (2.44m) long, together with associated mountings, gearing, and lubrication systems. In addition, the rear fuselage had to be strengthened to avoid the engine breaking free in a crash landing and flattening the pilot. The weight involved ensured that the Airacobra was seriously underpowered from the outset. Serviceability was also a problem; access to the engine for even quite routine tasks was difficult, and often involved a major dismantling operation.

The first major production variant, the P-39D, entered USAAF service early in 1941, and made its combat debut in the Pacific in the following year. It did not perform well against the agile Japanese Zero, and the "car door" access to the cockpit, rather than the more conventional sliding canopy, made baling out rather difficult. As a fighter it was not very popular. The RAF formed a single P-39 squadron in 1941, but the limitations of the type were such that it was used only for ground attack missions, and then for less than three months.

Of the 9,584 Airacobras built, the majority were optimised for ground attack, and over half were sent to the Soviet Union, where it found favour with the Russian pilots. Most air combat on the Eastern Front took place at relatively low level, where the P-39 was at its best. It was flown by many Russian aces, among them Alexsandr Pokryshkin, Grigorii Rechkalov, Nikolai Gulayev and Alexsandr Khubov, who amassed 159 victories between them with the type.

The P-39 was supplanted on the production lines from summer 1944, by the P-63 Kingcobra, a larger and more powerful variant.

Bereznyak-Isaev BI

Origin: Zhukovsky, Professor Viktor Bolkhovitinov, USSR.
Type: Single-seat, single-engined rocket fighter.
Engine: One Dushkin D-1A bifuel rocket motor rated at 2,425lb (1,100kg) thrust.
Dimensions: Span 21ft 3in (6.48m); length 20ft 11in (6.38m); height 6ft 9in (2.06m); wing area 75.34sq.ft (7.00m²).
Weights: Empty 1,742lb (790kg); normal takeoff 3,710lb (1,693kg).
Loadings (at normal takeoff weight): Wing 49lb/sq.ft (242kg/m²).
Performance: Maximum speed 621mph (965kph); initial climb 16,340ft/min (83m/sec); service ceiling n/a; maximum endurance 15min.
Armament: Two 20mm nose-mounted ShVAK cannon, each with 45 rounds.
History: The Bereznyak-Isaev BI was the world's first rocket-propelled fighter. The first powered flight took place on 15 May 1942, but problems with compressibility and the fuel system meant that the project was abandoned, although trials continued into 1945.
User: USSR, but failed to enter service.

Named after its designers, Aleksandr Bereznyak and Aleksei Isaev, working under the direction of Professor Viktor Bolkhovitinov at Zhukovsky, the BI was a small and pleasant-looking straight-winged monoplane. The engine, designed by L. S. Dushkin, used a bifuel combination of kerosene and nitric acid, although in practice the latter caused all sorts of corrosion problems. The airframe was of wooden semi-monocoque construction, and an unusual feature was endplates on the horizontal tail surfaces.

Bloch MB 152

Origin: Societe Nationale de Constructions Aeronautiques de Sud-Ouest (SNCASO), France.
Type: Single-seat, single-engined monoplane day fighter.
Engine: One 1,000hp Gnome-Rhône GR 14N-25 or -49 radial.
Dimensions: Span 34ft 7in (10.54m); length 29ft 10.25in (9.10m); height 9ft 11.33in (3.03m); wing area 186.43sq.ft (17.32m²).
Weights: Empty 4,758lb (2,158kg); normal takeoff 6,173lb (2,800kg).
Loadings (at normal takeoff weight): Wing 33lb/sq.ft (356kg/m²); power 6.17lb (2.80kg) per hp.
Performance: Maximum speed 316mph (509kph) at 14,765ft (4,500m); sustained climb 3min 24sec to 6,562ft (2,000m); service ceiling c31,000ft (9,448m); range 335 miles (540km).
Armament: Two 20mm Hispano-Suiza HS 404 cannon and two 7.5mm MAC 1934 M39 machine guns.
History: The Bloch MB 152 prototype first flew on 15 December 1938. Service with l'Armée de l'Air began in April 1939, the type saw brief action in the Battle of France. A total of 482 were built.
Users: France (*l'Armée de l'Air*), Romania.

Early attempts by Marcel Bloch, later famous as Marcel Dassault, designer of the post-war Mirage III, to produce a fighter, were not very promising. The first, the Avions Marcel Bloch (before the company was merged into what became SNCASO) MB 150 had to be extensively redesigned before it could be coaxed to leave the ground. This finally took place on 4 May 1937, more than 10 months late. Even then it was unsatisfactory, and two derivatives were put in

Above: Flown on 15 May 1942, the BI was the world's first rocket fighter.

The first, unpowered flight, took place on 10 September 1941 with Boris Kudrin at the controls, when the BI was towed aloft by a Pe-2. Development was disrupted by the German advance, and in that winter the project was relocated to Sverdlovsk. Due to illness, Kudrin was replaced by Grigorii Bakhchivandzhi, who made the first powered flight on 15 May 1942, climbing to 2,625ft (800m), but the flight lasted just 189 seconds. On 21 March 1943, he reached an altitude of 9,943ft (3,000m) in just 30 seconds, but was killed six days later when the third prototype dived into the ground during a low level pass. Compressibility appeared to be the problem, but little was known about it in those days.

An initial order for 50 aircraft was cancelled, but testing continued until the end of the war, during which Boris Kudrin achieved a climb rate of 16,340ft/min (83m/sec) on 9 March 1945.

Above: The Bloch MB 152 was a very ordinary fighter, and achieved little.

hand, the MB 151 and MB 152. Of these, the MB 151 proved disappointing, although it was used in combat by *l'Armée de l'Air* and *l'Aeronavale* in 1940.

Very similar in appearance, the MB 152 differed in having belt-fed rather than drum-fed machine guns, and an uprated engine which improved maximum speed, rate of climb and service ceiling by just under 10 per cent. Even then, performance was rated as poor, while wing loading was on the high side for the era, adversely affecting manoeuvrability.

Attempts were made to improve matters by installing American engines, either the Pratt & Whitney Twin Wasp or the Wright Cyclone 9, but their use in what became the Bloch MB 153 was overtaken by events. The final aircraft in the series was the extensively redesigned MB 155, but this showed little improvement and only 29 were built.

Blohm und Voss BV 40

Origin: Blohm und Voss, Germany.
Type: Single-seat, high-performance, high-wing monoplane glider fighter.
Engine: None.
Dimensions: Span 25ft 11in (7.90m); length 18ft 8.5in (5.70m); height 5ft 4in (1.63m); wing area 93.65sq.ft (8.70m^2).
Weights: Empty 1,821lb (826kg); normal takeoff 2,094lb (950kg).
Loadings (at normal takeoff weight): Wing 22lb/sq.ft (109kg/m^2); power n/a.
Performance: Estimated maximum speed in a 20deg dive 560mph (900kph); rate of climb on tow by Bf 109G 12min to 22,967ft (7,000m); service ceiling n/a; range n/a.
Armament: Two 30mm MK 108 cannon with 35 rounds each.
History: Selected for development, autumn 1943; 19 prototypes and 200 production aircraft ordered. First flight May 1944. Seven prototypes completed by August 1944, but abandoned shortly after.
Users: Germany, but failed to enter Luftwaffe service.

The BV 40 was the original "peanuts" fighter. Small, of basic configuration, and engineless, it cost peanuts to build. It was intended to be flown by glider pilots who cost peanuts to train.

Having said that, it was an interesting, if deeply flawed concept. One (or two) were to be towed into position between 2,461ft (750m) and 820ft (250m) above a USAAF bomber formation. Once there, it would cast off, make a 20deg diving attack, then disengage downwards.

Pilot protection was given high priority. To minimise the frontal area, the pilot lay

Boeing F3B-1

Origin: The Boeing Airplane Company, Seattle, USA.
Type: Single-seat, single-engined sesquiplane carrier fighter.
Engine: One 425hp Pratt & Whitney R-1340-80 Wasp radial.
Dimensions: Span 33ft 0in (10.06m); length 24ft 10in (7.57m) height 9ft 2in (2.79m); wing area 275sq.ft (25.55m^2).
Weights: Empty 2,179lb (988kg); maximum takeoff 2,945lb (1,336kg).
Loadings (at maximum takeoff weight): Wing 10.71lb/sq.ft (52.29kg/m^2); power 6.93lb (3.14kg) per hp.
Performance: Maximum speed 157mph (253kph) at sea level; initial climb rate 2,020ft/min (10.26m/sec; service ceiling 21,500ft (6,553m); range 340 miles (547km).
Armament: Two 0.30in (7.62mm) synchronized machine guns firing through the propeller. Provision for five 25lb (11.34kg) bombs.
History: Initially built as a private venture floatplane, the XF3B-1 first flew on 2 March 1927. Extensively rehashed as a carrier fighter, the F3B-1 had its first flight on 3 February 1928. Deliveries began in August 1928. Phased out of front line squadrons in 1932.
User: USA (USN).

Closely resembling the F2B-1 of 1926 vintage (Boeing's first carrier fighter), the XF3B-1 had provision for a single float with outboard stabilisers, and this was the form in which it first flew, on 27 March 1927. Having showed no real advantages over the earlier type, it was rejected by the US Navy.

It was then rebuilt, with a lengthened nose, completely new undercarriage, wings and tail, as the Model 77. Unlike previous Boeing designs, the wings

Right: The extraordinary BV 40 was the first and only unpowered fighter.

prone on a padded couch, with padded chin and brow rests. The cockpit was heavily armoured, the weight of which was about 26 per cent of the airframe weight. Pilot view was very restricted, the windshield and side panels being 4.75in (120mm) bullet-resisting glass. For the final attack, the side clear view panels could be covered by sliding armour.

A jettisonable trolley was used for takeoff, and landing was on an extendable skid. Flaps on the inboard trailing edge of the wing were lowered to 50deg for landing, but in emergencies this could be increased to 80deg.

The first flight took place in May 1944, with a Bf 110 as the towing aircraft. Further flights established that the prone pilot position was fatiguing. But by this time, long range Mustangs of the USAAF could escort the bombers all the way to Berlin, which made the proposed Bf 109G tow aircraft vulnerable, and thus rendered the BV 40 practically useless. The project was cancelled in autumn 1944.

Right: The Boeing F3B-1 could be configured for either land or water basing.

were of constant chord on upper and lower planes, with W- rather than N-shaped struts, and with the leading and trailing edges of the upper plane raked back at a shallow angle. The fin and rudder were a much more vertical shape.

Construction was mixed; the wings were of wood, but the ailerons were semi-monocoque metal with corrugated skinning. The fuselage was of fabric-covered steel tube, while the tail surfaces were also of semi-monocoque metal. This form of construction was a first for US fighters.

The first flight of the rebuilt F3B-1 took place on 28 February 1928, and the aircraft was almost instantly successful. The US Navy ordered 74, although this included the prototype, and all the production machines were delivered between August and December of the same year.

Shipboard service began on board the training carrier USS *Langley*, with operational squadrons with USS *Saratoga* and *Lexington*. Most F3B-1s had been phased out within four years, but a few were retained as administrative and command aircraft, usually fitted with a Townend ring engine cowling and wheel fairings.

Boeing P-12E

Origin: The Boeing Airplane Company, Seattle, USA.
Type: Single-seat, single-engined biplane fighter.
Engine: One 525hp Wright R-1340-17 Wasp radial.
Dimensions: Span 30ft 0in (9.14m); length 20ft 3in (6.17m); height 9ft 0in (2.74m); wing area 227.5sq.ft (21.13m^2).
Weights: Empty 1,999lb (907kg); normal takeoff 2,690lb (1,220kg).
Loadings (at normal takeoff weight): Wing 11.82lb/sq.ft (57.73kg/m^2); power 5.12lb (2.32kg) per hp.
Performance: Maximum speed 189mph (304kph) at 7,000ft (2,134m); sustained climb rate 5min 48sec to 10,000ft (3,048m); service ceiling n/a; range 475 miles (764km).
Armament: Two 0.30in (7.62mm) synchronized machine guns.
History: The Boeing P-12 series was built in relatively large numbers, 366 in total, in six basic variants. The first P-12 flew on 11 April 1929; deliveries of the P-12F model were completed in 1932.
User: USA (USAAC).

The US Army Air Corps evaluated the Boeing Model 89 (F4B-1 carrier fighter) in 1928 and ordered 10 essentially similar aircraft. This was the start of the very successful P-12 series.

Fabric-covered wooden wings were mated with a fuselage consisting of bolted aluminium box sections. After trials, the baseline aircraft was modified and improved. This resulted in the P-12B, of which 90 were built. The engine remained the 450hp Pratt & Whitney R-1340-7, but a ring cowling was introduced after it had entered service. The main difference from the first model was Frise-type balanced ailerons. The first P-12B was briefly fitted with a turbo-supercharged Y1SR-1340G/H engine to become the XP-12G, but no further progress was made. It soon reverted to standard P-12B configuration.

In June 1930 the P-12C emerged, first flown on 30 January 1931. This

Above: The P-12F seen here was the final major variant of this type.

was powered by the R-1340-9 engine of 525hp in a ring cowling, and a spreader bar undercarriage. In all, 131 aircraft were ordered, but the final 35 of these were fitted with the R-1340-17 engine, to become P-12Ds, externally indistinguishable from the P-12C, but with better performance.

The next step was to have a semi-monocoque fuselage, for which a P-12B was adapted as a prototype, taking to the air on 29 September 1930. Six months later, a contract for 135 P-12Es was placed, the first of which flew on 15 October 1931. The final 25 P-12Es ordered were completed as P-12Fs, powered by R-1340-19 engines rated at 600hp for takeoff and 500hp at 11,000ft (3,353m). This gave only a marginal improvement in maximum speed, but quite significant increases in climb rate and ceiling. The final P-12Fs were delivered late in 1932.

Several one-offs appeared in the P-12 series. The 33rd P-12D was temporarily fitted with the XGRS-1340-E engine, a geared version of the Wasp, to become the XP-12H. This proved to be another dead end; further development was abandoned, and the aircraft reverted to being a P-12D.

One P-12E was reconfigured with an SR-1340H engine rated at 575hp at 2,50Oft (762m), to become the XP-121. Considered worthy of further development, five standard P-12Es were then fitted with the fuel injected SR-1340E engine to become YP12Ks, as were the XP-12E and XP-12J. One of the distinguishing marks of the YP12K was a large fairing added behind the pilot's head. All seven served with the USAAC for a short while, and at least one was used with a combination wheel/ski undercarriage. At a later date, one YP-12K was fitted with an F-7 turbo-supercharger to become the XP-12L, but all were eventually returned to standard P-12E configuration. One other variant of note was a P-12F which was experimentally fitted with an enclosed cockpit with a sliding canopy, but this was not deemed a success. Deliveries ended in 1932, by which time Boeing had started to examine the advantages of monoplanes.

Left: The first production variant was the P-12B seen here; 90 were built.

Boeing P-26A

Origin: The Boeing Airplane Company, Seattle, USA.
Type: Single-seat, single-engined monoplane fighter.
Engine: One 600hp Pratt & Whitney R-1340-27 Wasp radial.
Dimensions: Span 27ft 11.63in (8.52m); length 23ft 7.25in (7.19m); height 10ft 5in (3.17m); wing area 149.5sq.ft (13.89m²).
Weights: Empty 2,194lb (995kg); normal takeoff 2,935lb (1,331kg).
Loadings (at normal takeoff weight): Wing 19.63lb/sq.ft (96kg/m²); power 4.89lb (2.22kg) per hp.
Performance: Maximum speed 234mph (367kph) at 7,500ft (2,286m); initial climb rate 2,360ft/min (11.99m/sec); service ceiling n/a; range 570 miles (917km).
Armament: Two fuselage-mounted 0.30in (7.72mm) machine guns; two 100lb (45kg) bombs.
History: Begun as a private venture; first flight 20 March 1932; production from 10 January to 30 June 1934. A handful remained in service in early 1942 and flew against the Japanese.
Users: China, Spain (1 only), USA (USAAC).

In the late 1920s, improvements in engine technology allowed significant increases in power, combined with large reductions in both engine weight per horsepower, and fuel consumption. This could obviously be used to improve performance, and even more so if drag could be reduced. One of the more obvious ways to reduce drag was to adopt a monoplane configuration, thereby cutting out a second wing with its struts and bracing wires.

In 1930, Boeing made two unsuccessful attempts at producing a monoplane fighter. The first was the XP-15, a parasol-wing design for the US Navy; The second was the XP-9, a shoulder-wing fighter for the USAAC. The first offered little performance improvement over existing types; the second was rejected due mainly to unpleasant handling.

For Boeing it was third time lucky. The Model 248 was begun in September 1931 as a private venture, and the first of three protoypes flew on 20 March 1932. As the XP-26, it was evaluated by the USAAC, and found favourable. The improved Model 266 was ordered as the P-26A, which became widely and affectionately known as the Peashooter. The first production aircraft flew on 10 January 1934, and the last of 111 machines ordered was delivered on 30 June of that year.

The Peashooter was a compact, rather portly fighter, powered by a 600hp Pratt & Whitney ring-cowled Wasp radial engine. The wing was low-set, but not cantilevered. Instead, it was wire-braced, with landing wires to the top of the forward fuselage, and flying wires to the main wheel frames. The main gears themselves were "trousered" as a drag-reducing measure at a slight penalty in weight. Wheel-braking was employed. The wing loading of the P-26 was nearly double that of the P-12, with, in the absence of flaps, a correspondingly high landing speed.

The P-26A was of all-metal construction, with a semi-monocoque fuselage, with two spar wings skinned with light alloy. Just aft of the open cockpit was a large hump, designed to protect the pilot in the event of a somersault on landing.

Armament for the P-26A was the then standard two rifle calibre machine guns, although on the P-26C one was supplanted by a 0.50in (12.7mm) heavy machine gun. An extremely long tubular sight was fitted, which must have been difficult to use in manoeuvring flight. P-26Cs, of which 25 were built, were later refitted with SR-1340-33 fuel-injected engines, to become P-26Bs.

An export version, the Model 281, was produced. Of these, 11 were bought by China, while one went to Spain for evaluation.

Left: The P-26A Peashooter was the first successful Boeing monoplane fighter.

Boeing X-32 Joint Strike Fighter

Origin: The Boeing Company, Seattle, USA.
Type: Single-seat, single-engined, multi-role fighter with CTOL (X-32A), STOVL (X-32B), and carrier-compatible (X-32C) variants.
Engine: One Pratt & Whitney JSF119-614 medium bypass ratio twin-spool afterburning turbofan rated at c42,000lb (19,051kg) maximum and c26,000lb (11,794kg) military thrust, with two-dimensional vectoring main nozzle.
Dimensions: Span X-32A and C 36ft 1in (11.00m), X-32B 30ft 0in (9.14m); length X-32A and C 47ft 3.5in (14.42m), X-32B 46ft 3.5in (14.03m); height X-32A and C 13ft 2.5in (4.02m), X-32B 13ft 3.5in (4.05m); wing area n/a.
Weights: Empty X-32A and C c22,000lb (9,979kg), X-32B c24,000lb (10,886kg); normal takeoff (CTOL) c38,000lb (17,236kg); maximum takeoff c50,000lb (22,680kg).
Loadings (at normal takeoff weight): Wing n/a; thrust 1.10.
Performance: Maximum speed (estimated) Mach 1.6 at altitude; operational radius X-32A c860 miles (1,380km), X-32B c690 miles (1,100km), X-32C c800 miles (1,300km). No other details released.
Armament: One internal 27mm BK-27 Mauser cannon for X-32A, possibly one 25mm cannon for other variants, either internal or in pods; four AIM-120C cropped Amraam in internal bays, plus four underwing pylons for other stores. Maximum ordnance load 17,000lb(7,711kg).
History: Inaugurated in 1986, what later became the Joint Strike Fighter concept called for an affordable all-singing, all-dancing fighter as a universal replacement for the F-15E, F-16, F-111 and F-117 (USAF), the F-14 and F/A-18 (USN), the AV-8B and F/A-18 (USMC), and the Harrier and Sea Harrier (RAF and RN). The Boeing X-32 was one of the two final candidates, but on 26 October 2001 it lost out to the Lockheed Martin X-35.
Users: None.

Like the F-14 and F-15 before it, the F-22 Raptor (which see) has proved to be unaffordable in the numbers required. To compensate, the Joint Strike Fighter was proposed, with a production run large enough to amortise development costs. Three basic types were required: a conventional takeoff and landing (CTOL) aircraft; a short takeoff vertical landing (STOVL) aircraft; and a carrier compatible aircraft. In November 1996, contracts were awarded to Boeing and Lockheed Martin to produce two (rather than three, to ensure a high degree of commonality) concept demonstrators each, one CTOL, the other STOVL. Boeing offered the CTOL X-32A and the STOVL X-32B. The X-32C would be a navalised CTOL X-32A.

The X-32A was massive. Overall dimensions were similar to those of the Harrier, but there the resemblance ended. Obviously shaped for stealth, it had an exceptionally deep fuselage. Since it had to have the engine located forward, make space for two lift nozzles more or less on the centre of gravity, house an enormous load of internal fuel, and carry its weapons in internal weapons bays, this was unavoidable.

A rather "beaky" chined nose surmounted a forward-swept chin inlet. This could be translated downwards to increase mass flow in jet-borne flight. A thick, shoulder-mounted delta wing with a 55deg leading edge sweep, but with the trailing edge raked 20deg forward, could accommodate plenty of fuel. At the tail were two orthodox outwardly canted fins and rudders.

For jet-borne flight, a direct lift system was adopted, in which the main nozzle closed off, and the efflux was diverted into two vectoring nozzles set beneath the centre of gravity. Developed by Rolls-Royce, these pivoted between 45deg aft and 15deg forward. Pitch and roll control was provided by Harrier-style puffers on the wingtips and at the rear.

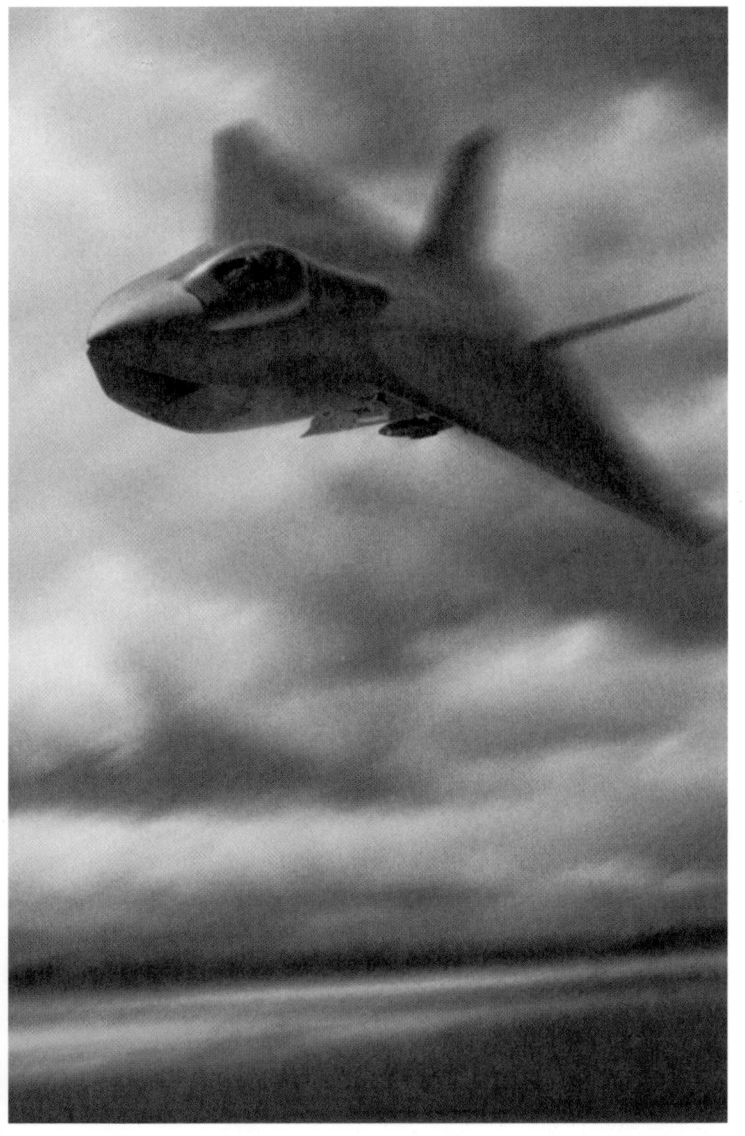

Above: The Boeing X-32 was the losing contender in the JSF competition.

In 1997 Boeing realised that they could not meet the evolving JSF requirements with the tail-less delta configuration. They switched to a broad chord swept wing with horizontal tail surfaces. But by this time, construction of the proof of concept aircraft was too advanced to change and, piloted by Fred Knox, the delta X-32A took to the skies on 18 September 2000. Jet-borne flight trials of the X-32B began on 13 April 2001. But, lacking the definitive article, the Boeing X-32 was unable to compete effectively.

Boulton Paul Defiant I

Origin: Boulton Paul Aircraft, Norwich, England.
Type: Two-seat, single-engined turret fighter.
Engine: One Rolls-Royce Merlin III liquid-cooled V-12 rated at 1,030hp at 16,250ft (4,953m).
Dimensions: Span 39ft 4in (11.99m); length 35ft 4in (10.77m); height 11ft 4in (3.45m); wing area 250sq.ft (23.22m²).
Weights: Empty 6,078lb (2,757kg); normal takeoff 8,318lb (3,773kg).
Loadings (at normal takeoff weight): Wing 33lb/sq.ft (162kg/m²); power 8.08lb (3.66kg) per hp.
Performance: Maximum speed 304mph (489kph) at 17,000ft (5,182m), 250mph (402kph) at sea level; initial climb rate 1,900ft/min (9.65m/sec); sustained climb 8min 30sec to 15,750ft (4,800m); service ceiling 30,350ft (9,250m); range 465 miles (748km).
Armament: Four .303in (7.7mm) Browning machine guns with 600 rounds each in a power-operated turret.
History: First flight (without turret) 11 August 1937. First production aircraft 30 July 1939. Production ceased in February 1943, total built 1,064, including 210 Defiant IIs. Later used as radar-equipped night fighters, target tugs and special duties.
User: Britain (RAF).

In the late 1930s, with war looming, the perceived threat to the British Isles was daylight formations of German bombers. These would be unescorted; the distance was far too great for the German fighters of the period. The result was that RAF Fighter Command evolved a series of set-piece fighter attacks. The tacticians however had far too much respect for the bomber gunners, and the pilots of orthodox fixed gun fighters were therefore trained to break off their attacks at a range where they might just have started to hit something.

Had the pundits been right, the Defiant would have been a massive success. Fighter Command Attacks A and B were written for the Defiant. Having caught the bombers, and the Defiant just about had the performance to do so, they would formate on them, typically 300ft (91m) below, either ahead or astern, but either way in the blind spot of the defending gunners. The range was determined by the "no-allowance" angle for the speed of the aroplanes and the muzzle velocity of the turret guns, which allowed the Defiant gunners to aim directly at their targets.

The Defiants were to be accompanied by Spitfires or Hurricanes, which would set about the bombers if they broke formation to defend themselves. This would force the bombers into the role of sitting ducks. It was a nice theory.

In practice it was a disaster. What no one had considered was that if France and the Low Countries were overrun, the bombers would be escorted by fighters. But this is precisely what happened. Defiants initially scored a few victories against German fighters when the latter failed to identify them correctly, and attacked from above and astern, directly into the teeth of the turret guns. But once it was identified, the slow, heavy, unmanoeuvrable Defiant was carved up by the agile Bf 109s, which attacked from below and astern. After several disastrous days in the summer of 1940, the Defiant was withdrawn from the daylight battle, having achieved little.

As a night fighter it was slightly better than the Blenheim because of its superior performance, but effectiveness was limited due to it having to operate as a "catseye" fighter. This was later amended by fitting AI Mk VI radar, with a pilot scope, from autumn 1941, but by this time the far better Beaufighter was in service in numbers. The final fighter variant was the Defiant II, with a more powerful Merlin engine.

Below: With no front guns, the Defiant turret fighter was a disaster.

Brandenburg D.I.

Origin: Phönix Flugzeugwerke, Vienna, Austria.
Type: Single-seat, single-engined biplane fighter.
Engine: One 185hp Austro-Daimler liquid-cooled inline.
Dimensions: Span 27ft 10.67in (8.50m); length 20ft 10in (6.35m); height n/a; wing area 257.80sq.ft (23.95m²).
Weights: Empty 1,481lb (672kg); normal takeoff 2,028lb (920kg).
Loadings (at normal takeoff weight): Wing 7.87lb/sq.ft (38.41kg/m²); power 10.96lb (4.97kg) per hp.
Performance: Maximum speed 116mph (187kph) at sea level; sustained climb 3min to 3,281ft (1,000m); service ceiling n/a.
Armament: One fixed 8mm Schwarzlose machine gun on the top plane to fire over the propeller.
History: Designed by Ernst Heinkel of Hansa- und Brandenburg for the Austro-Hungarian air force. First flight late 1916. A handful survived the war.
Users: Austro-Hungarian Empire (*Luftfahrttruppen*), and Austria (*Deutscheösterreichische Fliegertruppe*) post war.

Initially known as the KD (Kampf Doppeldecker), the D. I. was designed by Ernst Heinkel of Hansa- und Brandenburg specifically for Austro-Hungarian use. The prototype flew with the 160hp Mercedes DIII engine, but production aircraft built by Hansa- und Brandenburgische were fitted with the 150 and 160hp Austro-Daimler, while Phönix-built aircraft mounted the 185hp Austro-Daimler.

Of timber construction with fabric wing skins and plywood fuselage skins, the D.I. had two unusual features. The first was the arrangement of the

Brandenburg CC

Origin: Hansa- und Brandenburgische Flugzeugwerke, Germany.
Type: Single-seat, single-engined biplane flying boat fighter.
Engine: One 160hp Austro-Daimler liquid-cooled inline pusher.
Dimensions: Span 30ft 6.13in (9.30m); length 25ft 2.75in (7.69m); height 11ft 8.5in (3.57m); wing area 285.46sq.ft (26.52m²).
Weights: Empty 1,764lb (800kg); normal takeoff 2,381lb (1,080kg).
Loadings (at normal takeoff weight): Wing 8.34lb/sq.ft (40.72kg/m²); power 14.88lb (6.75kg) per hp.
Performance: Maximum speed 109mph (175kph); sustained climb 4min 48sec to 3,281ft (1,000m); service ceiling n/a; range 311 miles (500km).
Armament: One fixed 8mm Schwarzlose machine gun projecting through the windshield.
History: Prototype first flight 1916; deliveries commenced February 1917; total production 73.
Users: Austro-Hungarian Empire (Navy), Germany (Navy).

The Austro-Hungarian Navy had a requirement for a flying boat fighter to operate in the Adriatic, which the CC filled. The CC designation was for Camillo Castiglioni, the financier of Hansa- und Brandenburg, and there is sure to be a story there!

The Starstrutter wing configuration used on the D. I. was retained, although the gap between the upper and lower planes was much greater. Wing vibration could be severe in certain conditions and, to correct this, the German Navy, who were the second user, grounded the type pending fitting orthodox V-struts outboard. The lower plane carried outrigger floats .

Above: The Starstrutter took its name from the interplane strut arrangement.

interplane struts. Constructed of light-gauge steel tube with plywood fairings, these comprised four V-shaped struts on each side. These met at their apexes in a pattern which led the D.I. being dubbed the Starstrutter. The second feature was a very small rudder with almost no fin. This was unsatisfactory, as the rudder was often blanketed by the slab-sided fuselage. The horizontal tail was reminiscent of that of the Albatros series.

The Starstrutter was tricky to fly, lacking lateral stability, and difficult to recover from a spin. Be this as it may, it was flown by at least two high-scoring Austro-Hungarian aces in their early days, Godwin Brumowski (40 victories) and Frank Linke-Crawford (30 victories), both of whom were Polish-born.

Above: This is a German Navy CC, with V-struts outboard of the star struts.

A sleek boat-shaped hull made up the fuselage, with the pilot seated well forward. The pusher engine was mounted high, just below the upper plane. Austro-Hungarian aircraft were powered by either the 160hp Austro-Daimler or the 180hp Hiero; German machines were fitted with the 150hp Benz Bz III.

Late production aircraft had a slightly lengthened hull to improve flying characteristics, and two machine guns in the upper decking. The most successful CC pilot was Gottfried Banfield.

Brewster F2A-2 and Buffalo

Origin: Brewster Aeronautical Corporation, USA.
Type: Single-seat, single-engined carrier- and land-based monoplane fighter.
Engine: One 1,200hp Wright R-1820-40 Cyclone radial.
Dimensions: Span 35ft 0in (10.67m); length 25ft 11in (7.90m); height 12ft 1in (3.68m); wing area 208.9sq.ft (19.41m²).
Weights: Empty 4,576lb (2,076kg); normal takeoff 5,942lb (2,695kg).
Loadings (at normal takeoff weight): Wing 28.44lb/sq.ft (139kg/m²); power 4.95lb (2,25kg) per hp.
Performance: Maximum speed 323mph (520kph) at 16,500ft (5,029m); 285mph (459kph) at sea level; initial climb rate 2,500ft/min (12.7m/sec); service ceiling 30,500ft (9,296m); range 1,015 miles (1,633km).
Armament: Four 0.50in (12.7mm) Colt machine guns, two in the nose and two in the wings.
History: Prototype first flight December 1937. Deliveries to US Navy (F2A-1) June 1939, but only 11 accepted. The improved F2A-2 was delivered from June 1940 (43 aircraft). The land-based Buffalo was an export version, and production of the F2A-3 ceased in March 1942. The F2A saw only brief service with the USN/USMC.
Users: Australia (RAAF), Britain (RAF), Finland, Holland, New Zealand (RNZAF), USA (USN and USMC).

Design was begun in 1936 of an all-metal monoplane carrier fighter with a retractable undercarriage. It emerged as a rather rotund aircraft, although this was determined by the diameter of the Wright Cyclone engine as much as anything. The rather plain wing was midset, and one of the most memorable recognition features was the long, greenhouse-style cockpit canopy. Having evaluated the prototype XF2A-1, the US Navy ordered 54 examples of the developed production version, the F2A-1. This proved to be disappointing. Performance was sluggish and fell away rapidly with altitude; as a gun platform it was unstable; and manoeuvre was poor. Only 11 were accepted; the remainder were exported to Finland.

The F2A-2 followed, with 43 ordered to replace those sent to Finland. This had the more powerful -40 Cyclone engine, an electric variable pitch propeller instead of the former hydraulic article, a high pressure carburation system, and other detail changes. This was also unsatisfactory, manifesting all the previous faults, and exhibiting a tendency for the engine to overheat.

The final US Navy order was for 108 F2A-3s. This had greater fuel capacity, with a lengthened forward fuselage, and armour protection. Delivery took place between July and December 1941, but the added weight did nothing for performance.

Substantial export orders for the land-based Buffalo were placed in 1940 – 170 for the RAF, 72 for the Netherlands, and 28 for Belgium. The Buffalo differed from its predecessors in having a larger fuel tank, and the Wright GR-1820-G105A engine rated at 1,100hp. Belgium was overrun before the order could be fulfilled, and the aircraft went to Britain's RAF instead. The Dutch order was for the East Indies Army Air Division, and was completed with the final F2A off the production lines in March 1942.

Poor altitude performance made the Buffalo unsuitable for European operations, and the RAF transferred theirs to the Far East. The armament was replaced by four rifle calibre machine guns, while less ammunition and fuel were carried. This attempt to improve these Buffalos' performance by minimising weight availed them little: they were outmatched by the agile Japanese fighters. The same fate befell USMC F2As based on Midway, which lost 13 of 21 aircraft in their first and only major action.

The first Brewsters arrived in Finland in March and April 1940, although their combat debut did not occur until 25 July 1941. They were instantly successful, and by the end of the war had claimed 489 victories for 16 losses in air combat, although others were lost to ground fire and accidents. Seven aircraft survived, and were flown by the HQ Flight until 14 September 1948.

Below: Australian Brewster Buffaloes escorting a Blenheim over Malaya in 1942.

Bristol M.1C

Origin: British & Colonial Aeroplane Co., England.
Type: Single-seat, single-engined tractor monoplane fighter.
Engine: One 110hp Le Rhône rotary.
Dimensions: Span 30ft 9in (9.37m); length 20ft 5.5in (6.23m); height 7ft 9.5in (2.37m); wing area 145sq.ft (13.47m²).
Weights: Empty 896lb (406kg); normal takeoff 1,348lb (611kg).
Loadings (at normal takeoff weight): Wing 9.30lb/sq.ft (45.36kg/m²); power 12.25lb (5.56kg) per hp.
Performance: Maximum speed 130mph (209kph) at sea level, 127mph (204kph) at 5,000ft (15,239m); initial climb rate more than 1,000ft/min (5.08m/sec); sustained climb 10min 27sec to 10,000ft (3,048m); service ceiling 20,000ft (6,096m); endurance 1hr 45min.
Armament: One .303in (7.7mm) belt-fed Vickers machine gun.
History: First flight (M.1A) 14 July 1916; production order for 125 aircraft placed 3 August 1917; 33 aircraft sent to the Middle East 1917-18.
Users: Britain (RFC and RAF).

Designed by Frank Barnwell, the Bristol M.1A was a sleek monoplane with a fully faired cigar-shaped fuselage, its stylish lines accentuated by a large spinner. The braced wing was shoulder-mounted. First flown on 14 July 1916, it was aerodynamically advanced, as shown by a maximum speed attained of 132mph (121kph), more than any fighter in service at that time.

Be that as it may, official recognition was slow in coming, and the first and only order was not placed until well over a year had elapsed, by which time a

Bristol F.2B Fighter

Origin: British & Colonial Aircraft Co., England.
Type: Two-seat, single-engined tractor biplane fighter.
Engine: One 280hp Rolls-Royce Kestrel III liquid-cooled V-12.
Dimensions: Span 39ft 4in (11.99m); length 25ft 10in (7.87m); height 9ft 6in (2.89m); wing area 389sq.ft (36.14m²).
Weights: Empty 1,930lb (875kg); normal takeoff 2,848lb (1,292kg).
Loadings (at normal takeoff weight): Wing 7.32lb/sq.ft (35.75kg/m²); power 10.17lb (4.61kg) per hp.
Performance: Maximum speed 123mph (198kph) at 5,000ft (1,524m), 113mph (182kph) at 10,000ft (3,048m); sustained climb 6min 30sec to 6,500ft (1,981m), 11min 51sec to 10,000ft (3,048m); service ceiling 20,000ft (6,096m); endurance 3hr.
Armament: One belt-fed fixed .303in (7.7mm) Vickers machine gun and one swivelling drum-fed Scarff-mounted .303in (7.7mm) Lewis machine gun in the rear cockpit.
History: First flight of prototype 9 September 1916. Initial order for 50 F.2As, delivered in 1917. Combat debut April 1917. Quickly superseded by the improved F2B, powered successively by the Falcon I, Falcon II and Falcon III.
User: Britain (RFC/RAF).

First flown only nine weeks after the M.1, Frank Barnwell's next design was destined to eclipse the innovatory monoplane. Initially designed around a new 190hp Rolls-Royce 12-cylinder liquid-cooled engine, but with provision for a 150hp Hispano-Suiza, the Brisfit, as it affectionately became known, was of traditional tractor biplane configuration.

Above: The fast Bristol M.1C monoplane served only in Palestine and Macedonia.

whole new generation of fighters had entered service. This is generally ascribed to two factors: War Office prejudice against monoplanes, and a landing speed of 49mph (79kph), which was admittedly high for the time.

That there was prejudice against monoplanes can hardly be denied; even with slower landing aircraft, crash-landings were an everyday occurrence on Western Front airfields. The other factor not cited was the relatively high wing loading which, in spite of reports of excellent manoeuvrability, might have told against the M.1A.

Four M.1B evaluation aircraft were ordered, each with a single Vickers gun on the port wing root, and a clear vision cutout in the starboard wing, introduced to give the pilot a better downward view on landing. The M.1C as ordered differed only in that the Vickers was centrally mounted. The few that saw action served in Palestine and Macedonia; the remainder were used for training.

Above: Not a replica, but an original 1917 Brisfit, and still flying!

The Brisfit was large but, being a two-seater, there was little option. It was a two-bay biplane, of wooden construction and with two main spars in both upper and lower planes. Ailerons were located outboard, again in both upper and lower planes, but with one notable exception: whereas all previous biplanes mounted the lower planes on the fuselage structure, on the Bristol it was set lower, attached with short V-struts.

The fixed Vickers gun used the CC system developed by the Romanian George Constantinesco and G. C. Colley, which used oil pressure to synchronize firing through the propeller disc. The Lewis gun was mounted on a frame that allowed it to be elevated or depressed with ease, the whole on a circular Scarff ring which aided all-round movement.

The observer's cockpit was capacious enough to allow him free movement, and featured a sliding seat. It was placed very close to the pilot's seat, which minimised the difficulties of crew communication. A production order of 50 F.2A aircraft was placed even before first flight, and deliveries began early in 1917.

The first Brisfit unit was No 48 Squadron, which arrived on the Western Front in the spring of 1917. It was widely expected to make an immediate impact on the air fighting, and it was with high hopes that a flight of Brisfits, led by William Leefe Robinson, VC, took off for an offensive patrol between Douai and Valenciennes on 5 April 1917.

In terms of performance and manoeuvrability, the Bristol Fighter was the equal of any fighter then at the front. However, this was not appreciated by No 48 Squadron. The traditional use of two-seaters, as exemplified by the Sopwith Strutter, was to close formation and leave the shooting to the observers in the rear cockpits.

Leefe Robinson for one, knew no better. His Victoria Cross had been earned for shooting down a Zeppelin (it was actually a Schutte-Lanz) at night while on home defence several months earlier. He was therefore totally innocent of fighter tactics and their employment. When, at 11.15 am on that fateful morning, Manfred von Richthofen at the head of five Albatros D IIIs loomed out of the mist, Leefe Robinson took no offensive action, but left it to the guns of the observers. The result was a disaster. Four of the six Brisfits failed to return, two of them victims of the Red Baron, while the others limped back badly shot up. Wounded, Leefe Robinson ended the war as a prisoner. Nor was this the end; over the next eleven days, eight more Bristols went down.

Meanwhile the F.2A had been improved to become the F.2B. This had minor

Below: Although large, the Bristol Fighter outperformed many single-seaters.

modifications to improve the pilot's view, increased fuel capacity, more ammunition for the belt-fed Vickers, and slightly more area on the lower planes, while the span of the horizontal tail was increased. Delivery of the F.2B began on 17 April 1917.

Tactical usage was soon modified; Brisfit pilots soon learned to fly aircraft like single-seaters, using the Vickers as the main armament and leaving their observers to guard their tails. Despite its size and weight (compared to the Albatros D V, the span of the Brisfit was about one third larger, and it was 25 per cent heavier), it could hold its own in close combat, as well as outperforming the German fighter.

The leading exponent of the F.2B was Canadian Andrew McKeever, who arrived at the front to join No 11 Squadron in May 1917. A natural marksman, McKeever had always wanted to fly single-seaters, and from the outset he handled the F.2B like one. On 10 July 1917, he attacked nine Germans single-handed, and destroyed four. After this, in direct contravention of orders, McKeever had his aircraft painted white. Between 20 June 1917 and January 1918, he was credited with 30 victories. Various observers who flew with him claimed another eleven.

The first 150 F.2Bs were powered by the 190hp Rolls-Royce Falcon I, as it was now called. This was followed by the 220hp Falcon II, but most F.2Bs mounted the Falcon III, of 275hp. Of the final production batch, 153 were powered by the 200hp Sunbeam Arab, and 18 with the 230hp Siddeley Puma. Production ended in September 1919, with a delivery total of 4,747. Post-war the type was used for Army Co-operation, and remained in service until 1932.

Right: The F.2B was flown as a single-seater with the gunner guarding its tail.

Bristol Bulldog IIA

Origin: Bristol Aeroplane Co., England.
Type: Single-seat, single-engined biplane fighter.
Engine: One 490hp Bristol Jupiter VIIF radial.
Dimensions: Span 33ft 10in (10.31m); length 25ft 0in (7.62m); height 9ft 10in (2.99m); wing area 306.5sq.ft (28.47m²).
Weights: Empty 2,412lb (1,094kg); normal takeoff 3,530lb (1,601kg).
Loadings (at normal takeoff weight): Wing 11.52lb/sq.ft (56kg/m²); power 7.20lb (3.27kg) per hp.
Performance: Maximum speed 178mph (286kph) at 10,000ft (3,048m); sustained climb rate 14min 30sec to 20,000ft (6,096m); service ceiling 27,000ft (8,229m); range 350 miles (563km).
Armament: Two .303in (7.7mm) synchronized belt-fed Browning machine guns with 600 rounds per gun.
History: A private venture, the Bulldog I first flew on 27 March 1927, and was evaluated against Specification F.9/26. An improved version, the Bulldog II, first flew on 21 January 1928, and was selected for the RAF. Service entry June 1929. The major RAF type was the Bulldog IIA, which served until 1937. The final variants were the Bulldog IIIA and IVA. Total build, 377 aircraft.
Users: Britain (RAF), Denmark, Estonia, Finland, Latvia, Siam, Spain, Sweden, USA (USN).

The Bristol Aeroplane Company, as the British & Colonial Aircraft Company had now become, found the success of the F.2B a hard act to follow. The immediate post-war years saw a succession of fighter designs which failed to attract orders. Then in 1927 the tide turned with the Bulldog I. Powered by the 440hp

Above: Streamlining and radial engines did not mix, as on this Bulldog IIA.

Bristol Jupiter VII radial engine, construction was of fabric-covered high tensile steel strip.

Although not an official contender for Specification F.9/26, the Bulldog I was evaluated, and impressed sufficiently for an improved model to be ordered.

This, the Bulldog II, had a 24in (0.61m) longer fuselage, and was slightly taller. Armament consisted of two .303in (7.7mm) belt-fed Vickers guns, but export aircraft for Estonia and Latvia mounted two rifle calibre Oerlikons. These last also had Jupiter VI engines.

The definitive RAF fighter was the Bulldog IIA, which had a strengthened structure and undercarriage, and was powered by the 490hp Jupiter VIIF.

The quest for greater performance resulted in the Bulldog IIIA, powered by the 560hp Bristol Mercury IVS.2 radial, with a Townend ring cowling. The original airframe had been extensively redesigned, with a new and thicker upper plane to keep the fuel tanks completely within the wing section, narrow chord lower planes to improve downward view from the cockpit, and a deeper rear fuselage. Although significantly faster than the IIA, reaching 208mph (335kph)

Bristol Blenheim IF

Origin: Bristol Aeroplane Co., England.
Type: Three-seater, twin-engined long range monoplane day and night fighter.
Engines: Two 840hp Bristol Mercury VIII radials.
Dimensions: Span 56ft 4in (17.17m); length 39ft 9in (12.12m); height 9ft 10in (3.00m); wing area 469sq.ft (43.57m^2).
Weights: Empty 8,840lb (4,010kg); normal takeoff 12,200lb (5,534kg).
Loadings (at normal takeoff weight): Wing 26lb/sq.ft (127kg/m^2); power 7.26lb (3.29kg) per hp.
Performance: Maximum speed 278mph (447kph) at 15,000ft (4,572m); initial climb rate 1,540ft/min (7.82m/sec); sustained climb 3min 54sec to 5,000ft (1,524m); service ceiling 27,280ft (8,315m); range 1,050 miles (1,690km).

at 15,000ft (4,572m), the Bulldog IIIA failed to attract orders.

The second IIIA prototype (the first had crashed on 30 March 1933) was converted to become the four-gun Bulldog IVA. First flown in the spring of 1934, this competed for Specification F.7/30. The best performing of all Bulldog variants, the IVA could attain 225mph (362kph) at 16,000ft (4,877m), and reach 10,000ft (3,048m) in just 4min 40sec. Be this as it may, it lost out to the Gloster Gladiator, the fighter that by 1937 had supplanted the Bulldog IIA in RAF service.

This was not however the end of the road for the Bulldog; in April 1934 Finland ordered 17 examples of the Bulldog IVA, although these had only two Vickers machine guns. The type remained in the Finnish front line until spring 1940, having survived the Winter War, and remained in service, mainly in a training role, until 1944.

Armament: Four fixed forward-firing .303in (7.7mm) Browning machine guns in a ventral pack and one more in the wings; one .303in (7.7mm) Vickers K machine gun in a dorsal turret.
History: Developed from the fast light bomber, the prototype of which first flew on 25 June 1936 and entered service in December 1938. Became the first fighter in the world to carry airborne radar. Superseded by the Blenheim IVF from August 1939. The main RAF night fighter throughout 1940, but phased out in this role through 1941-42.
User: Britain (RAF).

Below: The Blenheim IF was the first night fighter to carry AI radar.

Most unusually for a fighter, the origins of the Blenheim lay in a fast commercial aircraft, the Bristol Type 142, which first flew on 12 April 1935, piloted by Cyril Uwins. Trials showed that it was significantly faster than the fighter recently ordered for the RAF, the Gloster Gladiator. Almost inevitably a military version, the Blenheim I, was ordered. This emerged as a fast light bomber, able to carry a 1,000lb (454kg) bomb load, and fitted with one fixed forward-firing Browning machine gun, and a Vickers K gun in a dorsal turret. With no need for a prototype, the first Blenheim took to the air on 25 June 1936.

A mid-wing monoplane, it was of all-metal stressed monocoque construction with the exception of the flying control surfaces, which were fabric-covered. Performance proved exceptional for the era; it was manoeuvrable and vice-free. By March 1937 the first Blenheim I light bomber squadron had formed.

A perceived need in the late 1930s was for a long range fighter, both for day and night operations. The Blenheim I, with its light wing loading, appeared to meet this requirement, and in December 1938 the Blenheim IF entered service. This differed from the light bomber in having a ventral gun pack with four Brownings, aimed via a reflector sight, and armour protection for the pilot. About 200 were converted from the bomber variant.

At the time, the Blenheim IF was potentially the best night fighter in RAF

Bristol Beaufighter IF

Origin: Bristol Aeroplane Co., England.
Type: Two-seat, twin-engined long range monoplane day and night fighter.
Engines: Two 1,500hp Bristol Hercules XI 14-cylinder radials.
Dimensions: Span 57ft 10in (17.63m); length 41ft 4in (12.60m); height 15ft 10in (4.82m); wing area 503sq.ft (46.73m^2).
Weights: Empty 14,069lb (6,382kg); normal takeoff 21,100lb (9,571kg).
Loadings (at normal takeoff weight): Wing 42lb/sq.ft (205kg/m^2); power 7.03lb (3.19kg) per hp.
Performance: Maximum speed 323mph (520kph) at 15,000ft (4,572m), 306mph (492kph) at sea level; initial climb rate 1,850ft/min (9.40m/sec); sustained climb 5min 48sec to 10,000ft (3,048m); service ceiling 28,900ft (8,808m); range 1,170 miles (1,883km).
Armament: Four under-nose-mounted 20mm drum-fed Hispano-Suiza cannon (later models belt-fed), and six .303in (7.7mm) Browning machine guns in the wings.
History: First flown by Cyril Uwins on 17 July 1939. Two weeks prior to this, an order for 300 aircraft had been placed. RAF trials commenced 2 April 1940. First production aircraft delivery 2 September 1940, and first squadron operational on 17 September. Other Beaufighters were the disappointing Merlin-powered IIF, and the thimble-nosed VIF, with AI Mk VII radar and two 1,635hp Hercules VI radials, which started to enter service at the beginning of 1942. The night fighter variants were largely replaced by Mosquitos from 1943. The last of more than 5,500 Beaufighters was retired on 12 May 1960.
Users: Australia (RAAF), Britain (RAF), New Zealand (RNZAF), USA (USAAF).

The world's first truly effective night fighter, the Beaufighter was only partly a new design. The remarkably short gestation period of just over eight months was achieved by using whole sections of the uninspiring Beaufort torpedo bomber. The outer wings, the entire rear fuselage and tail section, the landing gear and hydraulics, and the centre section were all from the Beaufort, only the latter needing minor modifications. The rest was new.

service, its performance exceeding that of the German bombers of the era, although not by much. Its main failing was the mass of transparent panels in the almost fully glazed nose, which produced myriad distracting reflections from the illuminated instruments.

The type was selected to carry the first airborne radar (AI), and operational trials began in September 1939, but success was a long time in coming. Not until the summer of 1940 was the first victory of an AI-equipped Blenheim recorded. But even before this, the lack of an adequate performance margin over German bombers had manifested itself. Many long and fruitless chases ensued.

The Blenheim IF was also used in daylight, but quickly proved vulnerable to the German fighters of the day. On 10 May 1940, six Blenheim IFs of No 600 Squadron attacked Waalhaven airfield near Rotterdam. Attacked by Bf 109s and BF 110s, all were shot down. The only real success was recorded by Dickie Haine, who claimed a Bf 109 destroyed and two Ju 52s damaged on the ground before force landing.

The Blenheim IF was followed by the IVF from 1939. Powered by two Mercury XV radials, and with a revised "long nose", this showed few advantages over its predecessor, and was effectively phased out by the end of 1942.

Above: "Built like a battleship" was the pilots' verdict on the Beaufighter IF.

The two enormous Hercules radials were set well forward of the wing leading edge to minimise vibration, but as this shifted the centre of gravity forward; the nose had to be cut back to compensate, at least in part. The pilot was seated right in the front, behind an optically flat armoured windshield. From the outset the Beaufighter was intended to carry the weight of radar and its operator without loss of performance, and the radar operator was seated under a shallow dome halfway down the fuselage. Also, as contacts at night might well prove fleeting, the Beaufighter IF carried the unprecedentedly heavy armament of four 20mm cannon and six rifle calibre machine guns, a brief burst from which could destroy a bomber in short order. At first the cannon were drum-fed, causing the radar operator to act as a powder monkey when replacing them, not the easiest task in an aeroplane in flight.

The Beaufighter was a big, strong brute of an aeroplane, with enough performance margins to catch bombers, but lacking manoeuvrability, although this mattered little at night. It was not however a good gun platform, as it wandered laterally at all speeds. No speed brakes were fitted, but the main gear could be lowered below 240mph (386kph), which slowed the aircraft as it came in behind a contact on a dark night. Gradually, experience was gained and the wayward AI Mk IV radar tamed, and victories increased. Total production of the IF was 914.

The Beaufighter IF was followed from March 1941 by the IIF. This was powered by two 1,260hp Rolls-Royce Merlin XX V-12s, but performance was disappointing, instability was worse, and only 450 were built. Next came the Beaufighter VIF, powered by two 1,635hp Hercules radials, and with a "thimble nose" housing the AI Mk VII radar, which began to enter service in 1942.

Beaufighters also served with Coastal Command and as torpedo fighters, but by 1943 the night fighter variant was being phased out in favour of the Mosquito.

British Aerospace Sea Harrier F/A 2

Origin: Hawker Siddeley Aviation, England.
Type: Single-seat, single-engined short takeoff vertical landing multi-role carrier fighter.
Engine: One Rolls-Royce Pegasus Mk 104 twin-spool vectoring nozzle unaugmented turbofan rated at 21,500lb (9,752kg) thrust.
Dimensions: Span 25ft 3in (7.70m); length 46ft 5in (14.15m); height 11ft 10in (3.61m); wing area 201sq.ft (18.67m^2).
Weights: Empty 14,050lb (6,373kg); normal takeoff 21,700lb (9,843kg); maximum 26,200lb (11,884kg).
Loadings (at normal takeoff weight): Wing 108lb/sq.ft (527kg/m^2): thrust 0.99.
Performance: Maximum speed 731mph (1,176kph) at sea level; maximum operating Mach number in dive Mach 1.25; initial climb rate c50,000ft/min (254m/sec); service ceiling c45,000ft (13,715m); interception radius 461 miles (741km).
Armament: Four AIM-120 Amraam radar-homing or two Amraam and four AIM-9M Sidewinder or Asraam heat-homing missiles. Provision for two 30mm Aden cannon in underfuselage pods. Seven hardpoints for external stores with maximum load of 8,500lb (3,856kg). A wide range of air-to-surface weapons can be carried, including Sea Eagle and Alarm.
History: The origins of the Sea Harrier date back to 21 October 1960, when the Hawker P.1127 made its first hovering flight. This evolved through the Kestrel to the Harrier close air support aircraft. The Sea Harrier FRS 1, which first flew on 20 August 1978, optimised for the fleet air defence role, saw action in the Falklands War in 1982. The F/A 2, with a much better radar and more AAMs, first flew on 19 September 1989.
Users: Britain (RN); India (FRS 51 only).

Above: Beaufighters served with Coastal Command on anti-shipping strikes.

Above: Sea Harrier FRS 1s aboard their carrier in the south Atlantic 1982.

The Cold War was at its height between 1950 and 1970, as was military aircraft technology. Tactical aircraft had become (with few exceptions) ever faster and ever heavier during this period, with increasing dependence on fixed bases with long runways, which were impossible to conceal. The advent of long and medium range ballistic missiles during this period, with and without nuclear warheads, exacerbated the problem, as did, much later, the Israeli pre-emptive strike in June 1967.

The answer appeared to be dispersed basing, which called for vertical takeoff and landing (VTOL), which would also give quick reaction. Many nations attempted to produce a VTOL aircraft in this period. There were three main approaches: the tail sitter, as pioneered by the Bachem Natter (which see) in 1945; lift jets plus a main engine; and vectored thrust.

The tail sitter posed extreme problems, both in piloting during landing, and in maintenance and servicing. Lift jets (and batteries of up to eight were used) plus a cruise engine, allowed a flat riser, which could also take off and land conventionally, but were penalised by weight and complexity, while the internal volume occupied by the lift engines would have been better used for other things.

The only VTOL aircraft to succeed in entering large-scale service was the Harrier, which used a unique combination of a large and powerful turbofan with four thrust-vectoring nozzles. These were chain-driven to swivel in unison. For vertical flight the thrust from the four nozzles had to be symmetrical, acting directly through the centre of gravity. The flow for the front nozzles was provided by an oversized fan, that for the rear from

***Below:* A Sea Harrier F/A 2 with Blue Vixen radar and AIM-120 Amraam AAMs.**

Above: Vertical landing proved the critical factor in the Falklands War.

the main engine efflux via a bifurcated duct. To achieve this, the engine had to be located centrally.

There were other problems. Conventional control surfaces were fine in wing-borne flight, but ineffective at very slow speeds or in the hover. For this, engine bleed air was fed through puffer ducts, to give zero-airspeed control in roll, yaw and pitch. These cut in when thrust vectoring was selected, but had to be linked to the flight control system.

The next problem was where to put the landing gear. With the nozzles situated on the fuselage sides, the wing had to be shoulder-mounted, which ruled out most orthodox locations. The solution eventually adopted was a bicycle main gear on the centreline, with castoring outriggers on the wingtips. It was forecast that these would give trouble. Finally, in the early days, with only one engine available, the excess of thrust over weight was marginal.

When it first appeared the prototype, the P.1127, was tiny. It could hardly have been otherwise. Designing an airframe which would allow an adequate margin of thrust over weight was far from easy. Starting with tethered hover trials, it first left the ground on 21 October 1960, piloted by Bill Bedford. The next step was the Kestrel, which flew on 7 March 1964, then the larger, more powerful Harrier for the RAF, which had meanwhile gone from VTOL to STOVL (short takeoff, vertical landing).

The retirement of the large aircraft

carriers of the Royal Navy had left the service without organic air power, but help was at hand in the form of what was known as through-deck cruisers, nominally helicopter carriers. The next step was the Sea Harrier, but this was not done without opposition. The intakes, sized for thrust at low airspeeds, ruled out supersonic flight, and a subsonic fighter was anathema to many. It was also range-limited. But at the end of the day it was the Sea Harrier or nothing.

It was navalised against corrosion, fitted with the Blue Fox air interception pulse radar, and armed with two (later four) Sidewinders. Externally, the main change was a raised cockpit to improve all-round vision, and to increase cockpit display area.

First flight of the Sea Harrier FRS 1 took place on 20 August 1978, and it entered service shortly after. But whereas its main function was expected to be intercepting Russian Tu-20 bombers far out over the North Atlantic, the Sea Harrier found itself embroiled with supersonic Argentinean Mirages and Daggers over the South Atlantic in 1982. Quickly establishing an ascendancy over its theoretically superior opponents, the subsonic wonder claimed a remarkable final score of 23 to nil.

The Falklands War exposed certain limitations in the FRS 1. The Blue Fox radar was inadequate, Sidewinders were too short-ranged at low level, while too few were carried. These points were corrected on the F/A 2, which first flew on 19 September 1989. It carried the multi-mode Blue Vixen pulse-Doppler radar, and provision for up to six AAMs, including the medium-range radar-homing AIM-120 Amraam. In total, 29 FRS 1s were upgraded to F/A 2 standard, plus 18 new-build aircraft.

Right: The Sea Harrier was the first aircraft to use ski-jump takeoffs.

BAe/McDonnell Douglas AV-8B Harrier II Plus

Origin: British Aerospace (UK) and McDonnell Douglas (USA).
Type: Single-seat, single-engined short takeoff vertical landing multi-role carrier- and land-based fighter.
Engine: One Pratt & Whitney F400-RR-408 twin-spool vectoring nozzle unaugmented turbofan rated at 23,800lb (10,769kg) thrust.
Dimensions: Span 30ft 4in (9.25m); length 47ft 9in (14.55m); height 11ft 8in (3.56m); wing area 230sq.ft (21.37m²).
Weights: Empty 14,867lb (6,744kg); normal takeoff c23,650lb (10,728kg); maximum takeoff 31,000lb (14,062kg).
Loadings (at normal takeoff weight): Wing 103lb/sq.ft (502kg/m²); thrust 1.01.
Performance: Maximum speed 674mph (1,083kph) at sea level, 600mph at 36,000ft (10,972m); initial climb rate c50,000ft/min (254m/sec); service ceiling c45,000ft (13,715m); endurance two hours at 115 miles (185km) radius with six AAMs and two drop tanks.
Armament: One 25mm GAU-12 cannon with 300 rounds; six AIM-120 Amraam and two AIM-9 Sidewinders, plus a wide range of air-to-surface munitions.
History: Derived from the British Harrier (see previous entry), and adopted by the US Marine Corps, initially as the AV-8A, then as the AV-8B close air support aircraft. The USMC still lacked a STOVL air combat fighter to cover its close air support operations. Consequently the Harrier II was given a multi-mode radar, glass cockpit, HOTAS, and a bagful of missiles to become the AV-

Above: The APG-65 multi-mode radar made the Harrier II Plus a true fighter.

8B Harrier II Plus. Service entry 1993.
Users: Italy, Spain, USA (USMC).

The US Marine Corps has always had a requirement for organic air cover for amphibious operations. This comes in two parts: quick reaction from ships close offshore, with the ability to move to semi-prepared land bases at the earliest opportunity. The USMC operated fast jets from USN carriers, but these were unable to comply with either condition. The Harrier, with its ability to operate initially from Marine commando assault ships, then from inland areas little larger than a tennis court, looked like the solution. At the Farnborough Air Show of September 1968, three USMC officers presented themselves at the Hawker Siddeley (as it then was) chalet, and asked to fly the Harrier. The rest is history!

McDonnell Douglas acquired a licence to build the Harrier as the AV-8A, which varied from the GR 3 in having a different nav/attack system, a Stencel ejection seat, and various other items of American equipment, including radios and IFF.

The next step was to improve payload/range performance, which resulted in the AV-8B Harrier II. The first full-scale development AV-8B flew on 15 November 1981. It differed from the AV-8A in having a raised canopy for better all-round visibility, and a completely redesigned wing with a greater span and increased area. This had leading edge root extensions, an increased thickness/chord ratio and huge double-slotted flaps, while the outriggers were moved inboard. Other devices were used to improve handling in the hover, which on the AV-8A had been a bit twitchy. Construction was largely of composite materials, including the entire wing, and the flight control system was fibre optic "fly-by-light", a world first. The AV-8B demonstrated the ability to carry twice the load for the same distance, or the same load for twice the distance.

While the AV-8B was excellent in the quick-reaction, close air support/battlefield air interdiction roles, its self defence capability was marginal, with just two Sidewinders and a cannon. In-house air defence was an obvious need, and to meet this a dedicated fighter was proposed: the AV-8B Harrier II Plus. This was given the APG-65 multi-mode radar as used by the Hornet, in a slightly bulged radome, and six to eight AIMs, some of which were beyond visual range weapons. The new aircraft was basically for defensive use, so the lack of supersonic speed was of less importance than it might otherwise have been. The USMC has 27 new-build aircraft, with 72 AV-8B being rebuilt to Plus standard; the Italian Navy ordered 16 aircraft, and the Spanish Navy, which had previously flown the EAV-8S as the Matador, a further eight.

Chengdu F-7MG

Origin: MiG OKB, Russia/Chengdu Aircraft Factory, China.
Type: Single-seat, single-engined limited all-weather jet fighter.
Engine: One Liyang WP-13F twin spool afterburning turbojet rated at 14,550lb (6,600kg) maximum and 9,920lb (7,540kg) military thrust.
Dimensions: Span 27ft 2.5in (8.32m); length 48ft 10in (14.885m); height 13ft 5.5in (4.10m); wing area 268sq.ft (24.88m^2).
Weights: Empty 11,667lb (5,292kg); normal takeoff 16,623lb (7,540kg); maximum takeoff 20,062lb (9,100kg).
Loadings (at normal takeoff weight)**:** Wing 62lb/sq.ft (303kg/m^2); thrust 0.88.
Performance: Maximum speed Mach 2.0 at altitude; 746mph (1,200kph) at sea level; initial climb rate 38,388ft/min (195m/sec); service ceiling 59,710ft (18,200m); operational radius 528 miles (850km).
Armament: Two 30mm Type 30-1 cannon with 60 rounds; four AIM-9P, R550 Magic, or PL-7 or PL-8 (Python 3) heat-homing AAMs. Usual range of "dumb" air-to-surface ordnance.
History: Originally developed from the MiG-21F-13, the J-7/F-7 series of fighters has been a continuous process of improvement. First flown 17 January 1966; development continuing into the 21st century. Total production believed to be about 1,000.
Users (all versions)**:** Albania, Bangladesh, China, Egypt, Iran, Iraq, Myanmar, Pakistan, Sri Lanka, Sudan, Tanzania, Zimbabwe.

Lacking advanced aerospace capability, China had for many years been reliant on licence-building and, in some cases, pirating Russian fighter designs. This process continued with the MiG-21, licence negotiations for which began in the early 1960s.

Above: The Harrier II Plus was the first fighter to "fly-by-light".

Above: The F-7M Airguard was the Chinese export version of the MiG-21.

Agreement was concluded, and work on the MiG-21F-13, the first variant to have missile armament, began in 1964. In Chinese service it became the Jianjiji-7 I (J-7 I, or F-7A for export versions). First flight took place on 17 January 1966.

A small tailed delta, the J-7 was, like its Russian forebear, simple in concept and construction, and perhaps the easiest of all supersonic fighters to fly, although like all Russian designs of the period it was very heavy on the controls. While this was a disadvantage for small-built Chinese pilots, who in the Korean War a decade or so earlier had had problems in flying the MiG-15, it at least made it difficult for them to overstress the airframe.

Co-operation with the Soviet Union ceased at an early stage. The Russians have long been notorious for screwing the last ounce of capability from a proven design, but the Chinese, left to their own devices with the J-7, far surpassed them. New variants are still appearing in the 21st century, long after the Russians ceased production of the MiG- 21. However, the Chinese do appear to have had problems; several later proposals have never come to fruition.

The J-7 I was followed by the J-7 II (F-7B). First flown on 30 December 1978, this differed from the J-7 I in having an aft-hinged cockpit canopy instead of the previous front-hinged type, a fully variable shock cone in the pitot intake, twin 30mm cannon, the more powerful WP-7B turbojet, and provision for a drop tank on the centreline. As an alternative to the Chinese PL-2 AAMs, it was compatible with French R550 Magic missiles.

An export version specifically for Sri Lanka was the F-7BS. This had four underwing missile pylons, and was reportedly powered by the WP-7C, rated at 13,625lb (6,180kg) maximum and 9,590lb (4,350kg) military thrust.

The J-7 II was followed rather more than five years later by the J-7 III, which first flew on 26 April 1984. The first J-7 to have more than a very limited all-weather capability, it had an advanced weapons control system, including the indigenous JL-7 radar, and various other avionic systems including IFF, RWR and ECM. Other changes were a head-up display and the HTY-4 ejection seat. The canopy was side-hinged. Powered by the WP-13 turbojet, it also featured blown flaps and increased internal fuel to improve range. Normal weaponry consisted of two heat-homing PL-7 AAMs, and a 23mm twin-barrel Type 23-3 cannon.

Several export variants appeared from about this time under the generic name of Airguard. Little is known about the F-7L, which does not appear to have found favour on the export market, but the F-7M Airguard was more successful. Completely modernized, this was fitted with mainly Western avionics, including the GEC-Marconi Skyranger multi-mode radar. A wide range of weaponry options increased its attraction for overseas air forces. The F-7P, often called the Skybolt, was produced specifically for the Pakistan Air Force. This was fitted with the Italian FIAR Grifo multi-mode radar, with four Sidewinder AAMs as main armament. The F-7MP is a much upgraded Skybolt, with improved avionics and cockpit layout.

The J-7E, which appeared in 1990, was a major departure, in that the wing shape was revised with a shallow reverse sweep outboard. Span and area were increased, the leading edge sweep was cranked from 57deg inboard to 42deg outboard, and with the trailing edge modified. It was powered by a Liming WP-7F turbofan rated at 14,330lb (6,500kg) maximum and 9,920lb (4,500kg) military thrust.

First flown in 1993, the J-7MG is very similar to the J-7E. It is fitted with the

Above: The F-7MG carries a wide variety of ordnance, as can be seen here.

GEC-Marconi Super Skyranger radar, and manoeuvre flaps on the wing leading and trailing edges. Armament consists of two 30mm cannon with 126 rounds each, and four AIM-9P, R550 or PL-7 AAMs. It remained in production in 2001.

The pitot nose intake proved eventually to be the weakest point of the basic MiG-21 design, since the radar had to be shoehorned into the shock cone. This limited its antenna size and, with it, its capability. An attempt to correct this was made with the Super-7, with a full-scale radar nose and side inlets. Overall dimensions were rather larger than the J-7 III. Plans to fit it with US avionics fell through in the wake of the Tiananman Square massacre, and development ceased before first flight.

The Super-7 was superseded by the FC-1, a tailed delta with an uncranked leading edge, a "solid" radar nose and cheek inlets, with the horizontal tail surfaces moun-ted on F-16-like shelves. Scheduled to fly in 2001, it reportedly has suffered from Western embargoes on avion-ics systems, and disagreement with Pakistan, the joint developer.

The latest variant is the F-7MF, developed as insurance against the failure of the FC-1. It has a radar nose coupled with a chin intake as tested by the J-7FS in 1998, and a similar wing to the F-7MG. Two small canard surfaces are placed forward of the wing but behind the cockpit. First flight was scheduled for 2001.

Right: The F-7MG is unmistakeably derived from the Russian-designed MiG-21.

Chengdu J-10

Origin: Chengdu Aircraft Factory, China.
Type: Single-seat, single-engined all-weather multi-role fighter.
Engine: One Klimov RD-93 afterburning turbofan rated at 17,985lb (8,158kg) maximum thrust, to be licence-built by Liyang.
Dimensions: Not available, but probably similar to those of the F-16C, apart from wing area, approximately 50 per cent greater.
Weights: Not available, but probably similar to those of the F-16C.
Loadings: Not available.
Performance (all speculative): Maximum speed Mach 1.8 at altitude; initial climb rate 50,000ft/min (254m/sec); service ceiling 55,000ft (16,763m); range 1,000 miles (1,609km).
Armament: One 23mm twin-barrel cannon; typically six or eight AAMs – PL-8 (Python 3), PL-9, PL-10, PL-11, possibly Vympel R-73 and R-77.
History: Design work begun in the early 1980s, with Israeli involvement. First flight March 1998. Service entry unlikely before 2008 at the earliest.
User: China, prototypes only at 2001.

Traditional Chinese secrecy has ensured that the J-10 remains shrouded in mystery, even though it first flew on 24 March 1998, piloted by Li Chen. Two brief glimpses have been afforded by poor quality pictures on the internet, but these were quickly removed, leaving the West with little more than guesswork plus satellite photographs dating back to 1994, to work on.

All that is certain is that the J-10 bears a distinct resemblance to the long-defunct Iraeli Lavi, although Israel denies involvement with the Chinese fighter. It is a tail-less canard delta with a chin inlet and twin canted ventral fins, and is

Above: The Chengdu J-10 is derived from the Israeli Lavi, seen here.

believed to be slightly larger than the Israeli fighter.

The J-10 is not the first attempt at producing a canard delta. The J-9 of lat 1960s vintage was an interceptor with a design maximum speed of Mach 2. Designed initially by Shenyang, development was transferred to Chengdu 1969, but succumbed to lack of interest. A canard delta without relaxed stabili and fly-by-wire, it would have been more comparable with the Saab JA.3 Viggen than the latest generation of European fighters.

Work began on the J-10 as an air superiority fighter in the early 1980 Initially it was intended to counter the Russian MiG-29 and Su-27, but it ha since become a multi-role aircraft. The canards are close-coupled and located the rear of the cockpit and above the wing, which is expected to feature variab camber. The powerplant is the Klimov RD-93, developed from the RD-33. It ha been suggested that production aircraft might be fitted with the indigenou Wopen WP15, rated at 26,700lb (12,111kg), but this engine is still und

Convair F2Y-1 Sea Dart

Origins: Consolidated Aircraft Co., USA.
Type: Single-seat, single-engined water-based jet fighter.
Engines: Two Westinghouse J46-WE-2 afterburning turbojets, rated at 6,100lb (2,767kg) maximum thrust.
Dimensions: Span 33ft 8in (10.26m); length 52ft 7in (16.03m); height 20ft 9i (6.32m); wing area 563sq.ft (52.30m²).
Weights: Empty 12,652lb (5,739kg); normal loaded 16,527lb (7,497kg).
Loadings (at normal loaded weight)**:** Wing 29lb/sq.ft (143kg/m²); thrust 0.74.
Performance (all projected)**:** Maximum speed Mach 1.25/825mph (1,328kph) at 36,000ft (10,972m); sustained climb 1min 42sec to 35,000ft (10,667m); service ceiling and range not available.

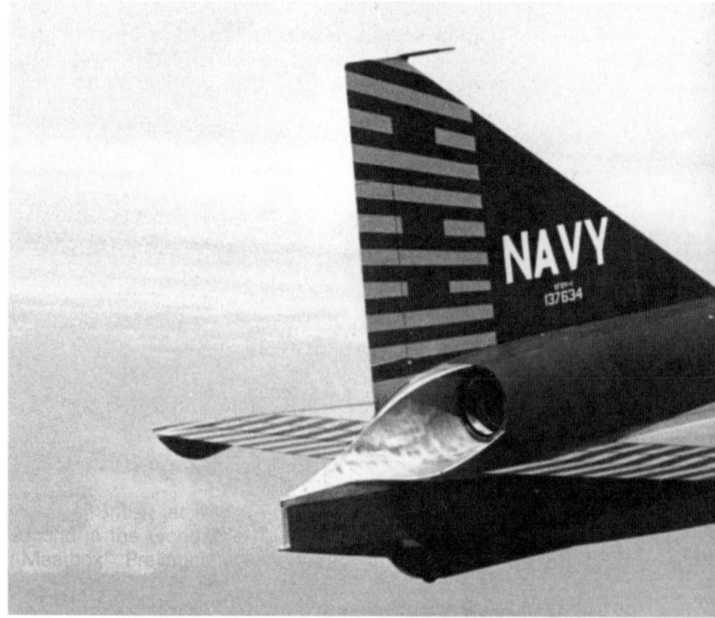

development, making its use unlikely. Construction is believed to incorporate a fair degree of composite material. Up to six prototypes had flown by 2001. At least one has crashed, reportedly due to problems with the digital fly-by-wire flight control system.

There are three contenders to supply the radar: the Russian Phazotron Zhemchug, with a reported maximum range of 98 miles (157km) and 10-target tracking; the Israeli Elta El/M-2035 as developed for Lavi but with a larger antenna; or the indigenous JL-10A, of which no details are available.

The cockpit has three head-down and one head-up multi-function displays, and will also have provision for a helmet-mounted sight. If Lavi influence has prevailed, the J-10 will have a central control column, and a not too steeply raked ejection seat.

Rumours persist that up to 300 J-10s could be produced for the Chinese Air Force. Future upgrades may include phased array radar, and a thrust vectoring nozzle.

Armament: Never finalised.
History: Taxi tests from 16 December 1952; first flight 9 April 1953; project abandoned 1956.
User (projected)**:** USA (Navy or possibly Marine Corps).

Probably the best thing that can be said about the Sea Dart is that it seemed like a good idea at the time. Floatplane fighters had been used in the island-hopping war in the Pacific, and in 1950 the US Navy was still interested in the concept.

Below: The F2Y-1 Sea Dart was the only transonic water-based fighter to fly.

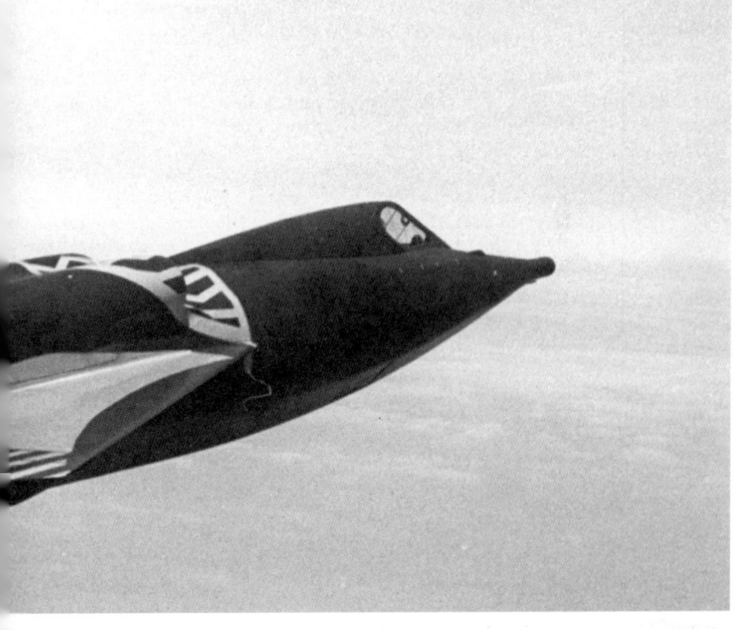

Convair had become enamoured of the tail-less delta layout for high performance fighters, and on June 1948, had flown the XF-92A experimental prototype. Now they began work on a water-borne aircraft, the F2Y Sea Dart. The main problem was how best to achieve supersonic speed and performance to match contemporary land-based fighters. Instead of bulky and draggy floats, Convair used retractable hydroskis to lift the aircraft out of the water prior to takeoff. To avoid water ingestion, twin engines were mounted high on the fuselage hull, fed by dorsal intakes above, and slightly back from, the wing roots. In 1952, when the Sea Dart first appeared, it looked tremendously futuristic, and its first takeoff, in the hands of Sam Shannon, was spectacular, with spray everywhere.

While the J46 was the engine of choice, it was unreliable, and the first prototype was powered by much less powerful J34s. This aircraft suffered from severe vibration from the twin hydroskis, although in the air it handled well. One of the advantages of hydroskis was that they allowed the aircraft to leave the water and taxi ashore.

Convair XFY-1

Origin: Consolidated Aircraft Co., USA.
Type: Single-seat, single-turboprop-engined tail-sitter VTOL fighter.
Engine (projected)**:** One Allison YT40-A-16 turboprop rated at 7,500shp (5,595kW), driving a 16ft (4.88m diameter) eight-bladed contra-rotating propeller,
Dimensions: Span 27ft 7.75in (8.43m); length (in horizontal flight) 34ft 11.75in (10.66m); vertical span 22ft 11in (6.98m); wing area 355sq.ft (32.98m^2).
Weights: Empty 11,742lb (5,327kg), normal takeoff 16,250lb (7,371kg).
Loadings (at normal takeoff weight)**:** Wing 46lb/sq.ft (223kg/m^2); power 2.17lb (0.98kg) per shp.
Performance (projected)**:** Maximum speed 610mph (982kph) at 15,000ft (4,572m); sustained climb 4min 36sec to 30,000ft (9,144m); service ceiling and range n/a.
Armament (projected)**:** Four 20mm cannon in wingtip pods, or two pods each with 24 2.75in (70mm) unguided rockets.
History: Three prototypes ordered March 1951. First vertical takeoff and landing (tethered) 1 August 1954. First transition from vertical to wingborne flight 2 November 1954. Programme terminated in 1956.
Users (projected)**:** USA (Navy).

For direct vertical takeoff, there were two choices. The first was to use a conventional jet engine to shift a small mass airflow downwards very quickly. The second was to use a turboprop to move a large mass airflow downwards relatively slowly. The latter solution eliminated the problems of ground erosion or deck heating attendant on the former, and was selected by the US Navy to explore the possibilities of providing limited air cover from small ships.

Three prototypes of the Convair XFY-1, unofficially known as the Pogo, were ordered, of which one was a static test vehicle. A tail-sitter, it had a large delta wing and almost equally large vertical tail surfaces, one dorsal, the other ventral. The landing gear consisted of four small castoring wheels on the trailing edges of wings and tails. In an emergency, such as engine failure, the ventral tail surface could be jettisoned, allowing a horizontal belly landing to be made.

On 2 November 1954, "Skeets" Coleman made the world's first VTOL fighter sortie, which sandwiched 20 minutes of conventional flight between a vertical takeoff and landing, a feat for which he was awarded the Harmon Trophy. The definitive engine never did materialise; the less powerful XT40-A-6, with a six-bladed contraprop, was used during trials.

A tail-sitter was always going to be taxing for the pilot, despite having a seat

The second Sea Dart was fitted with J46s and a single hydroski. While it demonstrated flight performance to match many land-based fighters of the day, one thing not easily overcome was the inherent shortcomings of the tail-less delta configuration. These made for much higher takeoff and landing speeds than might otherwise have been the case. For example, even with afterburning, the takeoff run was some 5,500ft (1,676m). The second prototype Sea Dart went supersonic on 3 August 1954, exceeding Mach 1 in a shallow dive at about 34,000ft (10,363m), but in the following November the same aircraft broke up during an air display at San Diego, killing the pilot.

The power output of the J46 failed to match predictions, and consequently so did aircraft performance, with maximum speed projected to be Mach 0.99. Low-rate testing continued until 1956, when the programme was finally abandoned. Convair continued design work on a variant powered by a single large engine; either the Pratt & Whitney J75 or the Wright J67, but this came to nought. The water-borne fighter concept was finally abandoned.

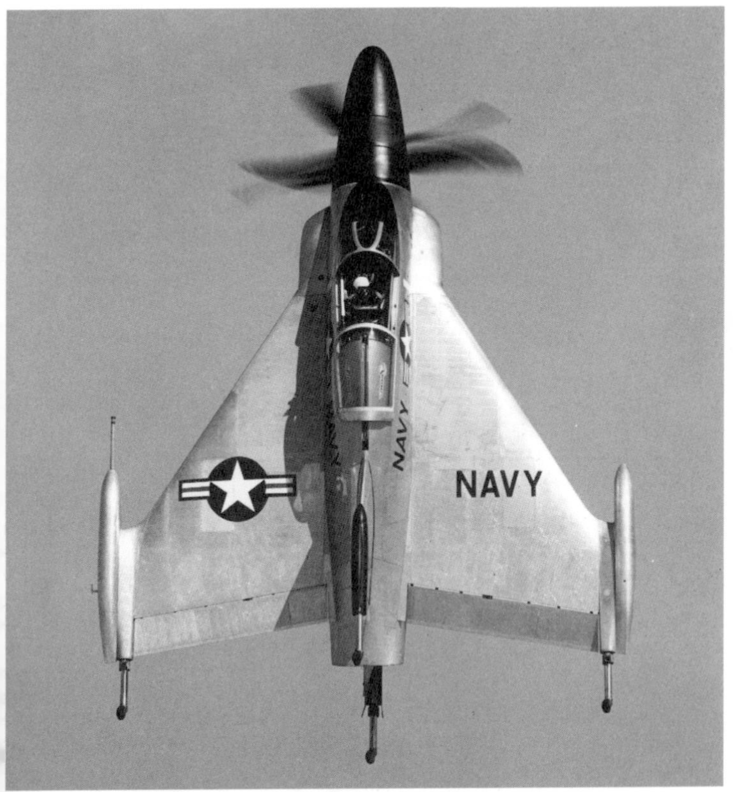

Above: Landing the XFY-1 was too demanding for the average squadron pilot.

that could rotate forward 45deg for vertical flight. After some 40 hours of flight time, the project was abandoned, only one prototype having flown.

Convair F-102 Delta Dagger

Origin: Consolidated Aircraft Co., USA.
Type: Single-seat, single-engined supersonic semi-automatic interceptor.
Engine: One Pratt & Whitney J57-P-23 two spool afterburning turbojet rated at 17,200lb (5,307kg) maximum and 11,700lb (5,307kg) military thrust.
Dimensions: Span 38ft 1.5in (11.60m); length 68ft 4.67in (20.83m); height 21ft 2.5in (6.45m); wing area 697.8sq.ft (64.83m²).
Weights: Empty 19,050lb (8,641kg); normal takeoff 27,765lb (12,594kg); maximum 31,500lb (14,288kg).
Loadings (at normal takeoff weight)**:** Wing 40lb/sq.ft (196kg/m²); thrust 0.62.
Performance: Maximum speed Mach 1.25 at 40,000ft (12,191m); initial climb rate 13,000ft/min (66m/sec); service ceiling 54,000ft (16,458m); range (with external tanks) 1,350 miles (2,172km).
Armament: 24 Mighty Mouse 2.75in (70mm) folding-fin unguided rockets in the weapons bay doors; six AIM-4 Falcon AAMs, three radar guided, three heat homing in an internal bay; later two AIM-26B Nuclear Falcons or one AIM-26B and three AIM-4s.
History: First flight YF-102 24 October 1953, but problems led to a major redesign. First flight YF-102A 20 December 1954. First service deliveries June 1955; operational mid-1956. Production ceased April 1958 after 875 aircraft built.
Users: Greece, Turkey, USA (USAF and ANG).

Widely known as the Deuce, the F-102A Delta Dagger set a whole hatful of firsts. It was the first tail-less delta fighter to enter production, the first supersonic all-weather interceptor, the first fighter to dispense with guns and carry an all-missile armament, the first fighter to carry AAMs in an internal bay, and the first fighter to feature a semi-automatic interception system. For its day, it was the most advanced interceptor in the world.

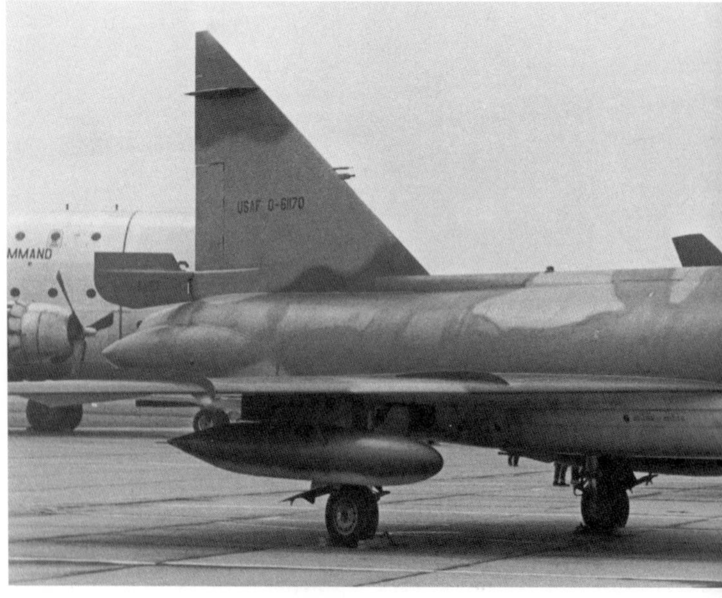

Previous Convair designs, notably the XF-92A and the Sea Dart had used the tail-less delta configuration. The F-102, its fuselage packed with the J57 engine, an internal weapons bay, and the black boxes for the collision course interception system, had no volume available for fuel. The delta wing solved this problem. It allowed relative depth for a low thickness/chord ratio, combined with a light but rigid structure, and the internal fuel load of the Deuce was housed within it. The other advantage was a large wing area for low wing loading.

When first flown by Dick Johnson on 24 October 1953, all was not well with the YF-102. Not only did handling leave much to be desired, it was firmly subsonic! Redesign was commenced, starting with conical camber on the wing leading edge, and a sharp-edged V-shaped windshield, but the solution was found with the newly discovered Area Rule. Briefly, this stated that a plot of cross-sectional area from nose to tail should be a smooth curve.

The fuselage length was extended by nearly 16ft (4.88m), making the Deuce almost as long as a World War II Lancaster bomber; the triangular fin was made taller, and large fairings, officially called Yellow Canary, but often referred to as Marilyn Monroe, were added to the rear fuselage. On 21 December 1954, the YF-102A reached Mach 1.2 quite comfortably.

The first Deuce unit was the 327th Fighter Interceptor Squadron, which became operational in mid-1956. Another two dozen squadrons followed over the next 18 months. The definitive fire control system was the Hughes MG-3. At interception, the pilot flew with his head in the radar viewing hood, with one hand on the control column and the other on the radar control stick.

The Deuce saw little action, although one was lost to a MiG over Vietnam, while there were rumours of an encounter between Greek and Turkish F-102s over Cyprus in 1974. In USAF service it was superseded by the F-106 Delta Dart.

Below: Bulged fairings on the rear fuselage identify this as an F-102A.

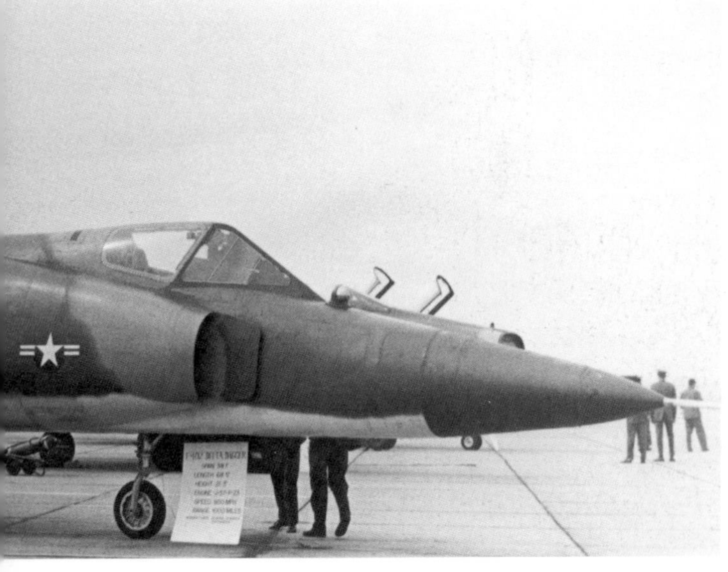

Convair F-106 Delta Dart

Origin: Consolidated Aircraft Co., USA.
Type: Single-seat, single-engined Mach 2 semi-automatic interceptor.
Engine: One Pratt & Whitney J75-P-17 two spool afterburning turbojet rated at 24,500lb (11,113kg) maximum and 17,200lb (7,802kg) military thrust.
Dimensions: Span 38ft 3.5in (11.67m); length 70ft 8.75in (21.55m); height 20ft 3.67in (6.18m); wing area 697.8sq.ft (64.83m²).
Weights: Empty 24,315lb (11,029kg); normal takeoff 35,500lb (16,103kg); maximum 39,915lb (17,779kg).
Loadings (at normal takeoff weight)**:** Wing 51lb/sq.ft (248kg/m²); thrust 0.69.
Performance: Maximum speed Mach 2.01 at altitude; initial climb rate 42,800ft/min (217m/sec); service ceiling 57,000ft (17,373m); combat radius (clean) 575 miles (925km).
Armament: Two AIR-2 Genie AAMs with nuclear warheads an four AIM-4 Falcons in an internal weapons bay.
History: First projected as the F-102B, first flight took place on 26 December 1956. Initial operational capability October 1960. Supplanted the Deuce with Air Defense Command, but was eventually replaced by the F-15. Production ceased in July 1961, with 277 F-106As and 63 F-106Bs, a combat-capable two-seat trainer. Finally retired from the Air National Guard in 1988.
Users: USA (USAF and ANG).

The "Six", as it was known, was a logical development of the Delta Dagger. Externally it looked very similar, but the designers had learned from the tribulations of the earlier aircraft. The main differences were the fin, which was broad chord and flat-topped, a redesigned fuselage which did away with the "Marilyn Monroe" fairings, and inlets set well back behind the cockpit.

Beneath the skin it was however a very different bird. The Pratt & Whitney J75 was much more powerful, and the thickness/chord ratio reduced to five percent, which was reflected in the performance figures. A longer fuselage

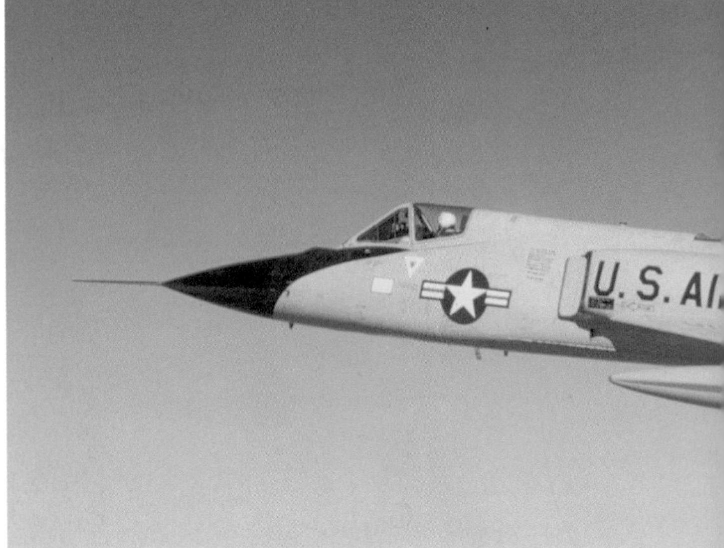

allowed a greater volume of internal fuel to be carried. With external tanks, operational radius increased to 729 miles (1,173km).

The Hughes MA-1 fire control system had by now reached maturity, which is to say that it worked well some of the time. The tie-in to the Semi-Automatic Ground Environment System (SAGE), now included the autopilot, and the early stages of an interception could now be controlled from the ground. In effect this made the pilot a systems manager, responsible for takeoff and landing; tactical decisions, and monitoring fuel state, while the Delta Dart flew a fully automated interception.

The Six was pleasant to fly, and like most deltas had no clearly defined point of stall. On landing approach, the angle of attack could be increased until it was in a full stall, in which case it continued to sink, without any tendency to drop a wing, until the nose was lowered just before touchdown. The power of the J75 meant that it was unlikely to get on the back side of the drag curve, while the low wing loading made it highly manoeuvrable in the thin air at altitude.

One of the more advanced gadgets was a tactical display indicator (TDI), low on the centre of the instrument panel. Linked to the radar, in combat this showed two little moving bugs; one representing the Six; the other its opponent. Working on film strips, the TDI at need also showed terrain, landmarks, airfields, and navigation data.

The Six had a shared fault with the Delta Dagger. While the V-shaped windshield reduced drag, it produced all sorts of annoying reflections from the cockpit instruments. This was in part reduced by a thin black shield on the centreline, but this was never very satisfactory.

The Six remained the mainstay of Continental Air Defence for two decades, until it was finally replaced by the F-15 Eagle and, to a lesser degree, a variant of the F-16 Fighting Falcon.

Below: A semi-autonomous interceptor, the F-106 replaced the F-102 from 1960.

Curtiss F9C-2 Sparrowhawk

Origin: Curtiss Aeroplane and Motor Co., USA.
Type: Single-seat, single-engined parasite fighter biplane.
Engine: One 438hp Wright R-975-E3 9-cylinder radial.
Dimensions: Span 25ft 5in (7.75m); length 20ft 7in (6.27m); height 10ft 11.5in (3.34m); wing area 173sq.ft ($16.07m^2$).
Weights: Empty 2,089lb (947kg); normal takeoff 2,770lb (1,256kg).
Loadings (at normal takeoff weight)**:** Wing 16.lb/sq.ft ($78kg/m^2$); power 6.32lb (2.87kg) per hp.
Performance: Maximum speed 176mph (284kph) at 4,000ft (1,219m); initial climb rate 1,700ft/min (8.63m/sec); service ceiling 19,200ft (5,952m); range 350 miles (563km).
Armament: Two 0.30in (7.62mm) Browning machine guns.
History: First flown as the XF9C-1 on 12 February 1931. Selected as parasite fighter for USN airships as F9C-2; first flight 14 April 1932. Only eight Sparrowhawks built. Retired from service 1936-37.
User: USA (Navy).

Airships had outstanding range and endurance, and were vulnerable to attack. The answer was of course parasite fighters, and the USN airships *Akron* and *Macon* were designed to have internal hangars large enough to house four small aircraft, which would be launched and recovered on a trapeze. The Curtiss F9C-2 Sparrowhawk was modified for the task. It was given a gullwing upper plane, and a hook, and the undercarriage and tail surfaces were also modified. Successful trials were held with the *Los Anqeles*, and the first hookup (to

Curtiss Hawk 75A-4

Origin: Curtiss Aeroplane and Motor Co., USA.
Type: Single-seat, single-engined monoplane fighter.
Engine: One 1,200hp Wright Cyclone R-1820-87 14-cylinder radial.
Dimensions: Span 37ft 4in (11.38m); length 28ft 10in (8.79m); height 9ft 6in (2.89m); wing area 236sq.ft ($21.92m^2$).
Weights: Empty 4,541lb (2,060kg); normal takeoff 5,750lb (2,608kg); maximum 6,662lb (3,022kg).
Loadings (at normal takeoff weight)**:** Wing 24.36lb/sq.ft ($119kg/m^2$); power 4.79lb (2.17kg) per hp.
Performance: Maximum speed 323mph (520kph) at 15,100ft (4,602m); sustained climb rate 4min 54sec to 15,000ft (4,572m); service ceiling 32,700ft (9,966m); maximum range 603 miles (970km).
Armament: Six 0.303in (7.7mm) Browning machine guns, two in the nose and four in the wings.
History: The Hawk 75 series, which included the RAF Mohawk, was developed from the Curtiss Model 75, which first flew on 15 May 1935. It was selected for the USAAC as the P-36A, of which 210 were ordered. More than 550 export Hawk 75s were produced, and were widely used in action by France and Britain, remaining in front line service with the latter country until January 1944.
Users: Argentina, Britain (RAF), China, Finland, France, Holland, Iran, Norway, Peru, Portugal, South Africa, Thailand, USA (USAAC).

The Curtiss Model 75 was designed by Donovan R. Berlin to participate in a USAAC fighter competition which was scheduled to commence on 27 May

***Above:* The Sparrowhawk was adapted as a parasite fighter to protect airships.**

Akron) was accomplished on 29 June 1932. This was aided-by means of an arm which swung down to steady the Sparrowhawk before it was hoisted into the hangar bay. But the loss of *Akron* in 1933, followed by *Macon* two years later, brought the airship/parasite fighter programme to an untimely end.

***Above:* The pleasant-handling curtiss P-36C lacked altitude performance.**

1935. An all-metal monoplane with a multi-spar wing and a monocoque fuselage, it first flew on 15 May 1935, just eight months after design work was commenced.

Initially it was powered by a 900hp Wright XR-1670-5 two-row radial engine with 14 cylinders, but this proved unreliable. This was replaced by a 700hp Pratt

& Whitney R-1535 Twin Wasp Junior, which also proved troublesome. Finally the aircraft it was fitted with a 950hp 9-cylinder Wright XR-1820-39 Cyclone, to become the Model 75B. In the competition, it came second to Seversky's SEV-1XP, which entered service as the P-35. This notwithstanding, the Model 75B showed promise, and on 7 August 1936, three evaluation aircraft were ordered, powered by 900hp Pratt & Whitney Twin Wasp radials, as the Y1P-36.

Further trials were successful, and on 7 July 1937 an order was placed for 210 aircraft as the P-36A, the first of which was delivered on 20 April 1938. The engine was standardised as the -17. Rearward vision had proved inadequate, and glazed tunnels aft of the cockpit were introduced, although these can have made little difference. A single machine was temporarily fitted with the 1,100hp R-1830-25 to become the sole example of the P-36B.

Initially armament consisted of one 0.50in (12.7mm) and one 0.30in (7.62mm) machine guns, but weight of fire was demonstrably inadequate. Two more 0.30in (7.62mm) machine guns were mounted in the wings to produce the P-36C. Experiments were made with even heavier armament, including two 23mm Madsen cannon mounted underwing, but these reduced performance and agility.

With an eye on the export market, Curtiss then introduced the Hawk 75, which had a fixed spatted main gear rather than the standard retractable item. Armament on these variants differed according to customer requirements. For example, Hawk 75-Os for Argentina carried four 0.30in (7.62mm) machine guns, while Hawk 75-Ns for Thailand were armed with two underwing Madsen

cannon and two fuselage-mounted rifle calibre machine guns.

Performance naturally suffered, due to the extra drag of the fixed main gear. Compared to the P-36C, maximum speed was about 10 per cent less, while climb rate and range were far worse. China was another customer for the Hawk 75-M, but a follow-up order was cancelled in favour of Hawk 75A.

Hawk 75A was the export version of the P-36 with retractable main gears. The first customer was France, which ordered 100 Hawk 75A-1s in May 1938. This model was fitted with two wing-mounted and two nose-mounted 7.5mm FN machine guns, and was powered by the 950hp Pratt & Whitney R-1830 Twin Wasp. Delivery was complete by April 1939, and a batch of 100 Hawk 75A-2s was ordered, the majority of which had two extra wing guns and the more powerful Twin Wasp rated at 1,050hp. Delivery was complete by July 1939, and was followed by 135 Hawk 75A-3s, with the 1,200hp Twin Wasp.

The stage was set for the combat debut of the Hawk. It was not long in coming. On 8 September 1939, four Bf 109Es encountered five Hawk 75As of GC II/4. One of the German victims was Werner Mölders, Condor Legion top scorer in the Spanish Civil War, who force-landed with a shot-up engine.

A notable encounter took place on 6 November 1939, when Hannes Gentzen, the Luftwaffe top scorer in Poland, led his whole *Gruppe* of Bf 109Ds down onto nine Hawk 75s of GC II/5. The German pilots had height, position, and a 3:1 advantage in numbers, but they lost. In the course of a frenzied

Below: Dutch Hawk 75s were outclassed by Japanese fighters in the Far East.

dogfight, four Bf 109s were destroyed; four more force-landed. The sole French casualty belly-landed, the pilot unhurt. In fact, two thirds of all French air combat victories up to 25 May 1940 were scored by Hawk units. This was a remarkable result, given that the Bf 109 went on to become one of the all time great fighters in World War II, while the Hawk 75A sank into obscurity. Why?

The P-36 was a much better fighter than its wartime record would suggest. Finely harmonised controls with a large mechanical advantage between stick and ailerons made it snappy in the rolling plane, especially at high speeds, where most contemporary fighters, and not a few later models, became sluggish. It also had an automatic variable pitch propeller, which meant that the engine was always working at maximum efficiency. Its main faults were that it was ineffective at higher altitudes; nor was it fast enough, at a time when performance mattered more than manoeuvrability.

A total of 227 Hawk 75As were acquired by Britain's RAF, mainly A-4 models intended for France, which were designated Mohawk IVs. Some of these were issued to 3 Sqn South African Air Force and used in East Africa, but most were sent to India, where three squadrons became operational from December 1941. They saw little air combat, and were withdrawn from operations in January 1944.

Right: HLeLv 32 of Finland flew the Hawk 75A-3 with great success in WWII.

Curtiss P-40M Kittyhawk III

Origin: Curtiss Airplane Division, Curtiss-Wright Corp, USA.
Type: Single-seat, single-engined monoplane fighter.
Engine: One 1,200hp Allison V-1710-81 liquid-cooled V-12.
Dimensions: Span 37ft 4in (11.38m); length 31ft 2in (9.50m); height 10ft 7in (3.23m); wing area 236sq.ft (21.92m^2).
Weights: Empty 6,400lb (2,903kg); normal takeoff 7,400lb (3,357kg); maximum 8,500lb (3,856kg).
Loadings (at normal takeoff weight)**:** Wing 31.35lb/sq.ft (153kg/m^2): power 6.17lb (2.80kg) per hp.
Performance: Maximum speed 362mph (582kph) at 5,000ft (1,524m); sustained climb rate 9min to 15,000ft (4,572m); service ceiling 30,000ft (9,144m); range on internal fuel 700 miles (1,126km).
Armament: Six 0.50in (12.7mm) wing-mounted machine guns; provision for bomb load of 1,000lb (454kg).
History: Developed from the P-36 with a series of Allison liquid-cooled V-12 engines. Prototype first flown as the XP-40 on 14 October 1938 and ordered in quantity in the following year as the P-40A. Wartime development was continuous, with heavier armament, pilot armour, self-sealing tanks, more powerful engines, and greater altitude capability. Production ceased in December 1944, with a total of 11,738 P-40s of all types.
Users: Australia (RAAF), Britain (RAF), Canada, China, Egypt, New Zealand (RNZAF), South Africa (SAAF), Soviet Union, Turkey, USA (USAAC, USAAF).

Right: Claire Chennault's Flying Tigers operated the P-40 in the Far East.

In the mid-1930s, the US Army Air Corps funded development of the Allison V-1710, a liquid-cooled V-12 engine. Although it was heavier and more complex than the radials used in the P-36, the USAAC rightly believed that the reduced drag would greatly improve performance, and also that the Allison offered more development potential. In February 1937, they ordered a P-36 modified to take the new engine, coupled with a General Electric turbo-supercharger. This combination promised far better altitude performance.

The XP-37 was far sleeker than the P-36, but the cockpit had been moved a long way aft to keep the centre of gravity within limits. First flown on 20 April 1937, this demonstrated better altitude performance, but the supercharger proved unreliable. Next came an order for 13 YP-37 service test aircraft with lengthened fuselages and new superchargers. These were no better; mechanical problems continued, and the project was abandoned.

Developed in parallel, an early production P-36 was fitted with an Allison V-1710-19 engine and, as the XP-40, first flew on 14 October 1938. This appeared promising, and a production order for 524 aircraft was placed on 27 April 1939. The first of these flew on 4 April 1940, as the P-40A. It was powered by a V-1710-33 engine which gave 1,040hp at takeoff. Armament consisted of two nose-mounted 0.50in (12.7mm) Browning machine guns.

By this time the lessons of World War II had become evident, and were applied to the P-40. From the 200th aircraft, pilot armour, self-sealing fuel tanks, and two 0.30in (7.62mm) wing guns were added, this variant becoming the P-40B. The P-40C, with two extra wing guns and provision for a drop tank, took its place in production from the 331st aircraft onwards. Many P-40Bs and Cs

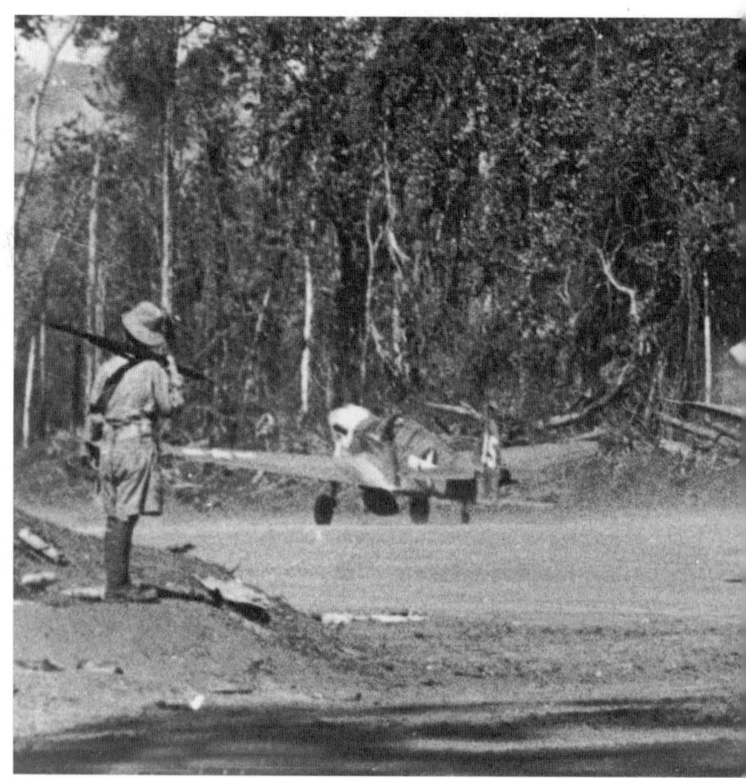

went to Britain as Tomahawk Is and IIs, although since they lacked altitude performance they were sent to North Africa, where most air combat took place at medium and low altitudes. They first became operational in June 1941 with No 112 Squadron, famous as the first RAF unit to paint shark mouths on their aircraft noses.

The P-40 had retained the pleasant handling of the P-36, but was not entirely fault-free. Landings were made with power on and tail up to avoid a tendency to ground-loop. A vicious wing drop at the stall came entirely without warning, and the Allison was less than reliable. Pilots quickly developed "oil temperature and pressure eyes" as a result.

In sheer performance, the Tomahawk was outclassed by the German Bf 109, but several pilots were successful with it. Top scorer was Australian Clive "Killer" Caldwell with 16 victories, eight of them Bf 109s, two of which were flown by high scoring *Experten*.

Meanwhile, on the far side of the world, early P-40s were in action with the American Volunteer Group, the Flying Tigers. Less agile than the Japanese fighters they opposed, they used dive and zoom tactics, and rarely stayed to fight. Also in action, in the Pacific were USAAF P-40 squadrons.

Efforts to improve altitude performance were still under way, and the Allison V-1710-39, rated at 1,150hp for takeoff, which was maintained at 11,700ft (3,566m), became available. This engine had an external spur reduction gear, which raised the thrust line. Overall length was reduced by 6in

Below: P-40Ns of the USAAF operating from a jungle airstrip in Burma, 1944.

(152mm), fuselage cross-section was reduced, the nose guns were removed, and a larger radiator was located under the nose. This was the P-40D, first flown on 22 May 1941. In RAF service it was known as the Kittyhawk. The addition of two more 0.50in (12.7mm) machine guns in the wings, with 281 rounds per gun, gave rise to the P-40E. The similar P-40K varied only in having the -73 Allison, with a higher takeoff rating, and a fuselage 19.5in (495mm) longer. This was followed by the P-40M, with the -81 Allison.

Attempts to achieve a decent altitude rating for the Allison having failed, Curtiss did the obvious and switched to the Roll-Royce Merlin 28 for the P-40F and P-40L Warhawk. This produced a fighter capable of 364mph (586kph) at 20,000ft (6,096m), which was a great improvement. The main problem was that Merlins were in such great demand that a spares shortage was created. This was so severe that in 1944 some 300 P-40Fs and Ls were re-engined with the Allison -81 to become P-40Rs.

The most numerically important P-40 variant was the P-40N Warhawk, known as the Kittyhawk IV in RAF service. With a new lightweight structure, and either four or six wing guns, it used successively the Allison V-1710-81, -99, and -115. The other major change was a frameless clear view canopy. In all, 5,216 P-40Ns were built, of a total P-40 production run of 17,378.

The final P-40 variant was the Q. Its -121 engine could put out 1,100hp at 25,000ft (7,620m), giving a maximum speed of 422mph (679kph) and a sustained climb of 4min 48sec to 20,000ft (6,096m). The rear fuselage was cut down to allow a bubble canopy for good all-round vision, and the wingtips were clipped. But by this time the superb Mustang was in widespread service, and no production of the P-40Q was undertaken.

Right: The P-40N Warhawk was numerically the most important P-40 variant.

Curtiss XP-55 Ascender

Origin: Curtiss Airplane Division, Curtiss-Wright Corp, USA.
Type: Single-seat, single-engined canard monoplane fighter.
Engine: One 1,275hp Allison V-1710-95 liquid-cooled V-12 engine, rear-mounted with a pusher propeller.
Dimensions: Span 44ft 0.5in (13.42m); length 29ft 7in (9.02m); height 10ft 0.75in (3.07m); wing area 235sq.ft (21.83m^2).
Weights: Empty 6,354lb (2,882kg); normal takeoff 7,330lb (3,325kg).
Loadings (at normal takeoff weight)**:** Wing 31lb/sq.ft (152kg/m^2); power 5.75lb (2.61kg) per hp.
Performance: Maximum speed 390mph (628kph) at 19,300ft (5,882m); sustained climb 7min 6sec to 20,000ft (6,096m); service ceiling n/a; range 635 miles (1,022km).
Armament: Four 0.50in (12.7mm) nose-mounted Colt-Browning M2 machine guns, with 200 rounds per gun.
History: Designed to explore unorthodox low drag confgurations; first flight 19 July 1943. Three prototypes built, but no production undertaken.
Users: USA (USAAF projected).

USAAC Specification XC-622 was issued on 27 November 1939, setting out stringent performance requirements for a new fighter, which were to be achieved by a drastic reduction in drag compared to conventional machines. Wind tunnel tests and a full-scale flying model occupied a great deal of time, and not until 10 July 1942 was an order placed for three prototypes. First flight took place on 19 July 1943.

A tail-less pusher configuration was chosen in an attempt to minimise the

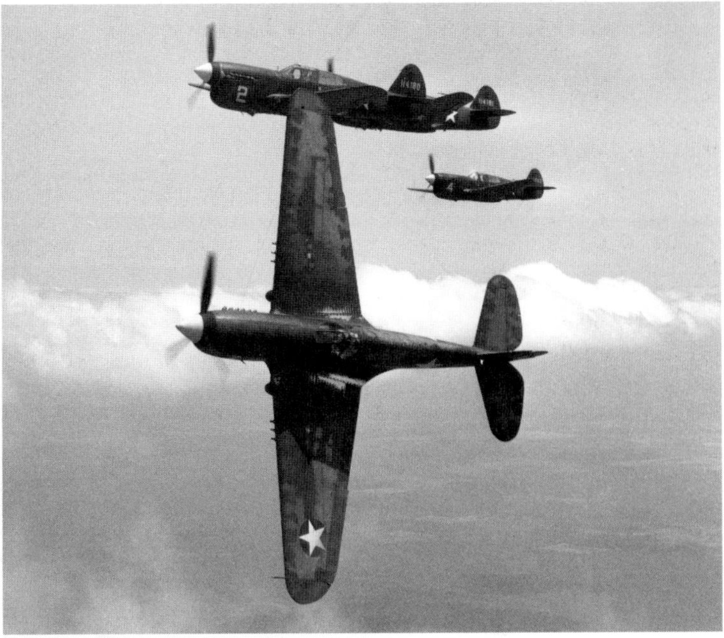

Above: The XP-55 Ascender was a tail-less pusher with canard foreplanes.

propeller slipstream effect, which meant that moveable canard foreplanes had to be used for pitch control. The wings were of laminar flow section, swept at 45deg, with a shallow dihedral. Twin fins and rudders were set outboard. Flaps occupied the inboard trailing edge, with ailerons outboard.

Stall characteristics were poor, and the first prototype was lost on 15 November 1943 when it pitched downwards through 180deg. Starved of fuel, the engine cut, allowing the pilot to bale out from an inverted position without being minced by the propeller. Trials continued into 1945, but it was evident that any advantages of the unconventional layout were not enough to justify further development. The main faults were an excessively long takeoff run, and poor stalling characteristics. The project was abandoned after the third prototype crashed at a military air show on 27 May 1945.

Dassault MD 450 Ouragan

Origin: Générale Aéronautique Marcel Dassault, France.
Type: Single-seat, single-engined subsonic jet fighter.
Engine: One Hispano-Suiza (Rolls-Royce) Nene 104B centrifugal flow turbojet rated at 5,070lb (2,300kg) military thrust.
Dimensions: Span 39ft 3.6in (11.98m); length 35ft 2.8in (10.74m); height 13ft 7in (4.17m); wing area 251.9sq.ft (23.40m^2).
Weights: Empty 9,131lb (4,142kg); normal takeoff 13,007lb (5,900kg); maximum 14,991lb (6,800kg).
Loadings (at normal takeoff weight)**:** Wing 52lb/sq.ft (252kg/m^2); thrust 0.39.
Performance: Maximum speed 578mph (930kph) at sea level, 503mph (810kph) at 39,372ft (12,000m); initial climb rate 7,480ft/min (38m/sec); sustained climb 3min 9sec to 9,843ft (3,000m); service ceiling 49,215ft (15,000m); range 520 miles (836km) with tip tanks; endurance 1hr 10min.
Armament: Four 20mm Hispano 404 cannon with 125 rounds per gun; 16 Matra T-10 rockets or two 1,000lb (454kg) bombs.
History: The first postwar jet fighter by Dassault, first flight 28 February 1949. Service entry early 1952; remained in front line French service until 1958. Combat debut 1961 with India; took part in the Six Day War of 1967 with Israel; served with the Salvadorean Air Force until the late 1980s.
Users: El Salvador, France, India (as Toofani), Israel.

Having survived the rigours of Buchenwald Concentration Camp, Marcel Bloch, prewar head of Avions Marcel Bloch, changed his name to Dassault and founded a new company. The MD 450 was his first foray into the field of jet fighters.

Dassault Super Mystére B.2

Origin: Générale Aéronautique Marcel Dassault, France.
Type: Single-seat, single-engined supersonic jet fighter.
Engine: One SNECMA Atar 101G-2 afterburning single-spool axial flow turbojet rated at 9,833lb (4,460kg) maximum and 7,441lb (3,375kg) military thrust.
Dimensions: Span 34ft 5.75in (10.51m); length 45ft 9in (13.95m); height 14ft 11.25in (4.55m); wing area 378.36sq.ft (35.15m^2).
Weights: Empty 15,282lb (6,932kg); normal takeoff 19,842lb (9,000kg).
Loadings (at normal takeoff weight)**:** Wing 52lb/sq.ft (256kg/m^2); thrust 0.50.
Performance: Maximum speed Mach 1.12, 739mph (1,189kph) at 39,372ft (12,000m); 645mph (1,038kph) at sea level; initial climb rate 10,827ft/min (55m/sec); service ceiling 55,777ft (17,000m); range (with maximum external fuel) 1,112 miles (1,790km).
Armament: Two 30mm DEFA 552 cannon with 125 rounds per gun; 35 68mm SNEB rockets; two AIM-9B Sidewinder AAMs; and bombs or rocket pods.
History: The last and most potent of the Mystére series; first flight of the prototype took place on 16 December 1953. The first of 180 production aircraft flew on 26 February 1957. Of these, 36 were delivered to Israel, where they served in three wars, 18 survivors being sold to Honduras in 1977, from where they were not retired until 1989.
Users: France, Honduras, Israel.

The development sequence from the Ouragan to the SMB 2, as this fighter was widely known, was a logical progression. Fitted with swept wing and tail surfaces, and re-engineered to take the axial flow Atar 101, the Ouragan became the Mystére II. The Mystére III was a night fighter with a radar nose

Right: The MD 450 Ouragan was Marcel Dassault's first jet fighter.

The Ouragan was a simple, low risk fighter, designed around the most powerful engine available, the Rolls-Royce Nene, fed by a pitot nose inlet. The straight low wing had a slightly swept leading edge, with provision for tip tanks, and the orthodox horizontal tail surfaces were set one third of the way up the fin. Speed brakes were set low on the sides of the rear fuselage.

The first of three prototypes flew on 28 February 1949. These were followed by 14 pre-series and 350 production aircraft for *l'Armée de l'Air.* A very sound, if uninspiring design, the Ouragan's very simplicity made maintenance easy. It was pleasant to handle, and a stable gun platform. It proved a suitable foundation for the swept-wing Mystére series which replaced it.

The Ouragan quickly established its export credentials with orders for 104 aircraft for India, and 75 for Israel. It saw action with both these nations. The combat record of the Ouragan was all as a ground attack aircraft, for which it carried rockets and bombs. Salvadorean aircraft were ex-Israeli.

Above: The SMB 2 was the first French fighter to be supersonic in level flight.

and lateral intakes, but failed to enter service. Next came the Mystére IVA which, although it had a similar layout to the Mystére II, was a rather different aircraft under the skin. An indifferent performer, it was exported to India and Israel. It was followed by the Mystére IVB, which was an aerodynamically refined model, and the first of the series to have afterburning. This was cancelled in favour of the much superior potential of the SMB 2.

Detail design of the SMB 2 began in October 1953. Initially known as the Mystére XX, this was firmly aimed at supersonic speed in level flight. The wing had a thickness/chord ratio of 6 per cent, and a quarter chord sweep angle of 45deg, the same as the slightly earlier North American F-100. But whereas the American fighter had inboard ailerons and no flaps, Dassault stayed with the orthodox solution of outboard ailerons and inboard trailing edge flaps. The horizontal tail surfaces, all-moving one-piece slabs, remained in the usual position one third of the way up the fin.

On 24 February 1954, the Mystére IVB prototype, powered by an afterburning Rolls-Royce Avon RA 7R, had gone supersonic in level flight; the first European fighter to do so. Dassault wanted the Rolls-Royce Avon RA 14 for the SMB 2, but was thwarted by officialdom. The SMB prototype, flown by Paul Boudier, made its first flight on 2 March 1955, powered by the RA-7R.

The definitive engine was the SNECMA Atar 101G, and the first production aircraft flew on 18 May 1956. At least 220 SMB 2s were planned, but the immense potential of the Mirage III, which flew later that year, caused a reduction to 180 aircraft, and saw the end of the line for the Mystére series.

Service entry was in 1957, and the SMB 2, with few modifications, remained with *l'Armée de l'Air* for 20 years. Of the 180 built, 24 were supplied to Israel. Used mainly for close air support, these gave valuable service, and in 1972 the survivors were re-engined with the non-afterburning Pratt & Whitney J52-P-8A. In 1977, Honduras received 18 admittedly tired SMB 2s from Israel and kept them on for 12 years, although in the later stages serviceability was almost nil.

Right: The Super Mystére B 2 (SMB 2), was the last of the Mystére series.

Dassault Mirage IIIC

Origin: Générale Aéronautique Marcel Dassault, France.
Type: Single-seat, single-engined supersonic jet and mixed-power fighter with limited adverse weather capability.
Engine: One SNECMA Atar 9B afterburning twin-spool turbojet rated at 13,320lb (6,042kg) maximum and 9,460lb (4,291kg) military thrust; 3,307lb (1,500kg) thrust SEPR 84 rocket motor optional.
Dimensions: Span 27ft 0in (8.23m); length 48ft 4in (14.73m); height 13ft 11.5in (4.26m); wing area 377sq.ft (35m^2).
Weights: Empty 13,040lb (5,915kg); normal takeoff 19,000lb (8,620kg); maximum 21,444lb (9,727kg).
Loadings (at normal takeoff weight, jet engine only)**:** Wing 50lb/sq.ft (246kg/m^2); thrust 0.70.
Performance: Maximum speed Mach 2.15 at altitude, Mach 1.14 at sea level; initial climb rate 16,405ft/min (83m/sec); sustained climb with rocket motor operating 6min 10sec to 59,058ft (18,000m); service ceiling without rocket motor 54,137ft (16,500m); operational radius on internal fuel 180 miles (290km).
Armament: Two 30mm DEFA 552 cannon with 125 rounds per gun (on aircraft without the rocket motor); one Matra R 511 or R 530 AAM; two R 550 Magics, Shafrir or Sidewinders.
History: Dassault turned to the tail-less delta configuration in 1954. After a couple of false starts, the Mirage III first flew on 12 May 1958. A process of development followed, and the first Mirage IIIC took to the skies on 9 October 1960, piloted by Jean Coreau. Service entry 10 July 1961. The Mirage IIICJ gained an enviable reputation as an air superiority fighter in Israeli service in 1967, and was widely exported as a result.

Above: The Mirage IIIC gained fame in Israeli service from 1967 onwards.

Users (Mirage III, 5, 50): Argentina, Australia, Belgium, Brazil, Chile, Colombia, Egypt, France, Gabon, Israel, Lebanon, Libya, Pakistan, Peru, Saudi Arabia, South Africa, Spain, Switzerland, United Arab Emirates, Venezuela, Zaire. In 2001, only 10 of these nations still operated the type, in small numbers.

Dassault's venture into the world of the tail-less deltas began in 1954, when a specification was issued for a small, all-weather supersonic point defence interceptor, able to reach an altitude of 59,058ft (18,000m) in six minutes. The result was the MD 550 Mirage I, initially called the Mystére-Delta. It was powered by two afterburning Armstrong Siddeley Viper turbojets each rated at 2,161lb (980kg) thrust, supplemented by an SEPR 66 bifuel rocket giving 3,307lb (1,500kg). The delta configuration was chosen for its low drag at high speed/altitude combinations, ease of construction, and also because it offered a large wing area, which conferred low wing loading and high altitude manoeuvrability.

First flown by Roland Glavany on 25 June 1955 the Mirage I performed well, but was too limited to be really useful. The rather larger Mirage II, which was never built, was sidelined for the same reason, and Marcel Dassault turned his attention to an even larger (but still smallish by contemporary fighter standards) project which, in addition to point defence interception, could fly conventional fighter missions. In a *tour de force*, the Mirage III was designed, built, and flown in just nine months.

In essence, the Mirage III was little more than a scaled-up Mirage I, tailored around the largest afterburning turbojet available, the Atar 101G, fed by semicircular plain side inlets. On 30 January 1957, the Mirage III reached Mach 1.52 in level flight. A couple of months later, translating shock half-cones (*souris*) were fitted and, with an SEPR 66 rocket pack installed, maximum speed rose to Mach 1.9.

The next step was the Mirage IIIA. Superficially similar to the Mirage III, the

uselage was reprofiled around the much more powerful Atar 9B. The wing was most totally redesigned. Area was increased by 17 per cent; thickness/chord ratio as reduced from 5 to an average of 4 per cent; and the leading edge was ambered, with a saw-cut in the leading edge (see English Electric Lightning). The n was reduced in height, and relocated further aft. A large radar nose was installed, or which *l'Armée de l'Air* selected the CSF Cyrano radar. In July 1957, 10 pre-roduction Mirage IIIAs were ordered.

The SEPR 84 rocket pack could be fitted for the interception mission, but fuel anks for this displaced guns and ammunition, leaving the sole air-to-air armament s a single Matra R 511 AAM. The rocket fuel was furaline and the intensely orrosive red fuming nitric acid, and pilots had to wear cumbersome protective lothing to guard against spillages. In practice, the rocket pack was soon bandoned.

With agreement from *l'Armée de l'Air*, Dassault proposed a range of pecialised aircraft with a more or less common airframe. The Mirage IIIC was an ll-weather interceptor; the IIIB was a two-seater conversion trainer; the IIIE was nitially a strike-optimised aircraft but became a dual role machine; and the IIIR was reconnaissance version. The IIIE mounted the more powerful Atar 09C-3 turbojet,

Below: Many export Mirage IIIs had a slimmer nose and canard foreplanes.

and featured an 11.8in (300mm) extension to the forward fuselage to house ext avionics.

Service entry with *l'Armée de l'Air* commenced in July 1961, and productic gradually built up, eventually to total more than 1,400. The export market was als busy, and the first and most important customer was Israel in 1961; not because the size of the order, but the use to which they were put.

The Six Day War in June 1967 first brought the Mirage IIIC to wor prominence. Of the 58 Israeli air combat victories over Russian-built fighters in th conflict, 48 were by Mirage pilots, and all were scored with cannon. Just on Mirage was lost in air combat. The Mirage was immediately hailed as a worl beater, despite the fact that the real difference between the two sides was pil quality. For the export market, no better recommendation could be sought tha "combat-proven". The Mirage legend was further enhanced during the War Attrition 1969-70, and the October War of 1973.

Even before these events, Israel had proposed a simplified Mirage III optimise for ground attack in clear weather. This became the Mirage 5, which first flew on 1 May 1967. This used basically the same airframe and engine as the Mirage IIIE, bu with a fined-down nose holding only a ranging radar. The spartan avionics fit allowe a larger internal fuel capacity and a greater air-to-surface weapons load. Politic considerations ruled out its export to Israel, and it eventually flew with *l'Armée d l'Air* and 10 other nations.

The final variant to reach service was the Mirage 50, the prototype of which fir flew on 15 April 1975. Powered by the Atar 9K-50, this outperformed previou models, but was operated only by Chile and Venezuela. Production of fir generation Mirages ended in 1991 with delivery of the 1,422nd aircraft.

Right: The re-engined Mirage 50 was operated only by Chile and Venezuela.

Dassault Mirage III overseas derivatives

Origin: Four nations have produced derivatives of the Mirage III: Atlas of South Africa with the Cheetah; ENAER of Chile with the Pantera; Israel Aircraft Industries with the Neshr, Kfir, Nammer and Dagger; and Switzerland with the Mirage IIIS. The following data apply to the Kfir C.7.
Type: Single-seat, single-engined bisonic jet fighter.
Engine: One IAI Bedek (General Electric) J79-IAI-J1E afterburning single-spoc turbojet rated at 18,750lb (8,505kg) maximum and 11,890lb (5,393kg) military thrust.
Dimensions: 26ft 11.5in (8.22m); length 51ft 4.25in (15.65m); height 14ft 11.25in (4.55m); wing area 375sq.ft (34.80m^2).
Weights: Empty 17,480lb (7,929kg); normal takeoff 23,540lb (10,678kg); maximum 36,376lb (16,500kg).
Loadings (at normal takeoff weight): Wing 63lb/sq.ft (307kg/m^2); thrust 0.80.
Performance: Maximum speed Mach 2.0 at altitude; Mach 1.14 at sea level; initial climb rate 45,866ft/min (233m/sec); service ceiling 58,074ft (17,700m); combat radius (with external fuel) 548 miles (882km).
Armament: Two 30mm DEFA 552 cannon with 125 rounds per gun; two AIM-9 Sidewinder, Shafrir, or Python heat-homing AAMs.
History: Adapted from a Mirage IIIC airframe modified to take a J79 turbojet; first flight took place on 19 October 1970. Deliveries of production Kfir C1s began in April 1975, followed by the C2, which had a dogtooth leading edge, canard foreplanes, and nose strakes. The C7 was an avionics upgrade from 1983.

Above: South Africa's Mirage III derivative was the Cheetah, seen here.

Users (all derivatives)**:** Argentina (Dagger/Neshr); Chile (Pantera); Colombia (Kfir); Ecuador (Kfir); Israel (Neshr/Kfir); South Africa (Cheetah); Switzerland (Mirage IIIS); USA (USMC/USN) (Kfir/F-21A).

The Swiss selected the Mirage III to be licence-built in 1961, but then proceeded to introduce modifications which turned into a production nightmare. Unsurprisingly, the DEFA cannon were dropped in favour of the Oerlikon 302 This was no great problem, but the Hughes Taran fire control system, coupled with the Hughes AIM-4 Falcon AAM, licence-built in Sweden, was. Nothing like this had ever been fitted to a Mirage, and enormous efforts were needed to make it work as advertised.

To improve short field performance, and this was never a Mirage strongpoint, the Swiss beefed up the main gear, added a tailhook, and made many other engineering changes. It all took time, and the first flight of the Mirage IIIS was delayed until October 1965 – two years late! The original plan for 100 aircraft was reduced to 58, only 36 of which were the "full-up" Mirage IIIS. It was the most expensive Mirage of all.

France having embargoed further Mirage deliveries, Israel promptly went ahead and produced an unlicensed home-brew. This was the Neshr, basically a Mirage 5 powered by an Atar 09C (also built in-house), and differing only in having a Martin-Baker JM6 ejection seat and some Israeli avionics. Deliveries commenced in 1971, and total production was 61, including two two-seaters. Some 39 Neshrs were later supplied to Argentina as Daggers.

IAI then proceeded to fit the licence-built General Electric J79 into a Mirage airframe, to produce the Kfir. First flown on 19 October 1970, it was first delivered in April 1975. The Kfir was longer and considerably heavier than the Mirage IIIC, and was less popular with Israeli pilots. From the C 2 model onwards, it was fitted with canard foreplanes, nose strakes, and dogtooth wing leading edges. The definitive article was the C 7. Some Kfirs were briefly used as adversary aircraft by the USN and USMC, as the F-21A.

The Atlas Aircraft Corporation upgraded 52 South African Mirage IIIEZs with Israeli assistance, as the Cheetah EZ, which became operational in 1987. It had the same canard foreplanes and dogtooth leading edges as the Kfir, but was powered by a licence-built Atar 9K-50 rated at 15,873lb (7,200kg) thrust maximum. The avionics were mainly of Israeli origin, including the multi-mode radar. Armscor V3B Kukri and V3C Darter AAMs were the main weapons.

The final Mirage overseas derivative is the Pantera, modified from the

Dassault Mirage IIIV

Origin: Générale Aéronautique Marcel Dassault, France.
Type: Single seat, nine-engined bisonic VTOL experimental jet fighter.
Engines: One SNECMA TF 306C twin-spool afterburning turbofan rated at 20,500lb (9,299kg) maximum and 11,700lb (5,307kg) military thrust, plus eight Rolls-Royce RB 162 lift engines rated at 4,409lb (2,000kg) thrust each.
Dimensions: Span 28ft 5in (8.72m); length 59ft 0.5in (18.00m); height 18ft 2in (5.55m); wing area n/a.
Weights: Empty c22,046lb (10,000kg); vertical takeoff 26,455lb (12,000kg); maximum (conventional takeoff) 37,000lb (16,783kg).
Loadings (at vertical takeoff weight)**:** Wing n/a; thrust 0.77.
Performance: Maximum speed Mach 2.04 at altitude; subsonic at sea level; initial climb rate n/a; service ceiling n/a; operational radius, subsonic, low altitude 280 miles (450km).
Armament: Projected, two 30mm DEFA cannon with 125 rounds per gun; 1,200lb (544kg) ordnance in internal bay.
History: The Mirage IIIV was preceded by the Balzac V 001 proof of concept aircraft, the first flight of which took place on 12 October 1962. The Mirage IIIV prototype, which first flew on 12 February 1965, was a much larger aircraft. It reached Mach 2.04 on 12 September 1966, but crashed on 28 November of that year, whereupon the programme lapsed.
User: France, experimental only.

Driven by the need for dispersed basing, Dassault proposed a tail-less delta supersonic aircraft with a single large propulsion engine, and a

Above: The Israeli-built Kfir C 7 was used by the USMC in the adversary role.

Mirage 50 by ENAER of Chile using kits supplied by IAI. It has non-moving canards and Israeli avionics and radar, and routinely carries Python 3 and Python 4 AAMs.

---

battery of lift engines mounted amidships. *L'Armée de l'Air* requirements were about 120 aircraft.

The new technology involved included three-axis electronic auto-

Below: Eight lift engines amidships penalised the design of the Mirage IIIV.

stabilization, jet reaction controls for the hover, and many other systems. To prove these, Dassault, together with Sud Aviation, modified the Mirage III prototype for vertical flight as the Balzac V. The propulsion engine was a Bristol-Siddeley Orpheus turbojet rated at 5,000lb (2,268kg) thrust, and eight Rolls-Royce RB 108 lift engines were mounted in pairs amidships, straddling the inlet duct of the Orpheus. Each of the RB 108s developed 2,210lb (1,002kg) of thrust which, despite 11 per cent being bled off for the jet reaction system, gave just enough power for a vertical takeoff at light weights.

Flown by Rene Bigand, the Balzac made its first tethered hop on 12 October 1962, a conventional flight on 18 March 1963, and the first complete cycle, vertical takeoff and landing, with wing-borne flight between, on 29 March. Later, it pioneered short rolling takeoffs. But on its 125th sortie, it crashed, killing test pilot Jacques Pinier. Rebuilt, it returned to the air, only to crash again on 8 September 1965, again killing its pilot.

Meanwhile, the Mirage IIIV was progressing fast. The volume occupied by the lift jets, combined with the extra fuel needed for them, and a planned internal weapons bay, ensured that it would be both large and heavy. Unlike

Dassault Mirage F.1C

Origin: Avions Marcel Dassault-Breguet Aviation, France.
Type: Single-seat, single-engined bisonic jet fighter.
Engine: One SNECMA Atar 9K50 two-stage afterburning turbojet rated at 15,873lb (7,200kg) maximum and 11,060lb (5,017kg) military thrust.
Dimensions: Span 27ft 6.75in (8.40m); length 50ft 2.5in (15.30m); height 14ft 9in (4.50m); wing area 269.1sq.ft ($25m^2$).
Weights: Empty 16,315lb (7,400kg); normal takeoff 25,353lb (11,500kg); maximum 35,714lb (16,200kg).
Loadings (at normal takeoff weight)**:** Wing 94lb/sq.ft ($460kg/m^2$); thrust 0.63.
Performance: Maximum speed Mach 2.2 at 39,372ft (12,000m); Mach 1.2 at sea level; initial climb rate 41,930ft/min (213m/sec); service ceiling 65,620ft (20,000m); endurance (with centreline tank) 2hr 15min.
Armament: Two 30mm DEFA 553 cannon with 135 rounds per gun; two Matra Super 530F SARH and two Matra R 550 Magic IR missiles.
History: Developed to replace the Mirage III. First flight of prototype 23 December 1966. Initial operational capability 1974. Air combat with Iraq and South Africa. Total production 731.
Users: Ecuador, France, Greece, Iraq, Jordan, Kuwait, Libya, Morocco, Qatar, South Africa and Spain. In 2001, it remained in service with all except Kuwait, Qatar, and South Africa.

The shortcomings of the Mirage III were evident from a very early stage: excessive takeoff and landing speeds, the need for long runways, poor ride quality at high speeds and low altitudes, and the too-rapid bleed-off of

Right: The Mirage F.1C was a move away from the tail-less delta format.

previous Mirages, twin landing wheels were used on all legs.

The first of two prototypes was powered by a SNECMA TF104B (modified Pratt & Whitney JTF10 turbofan), and the eight lift engines were RB 162-1s. The wing was larger and thinner, with a cranked leading edge, while the fin was taller.

Free hovering trials commenced on 12 February 1965, again flown by Rene Bigand, but there were many problems. Development of the propulsion engine proved difficult; the lift engines failed to give their expected thrust; and the airframe was considerably overweight. The propulsion engine was changed to the TF 306C, based on the Pratt & Whitney TF30, which later proved troublesome on the F-111 and the F-14.

Not until 24 March 1966 did the Mirage IIIV make its first full transitioning flight, but meanwhile the second prototype was being made ready. But by this time cost, and the problems of off-field basing, had made its chances of adoption look marginal, even though Jean-Marie Saget had reached Mach 2.04 on 12 September 1966. Then, on 28 November 1966, the second prototype crashed. Following this the programme was terminated.

energy during hard manoeuvring. To succeed the delta-winged aircraft, Dassault were awarded a contract for a single prototype of a conventionally configured aircraft. It was a two-seater, the Mirage F 2, to be powered by the TF-306 turbofan, which first flew on 12 June 1966. But even before this, Dassault, suspecting that the large and sophisticated F 2 might prove unaffordable started work on a scaled-down single-seat version as a private venture, the engine for which was the Atar 9K50. This was the Mirage F 1.

By comparison with the Mirage III, the appearance of the F 1 was unexciting. It had a moderately swept, shoulder-mounted wing, orthodox all-moving low-set horizontal tail surfaces, and twin fixed ventral fins beneath the tail. Thrust loading was similar to that of the Mirage III, but the wing loading was nearly double. This was however offset by a battery of high-lift devices on the wing: full-span leading edge flaps, which could double as combat manoeuvre flaps, and double-slotted trailing edge slats. These allowed the F 1 to turn rather tighter than the Mirage III and with less speed loss, but the main difference came in short field performance. Approach speed was reduced from the 210mph (338kph) of the delta to 160mph (257kph) for the F 1. Both landing and takeoff rolls were more than halved.

Dassault Mirage 2000C

Origin: Avions Marcel Dassault/Breguet Aviation, France.

Type: Single-seat, single-engined bisonic air superiority and multi-role jet fighter.

Engine: One SNECMA M53-P2 single-spool low-bypass afterburning turbofan rated at 21,400lb (9,707kg) maximum and 14,400lb (6,532kg) military thrust.

Dimensions: Span 29ft 11in (9.13m); length 47ft 1.5in (14.36m): height 17ft 1in (5.20m); wing area 441.32sq.ft (41m^2).

Weights: Empty 16,535lb (7,500kg); normal takeoff 25,928lb (11,761kg); maximum 37,478lb (17,000kg).

Loadings (at normal takeoff weight): Wing 59lb/sq.ft (287kg/m^2); thrust 0.83.

Performance: Maximum speed Mach 2.2 at altitude, Mach 1.2 at sea level; initial climb rate 58,000ft/min (295m/sec); sustained climb 2min 24sec to 49,215ft (15,000m); service ceiling 59,058ft (18,000m); interception radius (with drop tanks) 435 miles (700km).

Armament: Two 30mm DEFA 554 cannon with 125 rounds per gun; two Matra Super 530D and two R550 Magic AAMs, or four MICA and two Magics, or up to eight MICA.

History: The Mirage 2000 was unusual in that instead of being designed to a specification, the specification was written around it in March 1976. First flight 10 March 1978; initial operational capability July 1984. Like the Mirage

Right: Dassault reverted to the tail-less delta for the Mirage 2000C.

First flight of the prototype took place on 23 December 1966, piloted by Rene Bigand, and it exceeded Mach 2 on its fourth flight, on 7 January 1967. A hiatus occurred when the prototype broke up in the air on 18 May, killing Bigand, but by that time *l'Armée de l'Air* had decided that it wanted the F 1. Three pre-production aircraft were ordered in September 1967, but it was another 18 months before the first of these flew. A production order was placed later in 1969 for what became the F 1C, optimised for all-weather interception.

The first production F 1C was flown by Guy Miteaux-Maurouard on 15 February 1973, squadron deliveries began in October, and initial operational capability was achieved in 1974.

The F 1C had a Cyrano IVM multi-mode radar, and the weapons fit consisted of two 30mm DEFA 553 cannon with 135 rounds per gun, and initially a Matra 530 AAM on the centreline. Missile armament has since been increased to two Super 530s on underwing pylons, and two R550 Magics on wingtip rails.

The Mirage F 1 saw combat with Iraq, once against Iran, the second time in the Gulf War of 1991, where it failed to make an impact. South Africa also used it against Angola.

III before it, the 2000 has spawned a whole family of fighters, including two-seater strike aircraft. Total build 550; more to follow.
Users: Egypt, France, Greece, India, Peru, Qatar, Taiwan, United Arab Emirates.

After a brief flirtation with variable-sweep wings, France specified the Avion de Combat Futur (ACF), unofficially known as the Super Mirage. Twin-engined, this was to have a performance to match the F-15 Eagle. However, it soon became clear to Dassault that this was not only unattainable but unaffordable. In 1972 they commenced the Delta 2000 study, and when in December 1975 the ACF was cancelled, a compromise replacement was ready and waiting in the wings. In March 1976 an operational requirement was drafted around its projected performance, and the Mirage 2000 was born.

At a time when fighter agility reigned supreme, led by the F-16, *l'Armée de l'Air* wanted the top right hand corner of the flight performance envelope – maximum speed, maximum altitude – to counter the Russian MiG-25 Foxbat. The tail-less delta was optimum for these conditions, and recent technical advances, notably relaxed stability and computer-controlled fly-by-wire, appeared able to overcome the worst drawbacks of this configuration. Also optimised for the desired regime was the engine, the SNECMA M53 turbofan. Single-spool, and with a bypass ratio of only 0.4, it was really a

Dassault Super Mirage 4000

Origin: Avions Marcel Dassault/Breguet Aviation, France.
Type: Single-seat, twin-engined bisonic air superiority and multi-role canard delta jet fighter.
Engines: Two SNECMA M53-2P single-spool low-bypass afterburning turbofans each rated at 21,400lb (9,707kg) maximum and 14,400lb (6,532kg) military thrust.
Dimensions: Span 35ft 8.75in (11.93m); length 61ft 5in (18.72m); height 19ft 8.25in (6.00m); wing area 783sq.ft (72.70m^2).
Weights: Empty c30,313lb (13,750kg); normal takeoff 50,706lb (23,000kg); maximum 70,547lb (32,000kg).
Loadings (at normal combat weight)**:** Wing 65lb/sq.ft (316kg/m^2); thrust 0.84.
Performance: Maximum speed Mach 2.2 at altitude; initial climb rate 60,000ft/min (305m/sec); sustained climb 3min to 49,215ft (15,000m); service ceiling 65,620ft (20,000m); operational radius with external tanks 746 miles (1,200km).
Armament: Two 30mm DEFA 554 cannon with 125 rounds per gun; typically four Super 530D and six R 550 Magic AAMs.
History: A private venture, mainly for the export market, commenced in September 1976. First flew 9 March 1979 and supersonic on first flight. With no buyers, the programme lapsed, but was revived in 1987, with the same result.
User: None, but Saudi Arabia was viewed as the launch customer.

Dassault had already scaled up the Mirage III to produce the Mirage IV nuclear strike aircraft. In September 1976 they set about the same task with the Mirage 2000. First flown on 9 March 1979 by Jean-Marie Saget, it showed great promise.

A private venture for export, with Saudi Arabia touted as the launch customer, development costs had been minimised by the simple expedient of using technology and systems from the earlier aircraft. There were, however, certain innovations. More extensive use was made of composites and diffusion-bonded and super-plastic formed titanium components. A world first was a composite fin structure as a fuel tank. Internal fuel capacity was almost three times that of the Mirage 2000.

Apart from sheer size and two engines, the Super Mirage 4000 differed from leaky turbojet, but it delivered fast and high performance.

In appearance, the 2000 was clearly one of the Mirage delta family. although the wing leading edge sweep was 58deg rather than the 60deg of the earlier aircraft. But under the skin it was a very different bird. Full-span leading edge slats and full span two-piece trailing edge elevons combined to give variable camber, but the main key to enhanced manoeuvrability was relaxed static stability coupled with quadruplex fly-by-wire. With little or no inertia to overcome, control response was extremely rapid. An easy to overlook feature is the small strakes on the outside of the engine intakes, which produce vortices to clean up the airflow over the wing.

The Mirage 2000 is stressed for loadings of plus 9g and minus 3g, but the former can be overridden at need up to the full 13.5g. Under normal conditions, an alpha limiter gives carefree handling and ensures that the pilot does not stray into the area of lost control.

More recent fighter variants are the Mirage 2000-5 and the Mirage 2000-9. The former introduced HOTAS controls and a glass cockpit, one of the screens in which is, unusually, a look-level display, and an improved radar and weapons system. The -9 is essentially a machine with improved avionics. The Mirage 2000N is a two-seat strike aircraft with optimised mission avionics.

---

the 2000 externally in having a true bubble canopy with no dorsal spine, a different system of engine bleed doors, and moving canard foreplanes in lieu of strakes. The radome was more rounded, and sized to fit a 35in (900mm) diameter antenna for an unspecified radar, expected to provide a detection range in excess of 115 miles (185km). Otherwise, the projected avionics fit was very similar to that of the Mirage 2000.

Compared to the Mirage 2000, the two M53 afterburning turbofans provided a slightly better thrust/weight ratio across the board, while wing loading was only marginally increased. But in the event Saudi Arabia bought F-15s and Tornados, and the Super Mirage ended its career in 1987 as a test-bed for Rafale.

Below: Although very capable, the Super Mirage 4000 proved unaffordable.

Dassault Rafale F 2

Origin: Avions Marcel Dassault/Breguet Aviation, France.
Type: One/two-seat, twin-engined bisonic multi-role canard delta jet fighter; Rafale F 1 is a single-seat carrier variant.
Engines: Two SNECMA M88-2 two-spool afterburning turbofans each rated at 16,860lb (7,648kg) maximum and 11,243lb (5,100kg) military thrust.
Dimensions: Span 35ft 5in (10.80m); length 50ft 1in (15.27m); height 17ft 6in (5.34m); wing area 495sq.ft (46.00m²).
Weights: Empty 19,974lb (9,060kg); normal takeoff c32,430lb (14,710kg); maximum 47,399lb (21,500kg).
Loadings (at normal takeoff weight)**:** Wing 66lb/sq.ft (320kg/m²); thrust 1.04.
Performance: Maximum speed Mach 2 at altitude, Mach 1.14 at sea level; initial climb rate 60,000ft/min (305m/sec); operational ceiling 54,957ft (16,750m); range (with external tanks) 1,151 miles (1,850km); endurance 3hr.
Armament: One 30mm DEFA 719B cannon; eight MICA AAMs (four active radar, four heat-homing); wide range of air-to-surface ordnance.
History: Concept demonstrator Rafale A, powered by two General Electric F404-400s, first flown on 4 July 1986 piloted by Guy Mitaux-Maurouard. The first Rafale with the definitive M88 turbofan flew on 19 May 1991, and Rafale M, the carrier fighter, followed on 11 December of that year. Budgetary restraints have delayed service entry; the first Rafales were delivered to *l'Armée de l'Air* and *l'Aeronavale* in 2001.
Users: France (*l'Armée de l'Air, l'Aeronavale*).

If the origins of the Mirage F 1 and Mirage 2000 had been convoluted, those of Rafale were no less so. In 1983, Britain, France, Germany, Italy and Spain had more or less agreed on a common specification for a multi-role fighter, but in the case of France, this was less rather than more. Dassault demanded both design and industrial leadership, and wanted a rather smaller, cheaper, and more exportable aircraft than the others. This was unacceptable to the other

Below: Rafale F.1 is the single-seat carrier- based variant of this fighter.

Above: The Rafale F.2 is a multi-role fighter able to carry heavy loads.

four, and by 1985 France was left with no alternative but to go it alone. They had however already started; in April 1983, an Avion de Combat Experimentale (ACX) demonstrator had been authorised, followed shortly after by the M88 turbofan. The first requirement was as a replacement for the archaic F-8 Crusaders of *l'Aeronavale*, followed by Super Etendards of the same service, then *l'Armée de l'Air* Jaguars.

The ACX demonstrator, by now named Rafale, made what can only be described as a sporty maiden flight on 4 July 1986, when Guy Mitaux-Maurouard took it to Mach 1.3 at 29,529ft (9,000m) and put it through a series of 5g turns. The prototype Rafale, which was slightly larger and heavier than the service models, was powered by two General Electric F404-400s in lieu of the not yet ready SNECMA M88s.

Rafale's mid-set delta wing had two-piece leading edge slats and two-piece trailing edge elevons. The inlets were ingenious, of segmental shape, formed by constricting the forward fuselage. This combined the pressure recovery of side inlets with the high alpha traits of the chin inlet. The all-moving canard surfaces were mounted on the bulge formed above the constriction.

The cockpit was state of the art with HOTAS, a raked back ejection seat, sidestick controller, and multi-function displays with touch-sensitive screens. Voice control was also a feature; ironically the language is English. A helmet-mounted sight is planned for off-boresight missile launch. Radar is the RBE 2, with fixed phased array electronic scanning, a first in a European fighter.

Most *Armée de l'Air* machines are two-seaters optimised for attack, and will have a terrain-following mode. In the air superiority role they will be flown as single-seaters.

The carrier-compatible Rafale F 1 is rather heavier than its land based counterpart, as it is stressed for deck launches and landings, and has a tailhook and an integral boarding ladder.

Funding problems have delayed the service entry of Rafale and, given its history, it is ironic that in 2001 it had yet to attract a single export order.

de Havilland Mosquito NF XIX

Origin: de Havilland, England.
Type: Two-seater, twin-engined night fighter.
Engines: Two Rolls-Royce Merlin 25 liquid-cooled V-12s rated at 1,620hp for takeoff and 1,500hp at 9,500ft (2,895m).
Dimensions: Span 54ft 2in (16.51m); length 41ft 2in (12.54m); height 15ft 3in (4.65m); wing area 454sq.ft (42.18m²).
Weights: Empty 15,970lb (7,244kg); normal takeoff 20,600lb (9,344kg); maximum 21,750lb (9,866kg).
Loadings (at normal takeoff weight)**:** Wing 45lb/sq.ft (222kg/m²); power 6.36lb (2.88kg) per hp.
Performance: Maximum speed 378mph (608kph) at 13,200ft (4,023m); initial climb rate 2,700ft/min (14m/sec); operational ceiling 28,000ft (8,534m); range 1,400 miles (2,253km).
Armament: Four 20mm Hispano cannon.
History: The Mosquito, which first flew on 25 November 1940, was originally conceived as a fast, unarmed light bomber constructed mainly of non-strategic materials: i.e. wood. However, it excelled in many other roles, notably night fighting, for which it appeared in eight variants. Production continued until 1950 and totalled 7,781, of which more than 1,500 were night fighters.
Users: Australia (RAAF), Belgium, Britain (RAF), Canada (RCAF, Israel, New Zealand (RNZAF), Yugoslavia.

At the end of 1938, de Havilland proposed a fast, unarmed light bomber with a two-man crew, capable of 400mph (644kph), and a range of 1,000 miles (1,609km) with a 1,000lb (454kg) bomb load. It was accepted on 29 December 1939, and the first contract was placed on 1 March 1940. First flight, by

Below: The Mosquito was by far the most outstanding night fighter of WWII.

Above: First of many – an NF II with radar aerials on nose and wingtips.

Geoffrey de Havilland, Jr, took place on 25 November 1940.

By this time interest had grown in its potential as a long range fighter, the prototype of which was first flown, with the same pilot, on 15 May 1941. This differed from the bomber version mainly in having four 20mm Hispano cannon under the belly, with the breeches occupying the front part of the now redundant bomb bay, and four .303in (7.7mm) Browning machine guns in a solid nose. Thus was the Mosquito fighter born.

As the NF II, it entered squadron service in January 1942, with a matt black finish which reduced maximum speed by 16mph (26kph), although it still had an ample speed advantage over German bombers of the period. Fitted with AI IV or AI V radar, the NF II carried out its first operational night sortie on 27-28 April of that year, claimed its first probable one month later, and gradually supplanted the Beaufighter. Total production of the NF II was 466.

Plans for the NF VI and NF X were abandoned, and the next Mosquito night fighter, from March 1943, was the NF XII. This was the first aircraft to carry AI VIII centimetric radar, in a thimble nose which displaced the machine guns. The radar being the only difference, 97 NF XIIs were converted from NF IIs.

The next production variant was the NF XIII, also with AI VIII, which first flew in February 1944. It was powered by two Merlin 25s, which allowed all-up weight to be increased. In practice this was used for underwing tanks to extend endurance. Total production was 270.

At this point, the American SCR 720 centimetric radar became available in quantity. Its performance was slightly better than AI VIII, but it was not interchangeable with it. Consequently 100 NF IIs were converted to take AI X, as it was known in RAF service, to become NF XVIIs, while

220 aircraft were produced as NF XIXs, the first of which flew in May 1944.

Previously to this, a counter had been sought for the high-flying Junkers Ju 86P. To achieve altitudes in excess of 40,000ft (12,191m), a bomber variant of the Mosquito was converted. The wing span was extended to 59ft 0in (17.98m), high-altitude-rated Merlin 77s were fitted, a pressure cabin was installed, and a weight reduction programme instituted. This included smaller wheels, reduced tankage, deletion of the armour, AI VIII radar in a solid nose, and four .303in (7.7mm) machine guns in an underbelly blister. This resulted in the NF XV in 1943, which was able to reach 44,600ft (13,593m), but as high-altitude Spitfires soon became available only five NF XVs were built, serving with No 85 Squadron under future de Havilland Chief Test Pilot John Cunningham.

From the summer of 1944, some Mosquito squadrons were allotted to the bomber support role, ranging deep into Germany. Their task was to protect the bomber stream by harassing German night fighters. So effective were they that the prayer of *Nachtjagdflieger* pilots was commonly said to be: "*Lieber* Hermann, please give me a Mosquito."

The final night fighter Mosquito to see service in World War II was the NF 30, with high-altitude-rated Merlin 76s, which increased operational ceiling to 36,000ft (10,972m). Introduced in late 1944, this was to have been the most numerous of all the night Mosquitos, but production was curtailed to 230 by the end of the war.

Mosquito night fighter pilots claimed about 600 victories in defensive operations over Britain from 1942 onwards, but there were no high-scoring aces among them. The reason is not hard to find: opportunities were more plentiful in the early years, before the Mosquito was in widespread use. For example, John Cunningham, the top scorer on defensive operations with 20 victories, scored 16 of them with the Beaufighter. Opportunity was something that John "Ian" Allan had in spades over Sicily in 1943, when he claimed 13 German and Italian bombers in the space of just 18 nights with his NF XII, adding another just one month later. On offensive night operations, Branse Burbridge claimed 16 of his eventual 21 victories, including four in one night, in the course of 30 bomber support sorties. He flew the NF XIX and the NF 30. But, for most pilots, there were simply not enough targets to go round.

The side-by-side seating made for good crew co-operation, and the Mosquito would generally return safely to base on one engine. At night, the major problem was slowing up in time to avoid an overshoot. The first night fighter prototype was fitted with a "frill-type" speed brake around the fuselage, but this was not to become standard.

The Mosquito had been produced in Australia and Canada, but mainly in fighter-bomber versions. Production continued until November 1950, with the NF 36 and NF 38, which remained in service until the mid-1950s.

Below: The NF 30 was the final Mosquito variant to see action in WWII.

de Havilland Vampire F 3

Origin: de Havilland, England.
Type: Single-seat, single-engined subsonic jet day fighter.
Engine: One de Havilland H-1 Goblin centrifugal flow turbojet rated at 3,100lb (1,407kg) thrust.
Dimensions: Span 40ft 0in (12.20m); length 30ft 9in (9.37m); height 6ft 3in (1.91m); wing area 266sq.ft (24.71m^2).
Weights: Empty 7,134lb (3,236kg); normal takeoff 8,578lb (3,891kg); maximum 12,170lb (5,520kg).
Loadings (at normal takeoff weight)**:** Wing 32lb/sq.ft (157kg/m^2); thrust 0.36.
Performance: Maximum speed 531mph (854kph) at sea level, 505mph (813kph) at 30,000ft (9,144m); initial climb rate 4,375ft/min (22m/sec); service ceiling c40,000ft (12,191m); range (with drop tanks) 1,145 miles (1,842km).
Armament: Four 20mm Hispano cannon with 150 rounds per gun.
History: Designed around the H-1 Goblin turbojet as the second jet fighter for the RAF. First flight of prototype 20 September 1943. Service entry 1946. Developed through several variants, mainly for close air support, but also carrier fighters and two seater night fighters. Total production of all types 3,268.
Users (all types)**:** Australia, Britain (RAF and RN), Canada, Ceylon, Dominica, Egypt, Finland, France, India, Iraq, Italy, Jordan, Lebanon, Mexico, New Zealand, Norway, Rhodesia, South Africa, Sweden, Switzerland, and Venezuela.

Design of the DH 100, initially known as the Spider Crab, began in 1942 to take advantage of the new Halford H-1 turbojet. The H-1, later produced by de Havilland as the Goblin, had a single-sided centrifugal compressor which made for a small diameter engine, and in turn a small and light airframe. To minimise thrust losses, intake ducts and tailpipe were kept as short as possible by putting the pilot and engine in a short nacelle with wing root inlets, and carrying the tail surfaces on booms, high above the jet efflux. First flight, with Geoffrey de Havilland, Jr, at the controls, took place on 20 September 1943.

Development of what had become known as the Vampire was relatively trouble-free, and the first order was placed on 13 May 1944. Deliveries began in April 1945, too late to take part in World War II. It had always been intended to have a pressurised cockpit, and this was installed from the 51st aircraft onwards.

One F 1 was returned to de Havilland, where it was fitted with the more powerful Ghost turbojet and a metal canopy, and had the wing span extended by 8ft 0in (2.44m). In this guise, test pilot John Cunningham flew it to a new sustained altitude record of 59,446ft (18,118m) on 23 March 1948.

Greater endurance was soon demanded, and this was provided by the F 3. The original centre-section metal fuel tanks were replaced by Marflex bags, and three flexible fuel cells were added to each outer wing. At this point the tailplane was lowered and the fins and rudders revised. The low wing loading made handling very good, but the Vampire was outperformed by the Gloster Meteor, and the next main variants, the FB 5, FB 6, and FB 9, were optimised as fighter-bombers.

Meanwhile Britain's Royal Navy had been looking hard at jet fighters. Two fully navalised Vampire F 1 conversions were used for deck landing trials from 3 December 1945. Flown by Eric "Winkle" Brown, these were the first ever carrier operations by pure jet aircraft. Success brought an order for 30 Sea Vampire F 20s which, based on the FB 5, gave Fleet Air Arm pilots jet experience. These had larger flaps and speed brakes, and tailhooks on A-frames.

At much the same time, the powers that be came up with the potty idea of using flexible flight decks on carriers. To test this, three F 3s were converted to

Above: *The Vampire F.3 was the first British single-engined jet fighter.*

Below: *France licence-built the Nene-engined Vampire as the SE 532 Mistral.*

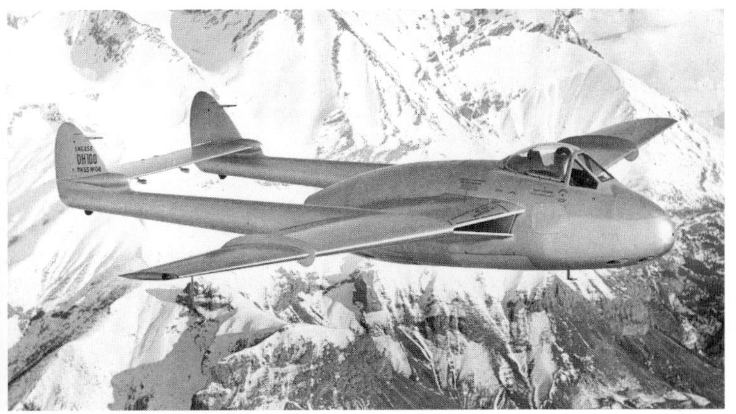

Sea Vampire F 21s with reinforced bellies. Trials soon proved that this idea was crazy. Why didn't they try a trampoline for vertical landing?

More power was always welcome, and the obvious engine to use was the Rolls-Royce Nene, of 5,000lb (2,270kg) thrust, probably the best engine never used by the RAF. Australia adopted the Nene for the Vampire, producing the FB 30, 31 and 32. These were retro-fitted with ejection seats, a glaring omission from RAF aircraft.

The other country to adopt the Nene-Vampire was France. After building 187 FB 5s, SNCASE mated the basic FB 5 airframe with the Hispano-built Nene as the SE 532 Mistral, the first flight of which took place on December 1951. The thrust of the Nene allowed a maximum sea level speed of 575mph

(925kph) as sea level. In all, 251 Mistrals were built, and the type remained in *l'Armée de l'Air* service between 1952 and 1961.

De Havilland also produced a night fighter, the Vampire NF 10, initially as a private venture. This was done by grafting on the modified front end a Mosquito NF 36, complete with AI X radar. To compensate for the extra weight and drag, the Goblin 3 was fitted, giving 3,300lb (1,497kg) thrust. Another change was the lengthened span of the horizontal tail. It was adopted by the RAF in 1951 as a stopgap pending delivery of the Meteor and Venom night fighters, but was withdrawn in 1954.

Below: The Vampire NF 10 utilised the front end of a Mosquito NF 36.

de Havilland Venom NF 3

Origin: de Havilland, England.
Type: Two-seat, single-engined subsonic jet all-weather fighter.
Engine: One de Havilland Ghost 105 centrifugal flow turbojet rated at 5,150lb (2,336kg) thrust.
Dimensions: Span 42ft 10in (13.06m) over tip tanks; length 36ft 8in (11.17m); height 6ft 6in (1.98m); wing area 280sq.ft (26m^2).
Weights: Empty 9,685lb (4,393kg); normal takeoff 12,417lb (5,632kg); maximum 14,400lb (6,532kg).
Loadings (at normal takeoff weight)**:** Wing 44lb/sq.ft (217kg/m^2); thrust 0.41.
Performance: Maximum speed 604mph (973kph) at sea level, 529mph (851kph) at 40,000ft (12,191m); initial climb rate 6,280ft/min (32m/sec); sustained climb 9min 30sec to 40,000ft (12,191m); service ceiling 45,000ft (13,715m); range 1,000 miles (1,609km).
Armament: Four 20mm Hispano cannon with 150 rounds per gun.
History: Developed from the Vampire and as a replacement for it, the Venom prototype first flew on 2 September 1949. The first variants in service were fighter-bombers, the FB 1 and FB 4, from 1952 to 1962. Next were night fighters, the NF 2 and NF 3, which served from 1953 to 1960, when they were replaced by the Javelin. The final fighter variant was the Sea Venom FAW 20-22, which was also licence-built by SNCASE as the Aquilon 201-203 for *l'Aeronavale*. Combat debut, Suez 1956. Total production 1,480, of which 671 were night or carrier fighters.
Users (all types)**:** Australia, Britain (RAF and RN), France, Iraq, Italy, Sweden, Switzerland, Venezuela.

Since the Vampire was designed for a predicted engine thrust of about 3,000lb (1,361kg), its wing thickness/chord ratio was 14 per cent, which gave a limiting Mach number of 0.75. But with ever more powerful engines becoming available, the obvious next step was to build a thin (10 per cent) wing Vampire, to raise the limit to Mach 0.84.

This duly emerged as the Venom FB 1. Although it looked like a Vampire, it was in fact rather different. The wing span was increased and the leading edge raked back at 17deg: not enough to be called swept, as this starts at 30deg. It was powered by the DH Ghost, and routinely carried wingtip fuel tanks. There were, however, problems with structural failures, and for much of its service the FB 1 was g-limited. The FB 1 was followed into service in 1955 by the FB

de Havilland Sea Vixen FAW 2

Origin: de Havilland, England.
Type: Two-seat, twin-engined swept-wing transonic jet all-weather carrier fighter.
Engine: Two Rolls-Royce Avon 208 axial-flow turbojets each rated at 11,230lb (5,094kg) military thrust.
Dimensions: Span 51ft 0in (15.54m); length 55ft 7in (16.94m); height 10ft 9in (3.28m); wing area 648sq.ft (60.19m^2).
Weights: Empty 27,952lb (12,679kg); normal takeoff 41,575lb (18,858kg); maximum 44,907lb (20,370kg).
Loadings (at normal takeoff weight)**:** Wing 64lb/sq.ft (313kg/m^2); thrust 0.54.
Performance: Maximum speed 690mph (1,110kph) at sea level; sustained climb rate 1min 30sec to 10,000ft (3,048m), 8min 30sec to 40,000ft (12,191m); service ceiling 48,000ft (14,630m); endurance 3hr 12min.

Above: This is the Aquilon, a French licence-built variant of the Sea Venom.

4, which had long overdue powered ailerons, air conditioning, and ejection seats. It also had a modified twin fin and rudder assembly.

Between the two fighter-bombers came two night fighters, the NF 2 and NF 3. The prototype NF 2 first flew on 22 August 1950, and it entered service in 1953. The front end was much the same as the Vampire, but curved dorsal fins with acorn fairings were added to the tail. The Venom was an interim night fighter, pending the arrival of the Javelin, and the final version was the NF 3. Radar was the Westinghouse APS-57, RAF designation AI 21. No ejection seats were fitted to the night fighters; the sole concession to crew escape was an enlarged roof hatch. But its main failing was an appallingly slow rate of roll.

Meanwhile the Royal Navy wanted an all-weather replacement for the Sea Hornet, and the two-seater Venom was the only British contender in sight. The Sea Venom, as it became, was navalised with anti-corrosion materials, fitted for arrested deck landings and catapult launches, and given a beefed-up landing gear and folding wings. The one surprise was that the horizontal tail extensions outboard of the booms were deleted. Late in its operational life, the Sea Venom FAW 22 carried Blue Jay AAMs, the first British fighter to be so armed. It was phased out in 1960.

The final fighter Venom was the Aquilon, licence-built by SNCASE. Based on the F 20, the first of 75 two-seater Aquilons flew on 25 March 1954. It had an ejection seat, a rearward sliding canopy, and air conditioning. Troubles with accommodating the radar led to 40 Aquilons being built as single-seaters, but the final batch were two-seaters with the Westinghouse APQ-65 radar. From 1956, Aquilons carried two Nord 5103 beam-riding AAMs, the first European missile to become operational.

Armament: Four Red Top all-aspect heat-homing AAMs.
History: Design work on the DH 110 commenced in 1946 as a carrier-based all-weather fighter, but first flight, by John Cunningham, did not take place until 26 September 1951. Development was delayed by a tragic accident at Farnborough in September 1952. Ten Sea Vixen FAW 1 production aircraft ordered in February 1955, and first flown on 20 March 1957, with service entry July 1959. Production switched to FAW 2 in 1963. Withdrawn from service 1972. Total production 145.
User: Britain (RN).

The Sea Vixen was the zenith of the twin-boom configuration for fighters. Initially it was to serve the RAF as a night fighter and the RN as a carrier strike fighter, but the RN, bothered by the thought of swept wing fighters aboard a carrier, pulled out in 1949 and settled for the very inferior Sea Venom. Two prototype DH 110s were retained by the RAF as insurance against the failure of the Javelin.

The DH 110 had several unusual features. As a swept-wing, twin-boom aircraft, the shape of the tail posed problems, as the wing sweep could not be matched without a really odd shape. In the event a straight horizontal tail of very thin section was selected. The radar displays of the day were very difficult to see in sunlight, and on the Sea Venom this had been enclosed in a hood. The solution adopted for the DH 110 was to bury the observer in a "coal-hole" on the starboard side of the fuselage, while the pilot's cockpit was offset to port.

On 9 April 1952, the DH 110 reached Mach 1.11 in a shallow dive; the first two-seater ever to do so, but the accident at Farnborough later that year, which killed 29 spectators, put the whole project on the back burner.

Navy interest gradually revived, and the Sea Vixen 20X prototype gradually took shape, despite literally hundreds of changes. It had more powerful Avon 208 engines, a longer nose, catapult spools and tailhook, restressed Fowler flaps in lieu of speed brakes, and modified wings with variable gear ailerons. The most unusual feature was ablative shoes to the underside of the rear booms. In the initial part of the landing roll, aerodynamic braking was used, hauling the nose up as high as possible. The shoes protected the booms if they touched the runway.

The Sea Vixen FAW 1 had wing folding, long-stroke main gear legs and a steerable nosewheel. Radar was the GEC AI 18, and the four 30mm Aden cannon proposed for the DH 110 had been dropped in favour of four Firestreak heat-homing AAMs. The first operational unit was No 892 Squadron, which embarked aboard HMS *Ark Royal* in March 1960.

Dewoitine D 501

Origin: SAF-Avions Dewoitine, France.
Type: Single-seat, single-engined low-wing monoplane fighter.
Engine: One 690hp Hispano-Suiza HS 12Xcrs liquid-cooled V-12.
Dimensions: Span 39ft 8in (12.09m); length 24ft 9.63in (7.56m); height 8ft 10.33in (2.70m); wing area 177.61sq.ft (16.50m²).
Weights: Empty 2,837lb (1,287kg); normal takeoff 3,940lb (1,787kg).
Loadings (at normal takeoff weight)**:** Wing 22.18lb/sq.ft (108kg/m²); power 5.71lb (2.59kg) per hp.
Performance: Maximum speed 288mph (367kph) at 16,405ft (5,000m); 196mph (315kph) at sea level; sustained climb rate 1min 21sec to 3,281ft (1,000m); service ceiling n/a; range 541 miles (870km).
Armament: One engine-mounted drum-fed 20mm Hispano-Suiza S7 (Oerlikon) cannon with 60 rounds, and two wing-mounted drum-fed 7.5mm Darne machine guns.
History: First flown (as the D 500) on 18 June 1932, and selected as the winner of the 1930 C1 single seat-fighter programme. Orders placed from November 1933, and delivery to *l'Armée de l'Air* from May 1935. Phased out of front line service by 1940.
Users: France (*l'Armée de l'Air* and *Aéronautique Navale*), Lithuania, Venezuela.

Emile Dewoitine was a prolific fighter designer between the two world wars, most of them parasol monoplanes. The D 500 was his first assay into the low-wing monoplane field. Angular, with an open cockpit and fixed undercarriage, it could accurately be described as attractively ugly.

The D 501 differed from the D 500 mainly in armament, having a 20mm cannon

Above: The Sea Vixen FAW 2 was the last of the de Havilland "twin-booms".

In 1963 production switched to the FAW 2. This involved a fire control system compatible with the Red Top all-aspect AAM, which would allow collision course interception rather than the tail-chase needed for Firestreak. The other major change was the extension of the forward portion of the tail booms to comply with the Area Rule. These were used to house more fuel.

In all, 29 FAW 2s were new production machines while 67 were converted from the original 114 FAW 1s. The last operational Sea Vixen unit was No 899 Squadron, aboard HMS *Eagle* until 1972.

Above: The D 501 marked the transition period from biplane to monoplane.

and two machine guns in lieu of four machine guns. The engine differed marginally to accommodate the cannon between the cylinder banks.

Not many D 500s/501s were actually built by Dewoitine. Lioré-et-Olivier produced 175, while Ateliers et Chantiers de la Loire turned out another 60. Reportedly pleasant to fly, the D 501 ended its service career as an advanced fighter trainer.

However, the story does not end there. Two of the first 15 D 500s were used as prototypes for the larger and heavier D 510, the first flying on 14 August 1934. It was very similar in appearance to the D 501 but had a smaller vertical tail and was slightly longer. It had underwing machine guns fed by 300-round drums. Powered by the HS 12Ycrs engine rated at 860hp, but with a takeoff weight some 313lb (142kg) heavier, the D 510 was slightly slower at altitude but 9mph (14kph) faster at sea level.

Dewoitine D 520

Origin: SNCAM-Emile Dewoitine, France.
Type: Single-seat, single-engined low-wing monoplane fighter.
Engine: One 935hp Hispano-Suiza HS 12Y45 liquid-cooled V-12.
Dimensions: Span 33ft 5.5in (10.20m); length 28ft 2.6in (8.60m); height 8ft 5.12in (2.57m); wing area 171.90sq.ft (15.97m^2).
Weights: Empty 4,686lb (2,123kg); normal takeoff (with wing tanks empty) 5,909lb (2,677kg); maximum 6,152lb (2,787kg).
Loadings (at normal takeoff weight)**:** Wing 34lb/sq.ft (168kg/m^2); power 6.32lb (2.87kg) per hp.
Performance: Maximum speed 264mph (425mph) at sea level, 332mph (534kph) at 18,046ft (5,500m); sustained climb rate 5 min 49sec to 13,124ft (4,000m), 14min 30sec to 26,248ft (8,000m); service ceiling 33,630ft (10,250m); range on full internal fuel 957 miles (1,540km).
Armament: One engine-mounted 20mm Hispano-Suiza HS 404 drum-fed cannon with 60 rounds; four wing-mounted belt-fed 1934-M39 MAC machine guns with 675 rounds per gun.
History: Two prototypes ordered 3 April 1938; first flight 2 October of that year. Production order placed 14 March 1939, and first production aircraft flew on 31 October. Operational from 13 May 1940. Production ended on 31 December 1942, with the 775th aircraft. Phased out 1945.
Users: France (*l'Armée de l'Air, Aéronautique Navale,* Vichy and Free French), Bulgaria, Germany (as fighter trainers), Italy, Romania.

Designed to meet a June 1936 specification, the D 520 was the best French fighter of World War II. An all-metal monoplane of monocoque construction and a monospar wing, the prototype was first flown by Marcel Doret on 2 October 1938. Initially it was disappointing, but replacing the two underwing radiators with a central single one reduced drag, while larger vertical tail surfaces increased stability. Later changes were a lengthened fuselage, two wing fuel tanks, and armou

Dornier Do 217N-2

Origin: Dornier-Werke GmbH, Germany.
Type: Three/four-seat, twin-engined radar-equipped night fighter.
Engines: Two 1,850hp Daimler-Benz DB 603A liquid-cooled V-12s.
Dimensions: Span 62ft 4in (19.00m); length 59ft 0.67in (18.00m); height 16ft 3.67in (4.97m); wing area 613.55sq.ft (57.00m^2).
Weights: Empty 22,665lb (10,270kg); normal takeoff 29,101lb (13,200kg).
Loadings (at normal takeoff weight)**:** Wing 47lb/sq.ft (232kg/m^2); power 7.87lb (3.57kg) per hp.
Performance: Maximum speed 320mph (515kph) at 19,686ft (6,000m), 267mph (430kph) at sea level; sustained climb rate 9min to 13,124ft (4,000m); service ceiling 29,201ft (8,900m); range 1,091 miles (1,755km).
Armament: Four nose-mounted 20mm Mauser MG 151 cannon with 200 rounds per gun and four nose-mounted 7.9mm MG 17 machine guns with 700 rounds per gun. Some aircraft carried two or four fixed upward-firing 20mm MG 151 cannon.
History: Derived from the Dornier Do 217M bomber, the Do 217N-2 was the last in a line of Dornier night fighters which had started with the Do 17Z-10. First flight 31 July 1942, with initial operational capability at the end of

Above: The D 520 was the best French-built fighter of World War II.

protection for the pilot. Placed in production, deliveries began on 14 January 1940.

Modifications delayed operational capability until 13 May 1940, but then the Dewoitine fighter showed its worth. It was slower but more manoeuvrable than the Bf 109, and D 520 pilots claimed 108 German and Italian aircraft shot down before the capitulation.

Production continued after the Armistice, and those built after May 1942 were powered by the HS 12Y49 engine, with improved altitude performance. Following the Battle of France, D 520s were active in Syria and North Africa, while on 19 August 1944, a *Forces Françaises de l'Interieur* unit with the Allies was outfitted with recaptured D 520s, which it flew until re-equipped with Spitfires on 1 March 1945.

The top-scoring D 520 pilot was probably Pierre Le Gloan who claimed seven Italian aircraft in June 1940, followed by four RAF Hurricanes and a Gladiator over Syria in June 1941.

Above: Like many other night fighters the Do 217N was adapted from a bomber.

that year. Production ended late in 1943, and the Dornier 217N-2 was phased out of service shortly afterwards.
Users: Germany, Italy.

The requirements of a night fighter in World War II were a means of finding the enemy in the dark, sufficient speed advantage to catch it, extended endurance, and preferably the range to operate over enemy bases. For the intruder mission, the choice fell on the Do 17, which made its combat debut during the Spanish Civil War as a fast bomber, but by mid-1940 it was being replaced by the He 111 and Ju 88, which could carry twice the bomb load. Fast enough, the Do 17Z was easy to fly and very manoeuvrable for a bomber.

To provide a sufficiently heavy punch, a solid nose from a Ju 88C long range fighter was grafted on. This contained two drum-fed 20mm Oerlikon MGFF cannon and four 7.9mm MG 17 machine guns. For target finding in darkness it was fitted with Spanner Anlage, an infra-red searchlight, but with a range of only 656ft (200m) this was next to useless. This aircraft became the Do 17Z-10 Kauz II, of which only nine were produced. They remained in service until 1943.

The next Dornier bomber to be modified was the better-performing Do 215B-5, which entered service late in 1940. Fitted with Lichtenstein airborne

---

Dornier Do 335A-1 Pfeil

Origin: Dornier-Werke GmbH, Germany.
Type: Single-seat, twin-engined day fighter.
Engine: Two 1,800hp Daimler-Benz DB 603E-1 liquid-cooled V-12 engines, one driving a tractor propeller, the other a pusher.
Dimensions: Span 45ft 3.33in (13.80m); length 45ft 5.25in (13.85m); height 16ft 4.88in (5.00m); wing area 414.42sq.ft (38.50m^2).
Weights: Empty 16,314lb (7,400kg); normal takeoff 21,160lb (9,598kg).
Loadings (at normal takeoff weight)**:** Wing 51lb/sq.ft (249kg/m^2); power 5.88lb (2.67kg) per hp.
Performance: Maximum speed 477mph (768kph) at 20,998ft (6,400m); climb rate n/a; service ceiling 37,403ft (11,400m); range 1,274 miles (2,050km); endurance 2hr.
Armament: One 30mm MK 103 cannon firing through the spinner and two 15mm MG 151 synchronised cannon in the upper engine cowling. An internal bomb bay was located behind and below the cockpit.
History: Potentially the fastest piston-engined fighter of World War II, the Do 335 prototype was first flown on 26 October 1943. Ten pre-production aircraft were built, and service evaluation began in July 1944. By the end of the war, only 11 production Do 335A-1s had been completed, plus two two-seater conversion trainers.
User: Germany.

First flown from Oberpfaffenhofen in October 1943, the Do 335 V1 was massive, and its appearance was most unusual. The DB 603E engine at the front was a V-12, but an annular radiator gave it the appearance of a radial. A second DB 603E was buried in the fuselage amidships with a ventral scoop radiator, and drove a pusher propeller at the rear via a long extension shaft. This arrangement promised several advantages: twin-engined power but with little more drag than a single-engined type. It allowed one engine to be shut down in flight to extend range and endurance, without the asymmetric handling problems normal with twin-engined types. For aerodynamic reasons the aircraft was actually slightly faster on the rear engine than the front one. But these radar, this scored the first radar "kill" on 9/10 August 1941 while on a defensive sortie. Only about 20 Do 215Bs entered service; the survivors remained operational until May 1944.

The next Dornier was a heavy bomber, the Do 217E. With a span 3ft 3in (1m) greater and an empty weight more than 3.5 tonnes heavier, it was an altogether larger machine. With two BMW 801ML radials rated at 1,580hp, it was rather underpowered, but handled well enough. Converted to night fighter configuration, this became the Do 217J. Armament consisted of four 20mm Oerlikon MGFF cannon (later replaced by four 20mm Mauser MG 151s), and four MG 17s in the nose, plus two 12.7mm MG 131s, one in a dorsal turret, the other in the ventral step. Radar remained the standard Lichtenstein. This model had virtually disappeared from service at the end of 1943.

The final Dornier night fighter was the Do 217N, derived from the Do 217M bomber. It differed from its predecessor in having 1,750hp Daimler-Benz DB603A liquid-cooled engines, which improved performance, while the dorsal turret and the ventral step gun were eliminated. Up to four upward-firing cannon were fitted to some aircraft. In all, 364 Do 217J and N fighters were built, and the latter served from the end of 1942 to the beginning of 1944. Two high scorers who flew Dorniers for part of their careers were Helmut Lent and Ludwig Becker.

Above: The Do 335A used a unique tractor/pusher layout to minimise drag.

advantages were not achieved without penalties. To enable the pilot to escape in an emergency, the rear propeller had first to be jettisoned. To prevent the rear propeller from touching the ground during takeoff and landing, a large ventral fin, with a sprung bumper at its base, was fitted, together with a tricycle undercarriage. All this, plus strengthening the fuselage around the amidships engine, increased structural weight. Finally, rearward vision was very poor. Delays in development ensured that the aircraft never saw action.

Douglas F3D-2 Skyknight

Origin: Douglas Aircraft Company, USA.
Type: Two-seat, twin-engined subsonic carrier-based jet night fighter.
Engines: Two Westinghouse J34-WE-36A single spool axial flow turbojets each rated at 3,400lb (1,542kg).
Dimensions: Span 50ft 0in (15.24m); length 45ft 5in (13.84m); height 16ft 1in (4.90m); wing area 400sq.ft (37.16m^2).
Weights: Empty 15,107lb (6,853kg); normal takeoff 23,575lb (10,694kg); maximum 26,731lb (12,125kg).
Loadings (at normal takeoff weight)**:** Wing 59lb/sq.ft (288kg/m^2); thrust 0.29.
Performance: Maximum speed 493mph (793kph) at 35,000ft (10,668m); initial climb rate 2,970ft/min (15m/sec); combat ceiling 39,400ft (12,009m); range on internal fuel 1,146 miles (1,844km); combat radius 400 miles (644km); endurance (with 4 drop tanks) 7hr.
Armament: Four 20mm M2 cannon with 200 rounds per gun; four Sparrow 1 beam-riding AAMs on 12 F3D-1M and 16 F3D-2M Skyknights.
History: First flight of the prototype 23 March 1948. First flight of production aircraft 13 February 1950. Service entry 1951. Combat debut Korea June 1952 on night escort missions. Used for electronic warfare in Vietnam from April 1965 until 1970. Production ceased October 1953, with a total of 265 built.
Users: USA (USMC and USN).

Affectionately known as "Willy the Whale", the Skyknight was designed to the first specification in the world (1946) to demand radar-guided interception at night at 500mph (805kph) at 40,000ft (12,191m). First flown by Russ Thaw on 23 March 1948, it had a straight wing in the mid position, and two turbojets set low on the fuselage beneath the wings, where they were easy to access. The fuselage was broad, mainly because the two-man crew were seated side by side, with an optically flat windshield in front of them. With no ejection seats, crew escape in an emergency was via a ventral chute, which was not a good idea at low level. The wide fuselage did however allow a huge internal fuel capacity.

Although grossly underpowered, the Skyknight showed no undesirable handling traits, and the first production order, for 28 F3D-1s, was placed in June 1948. Unfortunately the next batch, of F3D-2s, had to carry more than two tonnes of additional equipment, which made the thrust/weight ratio marginal. The planned engine for the F3D-2 was the Westinghouse J46, which gave 35 per cent more thrust, but this failed to enter service due to unreliability. Another feature of the -2 was the use of spoilers rather than ailerons. The ailerons of the day tended to twist the wing at high speeds, whereas spoilers, which extended from the upper surface of the wings, simply dumped lift, allowing the wing on that side to dip.

The Westinghouse APQ-35 radar was a nightmare, consisting of more than 300 thermionic valves, many of which needed matching by hand, and was very difficult to keep serviceable, although in this it was not a lot different to other contemporary radars.

Although designed as a carrier fighter, the lack of power and poor acceleration made the Skyknights marginal in this role, and few went to sea. Most were land-based, and served with the US Marine Corps. It was with this service that the Skyknight saw combat over Korea.

Marine Skyknights were used to fly barrier patrols between the MiG bases and the B-29 bombers of the USAF. Their first victory was a MiG-15, initially misidentified as a Yak-15, shot down on 3 November 1952 by William Stratton and his radar operator Hans Hoglind. This was the first ever jet-versus-jet night combat. Five more victories followed, four of them over MiG-15s. But the greatest success of the Skyknight was the fact that attacks on B-29s virtually ceased when they were operating.

Although a handful of Skyknights were fitted with the Westinghouse APQ-36 radar and Sparrow 1 beam-riding missiles, this was basically an operational experiment.

Below: Although underpowered, the Skyknight was successful over North Korea.

Douglas F4D-1 Skyray

Origin: Douglas Aircraft Company, USA.
Type: Single-seat, single-engined supersonic jet carrier interceptor.
Engines: One Pratt & Whitney J57-P-8B twin-spool axial flow afterburning turbojet rated at 16,000lb (7,258kg) maximum and 10,200lb (4,627kg) military thrust.
Dimensions: Span 45ft 8.25in (13.93m); length 33ft 6in (10.21m); height 12ft 11in (3.94m); wing area 557sq.ft (51.75m²).
Weights: Empty 16,024lb (7,268kg); normal takeoff 22,648lb (10,273kg); maximum 28,000lb (12,701kg).
Loadings (at normal takeoff weight)**:** Wing 41lb/sq.ft (198kg/m²); thrust 0.71.
Performance: Maximum speed Mach 1.05 at altitude, Mach 0.94 at sea level; initial climb rate 18,300ft/min (93m/sec); service ceiling 55,000ft (16,763m); combat radius c300 miles (483km).
Armament: Four 20mm Mk 12-0 wing-mounted cannon with 65 rounds per gun; either four 19-shot pods of 2.75in (70mm) FFARs, or four AAM-N-9 Sidewinder AAMs.
History: Designed as a fast-climbing interceptor, the prototype F4D was first flown by Larry Peyton on 23 January 1951. The first production Skyray, piloted by Robert Rahn, flew on 5 June 1954, and squadron service commenced in 1956. Production ceased December 1958 after 491 delivered. Finally phased out in 1964.
Users: USA (USMC and USN).

An order for two prototype XF4D-1s was placed on 16 December 1948. The Skyray was not a true delta, but a broad chord swept wing with automatic slats on the leading edge. The trailing edge had a much shallower sweep, with elevons. The broad wing chord made the aspect ratio exceptionally low, giving the very fast rate of roll of 500deg/sec. Plain wing root intakes were used, and to keep the thickness/chord ratio within bounds on this section, small trailing edge fillets were used at the junction with the fuselage.

The aerodynamics were sufficiently different to anything that had gone before to demand a new approach to the flight control system (FCS), with a computer and artificial "feel" to prevent the pilot from overstressing the airframe, and many other systems, many of which did not work as advertised.

In an attempt to minimise weight, a unique form of two layer structural skinning was used, most of which was only 0.03in (0.76mm) thick. This was a mistake; in service it was not "squaddy-proof", and dents and tears were all too frequent.

The engine of choice was the Westinghouse J40, but this was a major disaster. The first prototype, flown on 23 January 1951, was powered by the Allison J35 by default. With commendable foresight, Douglas designed the Skyray to take an

engine with a greater diameter. This finally emerged as the J57-P-8B.

Handling was, to say the least, interesting, sufficiently so that some were retained by the USN flight test school long after the type had left squadron service. Part of the problem was the broad chord. When transitioning from subsonic to supersonic flight, the centre of pressure shifted from quarter-chord to half-chord. This was not good, but the real problem came when decelerating from supersonic to subsonic flight, which produced a neck-breaking 4.5g pitchup. For a pilot already in a high-g turn, this resulted in instant overstress!

The Skyray had several soubriquets including the Ford, gained by contracting F4D; the Ten Minute Killer, from the time taken to carry out its basic interception mission, and Ensign Killer, from the fact that its safety record was terrible. That said, flying it was exciting. It could sustain a 70deg climb, which upset a lot of airline pilots. Then there were the world records. On 3 October 1953, Jimmy Verdin set a new air speed record of 752.9mph (1,211.64kph) in the second prototype, followed by Bob Rahn with the 100km closed circuit record 13 days later. Then in May 1958, it set five new time to altitude records, one of which was 2min 36.05sec to 15,000m (49,212ft). This was the more remarkable when one considers that the original specification of 5min to 40,000ft (12,191m) had been thought unreachable just a few years earlier. The F4D gave rise to the even better F5D Skylancer, but this failed to enter service.

Below: Radical in concept, the Skyray was almost too exciting for its pilots.

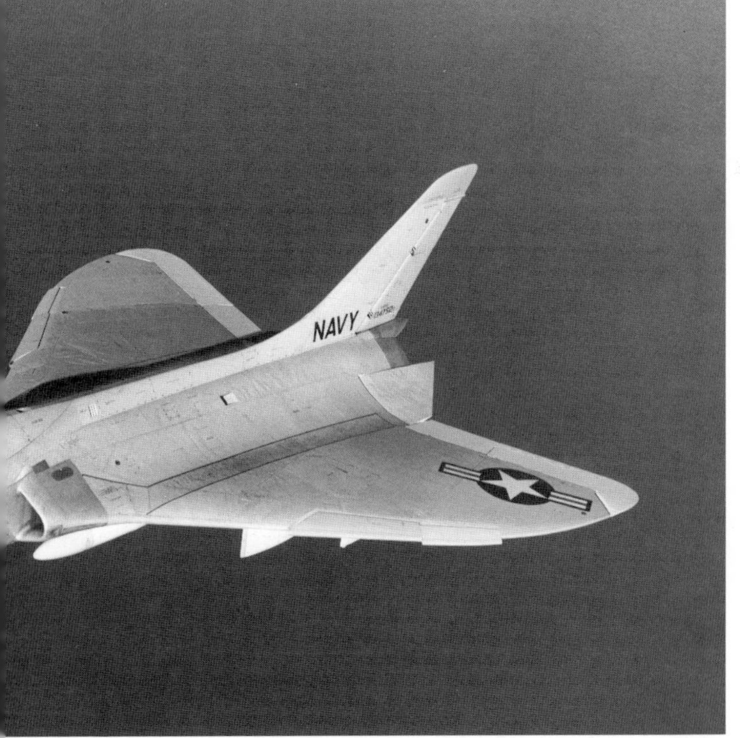

Dufaux Fighter

Origin: Armand Dufaux/CEA, France.
Type: Two-seat, single-engined biplane fighter.
Engine: One 110hp Le Rhône 9J rotary.
Dimensions: Span 26ft 1.4in (7.96m); length 20ft 0in (6.10m); height 9ft 1.25in (2.80m); wing area n/a.
Weights: Empty 1,168lb (530kg); normal takeoff 1,631lb (740kg).
Loadings (at normal takeoff weight)**:** wing n/a; power 14.83lb (6.73kg) per hp.
Performance: Maximum speed 87mph (140kph) at sea level; sustained climb rate 13min 9sec to 6,562ft (2,000m); service ceiling n/a; endurance 2hr.
Armament: One 0.303in (7.7mm) swivelling Lewis gun.
History: First flown early spring 1916, and commenced official testing at Chateaufort in April. Further development abandoned. Only one aircraft built.
User: None.

Way back in 1915, with air combat in its infancy, the design of fighting aircraft was in a state of flux. Tractor or pusher engine? Biplane or monoplane? Fixed guns or swivelling? One or two man crew? It was against this background that French designer Armand Dufaux set to work.

His approach was highly innovatory. His choice of a biplane was unsurprising, although a single streamlined interplane strut on each side was. He also concluded that the pilot had enough to do in flying the aeroplane, therefore a specialist gunner should be carried, sitting in the nose to have the widest possible field of fire, and armed with a swivelling machine gun. This was despite the weight and drag penalty involved. The gun chosen was a 0.303in (7.7mm) Lewis which, as it was drum-fed, could be kept in action much longer than a belt-fed gun. Gunner and pilot were seated almost side by side, but

English Electric Lightning F.6

Origin: The English Electric Company (later BAC), England.
Type: Single-seat, twin-engined bisonic all-weather interceptor.
Engines: Two Rolls-Royce Avon 301 afterburning turbojets each rated at 16,300lb (7,394kg) maximum and 13,220lb (6,000kg) military thrust.
Dimensions: Span 34ft 10in (10.61m); length over probe 55ft 3in (16.84m); height 19ft 7in (5.97m); wing area 474.5sq.ft (44.08m^2).
Weights: Empty 31,000lb (14,062kg); normal takeoff 39,940lb (18,117kg).
Loadings (at normal takeoff weight)**:** Wing 84lb/sq.ft (411kg/m^2); thrust 0.82.
Performance: Maximum speed Mach 2.14 at 36,000ft (10,972m); Mach 1.06 at sea level; initial climb rate 50,000ft/min (254m/sec); service ceiling 60,000ft (18,287m) plus; range 800 miles (1,287km).
Armament: Two 30mm Aden cannon with 130 rounds per gun; two Red Top or Firestreak AAMs.
History: Initially the P.1 supersonic research aircraft first flown on 4 August 1954. Developed as the P-1B fighter prototype which first flew, and went supersonic, on 4 April 1957. Mach 2 exceeded 25 November 1958. First order placed November 1956. Service entry 30 July 1960. Total production 338. Phased out in favour of F-4 Phantoms from 1974, and Tornados from 1986.
Users: Britain (RAF), Kuwait, Saudi Arabia.

To many contemporary observers, the English Electric Company seemed to have sprung from nowhere. Having spent World War II building aircraft designed by others, in 1949 they produced the world-beating Canberra bomber,

Above: An enclosed engine amidships caused problems for the Dufaux Fighter.

slightly staggered, with the gunner ahead.

Having put the gunner up front, how best to eliminate the drag caused by booms and rigging to carry the tail surfaces? In a truly unique solution, Dufaux placed the engine amidships inside the rectangular section fuselage, with an orthodox empennage carried on a substantial tubular beam passing through the centre of the crankshaft. Extra bracing for the tail was provided by rods from the wheel struts. Thus buried, the air-cooled rotary engine was prone to overheating, while structural problems were also encountered. No development work was undertaken.

Above: The P-1A Lightning prototype here shows its unique wing planform.

then followed this with the Lightning, the only all-British supersonic fighter.

The origin of the Lightning lay in ER 103, a specification for a supersonic research aircraft issued in May 1947. The English Electric team set to work, and by 1954 had produced the P.1, a large and rather brutal-looking aircraft.

The P.1 had several innovative features. The two Armstrong Siddeley Sapphire 5 engines were staggered one up, one down, with the upper engine aft of the lower. This eliminated asymmetric engine-out handling problems while the single shared nose inlet significantly reduced the fuselage cross-section and with it, profile drag. The wings were unique. Mid-mounted, they were swept at 60deg, with what for all practical purposes was a double trailing edge, the inboard section steeply swept with flaps, and the outboard section straight with ailerons. This demanded a rather heavy structure to resist bending moments at high loads.

The horizontal slab tail surfaces were all moving, with a similar planform to the wing and, unusually for the era, low-set. This helped avoid pitch-up, and prevented the tail from being blanketed by the wings at high angles of attack. The fin and rudder assembly was triangular. As befitted a high-speed research aircraft, the canopy was faired flush with the fuselage.

Piloted by fighter ace Bee Beamont, the P.1 first flew from Boscombe Down on 4 August 1954, and Mach 1 was exceeded a week later. As this was done with non-afterburning engines, it could be regarded as the first example

of supercruise, more than three decades before it became fashionable. It was another year before afterburning engines were fitted. By this time its potential as a fighter had been appreciated, and the second prototype, which first flew on 18 July 1955, carried two 30mm Aden cannon and had increased fuel capacity. Lack of endurance was in fact to bedevil the Lightning through much of its career. That said, handling qualities were benign and it was almost totally vice-free.

From January 1957 a modified wing was under test. This had a kinked leading edge, with conical camber on the outer sections, and cropped tips. Spanwise flow had long been a problem for swept wings; the usual solution was draggy wing fences. Instead English Electric used a sawcut to induce a vortex with the same effect.

Next came the P.1B, the first real fighter prototype. The fuselage was extensively redesigned to accommodate two Rolls-Royce Avons with four-stage afterburning. The canopy was set higher, with a dorsal spine running to the base of the fin. The intake was made annular, with a moveable centrebody housing the Ferranti AI 23 Airpass radar and attack system, which included, if one discounts reflector gunsights, what was probably the world's first head-up display. Optimised

Below: A Lightning F.3 of No 74 squadron RAF armed with two Firestreak AAMs.

for pursuit course interception, provision was made for two Firestreak AAMs.

The P.1B was flown on 4 April 1957, followed by two more prototypes and 20 development aircraft. The first production aircraft was the Lightning F 1, the first of 19 examples flying on 29 October 1959. The type entered squadron service from July 1960, by which time English Electric had become part of the British Aircraft Corporation. It has to be admitted that squadron service came as a terrible shock to the RAF, which had no previous experience of operating bisonic weapons systems. By comparison with previous RAF fighters, maintenance man-hours per flight hour were almost out of sight, and serviceability rates were poor. Next came 28 F 1As, powered by Avon 201s, and with bolt-on flight-refuelling probes. As an alternative to AAMs, 48 2in (51mm) unguided rockets could be carried. The F 1A was followed by the F 2 from 11 July 1961. An interim type, it varied little from its predecessor. The main difference was that it was powered by Avon 210s with fully variable

Eurofighter EF 2000 Typhoon

Origin: Eurofighter Jagdflugzeug GmbH, Multinational.
Type: Single-seat, twin-engined canard-delta bisonic air defence and multi-role fighter.
Engines: Two Eurojet EJ 200 two-spool afterburning turbofans each rated at 20,250lb (9,185kg) maximum and 13,500lb (6,124kg) military thrust.
Dimensions: Span 35ft 10.75in (10.95m); length 52ft 4in (15.96m); height 17ft 4in (5.28m); wing area 538sq.ft (50m^2).
Weights: Empty 21,500lb (9,752kg); normal takeoff c34,282lb (15,550kg); maximum 46,297lb (21,000kg).
Loadings (at normal takeoff weight)**:** Wing 64lb/sq.ft (311kg/m^2); thrust 1.18.
Performance: Maximum speed Mach 2 plus at altitude; Mach 1.20 at sea level; initial climb rate c50,000ft/min (254m/sec); operational ceiling c60,000ft (18,287m); radius of action 1,151 miles (1,852km); endurance 3.25hr.
Armament: One 27mm Mauser cannon with 150 rounds; 10 AAMs in a mix of Amraam, Aspide, Meteor, Asraam, or Sidewinder.
History: Feasibility studies commenced in 1983, and design weight was confirmed at about 10 tonnes. Britain and Italy combined to produce the Experimental Aircraft Programme (EAP), a concept demonstrator which first flew in August 1986. First EF 2000 prototype flown on 27 March 1994. First production aircraft flown 2001; squadron service entry scheduled from 2003.
Users (on order): Britain (RAF), Germany, Greece, Italy, Spain.

Spurred by the development of a new generation of agile Soviet fighters, notably the MiG-29 and the Su-27, several European nations commenced studies for a new fighter. Lured by the prospect of potentially huge savings accruing from a large production run, and equally anxious not to fall too far behind the USA in fighter technology, in 1983 four nations combined to develop an agile air superiority and multi-role fighter, with a weight of about 10 tonnes. They were Britain, France, Germany and Italy. France, having made demands that were unacceptable to her would-be partners, pulled out in 1985 to unilaterally develop Rafale, in which section the reasons are more fully explained. The remaining three nations continued, joined in 1985 by Spain, which needed to replace its ageing Phantoms and Mirage F 1s. In 1986 the Eurofighter consortium was founded.

The programme was triply high risk: airframe, engines, and radar and weapon system. Two more international consortia were formed to produce the latter two: Eurojet for the EJ 200 engine and Euroradar for the ECR 90 radar and weapon system.

Political and public relations considerations needed the new fighter to have an afterburners. Of the 42 aircraft delivered, 31 were later modified as F 2As, with an enlarged ventral fuel tank, extended and cambered wings, and a larger, square-tipped fin.

The Lightning F 3, which was first flown on 16 June 1962, was a next generation bird. Powered by Avon 301s, it could reach Mach 2 with ease, while the AI 23B radar was optimised for collision course interception, using large Red Top all-aspect AAMs. It was on this model that the square-topped fin, with its area increased by 15 per cent, was introduced. Another innovation was external fuel tanks mounted above the wing, with powered ejection. Outlandish in appearance, this was probably better than conventional underwing tanks in view of the low-set tail. In all, 72 F 3s were built.

The final Lightning was the F 6, which appeared in the sky on 26 June 1965. It had a modified wing and an enlarged ventral fuel tank. In all 55 new-build aircraft were produced, while nine were converted from F 3s.

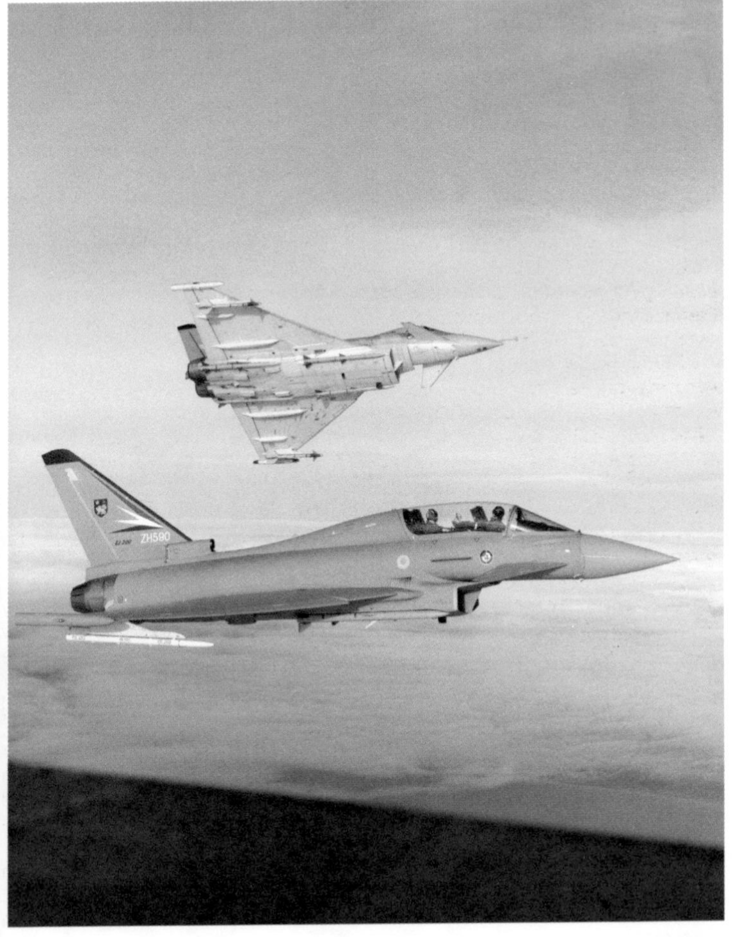

Above: EF 2000 Typhoon is being produced in single- and two-seater variants.

emotive name, but this was not done. At first it was known as the Eurofighter. Produced by Eurofighter GmbH, it thus became the Eurofighter Eurofighter! The next attempt was the uninspired EF 2000. Then in September 1998, it was named Typhoon, which is phonetically similar in German, Italian, and Spanish (Taifun, Tifone, etc). Even this caused controversy!

The new fighter was optimised for across the board combat: beyond visual range (BVR) and the close manoeuvring dogfight. The requirements for the former were long range detection and tracking, fast acceleration to give maximum energy, and thus range and manoeuvrability to the missiles when launched, and the ability to get the first shot in. As the saying goes, nothing makes an opponent more defensive than knowing that hostile missiles are already flying.

BVR has long been regarded as a panacea for all ills – every pilot an ace via technology, and kills before the enemy can get within range. Yet in December 1985, when the requirements were first laid down, the historical record was far from inspiring. The number of successful BVR engagements could be counted on the fingers of one hand; the number of unsuccessful attempts would have required the legs of several centipedes. The adoption of BVR on the grand scale was therefore a triumph of faith in future technology. One thing was certain: however good future BVR combat might become, sooner or later the fight would move to knife range. This demanded exceptional agility and high thrust/weight. The key to meeting the specification was the wing. A delta gives a high lift/drag ratio, low supersonic wave drag, and a high coefficient of lift. It also does not have a clearly defined stall point. Its traditional handicaps could be overcome by using canard foreplanes and variable camber with relaxed stability and an active computerised flight control system.

***Right:* ECM pod on the port wingtip; a towed radar decoy to starboard.**

***Below:* The canard foreplanes are set forward to increase the moment arm.**

To prove the concept, the Experimental Aircraft Programme (EAP) first took to the skies in August 1986. This had a cranked delta wing with automatic camber, quadruplex fly-by-wire, a chin inlet with a lower lip that could be drooped to improve airflow at high alpha, and an enormous vertical tail "borrowed" from a Tornado. Powered by two Turbo-Union RB 199s, it flew 259 sorties.

When the EF 2000 first flew on 27 March 1994, it differed considerably from EAP. The wing leading edge was now straight, with a 53deg sweep. Careful shaping reduced the radar cross-section, as did several other stealth features, including an upward-curved "smiling" inlet. After various metamorphoses, the fin was fairly tall, with a narrow chord. Unlike the other two European canard deltas, Rafale and Gripen, the canard foreplanes are not close-coupled, but set forward to give a long moment arm, and therefore greater effectiveness. More than 40 per cent of structural weight consists of

Fairey Flycatcher

Origin: Fairey Aviation Co Ltd., England.
Type: Single-seat, single-engined ship-board biplane fighter.
Engine: One 400hp Armstrong Siddeley Jaguar IV 14-cylinder radial.
Dimensions: Span 29ft 0in (8.84m); length 23ft 0in (7.01m); height 12ft 0in (3.66m); wing area 288sq.ft (26.76m²).
Weights: Empty 2,038lb (924kg); normal takeoff 3,028lb (1,375kg).
Loadings (at normal takeoff weight)**:** Wing 10.51lb/sq.ft (51kg/m²); power 7.57lb (3.43kg) per hp.
Performance: Maximum speed 134mph (216kph) at sea level, 110mph (177kph) at 17,000ft (5,181m); initial climb rate 1,090ft/min (5.53m/sec); sustained climb 25min 23sec to 17,000ft (5,181m); service ceiling 19,000ft (5,791m); range 263 miles (423km); endurance 1.82hr.
Armament: Two 0.303in (7.7mm) belt-fed synchronised Vickers machine guns.
History: Designed as either a floatplane, amphibian, land-based or carrier fighter. First flight 28 November 1922. In service from 1923. Total production 205, ceased June 1930. Phased out 1934.
User: Britain (FAA).

For many years the only front line fighter in the Fleet Air Arm, the Flycatcher was a small, mainly fabric-covered staggered biplane, with N-shaped interplane struts. First flown from Hamble on 28 November 1922, it carried out deck landing trials aboard HMS *Argus* in February 1923. For this it was fitted with two steel jaws on the undercarriage spreader bars to engage the fore and aft arrester wires then in use.

In squadron service from 1923, Flycatchers also served aboard capital ships, either flying off from small platforms above a gun turret, or later being catapulted. On the larger carriers of the day, *Courageous*, *Furious*, and *Glorious*, they were housed in a forward hangar below the main flight deck. This had a carbon fibre composites, giving a significant weight saving.

The first two development aircraft were powered by RB 199s, but since then the definitive EJ 200 has been fitted. It is possible that thrust-vectoring nozzles may be fitted at some future stage, to improve agility and short field performance.

The ECR 90 radar has a total of 31 modes, and is reported to simultaneously track up to 10 targets. It is supplemented by a "two-colour" Infra-Red Search and Track (IRST) system, and will have a helmet-mounted sight for off-boresight missile launch.

The cockpit is state of the art, with seven displays, HOTAS, and voice actuation for some functions. The Defensive Aids Sub-System (DASS), consisting of radar, missile approach and laser warning systems, together with active ECM, is housed in a pod on the port wingtip; the starboard wingtip carries towed radar decoys. Typhoon is scheduled to enter service with all four nations from 2003.

Above: The Flycatcher was for several years the FAA's front line fighter.

short runway, and the Flycatchers launched straight out over the bows.

Fitted with "boots" as a floatplane or amphibian, the Flycatcher's all-up weight was increased by 503lb (228kg); this and the added drag reduced performance and manoeuvrability considerably. It was also reported to be reluctant to leave the water on takeoff.

The nearest the Flycatcher ever got to action was with No 403 Flight, attached to the 5th Cruiser Squadron on the China Station. As floatplanes, the type operated from Hong Kong harbour against Chinese pirates. A single Fairey Flycatcher II was flown in 1926, but for all practical purposes it was no relation.

Fairey Firefly F 1

Origin: Fairey Aviation Co Ltd., England.
Type: Two-seat, single-engined long range monoplane carrier fighter.
Engine: One 1,990hp Rolls-Royce Griffon XII V-12 liquid-cooled engine.
Dimensions: Span 44ft 6in (13.56m); length 37ft 7in (11.46m); height 13ft 7in (4.14m); wing area 342sq.ft (31.77m²).
Weights: Empty 8,925lb (4,048kg), normal takeoff 12,131lb (5,503kg); maximum 14,288lb (6,481kg).
Loadings (at normal takeoff weight)**:** Wing 36lb/sq.ft (173kg/m²); power 6.10lb (2.77kg) per hp.
Performance: Maximum speed 319mph (513kph) at 17,000ft (5,181m), 284mph (457kph) at sea level: initial climb rate 2,300ft/min (11.68m/sec); sustained climb rate 5min 45sec to 10,000ft (3,048m); service ceiling 28,000ft (8,534m); range 1,364 miles (2,195km).
Armament: Four wing-mounted 20mm Hispano cannon with 160 rounds per gun; air-to-surface, eight 60lb (27kg) rocket projectiles or two 1,000lb (454kg) bombs.
History: Designed in 1939 to replace the Fulmar. First flight 22 December 1941. Deliveries commenced 4 March 1943. Operational from October 1943; combat debut July 1944. Mainly used for defence suppression. Production ended November 1946 after more than 850 built. Postwar saw a new generation of Fireflies emerge, but these were used for purposes other than air combat.
Users: Britain (FAA), Canada (Navy), Ethiopia, Netherlands (Navy), Thailand.

In the late 1930s, Britain's Fleet Air Arm shot itself in the foot by deciding that its new generation of monoplane fighters needed to be two-seaters. The thinking appeared to be that a pilot far out over the trackless ocean would be unable, without assistance, to find his way back to the carrier, which might have changed position by more than 50 miles (80km) since he launched. Therefore an observer would be provided, who would handle the radio and navigation. Carrier aircraft were already handicapped vis-a-vis their land-based counterparts by the extra weight of structure needed for deck landings and wing folding. A two-man crew simply increased the built-in headwind, with an aircraft designed for safety at the expense of fighting capability.

The first FAA two-seat monoplane fighter to enter service was the Fairey Fulmar, in June 1940. Essentially this was a scaled-down version of the Battle light bomber, although navalisation made it slightly heavier. Slow, and with a derisory rate of climb, it was not very effective even against unescorted bombers. Something far better was needed. That something was the Firefly, the name revived from a less than successful series of fighters in the 1920s. The prototype was first flown by C.S.Staniland on 22 December 1941, but development problems delayed service entry until mid-1943.

The Firefly F 1 carried a hefty punch in the form of four 20mm Hispano cannon which, compared to the eight Brownings of the Fulmar, could deliver four times the weight of fire in a one-second burst. The trailing edge of the shapely wing housed Fairey-Youngman flaps, which when extended improved range over the Fulmar by almost two-thirds, and enhanced manoeuvrability by effectively decreasing wing loading. Handling at the low end of the speed range was good, and it was engined by a Rolls-Royce Griffon of apparently more than adequate power.

It was not enough. The Firefly 1 was 38mph (61kph) faster than the Fulmar at sea level, and considerably better than this at altitude; it outclimbed it comfortably, and had a ceiling some 25 per cent higher. But by the time the Firefly 1 entered service it was outmatched in air combat by almost everything it was likely to encounter.

The FAA had meanwhile started to equip with American Hellcats and Corsairs, and the Fireflies were used primarily for defence suppression and anti-shipping strikes, commencing with attacks on the *Tirpitz* in July 1944. Only in the Far East did the type see any real air combat, and No 1770 Squadron registered nine victories against the Japanese.

Left: The two-seater, single-engined Firefly F.1 used manual wing folding.

Fiat CR 32quater

Origin: Fiat Aviazione, Italy.
Type: Single-seat, single-engined sesquiplane fighter.
Engine: One 600hp Fiat A 30 RA liquid-cooled V-12.
Dimensions: Span 31ft 2in (9.50m); length 24ft 4.5in (7.40m); height 8ft 7.5in (2.63m); wing area 238sq.ft (22.11m^2).
Weights: Empty 3,208lb (1,455kg); normal takeoff 4,222lb (1,915kg).
Loadings (at normal takeoff weight)**:** Wing 17.74lb/sq.ft (87kg/m^2); power 7.04lb (3.19kg) per hp.
Performance: Maximum speed 220mph (354kph) at 9,843ft (3,000m), 205mph (330kph) at sea level; initial climb rate 2,198ft/min (11.17m/sec); sustained climb 1min 35sec to 3,281ft (1,000m), 14min 25sec to 19,686ft (6,000m); service ceiling 25,264ft (7,700m); range 485 miles (780km).
Armament: Two 12.7mm belt-fed Breda-SAFAT synchronised machine guns in the upper cowling, with 375 rounds per gun.
History: First flown 28 April 1933. In service from March 1934. Combat debut Spanish Civil War August 1936. Used in early World War II over North and East Africa, and Greece. Total production 1,211; continued (in Spain) until 1943.
Users: Austria, China, Hungary, Italy, Paraguay, Spain, Venezuela.

Designer Celestino Rosatelli (the CR in CR 32) produced a line of sesquiplane

fighters commencing in 1923. The CR 32, which emerged in 1933, was a scaled-down version of the award-winning CR 30 of a year earlier. With a fabric-covered metal structure, its only unusual feature was the use of double Warren W-type interplane bracing, variations of which had appeared on all previous Rosatelli fighter designs. Not only did this almost completely eliminate bracing wires, it made for a very sturdy design. It was quickly ordered by the *Regia Aeronautica*, and deliveries began in March 1934. It was this version which saw service in the Spanish Civil War, with the *Aviacione Legionaria*, flown by Spanish Nationalists, and Italian "volunteer" pilots.

The CR 32 became a byword for agility in this conflict. There was little choice; once the Republicans had been equipped with the appreciably faster Polikarpov I-15 and I-16, both success and salvation lay in manoeuvrability. This had a pernicious influence on Italian fighter tactics in the global conflict to come; *Regia Aeronautica* had to unlearn the Spanish experience.

By far the most outstanding CR 32 pilot of the war was Spanish: Joaquin Garcia Morato y Castaño, who formed and led the famous *Patrulla Azul* (Blue Patrol) from December 1936. Of his 40 victories, 36 were scored with the little Fiat – not only the type but, amazingly, with the same aircraft! Only once was he shot down, by a stray bullet from a "friendly" Fiat, which caused minor engine damage.

The initial model was followed by the CR 32bis with an improved A 30 engine and two extra machine guns of 7.7mm calibre in the lower planes, plus a few minor "tweaks". Twelve 4.4lb (2kg) anti-personnel bombs could be carried on underwing racks. July 1937 saw the production of the CR 32ter, which reverted to the original 12.7mm gun armament, with an improved gunsight. The final model was the CR 32quater, literally Mk 4, which appeared late in 1936. Italian production ceased in 1939, in favour of the CR 42 Falco, although license production continued in Spain until 1943.

Although it was the second most numerous fighter type on Italy's entry into World War II in June 1940, the CR 32, by now obsolete, played little part, with the possible exception of East Africa, where the type accounted for several RAF aircraft. By mid-1941 they had all but vanished from the scene.

Left: The Fiat CR 32 was flown by the leading ace of the Spanish Civil War.

Fiat CR 42 Falco

Origin: Fiat Aviazione, Italy.
Type: Single-seat, single-engined sesquiplane fighter.
Engine: One 840hp Fiat A 74 R 1C 38 14-cylinder two-row radial.
Dimensions: Span 31ft 10in (9.70m); length 27ft 1.6in (8.27m); height 11ft 9.5in (3.59m); wing area 241.11sq.ft (22.40m²).
Weights: Empty 3,765lb (1,708kg); normal takeoff 5,033lb (2,283kg).
Loadings (at normal takeoff weight)**:** Wing 20.87lb/sq.ft (102kg/m²); power 5.99lb (2.72kg) per hp.
Performance: Maximum speed 267mph (430kph) at 17,488ft (5,330m); initial climb rate c2,500ft/min (12.70m/sec); sustained climb rate 9min 7sec to 19,686ft (6,000m); service ceiling 33,466ft (10,200m); range 482 miles (775km).
Armament: Two 12.7mm Breda-SAFAT belt-fed synchronised machine guns in the upper cowling, with 375 rounds per gun.
History: The last biplane fighter built by any of the combatants in World War II. First flight of the prototype 23 May 1938. Production commenced early 1939, and continued until 1944. Service entry from April 1939. Total production, including night fighters and fighter-bombers 1,781.
Users: Belgium, Germany (as night nuisance raiders), Hungary, Italy, Sweden.

The final Fiat fighter designed by Celestino Rosatelli, the CR 42 Falco was slightly larger and rather heavier than the CR 32, but retained much of the agility of the earlier fighter while offering considerably better performance across the board. It was arguably the best fighter biplane ever built, but this was simply not enough.

Compared with contemporary monoplane fighters of the other combatant nations, it was significantly slower, had a worse sustained climb rate, and was unable to dive as fast as they could. Unless circumstances were particularly favourable at the start of an engagement, it could neither force battle on an opponent, nor disengage at will. Even against bombers, it was hard pressed to achieve a good shooting position.

In fighter-versus-fighter combat, its best chance of survival lay in its agility, and its best chance of success lay in opportunistic attacks in the confusion of the dogfight. But even here it was handicapped. Its 12.7mm machine guns had a slow rate of fire and a low muzzle velocity, and the projectiles lacked penetration. Against opponents with self-sealing fuel tanks and armour protection, they were relatively ineffective. The Falco was obsolete even as it entered service.

The CR 42 Falco retained the unusual Warren W-type double interplane strut system and the spatted main wheels of the CR 32, but the main difference was the use of a radial engine with some 40 per cent more power. The tail surfaces were the only other feature to be radically altered, the large horn balances on the elevators being omitted. Perhaps surprisingly, wing area was only marginally increased.

Numerically the most important *Regia Aeronautica* fighter when Italy entered the war in June 1940, the Falco served in all theatres in the early years – the invasion of France, very briefly in the Battle of Britain, then in Greece, Malta, and the Aegean, North and East Africa, then as a night fighter over Italy. By early 1941 the shortcomings of the CR 42 as a fighter were apparent, and many units were converted to ground attack. The most successful CR 42 pilot was Mario Visentini, who flew mainly in East Africa.

The final fighter variant was the CR 42CN (*Caccia Notturna*). This had flame dampers on the exhausts, and carried a small searchlight pod under each wing, powered by a propeller-driven generator mounted on the upper plane centre-section. Without radar or effective ground control, it achieved little.

Left: The Fiat CR 42 was arguably the best biplane fighter ever built.

Fiat G 50bis Freccia

Origin: Fiat Aviazione, Italy.
Type: Single-seat, single-engined monoplane fighter.
Engine: One 870hp Fiat A 74 RC 38 14-cylinder two-row radial.
Dimensions: Span 36ft 0.25in (10.98m); length 25ft 7in (7.80m); height 9ft 8.5in (2.96m); wing area 196.44sq.ft (18.25m²).
Weights: Empty 4,579lb (2,077kg); normal takeoff 5,963lb (2,705kg).
Loadings (at normal takeoff weight)**:** Wing 30lb/sq.ft (148kg/m²); power 6.85l (3.11kg) per hp.
Performance: Maximum speed 294mph (473kph) at 19,686ft (6,000m); initial climb rate c2,600ft/min (13.21m/sec); sustained climb 3min 10sec to 9,843ft (3,000m); service ceiling 28,873ft (8,000m); range 621 miles (1,000km).
Armament: Two 12.7mm Breda-SAFAT belt-fed synchronised machine guns in the upper cowling, with 150 rounds per gun.
History: First flight of prototype 26 February 1937. Total of 45 pre-series aircraft built between October 1938 and July 1939. First G 50bis flown on 9 September 1940. Total production 684, plus 100 two-seater trainers.
Users: Finland, Italy.

Designed by Guiseppe Gabrielli, the G 50 Freccia was a move toward modernity. An all-metal low wing monoplane, with retractable main wheels an a fixed castoring tailwheel, in its early form it even had an enclosed cockpit However, it had three basic handicaps to overcome. The first was the lack of reliable high-powered engine, while the second was the insistence of the *Regi Aeronautica* on the best possible view for the pilot. To obtain this, he had to be

Fiat G 55 Centauro

Origin: Fiat Aviazione, Italy.
Type: Single-seat, single-engined monoplane fighter.
Engine: One 1,475hp Fiat RA 1050 RC 58 Tifone liquid-cooled V-12.
Dimensions: Span 38ft 10.5in (11.85m); length 30ft 9in (9.37m); height 10ft 3.25in (3.13m); wing area 227.23sq.ft (21.11m²).
Weights: Empty 5,798lb (2,630kg); normal takeoff c7,110lb (3,225kg); maximum 8,179lb (3,718kg).
Loadings (at normal takeoff weight)**:** Wing 31lb/sq.ft (153kg/m²); power 4.82lb (2.19kg) per hp.
Performance: Maximum speed 391mph (630kph) at 26,248ft (8,000m); sustained climb rate 7min 12sec to 19,686ft (6,000m); service ceiling n/a; range 746 miles (1,200km).
Armament: Three 20mm MG 151 cannon; two wing-mounted, one engine-mounted.
History: The first of three prototypes flown on 30 April 1942. The production G55/1 entered production in 1943, but only a handful had been built by the Armistice in September 1943. Total wartime production 311. Production resumed in 1947 as the G 55A. In all, 80 G 55As and two-seater G 55Bs were built.
Users: Argentina, Egypt, Italy (*Regia Aeronautica*, *Aeronautica Militare* and *Aviazione Nazionale Repubblicana*).

The dearth of suitable Italian fighter engines was solved in 1941 by a licence agreement with German company Daimler-Benz for their engines to be produced by Italian manufacturers. For the G 55, Fiat built the DB 605A as the Tifone, to power their new fighter, the Centauro. Three of the 37 pre-series aircraft were

Above: The Freccia was the first Fiat monoplane fighter to enter service.

sat up high, giving the Freccia a hump-backed, drag-inducing shape. The third was the pathetic Breda-SAFAT machine guns, which had to be nose-mounted since they were too heavy for carriage in the wings.

A dozen pre-production Freccias were sent to Spain for operational evaluation in 1939, but by this time there was little air combat in the civil war there. One change that did emerge was the deletion of the sliding canopy, the pilots objecting to anything that even slightly restricted their view. The vertical tail was also revised. A modified version, the G 50bis, first flown on 9 September 1940, had increased fuel capacity, a redesigned undercarriage, and a lengthened tailcone.

Like the CR 42, the G 50 served in most theatres during World War II, but its inferior engine and armament told against it, notably when faced with the Hurricane and P-40. The top-scoring Freccia pilot was Furio Lauri, with 11 of his total of 18 victories on the G 50.

Above: The Centauro was powered by a licence-built German DB 605A engine.

adapted to take the DB 603 engine, but this was at German request, and was not continued.

The Centauro was first flown on 30 April 1942, only 31 had been delivered when Italy changed sides, and most subsequent aircraft were delivered to the Axis-aligned *Aviazione Nazionale Repubblicana*, although opposed by Spitfires, Mustangs, and P-38 Lightnings they achieved little. Initial armament comprised two nose-mounted 12.7mm machine guns and two 20mm wing-mounted cannon.

Many Centauros survived the war, and in 1947 production was resumed as the G 55A. This differed from its predecessor only in instrumentation and radio, and was offered for export with either four 12.7mm Breda-SAFAT or Colt-Browning machine guns. At the same time a two-seater conversion trainer, the G 55B, was built. G 55As for the *Aeronautica Militare* were unarmed. Nineteen Centauros were delivered to Egypt and 45 to Argentina.

Focke-Wulf FW 190A-8

Origin: Focke-Wulf Flugzeugbau GmbH, Germany.
Type: Single-seat, single-engined monoplane fighter.
Engine: One 1,700hp BMW 801D-2 two-row 14-cylinder radial with methanol/water injection giving 2,100hp.
Dimensions: Span 34ft 5.5in (10.51m); length 29ft 4.25in (8.95m); height 12ft 11.5in (3.95m); wing area 196.98sq.ft (18.30m^2).
Weights: Empty 7,650lb (3,470kg); normal takeoff 9,656lb (4,380kg); maximum 10,803lb (4,900kg).
Loadings (at normal takeoff weight)**:** Wing 49lb/sq.ft (239kg/m^2); power (without m/w injection) 5.68lb (2.58kg) per hp.
Performance: Maximum speed 408mph (657kph) at 20,670ft (6,300m), 355mph (571kph) at sea level; initial climb rate 3,445ft/min (17.5m/sec); sustained climb 9min 54sec to 20,014ft (6,100m); service ceiling 37,403ft (12,000m); range 643 miles (1,035km).
Armament: Two 20mm MG 151 cannon in the wing roots and two more in the wing, two 13mm MG 131 machine guns in the upper cowling.
History: First flight of prototype 1 June 1939. Service entry and combat debut mid-summer 1941. The FW 190 was built in many variants, including fighter-bombers, dedicated bomber destroyers, and high altitude fighters. The final major variant was the FW 190D-9 which began to enter service in August 1944. Production continued until the end of World War II, with a total of about 20,000.
Users: France, Germany, Turkey.

Design work on the FW 190 began in 1938, some three years after the Messerschmitt Bf 109 had first flown, and the first flight of the prototype, by Hans Sander, took place on 1 June 1939. But, whereas the Bf 109 was a high-performance racehorse, Kurt Tank of Focke-Wulf designed his fighter as a rough and tough cavalry horse. This approach paid off handsomely.

Very unusually for the era, it had a radial engine, closely cowled, with an annular oil cooler with armour protection, and a 12-bladed cooling fan. The engine thrust line gave it a slightly nose-down attitude in level flight, which

Below: The final variant of the FW 190 was the D-9 "long nose" seen here.

Above: FW 190A-3s of 7/JG2, at Morlaix, France, in the summer of 1942.

improved pilot view forward. A single-piece sliding canopy gave good all-round vision in other directions. The seat was semi-reclining, with a high heel line, to improve g-resistance for the pilot. The sturdy wide track undercarriage was well suited to operating from grass fields. In a real return to simplicity, all trimming tabs were fixed. If all was not well after a test flight, they were bent slightly with an instrument rather like a tuning fork, until handling was just right. To reduce pilot workload there was an ingenious gadget called *Kommandgerät*, which automatically handled propeller pitch, fuel mixture, boost and engine revolutions to give optimum results. This allowed the pilot to concentrate on flying the aircraft in combat without unnecessary distractions. Finally, the ailerons were perfectly balanced, giving an exceptional rate of roll.

All this was not achieved without problems: engine and cockpit overheating, cowlings that blew off at high speeds, a few structural weaknesses, and inadequate firepower. However, these were soon overcome, and the initial production batch was completed in the spring of 1941. FW 190A-1s were delivered to the first operational unit, *6/JG 26*, in July of that year, and made their combat debut in September.

It came as a terrible shock to the British. Compared to the Spitfire V, the FW 190 was faster on the level and in a dive, climbed better, and rolled much faster. Only in a level turn was the more lightly loaded British fighter superior. But while the FW 190A initially outclassed the opposition, it was not without flaws. It was difficult to fly on instruments. The stall characteristics were unforgiving: without warning, the port wing dropped so violently that the aircraft almost inverted itself. If pulled into a high speed stall, it would flick out onto the opposite bank and probably spin. At low altitudes, with little room for recovery, this was bad news. It meant that at low level FW 190 pilots were often reluctant to use their aircraft to its full capacity. Nor was the FW 190 at its best at high altitude; here the Bf 109 reigned supreme.

The first major production model was the FW 190A-3, which entered service at the end of 1941. Next came the A-4, in 1942, the first to have methanol/water injection. There was also a tropical variant of this, and a long range fighter-bomber. The night fighter version of the A-5 had anti-glare panels and shrouded exhausts. Here its sheer sturdiness told against it. A hard landing by an inexperienced pilot at night in poor weather would often end with the FW 190 on its back. In similar circumstances the more flimsy Bf 109 would shear off its main gear and remain upright, with the pilot more or less intact.

As with every other fighter, the FW 190A suffered from creeping weight growth, as armament and fuel capacity were increased and other changes made. Wing loading of the A-8, which entered service at the end of 1943, had increased by more than 25 per cent compared to the A-3, and performance suffered equally.

By this time a means of countering daylight raids by massed formations of USAAF heavy bombers was needed. The only sure way to score was to approach from astern, in the teeth of crossfire from hundreds of heavy machine guns. This gave rise to the FW 190A-8/R8 Sturmbock, which had extra armour protection to the engine, cockpit, and gun magazines, with bullet-proof glass scabbed onto the quarterlights and canopy sides. To give it the necessary punch, it was armed with two 12.7mm machine guns in the cowling, two

20mm MG 151 cannon in the wing roots, and two 30mm MK 108 cannon under the wings. This version, the airborne equivalent of the tank, lacked performance and manoeuvrability, and needed fighter protection to keep the American escort fighters at bay.

The final variant of the FW 190 was the D-9, called by its Allied opponents the "long-nose", which entered service in the autumn of 1944. Still recognisably an FW 190, it was powered by a Junkers Jumo 213A V-12 with an annular radiator. Armament was two 20mm MG 151 cannon and two MG 131 machine guns. Compared to the FW 190A, it accelerated faster, was faster, and had a better climb and dive performance. Nor did it bleed off speed so quickly in hard turns. The one thing lacking was the sparkling rate of roll, while the lengthened fuselage made it sluggish in pitch.

The FW 190 sequel was the Ta 152 series. It was externally almost indistinguishable from the FW 190D, and only a handful of these saw service, the final one being the Ta 152H high altitude fighter.

Below: The FW 190A was the rough and tough "cavalry horse" of the Jagdwaffe.

Fokker E III Eindecker

Origin: Fokker Flugzeugwerke GmbH, Germany.
Type: Single-seat, single-engined monoplane fighter.
Engine: One 100hp Oberursel U 1 9-cylinder rotary.
Dimensions: Span 31ft 3in (9.52m); length 23ft 7.5in (7.20m); height 7ft 10.5in (2.40m); wing area 165.77sq.ft ($15.40m^2$).
Weights: Empty 880lb (399kg); normal takeoff 1,345lb (610kg).
Loadings (at normal takeoff weight)**:** Wing 8.11lb/sq.ft ($39.61kg/m^2$); power 13.45lb (6.10kg) per hp.
Performance: Maximum speed 87mph (140kph) at sea level; sustained climb rate 30min to 9,893ft (3,000m); service ceiling 11,812ft (3,600m); range 149 miles (240km), endurance 1hr 30min.
Armament: Two belt-fed 7.92mm Maxim LMG 08/15 synchronised machine guns mounted above the cowling.
History: Designed by Dutchman Anthony Fokker, the prototype M5 was first flown in the spring of 1914. The first fighter to be equipped with synchronisation gear which allowed it to fire through the propeller disc, the E 1 was ordered into production in 1915, with first deliveries in June of that year. It was followed by the up-engined E II and E III, with two machine guns. The final Eindecker was the E IV. Production ceased July 1916, with a total of 371 of all types delivered.
Users: Austro-Hungary, Germany.

The Fokker Eindecker set the trend for fighters for several decades, in that it was a single-engined, single-seater with fixed forward-firing machine guns aimed by pointing the aeroplane. A prewar design, it combined a welded steel tube fuselage structure with wooden wings, the whole being fabric-covered.

Lateral control was by wing-warping, which demanded a great deal of muscle on the part of the pilot.

Its real claim to fame lay in the development of a reliable form of gun synchronisation. Attempts had been made prewar, but were defeated by hang-fire rounds – faulty ammunition which fired a split-second late and hit the propeller. This was overcome by Frenchman Roland Garros, who fitted steel deflector plates to the propeller of his Morane Parasol. After a brief period of success, he was shot down by ground fire, enabling the Germans to examine his machine. They passed the problem to Anthony Fokker, who then devised a workable synchronisaton gear. The rest is history!

The Eindecker E 1, which was powered by an 80hp Oberursel rotary engine and armed with a single machine gun, started to arrive at the front in June 1915. It quickly established a deadly reputation, although based on cold figures this was hard to justify. The E 1 was not particularly fast, had a poor rate of climb, and did not behave well in steep dives. With wing warping, rate of roll was unexceptional which reduced manoeuvrability, despite the low wing loading. The E II and E III, the latter with the 100hp Oberursel engine and two machine guns, entered service at an early date, but performance-wise were little better than the original.

The first Eindecker victory was claimed by Kurt Wintgens on 1 July 1915, although since his victim fell on the wrong side of the lines it was not confirmed. One month later, Max Immelmann, "the Eagle of Lille", downed a BE 2c for the first confirmed Eindecker victory. This opened a period which has passed into folklore as the "Fokker Scourge!"

Below: The Fokker E.1 Eindecker had amazing impact on future air combat.

Like beauty, the Fokker menace was largely in the eye of the beholder. To British and French flyers, merely to be seen by one was to instantly be in mortal peril. Much of this impression was subjective: as a monoplane, the Eindecker was far more difficult to see from head-on than a biplane; consequently it suddenly appeared as if from nowhere. Its slim fuselage added to the illusion: the Eindecker often appeared to be much faster than it was. British ace James McCudden, flying as an observer in 1915, described an Eindecker as "fairly streaking across the sky".

However, the legend of the Fokker Scourge was not borne out by the facts. Initially it was distributed along the front in penny packets, the *Kampfeinsitzerkommando*, and flew only in ones or twos. Its greatest exponents were Oswald Boelcke and Max Immelmann, the greatest aces of the *Luftstreitkräfte* at that time. But even these two only managed to average slightly more than one victory a month each! In the final 61 days of the year, Britain's RFC losses in air combat were a mere 25 – one every two and a half days! By later standards, this was a mere bagatelle.

The main factor in the Fokker legend was inspired by a feeling of helplessness on the part of the Allied pilots: the Germans had a potent fighter, but they had nothing. On the other hand, pilot quality was paramount. On 29 December 1915, six Eindeckers, led by Boelcke and Immelmann, attacked two BE 2cs, aircraft widely regarded as turkeys. These defended themselves stoutly, and quickly drove off two German machines. Boelcke settled on one of

the BE 2cs and, after a wild fight lasting no less than 45 minutes, ran out of ammunition. At this point he was joined by Immelmann, but the RFC machine, piloted by Sholto Douglas (future head of RAF Fighter Command in World War II), escaped back to its own lines at low level.

The Eindecker did not reach the front in large numbers until 1916, and by this time the Allies had found an answer. The French had introduced the Nieuport Nie 11 Bébé, with a machine gun on the top wing firing over the propeller, while the British introduced two pusher biplane fighters, the single-seat DH 2 and the two-seat FE 2b. By the spring of 1915, these had taken the measure of the Eindecker, the final variant of which was the E IV, powered by the 160hp Oberursel U-III two-row 14-cylinder rotary, and armed with up to three machine guns. Although faster than its predecessors, with a maximum speed of 99mph (160kph), the E IV was less handy, and not very pleasant to fly. Boelcke for one preferred the E III. Only 49 examples of the E IV were delivered.

The Eindecker was remarkable in that it pointed the way to a true fighter configuration, which other nations followed. Its demise was heralded by the death of Max Immelmann, shot down by an FE 2b of No 25 Squadron on 18 June 1916. Oswald Boelcke, its greatest exponent with 18 victories, went on to raise his score to 40 by the time of his death on 28 October 1916.

Below: A Fokker E.III – the mainstay of the "Fokker Scourge" of 1915-16.

Fokker Dr 1

Origin: Fokker Flugzeugwerke GmbH, Germany.
Type: Single-seat, single-engined triplane fighter.
Engine: One 110hp Oberursel Ur II (Le Rhône) 9-cylinder rotary.
Dimensions: Span 23ft 7in (7.19m); length 18ft 11in (5.77m); height 9ft 8in (2.95m); wing area 200.86sq.ft (18.66m^2).
Weights: Empty 895lb (406kg); normal takeoff 1,292lb (586kg).
Loadings (at normal takeoff weight)**:** Wing 6.43lb/sq.ft (31.40kg/m^2); power 11.75lb (5.33kg) per hp.
Performance: Maximum speed 115mph (185kph) at sea level, 103mph (166kph) at 13,124ft (4,000m); sustained climb rate 2min 54sec to 3,281ft (1,000m), or 6min to 9,843ft (3,000m); service ceiling 20,014ft (6,100m); range 186 miles (300km); endurance 1.5hr.
Armament: Two 7.92mm belt-fed synchronised Maxim (Spandau) LMG 08/15 machine guns.
History: Arguably the most agile fighter in German service, the Dr 1 (*Dreidecker Eins*) was evaluated by Manfred von Richthofen's *Jasta 11* from August 1917, and entered unit service from October. Apart from rate of climb, it was outperformed by contemporary fighters, and relied on agility. Total production 320; it was phased out in June 1918.
User: Germany.

Inspired by the Sopwith Triplane, designer Reinhold Platz of Fokker set out to produce a super-agile fighter. His concept was to use three wings of narrow chord and short span to give at least the same lifting area as a similar biplane, but with less resistance in the rolling plane. This was combined with a rotary engine which, with the pilot sat up close, gave a very short moment arm about the centre of gravity. The engine selected was actually the 110hp Le Rhône rotary, built under license by Oberursal in Germany, and also in Sweden. While this lacked power compared with many contemporary units, overall dimensions

Below: The Fokker Dr 1 Dreidecker was designed for extreme manoeuvrability.

Above: Manfred von Ricthofen brings his Dr 1 in to land after a sortie.

were small, and the weight was light. The design configuration was intended to provide extreme manoeuvrability, and in this it succeeded.

A similar prototype was the V 4, first flown in May 1917, on which, unusually for the time, the wings were cantilevered. Flight trials showed an unacceptable amount of wing flexing, and single outboard interplane struts were fitted to cure this. Other modifications introduced after flight tests were aerodynamically balanced ailerons and elevators. The true prototype of the Dr 1 was actually the V 5, ordered in July 1917.

As an alternative, the Fokker V 6 was developed with a six-cylinder liquid-cooled Mercedes D III inline, with an increased span and wing area, but development was discontinued when it was found that the agility of the V 5 could not be equalled, even though it appears certain that the V 6 was the faster aircraft. Up to this point, the *Luftstreitkräfte* had preferred performance fighters, able to force battle on their opponents, or to disengage at will. The move to manoeuvre fighters, able to outfight their opponents in the dogfight, as typified by the Dr I, goes to show how deeply the high command had been impressed by the Sopwith Triplane. And not only the high command: many German aces – Manfred von Richthofen, Werner Voss, Eduard von Schleich, Kurt Wolff, and many others – all flew the Dr I.

Voss, whose final score was 48 victories, died in an epic combat against a horde of SE 5as, on 23 September 1917. James McCudden recalled that Voss turned amazingly quickly, in a sort of half-spin rather than a banked turn, and was almost impossible to follow. The German pilot was finally ground down by sheer weight of numbers.

Shortly after, the Dr I was grounded, since weaknesses had appeared in the wing structure. This was not corrected until the end of that year. Production ended in May 1918, and the type did not long survive von Richthofen, its greatest protagonist.

Fokker D VII

Origin: Fokker Flugzeugwerke GmbH, Germany.
Type: Single-seat, single-engined biplane fighter.
Engine: One 185hp BMW IIIa 6-cylinder liquid-cooled inline.
Dimensions: Span 29ft 2.33in (8.90m); length 22ft 9.75in (6.95m); height 9ft 0in (2.75m); wing area 217.44sq.ft ($20.20m^2$).
Weights: Empty 1,508lb (684kg); normal takeoff 2,006lb (910kg).
Loadings (at normal takeoff weight)**:** Wing 9.23lb/sq.ft ($45kg/m^2$); power 10.84lb (4.92kg) per hp.
Performance: Maximum speed 124mph (200kph) at sea level; sustained climb rate 2min 30sec to 3,281ft (1,000m), 16min to 16,405ft (5,000m); service ceiling 22,967ft (7,000m); endurance 1hr 30min.
Armament: Two 7.92mm belt-fed synchronised Maxim (Spandau) LMG 08/15 machine guns.
History: First flight of the V 11 prototype December 1917. Won the Adlershof fighter competition in the following month, and was ordered into large-scale production. Entered service late April 1918, and by the end of World War I it was the numerically most important German fighter. D VII production continued abroad after the war, and the type served with several nations, and remained in service with some until the early 1930s.
Users: Austro-Hungary, Belgium, Czechoslovakia, Germany, Hungary, Netherlands, Poland, Romania, Soviet Union, Sweden, Switzerland.

The final wartime biplane by Reinhold Platz, the V 11 prototype first flew in December 1917. Handling was far from perfect; among other faults it was directionally unstable, and the controls were far too sensitive for the average *Jasta* pilot to handle with any degree of confidence. Many modifications followed. The fuselage was lengthened, fin area increased, wing stagger was reduced, as was the gap between the wings. Perhaps surprisingly, no dihedral was added to the wings, which were absolutely straight. However, the problems were cured, and the D VII emerged as a

pleasant-handling and responsive fighter.

Powered by a 160hp Mercedes D 111 six cylinder inline engine with, unusually, a car-type radiator at the front, the Fokker D VII was structurally similar to the Dr I. It was of mixed tubular steel and wood, although the wings, which were of broader chord, differed in having two box spars rather than a single compound spar. It was fabric-covered except for the front, which was metal-clad back to the leading edge of the lower wing, and as far as the cockpit on the upper surface.

In the D-class (fighter) competition at Adlershof in January 1918, where it was evaluated by operational pilots, it was unanimously acclaimed a clear winner. This was apparently not on the basis of its performance, which in cold figures was not particularly outstanding, but on its handling. Even near its ceiling this remained responsive, and in a steep climb the D VII had an uncanny ability to "hang on its prop" at low airspeeds. Following Adlershof, it was ordered into large-scale production.

The first D VIIs entered service with *JG 1* in late April 1918, shortly after the demise of the Red Baron. These were closely followed by a variant powered by the 185hp BMW IIIa 6-cylinder liquid-cooled inline. In level flight this was 9mph (14kph) faster, nearly doubled the sustained climb rate to high altitude, and had a ceiling approximately 3,281ft (1,000m) higher. An instant favourite with its pilots, by the end of the war it equipped no fewer than 45 *Jastas*, had earned a formidable reputation, and was flown by almost every German ace to survive that far, including Ernst Udet. Much has been made of the fact that the Fokker D VII was singled out for special mention at the Armistice, but why this was is unclear.

The end of the war was not the end of the road for the D VII, which was subsequently produced in Holland and elsewhere, and saw much active service, mainly in Eastern Europe.

Below: The Fokker D VII was probably the best German fighter of WWI.

Fokker D XXI

Origin: N.V. Koninklijke Nederlandse Vliegtuigenfabriek Fokker, Holland.
Type: Single-seat, single-engined low-wing monoplane fighter.
Engine: One 825hp Bristol Mercury VIII 9-cylinder radial.
Dimensions: Span 36ft 1in (11.00m); length 26ft 10.75in (8.20m); height 9ft 8in (2.95m); wing area 174.38sq.ft (16.20m^2).
Weights: Empty 3,197lb (1,450kg); normal takeoff 4,519lb (2,050kg).
Loadings (at normal takeoff weight)**:** Wing 26lb/sq.ft (127kg/m^2); power 5.48lb (2.48kg) per hp.
Performance: Maximum speed 286mph (460kph) at 16,733ft (5,100m); sustained climb rate 1min 27sec to 3,281ft (1,000m); service ceiling n/a; range 578 miles (930km).
Armament: Four 7.9mm FN-Browning M.36 belt-fed wing-mounted machine guns.
History: Designed to meet a specification of the Royal Netherlands East Indies Army. First flight of prototype 27 February 1936. License-built in Finland, Denmark, and Spain. Total production 147. Saw combat in the Winter War and World War II. Withdrawn from service 1951.
Users: Denmark, Finland, Netherlands, Spain.

At the end of the Great War, Anthony Fokker moved back to Holland and continued to produce fighter aeroplanes, with a moderate degree of success, including an export order for 50 D XIIIs for the clandestine German aviation training centre at Lipetsk in the Soviet Union.

Designed by Erich Schatzki, and first flown on 27 February 1936, the D XXI was Fokker's first venture into the world of low-wing cantilever monoplanes, a trend which had been set more than two years earlier by the Polikarpov I-16. But, unlike the Soviet fighter, it did not feature retractable main wheels, although it did, in another first for the Dutch company, have an enclosed cockpit with a side-hinged canopy.

The engine of choice was the 825hp Bristol Mercury VIII radial with a three-bladed two-pitch propeller. The draggy radial combined with fixed spatted main wheels inevitably restricted performance. But since the specification had been drawn up to meet conditions in the Far East, this may have been considered not to matter too much. The D XXI was typical Fokker mixed structure, and the tailplane was braced by wires above and struts below.

Armament consisted of four 7.9mm FN-Browning machine guns mounted in the wings, firing outside the propeller disc, and aimed by an odd sort of half-ring and bead sight, both being mounted on a raised rod. This gave only half the firepower of the closely contemporary British monoplane fighters, which also had a reflector sight!

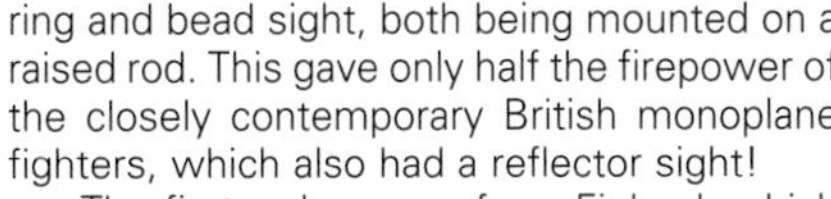

The first order came from Finland, which obtained a manufacturing licence, as did Denmark and Spain. Only 36 aircraft were ordered by the home air force, and in 1940 this proved to be far too few to deal with the *Luftwaffe* hordes. Finnish-built aircraft were fitted with the slightly more powerful Mercury VII with 840hp, license-built in Poland by PZL. The Danish-built machines also differed from standard: two of the machine guns were deleted and replaced by 20mm Madsen.

The combat debut of the D XXI came in the Winter War of 1939-40, when the Soviet Union invaded Finland. The lightweight armament proved adequate to deal with unarmoured Soviet bombers, and Jorma Sarvanto, the top-scoring ace of the conflict with 12 victories, claimed six bombers shot down in a single sortie.

Finnish production resumed later in 1940, but with the Pratt & Whitney Twin Wasp Junior radial of 825hp, and other minor changes. This first flew in January 1941, but showed a slight drop in performance and a marked reduction of manoeuvrability. Only 55 were built.

Left: The Dutch Fokker D XXIs were overwhelmed by the Luftwaffe in 1940.

Folland Fo 145 Gnat

Origin: Folland Aircraft Ltd., England.
Type: Single-seat, single-engined lightweight transonic jet fighter.
Engine: One Bristol-Siddeley Orpheus 701 single-spool turbojet rated at 4,520lb (2,050kg) military thrust.
Dimensions: Span 22ft 1in (6.73m); length 28ft 8in (8.74m); height 8ft 1in (2.46m); wing area 136.6sq.ft (12.69m²).
Weights: Empty 4,800lb (2,177kg); normal takeoff 6,650lb (3,016kg); maximum 9,040lb (4,101kg).
Loadings (at normal takeoff weight)**:** Wing 49lb/sq.ft (238kg/m²); thrust 0.68.
Performance: Maximum speed 714mph (1,149kph) at 18,000ft (5,486m); initial climb rate 20,000ftmin (102m/sec); sustained climb 5min 15sec to 45,000ft (13,715m); service ceiling 50,000ft (15,239m); endurance 1hr 15min; combat radius with external tanks 500 miles (805km).
Armament: Two 30mm Aden Mk 4 cannon in the intake fairings with 115 rounds per gun. Provision for two 500lb (227kg) bombs or 12 3in (76mm) rockets underwing.
History: The Fo 139 Midge proof of concept aircraft first flown 11 August 1954. First flight of prototype Gnat 18 July 1955. Six operational trials aircraft built. Exported to Finland, and India. Combat debut against Pakistan 1965. Developed by Hindustan Aeronautics Ltd (HAL) as the Ajeet, first flown 5 March 1975. Indian production terminated February 1982, and phased out of IAF service on 25 March 1991. Total production 314.
Users: Finland, India, Yugoslavia (evaluation only).

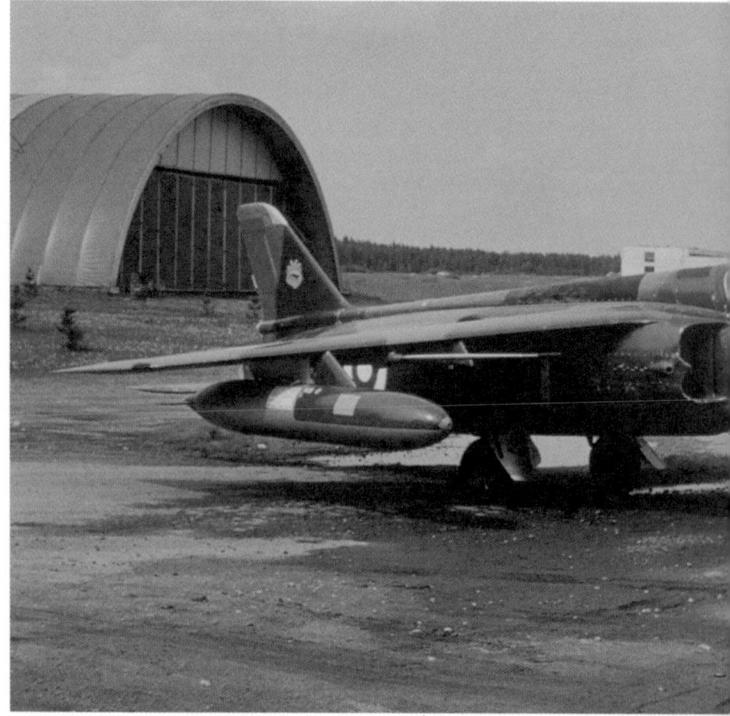

At a time when the trend was for bigger, heavier, more complicated, and more expensive fighters, Teddy Petter, of Canberra fame, made a gallant but unavailing attempt to reverse the trend. The Gnat was conceived as a small, simple, affordable, maintainable, fighter.

The engine originally selected was the Bristol-Siddeley Saturn, but when this was cancelled the Orpheus was substituted. Mindful of the delay caused by this, Petter went ahead with the Midge, a scaled-down version powered by an Armstrong Siddeley Viper, to prove the aerodynamics and systems. First flown by Teddy Tennant on 11 August 1954, this exceeded all expectations. The prototype Gnat followed on 18 July of the following year.

Tiny but chunky, the Gnat had a 40deg shoulder-mounted wing with a 40deg leading edge sweep. The pilot's seat was steeply raked to reduce frontal area, and not, as in the F-16 to increase g-resistance. The canopy was single piece, and front hinged like that of the MiG-21, faired into a dorsal spine which housed control runs. The engine was fed by side inlets, the outer portions of which housed the Aden cannon. Handling was superb, but the Gnat was not selected for the RAF as a fighter, possibly because such a small aircraft had little development potential. Instead, the two-seater version was adopted as an advanced trainer, and became the first mount of the Red Arrows aerobatic display team.

Nor did it do well on the export market: Yugoslavia bought two for evaluation, Finland a dozen for a single squadron, which served from July 1958 until 1973. The saving grace was India. Starting with an order for 23 aircraft and another 20 in kit form, HAL obtained a licence and churned out 193 Gnats.

In squadron service in India from March 1960, the Gnat made its combat debut on 3 September 1965, shooting down a Pakistani F-86F Sabre, the first of seven victories claimed during the 23-day conflict, against the loss of two Gnats. The greatest advantage of the Indian lightweight was its small size, which made it difficult to see, especially against a background of haze at low level, where most air fighting took place.

The Ajeet, developed by HAL from the Gnat, differed from it in having integral fuel tanks in the wings, improved control systems and avionics, and four underwing ordnance stations. The first production Ajeet flew on 5 March 1975, and low-rate production ended seven years later. By now obsolescent, the Ajeet soldiered on with No 2 Squadron IAF until March 1991.

Left: In Indian Air Force service, the Gnat was dubbed the Sabre Slayer!

General Dynamics F-16C Block 40 Fighting Falcon

Origin: General Dynamics, Fort Worth Division, USA.
Type: Single-seat, single-engined supersonic jet air superiority and multi-role fighter.
Engine: One General Electric F110-GE-100 two-spool afterburning turbofan rated at 28,982lb (13,146kg) maximum and 17,260lb (7,829kg) military thrust.
Dimensions: Span 31ft 0in (9.45m); length 49ft 3in (15.01m); height 16ft 8.5in (5.09m); wing area 300sq.ft (27.88m^2).
Weights: Empty 19,020lb (8,627kg); normal takeoff 28,500lb (12,928kg); maximum 42,300lb (19,187kg).
Loadings (at normal takeoff weight)**:** Wing 95lb/sq.ft (464kg/m^2); thrust 1.02.
Performance: Maximum speed Mach 2 at altitude, Mach 1.2 at sea level; initial climb rate 50,000ft/min (254m/sec); operational ceiling 50,000ft (15,239m); sustained ceiling 61,500ft (18,744m); operational radius 490 miles (788km) with four AAMs and one external fuel tank.
Armament: One 20mm M61A six-barrel rotary cannon with 511 rounds; six AIM-9 Sidewinders, AIM 120 Amraam, R550 Magic 2, MICA, or Python 3 AAMs, or in combination.
History: The winner of the USAF LWF competition, the prototype YF-16 first flew on 20 January 1974. First flight of a production F-16A took place on 7 August 1978. Operational from 1980. Combat debut 7 June 1981 (with Israel). Development has been continuous. In June 2001, the most recent variant was the F-16C Block 60, and production total was 4,028, with 257 still on order.
Users: Bahrain, Belgium, Chile, Denmark, Egypt, Greece, Holland, Indonesia, Israel, Jordan, Norway, Pakistan, Portugal, Saudi Arabia, Singapore, South

Below: In 1974, the YF-16 set new standards for fighter manoeuvrability.

Above: The F-16 is cleared to carry a variety of air-to-surface surface ordnance.

Korea, Taiwan, Thailand, Turkey, Venezuela, United Arab Emirates, USA (USAF – AFRES and ANG – and USN).

In the 1960s, had the Cold War in Europe turned hot, NATO tactical air forces would have been heavily outnumbered by hordes of austere but agile Warsaw Pact fighters. To achieve numerical parity was for many reasons not possible. The American reaction was to counter quantity with quality, to defeat superior numbers with technical superiority. But US experience over North Vietnam, where the sophisticated F-4 Phantom II was having a hard time against the basic MiG-17 and MiG-21, caused a rethink.

In the Pentagon, USAF Major John Boyd and analyst Pierre Sprey, began to address the problem, unofficially at first. Their solution was the hi-low mix, a few very capable and expensive fighters, backed by lots of austere, affordable aircraft optimised for close combat.

The hi-tech part of the mix was already underway, in the form of the very advanced F-14 Tomcat and F-15 Eagle. What was now needed was the lo-tech end of the mix. The USAF Light Weight Fighter competition was launched to explore the possibilities.

In order to give the designers a free hand, few performance minima and military requirements were specified. The need was for a close combat fighter with a high rate of turn and acceleration, and endurance rather better than that of the average lightweight. Five companies submitted schemes, and two – General Dynamics and Northrop – were given orders for two proof of concept machines each, in April 1972.

To develop the new fighter, General Dynamics set up a closed facility, housing about 250 people of all disciplines, under designer Harry Hillaker, who worked closely with Pierre Sprey. Progress was swift, and the first YF-16 was rolled out on 13 December 1973. The engine selected was the proven Pratt & Whitney F100-P-200, rated at 23,830lb (10,809kg) maximum thrust, which already powered the F-15. It was fed by a chin inlet located beneath the cockpit, which allowed the forebody to act as a compression wedge at high angles of attack. The F100 gave a thrust/weight ratio slightly in excess of unity at combat takeoff weight, giving outstanding acceleration and a high rate of climb.

The wing was swept at a 40deg angle, with a thickness/chord ratio of 4 per cent and an aspect ratio of 3. Leading and trailing edge flaps gave variable camber, computer controlled to give optimum lift for each flight condition.

Leading edge root extensions were used to form vortices which energized the sluggish boundary layer flow at high angles of attack. They were blended smoothly into the fuselage, which not only increased structural strength, but provided volume for internal fuel. These were carried aft to the tail, providing shelves on which differentially moving tailerons were mounted. Wing/body blending also proved advantageous in reducing the radar cross-sectional area, although this was fortuitous.

Armament was basic, a 20mm M61A six-barrel cannon in the port wing root extension, and two AIM-9 Sidewinders on wingtip rails. From the outset, Harry Hillaker recognized that something more that a ranging radar would be needed, and made provision for a more capable set to be fitted.

Of the few requirements laid down, two were a load factor of 7.33g (11g absolute) with 80 per cent internal fuel, and an operational radius of 575 miles (926km). The former was standard, but the latter was pushing the state of the art hard. Designing in sufficient internal fuel to meet this requirement would have incurred a significant weight penalty, which in turn would reduce performance and manoeuvrability. Since fighters almost invariably carry drop tanks, Hillaker reasoned that these could be used for the outbound leg of the mission. By allowing the YF-16 to arrive in the combat zone with full internal fuel, range could be stretched. Designed to a load factor of 9g (13.5g absolute) with full internal fuel, the YF-16 could fight on arrival with no g-restrictions.

YF-16 construction was almost entirely of aluminium alloy. The hi-tech lay under the skin. In a world first, the flight control system was quadruplex analogue fly-by-wire with no mechanical backup. Control commands were translated by computer to give the optimum for the flight conditions. Another first was a force transducer sidestick on the starboard console. The seat was raked back at a 30deg angle to increase g-resistance, and set high to give the best possible view "out of the window", which in this case was a single-piece canopy. The result was a close combat fighter which set new standards for manoeuvrability, and became a yardstick against which newer fighters were judged.

First flight, by Phil Oestricher, took place at Edwards AFB on 20 January 1974. The flyoff against the YF-17 took place later that year, and the YF-16 was declared the winner in January 1975. But, predictably, the USAF and the first four European customers wanted more capability. A Westinghouse APG-66 multi-mode radar was added, as well as carrying capacity for air-to-surface weapons. Wing and tail area were increased, the fin made taller and the fuselage longer. Weight increased by nearly 2,000lb (907kg).

This was to be a continuing trend with the F-16, and by 1980 the lightweight fighter had become a multi-role middleweight. Officially named

Above: Experiments with ventral control surfaces were made with an F-16.

Fighting Falcon, in US service it is known as the Electric Jet, or even more commonly, the Viper.

Many Viper variants have emerged. The F-16/79 was a down-market export version powered by the General Electric J79. It failed to attract orders. The F-16ADF was modified to carry AIM-7 Sparrow AAMs in the air defence role, while the US Navy adopted the F-16N as its adversary training aircraft. A tail-less cranked delta configuration was adopted for the F-16XL and F-16F, but neither entered service. In 1988, creeping weight growth was to be offset by the "big-wing" Agile Falcon, but this was cancelled in 1989.

The first major variant to enter service was the F-16C, with the advanced APG-68 multi-mode radar, and improved avionics and displays. To counteract creeping weight growth, later aircraft were powered by either the F100-P-229 or F110-GE-100 engines. While these restored the thrust/weight ratio, they did nothing for wing loading. Then, from Block 40 onwards, digital fly-by-wire replaced the analogue system.

The other thing that weight growth and more powerful engines had combined to erode was range. Block 60/62 Vipers are to have conformal fuel tanks along the fuselage above the wings. This again will do nothing for wing loading.

Although the Viper now operates mainly as a bomb truck, it has made its mark in its designed function, air combat. The first Viper air-to-air victory was a Syrian Mi-8 helicopter, downed on 28 April 1981 by a young Israeli. In all, Israeli fighters have claimed a total of 44 air combat victories; their top scorer, Amir Nahumi, has downed seven, making the first and so far only Viper ace.

Of other nations, Pakistani Vipers have claimed about 16 victories following violations of the border with Afghanistan, and USAF Vipers two Iraqi fighters and four Serbian Jastrebs. The most recent was a Serbian MiG-29 over Kosovo on 24 March 1999, the first by a Dutch pilot in more than 50 years.

Left: F-16As of Belgium, Denmark, the Netherlands, Norway, and the USAF.

Above: The Viper, as it is widely known, is larger than the WWII Mustang

276

Gloster Gladiator II

Origin: Gloster Aircraft Co Ltd., England.
Type: Single-seat, single-engined biplane fighter.
Engine: One 840hp Bristol Mercury VIIIA 9-cylinder radial.
Dimensions: Span 32ft 3in (9.83m); length 27ft 5in (8.36m); height 10ft 7in (3.22m); wing area 323sq.ft (30m^2).
Weights: Empty 3,444lb (1,562kg); normal takeoff 4,864lb (2,206kg).
Loadings (at normal takeoff weight)**:** Wing 15.06lb/sq.ft (73.53kg/m^2).
Performance: Maximum speed 257mph (414kph) at 14,600ft (4,450m); initial climb rate 2,430ft/min (12.34m/sec); sustained climb rate 4min 30sec to 10,000ft (3,048m); service ceiling 32,900ft (10,027m); range 444 miles (714km).
Armament: Two nose-mounted synchronized .303in (7.7mm) Browning machine guns with 600 rounds per gun; two underwing-mounted .303in (7.7mm) machine guns with 400 rounds per gun.
History: Developed from the Gauntlet, the prototype Gladiator first flew on 12 September 1934. Production began summer 1935; service entry February 1937. Sea Gladiators from 1939. Withdrawn from front line service 1942. Total production 746.
Users: Belgium, Britain (RAF and RN), China, Egypt, Eire, Finland, Greece, Iraq, Latvia, Lithuania, Norway, Portugal, South Africa, Sweden.

Obsolescent when it entered service, the Gladiator was an orthodox equal span biplane, its sole concessions to modernity being hydraulic flaps, a variable-incidence tailplane, and an enclosed cockpit. The original armament consisted of twin belt-fed Vickers machine guns and two Lewis guns under the wings, each with a 97-round

---

Gloster Meteor F 8

Origin: Gloster Aircraft Co Ltd., England.
Type: Single-seat, twin-engined subsonic jet day fighter.
Engine: Two Rolls-Royce Derwent 8 centrifugal flow turbojets each rated at 3,600lb (1,633kg) thrust.
Dimensions: Span 37ft 2in (11.32m); length 44ft 7in (13.59m); height 13ft 0in (3.96m); wing area 350sq.ft (32.51m^2).
Weights: Empty 10,684lb (4,846kg); normal takeoff 15,700lb (7,122kg); maximum 19,100lb (8,664kg).
Loadings (at normal takeoff weight)**:** Wing 45lb/sq.ft (219kg/m^2); thrust 0.46.
Performance: Maximum speed 598mph (962kph) at 10,000ft (3,048m); initial climb rate 7,000ft/min (35.55m/sec); service ceiling 44,000ft (13,411m); range 600 miles (965km).
Armament: Four nose-mounted 20mm Hispano Mk 5 cannon.
History: First flight of the prototype 5 March 1943. Operational from July 1944, and combat debut against V-1s in August. Final development the Meteor F 8, first flight 12 October 1948. Remained in RAF service until April 1957. Total production (all types including FR and PR variants) 2701.
Users: Argentina, Australia, Belgium, Brazil, Britain (RAF), Denmark, Ecuador, Egypt, Holland, Israel, Syria.

The first British jet fighter to enter service, and by a narrow margin only the second in the world to do so, was the Meteor, affectionately known as the "Meatbox". Preliminary design was begun late in 1940, under George Carter of Gloster Aircraft. It had of necessity to be twin-engined, given the predicted low thrust of the early jets, and like the German Me 262 carried them on the wings,

---

Right: The Gladiator was the last ever British biplane fighter.

drum, but these were soon changed for Brownings. The nose-mounted Brownings were set low, and fired from inside the engine cowling, the bullets passing perilously close to the plug leads! Their breeches protruded into the cockpit, and the pilot was provided with a mallet with which to hit the cocking handles.

The Sea Gladiator differed only in having an arrester hook, a dinghy in a fairing under the fuselage, and modified ejector chutes for guns.

Gladiators fought for China against Japan, and Finland and Sweden against the Soviet Union. In Allied service during World War II they fought over France and Belgium, Norway, North and East Africa, Greece and Syria against the Axis forces. Their greatest successes were against the Italians over North Africa and Greece. The Italian CR 42 was faster, and climbed and dived better, and its manoeuvrability was similar to that of the Gladiator. That notwithstanding, a dozen RAF Gladiator pilots became aces on the type. Two of them reached double figures: of "Pat" Pattle's 15 victories, 10 were CR 42s, while "Cherry" Vale's score of 10 included six CR 42s and a G 50.

Above: The F 8 was the last and best of the Meteor day fighters.

away from the fuselage. It did however have two advantages over its rival. First, Carter went for a nosewheel tricycle undercarriage from the start, whereas Willi Messerschmitt had it forced on him by experience. Second, the cockpit of the Meteor was located right forward, well ahead of the wing leading edge, giving the pilot a far better view "out of the window" than any other contemporary fighter.

An order for 12 prototype aircraft was issued in early 1941, and on 10 July 1942 test pilot Gerry Sayer lifted a Meteor off at Newmarket Heath. But with a mere 1,000lb (454kg) thrust from each of the Rover W2B engines, he had insufficient power to climb out safely, and so put it straight down again. More powerful engines were badly needed.

The true first flight was made by Michael Daunt at Cranwell on 5 March 1943, and the Meteor was ordered into production that summer. These were powered by Rolls-Royce Wellands rated at 1,700lb (771kg) thrust, and this, the Meteor F I, first flew on 12 January 1944, and entered squadron service in July, its first task to counter V-1 flying bombs. Derwent-powered Meteor IIIs were deployed to the European continent from February 1945, but the *Jagdflieger* proved elusive. This was perhaps just as well. In a dive the Meteor quickly reached its critical Mach number of 0.74, where buffeting made it uncontrollable. Dive brakes had to be used to contain the

Gloster (Armstrong Whitworth) Meteor NF 11

Origin: Sir W. G. Armstrong Whitworth Aircraft Ltd., England.
Type: Two-seat, twin-engined subsonic jet night fighter.
Engines: Two Rolls-Royce Derwent 8 centrifugal flow turbojets each rated at 3,600lb (1,633lb) thrust.
Dimensions: Span 43ft 0in (13.11m); length 48ft 6in (14.78m); height 13ft 11in (4.24m); wing area 374sq.ft (34.75m²).
Weights: Empty 12,019lb (5,452kg); normal takeoff 16,542lb (7,503kg); maximum 19,790lb (8,976kg).
Loadings (at normal takeoff weight)**:** Wing 44lb/sq.ft (216kg/m²); thrust 0.44.
Performance: Maximum speed 541mph (871kph) at 30,000ft (9,148m), 505mph (813kph) at sea level; initial climb rate 5,800ft/min (29.46m/sec); sustained climb 11min 30sec to 35,000ft (10,667m); service ceiling 40,000ft (12,191m); range 950 miles (1,529km).
Armament: Four wing-mounted 20mm Hispano Mk 5 cannon with 160 rounds per gun.
History: Based on the Meteor T 7 two-seat fighter trainer, the prototype first flew on 31 May 1950, followed by the first production aircraft on 13 November. Next came the NF 13 on 23 December 1952, the NF 12 (out of sequence) on 21 April 1953, and finally the NF 14 on 23 October. Production ended 31 May 1954, with a total of 547 of all types. Phased out August 1961.
Users: Belgium, Britain (RAF), Denmark, Egypt, France, Israel, Syria.

In the late 1940s, new RAF night and all-weather fighters were scheduled to replace the ubiquitous Mosquito in the mid-1950s. The Cold War then demanded something more urgently, and the Meteor NF 11 was born. Armstrong Whitworth were assigned the task, using the Meteor T 7 trainer as a basis. It was already a two-seater, so could carry a radar operator, and needed the addition of a radar and guns.

In practice things were a little more complicated. The nose was lengthened to accommodate AI 10 radar, but this occupied the space where the guns would have been. Where to put them? An undernose pack would have involved major redesign, while the inner wing section was already occupied by the main gear wells and other things. The only solution was the wings outboard of the engines. To make more room, the longer span wing of the F 3 was adopted, speed to within acceptable limits.

Next came the Meteor F IV. Powered by Rolls-Royce Derwent Vs, rated at 3,500lb (1,588kg) thrust each, this had a stronger airframe and a pressurized cockpit. Previous models had been sluggish in the rolling plane; to improve this the F IV had its span reduced by 5ft 10in (1.78m) and area reduced by 24sq.ft (2.23m2). Lengthened engine nacelles delayed the onset of buffet, raising the critical Mach number to 0.84. Postwar, Meteor IVs twice set new world air speed records, 616mph (991kph) being achieved on 7 September 1946.

The final dedicated fighter variant was the Meteor F 8, the prototype of which first flew on 12 October 1948. Structurally beefed up, the F 8 retained the small wing of the F IV, and had a totally revised empennage, an ejection seat, and a fuselage lengthened by 2ft 6in (0.76m). The F 8 was flown in Korea in 1952 by the RAAF against communist MiG-15s, which outclassed it.

Above: The Meteor NF 11 night fighter was developed from the T 7 trainer.

giving an extra 35in (89cm) on each side to play with. Other modifications were the empennage of the F 8 to offset the instability caused by the longer nose, larger tabs on the ailerons, and cockpit pressurisation.

The NF 11 prototype was first flown from Baginton by Eric Franklin on 31 May 1950. The only real trouble experienced was with the radar nose profile, but this was corrected. Production commenced, and the NF 11 started to reach the squadrons in 1951. Central Fighter Establishment commented quite favourably on its handling qualities, but that its main fault was the canopy. Taken directly from the T 7, it was single piece and side-opening, and consisted of lots of heavy metal framing which obscured the view. This was aggravated at high altitudes because the perspex over the pilot's head became encrusted with ice, blinding him to anything more than 25deg above. Also, rain obscured forward view during landing, making this hazardous.

The Meteor NF 12 had a 17in (43cm) longer nose housing the AI 21 radar (Westinghouse APS-57) and modifications to the fin. Although slightly heavier

Gloster Javelin FAW 8

Origin: Gloster Aircraft Co Ltd., England.
Type: Two-seat, twin-engined transonic jet all-weather fighter.
Engine: Two Armstrong Siddeley Sapphire ASSa 7R Mk 205/206 single-spool axial flow afterburning turbojets each rated at 12,300lb (5,579kg) maximum and 11,000lb (4,990kg) military thrust.
Dimensions: Span 52ft 0in (15.85m); length 56ft 3in (17.14m); height 16ft 0in (4.88m); wing area 927sq.ft ($86.12m^2$).
Weights: Empty c28,000lb (12,701kg); loaded 37,410lb (16,969kg); maximum 46,090lb (20,906kg).
Loadings (at normal takeoff weight)**:** Wing 40lb/sq.ft ($197kg/m^2$); thrust 0.66.
Performance: Maximum speed 701mph (1,128kph) at sea level, 620mph (998kph) at 37,000ft (11,277m); sustained climb rate 9min 15sec to 50,000ft (15,239m); service ceiling more than 50,000ft (15,239m); range 930 miles (1,496km); endurance 2hr plus.
Armament: Two wing-mounted 30mm Aden cannon (four in early models) and four Firestreak IR homing AAMs.

ıan the NF 11, this was offset by the Derwent 9, rated at 3,800lb (1,724kg) ırust. This, and the improved fineness ratio, marginally improved performance. ne NF 13 was a tropicalised variant, similar to the NF 11 but with air onditioning, and with enlarged intakes giving greater mass flow. The final ariant was the NF 14, with a clear vision canopy, a yaw damper on the rudder, nd spring tabs on the ailerons.

So far as is known, the only air combat victory scored by the type was ver an Egyptian Il-14 transport, which was shot down on the night of 28 ctober 1956 by an Israeli NF 13, flown by Chato Tsidon and Alyasheeb rosch.

History: Contract for two GA 5 prototypes on 13 April 1949. First flight 26 November 1951. Ordered into production as the Javelin in July 1952, and first flight of a production aircraft 22 July 1954. In squadron service spring 1956. Production ceased June 1960, with a total of 385 of nine different variants. Withdrawn from service April 1968.
User: Britain (RAF).

Two bomber interceptor prototypes made their first flights in 1951. Both designers were strongly influenced by Lippisch deltas, but the two aircraft could hardly have been more different. The Douglas Skyray was small, single-engined, short-legged and above all fast-climbing. The Gloster Javelin, designed by George Carter, was a huge two-seat, twin-engined monster with the accent on endurance, and high altitude performance and manoeuvrability.

The Javelin GA 5 prototype had a huge delta wing, which gave plenty of

Below: The Javelin was a tailed delta missile-armed all weather fighter.

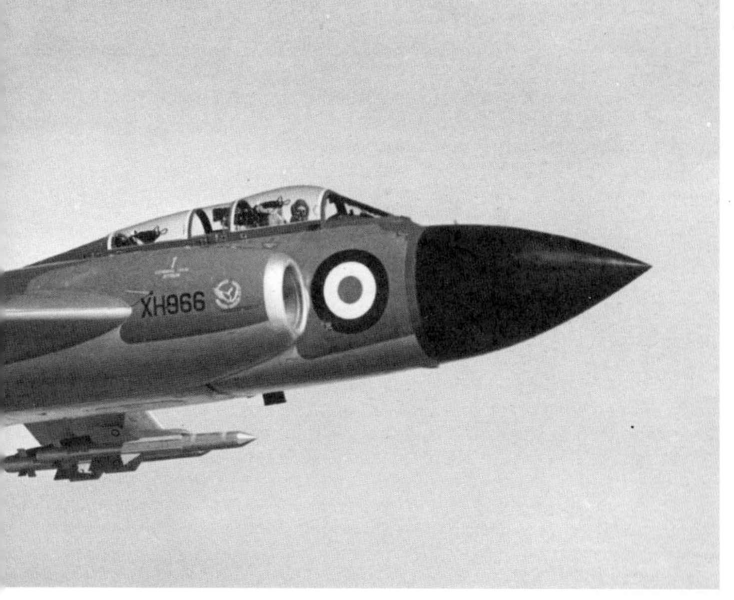

lifting area, with a 10 per cent thickness/chord ratio, and plenty of volume for fuel tanks. The down side was that the coefficient of lift was poor, and drag was high. Drag was not helped by an enormous broad-chord fin and rudder, with a huge wetted area, and a massive fuselage containing two widely spaced Sapphire turbojets. The basic appearance was rather odd which the fixed delta tailplane, perched on top of the fin, did nothing to dispel. Also unusual were the split flaps, which were located well in front of the wing trailing edges.

The GA 5 prototype was first flown by Bill Waterman from Moreton Valence on 26 November 1951. Troubles were experienced with turbulent airflow and buffeting, and these were only partly cured. The Javelin had started to earn its soubriquet of "Dragmaster". This notwithstanding, it was ordered for the RAF in preference to the DH 110, later the Sea Vixen, on the pretext that it had greater development potential. Given its sheer size, this was undeniable; there

Grumman F4F-4 Wildcat

Origin: Grumman Aircraft Engineering Corp., USA.
Type: Single-seat, single-engined carrier-based monoplane fighter.
Engine: One 1,200hp Pratt & Whitney R-1830-86 14-cylinder Twin Wasp radial.
Dimensions: Span 38ft 0in (11.59m); length 29ft 0in (8.84m); height 11ft 4in (3.45m); wing area 260sq.ft (24.15m²).
Weights: Empty 5,895lb (2,674kg); normal takeoff 7,975lb (3,617kg); maximum 8,762lb (3,974kg).
Loadings (at normal takeoff weight)**:** Wing 31lb/sq.ft (150kg/m²); power 6.65lb (3.01kg) per hp.
Performance: Maximum speed 320mph (515kph) at 18,800ft (5,730m), 274mph (441kph) at sea level; initial climb rate 2,190ft/min (11.12m/sec); sustained climb rate 5min 36sec to 10,000ft (3,048m), 12min 24sec to 20,000ft (6,096m); service ceiling 34,000ft (10,363m); range 770 miles (1,239km).
Armament: Six 0.50in (12.7mm) wing-mounted Browning M2 machine guns with 240 rounds per gun, plus two 100lb (45kg) bombs.
History: First flight of the XF4F-2 on 2 September 1937, then XF4F-3 on 12 February 1939. First production aircraft flown in February 1940, and entered service in December. The type remained in front line service and in production until 1945, with 7,722 built.
Users: Britain (FAA), USA (USN and USMC).

The Wildcat was unusual in that its origins lay in a biplane, the XF4F-1, but the US Navy soon concluded that a more modern fighter was needed. This duly emerged as the XF4F-2, a rotund mid-wing monoplane which, piloted by Robert Hall, first flew at Bethpage on 2 September 1937. Non-critical technical problems, coupled with ill fortune in the evaluation phase, resulted in it losing out to the Brewster F2A Buffalo.

An extensive redesign resulted in the XF4F-3, with a more powerful engine and a revised squared-off wing with greater span and wing area. First flown on 12 February 1939, it was evaluated by the Navy, and after a few tweaks, such as a taller fin and smaller ailerons, was ordered into production on 8 August. The revised aircraft was first flown in February 1940, was re-evaluated, and after a few problems had been overcome was found satisfactory. Grumman had a reputation for building almost unbreakable fighters, popularly supposed to be carved out of the solid, which had earned the company the soubriquet of "The Iron Works". This tradition was perpetuated by the Wildcat, and many was volume to spare for anything the RAF might want to fit in it.

Development proved a two-edged sword. No sooner were a few aircraft out of the door when a new model was introduced. In all, eight fighter variants entered service, making it all but impossible to equip more than a couple of squadrons with the same type. A new wing with a kinked leading edge drooped outboard, and squared-off tips, powered ailerons and a pen-nib fairing beneath the rudder, an all-flying tailplane, and increased fuel tankage were just some of the improvements introduced. Radars alternated between AI 17 and the AI 22 (Westinghouse APQ-43), and Firestreak AAMs were fitted.

The modifications really needed were a much thinner wing, lavishly equipped with high lift devices, and proper afterburners for the 200 series Sapphire turbojets rather than the feeble attempts that were made. This could have resulted in a supersonic Javelin which would have remained in service for many more years. But it was not to be!

Above: The F4F Wildcat cockpit was set high to aid deflection shooting.

pilots owed their lives to its ability to absorb battle damage.

The large radial engine, which drove an automatic variable-pitch propeller, gave the Wildcat its characteristic tubby form, accentuated by the fact that the US Navy was at this time about the only air arm in the world to teach and practise deflection shooting. To aid this, the cockpit was set high, giving an eight degree angle of sight over the nose. As with previous Grumman fighters, the main gears retracted into the fuselage beneath the mid-set wing. While this gave a narrow track, it meant that the stresses of deck landings were absorbed by the main structure rather than that of the wings.

France placed an order for Wildcats powered by the Wright Cyclone G-205A, but surrendered before these could be delivered. They were transferred to Britain, with a conventional throttle instead of the standard French "back-to-front" system, and with four 0.50in (12.7mm) wing guns. Entering Fleet Air

Arm service on 8 September 1940 as the Martlet I, they were land-based as they lacked wing folding. The first air combat victory scored by the type came on 25 December of that year, a Ju 88 shot down over Scapa Flow.

The US Navy and Marine Corps began to equip with F4F-3s from December 1940. In December 1941, Marine Wildcats put up an epic defence of Wake Island before being swamped by superior force. Carrier-based aircraft were soon in action against the Japanese, but experienced problems against the outstanding manoeuvrability of the Zero. At this point the F4F-4 was entering service in numbers. This had manually folding wings, six rather than four heavy machine guns, self-sealing fuel tanks, a bullet-proof windshield, and 139lb

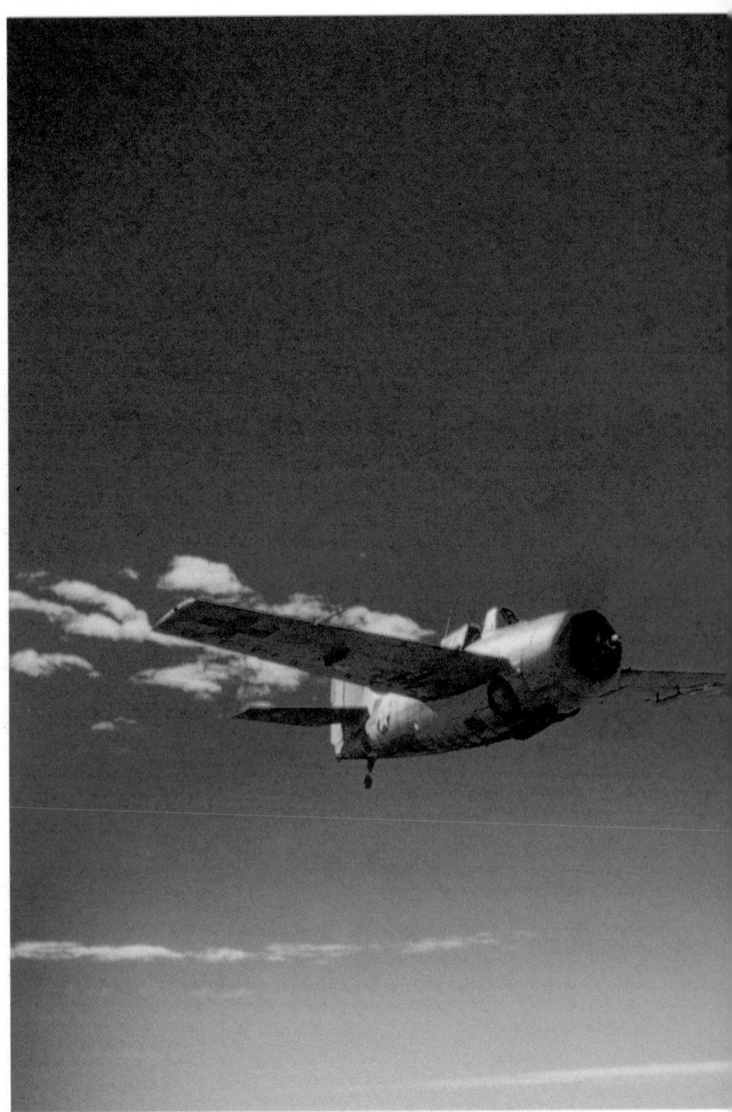

(63kg) of armour protection. This version made its operational debut at the Battle of Midway in June 1942.

Against the Zero, the Wildcat was outclassed. It was slightly slower at all altitudes, with a much lower initial climb rate, accelerated more sluggishly, and with a wing loading almost 50 per cent greater was totally unable to compete in turn radius. The Wildcat had just two advantages. It could absorb far more damage than its Japanese opponent, and once speed exceeded 250mph

Below: The F4F-4 made its combat debut at the Battle of Midway in June 1942.

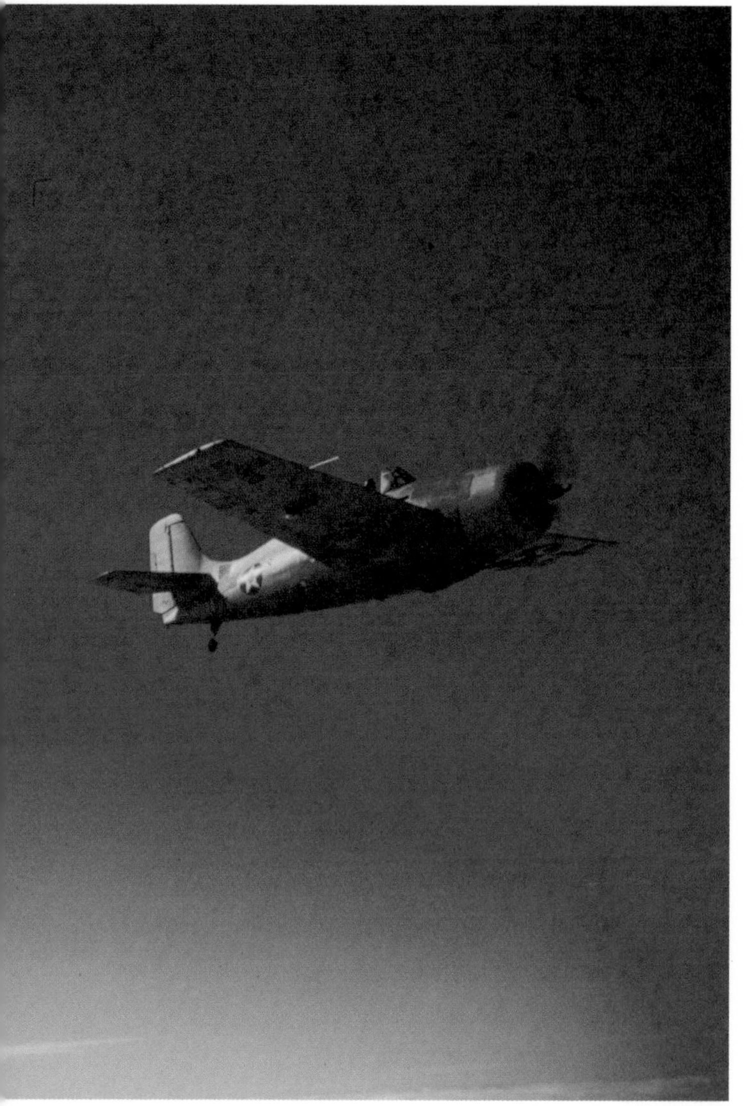

(402kph) its rate of roll became progressively superior, which allowed it to reverse its turn faster than the Zero could follow. Other measures used by Wildcat pilots were dive and zoom tactics, mutual cover at all times and, when all else failed, reliance on the fact that they were hard to shoot down.

Meanwhile Grumman had begun work on the Hellcat to succeed the Wildcat. However, it was not to succeed it entirely; the Wildcat could operate from small escort carriers, and so it was necessary to keep it in production. This was switched to General Motors as the FM-1, which varied from the F4F-4 only in having four heavy machine guns with 430 rounds per gun. In British service the FM-1 became the Martlet V.

Next came the XF4F-8, a lightweight variant specifically designed to operate from small carriers. While it retained the four machine gun armament, the engine was a Wright R-1820-56 Cyclone with a single stage two-speed supercharger, giving 1,350hp for takeoff, although weighing less than the Pratt & Whitney. At first slotted flaps were fitted, but these were later replaced by standard split flaps, and the vertical tail was increased in height. This became the FM-2, which was mainly used for close air support, and 4,777 were built.

The Wildcat held the ring in the early years of the Pacific war against far more agile fighters. The top-scoring Wildcat ace was a Marine, "Swivel-neck Joe" Foss with 26, scored between 9 October 1942 and 15 January 1943. Flying from land bases, Marines had more opportunities than carrier pilots to score, reflected in the fact that 15 racked up double figures.

Grumman F6F-3 Hellcat

Origin: Grumman Aircraft Engineering Corp., USA.
Type: Single-seat, single-engined carrier-based monoplane fighter.
Engine: One 2,200hp Pratt & Whitney R-2800-10W 18-cylinder Double Wasp radial.
Dimensions: Span 42ft 10in (13.05m); length 33ft 4in (10.16m); height 14ft 5in (4.40m); wing area 334sq.ft (31.03m²).
Weights: Empty 9,042lb (4,101kg); normal takeoff 12,186lb (5,528kg); maximum 13,221lb (5,997kg).
Loadings (at normal takeoff weight)**:** Wing 36lb/sq.ft (178kg/m²); power 5.54lb (2.51kg) per hp.
Performance: Maximum speed 376mph (605kph) at 22,800ft (6,949m), 324mph (521kph) at sea level; initial climb rate 3,650ft/min (18.54m/sec); sustained climb rate 7min 42sec to 15,000ft (4,572m); service ceiling 37,500ft (11,429m); range 1,085 miles (1,746km).
Armament: Six 0.50in (12.7mm) wing-mounted Browning M2 machine guns with 400 rounds per gun.
History: First flight of prototype XF6F-1 on 26 June 1942. First flight of production F6F-3 on 3 October 1942, and service entry early 1943. Operational debut 31 August 1943. Production switched to the F6F-5 on 21 April 1944, with only minor improvements. Both the -3 and -5 had radar-equipped night fighter variants. Production ended in November 1945, with a grand total of 12,275 built. Finally retired mid-1954.
Users: Britain (FAA), France (Aeronavale), USA (USN and USMC),

Concerned in 1941 that the F4F was outmatched by its land-based

Above: The rugged Wildcat remained in production until the end of WWII.

Above: An F6F-3 Hellcat of VF-12 prepares for carrier launch in 1944.

contemporaries, on 30 June the USN ordered two prototype XF6Fs from Grumman, partly as insurance against the failure of the F4U Corsair, ordered into production on the same day. Initially the XF6F was expected to be little more than a developed Wildcat, but things turned out very differently. Requirements were more speed, greater climb, high manoeuvrability, plenty of protection, and increased combat persistence in the form of more ammunition and increased endurance.

In attaining all of these, the Hellcat grew until empty weight was almost double that of the Wildcat. Externally the family resemblance remained, with low-set wings and wing-mounted aft-retracting main gear legs the main differences. Less obvious was the negative thrust line of the Double Wasp engine, adopted to maximise level flight acceleration by giving the angle of attack for minimum drag. Protection for the pilot and oil system was provided by no less than 212lb (96kg) of armour plating.

The first production Hellcat reached the squadrons on 16 January 1943, starting to replace the Wildcat on USN fleet carriers, and its rugged construction and viceless handling made it ideal for shipboard operations. As 23-victory Hellcat ace Gene Valencia commented: "If they could cook, I'd marry one!".

The Hellcat made its combat debut over Marcus Island on 31 August 1943. While it could not stay with the Zero in a level turn, it out-climbed, out-dived and out-accelerated it, while its six 0.50in (12.7mm) guns chewed up its lightweight opponent in short order. In combat it quickly gained ascendancy by day, and in what became known as "The Great Marianas Turkey Shoot" on 19 June 1944, no fewer than 243 Japanese carrier aircraft of a total of 328 were shot down. USN losses amounted to just 28 from all causes. The top-scoring Hellcat pilot was USN ace David McCampbell, with 34 victories, nine of them scored in a single mission over Leyte Gulf on 23 October 1944.

The British Fleet Air Arm also operated Hellcats from July 1943, and these were initially used to cover anti-shipping strikes off Norway. From late 1944 FAA Hellcats were deployed to the Pacific, but by now opportunities were few. The top-scoring FAA Hellcat pilot was South African Edward Wilson, with three victories.

Interestingly, F6F-3N and -5N Hellcats conclusively proved that radar-

Grumman F9F-5 Panther

Origin: Grumman Aircraft Engineering Corp, USA.
Type: Single-seat, single-engined subsonic jet carrier fighter.
Engine: One Pratt & Whitney J48-P-6A centrifugal flow turbojet rated at 7,000lb (3,175kg) thrust with water injection.
Dimensions: Span 38ft 0in (11.58m) over tip tanks; length 39ft 1.5in (39ft 1.5in (11.92m); height 12ft 3.5in (3.75m); wing area 250sq.ft (23.23m²).
Weights: Empty 10,178lb (4,617kg); normal takeoff 17,818lb (8,082kg); maximum 19,261lb (8,737kg).
Loadings (at normal takeoff weight)**:** Wing 71lb/sq.ft (348kg/m²); thrust 0.39.
Performance: Maximum speed 614mph (988kph) at sea level, 579mph (932kph) at 25,000ft (7,620m); initial climb rate 6,280ft/min (32m/sec); service ceiling 42,800ft (13,045m); range 1,300 miles (2,092km) with tip tanks.
Armament: Four nose-mounted 20mm M2 cannon with 190 rounds per gun. Two 1,000lb (454kg) bombs or six 5in (127mm) rockets.
History: First flight of XF9F-2 prototype 24 November 1947. First flight of production aircraft November 1948. With operational units from 8 May 1949. Combat debut 3 July 1950. Total production 1,346. Withdrawn from service 1962.
Users: Argentina, USA (USMC, USN).

Oddly, the F9F Panther began life as a night fighter, with radar in the nose, a two-man crew seated in tandem, and with four rather feeble Westinghouse J30 axial flow turbojets in the wing roots. This arrangement caused design problems, and Grumman switched to a single large turbojet. This was the Rolls-Royce Nene, which was arguably the best jet engine in the world at that time,

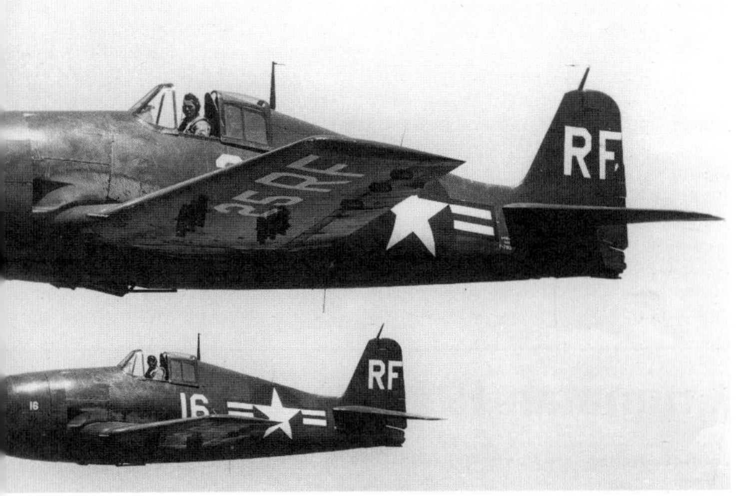

Above: Hellcats scored more air victories in the Pacific than any other fighter.

equipped single-seaters could be effective at night, with top-scoring night ace Bill Henry claiming 12 victories.

Above: In Korea Panthers claimed six victories for one loss in air combat.

combining 5,000lb (2,268kg) of thrust with reliability. License-built by Pratt & Whitney as the J42, this was installed in the aft fuselage, with the jet pipe ending under the tail, in what was nearly, but not quite, a pod and boom arrangement. At this point the F9F became a single-seater day fighter without radar.

The wing was straight, with a leading edge flap to give variable camber, and trailing edge flaps inboard and hydraulically powered ailerons outboard. Fixed tip tanks were standard. The engine was fed by wing root inlets; these obviously increased the thickness, and to keep the thickness/chord ratio within bounds a large trailing edge fillet was added. The horizontal tail was set high on a large triangular fin, and the pilot was located on an early Martin Baker ejection seat at a time when the RAF was not using them.

First flight, by test pilot Corky Meyer, took place from Bethpage on 24 November 1947, and all went well. Carrier qualification was completed in September 1949, but more power was obviously needed. Two engines were

Grumman F9F-8 Cougar

Origin: Grumman Aircraft Engineering Corp, USA.
Type: Single-seat, single-engined transonic jet carrier fighter.
Engine: One Pratt & Whitney J48-P-8A centrifugal flow turbojet rated at 8,500lb (3,856kg) thrust with water injection.
Dimensions: Span 34ft 6in (10.52m); length 42ft 2in (12.85m); height 12ft 4in (3.76m); wing area 337sq.ft (31.31m^2).
Weights: Empty 11,866lb (5,382kg); normal takeoff 20,600lb (9,344kg); maximum 24,763lb (11,232kg).
Loadings (at normal takeoff weight)**:** Wing 61lb/sq.ft (298kg/m^2); thrust 0.41.
Performance: Maximum speed 643mph (1,035kph) at sea level; initial climb rate 4,800ft/min (24.38m/sec); service ceiling 42,000ft (12,801m); range 1,050 miles (1,690km).
Armament: Four nose-mounted 20mm M2 cannon with 190 rounds per gun. Four Sidewinder AAMs on late models. Two 1,000lb (454kg) bombs or six 5in (127mm) rockets.
History: First flight of XF9F-6 prototype 20 September 1951. Entered service late 1952. The F9F-8, with an enlarged wing and greater internal fuel capacity, first flown 18 January 1954 by Corky Meyer. Production ceased in 1959 with a total of 1,985, including photo-reconnaissance aircraft and two-seater F9F-8T advanced trainers. The latter was finally retired in February 1974.
Users: Argentina, USA (USMC ,USN).

For all practical purposes, the Cougar was a Panther with swept wings and horizontal tail surfaces. The wing, swept back at 35 degrees, had a broader chord and greater area than that of the Panther, with a larger trailing edge fillet. Fences were fitted to guard against spanwise flow, and slats occupied the leading edge. Large flaps were fitted to the trailing edge, and, instead of ailerons, which at high speeds tended to twist the wings under heavy loads, spoilers were used to dump lift on one side or the other. The first F9F-6 Cougars entered service in November 1952.

It was felt necessary to use a second source engine, and the F9F-7 powered by the Allison J33-A-16A rated at 7,000lb (3,175kg) with water tried: the Allison J33-A-16, which was not adopted, and the Pratt & Whitney J48-P-2, actually a license-built Rolls-Royce Tay.

Access to the engine was achieved by unbolting the rear fuselage and wheeling it clear on a dolly. Navy aircraft were midnight blue, whereas Marine aircraft were gray. On one occasion a USMC Panther was fitted with the rear end of a Navy machine, with which it flew 13 sorties and earned the soubriquet of "The Blue-Tailed Fly". A lesser-known incident saw a Navy Panther with a gray rear end. This became known as "Vice-Versa!". Pleasant to fly, the Panther became the mount of the US Navy aerobatic team, the Blue Angels.

First into combat, over Korea, was the F9F-2, flying from USS *Valley Forge*. Mainly used for ground attack and interdiction, Panthers saw little air combat, but managed to knock down six MiG-15s for one loss. The first victory, scored by Bill Amen, took place on 9 November 1950; the next three came in November 1951; and the final two, Russian aircraft flying from Vladivostok, on 18 November 1952.

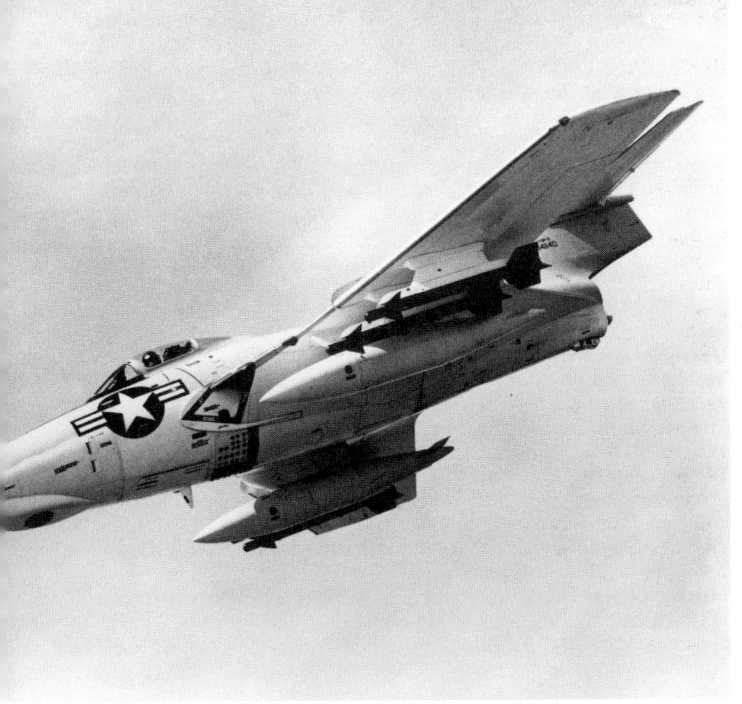

Above: The F9F-8 Cougar was essentially a Panther with swept wings and tail.

injection, was the result, although only 168 of this type were delivered. The final fighter Cougar was the F9F-8, with a wing area 40 per cent larger than the original Panther; this significantly reduced wing loading despite a considerable increase in normal takeoff weight, in part caused by increased fuel capacity. Other changes were a fixed drooped wing leading edge, and the even more powerful -8A engine.

Grumman F11F-1 Tiger

Origin: Grumman Aircraft Engineering Corp, USA.
Type: Single-seat, single-engined supersonic jet carrier fighter.
Engine: One Wright J65-W-18 afterburning single-spool axial flow turbojet rated at 10,500lb (4,763kg) maximum and 7,450lb (3,379kg) military thrust.
Dimensions: Span 31ft 7.5in (9.64m); length 44ft 6in (13.56m); height 13ft 2.75in (4.03m); wing area 250sq.ft (23.22m²).
Weights: Empty 13,307lb (6,036kg); normal takeoff 19,600lb (8,891kg); maximum 23,459lb (10,641kg).
Loadings (at normal takeoff weight)**:** Wing 78lb/sq.ft (383kg/m²); thrust 0.54.
Performance: Maximum speed Mach 1.3 at altitude, Mach 0.99 at sea level; initial climb rate 5,130ft/min (26m/sec); service ceiling 41,900ft (12,770m); range 1,108 miles (1,783km).
Armament: Four 20mm underfuselage-mounted Colt-Browning Mk 12 cannon with 125 rounds per gun; up to four Sidewinder AAMs, plus slick bombs and unguided rockets.
History: First flight of the prototype 30 July 1954. Squadron service from March 1957, but withdrawn from front line units in April 1961 to become an advanced trainer. Served with the Blue Angels aerobatic team 1957-1968. Production ceased in December 1958, with 201 aircraft delivered.
Users: USA (USN).

The F11F-1 Tiger clocked up an amazing amount of "firsts". First flown (as the XF9F-9) by Corky Meyer from Bethpage on 30 July 1954, it was the first fighter designed from scratch to the newly discovered area rule; the first ever

Grumman F-14D Tomcat

Origin: Grumman Aircraft Engineering Corp, USA.
Type: Two-seat, twin-engined bisonic all-weather variable-sweep jet carrier interceptor fighter.
Engine: Two General Electric F110-GE-400 two-spool afterburning turbofans each rated at 27,080lb (12,283kg) maximum and 16,610lb (7,534kg) military thrust.
Dimensions: Span 64ft 1.5in (19.55m) at minimum sweep, 38ft 2.5in (11.65m) at maximum sweep; length 61ft 11in (18.87m); height 16ft 0in (4.88m); wing area 565sq.ft (52.50m²).
Weights: Empty 41,780lb (18,951kg); normal takeoff 61,200lb (27,760kg); maximum 70,000lb (31,752kg).
Loadings (at normal takeoff weight)**:** Wing 108lb/sq.ft (529kg/m²); thrust 0.88.
Performance: Maximum speed Mach 2.34 at altitude with four AIM-120 Amraam, but limited to Mach 1.88 with full external stores, Mach 1.2 at sea level; initial climb rate c48,000ft/min (244m/sec); operational ceiling 53,000ft (16,154m); tactical radius 510 miles (821km).
Armament: One 20mm six-barrel M61A-1 cannon with 675 rounds; typically four AIM-120 Amraam and four AIM-9 Sidewinders. Early models carried up to six AIM-54 Phoenix long range AAMs. Air-to-surface weaponry also carried.
History: Prototype first flight 21 December 1970. F-14A entered service in 1973, and initial operational capability in 1974. Combat debut in the Gulf of Sidra August 1981. Followed by F-14B from November 1989, and F-14D from March 1990. Production ceased July 1992, with a grand total of 723, including prototypes.
Users: Iran, USA (USN).

From the late 1950s, the perceived threat to the US Navy was the long range anti-

***Right:* The F11F-1 Tiger was the world's first supersonic carrier fighter.**

supersonic carrier fighter; the first service aircraft to have titanium firewalls; and the first to have a "wet" fin. A "first" that it could have done without occurred when test pilot Tom Attridge carried out a high speed guns test on 21 September 1956. Ballistically faulty shells tumbled in flight. They were ingested by the engine as the Tiger caught up with them, in the only recorded case of a fighter shooting itself down without benefit of a ricochet.

The F11F-1 Tiger was a simple design. It had a mid-set wing with a 35deg quarter-chord sweep and a thickness/chord ratio of 6.5 per cent, with leading edge slats and trailing edge flaps. Roll control was via spoilers; the variable incidence tailplane was set low to avoid being blanketed by the wings at high angles of attack. Its weakness was however the J65 engine (a license-built Bristol Siddeley Sapphire), which Wrights had somehow managed to foul up. Otherwise, handling was benign. Grumman then produced the F11F-1F Super Tiger, powered by the General Electric J79. Although this set new world records for absolute speed and absolute altitude, only two were built.

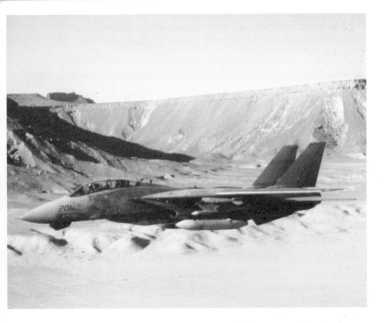

***Above:* A Tomcat sweeps low over the desert during operation Desert Shield.**

shipping missile launched from fast jet bombers. The best solution was to destroy the bombers before they could launch their weapons, but this was easier said than done. What was needed was a carrier-compatible interceptor able to loiter for extended periods far from the fleet, with a weapon system able to destroy multiple targets at unprecedentedly long ranges. It needed supersonic speed in order to reinforce existing patrols quickly. As a secondary requirement it needed performance and agility to allow it to carry out combat air patrols and the escort of air strikes.

In 1961 the USAF was on the brink of ordering the F-111A interdictor. It was fast, it was large enough to carry a heavy warload for long distances, and it was a two-seater. At this point Robert McNamara, arguably the most disastrous Defense Secretary in American history, intervened. Although told that the USAF and USN requirements were incompatible, he forced the USN to proceed with the purchase of F-111As

The F-111A was a General Dynamics product. Grumman, with a wealth of experience of carrier fighters, and knowledgeable about variable-sweep wings, were given the task of navalising the F-111 in December 1962. The F-111B, as the carrier variant was known, first flew on 18 May 1965. It was too heavy, unmanoeuvrable, inferior to the F-4 Phantom in all departments, and suffered from engine problems. A carrier fighter it could never be! The programme was finally terminated in December 1968.

With commendable foresight, the USN and Grumman had anticipated this, and had begun studies for an advanced carrier fighter in January 1966, to be designed around the weapon control system developed for the F-111B. A contract was awarded on 14 January 1969 for what was now the F-14A Tomcat. The name was fortuitous. Grumman fighters traditionally had been named after felines, and the involvement of Vice Admiral Tom Connolly had inevitably led to the unofficial name Tom's Cat, later formalised as Tomcat.

Flown by Robert Smythe and Bill Miller, the prototype made its successful first flight on 21 December 1970. It was a big aircraft, and unusually configured. Like the F-111, it had a variable-sweep wing, pivoting on spherical bearings. Slats and flaps occupied most of the leading and trailing edges, with spoilers on the upper surfaces. These were mainly used for direct lift control on landing, as roll control

Below: This Tomcat has wings at minimum sweep for cruising flight.

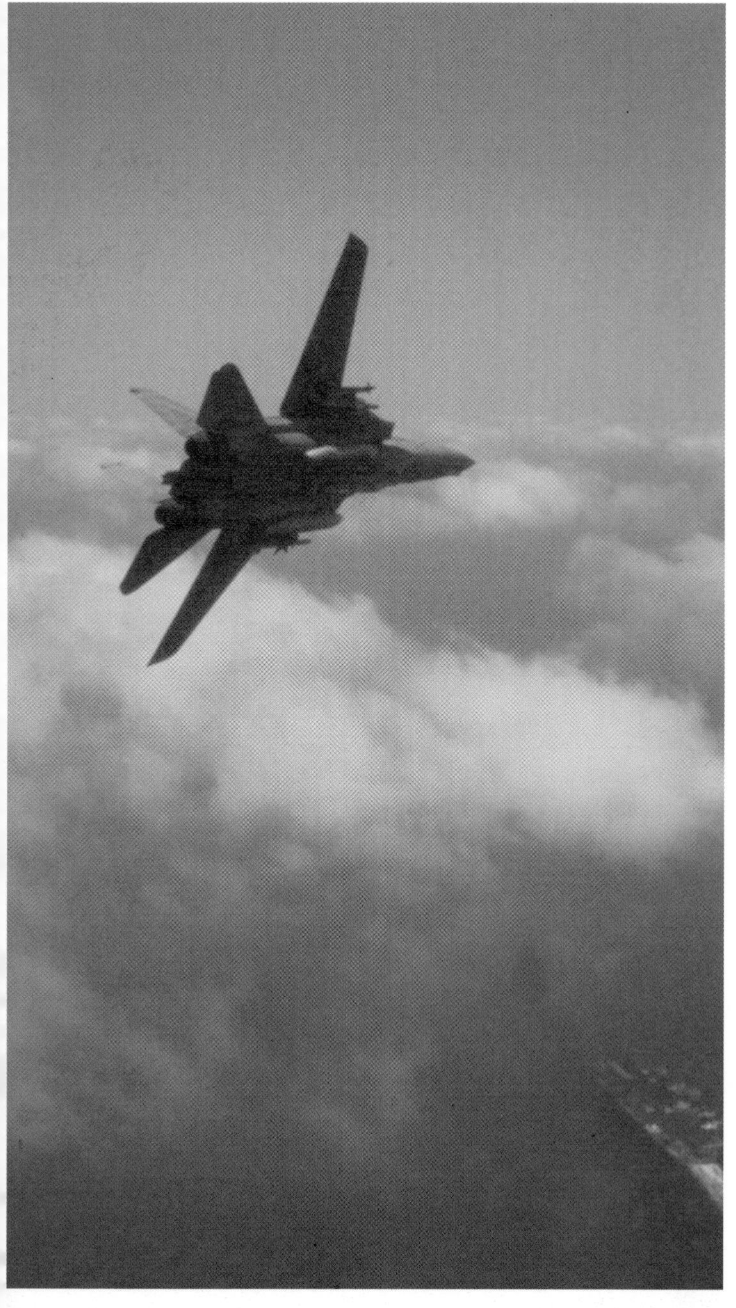

Above: Minimum sweep gives best turning performance at subsonic speeds.

was mainly provided via differentially moving tailerons. Sweep angle automatically varied to give optimum performance according to flight regime. At supersonic speeds, vanes deployed from the wing gloves to give a destabilizing effect, improving high-speed manoeuvrability. No wing folding was needed, since an oversweep angle was used to reduce parking area.

In theory, wing loading was distinctly on the high side, but this was to a degree compensated for by the planform. The engines, Pratt & Whitney TF30-P-412 turbofans, the same as those that had proved so troublesome on the F-111, were sensitive to disturbed airflow. Grumman largely, but not completely, overcame this by setting the nacelles out from the forebody, with a straight line from inlet to nozzle. The rear fuselage therefore took the form of a large "pancake", which not only provided plenty of space for fuel, but gave a 40 per cent increment to the total lifting area. In the lower speed range, the F-14 proved remarkably agile; as F-15 pilot Dito Ladd commented to the writer; "We don't get slow against the gents in the F-14s!" Twin fins were set atop each engine, with small ventral strakes below.

The fire control system was the Hughes AWG-9, which could not only detect targets at previously unheard-of distances, but could guide up to six AIM-54 Phoenix long range missiles at one time. Other weapons loads were up to six AIM-7 Sparrow medium range and four AIM-9 Sidewinder short range AAMs.

Initially the TF30 was intended as no more than an interim engine; the definitive article was to be the General Electric F101. But soaring costs prevented this; at one point the entire F-14 programme was endangered, and was rescued only by an export order from Iran. F-14A pilots were stuck with having to fly the engines as well as the airframe; a most unsatisfactory state of affairs.

This was not rectified until April 1987, when production began of the F-14A Plus, later redesignated F-14B. This was powered by the General Electric F110-GE-400, a far sturdier and less sensitive engine. In all, 70 F-14Bs were produced. The

HAL Light Combat Aircraft

Origin: Aeronautical Development Agency, India.
Type: Single-seat, single-engined supersonic lightweight multi-role fighter.
Engine: One Gas Turbine Research Establishment Kaveri two-spool afterburning turbofan rated at 18,750lb (8,505kg) maximum and 11,530lb (5,230kg) military thrust.
Dimensions: Span 26ft 10.5in (8.20m); length 43ft 3.5in (4.40m); height 14ft 5in (4.40m); wing area c413sq.ft (38.40m^2).
Weights: Empty c12,125lb (5,500kg); clean takeoff 18,739lb (8,500kg); maximum c27,558lb (12,500kg).
Loadings (at clean takeoff weight)**:** Wing c45lb/sq.ft (221kg/m^2); thrust 1.00.
Performance: Maximum speed Mach 1.6 at altitude, supersonic at sea level; service ceiling 50,000ft (1,5239m); g limits plus 9, minus 3.5; no other details available.
Armament: One 23mm GSh-23 twin-barrel cannon with 220 rounds; two each of unspecified BVR and short range AAMs; wide variety of air-to-surface weapons.
History: Project begun 1983; initial design completed 1990; roll- out 17 November 1995; first flight 4 January 2001. Continuing delays make service entry unlikely before 2012.
Potential users: India, about 200 required.

The Light Combat Aircraft (LCA) programme was initiated at a time when two homebrew aircraft were still in service, the Marut and the Ajeet, withdrawn in 1985 and 1991 respectively. The LCA, which is scheduled to have an Indian engine and an Indian multi-mode pulse-Doppler radar, would give a near total

Above: This angle shows the undernose sensors of the F-14B and F-14D Tomcat.

final variant was the F-14D, first flown in September 1990, with 60 per cent new avionics, including the Hughes APG-71 radar and a glass cockpit. Only 55 F-14Ds, some new, others rebuilds, were produced. In air combat, success has been meagre, due to lack of opportunity. Two Libyan Su-22 Fitters were shot down over the Gulf of Sidra in 1981; two Libyan MiG-23 Floggers in the same area in January 1989; and an Iraqi Mil Mi-8 in the Gulf in 1991, which hardly counts.

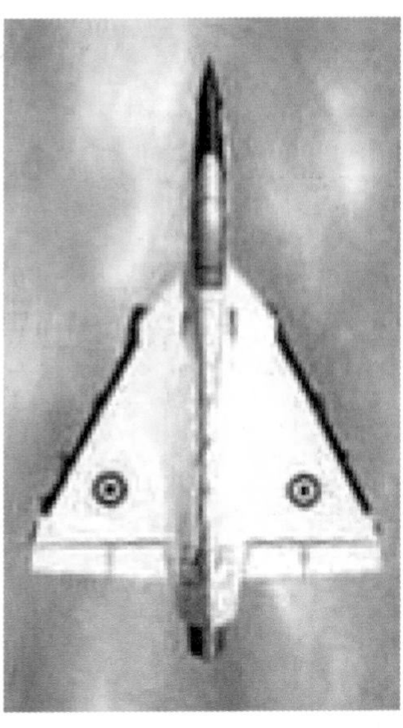

Right: The LCA has flown but whether it will ever enter service is dubious.

indigenous fighter capability for the first time. However, the proposed Kaveri engine has been beset by problems and is unlikely to be ready before 2004. Meanwhile the General Electric F404 powers the prototypes. Other delays have been caused by development of the digital quadruplex fly-by-wire system.

The LCA has a shoulder-mounted cropped compound delta wing, unusually having a shallower sweep inboard than outboard. Mainly of carbon fibre composite construction, it has three-piece leading edge slats and two-piece trailing edge elevons. The engine is fed by fixed geometry cheek intakes located under the wing. Of the seven hardpoints, five are plumbed for drop tanks.

Piloted by Rajiv Kothiyal, the LCA made its first flight from Bangalore on 4 January 2001, 17 years after the project was initiated, which may be a record for protracted gestation. A two-seat conversion trainer and a carrier-compatible variant are also planned.

Hanriot HD 1

Origin: SA des Appareils d'Aviation Hanriot, France.
Type: Single-seat, single-engined biplane fighter.
Engine: One 120hp Le Rhône 9Jb rotary.
Dimensions: Span 28ft 6.5in (8.70m); length 19ft 2.25in (5.85m); height 9ft 7.5in (2.94m); wing area 196sq.ft (18.20m²).
Weights: Empty 983lb (446kg); normal takeoff 1,437lb (652kg).
Loadings (at normal takeoff weight)**:** Wing 7.33lb/sq.ft (36kg/m²).
Performance: Maximum speed 114mph (184kph) at sea level, 111mph (184kph) at 6,562ft (2,000m); sustained climb rate 2min 58sec to 3,281ft (1,000m); service ceiling 19,686ft (6,000m); range 224 miles (360km); endurance 2hr 30min.
Armament: One 7.7mm synchronised belt-fed Vickers machine gun.
History: First flown 1916 and entered service the following year. Production continued into 1919, with a total of 980. Served with Switzerland until 1930.
Users: Belgium, France (few only, Navy), Italy, Switzerland.

Designed by Emile Dupont, the HD 1 was a compact and agile fighter, but its timing was unfortunate. It was preceded by the fast and rugged SPAD S VII, which had been ordered in quantity by *l'Aviation Militaire*. Consequently, the only order it attracted from its country of origin was a handful of aircraft for the French Navy, and then not until 1918.

Initially the HD 1 was powered by a 100hp Le Rhône, but this was soon found to be inadequate, and the 120hp Le Rhône 9Bj was substituted.

The single Vickers gun was somewhat on the light side for the later years of the war, but while experiments with twin Vickers, or single larger-calibre machine guns were made, they caused an unacceptable drop in performance.

Hawker Fury I

Origin: Hawker Aircraft Ltd., England.
Type: Single-seat, single-engined biplane fighter.
Engine: One 575hp Rolls-Royce Kestrel IIS V-12 liquid-cooled supercharged engine.
Dimensions: Span 30ft 0in (9.15m); length 26ft 3.75in (8.00m); height 9ft 6in (2.89m); wing area 252sq.ft (23.40m²).
Weights: Empty 2,623lb (1,190kg); normal takeoff 3,490lb (1,583kg).
Loadings (at normal takeoff weight)**:** Wing 13.85lb/sq.ft (68kg/m²); power 6.07lb (2.75kg) per hp.
Performance: Maximum speed 207mph (333kph) at 14,000ft (4,267m), 192mph (309kph) at 5,000ft (1,524m); initial climb rate 2,380ft/min (12.09m/sec); sustained climb rate 4min 30sec to 10,000ft (3,048m); service ceiling 28,000ft (8,534m); range 305 miles (492km).
Armament: Two 0.303in (7.7mm) belt-fed synchronised Vickers machine guns.
History: Prototype first flight March 1929. First order placed August 1930. Operational May/June 1931. Air combat debut Spanish Civil War 1936. Production ceased 1937, with a total of 328. Withdrawn from RAF squadron service Jun 1937
Users: Britain (RAF), Iran, Norway, Portugal, South Africa, Spain, Yugoslavia.

The first production fighter able to exceed 200mph (322kph) in level flight, the Fury was developed from the radial-engined F20/27 experimental fighter which flew in August 1928. Fitted with a 480hp Rolls-Royce V-12 as a private venture, it became the Hornet, which took to the air in March 1929. Bought by the Air Ministry six months later, and after competitive trials against the Fairey Firefly IIM, it was

Above: Switzerland was the last nation to operate Hanriot HD1s until 1930.

Production by Hanriot was relatively limited – 125 aircraft for Belgium and Italy. The latter country however undertook license-production, and turned out many hundreds of the type. Agile, reliable, and pleasant to fly, in Belgian service the HD 1 became the mount of ace balloon buster Willy Coppens. Offered the Sopwith Camel in 1918, many Belgian pilots preferred to retain the HD 1, which was equally popular with its Italian pilots. It remained in service with both nations until the mid-1920s, and with Switzerland until 1930.

Above: In 1931, the Fury I was the world's fastest production fighter.

renamed Fury and orders were placed for 117 aircraft for the RAF.

A single-bay biplane of slightly unequal span and a steeply staggered lower wing, the Fury was the sleekest fighter in the skies at that time. In part this was due to the low frontal area of the Rolls-Royce Kestrel, which was marred only by the fitting for the Hucks starter on the spinner, and the deep underslung radiator. It was of all-metal construction, with fabric covering to the wings, rear fuselage and empennage.

The first unit to receive the Fury I (as it became) was No 43 Squadron at Tangmere, in May and June 1931, followed by No 1 and No 25 Squadron. All three formed aerobatic teams, although despite crisp handling the Fury was not the easiest aircraft in which to fly tight formation due to its low drag. Throttling back did not have the same instant deceleration as it had in a radial-engined fighter.

Not content to rest on their laurels, Hawker then produced the Fury II powered by the even more potent Kestrel VI which gave 640hp. Externally the Fury II was almost identical to the Fury I, the main difference being spats on the wheels. Internally it had increased fuel capacity. The weight increase was no

Hawker Hurricane I

Origin: Hawker Aircraft Ltd., England.
Type: Single-seat, single-engined monoplane fighter.
Engine: One 1,050hp Rolls-Royce Merlin II V-12 liquid-cooled engine.
Dimensions: Span 40ft 0in (12.19m); length 31ft 5in (9.58m); height 12ft 11.5in (3.95m); wing area 258sq.ft (23.97m^2).
Weights: Empty 5,085lb (2,307kg); normal takeoff 6,661lb (3,021kg).
Loadings (at normal takeoff weight)**:** Wing 26lb/sq.ft (126kg/m^2); power 6.34lb (2.88kg) per hp.
Performance: Maximum speed 316mph (508kph) at 17,750ft (5,410m); initial climb rate 2,300ft/min (11.68m/sec); sustained climb rate 6min 18sec to 15,000ft (4,572m); service ceiling 35,600ft (10,850m); range 425 miles (684km).
Armament: Eight 0.303in (7.7mm) wing-mounted Colt-Browning machine guns with 300 rounds per gun.
History: First flight 6 November 1935. Ordered on 20 July 1936, and first flight of production Hurricane 12 October 1937. In squadron service from December 1937. First air combat victory 30 October 1939. Bore the brunt of the French campaign and the Battle of Britain in 1940. Developed through several variants, including the four-cannon Hurricane IIB, but from late 1941 was used more as a fighter-bomber. Navalised for carrier operations, it became the Sea Hurricane. Production ceased in September 1944, after 14,231 aircraft. Hurricanes remained in service with the RAF until January 1947.
Users: Australia, Belgium, Britain (RAF and FAA), Canada, Finland, Free France, India, Iran, New Zealand, Portugal, Romania, South Africa, Soviet Union, Turkey, Yugoslavia.

In 1934, Hawker Aircraft were working on a project provisionally known as the Fury Monoplane. The engine selected was the Rolls-Royce PV-12, later to become the Merlin. The design was finalised and a mockup prepared, on the strength of which the Air Ministry ordered a single "high speed monoplane". Piloted by Percy "George" Bulman, this, the prototype Hurricane, first flew from Brooklands on 6 November 1935.

A low wing monoplane, its construction was traditional Hawker, with metal tube framing, fabric-covered from aft of the cockpit. Initially the wings were also fabric-covered, but this was replaced by light alloy skinning at an

Right: One of a handful of Hurricane Is exported to Yugoslavia prewar.

great, and was more than compensated for by increased performance. The Fury II could attain 223mph (359kph) at 16,400ft (4,998m), some 16mph (26kph) faster; initial climb rate was more than a third better; and it could reach 10,000ft (3,048m) in 42 seconds less, an improvement of nearly 20 per cent.

The Fury II equipped five front line RAF squadrons, and was used as an advanced trainer by several training schools. It was replaced by Gladiators in 1937. Some 48 Fury IIs remained in service with RAF training units well into 1939, and still later in South Africa.

Few Furies were exported, and many of these had different engines. Iran took 24 (as the Nisr), powered by either Pratt & Whitney Hornets or Bristol Mercuries; one of these aircraft was shot down by a Hurricane flown by "Imshi" Mason on 26 August 1941. One Fury went to Norway with a Panther IIA, and three to Spain with the HS 12Xbr. These last were used by the Republican Air Force in the Civil War. Finally, 40 were license-built in Yugoslavia.

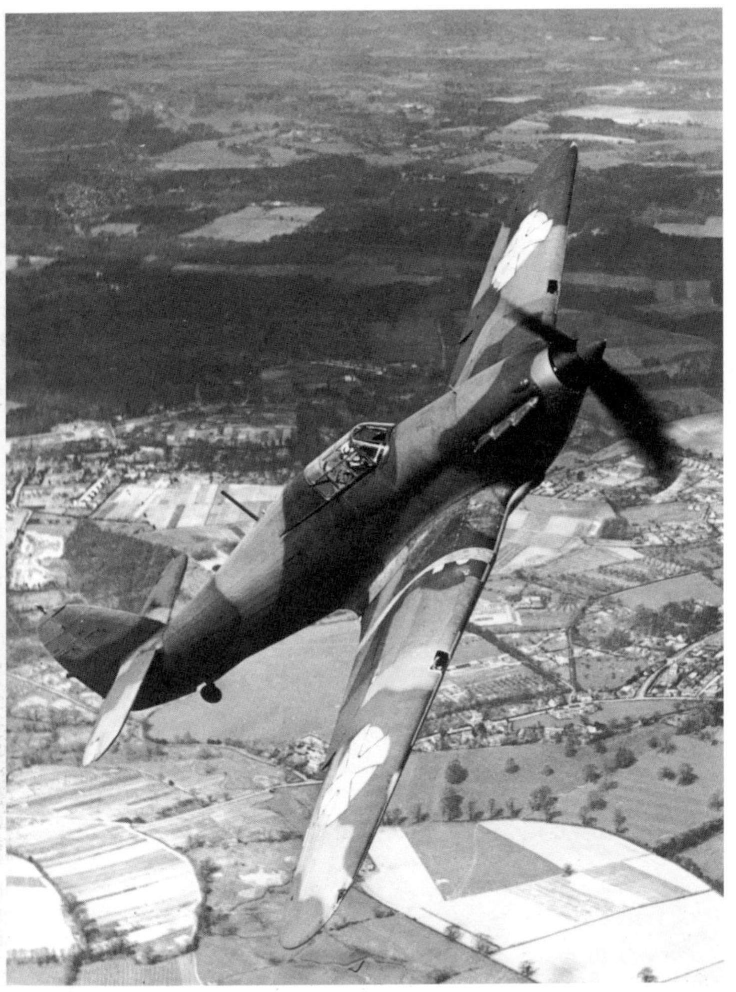

early stage. The shape of the tail surfaces instantly identified the Hurricane as a Hawker product. The cockpit was enclosed, and set slightly high, giving the fighter its characteristic hump-backed look, although this was not as extreme as its Italian contemporaries. It also gave a slightly better view over the nose than the Spitfire. The inward-retracting main wheels were located beneath the wings, giving a fairly wide track, and armament consisted of eight wing-mounted machine guns.

In February 1936 the prototype was delivered to Martlesham Heath for official trials. These proved satisfactory, and in a bold move Hawker Aircraft started to prepare for mass production three months before the first official order was issued, on 3 June 1937. The first production aircraft flew on 12 October, and deliveries to No 111 Squadron commenced before the end of the year; a remarkable performance.

With war looming, production was accelerated, and by September 1939 some 18 squadrons had been equipped. A year later this had risen to 32 squadrons. Hurricanes were sent to France on the outbreak of war, and the first air combat victory, over a Dornier Do 17, was claimed by "Boy" Mould of No 1 Squadron on 30 October.

Although outperformed by the opposing Messerschmitt Bf 109E, the Hurricane I had many strengths. It had no vices; in fact German ace Werner Mölders, who flew a captured Hurricane in the summer of 1940, commented that it was "very good-natured!" Although somewhat slow in roll acceleration, once the angle of bank was established speed for speed it out-turned the higher-wing-loaded German fighter with ease. The wide track undercarriage made operations from semi-prepared airstrips, which were

the norm in France, quite easy, while the sturdy construction made it able to absorb a great deal of battle damage. In fact, Jim Lacey of No 501 Squadron (23 victories with the Hurricane, five of them in France), commented that it was a collection of inessential parts! It was a stable gun platform, and its thick wings were less prone to flexing when the guns were fired in manoeuvring flight than were those of the Spitfire, reducing shot dispersion. Finally, the view "out of the window" was much better than that of its German opponent, which was obstructed by heavy framing.

The *Blitzkrieg* opened on 10 May 1940. No effective early warning was available, and most engagements were co-incidental. The Hurricane pilots largely held their own against superior numbers in the air, but lost heavily due to the situation on the ground. Forced to continually retire by advancing German armour, many damaged Hurricanes were abandoned or destroyed.

The Battle of Britain, which officially commenced in July 1940, saw a complete change of circumstance. Flying from bases which could not be over-run by ground forces, and with a well-honed early warning, detection, and control system in the air, the 28 Hurricane squadrons that took a substantial part in the fighting acquitted themselves well, destroying a total of 638 German aircraft.

Two things were badly needed: greater performance and more hitting power. The first point was addressed by the Hurricane IIA powered by the Merlin XX, rated at 1,460hp, which entered service from September 1940.

Below: Four 20mm Hispano cannon gave the Hurricane IIc unequalled firepower.

This was followed by the Hurricane IIB with 12 wing-mounted Brownings, and the IIC with four 20mm Hispano-Suiza wing-mounted cannon. But in 1941, improved versions of the Bf 109 were in service, and towards the end of that year the Hurricane switched mainly to ground attack, although it continued as a fighter in the Middle and Far East, and in Russia.

Hurricanes also served as "cats eye" night fighters from the autumn of 1940, fitted with shields to mask the glare from the exhausts which would otherwise have interfered with the pilots' night vision. But with the radar-equipped Beaufighter entering service, this was no more than a temporary measure.

Fitted with a tailhook, and with local strengthening, the Sea Hurricane was embarked aboard HMS *Furious* in July 1941. Superior to the Fulmar, it greatest failing was the lack of wing folding, which although proposed was never implemented. The last was delivered in August 1943, and by the end of that year it had largely been replaced by the Seafire and Hellcat.

Finally, mention must be made of the Hurricat. These were one-shot aircraft, catapulted from a ramp on a merchant ship to drive away shadowers, after which the pilot was forced, if he could not reach land, to ditch. Escort carriers soon made this hazardous procedure unnecessary.

Right:* *The Hurricane IIb fighter-bomber had twelve Browning machine guns.

Hawker Typhoon IB

Origin: Hawker Aircraft Ltd., England.
Type: Single-seat, single-engined monoplane heavy fighter.
Engine: One 2,180hp Napier Sabre IIA cylinder horizontal-H liquid-cooled engine.
Dimensions: Span 41ft 7in (12.67m); length 31ft 10in (9.70m); height 14ft 10in (4.52m); wing area 278sq.ft (25.83m^2).
Weights: Empty 8,690lb (4,064kg); normal takeoff 11,780lb (5,343kg); maximum 13,250lb (6,010kg).
Loadings (at normal takeoff weight)**:** Wing 42lb/sq.ft (207kg/m^2); power 5.40lb (2.45kg) per hp.
Performance: Maximum speed 412mph (663kph) at 19,000ft (5,791m), 374mph (602kph) at 5,500ft (1,676m); sustained climb rate 5min 54sec to 15,000ft (4,572m); service ceiling 34,000ft (10,363m); range 690 miles (1,110km).
Armament: Four 20mm wing-mounted Hispano-Suiza cannon with 140 rounds per gun. Two 1,000lb (454kg) bombs or eight 3in (76mm) rockets.
History: First flight of prototype 24 February 1940. First squadron delivery 11 September 1941. Operational debut 28 May 1942. As D-Day approached (June 1944), the Typhoon was increasingly switched to ground attack. Production ceased November 1945, with a total of 3,315, but by this time the Typhoon had been withdrawn from service.
Users: Australia, Britain (RAF).

In 1937, Hawker chief designer Sydney Camm commenced work on a high-speed fighter to be powered by the 2,000hp Napier Sabre engine. Construction of what became the Typhoon started in March 1938, but engine hold-ups delayed the first flight until 24 February 1940. It was not a good start. Low-speed handling left much to be desired, rate of climb and high altitude performance were disappointing, and manoeuvrability was poor by

Above: Very fast at low level, the Typhoon Ib was not much of a fighter.

contemporary standards. Rearward view from the cockpit was also unacceptable. By mid-1940, the priority was to produce existing fighters, and Typhoon development was all but halted. The second prototype did not fly until 3 May 1941.

In its final form, the Typhoon looked big and brutal, with a massive chin radiator. The traditional Hawker tubular metal structure was retained for the front and middle fuselage, but the rear fuselage was metal monocoque. Only the rudder was fabric. The wings were thick and slightly cranked, with the main gear legs located at the crank, giving a sturdy, wide-track undercarriage. Early models had "car-door" cockpit access, with a folding roof hatch, but late production machines had a sliding bubble canopy, giving excellent all-round vision.

The first production Typhoon IA flew just 24 days after the second prototype, differing from the IB in having an armament of 12 machine guns rather than four cannon. But problems persisted, and its future hung in the balance. It was saved from oblivion by its sheer speed at low and medium levels, and was ordered into service to counter the FW 190A, which at that

Hawker Tempest V

Origin: Hawker Aircraft Ltd., England.
Type: Single-seat, single-engined monoplane heavy fighter.
Engine: One 2,400hp Napier Sabre IIB cylinder horizontal-H liquid-cooled engine.
Dimensions: Span 41ft 0in (12.49m); length 33ft 8in (10.26m); height 16ft 1in (4.90m); wing area 302sq.ft (28.06m^2).
Weights: Empty 9,250lb (4,196kg); normal takeoff 11,400lb (5,171kg); maximum 13,640lb (6,187kg).
Loadings (at normal takeoff weight)**:** Wing 38lb/sq.ft (184kg/m^2); power 4.75lb (2.15kg) per hp.
Performance: Maximum speed 435mph (700kph) at 17,000ft (5,181m); 392mph (631kph) at sea level; initial climb rate 4,700ft/min (24m/sec); sustained climb rate 2min 42sec to 10,000ft (3,048m), 6min 6sec to 20,000ft (6,096m); service ceiling 34,800ft (10,607m); range 740 miles (1,191km).
Armament: Four 20mm wing-mounted Hispano-Suiza V cannon with 150 rounds per gun. Two 1,000lb (454kg) bombs or eight 3in (76mm) rockets.
History: Developed from the Typhoon. Prototype first flight 2 September 1942, first production aircraft 21 June 1943, and service entry April 1944. Air combat debut 8 June 1944. Total production 1,007. Retired from RAF front line service in 1949.
Users: Tempest V, Britain (RAF), New Zealand. Tempest II, radial engined, Britain (RAF), India, Pakistan.

Many of the problems of the Typhoon stemmed from the thick wing; the thickness/chord ratio of which varied from 19.5 per cent at the root to 10 per cent at the tip, with the greatest thickness at 30 per cent chord. An altogether thinner wing was needed, and design of this commenced in September 1941, resulting in a semi-elliptical planform. Philip Lucas took the prototype aloft a year later. Subsequent flights confirmed that performance and handling were greatly improved.

The thinner wing reduced fuel capacity, and to restore, and even increase, this the engine was moved 21in (533mm) forward to allow for a new tank in front of the firewall. To compensate for the extra length, all tail surfaces were increased in size. Various other refinements followed, including the bubble canopy developed for the Typhoon, and the new short barrel Hispano V cannon, which was not only 25lb (11kg) lighter, but had a rate of fire 15 per cent faster, albeit with a slightly lower muzzle velocity. What emerged was the Tempest V, a superb medium and low altitude air combat fighter, which was rushed into service in mid-1944. It was however regarded as an interim type pending the

time outclassed the Spitfire V.

In service, more problems manifested themselves. Carbon monoxide seepage into the cockpit could be countered by wearing an oxygen mask throughout the flight, but a tendency to shed its tail was much more serious, as was the unreliability of the Sabre engine. The latter was eventually cured, but structural failures, although reduced in frequency, continued into 1945, by which time the Typhoon was being withdrawn.

At low level, the Typhoon was significantly faster than the FW 190A, and made fighter-bomber raids by the latter distinctly risky. But when in 1944 its stablemate the Tempest entered service, it was switched to tank-busting and close air support, in which it gained an enviable reputation. A few Typhoon pilots did well in the air combat arena, notably Johnny Baldwin with 15 confirmed victories prior to August 1944.

Above: The Tempest V was developed from the Typhoon to become a superb fighter.

service entry of the Tempest II, due to the vagaries of the Napier Sabre engine.

First flown in prototype form on 28 June 1943, the Tempest II was powered by the Bristol Centaurus IV 18-cylinder radial engine, which gave 2,520hp. Much sleeker (no chin radiator) than the Tempest V, it was faster, climbed better, had a higher ceiling, and was less tiring to fly. The first production Tempest IIs came off the line in October 1944, but with the war in Europe nearing its end, it was earmarked for Tiger Force in the Far East. However, Japan surrendered before it could be used operationally, and its only active service was for both India and Pakistan at independence.

The first air combat victories (Tempest V) came on 8 June 1944, when three Bf 109Gs were claimed north of Rouen. Shortly after, they were diverted to deal with the V-1 threat and not until late September did they once more engage in air combat. By the end of the war, Tempest pilots claimed 240 enemy aircraft destroyed in the air and on the ground, including seven Me 262 and three Ar 234 jets. Tempest losses were high. Most fell to flak and engine failure, and only 23 in air combat. Only five Tempest pilots became aces, reflecting, like the low figure of air-to-air losses, lack of opportunity. Top scorer was American David Fairbanks, with 11 Tempest victories out of his total of 12, before he was shot down and taken prisoner.

Right: The sleek lines of the Tempest V are belied by the large chin inlet.

Hawker Sea Fury FB 11

Origin: Hawker Aircraft/Boulton & Paul Aircraft Ltd., England.
Type: Single-seat, single-engined carrier fighter.
Engine: One 2,480hp Bristol Centaurus 18-cylinder radial.
Dimensions: Span 38ft 4.75in (11.69m); length 34ft 8in (10.56m); height 15ft 10.5in (4.84m); wing area 280sq.ft (26.01m^2).
Weights: Empty 9,240lb (4,191kg); normal takeoff 12,500lb (5,670kg); maximum 14,650lb (6,645kg).
Loadings (at normal takeoff weight)**:** Wing 45lb/sq.ft (218kg/m^2); power 5.04lb (2.29kg) per hp.
Performance: Maximum speed 460mph (740kph) at 18,000ft (5,486m), 415mph (668kph) at 30,000ft (9,144m); initial climb rate 4,320ft/min (22m/sec); sustained climb rate 10min 48sec to 30,000ft (9,144m); service ceiling 35,800ft (10,911m); range 700 miles (1,126km).
Armament: Four wing-mounted 20mm Hispano-Suiza V cannon with 150 rounds per gun. Two 1,000lb (454kg) bombs or 12 3in (76mm) 60lb (27kg) rockets.
History: First flight of prototype 21 February 1945, and first production aircraft 7 September 1946. Operational from 1948. Combat debut Korea 1950. Production ceased November 1952 with a total of 665. Replaced in FAA service from 1953.
Users: Australia, Britain (FAA), Burma, Canada, Cuba, Holland, Iraq, Pakistan.

In the quest for greater performance and agility, Hawker scaled down the Tempest II for the RAF, producing the Fury. At the same time, Boulton & Paul undertook navalisation – arrester hook with local strengthening, and wing

Right: The Sea Fury was a scaled-down, radial-engined, navalized Tempest II.

folding – as the Sea Fury carrier fighter for the Fleet Air Arm. The RAF Fury was cancelled at the end of the war, but the Sea Fury went on to enter service with the Royal Navy.

The main difference between the Sea Fury and the Tempest was a reduction in both span and wing area, mainly by omitting the centre section of the original wing. While this increased wing loading and thus turning radius, it considerably improved rate of roll, an area in which the Tempest was notoriously lacking. Of course, the extra weight of the tailhook and wing folding, a total of 625lb (283kg), did nothing to help matters, but this was unavoidable.

The first Sea Fury was the F 10, of which 50 were built, but the definitive model was the FB 11, which had a significant attack capability. This was its main function in the Korean War, in which it served with distinction. On rare occasions it encountered the fast MiG-15, which it outmanoeuvred with relative ease. Peter Carmichael gave the Sea Fury its first victory over the MiG on 9 August 1952. But, with the onset of the jet age, the Sea Fury's days were numbered.

Hawker Sea Hawk F1

Origin: Hawker Aircraft Ltd., England.
Type: Single-seat, single-engined jet carrier fighter.
Engine: One Rolls-Royce Nene 101 centrifugal flow turbojet rated at 5,000lb (2,268kg) military thrust.
Dimensions: Span 39ft 0in (11.89m); length 39ft 8in (12.09); height 8ft 8in (2.64m); wing area 278sq.ft (25.83m²).
Weights: Empty 9,091lb (4,124kg); normal takeoff 13,220lb (5,997kg); maximum 15,030lb (6,818kg).
Loadings (at normal takeoff weight)**:** Wing 48lb/sq.ft (232kg/m²); thrust 0.38.
Performance: Maximum speed 602mph (969kph) at low level, 587mph (945kph) at 20,000ft (6,096m); initial climb rate 5,900ft/min (30m/sec); service ceiling 44,500ft (13,563m), reached in 11min 50sec; range 480 miles 772km).
Armament: Four nose-mounted 20mm Hispano-Suiza V cannon with 200 rounds per gun. Two 500lb (227kg) bombs or 10 3in (76mm) rockets on later models.
History: Prototype first flight 2 September 1947, and first production aircraft 14 November 1951. Squadron entry March 1953. Combat debut Suez November 1956. Production ended 1961 with a total of 542 of all variants. Phased out of FAA service December 1960, but served with the Indian Navy until May 1983.
Users: Britain (FAA), Germany, Holland, India (navies).

One of the most beautiful aircraft ever flown, the Sea Hawk design was begun in 1944. It had exceptionally clean lines, and the cockpit, located right in the nose and well ahead of the wings, gave its pilots an excellent all-round view. The Rolls-Royce Nene engine was located on the centre of gravity, well behind the cockpit, and was fed by wing-root inlets, thus avoiding the need for long inlet ducts, with their attendant problems. A long tailpipe was also avoided by the neat idea of a bifurcated efflux exhausting on both sides of the fuselage.

Hawker Hunter F 6

Origin: Hawker Aircraft Co Ltd., England.
Type: Single-seat, single-engined transonic day fighter.
Engine: One Rolls-Royce Avon 203 axial-flow turbojet rated at 10,000lb (4,536kg) military thrust.
Dimensions: 33ft 8in (10.25m); length 45ft 10.5in (13.98m); height 13ft 2in (4.00m); wing area 349sq.ft (32.42m²).
Weights: Empty 14,122lb (6,406kg); normal takeoff 17,750lb (8,051kg); maximum 23,800lb (10,796kg).
Loadings (at normal takeoff weight)**:** Wing 51lb/sq.ft (248kg/m²); thrust 0.56.
Performance: Maximum speed Mach 0.938, 714mph (1,149kph) at sea level; Mach 0.95, 627mph (1,009kph) at 36,000ft (10,972m); sustained climb rate 5min 30sec to 40,000ft (12,191m); service ceiling 51,500ft (15,696m); operational radius 318 miles (511km); endurance 1hr 18min.
Armament: Four 30mm Aden revolver cannon under the nose, with 100 rounds per gun. Up to four drop tanks, bombs and rockets.
History: First flight of prototype 21 July 1951. First production aircraft 16 May 1953. World speed record 7 September 1953. Service entry 1956, with combat debut over Suez in November. Served into the 1980s with several air forces. Production ceased in 1959 with a total of 1,972 of all types.
Users: Abu Dhabi, Belgium, Britain (RAF and FAA), Chile, Denmark, Holland,

Above: Smoke billows from the cartridge starters of a squadron of Sea Hawks.

While this inevitably resulted in thrust losses, this might equally have been the case with a conventional tailpipe. It also had the advantage of freeing some of the aft fuselage for fuel.

First flight took place on 2 September 1947, at Boscombe Down, piloted by Bill Humble. The only "quick fix" needed was the addition of pen-nib fairings aft of the effluxes, although later an increased wing span, a larger tailplane, an acorn at the junction of fin and tailplane, powered ailerons, an all-flying tail, and a Martin-Baker ejection seat, were all added.

The greatest failing of the Sea Hawk was its straight wing, which restricted performance. From a fighter, the Sea Hawk was increasingly developed as a bomb truck, ending with the FGA 6.

Right: This Hunter F 6 of 54 Squadron was later converted to become an FGA 9.

India, Iraq, Jordan, Kenya, Kuwait, Lebanon, Peru, Qatar, Rhodesia, Saudi Arabia, Singapore, Sweden, Switzerland.

Towards the end of 1947, Hawker began work on a swept-wing fighter designed around either the Rolls-Royce Avon or the Armstrong Siddeley Sapphire engines. An order for three prototypes was placed in June 1948, and the design of what became the P 1067 was finalised in April 1949. With the Korean War raging, a production order was placed even before Chief Test Pilot Neville Duke lifted the prototype off the ground from Boscombe Down on 20 July 1951.

The Hunter had a mid-set 40deg wing sweep at quarter chord, and a thickness/chord ratio of 8.5 per cent. Wing root inlets similar to those on th Sea Hawk were used, but the tail pipe was "straight-through", which occupie much of the rear fuselage. The canopy was faired into a dorsal spine which extending back to the steeply swept fin, housed control runs to the rudder an elevators. The horizontal tail was mounted about one third of the way up the fin with an acorn fairing at the rear junction.

Aerodynamically very clean, the Hunter amazingly lacked speed brakes Flaps were tried, but these produced unacceptable trim changes. Eventually ventral brake was scabbed on, looking like the afterthought that it was.

Early Hunters were not fault-free. It was chronically short on endurance; on one occasion six out of eight experienced pilots ran out of fuel and ejected while the other two belly-landed, after a flight time of less than 40 minutes. On the Avon-powered F 1, firing the guns caused engine surging, leading to the imposition of limits which made it useless as a fighter. As it happened, this was

Heinkel He 51B-1

Origin: Ernst Heinkel AG, Germany.
Type: Single-seat, single-engined unequal span biplane fighter.
Engine: One 750hp BMW VI 7,2Z liquid-cooled V-12.
Dimensions: Span 36ft 1in (11.00m); length 27ft 6.75in (8.40m); height 10ft 6in (3.20m); wing area 293sq.ft (27.20m^2).
Weights: Empty 3,247lb (1,473kg); normal takeoff 4,189lb (1,900kg).
Loadings (at normal takeoff weight)**:** Wing 14.30lb/sq.ft (70kg/m^2); power 5.59lb (2.53kg) per hp.
Performance: Maximum speed 205mph (330kph) at sea level, 193mph (310kph) at 13,124ft (4,000m); sustained climb rate 1min 24sec to 3,281ft (1,000m); service ceiling c22,967ft (7,000m); range 435 miles (700km).
Armament: Two 7.9mm nose-mounted synchronised MG 17 belt-fed machine guns with 500 rounds per gun.
History: Prototype first flight summer 1933. Production aircraft from April 1935. Combat debut Spanish Civil War 1936. Withdrawn from front-line service 1938 and used as advanced trainer. Total production 709.
Users: Germany, Spain.

The first design for Heinkel by the Günther brothers was the He 49, the first prototype of which flew in November 1932. A process of development led to the fourth prototype being sufficiently different to be redesignated the He 59, which first flew in the summer of 1933. Nine pre-series He 51A-0 evaluation aircraft followed, and the type was ordered into production as the He 51A-1, the first of which flew in April 1935.

It was followed by the He 51B-1, the main difference being provision for a drop tank beneath the cockpit, and the He 51B-2, fitted with floats, which served briefly with the *Küstenflieger*. The final variant not a problem with the Sapphire-powered F 2. It was also found that spent links and cases could cause damage, so bulged housings were fitted to retain them. These were called Sabrinas, after a well-endowed young lady of the era.

Next generation Avons were untroubled by gun firing, and these powered the F 4 and F 6. These and the Sapphire-powered F 5 had integral wing tanks to increase internal fuel capacity, an all-flying tail, and on the F 6 a dogtooth wing leading edge and a 200-series Avon.

The Hunter made its air combat debut for India against Pakistan in 1965, where it was largely unable to use its superior speed and acceleration against the slower but better-turning, Sidewinder-armed F-86 Sabre, although five Sabres were claimed. In the 1971 replay, Hunters claimed at least five more Sabres and a supersonic MiG-19.

Hunters saw action against Israel for Jordan in November 1966; for Jordan and Iraq in the Six Day War of 1967; and for Iraq in the October War of 1973.

---

was the He 51C, which was optimised for close air support, and carried racks of 22lb (10kg) bombs.

Heinkel 51s were supplied to the Spanish Nationalists, and the first air combat victory for the type was claimed by future ranking ace Joaquin Morato – a Republican Potez 540 bomber, on 18 August 1936. Shortly after, Julio Benjumea claimed a NiD 52 fighter and a Breguet Br XIX. German pilots of the Condor Legion also flew the type, and notched up a handful of victories, but when later in 1936 the Republicans started to receive Russian-built Polikarpov I-15s and I-16s, the German fighter was outclassed and relegated to close air support.

Below: He 51B pilots claimed a few victories in the Spanish Civil War.

Heinkel He 100D-1

Origin: Ernst Heinkel AG, Germany.
Type: Single-seat, single-engined monoplane fighter.
Engine: One 1,175hp Daimler-Benz DB 601 liquid-cooled V-12.
Dimensions: Span 30ft 10in (9.40m); length 26ft 10.8in (8.20m); height 11ft 9.75in (3.60m); wing area 157.15sq.ft (14.60m²).
Weights: Empty 3,990lb (1,810kg); normal takeoff 5,511lb (2,500kg).
Loadings (at normal takeoff weight)**:** Wing 35lb/sq.ft (171kg/m²); power 4.69lb (2.13kg) per hp.
Performance: Maximum speed 416mph at 16,405ft (5,000m), 358mph (576kph) at sea level; sustained climb rate 2min 12sec to 6,562ft (2,000m); service ceiling 34,451ft (10,500m); range 628 miles (1,010km).
Armament: One Oerlikon 20mm MG FF cannon firing through the propeller hub; two 7.9mm MK 17 wing-mounted machine guns.
History: First flight of prototype 22 January 1938. World air speed record of 463.92mph (746.61kph) set 30 March 1939 by a heavily modified aircraft. Total production nine prototypes, three pre-series He 100D-0s, and 12 He 100D-1s.
User: Heinkel Factory Defence Flight only, although six prototypes sold to the Soviet Union and three D-0s to Japan.

Annoyed by the failure of his He 112 to be preferred to the Bf 109, Ernst Heinkel set out to produce a fighter that would outperform the Messerschmitt. First flown on 22 January 1938 by Gerhard Nitschke, the He 100 showed promise from the outset. In He 100D-1 production form, it was outstandingly fast for its day. Furthermore, it was designed for ease of construction, which at that time was

---

Heinkel He 162A-2 Salamander (Volksjäger)

Origin: Ernst Heinkel AG, Germany.
Type: Single-seat, single-engined subsonic basic jet fighter.
Engine: One BMW 003E axial-flow turbojet rated at 1,764lb (800kg) military thrust.
Dimensions: Span 23ft 7.5in (7.20m); length 29ft 8.25in (9.05m); height 8ft 6.5in (2.60m); wing area 120.56sq.ft (11.20m²).
Weights: Empty 3,666lb (1,663kg); normal takeoff 6,184lb (2,805kg).
Loadings (at normal takeoff weight)**:** Wing 51lb/sq.ft (250kg/m²); thrust 0.29.
Performance: Maximum speed 562mph (905kph) at 14,686m), 553mph (890kph) at sea level; initial climb rate 4,615ft/min (23.45m/sec); service ceiling c36,091ft (11,000m); range 606 miles (975km); endurance 57min high, 20min at sea level.
Armament: Two 20mm Mauser MG 151 cannon.
History: Prototype first flight 6 December 1944. Production aircraft to operational units from January 1945. Total production about 300.
User: Germany.

A desperation measure, the He 162 was to be churned out in thousands, and to be so easy to fly that it could be fought by Hitler Youth glider pilots. It might have worked with the *Volkswagen*; it didn't work with the *Volksjäger*!

Speed was of the essence. Proposals were requested on 8 September 1944, an order was placed later that month, work began at once, and the first

Above: *Although faster than the Bf 109E, the He 100D failed to enter service.*

unusual. The question is posed: why was it not ordered by the *Luftwaffe*?

There were several reasons. Such a blatant move to upstage the Messerschmitt fighter would have earned Heinkel no prizes in a popularity contest, and may well have worked against him. More relevant was the fact that the He 100 was closely tailored to the DB 601 engine, almost the entire output of which was committed to the Bf 109. Finally, *Rechlin* test pilots reported that it was tricky to handle, and that the landing speed was too high.

Nazi propaganda portrayed the record-breaking He 100D as the mythical He 113. Not only did the Allies come to believe that this was in large scale service, but RAF pilots reported encountering it over Southern England in the summer of 1940.

Above: *Although cheap and quick to produce, the He 162 was not easy to fly.*

flight took place on 6 December. It had a high-set wing with down-turned tips, twin inward-canted fins, necessary to keep them clear of the efflux from the dorsally mounted engine. Adopted mainly for ease of access, this engine location had three disadvantages. The intake caught the disturbed airflow during manoeuvring flight; it blocked the rear view from the cockpit; and it made escape hazardous.

Aerodynamically unstable, the He 162 was a hot ship, and snaked badly at high speed. The controls were poorly harmonised and it had a tendency to tip stall. Pilots also had to "fly the engine", making their manoeuvres smooth to avoid compressor stalls. The He 162 never became operational, although it had a few brief encounters with Allied fighters in the spring of 1945. *Leutnant* R Schmitt of *I/JG 1* claimed a Typhoon on 4 May 1945, although this may have been a Tempest of No 486 squadron.

Heinkel He 219A-7 Uhu

Origin: Ernst Heinkel AG, Germany.
Type: Two-seat, twin-engined radar-equipped night fighter.
Engine: Two 1,900hp Daimler-Benz DB 603G liquid-cooled V-12s.
Dimensions: Span 60ft 8.5in (18.50m); length 50ft 11.75in (15.54m); height 13ft 5.5in (4.10m); wing area 479sq.ft (44.50m²).
Weights: Empty 24,692lb (11,200kg); normal takeoff 33,730lb (15,300kg).
Loadings (at normal takeoff weight)**:** Wing 70lb/sq.ft (344kg/m²); power 8.88lb (4.03kg) per hp.
Performance: Maximum speed 416mph (670kph) at 22,967ft (7,000m); initial climb rate 1,810ft/min (9.19m/sec); sustained climb rate 11min 30sec to 19,686ft (6,000m), 18min 48sec to 32,810ft (10,000m); absolute ceiling 41,669ft (12,700m); range 963 miles (1,550km).
Armament: Two 30mm Mauser MK 108 cannon in wing roots with 100 rounds per gun, two 30mm Mauser MK 103 cannon with 100 rounds per gun and two 20mm Mauser MG 151 cannon with 300 rounds per gun in a ventral tray. Two 30mm drum-fed Mauser MK 108 cannon in rear fuselage, slanted upwards at 65deg (*Schräge Musik*) and aimed through a sight in the cockpit roof.
History: Prototype first flight 15 November 1942. Comparative trials against the Dornier Do 217N and Junkers 188 early 1943. First operational sortie 11/12 June 1943. Operational with regular units from January 1944. Total production 268.
User: Germany.

Towards the end of 1941, Ernst Heinkel was asked to develop the Heinkel He 219 *Uhu* (Owl) heavy fighter project into a night fighter. Design was transferred to Vienna when RAF bombing raids destroyed the completed drawings, although the partly built prototype was untouched. To speed development, 130 pre-series aircraft were ordered, with the impossible deadline for service entry of 1 April 1943!

The first flight of the prototype took place on 15 November 1942. During the comparative trials in early 1943, the He 219 had been flown by night fighter

ace Werner Streib, *Kommandeur* of *I/NG 1* at Venlo. At his request, a small batch of pre-series aircraft was delivered to this unit in April 1943.

The developed He 219A was large, and exceptionally heavily armed. The crew sat in tandem on primitive ejection seats. To afford the best possible view, the cockpit was located ahead of the shoulder-mounted wing. The windshield and nose formed a single blunt curve, broken only by the "antler" aerials of the FuG 202 Lichtenstein SN 2 radar. At the other end it had twin "endplate" fins. The Daimler-Benz engines were underslung, with annular radiators giving the appearance of radials. The nacelles for these housed twin-wheeled main gears. The landing gear was completed by a nose leg to form a tricycle undercarriage.

Streib himself took the *Uhu* on its first war sortie, on the night of 11/12 June. In the space of half an hour, he shot down five Lancaster bombers, although this outstanding operational debut was marred when the *Uhu* was wrecked on landing after its flaps failed. In the next month, the small He 219A detachment accounted for 20 more RAF aircraft, including six fast and elusive Mosquitos. The obvious next step was to order the *Uhu* into mass production with a high priority, but this was not done.

The reason for this has often been quoted as a mixture of German mismanagement and internal politics. The truth is more prosaic. The impressive brochure figures could not be matched by production aircraft. With the exception of climb rate, could an aircraft with such a modest power loading really outperform the contemporary Mosquito to such a degree? Also, the exceptionally high wing loading and aspect ratio would be unlikely, despite reports to the contrary, to give outstanding manoeuvrability.

This may have been a factor in the death of 65-victory ace Manfred Meurer on 21/22 January 1944. After attacking a bomber from below with *Schräge Musik*, he was unable to get clear of his stricken victim. Be that as it may, production of the He 219A was halted on 25 May 1944.

***Below:* The He 219A failed to achieve its full potential as a night fighter.**

Heinkel He 280A

Origin: Ernst Heinkel AG, Germany.
Type: Single-seat, twin-engined subsonic jet fighter.
Engine: Two Heinkel-Hirth HeS 8A centrifugal-flow turbojets each rated at 1,653lb (750kg) military thrust.
Dimensions: Span 40ft 0.25in (20.20m); length 34ft 1.5in (10.40m); height 10ft 1.5in (3.06m); wing area 231.43sq.ft (21.50m²).
Weights: Empty 6,735lb (3,055kg); normal takeoff 9,482lb (4,310kg).
Loadings (at normal takeoff weight)**:** Wing 41lb/sq.ft (200kg/m²); thrust 0.34.
Performance: Maximum speed 559mph (900kph) at 19,686ft (6,000m), 541mph (870kph) at sea level; initial climb rate 3,760ft/min (19.10m/sec); service ceiling c37,732ft (11,500m); range 603 miles (970km).
Armament: Three nose-mounted 20mm Mauser MG 151 cannon.
History: First flight (unpowered) 22 September 1940. First powered flight 30 March 1941. First successful ejection 13 January 1943. Project cancelled 27 March 1943. Production, eight prototypes only.
Users: None.

The Heinkel He 280 has two main claims to fame: it was the first jet aircraft specifically designed as a fighter, and it was the first to be designed from the start with an ejection seat. Given the limited thrust of early jets, two engines were needed.

As still is traditional, engine development was a far slower process than that of airframes. The first prototype He 280 was completed in September 1940, with four others in various build stages, but the Heinkel-Hirth turbojets were lagging well behind. To keep the programme moving, 41 unpowered flights were made over the next few months, the fighter first being towed to altitude by an He 111. Handling in this condition was generally good.

Finally, two HeS 8 turbojets were ready, although not yet delivering the power predicted, and the first brief powered flight was made by Fritz Schäfer at Marienehe on 2 April 1941. As the engines tended to leak fuel, the cowlings were left off for this flight as a safety measure, but these were in place for an official demonstration four days later.

The wing leading edge was absolutely straight, but the trailing edge followed a curve outboard. The engine nacelles were underslung for ease of access, and the He 280 had a tricycle undercarriage from the outset, thus sparing itself the takeoff tribulations experienced by the Me 262. Its most unusual feature was the tailplane, mounted on a stub fin above the rear fuselage to clear the engine exhausts, which had a full-span elevator and twin end-plate fins and rudders.

Many of the problems of the HeS 8 engine stemmed from the attempt to minimise frontal area. Axial-flow engines were tried during the test programme: Jumo 109-004s and BMW 109-003s. Using Jumos, the He 280 was faster, climbed better, and had a higher ceiling than the similarly powered Me 262. It lost out in being relatively undergunned, in having far less endurance, and having tail flutter problems.

The remaining He 280s ended as research vehicles, and it was one of these that gave it its final claim to fame. The first prototype was fitted with four Argus 109-014 pulse-jets for trials. On 13 January 1943, it was towed into the air by two Bf 110s, but when Argus test pilot Schenk at 7,874ft (2,400m) cast off ready to start the motors, he found that he was unable to jettison the towline. Wisely, he abandoned the aircraft, thereby becoming the first man to successfully eject.

Below: In some areas, the He 280A was superior to the Me 262 jet fighter.

IG JAS 39A Gripen

Origin: Industri Gruppen JAS AB, Sweden.
Type: Single-seat, single-engined supersonic canard delta multi-role fighter.
Engine: One Volvo Flygmotor RM12 afterburning two-spool turbofan rated at 18,105lb (8,212kg) maximum and 12,141lb (5,507kg) military thrust.
Dimensions: Span 27ft 7in (8.40m); length 46ft 3in (14.10m); height 14ft 9in (4.50m); wing area c275sq.ft (25.54m²).
Weights: Empty 14,595lb (6,620kg); normal takeoff c19,224lb (8,720kg); maximum 30,864lb (14,000kg).
Loadings (at normal takeoff weight)**:** Wing 70lb/sq.ft (341kg/m²): thrust 0.94.
Performance: Maximum speed Mach 1.8 at altitude, supersonic at low level; initial climb rate c50,000ft/min (254m/sec); operational ceiling 50,000ft (15,230m); range 497 miles (800km).
Armament: One 27mm Mauser BK 27 cannon; two AIM-120 Amraam and four Rb 74 Sidewinders, or MICA. Cleared to carry a wide variety of air-to-surface ordnance.
History: Prototype first flight 9 December 1989. Batch 2 production ordered 26 June 1992. First Gripen handed over to Swedish Air Force June 1996. Initial operational capability late 1997. Total orders 200 plus and counting.
Users: Czechoslovakia, Hungary, South Africa, Sweden.

In 1980, a consortium was formed by Saab-Scania, Volvo Flygmotor, Ericsson, and FFV Aerotech. Its sole purpose was to develop a new combat aircraft to fulfil the air superiority fighter, attack and reconnaissance mission. In Swedish, this is *Jakt, Attack, Spaning*, from which the consortium drew its name of Industri Gruppen JAS AB.

The then-current Swedish fighter was the Viggen, which had been built in different variants to cover the three missions, plus a trainer. A product of 1960s technology and operational requirements, the Viggen was already dated by 1980, and would be still more so before a replacement came on line.

For such a numerically small population, the Swedes had long established their independence from foreign aircraft producers by turning out a long line of fine jet fighters. But times and technology had moved on; costs had gone through the roof. Could they do it again? The keynote was affordable capability.

In the military aircraft field, there is a direct link between weight and cost. The lighter the aircraft, the less it weighed and the less it cost. On the other hand the new fighter had to at least match the payload/range capability of the Viggen, while outperforming it in other areas, notably in air combat. Nor could it afford to appear in any way inferior to foreign fighters such as the trend-setting F-16.

Initial studies showed that although it was difficult, the task was not impossible. The latest technology in engines, in radar and avionics, allied to fly-by-wire control systems, weight saving using advanced composite construction, and state of the art design, would give payload/range equal to that of the Viggen for half its takeoff weight, while for air combat agility would be far superior.

A target weight of what would become the JAS 39 Gripen was set at eight tonnes. With this settled an engine could be chosen, and this fell on the General Electric F404 turbofan. Developed by Volvo Flygmotor with GE assistance, this became the RM12, with maximum thrust increased by 2,000lb (907kg).

The requirement for small size constrained airframe design. A chin inlet like that of the F-16 would have been ideal in many ways, but minimal ground clearance would have made this a foreign object damage (FOD) hazard. Instead fixed-geometry cheek inlets were used, accepting that sideslip would cause disturbed airflow. Ground clearance was also a factor in the mid-set wing position, selected as the optimum for the loading and carriage of external stores.

Below: Gripen offers outstanding multi-role capability in a small fighter.

A canard delta configuration was selected to give maximum agility combined with acceleration. The all-moving canards were located at the top of the inlet ducts, where they caused minimal obstruction to the pilot's vision, and like Rafale were close coupled. On landing they have a secondary function. Deflected down at a steep angle, they not only provide a download to assist the wheel brakes, but give aerodynamic braking to help ensure a short landing run.

The wing itself has two-piece slats on the leading edge with a dogstooth discontinuity, and two-piece elevons to the trailing edge, computer-controlled to give optimum camber for all flight conditions. Redundancy is built in; Gripen can return to base with any two control surfaces out of action.

Composite construction is used for the wing, canards and fin, and part of the fuselage. The cockpit is state-of-the-art, with HOTAS, three multi-function displays, a wide-angle HUD, and a raked seat. Radar is the Ericsson PS-05 multi-mode pulse-Doppler, and the same company makes the electronic warfare suite.

A great deal of time was spent validating the software for the automatic flight control system. Chief test pilot Stig Holmström spent about 1,000 hours in the simulator before making the first flight, on 9 December 1988, commenting afterwards that handling was a bit too sensitive. There were bugs

n the software and when Lars Rådeström came in to land on 2 February 1989, the aircraft pitched, hit the runway hard, and turned over. Fortunately he suffered only minor injuries.

The flight control software was to cause further delays. The test programme resumed in May, and just when all seemed well, Rådeström again drew the short straw. During a public display over Stockholm on 8 August 1993, his Gripen became uncontrollable. It felt, as Rådeström put it, "like butter sliding down a hot potato!", and he ejected.

Although flight testing resumed on 29 December, it was not until 1995 that the new P11 software was finally accepted. Gripen entered service in 1996 and became operational during the following year, accompanied by the JAS 39B, a fully combat-capable two-seat conversion trainer. Projected is the JAS 39C, which will have a more powerful engine to counteract creeping weight growth. The engine choice lies between the Eurojet EJ 2000, the SNECMA M88-3, the General Electric F414, and the RM12 Plus. Thrust vectoring is also a future possibility.

Below: Affordable without being austere, Gripen is eminently exportable.

Junkers Ju 88G-7b

Origin: Junkers Flugzeug und Motorenwerke AG, Germany.
Type: Three-seat, twin-engined radar-equipped night fighter.
Engines: Two 2,250hp (emergency with water/methanol injection) Junkers Jumo 213E V-12 liquid-cooled, rated at 1,880hp for takeoff.
Dimensions: Span 65ft 10.5in (20.08m); length 51ft 0.25in (15.55m); height 15ft 11in (4.85m); wing area 587sq.ft (54.50m²).
Weights: Empty c20,944lb (9,500kg); normal takeoff 28,902lb (13,110kg), maximum 32,350lb 14,674kg).
Loadings (at normal takeoff weight)**:** Wing 49lb/sq.ft (241kg/m²); power (emergency) 6.42lb (2.91kg) per hp.
Performance: Maximum speed 389mph (626kph) at 29,857ft (9,100m), 270mph (434kph) at sea level; initial climb rate 1,655ft/min (8.41m/sec); sustained climb 26min 24sec to 30,185ft (9,200m); service ceiling 32,810ft (10,000m); endurance 3hr 43min.
Armament: Four 20mm Mauser MG 151 fixed forward-firing cannon in ventral housing with 200 rounds per gun; two 20mm Mauser MG 151 fixed upward-firing cannon in rear fuselage (*Schräge Musik*) with 200 rounds per gun; one 13mm MG 131 swivelling machine gun with 500 rounds firing aft.
History: Developed from a high speed bomber, the first fighter variant was the Ju 88C, which appeared in 1940. After development through several subtypes, this was joined early in 1943 by the Ju 88R. The final main variant was the Ju 88G, which remained in service until the end of the war. Total production of Ju 88 fighters exceeded 4,000.
User: Germany.

The Ju 88 was conceived as a fast bomber, the prototype of which first flew on 21 December 1936. Stressed for dive bombing, its potential as a heavy fighter was immediately obvious, and the seventh prototype (Ju 88 V7) was given an unglazed nose which housed guns. This became the Ju 88C-2, with a 20mm Oerlikon MG FF cannon and three MG 17 machine guns in the nose. Converted from the Ju 88A bomber, it entered service as a night fighter in the summer of 1940, mainly for intruder missions.

The first bespoke fighter variant was the Ju 88C-4. This had a greater wing span and area, more armour protection, beefed-up landing gear, and two extra 20mm cannon in the gondola. Only about 100 were built before it was supplanted in production in 1942 by the Ju 88C-6, with uprated Jumo 211J engines. The -6a was a long range day fighter, used mainly for coastal patrols, while the -6b was fitted with FuG 202 Lichtenstein radar for night operations. The -6b was also the first variant to be fitted with *Schräge Musik*. In October 1943 it was followed into service by the -6c, with FuG 121 Lichtenstein C-1 radar, and a single aft-firing MG 131 heavy machine gun.

At various times, radial engines had been proposed; since the Jumo had annular radiators this involved minimal changes. This now came to fruition with the Ju 88R-1 powered by 1,600hp BMW 801C radials. The MG FF cannon in the "solid" nose was replaced by the more potent MG 151/20; radar was the Lichtenstein BC. The R-2 had 1,700hp BMW 801D radials, Neptun tail warning radar, and some carried Naxos Z radar homing.

Like all military aircraft, the Ju 88 had suffered creeping weight growth, and despite increases in engine power was beginning to creak a bit. This manifested itself in handling, either at low speed or high altitude. Even the Ju 88A had been regarded as a "hot ship". Former test pilot Peter Stahl likened it to a temperamental and capricious *diva*: "It is capable of suddenly doing quite surprising things without the slightest warning." Takeoff and landing accidents were frequent. Bomber ace Werner Baumbach crashed on landing twice in less than six weeks, and only an experienced pilot could hope to control it with one engine out. The fighter variants were no better.

The final night fighter variant was the Ju 88G, which appeared in mid-1944. To improve handling, this had the more angular tail surfaces of the Ju 188, the assymetrical gondola was deleted and the frontal armament housed in a ventral bulge. It was flown by Helmut Lent (102 victories), Heinz Rökker (63), Paul Zorner (59), Martin Becker and Gerhard Raht (58), and Heinz Strüning (56), among others.

Below: By 1945, the Ju 88 was the most numerous German night fighter.

Kawanishi N1K2-J Shiden-Kai Model 21

Origin: Kawanishi Kokuki Kabushiki Kaisha, Japan.
Type: Single-seat, single-engined monoplane fighter.
Engine: One 1,990hp Nakajima NK9H Homare Ha 45 18-cylinder radial.
Dimensions: Span 39ft 4.5in (12.00m); length 30ft 8in (9.34m); height 13ft 0in (3.96m); wing area 253sq.ft (23.50m²).
Weights: Empty 5,858lb (2,657kg); normal takeoff 8,818lb (4,000kg).
Loadings (at normal takeoff weight)**:** Wing 35lb/sq.ft (170kg/m²); power 4.43lb (2.01kg) per hp.
Performance: Maximum speed 416mph (669kph) at 19,030ft (5,800m)*, 358mph (576kph) at sea level*; sustained climb rate 6min 6sec to 20,014ft (6,100m)* service ceiling 39,700ft (12,100m); combat radius 350 miles (5,63km).* NB: the asterisk denotes figures attained by captured aircraft which exceed those usually quoted.
Armament: Four 20mm wing-mounted cannon.
History: Landplane Navy fighter derived from the floatplane N1K1 *Kyofu*; first flight of the prototype N1K1-J 27 December 1942. Production deliveries from July 1943. Major redesign led to the N1K2-J, which first flew on 31 December 1943. Production deliveries from July 1944. Total deliveries of all Shidens 1,413.
User: Japan (Navy).

Given the Allied reporting name "George", the N1K1-J *Shiden* (Violet Lightning) was unusual in that it was derived from the *Kyofu* (Mighty Wind) floatplane fighter, which had entered service in July 1943. The *Kyofu* was not very suitable for conversion to a landplane fighter in that the wings were mid-mounted to keep them clear of spray on takeoff and landing. This resulted in very long undercarriage legs with a complicated retraction procedure. However, the Japanese, opposed by the P-38 Lightning urgently needed a high altitude fighter. While new designs were on the drawing board, they were all taking far

too long. On the other hand, the *Shiden*, divested of "boots" and up-engined, looked as though it could deliver.

The Mitsubishi MK4D Kasei 13 14-cylinder radial engine was replaced by the more powerful Homare and two extra wing cannon were added. The X-1 prototype first flew on 27 December 1942, and production deliveries of the N1K1-J *Shiden* began in June 1943.

Even as the *Shiden* entered service, Kawanishi undertook a major redesign. The wings were moved to a low-set position, which allowed much shorter main gear legs. The fuselage was extensively redesigned and lengthened by 18.5in (47cm). The fin-and-rudder was reshaped, with a narrower chord. Remarkably, empty weight of the N1K2-J was actually 529lb (240kg) lighter than that of the N1K1-J, while normal takeoff weight showed the even greater advantage of 708lb (321kg). This reduced wing loading while, uniquely, automatic combat flaps were fitted, greatly enhancing manoeuvrability. Designated N1K2-J *Shiden-Kai*, the first of eight prototypes flew on 31 December 1943, and production commenced at once, the first deliveries taking place in July 1943.

Although it was an outstanding fighter, its centre of gravity was too far aft, and this made handling characteristics treacherous. Japanese Navy ace Saburo Sakai, who test flew the *Shiden-Kai* in September 1944, commented that far too many men failed to survive their familiarisation flights on the type, although in the hands of an experienced pilot it was a deadly opponent. On 19 March 1945, Imperial Japanese Navy ace Shoichi Sugita (70 victories) claimed four Hellcats destroyed and three more as probables in a huge dogfight near the Kure naval base.

In the spring of 1945, two *Shiden-Kai*s were modified by moving the Homare engine forward to correct the centre of gravity position, and this allowed two 13.2mm machine guns to be fitted in the nose. This was the N1K3-J, but it was too late to enter production.

Left: The aft centre of gravity of the Shiden-Kai made it tricky to fly.

Kawasaki Ki-61-I-Kai-Hei Hien

Origin: Kawasaki Kokuko Kogyo Kabushiki Kaisha, Japan.
Type: Single-seat, single-engined monoplane fighter.
Engine: One 1,175hp Kawasaki Ha 40 liquid-cooled V-12.
Dimensions: Span 39ft 4.5in (12.00m); length 29ft 2.75in (8.94m); height 12ft 1.75in (3.70m); wing area 215sq.ft (20.00m^2).
Weights: Empty 5,798lb (2,630kg); normal takeoff 7,650lb (3,470kg).
Loadings (at normal takeoff weight)**:** Wing 36lb/sq.ft (174kg/m^2); power 6.51lb (2.95kg) per hp.
Performance: Maximum speed 360mph (580kph) at 16,405ft (5,000m); sustained climb rate 7min to 16,405ft (5,000m); service ceiling 32,810ft (10,000m); range 901 miles (1,450km).
Armament: Two 20mm nose-mounted synchronised Ho 5 cannon and two 12.7mm wing-mounted Ho 103 machine guns.
History: Prototype first flight December 1941. First delivery of production aircraft August 1942. Combat debut in New Guinea April 1943. Production ended spring 1945 with a total of 2,783.
User: Japan (Army).

The Ki-61 *Hien* (Swallow), Allied reporting name "Tony", was designed for performance rather than manoeuvrability. To optimise performance, a liquid-cooled V-12 engine was adopted, rather than a standard Japanese radial. This was the Ha 40, a lightened derivative of the Daimler-Benz DB 601A. The Ha 40 was however to prove a source of weakness, as poor quality control made it very unreliable in service.

Lavochkin LaGG-3

Origin: Lavochkin OKB with Gorbunov and Gudkov, Soviet Union.
Type: Single-seat, single-engined monoplane fighter.
Engine: One 1,210hp Klimov M-105PF liquid-cooled V-12.
Dimensions: Span 32ft 2in (9.80m); length 28ft 11in (8.81m); height 14ft 5in (4.40m); wing area 188sq.ft (17.51m^2).
Weights: Empty 5,776lb (2,620kg); normal takeoff 7,032lb (3,190kg); maximum 7,231lb (3,280kg).
Loadings (at normal takeoff weight)**:** Wing 37lb/sq.ft (182kg/m^2); power 5.81lb (2.64kg) per hp.
Performance: Maximum speed 354mph (570kph) at 13,124ft (4,000m), 308mph (495kph) at sea level; sustained climb rate 5min 36sec to 16,405ft (5,000m); service ceiling 31,498ft (9,600m); range 410 miles (660km).
Armament: One 20mm ShVAK cannon with 650 rounds, and two 7.62mm ShKAS machine guns with 200 rounds per gun, all nose-mounted.
History: First flight as I-22 (LaGG-1) prototype 30 March 1940, piloted by P.N.Nikashin. In production from early 1941. Combat debut June 1941. Production ceased late summer 1942 with 6,528.
User: Finland (captured aircraft), Soviet Union.

When in 1939 a replacement was wanted for the Polikarpov I-16, Semyon Lavochkin's newly formed design bureau (OKB) began work on a prototype designated I-22. This duly emerged as the LaGG-1, a low-wing monoplane fighter. It was not a success; range and ceiling were inadequate, manoeuvrability was poor, and in some flight regimes handling was actually dangerous.

Above: The Ki-61 Hien was a move towards performance rather than agility.

First encountered by the Allies over New Guinea in 1943, the *Hien* proved a formidable opponent. Eschewing the classic turning fight, *Hien* pilots fought in the vertical. It could outdive the Wildcat and match the Hellcat in most departments, while armour protection for pilot and fuel made it able to absorb considerable battle damage. The first variants carried two 7.7mm and two 12.7mm machine guns, but these were found to be inadequate against the tough American fighters, and the 7.7mm weapons were replaced by 20mm cannon.

The Ki-61-II, which first flew in December 1943, had the more powerful Ha 140 engine, but this was not a success, and the aircraft was redesigned as the Ki-61-II-*Kai* with a strengthened airframe and a larger fin, but engine problems persisted. Finally it was modified to take the Ha 112-II radial, making a superb fighter, but was then redesignated Ki 100.

Above: A captured Soviet LaGG-3 in Finnish markings about to be test-flown.

Remarkably, construction was mainly of delta-drevesina, a bakelite/plywood sandwich, including wing box spars. With the exception of the dural-clad nose and fabric-covered control surfaces, the entire skin of the aircraft was plywood.

With war looming, the Lavochkin OKB attempted to cure the worst faults; not the least to trim excess weight. Wings were modified to have slats, and also fuel tanks, and lighter armament was fitted. The result was the LaGG-3.

The LaGG-3 was not popular with its pilots. Acceleration was poor, handling less than crisp, and it tended to spin off a tight turn, although lowering the flaps was later found to be a partial cure. In Russian conditions, the wooden construction did not last long: about 80 flying hours. But in combat, few aircraft lasted that long! The LaGG-3 helped hold the ring until 1943.

Lavochkin La-5FN

Origin: Lavochkin OKB, Soviet Union.
Type: Single-seat, single-engined monoplane fighter.
Engine: One 1,850hp Shvetsov ASh-82FN 14-cylinder two row radial.
Dimensions: Span 28ft 7in (8.71m); length 28ft 2.5in (8.60m); height 8ft 4in (2.54m); wing area 188sq.ft (17.51m^2).
Weights: Empty 6,173lb (2,800kg); normal takeoff 7,407lb (3,360kg).
Loadings (at normal takeoff weight)**:** Wing 39lb/sq.ft (192kg/m^2); power 4.00lb (1.82kg) per hp.
Performance: Maximum speed 403mph (648kph) at 20,998ft (6,400m), 342mph (550kph) at sea level; sustained climb rate 4min 42sec to 16,405ft (5,000m); service ceiling 31,170ft (9,500m); range 475 miles (765km).
Armament: Two 20mm nose-mounted synchronised ShVAK cannon with 200 rounds per gun.
History: The La-5 prototype, which first flew in March 1942, was a LaGG-3 airframe modified to take a Shvetsov radial engine. Production commenced July 1942. Combat debut September 1942 over Stalingrad. La-5FN combat debut over Kursk in July 1943. Production ceased late 1944, with a total of 9,920.
Users: Czechoslovakia, Soviet Union.

In 1942, with the Soviet Union fighting for its life against the Nazi invader, factories were pouring out mediocre LaGG-3s at an astonishing rate. They were badly needed. The question was how best to improve them with minimal disruption to production.

The first step was to fit the powerful new Shvetsov radial engine, with a minimum of modifications. The conversion first flew in March 1942, a state flight test programme was begun in April, production was ordered in July, and flown by factory pilots, what had now become the La-5 made its combat debut over Stalingrad in September 1942.

The LaGG-3s at an advanced stage on the production line were simply modified to accept the new engine; after that a gradual series of modifications was introduced. The most radical of these was lowering the aft fuselage to allow a semi-bubble canopy, allowing clear all-round vision. To protect the pilot while not blocking his view astern, the uniquely Russian solution of a 10mm thick armoured glass plate was fitted inside the rear canopy bow and above the steel back armour to the seat.

The ASh-82F engine became available late in 1942, giving a useful power increment and improved performance at low and medium altitudes. In this connection it should be noted that because the air war on the Eastern Front was mainly tactical in nature, in support of the ground forces, most air combat took place below 14,765ft (4,500m), and often a good deal lower. This was in direct contrast to the situation in the West, where operations at this time were largely divorced from the surface, and where the "ever faster, ever higher" trend was in full swing.

The final variant was the La-5FN, which took its suffix from the ASh-82FN (*forsirovannie neprosredstvennyi* – direct boost) engine, the most obvious external change being an extended air intake trunk to the supercharger. Weight reduction measures were also made on this model, notably the use of metal wing spars instead of wood, which saved some 379lb (172kg), and new automatic leading edge slats were fitted.

The La-5FN appeared at the front over Kursk in July 1943. Its controls were well harmonised; it was snappy in the rolling plane, and it could generally out-turn the Bf 109G and FW 190A. Two notable Soviet aces who flew the type were Ivan Khozhedub (62 victories) and Alexei Marase'ev, most of whose 19 victories were gained while flying with two artificial feet.

Below: The La-5FN made its combat debut during the Battle of Kursk in 1943.

Lockheed P-38L Lightning

Origin: The Lockheed Aircraft Corporation, USA.
Type: Single-seat, twin-engined long range monoplane fighter.
Engines: Two 1,600hp Allison V-1710-111/113 turbo-supercharged liquid-cooled V-12s.
Dimensions: Span 52ft 0in (15.85m); length 37ft 10in (11.53m); height 12ft 10in (3.91m); wing area 328sq.ft (30.47m²).
Weights: Empty 14,100lb (6,396kg); normal takeoff 17,500lb (7,938kg); maximum 21,600lb (9,798kg).
Loadings (at normal takeoff weight)**:** Wing 53lb/sq.ft (261kg/m²); power 5.47lb (2.48kg) per hp.
Performance: Maximum speed 414mph (666kph) at 25,000ft (7,620m), 360mph (579kph) at 5,000ft (1,524m); initial climb rate 3,800ft/min (19.30m/sec); sustained climb rate 7min to 20,000ft (6,096m); service ceiling 40,000ft (12,191m); range 2,260 miles (3,637km); endurance 12 hrs with external fuel.
Armament: One 20mm Hispano AN-M-2C cannon with 150 rounds, and four 0.50in (12.7mm) Browning M2 machine guns with 500 rounds per gun, all nose-mounted. Provision for rockets and bombs underwing.
History: First flight of XP-38 prototype 27 January 1939. First production order September 1939. Service entry 1941. Combat debut 7 December. Production ended August 1945 at a total of 9,923.
User: USA (USAAF).

Designed to a 1937 specification for a high-altitude interceptor, the P-38 Lightning was an extremely innovative design. The performance requirements were stringent, and to meet them two Allison V-1710 (the number was a reference to its cubic capacity in inches while the V was the cylinder configuration) liquid-cooled engines were selected. As the Allison was not

Below: The twin booms of the Lightning housed the turbo superchargers.

Above: An excellent view of the radiators on the twin booms of this P-38.

normally renowned for its high-altitude performance, turbo-supercharging was needed.

This virtually determined the configuration. Turbo-superchargers were large and heavy. Driven by very hot exhaust gases, they compressed air from the intake before feeding it to the engine. Needing a twin-engined design to obtain the necessary power, Lockheed had little choice but to settle for a twin-boom layout with a turbo-supercharger behind each engine, with a radiator astern of both. This left the pilot in a central nacelle, with the main armament in the nose in front of him. It also permitted, if it did not positively dictate, the use of a tricycle landing gear. Similarly, twin fins and rudders could hardly be avoided.

Given all this, the Lightning could hardly have been other than dimensionally large; it was actually rather heavier than the standard British medium bomber of the era, the Blenheim. Wing loading was enormous, double that of contemporary single-seater fighters. In an attempt to offset this, Fowler-type flaps were developed, but these had problems due to pressure reversal. Firepower was also high, more than triple the usual USAAC norm. Initially the projected armament was one 23mm Madsen cannon with 50 rounds, and four 0.50in (12.7mm) Colt MG-53 machine guns with 1,000 rounds per gun. These were electrically heated to prevent freezing at high altitudes. A further interesting idea was to use "handed" engines, with both propellers rotating inwards. This was adopted to eliminate torque in normal flight, and to minimise the effect of asymmetric thrust with one engine out.

An official contract for a single XP-38 prototype was issued in June 1937. Piloted by Ben Kelsey, it had its maiden flight from March Field, California, on 27 January 1939. Just 15 days later, aided by a strong tailwind, it made a transcontinental flight to New York in just over seven hours, with two refuelling stops. This feat was rather degraded by the fact that on arrival it was destroyed in a crash landing!

An order was then placed for 13 pre-production YF-38s, the first of which arrived for evaluation by the USAAC in March 1941. These differed from the prototype in having outwardly rotating propellers, a raised thrust line, and a 37mm Madsen cannon. But even before this, a production order was placed for 66 aircraft.

The first truly operational Lightning was the P-38D, which had armour protection for the pilot, and self-sealing fuel tanks. When the USA entered the war in December 1941, only a handful of these were on strength, but an Iceland-based aircraft scored the first victory by the type, shooting down an FW 200 Condor only minutes later.

Lightnings were the first single-seat fighters to fly the Atlantic, staging through Labrador, Greenland and Iceland, using B-17s as navigational escorts. Other models had by now appeared: the P-38F, G, and K. The type's first experience against the *Luftwaffe* was in North Africa late in 1942, but this was not an entirely happy event. Most combat took place at medium or low levels, where it was outmatched by the Bf 109G and FW 190A, especially in a turning fight. A combat flap setting of 8deg improved the Lightning's turn radius, especially with the inner engine throttled back, but to gain any real advantage it first had to establish itself in the turn. This was not easy. Matters were not helped by the yoke-type control column, which was unique for a fighter, while it was also a rather "busy" aircraft to

fly, with engine and oil temperatures that needed continual watching.

The long range of the Lightning saw it used in the bomber escort role from October 1943, but its large span and high wing loading made it easily outmanoeuvred by its German opponents. In Northern Europe it was beset by a variety of mechanical problems, most caused by the un-Californian climate. By September 1944 it had been withdrawn from bomber escort, although it was still used tactically by the 9th and 15th Air Forces. Top scorer in North Africa was William Sloane with 12 victories, equalled by Michael Brezas over Italy and Southern Europe.

The Lightning was most successful in the Pacific, where its long legs made it invaluable in the island-hopping campaign. Almost invariably its altitude performance allowed it to take a high perch prior to engaging, and the standard tactic was the dive and zoom, its firepower chewing up the Japanese lightweights in short order. The American top scorer of the war, Dick Bong, claimed 35 of his 40 victories with the Lightning. He was closely followed by Tommy McGuire (38), who was killed when he slowed down to dogfight with a Zero in the Philippines.

Below: In the Pacific, the Lightning outclassed most Japanese fighters.

Lockheed P-80C Shooting Star

Origin: The Lockheed Aircraft Corporation, USA.
Type: Single-seat, single-engined subsonic jet fighter.
Engines: One Allison J33-A-35 centrifugal flow turbojet rated at 5,400lb (2,449kg) military thrust.
Dimensions: Span 38ft 10.5in (11.85m); length 34ft 6in (10.52m); height 11ft 4in (3.45m); wing area 238sq.ft (22.11m^2).
Weights: Empty 8,240lb (3,738kg); normal takeoff 12,650lb (5,738kg); maximum 16,856lb (7,646kg).
Loadings (at normal takeoff weight)**:** Wing 53lb/sq.ft (260kg/m^2); thrust 0.43.
Performance: Maximum speed 580mph (933kph) at sea level; initial climb rate 7,000ft/min (35.56m/sec); service ceiling 39,500ft (12,039m); range 716 miles (1,152km).
Armament: Six 0.50in (12.7mm) Browning M-2 machine guns with 300 rounds per gun. Eight 5in (127mm) unguided rockets, or two 1,000lb (454kg) bombs, or six napalm tanks.
History: First flight 8 January 1944. Entered service from February 1945. Combat debut Korea July 1950. Production ceased 1949 with a total of 1,714. Served with ANG until 1961.
Users: Brazil, Chile, Colombia, Ecuador, Peru, Uruguay (the latter until 1975), USA (ANG, USAAF/USAF, USMC and USN).

The first American jet fighter to enter service, the XP-80 Shooting Star, was designed and built in the astonishingly short time of 143 days. The engine was the British-built Halford H-1B, to become known in its land of origin as the De Havilland Goblin. But on the final engine test run, on 15 November 1943, the inlet ducts collapsed, wrecking the only available engine. This delayed the Shooting Star's first flight until 8 January 1944, when Milo Burcham lifted the new jet, named Lulu-Belle, off from Muroc Dry Lake.

The H-1B engine had been supplied by the British to get American jet fighter progress underway, but with a mere 2,200lb (998kg) thrust it was not to be the definitive powerplant. Designer Kelly Johnson modified the XP-80 to house the General Electric I-40, of nearly double the thrust. Two XP-80As were built, followed by 13 YP-80As, and the first production order, for the P-80A, was placed on 4 April 1944. Service entry was in February 1945, but although four aircraft were rushed to Europe they were too late to see combat there.

The P-80A was dimensionally larger and significantly heavier than the XP-80, and was powered by the J33-GE-11 and the J33-A-9, located amidships in the fuselage, and fed by cheek intakes. It was conventional in all respects except one: the wing section was an untried laminar flow type. Fortunately this worked well, but other problems were encountered during development. Test pilot Milo Burcham and top American ace Dick Bong both lost their lives after fuel system failures, and test pilot Tony LeVier was badly injured after baling out.

Above: The P-80 Shooting Star was the first American jet fighter in service.

Although several subtype suffixes were allocated, only three major variants entered service. Jacksel Broughton, who flew the Shooting Star extensively in the late 'forties and also in Korea, described them thus: "The A was the fun machine... She was small, the cockpit was tight, and when you manually cranked that cockpit closed and locked yourself in, there was no doubt that you and the bird were one. The B was a limited edition hybrid [*it had a thinner wing and upgraded equipment and armament; only 240 B models were built*]. The Cs were the Cadillacs of the fleet, with more power, ejection seats, and improved fuel controls".

It was the F-80C, as it was now redesignated, that went to war in Korea, and Russell Brown scored the first jet-versus-jet victory against a MiG-15 on 8 November 1950. In all, Shooting Stars claimed 37 victories in air combat, including six MiG-15s. They were however outclassed by the Russian fighter and, lacking manoeuvrability and endurance for close air support, were withdrawn from Korea in 1951.

Lockheed F-94C Starfire

Origin: The Lockheed Aircraft Corporation, USA.
Type: Two-seat, single-engined subsonic jet all-weather fighter.
Engines: One Pratt & Whitney J48-P-45 axial-flow afterburning turbojet rated at 8,750lb (3,969kg) maximum and 6,350lb (2,880kg) military thrust.
Dimensions: Span 37ft 4in (11.38m); length 44ft 6in (13.56m); height 14ft 11in (4.55m); wing area 233sq.ft (21.65m^2).
Weights: Empty 12,708lb (5,764kg); normal takeoff 18,300lb (8,301kg); maximum 27,000lb (12,247kg).
Loadings (at normal takeoff weight)**:** Wing 79lb/sq.ft (383kg/m^2); thrust 0.48.
Performance: Maximum speed 646mph (1,039kph) at sea level, 585mph (941kph) at 35,000ft (10,776m); initial climb rate 7,975ft/min (40.51m/sec); service ceiling 51,400ft (15,666m); range 805 miles (1,295km).
Armament: 24 2.75in (70mm) Mighty Mouse folding-fin aircraft rockets (FFARs) in the nose, and 24 FFARs in two leading edge wing pods.
History: Developed from the T-33 two-seat trainer variant of the F-80. First flight 16 April 1949. F-94A operational from May 1950 and F-94B from April 1951. Combat debut F-94B, Korea March 1952. Production ceased in May 1954, with a total of 851. Withdrawn from USAF service February 1959, and ANG summer 1960.
Users: USA (ANG , USAF).

Intended as a stopgap night fighter, the Starfire was based on the T-33 tandem-seat trainer. The Hughes E-1 weapon system, which included the APG-32 radar, was shoehorned into the nose, together with four 0.50in (12.7mm) Browning machine guns. Weight inevitably increased, and performance could be maintained only by using afterburner. This had a variable eyelid nozzle, the development of which took time.

The F-94A became operational in June 1950, and first flew a combat

Lockheed F-104A Starfighter

Origin: The Lockheed Aircraft Corporation, USA.
Type: Single-seat, single-engined bisonic jet fighter.
Engines: One General Electric J79-GE-3B single-spool axial-flow afterburning turbojet rated at 14,800lb (6,713kg) maximum and 9,600lb (4,355kg) military thrust.
Dimensions: Span 21ft 11in (6.68m); length 54ft 9in (16.69m); height 13ft 6in (4.11m); wing area 196sq.ft (18.21m^2).
Weights: Empty 13,384lb (6,071kg); normal takeoff 22,614lb (10,258kg); maximum 25,840lb (11,721kg).
Loadings (at normal takeoff weight)**:** Wing 115lb/sq.ft (563kg/m^2); thrust 0.65.
Performance: Maximum speed Mach 2.2 plus at altitude, Mach 1 plus at sea level; initial climb rate 60,395ft/min (307m/sec); service ceiling 64,795ft (19,749m); range 730 miles (1,175km) with tanks.
Armament: One 20mm M61-A six-barrel Vulcan rotary cannon with 725 rounds; two or four AIM-9 Sidewinders, late models two AIM-7 Sparrow or Aspide with two Sidewinders.
History: First flight 4 March 1954. Service entry 26 January 1958. Combat debut Pakistan September 1965. Withdrawn by USAF December 1969 and by the ANG in July 1975. Still in service with Italy in 2002. Production ended 1975, with a total of 2,171.
Users: Belgium, Canada, Denmark, Germany, Greece, Holland, Italy, Japan,

***Above:** Based on the T-33 trainer, this is the all-rocket armed F-94C Starfire.*

mission in Korea in March 1952. Only in November was it released to operate over enemy territory, claiming its first (of four) victories on 28 January 1953. There is however a strange account from the other side. Russian MiG-15 ace Eugeny Pepelyaev, backed by Boris Abakumov, records encountering eight Starfires during July 1951, over Mukden (Shenyang), seven of which were shot down. The Starfire was short on range, and would have been hard-pressed to get this far inland, even more so as it was not supposed to be in the theatre at this time.

The final Starfire variant was the F-94C, with a thinner wing, swept tail surfaces, the E-5 fire control system optimised for collision course interception, and all-rocket armament. At maximum all-up weight, wing loading was a horrendous 116lb/sq.ft (566kg/m2).

***Above:** The Starfighter had an incredibly small and thin unswept wing.*

Jordan, Norway, Pakistan, Spain, Taiwan, Turkey USA (ANG and USAF).

During the Korean War, the high-altitude capability of the MiG-15 had F-86 Sabre pilots clamouring for greater performance. Lockheed chief designer Kelly Johnson took them at their word. With the F-104 Starfighter he delivered what was called "a missile with a man in it". But performance was gained at the expense of manoeuvrability.

The Starfighter was designed around the new and unproven General Electric J79, the first production powerplant to use variable stators. Housed in a sleek cylindrical fuselage with a good fineness ratio, it was fed by side inlets with fixed shock half-cones. The wings were amazing. Unswept at a time when swept wings were *de rigeur*, they were incredibly tiny and incredibly thin: just 4.2in (107mm) thick at the root, with a thickness/chord ratio of 3.36 per cent

This resulted in an extremely high wing loading, limited manoeuvrability, and exceptionally high takeoff and landing speeds. To offset this a little, the leading edge hinged down as a slat, while the trailing edge flaps had boundary layer control using engine bleed air. Outboard, the ailerons were powered by hydraulic boosters only 1.10in (28mm) thick! Bolted to the fuselage

Lockheed YF-12A

Origin: The Lockheed Aircraft Corporation, USA.
Type: Two-seat, twin-engined trisonic interceptor.
Engines: Two Pratt & Whitney J58 axial-flow turbo-ramjets each rated at 32,500lb (14,742kg) maximum thrust.
Dimensions: Span 55ft 7in (16.94m); length 101ft 8in (30.99m); height 18ft 3in (5.56m); wing area 1,605sq.ft ($149m^2$).
Weights: Empty 60,730lb (27,547kg); normal takeoff 127,000lb (57,607kg).
Loadings (at normal takeoff weight)**:** Wing 79lb/sq.ft ($387kg/m^2$); thrust 0.51.
Performance: Maximum speed Mach 3.35 at 80,000ft (24,383m); climb rate n/a; operational ceiling 85,000ft (25,907m); range 2,500 miles (4,023km).
Armament: Six AIM-47 long-range radar-homing AAMs.
History: First flight 7 August 1963. Only three built. Final flight 7 November 1969.
User: USA (USAF trials only).

From the late 1950s, Kelly Johnson of Lockheed was working on the A-12; a long-range single-seat reconnaissance aircraft able to reach Mach 3.35 and 95,000ft (28,955m). Given the speed/range requirement, it could hardly have been otherwise than large. The configuration chosen was a tail-less delta powered by two turbo-ramjets optimised for trisonic cruising. For technical reasons, these were located in nacelles outboard on the wings, which left virtually the whole of the fuselage free to carry an enormous amount of fuel. To withstand the extreme kinetic heating of Mach 3 flight, most of the structure and virtually all the skin were of titanium, then a difficult metal to work. The very thin wing, with a thickness/chord ratio of just 2.5 per cent, was swept at 57.5deg,

ainframes, with no carrythrough structure, the wing had 10deg of anhedral. e high-set tailplane was a single-piece all-moving slab on top of the fin, and s caused a downward-ejecting seat to be fitted.

First flight, by Tony LeVier, took place from Edwards AFB on 4 March 1954, an XF-104 powered by a Wright J65, a license-built Sapphire. With the J79 ailable, the YF-104 was flown by Hermann Salmon on 17 February 1956. oblems were encountered, with the engines, with pitchup caused by the h-set tail, and with inertia coupling. The downward ejection seat quickly came unpopular, and all too many pilots died because of it.

As a fighter, the F-104 was a disaster. It could not turn tightly and its radar d avionics were totally mismatched with its performance. On the other hand, vas a superb flying machine, highly regarded by former Spitfire pilots Johnnie hnson and John Nicholls, the latter of whom was to become RAF Vice-Chief. t both added the stricture: "But not to go to war in!"

This is borne out by its combat record. In Vietnam, it was handicapped by ort endurance. In the Indo-Pakistan War of 1965, Starfighter pilots scored ee victories for one loss; then in 1971 they claimed another four, but lost four MiG-21s.

Above: Derived from the A-12, the YF-12A was the fastest fighter ever.

with differentially moving elevons over the entire trailing edge. The fins were equally unorthodox: twin all-moving surfaces mounted above the engines and canted inwards at about 15deg. The A-12 had other unusual features: it was designed from the outset to have a low radar signature, or stealth. The most obvious external signs of this were wing-body blending, chines extending from the wing leading edges to the tip of the nose, and black radar-absorbent paint.

Prior to this, North American was developing the F-108 Rapier trisonic fighter, but for various technical and budgetary reasons this was cancelled in September 1959. However, its advanced fire control system, the Hughes ASG-18, which included the first ever coherent pulse-Doppler radar, and the GAR-9 (later AIM-47) long-range AAMs, also a Hughes product, were at a very advanced stage. Even before the A-12 had flown, it was decided to modify three examples as proof-of-concept fighters. Thus was born the YF-12A,

Lockheed Martin F-22A Raptor

Origin: Lockheed Martin Aeronautics, USA.
Type: Single-seat, twin-engined bisonic air superiority fighter.
Engines: Two Pratt & Whitney F119-PW-100 twin-spool axial-flow afterburning turbofans each rated at 35,000lb (14,742kg) maximum thrust; military thrust classified, with pitch-vectoring nozzles.
Dimensions: Span 44ft 6in (13.56m); length 62ft 1in (18.92m); height 16ft 8in (5.08m); wing area 840sq.ft (78.04m^2).
Weights: Empty 31,670lb (14,365kg); normal takeoff classified; maximum 55,000lb (24,948kg).
Loadings (at maximum takeoff weight)**:** Wing 65lb/sq.ft (320kg/m^2); thrust 1.27.
Performance: Maximum speed Mach 2 at altitude, Mach 1.21 at sea level, supercruise Mach 1.58; initial climb rate classified; service ceiling classified but in excess of 50,000ft (15,239m); range 2,000 miles (3,218km).
Armament: One 20mm M61A-2 six-barrel rotary cannon with 460 rounds; six AIM-120C Amraam and two AIM-9T Sidewinder AAMs in internal bays. More weapons can be carried externally.
History: First flight 29 September 1990. EMD contract awarded August 1991. First flight of development aircraft 7 September 1997. Service entry late 2005. Anticipated production 339.
User: USA (probably USAF only).

In 1983, the Soviet Union not only still posed a major threat, but was also developing a whole new generation of agile fighters. By this time, the premier USAF fighter, the F-15 Eagle, had been in service for eight years. Concept definition studies for its replacement were commenced. The new fighter had to outfly and outfight the opposition, operate deep into hostile airspace, be easily maintainable, operable from damaged or austere bases and, with the lessons of the F-14 and F-15 still fresh, be affordable. Priorities soon emerged: stealth, speed, and agility for the mission, hi-tech for maintenance, and a maximum weight limit of 50,000lb (22,680kg) for affordability. This was the basis of the Advanced Tactical Fighter (ATF).

Stealth was necessarily a tradeoff. It could not be allowed to compromise the traditional fighter virtues of speed, agility, acceleration, and rate of climb, because once within visual range it counted for little. It could however be used to complement them. In air combat, the priority is detect first, shoot first. A high level of stealth would enable the ATF to do this. Stealth would also crimp in the engagement envelopes of surface-to-air weapons and hopefully foil hostile early warning systems. Stealth would also reduce the need for differing from the A-12 in having a longer fuselage, a second cockpit for the weapons system operator, a differently shaped nose to house the radar, with the chines cut back and infra-red sensors installed, internal weapons bays to house the missiles, fixed ventral fins beneath the engine nacelles, and a large side-folding fin beneath the rear fuselage.

First flight, by Jim Eastham, took place from Groom Lake on 7 August 1963. Weapons tests went well, with launch ranges of up to 120 miles (193km) and the fire control system was soon proven. The YF-12A also set a hatful of world records in 1965, including absolute speed, and sustained altitude. But as a fighter it had severe limitations. It was structurally limited to +3/-1g which meant that radical course changes took forever. Even worse, its specialised fuel precluded a rapid scramble. But, at the end of the day, the YF-12A was the world's fastest fighter!

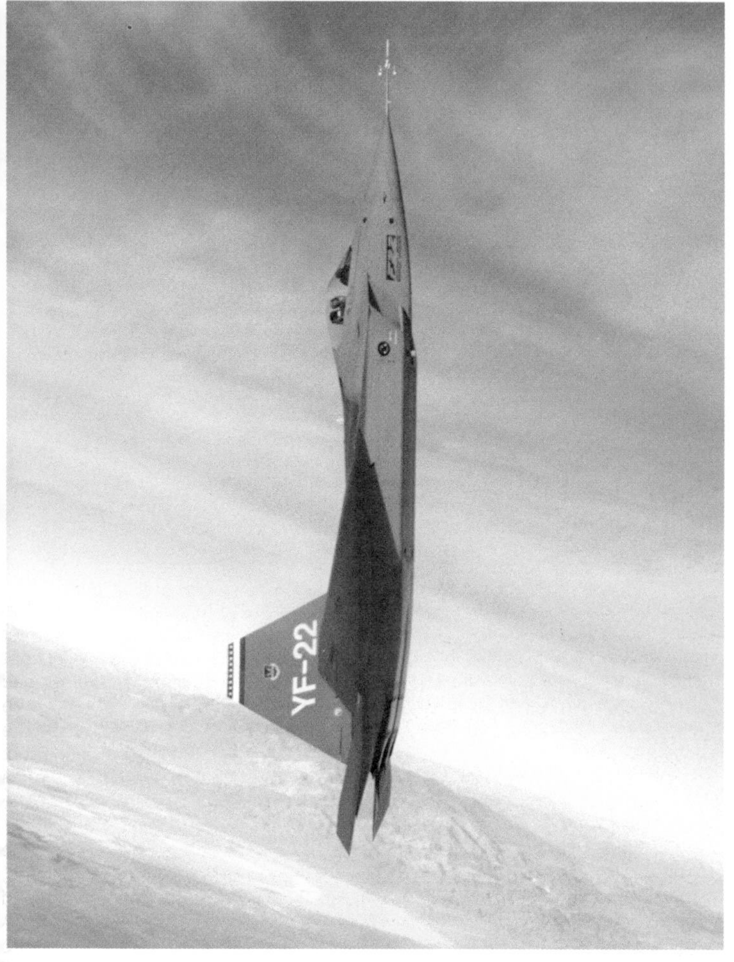

Above: The design of the F-22A is a compromise between stealth and agility.

electronic countermeasures, which, as emitters, betray the position of the parent aircraft.

Speed is another essential. It reduces the reaction time of the defences, makes tracking more difficult, allows rapid closure on a target and, when needs be, permits a hasty exit from the arena. It has one other important function: against an attacker trapped at six o'clock, it shrinks his missile launch envelope. Studies showed that Mach 1.4 was about the minimum required.

The problem was that speeds appreciably above Mach 1 needed afterburning, and this was effectively a large heat beacon in the sky. It was unstealthy. What was needed was supercruise, the ability to exceed Mach 1 by a significant margin in military thrust only. For this, a totally new engine was needed. A spin-off effect here was fuel economy; supercruise would greatly extend both operational radius and combat persistence. This was particularly important. While external tanks could be carried for ferry flights, or possibly even in a benign combat situation, in a truly hostile scenario stealth requirements ruled out the carriage of drop tanks; all fuel had to be carried internally.

Above: The Raptor has been shaped to deflect hostile radar emissions away.

Stealth impinged on almost every aspect of the design. A minimum of eight AAMs would be needed to give sufficient combat persistence, but these had to be carried in internal bays – six Amraam ventrally, pneumatically expelled on launch, and two Sidewinders in side bays which swung out on trapezes. This, plus the need to carry all fuel internally, inevitably resulted in a big aircraft, but size is little to do with stealth. What matters most is shaping, and a very precise external finish. All of the new fighter's surfaces were carefully angled to deflect incoming radar impulses away from the emitter.

Piloted by Dave Ferguson, the YF-22 first flew from Edwards AFB on 29 September 1990. The wing planform was a rhomboid with a 48deg sweep on the slatted leading edge, and a 17deg reverse sweep on the trailing edge, with ailerons outboard and flaperons inboard. The angles of the all-moving tailerons were matched to the wing, and twin fins and rudders were outward-canted. As the original Mach 2.5 requirement had been dropped, the engine inlets were plain, trapezoidal in shape, and raked to match the wing leading edge. The inlet ducts were serpentine and lined with radar-absorbent material, to prevent hostile radar emissions from reaching the compressor face. One area where agility took precedence over stealth was the use of pitch-only vectoring nozzles.

After a flyoff against the rival Northrop YF-23, Lockheed was awarded an Engineering/Manufacturing/Development (EMD) contract in August 1991. Several changes were made, notably the reduction of leading edge sweep to 42deg, and to reduce the radar cross-section. By now officially named Raptor, the first EMD aircraft flew on 7 September 1997, piloted by Paul Metz, formerly of Northrop, who had made the first flight in the YF-23.

The Raptor is the most heavily computerised fighter in the world. Fast response is given by a three-stage programme, compared to about 17 in most other aircraft. The flight control system is triplex digital FBW. Radar is the APG 77 active array fixed-antenna multi-mode, with a low probability of intercept. The cockpit has four active-matrix liquid crystal displays, two up-front displays and a wide-angle HUD, while a helmet-mounted sight looks certain for the future. Pilot's Associate is another new feature: this gives aural advice on the tactical situation, while voice recognition reduces the manual workload. Finally there is the LMAS ALR-94 EW suite, which gives all-round coverage of radar emissions, and heat missile launch warnings. All that is lacking is an IRST, and this could be added at a later date.

Right: Stealthy thrust-vectoring nozzles are a feature of the Raptor.

Lockheed Martin F-35A

Origin: Lockheed Martin Corporation, USA.
Type: Single-seat, single-engined supersonic multi-role fighter.
Engine: One Pratt & Whitney F135 two-spool afterburning turbofan rated at 35,000lb (15,876kg) maximum; military thrust classified.
Dimensions: Span 35ft 1.25in (10.70m); length 50ft 10in (15.50m); height n/a; wing area 460sq.ft (42.70m^2).
Weights: Empty 26,477lb (12,010kg); maximum takeoff 50,000lb (22,680kg).
Loadings (at 42,000lb/19,051kg weight)**:** wing 91lb/sq.ft (446kg/m^2); thrust 0.83.
Performance: Maximum speed Mach 1.7; supercruise Mach 1.4; rate of climb classified; service ceiling classified but probably about 50,000ft (15,239m); operational radius 620 miles (1,000km).
Armament: One 20mm M61A-2 cannon with 400 rounds or one 27mm Mauser BK 27 cannon; four AIM-120C Amraam or Asraam AAMs in internal bay.
History: First flight X-35A 24 October 2000; first flight X-35C 16 December 2000; first full short takeoff, supersonic flight and vertical landing by X-35B 20 July 2001. Declared winner of JSF competition 26 October 2001. Potential production c3,000 plus exports. Projected in-service date 2010.
Users (proposed): Britain (RAF, RN), USA (USAF, USMC, USN).

Having defeated the Boeing X-32 in the Joint Strike Fighter competition, the consortium headed by Lockheed Martin appears to have succeeded in that most difficult of tasks: the development of a single aircraft type to satisfy the needs of five different services. Over the next three decades the F-35 is

Above: The F-35 was the winner of the Joint Strike Fighter competition.

scheduled to replace such widely disparate types as the F-15E, F-16C and F-117 for the USAF to give that service an all-stealth strike force; the F-14 and F/A-18C/D for the USN; the F/A-18C/D and the AV-8B Harrier II for the USMC; and the Harrier and Sea Harrier for the RAF and RN.

Affordability drove the quest for commonality; a large production run would help to amortise development costs, but even then, three distinct variants of the baseline aircraft were needed. Easiest and most numerous was the

Conventional Take Off and Landing (CTOL) version for the USAF; this was the F-35A. Next in numerical priority was a carrier-compatible CTOL aircraft, the F-35C, mainly for the USN, but with some for the USMC. Smallest in numbers heaviest, most complex and most expensive, was the F-35B Short Take Off Vertical Landing (STOVL) Harrier replacement for the USMC, RAF and RN.

Historically, the only operationally successful fixed wing STOVL aircraft has been the Harrier, but its engine and vectoring nozzle layout had, despite repeated attempts, proved incompatible with supersonic flight. The basic problem was in getting enough vertical lift to power an aircraft large enough to do a worthwhile job, without unacceptable ground erosion, melting tarmac runways, or burning holes in carrier decks.

The solution adopted by Lockheed Martin, with assistance from Rolls Royce, was not new, but was complex, heavy, and high risk. Vertical lift is provided by a three-piece lobsterback vectoring nozzle at the rear, similar to that of the Yak-141, balanced by a large shaft-driven fan aft of the cockpit. By providing a large volume of low-energy, low temperature air, the problems inherent in plenum chamber burning or separate lift engines, have largely been avoided, although the wasted fuselage volume has to be accepted. Trials have shown that this solution is better than the more orthodox system adopted by the Boeing X-32.

The basic F-35A is in many ways similar to that of the F-22A Raptor which is not surprising, and externally the F-35B differs little. The carrier-compatible F-35C has a larger wing area with wing folding, beefed-up main gear, catapult and arrester hook attachments, and a refuelling probe rather than the receptacle of the F-35A.

Right: The F-35 will be built in conventional, carrier, and STOVL variants.

Macchi MC 200 Saetta

Origin: Aeronautica Macchi, Italy.
Type: Single-seat, single-engined monoplane fighter
Engine: One 870hp Fiat A.74 RC 38 14-cylinder radial.
Dimensions: Span 34ft 8.5in (10.58m); length 26ft 10.5in (8.19m); height 11ft 5.75in (3.51m); wing area 181sq.ft (16.80m²).
Weights: Empty 4,451lb (2,019kg); normal takeoff 5,597lb (2,339kg).
Loadings (at normal takeoff weight)**:** Wing 31lb/sq.ft (139kg/m²); power 6.43lb (2.92kg) per hp.
Performance: Maximum speed 312mph (503kph) at 14,765ft (4,500m); sustained climb rate 3min 24sec to 9,843ft (3,000m), 7min 33sec to 19,686ft (6,000m); service ceiling 29,201ft (8,900m); range 354 miles (570km).
Armament: Two 12.7mm Breda-SAFAT nose-mounted synchronised machine guns with 370 rounds per gun.
History: First flight 24 December 1937. In service from spring 1939. Combat debut late 1940. Production ceased 1942 with a total of 1,153. A few survived into 1947 as fighter trainers.
Users: Italy.

The Saetta was designed by Mario Castoldi to meet the same requirement as the Fiat G 50, and suffered the same handicaps – the low-powered Fiat radial engine, inadequate armament, and the raised cockpit which, while it gave a good view over the nose, caused unnecessary drag. First flight, by Giuseppe Burei, took place on 24 December 1937, some 10 months later than the G 50.

The Saetta was an all-metal low wing monoplane of monocoque construction. An inherent fault of the high-set cockpit, which was full

Above: The MC 200 was underpowered and undergunned, but handled superbly.

enclosed, was that if the aircraft turned over on landing, the pilot was at risk. To offset this, a pylon structure was fitted just behind the seat. The MC 200 was rather faster than the G 50, and its handling was superb; light and crisp across the board, while during official trials it reached 500mph

(805kph) in a dive while under full control.

Unusual features for the time were a retractable tailwheel – although on late production machines this was fixed – and ammunition indicators in the cockpit. The variable-incidence tailplane moved between plus 1deg 45min and minus 5deg 30min. From the outset, the Saetta had a constant-speed propeller, which was more than could be said for its contemporaries, the Spitfire, Hurricane, and Bf 109.

Production orders were placed in 1938, and deliveries began in spring 1939 to the pilots of *1O Stormo Caccia*, veterans of the Spanish Civil War. There were however initial problems, including a tendency to spin without warning, while two pilots were lost in unexplained crashes. The future of the Saetta hung in the balance until the causes were found, when a simple wing modification cured the fault.

Macchi MC 202 Folgore

Origin: Aeronautica Macchi, Italy.
Type: Single-seat, single-engined monoplane fighter.
Engine: One 1,175hp Alfa Romeo RA 1000 RC41-I Monsoni liquid-cooled V-12.
Dimensions: Span 34ft 8.5in (10.58m); length 29ft 0.5in (8.85m); height 9ft 11.5in (3.04m); wing area 181sq.ft (16.80m^2).
Weights: Empty 5,181lb (2,350kg); normal takeoff 6,459lb (2,930kg); maximum 6,636lb (3,010kg).
Loadings (at normal takeoff weight)**:** Wing 36lb/sq.ft (174kg/m^2); power 5.50lb (2.49kg) per hp.
Performance: Maximum speed 373mph (600kph) at 18,374ft (5,600m), 309mph (497kph) at sea level; sustained climb rate 2min 28sec to 9,843ft (3,000m), 4min 4sec to 16,405ft (5,000m); service ceiling 37,732ft (11,500m); range 475 miles (765km).
Armament: Two 12.7mm Breda-SAFAT nose-mounted synchronised machine guns with 400 rounds per gun, and two 7.7mm Breda-SAFAT wing-mounted machine guns with 500 rounds per gun.
History: Essentially a minimal redesign of the MC 200 to take the more powerful V-12 engine. First flown 10 August 1940. First deliveries April 1941. Combat debut Malta November 1941. Total production MC 202 and MC 205V c1,400.
Users: Egypt (MC 205V from 1949), Italy (*Regia Aeronautica*, Co-Belligerent Air Force, *Aviazione della Repubblica Sociale Italiana*).

Undoubtedly the best Italian fighter of World War II, the MC 202 Folgore was made possible by the licence-manufacture of the Daimler-Benz DB 601A liquid-cooled V-12 engine by Alfa

Combat debut was over Malta in the late summer of 1940, where the main opponent was the Hurricane. Of comparable speed, the Macchi could handily outclimb and outdive the much larger British fighter and was agile enough to give it problems in a turning fight. It was seriously outgunned, however.

The Saetta was very similar in appearance to the Freccia, and it is fair to say that often its opponents didn't know which type they were up against. Like the latter, the enclosed cockpit was unpopular, and the canopy was often removed to improve all-round vision, thus adding to the general confusion.

Some late production Saettas carried two wing-mounted 7.7mm Breda-SAFAT machine guns with 500 rounds per gun, but when the superior Folgore started to enter service, the MC 200 was increasingly diverted to the close air support mission.

Romeo. Having acquired an example of the German engine in 1940, Mario Castoldi of Aeronautica Macchi modified the MC 200 to accept it. First flown from Varese on 10 August 1940, the Folgore was an instant success. Castoldi had achieved the near-impossible in installing a far more powerful and much heavier engine in what was a fairly minimally modified Saetta airframe, gaining the expected performance improvements while retaining the excellent handling qualities of the original.

The main change in appearance was of course due to the new engine, which gave a much sleeker line to the fuselage, broken only by a ventral radiator bath. The cockpit was low-set to reduce drag, bringing the MC 202 into

Below: Even Spitfire pilots treated the MC 202 Folgore with respect.

line with contemporary European fighters. Castoldi had already done this on the radial-engined MC 201, which had failed to show sufficient advantages over the MC 200 to enter production. The lowered cockpit made the crash pylon unnecessary; it was replaced by a strengthened rear canopy frame, with a slender fairing behind the pilot's head.

Other changes were increased-capacity fuselage fuel tanks, and a small supplementary tank in each inboard wing section, while the ammunition supply to the two 12.7mm machine guns was increased to 400 rounds each. Later production aircraft were fitted with a 7.7mm machine gun in each wing, while a small batch carried two 20mm Mauser MG 151 cannon in underwing gondolas.

The Folgore made its combat debut over Malta with 1° *Stormo* early in November 1941, but after a matter of days this unit was transferred to Libya.

McDonnell F2H-3 Banshee

Origin: McDonnell Aircraft Company, USA.
Type: Single-seat, twin-engined subsonic all-weather jet carrier fighter.
Engines: Two Westinghouse J34-WE-34 single-spool axial-flow turbojets each rated at 3,250lb (1,474kg).
Dimensions: Span 41ft 9in (12.73m); length 48ft 3in (14.71m); height 14ft 6in (4.42m); wing area 294sq.ft (27.31m²).
Weights: Empty 13,183lb (5,980kg); normal takeoff 21,013lb (9,531kg); maximum 25,214lb (11,437kg).
Loadings (at normal takeoff weight)**:** Wing 71lb/sq.ft (349kg/m²); thrust 0.31.
Performance: Maximum speed 541mph (871kph) at sea level; initial climb rate 5,150ft/min (26m/sec); sustained climb rate 8min 12sec to 30,000ft (9,144m); service ceiling 47,000ft (14,325m); combat radius 478 miles (769km); range 1,169 miles (1,881km).
Armament: Four 20mm Mk 16 cannon with 150 rounds per gun.
History: First flight prototype XF2D-1 11 January 1947. Production deliveries from August 1948; squadron service from March 1949. Combat debut Korea 23 August 1951. Production ceased 31 October 1953 with a total of 867. Phased out of front line service 30 September 1959, and reserve 1964.
Users: Canada, USA (USMC, USN, USNR).

The first jet fighter produced by McDonnell Aircraft was the XFD-1 Phantom, the first prototype of which flew from Lambert St. Louis on 26 January 1945, piloted by Woodward Burke. Straight-winged, it was powered by two small-diameter Westinghouse axial-flow jets located in the wing roots. Although a small order was placed, the Phantom {not to be confused with the Phantom II by the same company}, was somewhat marginal in many ways. Work began on its successor, the XFD-2 Banshee, which was little more than a scaled-up and aerodynamically refined Phantom, with two much more powerful engines.

With Robert Edholm at the controls, the Banshee prototype took to the air at Lambert St. Louis on 11 January 1947. At this stage the fact that the "D" designator would cause confusion with Douglas had not been realised; only

There it outclassed the Allied Hurricanes and P-40s. When in 1942 Spitfires began to arrive in the theatre, even these were forced to treat the Macchi fighter with respect. Confident in the agility of the mount, Folgore pilots were often willing to mix it, unlike German Bf 109 pilots who preferred to fight in the vertical. At least one Italian complained that the Germans left all the real fighting to them! Top scorer was Franco Lucchini, who claimed 16 of his 26 victories with the Folgore.

The final development to see action was the MC 205V Veltro, powered by the 1,475hp Fiat RA 1050 RC 58 Tifone (DB 605). First flown on 19 April 1942, the Veltro's had its combat debut over Pantelleria on 8 July 1943. After Italy's capitulation, it flew for the RSI. Postwar, 42 aircraft were delivered to the Royal Egyptian Air Force, and flew against Israel in 1948-49.

later was MAC allotted the letter "H", and the Banshee became the F2H. The flight test programme was singularly trouble-free, and 56 F2H-1s were ordered. For its day, the Banshee had a high degree of electrics: wing folding, the sliding canopy, six-segment split flaps and the speed brakes were all electrically

Below: The F2H-3 Banshee carried a search radar in a lengthened nose.

operated. The first squadron to receive the type was VF-171 in March 1949, and carrier trials were completed on 8-9 May of that year.

Next came the F2H-2, which varied from the original in having greatly increased fuel capacity, partly by a fuselage stretch, and partly by using tip tanks; improved -34 turbojets, and four underwing stores stations. A handful of -2N night fighters were also produced, with the Westinghouse APS-46 radar, to make room for which the nose was extended.

The -2 was the first Banshee to go to war, on 23 August 1951, when VF-172 Blue Bolts, flying from USS *Essex*, dive-bombed bridges in Korea. The Banshee had an outstanding high-altitude performance – the -2 could get up to

McDonnell XF-85 Goblin

Origin: McDonnell Aircraft Company, USA.
Type: Single-seat, single-engined subsonic jet parasite fighter.
Engines: One Westinghouse J34-WE-22 single-spool axial-flow turbojet rated at 3,000lb (1,361kg) military thrust.
Dimensions: Span 21ft 1.5in (6.44m); length 14ft 10.5in (4.53m); height 8ft 3.25in (2.56m); wing area 90sq.ft ($8.36m^2$).
Weights: Empty 3,740lb (1,696kg); drop weight 4,550lb (2,064kg).
Loadings (at drop weight)**:** Wing 51lb/sq.ft ($247kg/m^2$); thrust 0.66.
Performance (all estimated)**:** Maximum speed 648mph (1,043kph) at sea level; service ceiling 48,200ft (14,691m); endurance 30min.
Armament: Four 0.50in (12.7mm) Colt Browning machine guns.
History: Letter of Intent for two prototypes issued 9 October 1945. First free flight 23 August 1948. Programme terminated mid-1949.
Users: None.

Parasite fighters had long been considered a possible way of providing protection to long range strategic bombers, and in 1944 a Request For Proposals (RFP) was issued for a fighter to be carried in the front bomb bay of the gigantic Convair B-36 intercontinental bomber. Size was the problem. The bay was just 16ft (4.88m) long, but while it was 9ft (2.74m) wide the useable width between the open bay doors was a mere 6ft (1.83m).

Only McDonnell Aircraft responded to the RFP, although further studies delayed progress until February 1947, when two XF-85 Goblin prototypes were ordered. The design was ingenious. To overcome the access width restrictions, the wings folded vertically upwards from the root, and there were multiple short-span tail surfaces two of which had vertical surfaces, and fins on the wingtips. A huge retractable hook was located immediately in front of the pilot, and this connected with a trapeze which lowered the XF-85 for launch and raised it on recovery.

52,000ft (15,849m) – and its pilots fancied their chances against the MiG-15. Unfortunately for them the opportunity never occurred.

The definitive Banshee was the F2H-3, which was designed from scratch to carry the Westinghouse APQ-41 search radar. This was accommodated by stretching the nose 25in (635mm) and relocating the cannon well back under the fuselage. Other modifications were an ejection seat, and a vastly increased internal fuel capacity. And weight! Speed, climb, and ceiling were all significantly reduced. The final variant was the -4, powered by -38 turbojets, and with a Hughes APG-37 radar.

Above: The XF-85 parasite fighter was designed to fit a B-36 bomb bay.

After five captive flights under an EB-29A, pilot Ed Schoch disengaged on 23 August 1948. All went well until he attempted to hook back on. Chuck Yeager, flying chase, watched horrified as Schoch first failed to connect, then hit the trapeze with his canopy, losing his helmet and mask in the process. Yeager managed to escort him down to a belly landing on a dry lake bed. Three successful hookups were eventually made, but the programme was terminated after a mere 2hr 19 min of flight time.

McDonnell F3H-2 Demon

Origin: McDonnell Aircraft Company, USA.
Type: Single-seat, single-engined subsonic jet carrier fighter.
Engines: One Allison J71-A-2E single-spool axial-flow afterburning turbojet rated at 14,250lb (6,464kg) maximum and 9,700lb (4,400kg) military thrust.
Dimensions: Span 35ft 4in (10.77m); length 58ft 11.5in (17.97m); height 14ft 6.5in (4.43m); wing area 519sq.ft (48.22m²).
Weights: Empty 21,287lb (9,656kg); normal takeoff 31,145lb (14,127kg); maximum 38,997lb (17,689kg).
Loadings (at normal takeoff weight)**:** Wing 60lb/sq.ft (293kg/m²); thrust 0.46.
Performance: Maximum speed 693mph (1,116kph) at sea level, 625mph (1,006kph) at 35,000ft (10,667m); initial climb rate 12,410ft/min (63m/sec); sustained climb rate 7min 12sec to 20,000ft (6,096m); combat ceiling 42,880ft (13,069m); range 1,025 miles (1,899km).
Armament: Four 20mm Mk 12 cannon with 150 rounds per gun. F3H-2M, four Sparrow III or four Sidewinder AAMs.
History: Prototype first flight 7 August 1951. First production aircraft from 23 April 1955. Squadron service from 7 March 1956. Production ended November 1959, with a total of 519. Withdrawn from service August 1964.
User: USA (USN).

Robert Edholm made the first flight of the Demon prototype from Lambert St. Louis on 7 August 1951. The fuselage was portly, due to a large internal fuel capacity. The inlets to the ill-fated Westinghouse J40 turbojet were curved to conform to the fuselage, with sharp lips meeting a sharp ramp at the bottom. Steeply swept tail surfaces were mounted on a boom above the jetpipe. The wings were distinctive: a 45deg sweep with a very broad chord, just thick enough to house the inward retracting main gears.

The flight test programme was beset with explosions, crashes, and engine

failures. The first production variant, the F3H-1N, failed to enter service, and many ended up as ground instructional airframes. The adoption of the J71 solved some of the problems, but there were others. Rate of roll was inadequate, the ailerons were moved to the midspan position, and wing area was increased by 17.5 per cent. But this was not enough. When rolling at high speed, the forces exerted by the ailerons bent the wings out of shape. The solution was to use spoilers, which took over from the ailerons above a certain speed. Nor was this all. Firing the guns at high altitudes caused compressor stalling and flameout, while high-altitude manoeuvres often resulted in pitchup. Meanwhile attitudes were changing. The cannon armament was to have been supplemented by four pods of 2in (51mm) Mighty Mouse folding fin aircraft rockets, to be used in collision course interception, but these were now dropped.

Not until March 1956 was the Demon ready for squadron service, a delay of 54 months since first flight, which itself had been delayed by several months. This was the F3H-2N. It saw active service in 1958 over Quemoy (off southeast coast of China, administered by Taiwan but claimed by PRC) and Lebanon.

Although internal fuel capacity was 10,241lb (4,647kg), the Demon was still short on range, but experiments with external tanks gave the surprising result that, due to excessive interference drag, they reportedly reduced range! Finally a bolt-on refuelling probe was fitted.

The radar was the Hughes APG-51, which could illuminate targets for the new Sparrow III SARH missile, which achieved initial operational capability in July 1956, just in time for the F3H-2M Demon. Four Sparrows could be carried, although the usual fit was two Sparrows and two Sidewinders. But when production ceased at the end of 1959, the firmly subsonic Demon was regarded as nearing obsolescence.

Below: The Sparrow I armed F3H-2M was the final Demon variant in service.

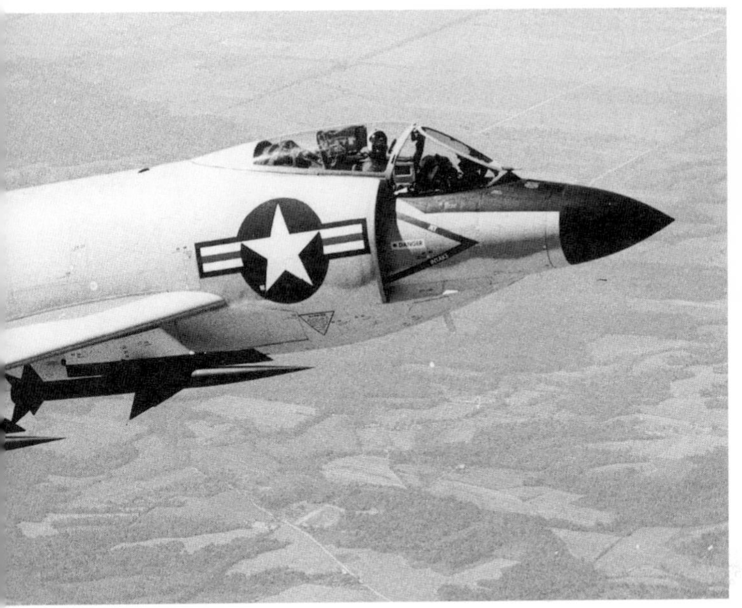

McDonnell F-101B Voodoo

Origin: McDonnell Aircraft Company, USA.
Type: Two-seat, twin-engined supersonic all-weather interceptor.
Engines: Two Pratt & Whitney J57-P-55 two-spool axial-flow afterburning turbojets each rated at 16,900lb (7,666kg) maximum and 10,700lb (4,853kg) military thrust.
Dimensions: Span 39ft 8.4in (12.10m); length 67ft 5in (20.55m); height 18ft 0in (5.49m); wing area 368sq.ft (34.19m²).
Weights: Empty 28,492lb (12,924kg); normal takeoff 45,461lb (20,621kg); maximum 51,724lb (23,462kg).
Loadings (at normal takeoff weight)**:** Wing 124lb/sq.ft (603kg/m²); thrust 0.74.
Performance: Maximum speed 1,094mph (1,760kph) at 35,000ft (10,667m), Mach 1.63; initial climb rate 36,500ft/min (185m/sec); sustained climb rate 2min 36sec to 40,000ft (12,191m); combat ceiling 51,000ft (15,544m); combat radius 852 miles (1,371km).
Armament: Four AIM-4 Falcon AAMs and two AIR-2A Genie unguided nuclear rockets.
History: Prototype XF-101A first flight 29 September 1954. In service from May 1957. World speed record 12 December 1957. First flight of two-seater F-101B 27 March 1957. Production ceased March 1961, with a total of 805 of all variants. Withdrawn from first line USAF units spring 1971, but served with ANG until 1983 and Canada until 1985.
Users: Canada, USA (USAF and ANG).

Enthused by the success of the P-51 Mustang, the USAF sought a long range escort fighter in the postwar era. This was doomed from the start; there was no way a jet fighter could even begin to approximate the range of the next generation of strategic bombers. This notwithstanding, the McDonnell XF-88 first flew on 20 October 1948. It had however sufficient potential for further development.

An initial production order for 29 aircraft was placed on 28 May 1953, and

the F-101A Voodoo was first flown from Edwards AFB by Bob Little on 29 September 1954. It was massive, partly due to a vast internal fuel capacity of 2,084 US gal (7,894l). Fed by sharp-lipped wing root inlets, the two J57s, at that time the most powerful engines available, had variable nozzles. They were set low, side by side, and the fuselage was carried past above them, carrying the fin and high-set tail. The moderately swept wing had its chord increased inboard to give a cranked trailing edge, which allowed very large flaps to be fitted. But the area was moderate, which gave a simply enormous wing loading.

This last, with its low gust response, made the F-101A eminently suitable for high-speed low-level penetration, and it commenced its service career as a bomb truck, albeit with a single USAF Wing. The F-101C, with a beefed-up wing, was similarly employed. The RF-101A camera ship which followed was built in greater numbers than both the standard A and C together.

The two-seater F-101B all-weather interceptor was begun in 1955, and the first example flew on 27 March 1957. Basically it was a new front end grafted on to the standard F-101A airframe, although more powerful -55 turbojets were fitted. The 20mm M-39 cannon of the A were displaced by the Hughes MG-13 fire control system and radar. The internal weapons bay of the A model was retained, and housed an all-missile armament of four AIM-4 Falcon AAMs – typically two with SARH and two with IR homing. Two AIR-2A Genie unguided rockets with nuclear warheads could be carried underwing. Range could be extended by in-flight refuelling.

Supplementing the F-102, the F-101B was rather more autonomous in operation, but at high altitude it was tricky to fly, and restricted to 1.2g turns at 50,000ft (15,239m). Handling has been described as like trying to balance on the point of a pencil without ever finding the right place. As frosting, rain penetration did on occasion cause a short circuit which jettisoned the canopy. The Voodoo did however do a useful job for both the USAF and Canada.

Below: The F-101B Voodoo was a missile-armed all-weather interceptor.

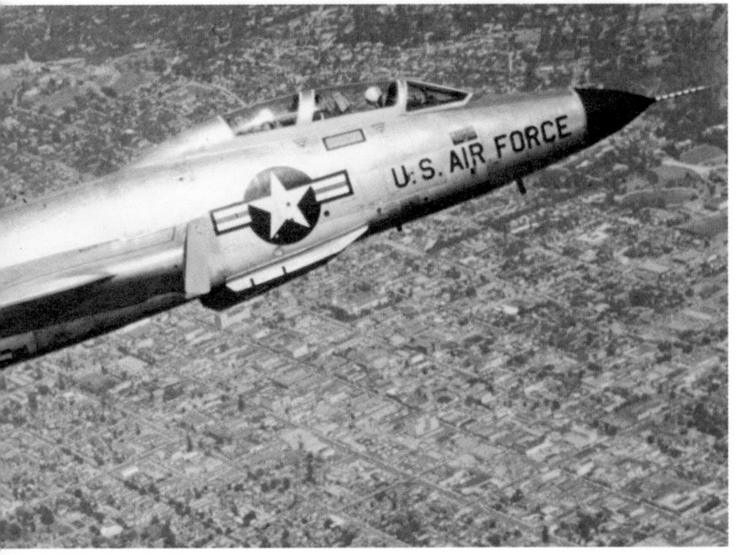

McDonnell F-4E Phantom II

Origin: McDonnell Aircraft Company, USA.
Type: Two-seat, twin-engined bisonic all-weather multi-role land-based fighter.
Engines: Two General Electric J79-GE-17 two-spool axial-flow afterburning turbojets each rated at 17,900lb (8,119kg) maximum and 10,900lb (4,944kg) military thrust.
Dimensions: Span 38ft 4in (11.68m); length 63ft 0in (19.21m); height 16ft 3in (4.95m); wing area 530sq.ft (49.26m²).
Weights: Empty 29,535lb (13,400kg); normal takeoff 45,750lb (20,752kg); maximum 61,795lb (28,030kg).
Loadings (at normal takeoff weight)**:** Wing 86lb/sq.ft (421kg/m²); thrust 0.78.
Performance: Maximum speed Mach 2.04 at 40,000ft (10,667m), Mach 1.10 at sea level; initial climb rate 28,500ft/min (142m/sec); combat ceiling 55,000ft (16,763m); combat radius 500 miles (805km) plus.
Armament: One M61A-1 six-barrel cannon with 639 rounds; typically four AIM-7 Sparrow and four AIM-9 Sidewinder AAMs interchangeable with Skyflash and Shafrir. Almost every air-to-surface weapon in the U.S. inventory.
History: Initial production order placed before first flight of XF4H-1 prototype 27 May 1958. First delivery to USN 30 December 1960. F4H redesignated F-4 September 1962. IOC of F-4C with USAF December 1963. Combat debut (F-4B) 5 August 1964. First flight of F-4D 9 December 1965. First flight of F-4J 27 May 1966. First flight of F-4E 30 June 1967. U.S. production ceased October 1979; Japanese production ended 20 May 1981. Total 5,195 of all variants.
Users: Australia, Britain (RAF and RN), Egypt*, Germany*, Greece*, Iran*, Israel*, Japan*, South Korea*, Spain*, Turkey*, USA (USAF, USMC, USN, ANG).
* denotes still in service end of 2001, mainly F-4Es and RF-4Es.

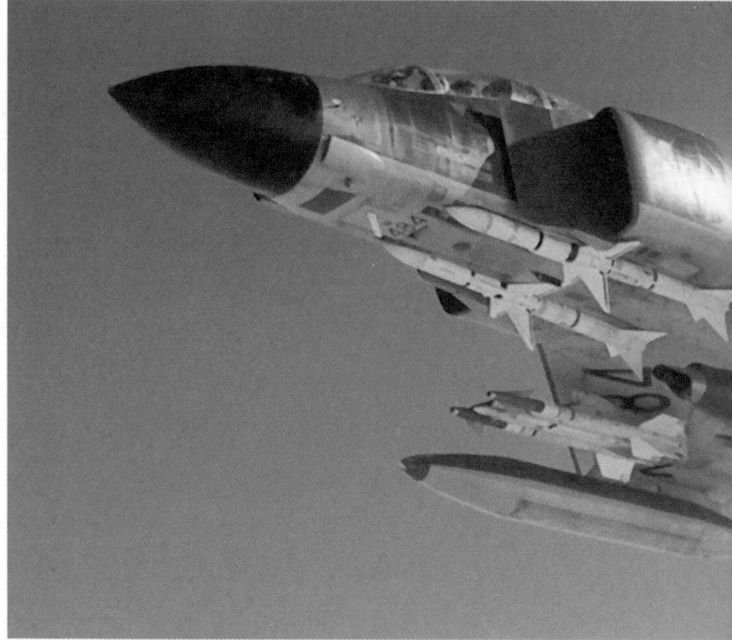

That the Phantom became the most versatile tactical aircraft of its generation is hardly surprising; the F3H-G, from which it was descended, was a series of solutions looking for the right problem. On 18 October 1954, the US Navy issued a Letter of Intent for two prototype single-seat attack aircraft, designated AH-1. In April 1955, this was changed to a fleet air defence interceptor, with long endurance, all-missile armament, powered by two General Electric J79s.

In appearance the F3H-G was unexceptional. The twin engines were mid-mounted, with side inlets, and the rear fuselage was high-set above the line of the effluxes. On this were mounted horizontal stabilizers, and a broad-chord fin and rudder. The low-set wing was swept at 45deg, with flaps on both leading and trailing edges, with ailerons outboard on the latter.

The next three years saw wholesale changes. To reduce pilot workload the aircraft was made a two-seater. The outboard wing panels were increased in chord to give a dogtooth leading edge, and cranked up at 12deg to improve stability, while boundary layer control was applied to both flaps and slats. The stabilizers were cranked down at 23deg to keep them clear of the wing downwash at high angles of attack. To minimise drag, four bulky Sparrow AAMs were carried semi-submerged beneath the fuselage, and the second cockpit was flush with the fuselage. Before first flight, but too late to affect the first production batch, the cockpit canopy was raised, and the larger APQ-72 radar was selected, which needed a larger, drooped radome, under which was an IR sensor.

The F-4 eventually went through 12 fighter variants, but from the F-4B on

Below: British F-4K and F-4M Phantoms were powered by Rolls-Royce turbofans.

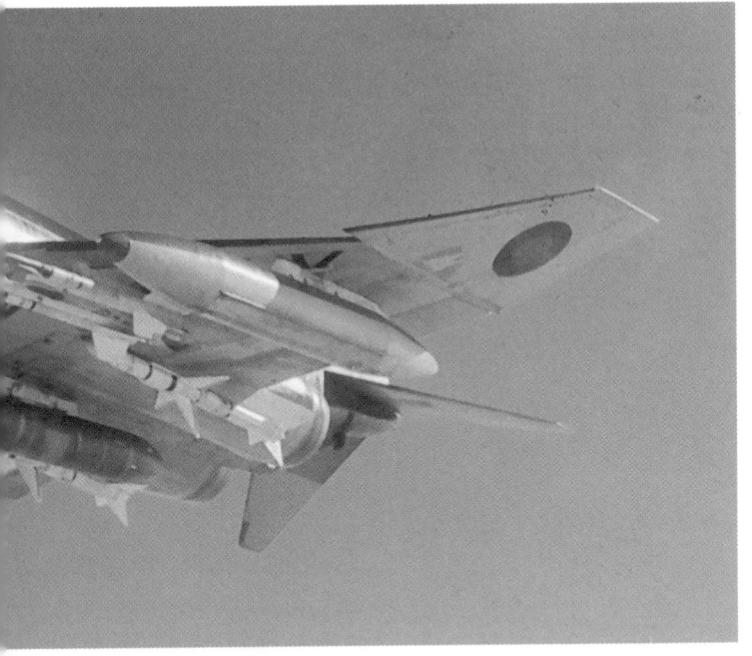

altered so little in external appearance that care was needed for correct identification – a tribute to the soundness of the basic design. Large and angular, it was often called "Big Ugly" by its crews.

Bob Little took the XF4H-1 aloft for the first time from Lambert St. Louis on 27 May 1958. The US Navy placed an order in February 1959, and on 3 July it was officially named Phantom II. In December that year, the second prototype set a new absolute altitude record of 98,557ft (30,038m), then in 1960 it took two closed circuit speed records. The next year saw two world speed records set: 902.769mph (1,453kph) at low level on 28 August, and absolute of 1,606.3mph (2,585kph) at altitude on 22 November. In early 1962 it set eight new records for time to altitude. In September, the USN F4H-1 was redesignated F-4A.

The first Phantoms were delivered to training outfit VF-121 at Miramar on 30 December 1960, but the first line squadron, VF-74, did not become operational until October 1961. In that same month, following extensive evaluations against existing aircraft, the USAF took the unprecedented step of ordering the F4H, a Navy aircraft, as the F-110A.

The first Air Force variant was the F-4C. It differed from the Navy F-4B in having larger wheels and tyres, which needed a slight bulge in the wing to accommodate them, and a receptacle for flight refuelling to replace the Navy-style probe. Other changes were mainly to the avionics, while AIM-4 Falcons replaced AIM-9 Sidewinders on the underwing pylons. F-4C deliveries commenced 20 November 1963.

Meanwhile F-4Bs of VF-41 had been on active service during the Cuban crisis in November 1962. The F-4B was also the first Phantom to fire shots in anger, off the coast of Vietnam on 5 August 1964, and the first to claim air combat victories, two MiG-17s downed by VF-21 on 17 June 1965.

The Vietnam experience hastened Phantom development. The USAF F-4D was basically an improved bomb truck, although of course it still had to fight other aeroplanes when needed. Then there were operational problems.

The Phantom had been designed as a fleet air defence fighter and little thought had been given to close combat, or the need to evade SAMs.

Below: The USAF F-4D was a compromise between a fighter and a bomb truck.

Manoeuvring at high all-up weights or low speeds, the Phantom could easily stray into the area of lost control. If this happened, it was difficult to recover, and below 10,000ft (3,048m) virtually impossible.

Similarly, its "magic missiles", designed to destroy unmanoeuvring targets, were equally unsuitable for close combat, as well as suffering from chronic unreliability. Lack of a gun was also a tremendous handicap. While a 20mm gun pod could be hung on the centreline, for technical reasons this was unsatisfactory.

Little could be done about the missiles, but the USAF addressed the other two problems with the F-4E. This had a revised nose, housing an internal 20mm cannon, displacing the IR sensor; and modified wing leading edges and stabilizers. With the exception of the gun, this was echoed by the USN F-4J. Both had uprated J79 turbojets, and look-down pulse-Doppler radars.

Two other fighter variants are radical enough to warrant a mention. These are the F-4K and F-4M Phantoms for Britain, and the F-4F for Germany.

British Phantoms were powered by two Rolls-Royce Spey turbofans, each rated at 20,515lb (9,306kg) maximum thrust. This should have given improved acceleration and climb, lower fuel consumption, and better handling.

Below: The USN and USMC both operated the carrier-compatible F-4J.

Unfortunately difficulties were encountered in matching the engines to the airframe, and the promised performance increments failed to materialise. Neither British types carried an internal gun.

The German F-4F was a weight-reduced F-4E, minus in-flight refuelling, the slotted stabilizer and No 7 fuel cell; it had a simplified APQ-120 radar, and no Sparrow capability. Total armament was the 20mm nose cannon and four Sidewinders.

Phantoms have served in several conflicts, in South-East Asia and the

McDonnell Douglas F-15C Eagle

Origin: McDonnell Douglas Corporation, USA.
Type: Two-seat, twin-engined bisonic all-weather air superiority fighter with secondary attack capability.
Engines: Two Pratt & Whitney F100-P-220 two-spool axial-flow afterburning turbofans each rated at 23,770lb (10,782kg) maximum and 14,590lb (6,618kg) military thrust.
Dimensions: Span 42ft 9.5in (13.05m); length 63ft 9in (19.43m); height 18ft 5.5in (5.63m); wing area 608sq.ft (56.50m^2).
Weights: Empty 28,600lb (12,973kg); normal takeoff 44,500lb (20,185kg); maximum 68,000lb (30,845kg).
Loadings (at normal takeoff weight)**:** Wing 73lb/sq.ft (357kg/m^2); thrust 1.07.
Performance: Maximum speed Mach 2.50 at 40,000ft (10,667m), Mach 1.20 at sea level; initial climb rate 50,000ft/min (254m/sec); combat ceiling 65,000ft (19,811m); combat radius 740 miles (1,191km).
Armament: One M61A-1 six-barrel cannon with 675 rounds; typically four AIM-120 Amraam or AIM-7 Sparrow, and four AIM-9 Sidewinder or Shafrir AAMs. Most air-to-surface weapons in the U.S. inventory.
History: First flight 27 July 1972. Service entry F-15A November 1974. Eight new time to altitude records set January/February 1975. Production of F-15C/D from 1978 to 1992. First flight of production F-15C 27 February 1979. Combat debut 27 June 1979. Production of F-15E from 1989. Total production all variants exceeds 1,500.
Users: Israel, Japan, Saudi Arabia, USA (USAF, ANG).

In July 1967 the Soviet Union revealed the MiG-25 Foxbat to the world. Three

Middle East, as a bomb hauler, a Wild Weasel defence suppression aircraft, and as a fighter. In the latter role, it has notched up at least 282 air combat victories, the majority of them over Russian designs. Known victims include 53.5 MiG-17s, 10 MiG-19s, 109.5 MiG-21s, and a couple of An-2 light transports. Iranian Phantoms may also have scored against Iraqi aircraft in the first Gulf War, but no details are available.

Below: The F-4E was the first Phantom II to be fitted with an integral gun.

Above: The F-15C Eagle was arguably the most potent fighter of its era.

months later, it took two closed circuit speed records previously held by the YF-12A. Performance was obviously outstanding. Western intelligence jumped to two erroneous conclusions: first that it was a manoeuvrable air superiority fighter; also that it had been ordered in large numbers. If these assumptions were correct, the Phantom was hopelessly outclassed. A replacement was urgently needed.

McDonnell Douglas (MAC and Douglas had merged some years earlier) responded to the FX specification that was issued to industry in September 1968. Their proposal was approved in December 1969, and 20 Full Scale Development (FSD) F-15s were ordered, the first of which was flown by Irving Burroughs on 27 July 1972, at Edwards AFB.

Designed to carry the same missile armament as the Phantom, it was large. The maximum speed originally specified was Mach 3, but as this conflicted with manoeuvre requirements it was relaxed to Mach 2.5. It was powered by two afterburning Pratt & Whitney F100 turbofans, which at that time were pushing the state of the art very hard indeed. Located in the rear fuselage, these had convergent-divergent nozzles. They were fed by sharply raked two-dimensional variable-ramp side inlets, with one most unusual feature. The inlet fronts were hinged, and automatically "nodded" 4deg up and 11deg down to smooth the airflow into the compressor face. The cockpit was roomy, its width influenced by the antenna diameter of the Hughes APG-63 radar. A bubble canopy gave excellent all-round vision.

The shoulder-mounted wing was remarkably simple. Swept at a modest 45deg, it had a plain leading edge with conical camber outboard. The trailing edge had simple flaps inboard and ailerons outboard. Thickness/chord ratio varied between 5.9 and 3 per cent and, innovatively, incidence was zero. This was to minimise drag in level flight, thus aiding acceleration. Wing area was a massive 608sq.ft (56.50m2), to give a moderate wing loading for manoeuvrability. The 20mm M61A cannon was housed in the starboard wing root.

The tail surfaces were mounted on shelves outboard of the engines. All-moving tailerons were set low, out of the wing wake, and twin fins and rudders were used to offset instability at high speeds. The other moveable surface was a dorsal speed brake.

The cockpit was conventional "steamgauge", with a plethora of dials and instruments, and a small radar screen in the top left corner. It did however have an innovation which has been copied by all fighter designers since: Hands On Throttle And Stick, or HOTAS. It had long been of concern that pilot workload was too high for comfort and, in some cases, for safety. For the F-15, the solution was to place all flight or combat-critical switches on either the control column or the throttle levers. While this made great demands on manual dexterity, the only answer was practice.

Flight testing went fairly smoothly, although a few bugs had to be fixed. Buffet due to spanwise flow was eliminated by an inward crop of the wing tips. Tailplane flutter was cured by extending the chord outboard, to give a notched leading edge. The speed brake area had to be increased by more than 50 per cent. More difficult to fix was a tendency to weathercock on landing.

The first USAF unit to receive the Eagle was the 555th Training Squadron, and the first operational units were the 27th and 71st Fighter Squadrons at Langley AFB, at the end of 1976. In squadron service, other problems were found. Some involved the weapons system; others, more serious, affected the engines.

In previous fighters, power settings were left high in combat. In the F-15, the pilot worked the engines much harder by continually throttling up and down. Turbine failures and stagnation stalls were common. Pratt & Whitney

Right: Variable raked intakes allow a speed of Mach 2.5 at altitude.

Above: The original "feathers" around the engine nozzles were removed.

finally overcame the problems with the -220 engine. The afterburner was also unreliable, and pilots tended to leave their engines on minimum 'burner rather than have them fail to light when needed. This resulted in heavier than predicted fuel burn, and reduced endurance.

The design philosophy had started as "not a pound for air to ground", but it was not long before air-to-surface weaponry was introduced. The endurance problem was addressed by extra fuel tanks in the wings, and by conformal fuel tanks (CFTs) along the sides of the fuselage. Although the CFTs held 17 per cent less fuel than three 600gal (6,818l) drop tanks, this was more than offset by far less drag and also the fact that the three hardpoints were freed for ordnance. The resulting maximum weight increase demanded structural strengthening and a beefed-up landing gear. This was the F-15C/D, which also featured improved radar capability. The final Eagle variant was the F-15E, a two-seater interdictor, with more powerful engines and the huge maximum takeoff weight of 81,000lb (36,741kg).

By the end of 2001 Eagle pilots had claimed 102.5 air combat victories for no losses. Of successes, USAF pilots have claimed 36, Saudi Arabian pilots four, and Israeli pilots the remaining 62.5.

Right: Conformal fuel tanks are clearly visible on both these F-15Cs.

McDonnell Douglas F/A-18C Hornet

Origin: McDonnell Douglas Corporation (now Boeing), USA.
Type: Single-seat, twin-engined multi-mission carrier fighter.
Engines: Two General Electric F404-GE-402 two-spool axial-flow afterburning turbofans each rated at 17,700lb (8,029kg) maximum and 10,860lb (4,925kg) military thrust.
Dimensions: Span 37ft 6in (11.43m); length 56ft 0in (17.07m); height 15ft 3.5in (4.66m); wing area 400sq.ft (37.16m²).
Weights: Empty 23,000lb (10,433kg); normal takeoff 36,970lb (16,769kg); maximum 56,000lb (25,401kg).
Loadings (at normal takeoff weight)**:** Wing 92lb/sq.ft (451kg/m²); thrust 0.96.
Performance: Maximum speed Mach 1.7 at altitude, Mach 1.01 at sea level; initial climb rate c50,000ft/min (254m/sec); operational ceiling c50,000ft (15,239m); operational radius in excess of 460 miles (740km).
Armament: One 20mm M61A six-barrel cannon with 570 rounds; maximum 10 AIM-120 Amraam and two AIM-9 Sidewinders. Full range of U.S. air-to-surface weapons.
History: First flight (as YF-17) 9 June 1974. First flight as F/A-18 FSD aircraft 18 November 1978. Service entry F/A-18A/B February 1981; operational from January 1983. Production F/A-18C/D September 1987. Air combat debut 17 January in the Gulf War of 1991. The larger and heavier F/A-18E/F Super Hornet entered service from November 1999. Projected production all types in excess of 1,500.

***Above:* Huge flaps deployed and without burner, a Hornet deck launches.**

Above: This F/A-18C Hornet carries HARMs for a defence suppression sortie.

Users: Australia, Canada, Finland, Kuwait, Malaysia, Spain, Switzerland, USA (USMC, USN).

First produced by McDonnell Douglas, then by Boeing, the Hornet started life as a Northrop product, the YF-17, which lost the LWF competition to the F-16 in 1972. The margin was smaller than most people realised, and when the USN and USMC looked for an affordable replacement for 24 squadrons of F-4 Phantoms and 30 squadrons of A-7 Corsairs, they chose the YF-17.

Unofficially called the Cobra, the YF-17 was twin-engined. In the LWF competition, the added structure, complexity, volume, and inevitably weight of two engines, had been a disadvantage against the single engined F-16. This was compounded by the undeveloped state of the Cobra's very low bypass YJ-101 turbofans used, whereas the F100 of the F-16 was a relatively mature engine. Two engines were however considered an advantage by the US Navy

Above: These Hornets are from the operational evaluation squadron VX-5.

in terms of safety, and also of potential development.

As Northrop had no experience of carrier aircraft, the project was turned over to McDonnell Douglas, leaving Northrop as a major subcontractor. The baseline aircraft was almost straight-winged, with a 20deg sweep at quarter-chord, and computerised variable camber. Huge leading edge root extensions were used to offset trim drag at supersonic speeds, and to act as compression wedges above the intakes, the hooded effect of which gave rise to the name Cobra. By contrast the tail surfaces were steeply swept, with outboard-canted twin fins set forward in the gap between the wing trailing edge and the leading edge of the horizontal tail surfaces. Construction was mainly of aluminium, but with a great deal of carbon fibre composites in the skin. The flight control system was quadruplex analogue fly-by-wire, with a mechanical backup to the stabilisers.

As developed by McDonnell Douglas, the Hornet was a scaled-up Cobra, with a 50 per cent increment in gross weight. Much of this was in carrie compatibility; greater structural strength, tailhook, wing folding etc, plus 70 pe cent more internal fuel, and a flight refuelling probe. One of the great succes stories was the engine. The YJ 101 was developed into the F404-GE-400, wit increased thrust, improved fuel consumption, and outstanding reliability.

Initially the Hornet was to be produced in air superiority and attack variants but the versatility of the Hughes APG-65 multi-mode radar changed that. Th first production radar in the world to have a programmable signal processor, had nine air-to-air and as many air-to-surface and navigation modes. McDonne Douglas had pioneered HOTAS on the F-15; now they introduced the "glas cockpit", with virtually all dials and instruments replaced by three colour multi function displays, on which information could be called up at the touch of button. This convinced the US Navy that one man and one aircraft could fly th air combat and attack missions equally well.

Whereas the F-15 and F-16 had carried the M61A cannon in the wing root this was not possible for the Hornet, since it would have spoiled the lines of th root extension. Instead, it was mounted high in the nose. Other air-to-ai weaponry initially consisted of two AIM-9 Sidewinders on wingtip rails, and tw AIM-7 Sparrows mounted semi-conformally on the lower fuselage corners. Thi last needed an extremely complex retraction system for the main gears. Th final major change was a digital rather than analogue FBW system, the firs production aircraft in the world so equipped.

The first flight of the Hornet was at Lambert St. Louis on 18 Novembe

Messerschmitt Bf 109G-6

Origin: Bayerische Flugzeugwerke GmbH, Germany.
Type: Single-seat, single-engined monoplane air superiority fighter.
Engine: One 1,475hp Daimler-Benz DB 605A liquid-cooled V-12 with water methanol injection.
Dimensions: Span 32ft 6.5in (9.92m); length 29ft 7in (9.02m); height 11ft 2in (3.40m); wing area 173sq.ft (16.05m^2).
Weights: Empty 5,952lb (2,700kg); normal takeoff 6,944lb (3,150kg).
Loadings (at normal takeoff weight)**:** Wing 40lb/sq.ft (196kg/m^2); power 4.71lb (2.14kg) per hp.
Performance: Maximum speed 387mph (623kph) at 22,967ft (7,000m), 338mph (544kph) at sea level; sustained climb rate 6min to 18,287ft (6,000m); service ceiling 38,552ft (11,750m); absolute ceiling 39,700ft (12,100m); range 451 miles (725km).
Armament: One 30mm Rheinmetall Borsig MK 108 cannon firing through the spinner, two 20mm Mauser MG 151 cannon underwing, and two Rheinmetall Borsig 13mm MG 131 synchronised machine guns above the engine. Some models, two 21cm mortars.
History: First flight September 1935. Service evaluation spring 1937. Combat debut Spain July 1937. Built continuously until May 1945, with total production of all variants exceeding 31,000.
Users: Bulgaria, Croatia, Finland, Germany, Hungary, Italy, Japan*, Romania, Slovakia, Soviet Union*, Spain, Switzerland*, Yugoslavia.
* did not enter service with these.

By far the most prolific fighter in history, the Bf 109 predated the Britisl Hurricane and Spitfire by a few months. Continually updated in both engines and armament, the type ended World War II hopelessly overweight, and its handling characteristics, never benign, became downright malicious. Yet it was flown by most of the top-scoring *Luftwaffe* fighter aces.

1978, piloted by Jack Krings. The scaling up of the YF-17 was not without problems, but these were finally overcome. The Hornet entered service with VFA-125 Rough Raiders in February 1981, and the first operational squadron was VMFA-314 Black Knights from January 1983.

Operationally, the main problem was that while the Hornet was dual-mission capable, its pilots were not. This was solved by assigning some squadrons to air superiority and others to ground attack. Two-seaters were fully combat-capable, but with 600lb (272kg) less internal fuel.

Virtually indistinguishable from the F/A-18A/B, the F/A-18C/D was rolled out in September 1987. Most changes were beneath the skin: computers of greater capacity, provision for Amraam, and ACES ejection seats. From 1992 the more powerful -402 engines were installed, then from May 1994 the APG-65 radar was replaced by the APG-73, with tripled memory and processing speed. The Marines have a dedicated two-seater F/A-18D optimised for night missions with TINS and FLIR.

In the Gulf War of 1991, Hornets were mainly used in the attack role. Their only air combat came on 17 January, when two F/A-18Cs, loaded with air-to-surface ordnance, were intercepted by two Iraqi MiG-21s. A couple of quick switch changes enabled them to launch two Sidewinders, destroy both MiGs, and carry on to hit their targets.

The final Hornet is the F/A-18E/F, a much larger and heavier variant powered by two F414-GE-400 turbofans, which entered service with VFA-122 in November 1999. This has various stealth features, and a projected active array radar.

Above: An early subtype of the Bf 109E; possibly a pre-series aircraft.

In the summer of 1934, the *Luftfahrtministerium* issued a requirement for a monoplane fighter to replace the He 51 and Ar 68 biplanes. The Bayerische Flugzeugwerke entry was the Bf 109, which first flew at Augsburg in mid-

September 1935, piloted by "Bubi" Knötsch. As the Junkers Jumo 210A was not ready in time, the first prototype was powered by a Rolls-Royce Kestrel V engine.

In the quest for performance, the Bf 109 was the smallest and lightest airframe that could be wrapped around the most powerful engine then under development. It was angular, with squared-off wingtips and a rectangular braced tailplane. The canopy enclosing the cockpit was of heavy metal framing, side-hinged. This made it rather unpopular with pilots, many of whom preferred the open cockpit of the rival He 112, which had a very similar performance.

Wing loading was comparable with the Spitfire and Hurricane but, with an eye to future weight increases, automatic slats were fitted to the outboard section of the wing leading edge, with large slotted flaps to the trailing edge, supplemented by slotted ailerons which drooped when the flaps were lowered. The mainwheel legs were located at the fuselage/wing junction, retracting outward. This gave a very narrow track with poor ground handling; this bedevilled the '109 during its entire life.

The second '109 prototype was powered by the Jumo 210A, and was flown from January 1936. The flight test programme uncovered problems with wing flutter, tail buffet, a tendency to drop the port wing before touchdown, a strong tendency to swing on takeoff and landing, leading edge slat malfunctions, and the inherently weak undercarriage. Despite these faults, the Bf 109 was selected as the future *Luftwaffe* fighter, and for the most part its pilots had to learn to live with its shortcomings.

The first series production type was the Bf 109B, powered by the 635hp Jumo 210D and armed with three 7.9mm MG 17 machine guns. Used by the Condor Legion in Spain from July 1937, it was soon found to lack hitting power. Experiments were made with a 20mm Oerlikon MGFF cannon firing through the propeller hub, but this proved unreliable. The C model which followed was powered by the fuel-injected 730hp Jumo 210G and armed with four 7.9mm machine guns, while the parallel D model had the conventionally aspirated Jumo 210D.

Above: Sixty-nine air combat victories are recorded on the rudder of this Bf 109E-3.

Below: The Bf 109E also saw extensive action in the Middle East and Malta.

The search for greater performance led to the installation of the 1,100hp Daimler-Benz DB 601A engine with fuel injection, and two wing-mounted MGFF cannon supplementing the two nose-mounted synchronised MG 17s. This, the Bf 109E, first flew in the summer of 1938, and by September 1939 it was rapidly replacing all previous models in *Luftwaffe* service. Production of the Emil, as it was known, continued until early 1942 in several variants.

The Emil handled well in the low- and mid-speed range, although above 300mph (483kph) the controls became progressively heavier; the ailerons in particular becoming almost immovable at 400mph (644kph). During hard manoeuvring the leading edge slats tended to open asymmetrically, which did nothing for precision gun tracking. In combat, its greatest advantage was fuel injection, which allowed it to perform negative-g manoeuvres without loss of power. However, it remained touchy on takeoff and landing, and the accident rate, both in training units and operational formations, was horrendous. Bf 109 ace Werner Mölders tested a captured Spitfire and a Hurricane in 1940; he described them as childishly simple to fly, unwittingly making an adverse comparison with the Emil.

An interesting variant was the Bf 109T carrier fighter. This had increased wing span and area with spoilers, manual wing folding, a beefed-up structure with a tailhook, and strengthened main gear legs. Denavalised, these remained in service until the end of 1944, operating from land bases.

The best flying machine of the entire breed was the Bf 109F, or Franz, which began to enter operational service in January 1941. Designed around a more powerful series of Daimler-Benz engines; typically the DB 601E of 1,300hp, it had a much sleeker nose with a larger spinner. The wings were redesigned, with rounded tips, shallower underwing radiators, Frise-type aileron surfaces and plain flaps. The bracing struts to the tailplane vanished, and the tailwheel was made retractable. Surprisingly, armament was reduced. The two nose-mounted MG 17s were initially supplemented by a single 20mm MGFF cannon firing through the spinner. In some later models, this was replaced by a 15mm MG 151 cannon, which had a faster rate of fire and a higher muzzle velocity than the Oerlikon. The later F-4 had a 20mm MG 151 cannon, and for tackling heavy bombers some had two 20mm MG 151 cannon in underwing gondolas.

Performance was given priority over manoeuvrability. Creeping weight growth had set in, and while greater engine power allied to a cleaner aerodynamic design gave the Franz a far better performance than the Emil, increased wing loading (about 40 per cent greater than that of the Bf 109 prototype), adversely affected turn radius. This last was not particularly important so long as the Messerschmitt pilots stuck to dive and zoom tactics, and avoided mixing it.

In late 1942, production switched to the Bf 109G, or Gustav, the main feature of which was the more powerful and considerably heavier DB 605A-1 engine with GM-1 boosting. More than a dozen Gustav subtypes were produced, variations being mainly in the powerplant – the DB 605D of the G-10 reached 1,850hp – and the armament. Weaponry variously consisted of a 30mm MK 108 cannon firing through the spinner; two 30mm MK 108s or two 20mm MG 151s in underwing gondolas; two 21cm WG 21 mortars carried underwing; and either two 7.7mm MG 17 or 13mm MG 131 machine guns in the engine upper decking. These last needed large bulges to house their breeches, which did nothing for streamlining.

The G-6/U4N was optimised for *Wilde Sau* night fighting by the addition of Naxos-Z radar detection gear. This was one case in which the flimsy

Below: Romanian Bf 109G-2s prepare to take off from Otopeni, Bucharest.

undercarriage proved an advantage. A heavy landing by a pilot unused to night flying tended to sheer the legs off rather than overturn.

A feature introduced on late G models was the "Galland Hood", which gave a far better view from the cockpit. As a generalisation, most Gustavs gave few performance advantages over the Franz, while handling became even more tricky, especially at takeoff and landing. The more heavily armed variants were

Messerschmitt Bf 109 derivatives, S 199 and HA-1112-M

Origin: S 199 Avia (Czechoslovakia); Ha-1112-M Hispano Aviacion (Spain).
Type: Both single-seat, single-engined air superiority fighters.
Engine: S 199, one 1,350hp Junkers Jumo 211F liquid-cooled V-12; Ha-1112-M, one 1,610hp Rolls-Royce Merlin 500 liquid-cooled V-12.
Dimensions: Span (both) 32ft 6.5in (9.92m); length (S 199) 29ft 4in (8.94m), (Ha 1112) 29ft 7in (9.02m); height (both) 8ft 6.5in (2.60m); wing area (S 199) 178 sq.ft (16.54m2), (Ha 1112) 173sq.ft (16.05m^2).
Weights: Empty (S 199) 6,305lb (2,860kg), (Ha 1112) 5,461lb (2,477kg); normal takeoff (S 199) 7,716lb (3,500kg), Ha-1112 6,382lb (2,895kg).
Loadings (at normal takeoff weight)**:** Wing (S 199) 43lb/sq.ft (212kg/m2), (Ha 1112) 37lb/sq.ft (180kg/m^2); power (S 199) 5.72lb (2.59kg) per hp; (Ha 1112) 3.96lb (1.80kg) per hp.
Performance: Maximum speed (S 199) 371mph (598kph) at 19,686ft (6,000m), 328mph (528kph) at sea level, (Ha 1112) 419mph (674kph) at 13,124ft (4,000m); initial climb rate (S 199) 2,697ft/min (13.70m/sec), (Ha 1112) 5,807ft/min (29.50m/sec); service ceiling (S 199) 31,170ft (9,500m), (Ha 1112) 33,466ft (10,200m); range (S 199) 528 miles (850km), (Ha 1112) 476 miles (766km).

bomber destroyers. The fact was that the Bf 109 had reached the limit of its growth potential. However, it had to remain in service for the simple reason that at high altitude it was superior to the FW 190A.

The final variant to enter service was the Bf 109K. With a souped-up DB 605 engine putting out 2,000hp, it was the fastest '109 of all, but only a few hundred reached the *Luftwaffe* before the end of the war.

Armament: (S 199) Two synchronised nose-mounted 13mm MG 131 machine guns and two 20mm Mauser MG 151 cannon in underwing gondolas; (Ha 1112) two wing-mounted 20mm Hispano cannon.
History: Both developed from the Bf 109G. First flight of S 199 25 March 1947. Combat debut Israel 29 May 1948. Production ended 1951 with a total of 551. Ha 1112 first flight May 1951. In service from 1952-1967. Production ended 1958 with a total of 239.
Users: S 199 Czechoslovakia, Israel. Ha 1112 Spain.

The advent of both Bf 109 derivatives was fortuitous; at the end of the war, the Avia factory in Prague had large stocks of components; Spain was licence-building the type. Both continued production, but DB 605 engines were unavailable.

Avia adapted the basic airframe to accept the Junkers Jumo 211F engine, which happened to be available in quantity. It was not the best of choices; the

Below: The Spanish HA-1112-M Buchon was a Rolls-Royce engined Bf 109G.

211 was basically a bomber engine, widely used in Ju 87s and He 111s. Shoehorning it in was a major undertaking, and the bumps and lumps resulted in the ugliest Bf 109 ever. Even more important, handing – never good – became absolutely appalling.

Despite this, production for the Czechoslovakian Air Force was commenced, with the first delivery made in February 1948. Israel, desperate for any sort of fighter, acquired 25 in 1948, and these, flown by volunteer pilots, scored a handful of air combat victories against Egyptian aircraft. By autumn they were all out of commission, mainly due to accidents.

The Spanish process was much slower. Initially the Bf 109Gs were fitted with the 1,300hp Hispano-Suiza 12Z 89, but this was not very suitable

Messerschmitt Bf 110G-4

Origin: Bayerische Flugzeugwerke GmbH, Germany.
Type: Three-seat, twin-engined radar-equipped night fighter.
Engine: Two 1,475hp Daimler-Benz DB 605B-1 liquid-cooled V-12 engines with water methanol injection.
Dimensions: Span 53ft 4in (16.25m); length 39ft 7.25in (12.07m); height 13ft 8.5in (4.18m); wing area 413sq.ft ($38.40m^2$).
Weights: Empty 11,230lb (5,094kg); normal takeoff 20,701lb (9,390kg); maximum 21,799lb (9,888kg).
Loadings (at normal takeoff weight)**:** Wing 50lb/sq.ft ($245kg/m^2$); power 7.02lb (3.18kg) per hp.
Performance: Maximum speed 342mph (550kph) at 22,967ft (7,000m),

The next stage was preparation to manufacture 200 Ha 1109s, the selected engine being the French-built HS 12Z 17. First flight took place in May 1951 and, modified to become Ha 1112-Ks, production began in 1952. Only 69 were completed.

Hispano then extensively reshaped the nose to house the Merlin, doing a far more professional job than had Avia. First flown in 1954, the Ha 1112-M, dubbed Buchon, had rather better performance than the original Bf 109G, while handling was greatly improved. With two wing-mounted 20mm Hispano-Suiza cannon and provision for eight 80mm rockets, the Buchon became the standard Spanish fighter for several years. It was phased out just in time to double as the Bf 109E in the Battle of Britain film of 1968.

311mph (500kph) at sea level; initial climb rate 2,165ft/min (11m/sec); sustained climb rate 7min 54sec to 18,287ft (6,000m); service ceiling 26,248ft (8,000m); range 559 miles (900km).

Armament: Nose armament two 30mm Rheinmetall Borsig MK 108 cannon with 135 rounds per gun, and two 20mm Mauser MG 151 cannon with 300 and 350 rounds. One 7.9mm MG 81Z twin swivelling machine gun with 800 rounds at rear of cabin. Some aircraft, two 20mm Mauser MG 151 or 20mm Oerlikon MGFF drum-fed cannon in *Schräge Musik* installation firing upwards.

History: Prototype first flight 12 May 1936. In service early 1939, and combat

Below: A long range heavy fighter, the Bf 110 was no match for single seaters.

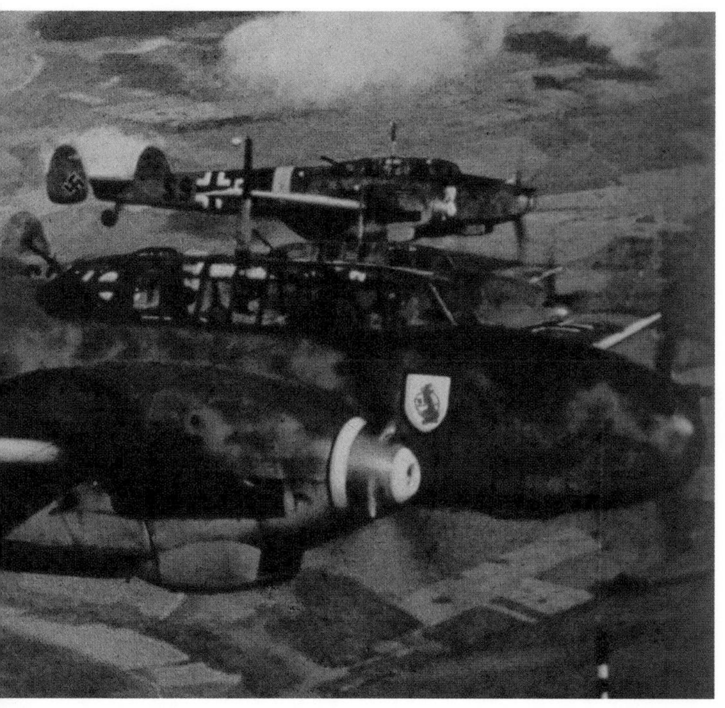

debut over Poland 1 September as long-range day fighter. Conversion to ground attack and night fighting began mid-1940. Airborne radar carried from summer 1942. Production ceased March 1945 with an approximate total of 6,050 of all variants.
Users: Germany, Hungary, Italy, Romania.

In the 1930s, heavy long-range fighters became fashionable in many countries, two of the reasons being the need to escort strategic bombers in daylight, and to project air power at greater distances than was possible with the traditional single-engined single seater. They had of necessity to be large enough to carry sufficient fuel to meet the range requirements, while two engines were needed for adequate performance.

By September 1939, heavy fighters were in service with four nations. Britain had the Blenheim, admittedly a makeshift adaptation of a light bomber; France the Potez 631; and Holland the Fokker G-1. Best of all, and the only one to remain in service until the end of the war, was the German Bf 110.

The prototype Bf 110 was first flown at Augsburg on 12 May 1936. Rate of climb, manoeuvrability and acceleration were poor, but it was faster than the single-engined Bf 109B, then entering service. This was impressive, and after initial problems had been ironed out it was ordered into production in 1938.

The first production variant was the Bf 110B, of which only a handful were built. It was succeeded by the Bf 110C, deliveries of which began in January 1939. The original (and troublesome) conventionally aspirated DB 600A engines had been replaced by fuel-injected DB 601As, each rated at 1,100hp.

The Bf 110 was a twin-engined low-wing monoplane with a lengthy two-seat cabin to house the pilot and his radio operator. It was distinguished by

rather angular (typically Messerschmitt) wings, with automatic leading edge slats outboard of the engines, which like those on the Bf 109, tended to open asymmetrically. Ailerons and slotted flaps occupied the trailing edges. The tailplane was set atop the empennage, with endplate twin fins and rudders. The main gears were housed in the engine nacelles, giving a wide track and good ground handling. In the air, handling was generally good, with no unpleasant surprises for the inexperienced, although directional control on takeoff was poor, and it was advisable that the flaps should not be raised at less than 492ft (150m). It was popular with its pilots, until the day came when the aircraft were opposed by agile modern day fighters.

The Bf 110C Zerstörer (Destroyer) was heavily armed, with two 20mm Oerlikon MGFF cannon and four 7.9mm MG 17 machine guns in the nose. The rear-facing radio operator protected the tail with a single swivelling MG 17.

In air combat it performed well enough over Poland, although this was against second rate opposition. In the French campaign its limitations had begun to show, although these were masked to a degree by the speed of the French collapse. But in the summer of 1940, over southern England, against a determined foe with first class equipment and a ground control system which more often than not positioned the defenders where they were needed, Bf 110's faults were ruthlessly exposed. The fact was that the heavy fighter itself needed a fighter escort! At the end of the year it was withdrawn from the Channel coast.

From this point on, the Bf 110 was a solution in search of a problem. It was developed as a ground attack aircraft, a fast bomber, a reconnaissance

Below: This Bf 110G-2/R3 carries 21cm mortars to destroy USAAF heavy bombers.

machine, and more or less by default a makeshift night fighter. It was fast enough to overhaul RAF bombers, had adequate endurance, was heavily armed, large enough to accommodate extra kit, and its handling was adequate for night operations.

Scheduled to be replaced from early 1942, it appeared to have little future, and production ceased in December 1941. But the disastrous Bf 210 which was to replace it was cancelled, and the Bf 110 production lines reopened in February 1942.

The Bf 110C made its debut as a night fighter in July 1940, but as a "catseye" fighter, or with searchlight cooperation, achieved little. A system of close ground control improved matters, although the Bf 110E-1/U2 had an extra crewman squeezed in to aid communications. This was followed by the Bf 110F-4, with 1,350hp DB 601F engines, increased crew protection, FuG 202 radar, and a ventral tray with two 30mm MK 108 cannon. In some F-4 subtypes the 20mm MGFF cannon were replaced by 20mm MG 151s, while in others the MK 108s from the ventral tray were modified in the field to become upward-firing *Schräge Musik*. The final variant was the Bf 110G-4, with 1,475hp DB 605B-1 engines and either the FuG 212 or FuG 221a radar. When these were jammed by Window, they were replaced by Lichtenstein SN-2. Also fitted were Flensburg and Naxos, devices which could home on British bomber emissions, thus minimising German use of airborne radar.

Creeping weight growth had eroded performance. By this time endurance was more important than speed, and at operational altitude the Bf 110G was

Messerschmitt Me 163B Komet

Origin: Messerschmitt AG, Germany.
Type: Single-seat, single-engined point defence interceptor.
Engine: One Walter HWK 109-509A-1 bifuel rocket motor giving 3,748lb (1,700kg) thrust.
Dimensions: Span 30ft 7.33in (9.33m); length 19ft 2.5in (5.85m); height 9ft 0.5in (4.18m); wing area 199sq.ft (18.50m²).
Weights: Empty 4,206lb (1,908kg); normal takeoff 9,502lb (4,310kg).
Loadings (at normal takeoff weight)**:** Wing 48lb/sq.ft (233kg/m²); thrust 0.39.
Performance: Maximum speed 593mph (955kph) above 9,843ft (3,000m), 516mph (830kph) at sea level; initial climb rate 15,946ft/min (81m/sec); sustained climb rate 3min 21sec to 39,700ft (12,100m); service ceiling 39,700ft (12,100m); range c50 miles (80km).
Armament: Two 30mm Rheinmetall Borsig MK 108 short-barrel cannon with 60 rounds per gun.
History: First flight of prototype Me 163V-1 (unpowered), spring 1941. First powered flight August 1941 and first production order December. First powered flight of the prototype Me 163B August 1943. In service from May 1944; combat debut 28 July. Total production c370, with 279 delivered.
User: Germany.

Rocket propulsion for fighters promised outstanding gains in performance. In 1937, aerodynamics pioneer professor Alexander Lippisch was recruited for the task of designing what later became the Me 163B, unofficially called the Komet. The first step was the DFS 194 glider, to provide data on low and moderate speed handling. This was later modified to take a low powered rocket

***Above:* The nose of the Bf 110G-4 night fighter bristles with radar aerials.**

hard-pressed to catch a bomber in a hurry. Overtaken by events, the Bf 110 was gradually replaced by the Ju 88, and by April 1945 barely 50 remained operational.

The greatest exponent of the Bf 110 at night was Heinz-Wolfgang Schnaufer, with 121 victories, 64 of them during 1944 alone, at a time when the German night fighters were outnumbered and technically overmatched. Production ceased in March 1945; more than three years later than had originally been scheduled.

***Above:* The rocket-powered Me 163B Komet was a point defence interceptor.**

motor, to become the Me 163V-1.

For security reasons, the project was switched to Peenemünde where Heini Dittmar made the first powered flight in August 1941. In October he recorded a speed of 624mph (1,004kph), but then encountered compressibility, at that time a barely known phenomenon, which caused an uncommanded steep dive. This notwithstanding, the status of the project was changed from high-speed research to point defence interceptor.

Redesign began in December, based around a new rocket motor powered by hydrazine hydrate/methyl alcohol, and high-test hydrogen peroxide. Both were highly unstable; peroxide was also extremely corrosive to all organic matter, including the pilot. When mixed, these fuels reacted hypergolically to produce thrust. It was a potentially lethal combination.

Technical problems delayed the first flight of the Me 163B until August 1943, and the first Komets were not received by the operational units until several months later. The Komet was a chunky tail-less fighter, with a mid-set wing swept at 22.3deg. It had low-drag anti-spin fixed slots on the leading edge, with elevons outboard and trimming flaps inboard on the trailing edge. Landing flaps were fitted underwing. Takeoff was made on a wheeled dolly, and landing on an extendable skid.

Despite its tail-less configuration, the Komet handled well. Its greatest weakness was lack of endurance; just eight minutes of powered flight if the throttle was used sparingly. However, it could be held on the ground until the USAAF heavy bombers were almost in sight and, when launched, could reach their altitude in about two minutes. Its speed enabled it to penetrate the escort fighter screens with ease, but against bombers at 180mph (290kph) the rate of overtake was too high to give more than a fleeting shooting chance. Once out of fuel, it then had to glide back to base, but since the Komet could be dived at more than 500mph (805kph), this was not quite as suicidal as it sounds.

In practice, the Komet claimed only nine victories, and its attrition rate was horrendous. Explosions were common, mainly on takeoff and on landing; inadvertently exceeding the critical Mach number could lead to an uncontrollable dive; and the need to land first time, with no second chance, did

Messerschmitt Me 262A-1a Schwalbe

Origin: Messerschmitt AG, Germany.
Type: Single-seat, twin-engined subsonic jet fighter.
Engine: Two Junkers Jumo 109-004B single-spool axial-flow turbojets each rated at 1,980lb thrust.
Dimensions: Span 41ft 0.5in (12.51m); length 34ft 9.5in (10.60m); height 12ft 6.75in (3.83m); wing area 234sq.ft (21.70m^2).
Weights: Empty 9,742lb (4,420kg); normal takeoff 14,101lb (6,396kg).
Loadings (at normal takeoff weight)**:** Wing 60lb/sq.ft (295kg/m^2); thrust 0.28.
Performance: Maximum speed 541mph (870kph) at 19,686ft (6,000m), 500mph (805kph) at sea level; initial climb rate 3,937ft/min (20m/sec); service ceiling 37,565ft (11,450m); range 653 miles (1,050km).
Armament: Four nose-mounted 30mm Rheinmetall Borsig MK 108 cannon, two with 100 rounds per gun and two with 80 rounds per gun. Towards the end of the war, about 40 aircraft carried 24 55mm R4M unguided rockets on underwing racks.
History: First flight of prototype 18 April 1941 with Jumo piston engine. First flight with turbojets alone 18 July 1942. First production order May 1943. Service entry May and combat debut July 1944. Total production 1,442, including 12 built postwar in Czechoslovakia as the Avia S 92 Turbina.
Users: Czechoslovakia (S 92), Germany.

Above: An Me 163 lookalike, the Japanese Shusui crashed on its only flight.

not help matters. The Komet killed far more of its own pilots than ever did the enemy.

Above: Only a few radar-equipped two-seater Me 262Bs became operational.

The first jet fighter to fly was the Heinkel He 280 (see page 210), but the Me 262 was the first to enter operational service. There had been little to choose between them, and the selection of the Schwalbe owed at least as much to political infighting as technical merit.

The German jet engine programme of 1938 was parallelled by an airframe development group, and before the end of that year an order was placed with Messerschmitt for a jet fighter, to be based on theoretical data for the proposed turbojets. A twin-engined configuration was adopted for two reasons: lack of thrust of the early engines, and greater design flexibility. Initially the engines were to be integral with the wings, as with the Gloster Meteor, but by May 1940 this was changed to an underslung position. This not only simplified wing design, but provided ease of access to the so-far undeveloped new engines. Three prototypes were ordered, and while these were complete in April 1941, the proposed BMW turbojets were not. Producing little more than one third of their designed thrust, they were completely inadequate. In order to explore low-speed handling, a Jumo 210G reciprocating engine was installed in the nose of the first prototype and, although the aircraft was significantly underpowered, on 17 April Fritz Wendell made the first of seven flights in this configuration. For the record, the similarly sized but much lighter He 280 had already flown on the power of two small Heinkel turbojets.

By November, BMW had managed to double the original thrust of the 109

turbojet. Two of these were installed alongside the Jumo 210, and on 25 November a flight was attempted, only for the turbines of both jets to fail on takeoff. Not until 18 July 1942 did the Me 262 fly on jet power alone, when flight-cleared Jumo 004s became available.

Reasons for the delays were threefold. First, the engine designers were exploring uncharted territory. Second, the jet fighter programme had a low priority, as it was thought that the aircraft could not be ready before the war was won. Third, there was a dearth of chromium and nickel; both were needed to make high temperature alloys. This led to the use of unsuitable expedients.

However, the potential of the new aircraft was evident, and in October 1942 an order was placed for 30 development aircraft. As it emerged, the Me 262 had a sleek fuselage of rounded triangular section, with the cockpit aft of the leading edges, unlike the forward position of the Meteor. The wings were swept at a shallow angle, with three-piece leading edge slats on the leading edge and two-piece Frise-type ailerons and two-piece flaps on the trailing edge.

Below: The Me 262A Schwalbe engines were underslung to ease maintenance.

The tailplane was high-set on a triangular fin and rudder. The main gears were wing-mounted just inboard of the engine nacelles, and at first it had a tailwheel. The nose-up sit produced meant that the horizontal tail was blanketed by the wings on takeoff; getting the tail up was a problem. This was finally overcome by fitting a nosewheel, thus copying the He 280.

Mass production was finally approved in November 1943, with a target of 60 per month from May 1944. Hitler's intervention in insisting it be adapted as a fighter-bomber came at this point, but does not seem to have delayed the project much, despite reports to the contrary. The first production aircraft reached the evaluation unit in May 1944, and made its air combat debut with *Kommando Nowotny* in July.

In the air, the Me 262A handled very well but for one thing. In a dive it quickly reached its limiting Mach number of 0.86, but its greatest weakness was its engines. Acceleration was poor and, after takeoff, speed built up only slowly. Deceleration was also lacking; landing consisted of a long straight approach, slowly bleeding off speed. This made it vulnerable to fighters.

Me 262 pilots had to learn to fly the engines. Apart from their chronic unreliability, mishandling the throttles often resulted in compressor stalls, flameouts, and engine fires.

The speed of the jet was also a two-edged sword. It enabled the Schwalbe to penetrate the screen of escort fighters with relative ease, but against the lumbering bombers, shooting opportunities were fleeting. Nor were matters helped by the relatively short range of the 30mm cannon, which took the Me 262 well within the range of the bomber gunners. Losses to this cause were high. In the final months of the war, batteries of R4M rockets were carried to allow stand-off attacks to be made.

The Me 262 could not turn with Allied fighters, and any attempt to do so

Mikoyan-Guryevich MiG-3

Origin: Mikoyan-Guryevich OKB, Soviet Union.
Type: Single-seat, single-engined high-altitude monoplane fighter.
Engine: One 1,350hp Mikulin AM-35A liquid-cooled V-12.
Dimensions: Span 33ft 5.5in (10.20m); length 27ft 1in (8.25m); height 10ft 10in (3.30m); wing area 188sq.ft (17.44m^2).
Weights: Empty 5,950lb (2,699kg); normal takeoff 6,900lb (3,130kg); maximum 7,385lb (3,350kg).
Loadings (at normal takeoff weight)**:** Wing 37lb/sq.ft (179kg/m^2); power 5.11lb (2.32kg) per hp.
Performance: Maximum speed 398mph (640kph) at 25,592ft (7,800m), 314mph (505kph) at sea level; sustained climb rate 10min 17sec to 26,248ft (8,000m); service ceiling 39,372ft (12,000m); range 510 miles (820km).
Armament: One 12.7mm UBS machine gun with 300 rounds; two 7.62mm ShKAS machine guns with 375 rounds per gun, all nose-mounted and synchronised. Sometimes, eight RS-82 unguided rockets.
History: First flight of prototype (I-200) 5 April 1940. First production aircraft December 1940. Into service from April 1941. Production terminated 23 December with a total of 3,120, plus 50 more during 1942 from components.
User: Soviet Union.

The MiG-3 was designed by the newly formed Mikoyan-Guryevich OKB in 1939 as a high-altitude interceptor to counter overflights by German Ju 86Ps. The need was urgent, and barely 100 days elapsed between completion of production drawings and the first flight of the I-200 prototype, by A.N.Yekatov at Khodinka on 5 April 1940. Longitudinal stability was poor; the controls were

Above: The Me 262A-1a made its combat debut in July 1944 with Kdo Nowotny.

resulted in an alarming speed loss, rendering it vulnerable to counterattack. The leading German jet ace in the type was Heinz Baer, with 16 victories.

Postwar, many Me 262 components, jigs and tools, ended up in Czechoslovakia. A dozen aircraft were completed by Avia as the S 92 Turbina, and formed a fighter squadron in the summer of 1950, but this was disbanded during the following year.

Right: A high altitude fighter, the MiG-3 was unsatisfactory lower down.

heavy, it stalled without warning and the ensuing spin was difficult to recover. However, it was accepted for service in September on the basis of sheer speed, and entered production as the MiG-1, of which only 100 were built.

A programme to minimise its faults resulted in the very similar MiG-3, which entered service concurrently with the MiG-1. With the Nazi invasion, most air combat took place at medium and low altitudes, where the MiG-3 proved greatly inferior to the Bf 109F in all departments. The exceptionally heavy AM-35A engine, which had been designed for bombers and had only a single-stage supercharger, did not help. Other engines were tried, but in the event these were reserved for the Il-2 Shturmovik. With no alternative engine available, the MiG-3 programme was terminated.

The MiG-3 had no high-scoring aces, although Aleksandr Pokryshkin scored the first of his 59 victories on the type.

Mikoyan-Guryevich MiG-9FS

Origin: Mikoyan-Guryevich OKB, Soviet Union.
Type: Single-seat, single-engined subsonic jet fighter.
Engine: Two Kazan RD 20 (BMW 003A) single-spool axial-flow turbojets each rated at 1,764lb (800kg) military thrust.
Dimensions: Span 32ft 9.75in (10.00m); length 32ft 3in (9.83m); height 10ft 7in (3.23m); wing area 196sq.ft (18.20m^2).
Weights: Empty 7,540lb (3,420kg); normal takeoff 7,540lb (3,420kg).
Loadings (at normal takeoff weight)**:** Wing 38lb/sq.ft (188kg/m^2); thrust 0.47.
Performance: Maximum speed 566mph (911kph) at 14,765ft (4,500m), 537mph (864kph) at sea level; sustained climb rate 4min 18sec to 16,405ft (5,000m); service ceiling 44,294ft (13,500m); range 497 miles (800km).
Armament: One 37mm N-37 cannon with 40 rounds in the intake splitter; two 23mm NS-23 cannon with 80 rounds per gun beneath the intake.
History: First flight of prototype (I-300) 24 April 1946. First pre-series aircraft flown 26 October, and accepted for service at the end of the year. Service entry early 1947. Production ceased July 1948, with a total of 604 of all variants.
User: Soviet Union.

When on 24 April 1946 test pilot Alexei Grinchik took the MiG-9 into the air, it was the first flight by a Soviet jet. Lacking an indigenous turbojet, it was at first powered by two BMW 003As, but for production aircraft these were reverse-engineered at the Kazan factory as RD 20s. With the mineral riches of Siberia to call upon, heat-resistant alloys were available, thus avoiding the problems encountered by the Germans.

Mikoyan-Guryevich MiG-15bis/SD

Origin: Mikoyan-Guryevich OKB, Soviet Union.
Type: Single-seat, single-engined subsonic jet fighter.
Engine: One Klimov VK-1 centrifugal-flow turbojet rated at 5,952lb (2,700kg) military thrust.
Dimensions: Span 33ft 1in (10.09m); length 33ft 2in (10.10m); height 12ft 2in (3.70m); wing area 222sq.ft (20.60m^2).
Weights: Empty 8,115lb (3,681g); normal takeoff 11,861b (5,380kg); maximum 13,461lb (6,106kg).
Loadings (at normal takeoff weight)**:** Wing 53lb/sq.ft (261kg/m^2); thrust 0.50.
Performance: Maximum speed 688mph (1,107kph) at 9,843ft (3,000m), 669mph (1,076kph) at sea level; limiting Mach number 0.92; initial climb rate 9,055ft/min (46m/sec); sustained climb rate 1min 57sec to 16,405ft (5,000m), 4min 54sec to 32,810ft (10,000m); service ceiling 50,856ft (15,500m); range 702 miles (1,130km) with external tanks.
Armament: One 37mm N-37 cannon with 40 rounds; two 23mm NS-23KM cannon with 80 rounds per gun.
History: First flight of prototype (I-310) 30 December 1947. Ordered into production 20 May 1949. To operational units winter 1949-50. Combat debut Korea 1 November 1950. Production ceased 1968, with a total of about 12,000 of all variants.
Users: Afghanistan, Albania, Algeria, Angola, Bulgaria, Cambodia, China (People's Republic), Cuba, Czechoslovakia, East Germany, Egypt, Finland, Guinea, Hungary, Indonesia, Iraq, Libya, Madagascar, Mali, Mongolia, Morocco, Mozambique, Nigeria, North Korea, North Vietnam, North Yemen, Pakistan, Poland, Romania, Somalia, South Yemen, Soviet Union, Sri Lanka, Sudan, Syria, Tanzania, Uganda.

Above: The MiG-9 had two Kazan RD 20 turbojets mounted about the centreline.

The MiG-9 was of pod and boom configuration, the engines mounted side by side on the centre of gravity, which minimised the problems of asymmetric thrust in single-engined flight. Aft of the jetpipes, the fuselage tapered to a high-set boom with a stainless steel sandwich to protect it from the hot exhaust. This carried the tail surfaces. The straight wing, of 9 per cent thickness/chord ratio, was in the mid-position, and had Frise-type ailerons outboard and slotted flaps inboard. The nosewheel landing gear was a Soviet first.

The MiG-9 became the first Soviet jet to be fitted with ejection seats, and the first to have a two-seater trainer variant. Handling was pleasant; the one real problem was that firing the guns above 24,608ft (7,500m) caused the engines to flame out. But it was soon surpassed by the swept-wing MiG-15.

Above: The MiG-15bis was licence-built in Poland as the Lim-2, seen here.

The MiG-15 was designed as a bomber destroyer. Its requirements were a maximum speed of Mach 0.9, a high rate of climb, good high-altitude manoeuvrability, a minimum endurance of one hour, and exceptionally heavy armament. The latter was no problem; Soviet calculations showed that on average the American B-29, then seen as the major threat, could be destroyed by just two hits by 37mm shells, or eight hits by 23mm shells. Armament could therefore be lifted unchanged from the MiG-9, the only difference being that the three cannon and their ammunition were arranged on a tray which could be winched in and out of the aircraft, thus easing servicing.

The greatest problem was finding a suitable engine, but this was fortuitously solved by the British Labour government of the time, which stupidly supplied Russia a batch of Rolls-Royce Derwent and Nene turbojets. The Nene, a centrifugal-flow engine, was arguably the best engine in the world at that time, and was reverse-engineered to become, with the addition of water injection, the RD-45F (F = *forsirovanni*, or boosted), manufactured in factory No 45 in Moscow. All that remained was to design a suitable airframe.

Swept wings were known to delay the onset of compressibility and an angle of 35deg was chosen, with two fences per side to reduce the effects of

spanwise flow. Two degrees of anhedral were used to aid stability, and the wing was set in the mid-position. The cockpit was pressurized and air conditioned, not that either worked very well, with an ejection seat, and a bubble canopy gave good all-round vision. The horizontal tail was set high on the fin. By Western standards the MiG-15 was a no-frills fighter.

First flight was made by Valery Yuganov on 30 December 1947, and after a few tweaks state acceptance trials were completed in a few months. Both stability and manoeuvrability were praised, and production was initiated in August 1948, and confirmed in May 1949. The first MiG-15s started to reach operational units during the following winter.

The basic MiG-15 was followed by the MiG-15bis/SD, which differed from the original primarily in having the Klimov VK-1 powerplant which had been developed from the RD-45F. It was this variant that took the brunt of the fighting over North Korea between 1950 and 1953.

While the MiG-15, which was given the unflattering NATO reporting name of Fagot, occasionally encountered the B-29, its original designated foe, over North Korea, most action was against the American F-86 Sabre. Although the

Below: Czechoslovakia also licence-built the MiG-15SD as the S-103.

thrust of the turbojets of both aircraft was similar, the MiG-15 was slightl smaller and considerably lighter than its American opponent, giving it a bette thrust/weight ratio. This, plus other factors, gave the Soviet fighter a far bette climb rate, especially at altitude, and a much higher ceiling.

The MiGs, for the most part flown by Russian pilots, were mainly based i China. With the advantage of radar early warning, they could gain height befor crossing the border to engage the American fighters. Plummeting down t attack, they immediately grabbed for height afterwards, hoping to lure th Sabres to an altitude where the MiGs had the advantage. By contrast, th Sabres tended to dive away, hoping to lure the MiGs down to where thei Russian opponents' advantages were lost. In many cases, the engagement wa over before it had really begun. But on occasion, they mixed it.

In this situation, the MiGs found that their armament was not really suite to dogfighting. While only one or two hits were enough to destroy a Sabre, th problem was getting them. While the muzzle velocities of the 37mm and 23mn cannon were similar, the rate of fire, seven 37mm shells per second and abou double this for 23mm shells, was insufficient against hard manoeuvring targets The ballistic qualities, and thus the trajectories of the shells, also varied. Som American reports described 23mm shells going over them while the 37mn shells passed below.

Another deficiency was that the MiG-15 was a poor gun platform. It wa unstable and snaked laterally at speeds above Mach 0.86, and at Mach 0.92 th speed brakes automatically deployed, which in combat was embarrassing Other problems were that it stalled with no warning and spun at the slightes provocation. So bad was this that a vertical white line was painted on the dash to aid pilots to centre the control column.

Despite its faults, the MiG-15's high-altitude performance gained it ar

Mikoyan-Guryevich MiG-17F

Origin: Mikoyan-Guryevich OKB, Soviet Union.
Type: Single-seat, single-engined transonic jet fighter.
Engine: One Klimov VK-1F centrifugal-flow afterburning turbojet rated at 7,452lb (2,600kg) maximum and 5,952lb (2,700kg) military thrust.
Dimensions: Span 31ft 7in (9.63m); length 36ft 11.5in (11.26m); height 12ft 5.5in (3.80m); wing area 243sq.ft (22.60m^2).
Weights: Empty 8,664lb (3,930g); normal takeoff 11,773lb (5,340kg); maximum 13,380lb (6,069kg).
Loadings (at normal takeoff weight)**:** Wing 48lb/sq.ft (236kg/m^2); thrust 0.63.
Performance: Maximum speed 712mph (1,145kph) at 9,843ft (3,000m), 684mph (1,100kph) at sea level; limiting Mach number 1.15; initial climb rate 12,796ft/min (65m/sec); sustained climb rate 3min 42sec to 32,810ft (10,000m); service ceiling 54,465ft (16,600m); range 584 miles (940km) with external tanks.
Armament: One 37mm N-37 cannon with 40 rounds; two 23mm NR-23 cannon with 80 rounds per gun. Sometimes, two K-13 AAMs.
History: First flight of prototype (I-330) January 1950. Ordered into production September 1951. Operational from October 1952. Combat debut Middle East 1960. Production ceased 1986, with a total of nearly 10,000 of all variants.
Users: Afghanistan, Albania, Algeria, Angola, Bangladesh, Bourkina Faso, Bulgaria, Cambodia, China (People's Republic), Congo, Cuba, Czechoslovakia, East Germany, Egypt, Ethiopia, Finland, Guinea-Bissau, Hungary, India, Indonesia, Iraq, Madagascar, Libya, Mali, Mongolia, Morocco, Mozambique, Nigeria, North Korea, North Vietnam, Pakistan, Poland, Romania, Somalia, Soviet Union, Sri Lanka, Sudan, Syria, Uganda, Yemen, Yugoslavia.

Above: This MiG-15bis was delivered into US hands by a North Korean defector.

enviable reputation among its opponents, and started a period of four decades in which MiG was synonymous with Soviet fighter. Its main exponents in Korea were Eugeny Pepelyaev with 23 victories, and Nikolai Sutyagin with 20. It was licence-built in Czechoslovakia as the S-103, Poland as the Lim-2, and China as the J-2. Surprisingly, it remained in service into the mid-1980s with no fewer than 19 nations, mainly as two-seat trainers.

Above: The MiG-17F. showing its three wing fences and cranked leading edge.

The MiG-17, NATO reporting name Fresco, used the MiG-15bis as a starting point. With engine development temporarily stalled, the challenge was to improve performance and capability by aerodynamic means alone.

The main feature was a totally new wing, with greater area but reduced span. As it had to house the main gears, thickness remained the same, but increased breadth reduced the thickness/chord ratio, effectively minimising compressibility effects. The leading edge sweep was increased to 49deg, reducing outboard to 45.5deg, giving a noticeable kink. This last however was not done for aerodynamic benefits, but for the more prosaic reason that the wing structure had to fit a section of fuselage which was common to the MiG-15! Unofficially, the expression "sickle wing" was adopted. Wing skinning was thicker, and the tips were made rounded. Spanwise airflow was contained by three fences on each side, and anhedral was increased from 2deg to 3deg.

Whereas the trailing edge sweep of the MiG-15 had been a constant 25deg, on the MiG-17 this was increased to 40deg, although a narrow inboard section met the fuselage at 90deg.

To maintain trim, commensurate with the increase in wing sweep, the fuselage was lengthened by 35.5in (900mm), giving an improved fineness ratio. The speed

brakes were increased in size. The tail surfaces appeared very similar to those of the MiG-15, but were in fact modified considerably. At a later date, afterburning was introduced to give added thrust. Since this reduced range and endurance, drop tanks were routinely carried.

The result was a fighter which closely resembled the MiG-15. First flown by Ivan Ivashchenko in January 1950, it quickly demonstrated improved performance and handling, but on 20 March it dived out of control and crashed, killing Ivashschenko. This delayed the programme by more than a year. Not until 1 September 1951 was it ordered into production, the first units achieving initial operational capability in October 1952. Less than a month later, flight testing commenced on the MiG-17F, with the afterburning VK-1F turbojet, and this variant

Below: The intake shows this to be a MiG-17PF limited all-weather fighter.

entered production at the end of 1952.

In combat the MiG-17 had two main failings. The first was poor vision from the cockpit, which it inherited from the MiG-15, and which was to become a feature of MiG fighters for decades to come. The pilot was buried deep in the fuselage, with only his head above the cills, restricting his view sideways and downwards. Forward vision was inadequate for the same reason, made worse by the heavy metal framing of the windshield and canopy bow. As partial compensation, a periscope giving 360deg coverage was fitted later.

The second failing was the mechanical linkage to the control surfaces. Stick forces increased with speed, which made extreme physical demands on the pilot. In particular, rate of roll was badly degraded. Oddly, this held one advantage. The absence of hydraulic control runs significantly decreased vulnerability to battle damage. This apart, the MiG-17 was pleasant to fly, and at lower speeds was extremely manoeuvrable.

While several further variants of the MiG-17 were developed, the MiG-17F (Fresco C), saw nearly all the action. In 1960 there were a few mainly inconclusive encounters between Egyptian MiGs and Israeli fighters. By 1967, more modern Soviet fighters were available to the Arab nations, and the MiG-17 was largely relegated to ground attack. It was used in this role by Nigeria against Biafra between 1968 and 1970, in the Uganda/Tanzania conflict in 1972, and by both Afghanistan and Mozambique against rebels. But as a fighter, it is mainly remembered for its part in the Vietnam conflict.

For all its faults, the MiG-17 had to be treated with respect. It could handily out-turn the large and heavy U.S. fighters, and the hitting power of its heavy cannon armament could not be ignored. Operating in a close ground control environment, its small size, coupled with poor visibility, often enabled it to make hit and run attacks. In the later stages of the war, MiG-17s were often ordered to form a circle (the wagon wheel) at low level, from which they were vectored to intercept.

In the period 1965-1968, MiG-17s shot down 23 American air-craft, but lost about 87 of their number in the process. Then in 1972, 14 MiG-17s fell to US Navy Phantoms for almost no return. How-ever, its effectiveness should not be measured by its meagre victory score, but more in terms of how many strike aircraft it forced to jettison their bombs and abort their attacks.

Several more variants of the MiG-17 were developed, notably the MiG-17P. This

Mikoyan-Guryevich MiG-19S

Origin: Mikoyan-Guryevich OKB, Soviet Union.
Type: Single-seat, twin-engined supersonic jet fighter.
Engines: Two Mikulin AM-9B single-spool axial-flow afterburning turbojets each rated at 7,165lb (3,250kg) maximum and 5,732lb (2,600kg) military thrust.
Dimensions: Span 29ft 6.33in (9.00m); length 41ft 4in (12.60m); height 12ft 9in (3.89m); wing area 269sq.ft (25.00m^2).
Weights: Empty 11,402lb (5,172kg); normal takeoff 16,667lb (7,560kg); maximum 19,471lb (8,832kg).
Loadings (at normal takeoff weight)**:** Wing 62lb/sq.ft (302kg/m^2); thrust 0.86.
Performance: Maximum speed 902mph (1,452kph) Mach 1.34 at 32,810ft (10,000m), 715mph (1,150kph) Mach 0.94 at sea level; initial climb rate 35,435ft/min (180m/sec); sustained climb rate 1min 6sec to 32,810ft (10,000m), 2min 36sec to 49,215ft (15,000m); service ceiling 57,418ft (17,500m); range 864 miles (1,390km) with external tanks.
Armament: Three 30mm NR-30 cannon, one under the nose with 55 rounds; two in the wing roots each with 73 rounds, possibly with two K-13 AAMs.
History: First flight of prototype (I-360) 5 January 1954. Mass production ordered 17 February. First deliveries March 1955. Operational from mid-1956. Soviet

***Above:* All MiG-17s have rounded wing tips, like this Polish Lim-5.**

had an Izumrud RP-1 radar mounted on the upper lip of the intake, which gave it a limited night and adverse weather capability. This was followed by the MiG-17PF, which had no cannon, but was armed with four K-5 beam-riding missiles.

At the end of 2001, a few MiG-17s/J-5s were still on strength with nine nations, although few were considered serviceable.

***Above:* The MiG-19S was the first supersonic Soviet fighter to enter service.**

production ceased in 1958 but continued in Czechoslavakia and China (as the J-6), in the latter until past 1980. Total production of all variants c5,000.
Users: Afghanistan, Albania, Angola, Bulgaria, China (People's Republic), Cuba, Czechoslavakia, East Germany, Hungary, Indonesia, Iraq, North Korea, North Vietnam, Pakistan, Poland, Romania, Soviet Union, Tanzania, Yugoslavia, Zambia.

In 1947, turbojet specialist Lyulka commenced work on the AI-5, an axial-flow engine expected to achieve a thrust of 9,921lb (4,500kg) without afterburning. This opened up the possibility of supersonic speed in level flight if a suitable airframe could be designed around it.

Three OKBs entered the ring: Lavochkin with the La-190, Yakovlev with the Yak-1000, and Mikoyan (from the early 1950s Guryevich was increasingly sidelined by ill health, but the G in MiG was retained even after his retirement in 1964) with the I-350. None succeeded. The large and complex La-190, the first fighter to have an entirely wet wing and bicycle undercarriage, was beset by problems, not least of which was the engine. In the course of eight flights, it barely managed to squeeze past Mach 1 on a single occasion, and the programme was then terminated. The Yak-1000 was a tailed cropped delta with a tiny wing, and also had a bicycle main gear. Ground tests showed such appalling handling characteristics that it was never flown.

This left the I-350. This had the typical MiG pitot intake and high-set tailplane, but was otherwise totally new. The mid-set wing was swept at 60deg, and initially had four fences on each side. A small ventral fin was fitted, with a bumper. Armament was the same as the MiG-17F. First flight, by Gregoriy Sedov, took place on 16 June 1951, but engine unreliability, and the inability of the I-350 to significantly exceed Mach 1, caused the programme to be terminated after seven flights.

At this point, Uncle Joe Stalin issued a directive to the MiG OKB, demanding a supersonic fighter prototype. He was not a forgiving man; the

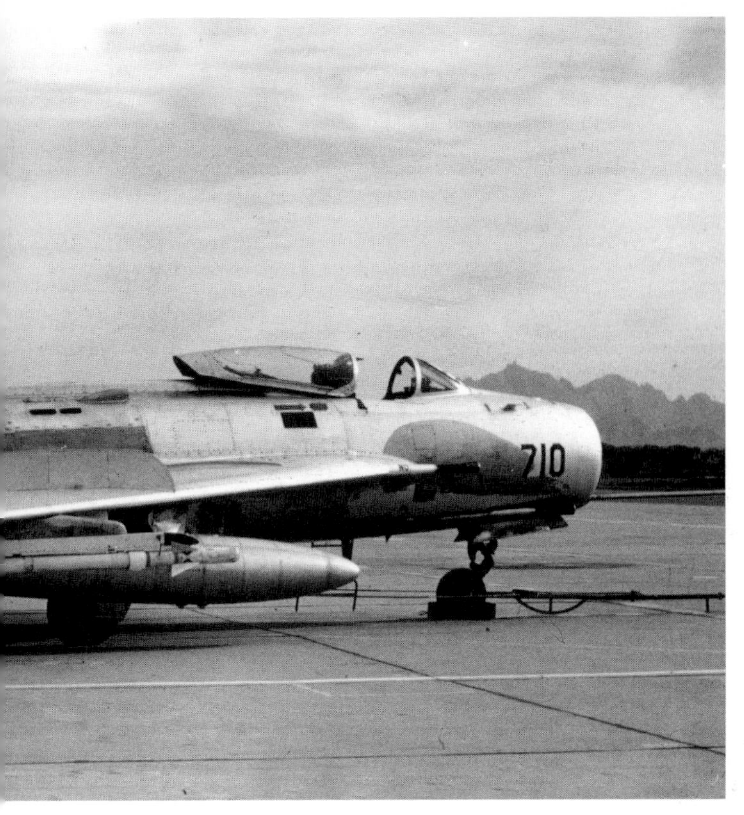

Above: The F.6 was the Chinese licence-built version of the MiG-19S.

implied reward for failure was probably a holiday home in the Gulags. This concentrated the collective mind of the MiG OKB wonderfully. The I-350 airframe was good enough; the problem then became one of providing sufficient power.

The choice fell on the Mikulin AM-5A, a compact axial flow turbojet. Two were needed to provide adequate thrust. A major redesign of the fuselage was undertaken to accommodate them, fed by an enlarged pitot inlet, to achieve which the two 23mm cannon were moved to the wing roots. Profile drag was little more than that of the single-engined I-350.

Extreme stick forces at high speeds could no longer be ignored, and a hydraulic flight control system was developed, duplicated to guard against either failure or battle damage. To prevent an over-enthusiastic pilot from pulling the wings off during hard manoeuvres, this was given artificial feel. Other changes were AM-9B turbojets which had afterburning, while the variable-incidence tailplane and elevators were replaced by an all-moving slab surface. This was not all done at once; the MiG OKB was exploring uncharted territory.

Grigoriy Sedov took the I-360 (MiG-19) prototype into the air on 5 January 1954, and reached Mach 1.3 on only its second flight. There were still problems to be overcome with both engines and airframe, but these were eventually solved. The most notable change was the tailplane, which was moved from the top of the fin, where it could be blanketed by the wing at high angles of attack, to the fuselage just below the fin. Unusually, mass production was ordered just over six weeks later, before the production drawings were complete.

Development continued. Spoilers linked to the ailerons were located just ahead of the wing flaps to improve roll control at high Mach numbers. The flight control system was fine-tuned, and a single huge wing fence was added on each side. Armament became three 30mm NR-30 cannon. Deliveries to the Soviet Air Force began in March 1955, and the first MiG-19 fighters, NATO reporting name Farmer, became operational a year later.

The extreme wing sweep meant that its structure had to be heavy to resist the bending moments in manoeuvring flight, but despite this the MiG-19S was a very manoeuvrable fighter, with a rapid rate of roll and a small turning radius. Acceleration and rate of climb were good. If it had a fault, it was its extremely short operational radius. At low level, using afterburning, the pilot had to consider where he was going to land literally within minutes of taking off.

The MiG-19 saw action with Egypt against Israel, Pakistan versus India, and North Vietnam (as the Chinese J.6) against the USA. Poorly flown, it achieved little in Egyptian service, but Pakistani ace Sayed Sa'ad Hatmi scored three of his five victories with the type. Cleverly handled by the North Vietnamese, it proved a formidable opponent to the Phantom, especially when armed with K-13A AAMs.

The MiG-19P carried an RP-1 Izumrud AI radar in the nose, and only two 30mm cannon. The final major variant was the MiG-19PM, in which the cannon were deleted. Armament consisted of four beam-riding K-5M AAMs on underwing pylons. Much development of the MiG-19 was rendered void by the advent of the MiG-21.

Right: The MiG-19PM was armed with four beam-riding K-5M missiles.

Mikoyan-Guryevich MiG-21bis

Origin: Mikoyan-Guryevich OKB, Soviet Union.
Type: Single-seat, single-engined bisonic jet fighter.
Engine: One Tumansky R-25-300 twin-spool axial-flow afterburning turbojet rated at 15,653lb (7,100kg) maximum and 9,039lb (4,100kg) military thrust. Plus a special afterburning rating of 21,826lb (9,900kg) for short periods below 13,124ft (4,000m).
Dimensions: Span 23ft 5.5in (7.15m); length 48ft 2.3in (14.70m); height 13ft 6.5in (4.13m); wing area 248sq.ft (23.00m^2).
Weights: Empty 13,492lb (6,120kg); normal takeoff 19,235lb (8,725kg); maximum 21,605lb (9,800kg).
Loadings (at normal takeoff weight and normal max thrust)**:** Wing 78lb/sq.ft (379kg/m^2); thrust 0.81.
Performance: Maximum speed 1,352mph (2,175kph) Mach 2.05 at 42,653ft (13,000m), 808mph (1,300kph) Mach 1.22 at sea level; initial climb rate 45,278ft/min (230m/sec); sustained climb rate 8min 30sec to 55,777ft (17,000m); service ceiling 57,418ft (17,500m); range 761 miles (1,225km).
Armament: One 23mm GSh-23 cannon with 200 rounds; two or four K-60 AAMs.
History: First flight of prototype (I-500) 16 June 1955. Service introduction (MiG-21F) 1958. First missile-armed variant MiG-21F-13, with two K-13. Combat debut 1963. Produced in 15 main variants in the Soviet Union between 1958 and 1987. Licence-built in Czechoslovakia, India, and China. Chinese production continued through 2001 as the J.7MG. Total production of all variants c13,500.
Users: Afghanistan, Albania, Algeria, Angola, Azerbaijan, Bangladesh,

***Above:* First flown almost 50 years ago, the MiG-21 remains in widespread service.**

Bourkina Faso, Bulgaria, Cambodia, China (People's Republic), Congo, Croatia, Cuba, Czech Republic, East Germany, Egypt, Ethiopia, Finland, Hungary, India, Iran, Iraq, Laos, Libya, Madagascar, Mongolia, Mozambique, Myanmar,

Nigeria, North Korea, Pakistan, Poland, Romania, Slovakia, Somalia, Soviet Union, Sri Lanka, Sudan, Syria, Tanzania, Turkmenistan, Uganda, Vietnam, Yemen, Yugoslavia, Zambia, Zimbabwe.

The MiG-21, NATO reporting name Fishbed, arose from a 1954 programme for an interceptor capable of catching fast and high-flying nuclear-armed bombers. The requirements were a speed of Mach 2, a high rate of climb, an operational ceiling of about 65,620ft (20,000m), missile compatibility, and range only radar. It had to be easily maintainable (a fault of the MiG-19), easy to fly, and affordable in large numbers.

It is therefore ironic that what emerged is best known as an austere and agile tactical fighter. The MiG-21 has served with more air forces and nations than any other fighter, has taken part in more conflicts than any other, and has almost invariably ended up on the losing side. Despite this unenviable reputation, which brands it as a turkey, more than 3,000 remain in the inventories of 37 nations, making it a prime target for upgrading. Why was it so popular?

The answer is complex. In the 1950s and 1960s, Mach 2 was regarded as essential, especially for interception. Be that as it may, combat experience in limited wars over the past four decades has shown that not only was Mach 2 never approached, but that little time was spent at speeds in excess of Mach 1.2. The lines of thrust versus drag crossed at slightly above Mach 2, but the short-legged early versions of the MiG-21 would probably have run out of fuel before getting there.

The fact was that Mach 2 was fashionable, and national self-esteem demanded a bisonic fighter, even though some defence needs might have been better served by attack aircraft such as the A-7 Corsair or the Su-25 Frogfoot. In practice, the Soviet Union and China made the MiG-21 widely available on favourable terms, to those nations that they sought to influence.

In 1954, the MiG OKB was initially unable to decide which wing was best: thin and highly swept, or a delta. To resolve this, a series of prototypes with both wing types were built. The delta I-500 (Ye-4) was first flown by Grigoriy

Below: Poland is just one of 47 countries to have operated the MiG-21.

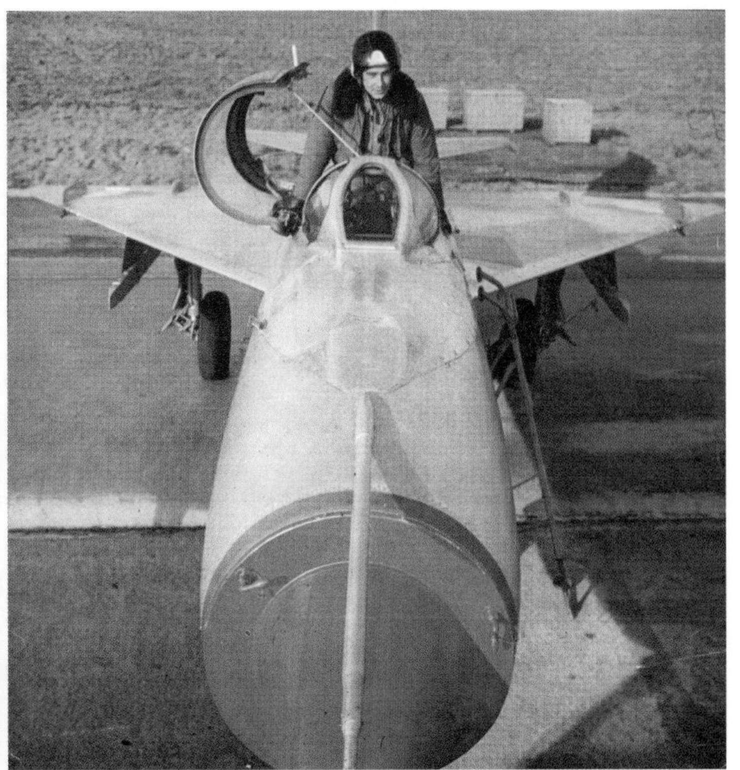

Above: The thick windshield framing severely restricts the pilot's view.

Sedov on 16 June 1955, a few months later than the swept-winged Ye-2. It was joined in flight test from January 1956 by the similar Ye-5. This was powered by the Mikulin AM-11 afterburning turbojet rated at 11,243lb (5,100kg) thrust. After an evaluation lasting until 20 September 1956, the delta wing was selected.

The next step was three Ye-6 prototypes, which were built and flight tested in 1957-58. They were powered by the Tumansky R-11F-300, rated at 12,654lb (5,740kg) maximum and 8,554lb (3,880kg) military thrust. The first Ye-6 reached Mach 2.05 at 39,536ft (12,050m), but on its seventh flight crashed on landing, killing test pilot Vladimir Nefyedov.

The third Ye-6 first flew in December 1958, and as the Ye-66 set a new absolute speed record of 1,484mph (2,388kph) Mach 2.24, flown by Georgiy Mosolov. This was the first of a hatful of records set over the years by modified MiG-21s.

The first production model was the MiG-21F (Ye-6T). The delta wing had a 57deg leading edge sweep, and Fowler flaps inboard of the ailerons. The pitot intake contained a three-position shock cone, which in turn housed an SRD-5 ranging radar, and armament consisted of two 30mm NR-30 cannon with 60 rounds per gun. Only 40 MiG-21Fs were built.

The MiG-21F was replaced on the production lines in 1960 by the MiG-21F-13, which carried two K-13 AAMs on underwing pylons. Other differences were a broader fin, fully variable afterburner, and the SRD-5M Kvant ranging radar.

This variant was produced in the Soviet Union until 1965, in Czechoslovakia until 1972, and formed the basis of the Chinese J-7.

Production of the MiG-21P commenced in June 1960. This had a limited night and adverse weather capability. The TsD-30T radar was housed in an enlarged fixed centrebody, causing the nose to be lengthened and widened to provide the same mass flow. The cannon were deleted, leaving only two K-13 AAMs. An extra fuel tank was inserted behind the cockpit. Next came the MiG-21PF. This had a translating shock cone housing the new RP-21 Sapfir radar, and the R-11F2-300 turbojet rated at 13,492lb (6,120kg) maximum and 8,708lb (3,950kg) military thrust. An enlarged dorsal spine housed more fuel, at the expense of rearward visibility, which went from appalling to non-existent. Provision was made for a GP-9 gun pack, holding a 23mm GsH-23 twin-barrel cannon.

A downgraded MiG-21PF, known as a "monkey" variant, was produced for export. This was the MiG-21FL. It had the inferior R-2L radar, and the same powerplant as the MiG-21F. The FL was also licence-built in India by HAL until 1968. Other "monkey" variants were exported, including the MiG-21PFS.

The MiG-21PF was replaced on the production lines by the MiG-21PFM from 1965. This had an enlarged fin, a tail parachute as standard, blown flaps, and the slightly more powerful R-11F2S-300 turbojet. Radar was the RP-21M, and standard armament was two K-5M beam-riding AAMs. Whereas the windshield and canopy on previous models had opened forwards to protect the pilot in the event of an ejection, on the PFM the windshield was fixed and the canopy hinged sideways.

Between 1965 and 1968, the MiG-21S was an interceptor powered by the R-11F2S-300 and flap blowing. To improve all-weather capability it had the

Lazur-M guidance system, the RP-22S radar, and for the first time a three-axis autopilot. It was succeeded by the MiG-21SM from 1968. This had an integral gun, the twin-barrel 23mm GsH-23L cannon with 200 rounds, and a gunsight designed to cope with hard manoeuvring targets. Its "monkey" version was the 21M, and, unusually, this itself was upgraded as the MiG-21MF, powered by the Tumansky R-13-300 and able to carry four K-13 AAMs. Up to this point all MiG-21s had been lacking in speed at low level; this engine corrected the deficiency. It came as a nasty surprise to American flyers over Vietnam in 1972.

In 1971, an attempt to increase internal fuel capacity by 20 per cent, most of it in an enormous dorsal spine, resulted in the MiG-21MT. A transitional type, only 15 were built, and the next step was to combine the airframe and weapons system of the MF and the engine and fuel capacity of the MT to give the SMT. This had stability problems, which were cured only by reducing fuel in the spine by one third.

The definitive Fishbed was the MiG-21bis, with the R-25-300 turbojet, improved avionics, and four AAMs, typically two K-60Ms and two K-13Ms. This was produced in the Soviet Union between 1972 and 1975, and under licence by HAL until 1987.

The overall kill/loss ratio of the MiG-21 makes depressing reading. It was fast and agile. Why did it not do better? The main reason is probably the appalling view from the cockpit. A pilot could just about see the leading edges of his wings, but nothing astern of that, and, like the MiG-17, the view over the nose and sideways and downwards was far from adequate. It was therefore easy to surprise. The controls were heavy, and it was difficult to manoeuvre

Below: The MiG-21 PFM had a greatly enlarged vertical tail as seen here.

below 248mph (398kph) or above 587mph (945kph). The afterburner took between five and seven seconds to light. Finally, the gunsight was inadequate at more than 3g. Agile or not, it was an inferior weapons system. Oddly, the short range was not a disadvantage over Vietnam; rarely did a MiG stray more than 40 miles (64km) from its base.

Given the combat record, why bother to upgrade such an obvious turkey? The short answer is that for many nations, buying new is unaffordable, but zero-lifing the airframe and installing a whole new avionics and weapons package should produce a much more capable fighter. Typical is the Romanian/Israeli Lancer package, with a "glass cockpit", HOTAS, a multi-mode radar, and state of the art avionics. And if you must have something new, go to China for the latest J-7!

Right: The definitive Fishbed was the MiG-21bis, seen here with four AAMs.

Mikoyan-Guryevich MiG-23MF

Origin: Mikoyan-Guryevich OKB, Soviet Union.
Type: Single-seat, single-engined bisonic variable-geometry jet fighter.
Engine: One Khachaturov R-29-300 twin-spool axial-flow afterburning turbojet rated at 27,558lb (12,500kg) maximum and 18,298lb (8,300kg) military thrust.
Dimensions: Span 45ft 9.8in (13.97m) at 16deg sweep, 25ft 6.25in (7.78m) at 72deg sweep; length 55ft 6in (16.92m); height 14ft 4in (4.37m); wing area at 16deg sweep 402sq.ft (37.35m²), at 72deg sweep 368sq.ft (34.16m²).
Weights: Empty 23,909lb (10,845kg); normal takeoff 34,722lb (15,750kg); maximum 45,569lb (20,670kg).
Loadings (at normal takeoff weight and 72deg sweep)**:** Wing 94lb/sq.ft (461kg/m²); thrust 0.79.
Performance: Maximum speed 1,547mph (2,490kph) Mach 2.35 at 41,013ft (12,500m), 839mph (1,350kph) Mach 1.1 at sea level; initial climb rate 45,278ft/min (230m/sec); service ceiling 60,042ft (18,300m); range 1,181 miles (1,900km).

Right: The MiG-23 had variable-sweep wings for good short field performance.

Armament: One 23mm GSh-23L cannon with 200 rounds; typically two R-23 and four R-60 AAMs.
History: First flight of prototype 23-11 10 June 1967. First flight of production aircraft (MiG-23S) 28 May 1969. Service introduction 1971. Combat debut probably Beka'a 1982. Production ceased in 1985, with a total of 5,047 of all types, including two-seater trainers. Withdrawn from Russian service 1994.
Users: Algeria, Angola, Belarus, Bulgaria, Cuba, Czechoslovakia, East Germany, Egypt, Ethiopia, Finland, Hungary, India, Iraq, Kazakhstan, Libya, North Korea, Poland, Romania, Soviet Union/Russia, Sudan, Syria, Turkmenistan, Zimbabwe.

In the early 1960s, during the uneasy standoff between NATO and the Warsaw Pact, military aircraft were totally dependent on fixed bases with long, vulnerable runways. If these could be put out of commission, the aircraft on them would be grounded. The Soviet solution was improved short field performance. The Mikoyan OKB, under the direction of Grigoriy Sedov, by now chief designer, attacked the problem on two fronts.

First to fly was the 23-01, on 3 April 1967, with Piotr Ostapyenko at the controls. This was a tailed delta wing with a turbojet for conventional flight, and two lift-jets amidships. There was no attempt at VTOL; the lift-jets were to reduce takeoff and landing runs. In this it succeeded; takeoff distance was no more than 656ft (200m), and landing roll 820ft (250m). But after extensive testing, the OKB concluded that it had little potential as a combat aircraft, and the programme was terminated.

Mikoyan-Guryevich MiG-25P

Origin: Mikoyan-Guryevich OKB, Soviet Union.
Type: Single-seat, twin-engined, high-speed, high-altitude interceptor.
Engines: Two Tumanskiy R-15B-300 single-spool axial-flow afterburning turbojets each rated at 22,509lb (10,210kg) maximum and 16,535lb (7,500kg) military thrust.
Dimensions: Span 46ft 0in (14.02m); length 64ft 9.5in (19.75m); height 18ft 6in (5.64m); wing area 661sq.ft (60.40m^2).
Weights: Empty c44,000lb (19,960kg); takeoff with four R-40 AAMs 80,953lb (36,720kg).
Loadings (at takeoff weight)**:** Wing 122lb/sq.ft (608kg/m^2); thrust 0.56.
Performance: Maximum speed 1,864mph (3,000kph) Mach 2.83 at 42,653ft (13,000m), 746mph (1,200kph) Mach 0.98 at sea level; sustained climb rate 8min 54sec to 65,620ft (20,000m); service ceiling 78,088ft (23,800m); range 777 miles (1,250km).
Armament: Typically four R-60 AAMs, two SARH and two IR homing.
History: Studies commenced c1960. Prototypes ordered February 1962. First flight of interceptor prototype Ye-155P-1 on 9 September 1964. Service entry 1973. Mass production 1969 to 1985; total of 1,186. Withdrawn from Russian service 1994.
Users: Algeria, Armenia, Azerbaijan, India, Iraq, Kazakhstan, Libya, Soviet Union/Russia, Syria, Turkmenistan.

Between July 1956 and May 1960, the Soviet Union had to bear the humiliation of high-altitude overflights by the American U-2 reconnaissance aircraft. Barely did it seem that they had found a solution to this when they became aware that the USA was working on Project Oxcart, the A-12, which would not only fly much higher than the U-2, but was to be trisonic. This could not go unchallenged, but the problems of intercepting an aircraft travelling at more

Developed in parallel, the 23-11, first flown by Alexsandr Fedotov on 10 April 1967, showed more promise. It had variable-sweep wings, lavishly equipped with flaps on both leading and trailing edges. At minimum sweep it created a lot of lift, which permitted takeoff and landing distances short enough to allow it to be operated from damaged runways, or even semi-prepared strips. Where it really scored was in potential payload/range, an area in which the 23-01, handicapped by the weight and volume of two lift engines, could not compete. The aircraft was ordered into production as the MiG-23, NATO reporting name Flogger.

Three sweep angles were used: 16deg for takeoff, landing, and economic cruise; 45deg for combat manoeuvre, for which it was stressed to 8g; and 72deg for acceleration and high speed flight. Roll control was provided by differentially moving tailerons and spoilers. Variable-geometry side intakes were used, leaving the nose free for the capable Sapfir-23D-Sh radar, which was compatible with semi-active homing missiles.

The first major production variant was the MiG-23MF, produced between 1970 and 1976, followed by the rather better MiG-23ML until 1981. Its weapons system was good, but it had the typical MiG fault – a poor view from the cockpit. Nor did it turn well: an instantaneous rate of 11.5deg/sec at Mach 0.9 at 15,093ft (4,600m), reducing to 8.6deg/sec at Mach 0.5 at the same altitude.

The fighter's air combat record is abysmal, approaching 50 to nil at the end of 2001, and its main claim to fame is in the attack role and as progenitor of the MiG-27. About 1,400 remain in the inventories of 18 air forces, but at least half are unserviceable or in storage.

Above: The MiG-25 Foxbat was the fastest fighter ever to enter service.

than a mile (1.74km) every two seconds were extreme.

The MiG OKB immediately began the preliminary design of an ultra-high-speed, ultra-high-altitude interceptor with an exceptional rate of climb. The *modus operandi* was to cut the intruder off with a front quarter attack; the speeds involved made jockeying for the traditional attack from astern impossible, even with missile armament. But from the front quarter, with closing speeds in excess of 50 miles (80km) per minute, the timing had to be near-perfect. As with the American F-106 Delta Dart, automatic control from the ground was the only possible solution, leaving the pilot responsible for takeoff, fuel and systems monitoring, target acquisition and weapons release, and return to base and landing. Also needed was a medium-range radar which would be impervious to jamming, and very large medium-range AAMs, to give an intruder no second chance.

At the time, Soviet technology was at least ten years in arrears of the USA in all fields. There were no suitable engines; titanium alloys were known but were very difficult to work; the miniaturisation of electronics and missile technology were still in the stone age. The Mikoyan designers had to make do with what was available. They succeeded remarkably well!

The engines were based on those used by a high-altitude reconnaissance drone. Optimised for maximum performance in the top right hand corner of the envelope, they were single-spool, cooled by water/methanol injection, backed by a huge afterburner. The penalty was that they were extremely inefficient at low altitudes and subsonic speeds.

Using full 'burner for takeoff, climb, and the interception meant that fuel consumption was enormous, even using special high-density T-6. The answer was to pack fuel into every conceivable space. Occupying 70 per cent of the total volume, internal fuel weighed an enormous 32,120lb (14,570kg). This was used so rapidly that an automatic fuel transfer system was needed to keep the centre of gravity within limits.

The greatest problem was kinetic heating, which in certain areas could reach 300deg Celsius. This ruled out the use of aluminium alloy, except in a few non-critical places. Given the Soviet state of the art, titanium could be used only in simple applications such as wing leading edges and around the tailpipes. By default, most of the structure was welded nickel steel, even for the integral fuel tanks. The weight penalty was potentially excessive but, to minimise this, structural strength was limited to a maximum load factor of 4.5g at supersonic speed.

Other heating problems were encountered. The original canopy softened at high speed, and needed a new material, as did the dielectric radome. As the biggest single heat source, the engines were insulated with silver-plated steel sheets wrapped in fibreglass.

Below: At maximum speed and altitude, these MiG-25Rs are hard to intercept.

Radar was the Smertch-A. Since interception was primarily the province of ground control, it did not need a long detection range. With a tracking range of 31 miles (50km), the main priority was to defeat hostile jamming. This it did by "burning through" with sheer power, of the order of 600 watts, using old-fashioned thermionic valves. Reputed to be able to kill a rabbit at 650ft (200m), the microwave effect was such that using it close to the ground was a court-martial offence.

The first flight of the MiG-25, NATO reporting name Foxbat, took place on 6 March 1964, piloted by Aleksandr Fedotov. This was actually a reconnaissance variant; the interceptor prototype first flew on 9 September, piloted by Piotr Ostapyenko. Having pushed the state of the art so hard, development was slow, and Foxbat was not certified until 1970, and did not enter service until 1973.

The MiG-25 was a huge and rather brutal-looking aeroplane. The engines were fed by steeply raked variable lateral intakes; the 5deg anhedral wing had a compound leading edge sweep, 42.5deg inboard and 41deg outboard, with two small fences per side. The differentially moving tailerons were swept at 50deg and the twin fins were cropped and outwardly canted at 11deg.

Between 1965 and 1973, the Ye-266 (stripped MiG-25), set 16 world records, including that for absolute altitude, 118,867ft (36,240m). From 1979, all MiG-25Ps were upgraded to PD standard. These had more powerful engines, the Sapfir-25 radar with a look-down, shoot-down capability, and an infra-red sensor.

Foxbats have seen little action. In 1973 one was tracked over Sinai at Mach 3.2, although it was later discovered that it had wrecked its engines in the process. Otherwise its air combat record is an uninspiring 0-5.

Right: This MiG-25P Foxbat E carries four enormous R-60 air-to-air missiles.

Mikoyan-Guryevich MiG-29SM

Origin: Military-Industrial Group (MiG) MAPO, Russia.
Type: Single-seat, twin-engined bisonic air superiority fighter.
Engines: Two Klimov RD-33K twin-spool axial-flow afterburning turbofans each rated at 19,400lb (8,800kg) maximum and 12,125lb (5,500kg) military thrust.
Dimensions: Span 37ft 3.25in (11.36m); length 56ft 10in (17.32m); height 15ft 6.25in (4.73m); wing area 409sq.ft (38.00m^2).
Weights: Empty 24,030lb (10,900kg); normal takeoff with 6 AAMs 34,392lb (15,600kg); maximum 44,092kg (20,000kg).
Loadings (at normal takeoff weight)**:** Wing 84lb/sq.ft (411kg/m^2); thrust 1.13.
Performance: Maximum speed 1,518mph (2,445kph) Mach 2.30 at 39,372ft (12,000m), 808mph (1,300kph) Mach 1.06 at sea level; initial climb rate 64,964ft/min (330m/sec); service ceiling 55,777ft (17,000m); range 932 miles (1,500km).
Armament: One 30mm GSh-30-1 single-barrel cannon with 100 rounds. Typically six R-77, or four R-27 and four R-73 or R-60 AAMs.
History: First flight of prototype 6 October 1977. Service entry July 1983. Mass production from 1982; total continuing as at 2002 c1,600. Combat debut, Gulf War 1991.
Users: Algeria, Bangladesh, Belarus, Bulgaria, Cuba, Eritrea, Hungary, India, Iran, Kazakhstan, Malaysia, Moldova, Myanmar, North Korea, Peru, Poland, Romania, Slovakia, Soviet Union/Russia, Syria, Turkmenistan, Ukraine, Uzbekistan, Yugoslavia.

Above: A near-perfect plan view of the MiG-29 seen at Farnborough 1988.

The performance versus agility debate, which had commenced in 1917, had still not been conclusively settled 50 years later, despite astounding advances in weaponry and systems. The austere and agile MiG-21 had singularly failed to gain a decisive ascendancy over the powerful and sophisticated but unhandy F-4 Phantom in Vietnam and the Middle East. The Soviet Air Force had then switched to the performance-oriented MiG-23 which, although it turned like a tram, had a true "shoot 'em in the face" beyond visual range (BVR) capability. Meanwhile the USA, unhappy with the war record of the Phantom, sought greater agility combined with capability. This resulted in the F-15 Eagle although, as related, the American superfighter was designed to counter an erroneous intelligence appreciation of the MiG-25 Foxbat.

With the F-15 unaffordable in sufficient quantities, the USA then commenced the Lightweight Fighter (LWF) programme, which led to the F-16 Fighting Falcon, and still later to the F/A-18 Hornet carrier fighter.

From the Soviet viewpoint, the threat was about to change dramatically, and their latest and greatest, the MiG-23, while adequate for BVR slashing attacks, was a turkey in a dogfight situation. With something better badly needed, the front line light fighter (*Legkiy Frontovoy Istrebityel*) project, with agility paramount, commenced in 1971.

The Central Institute of Aero-Hydrodynamics (TsAGI) produced an optimised layout which formed the basis of the LFI, later the MiG-29, NATO reporting name Fulcrum. Radically different from anything that the MiG OKB had produced before, it was arguably a middleweight rather than a lightweight fighter. The first flight of the prototype, by Alexsandr Fedotov, took place on 6 October 1977. Progress was slow and, in all, 19 prototypes were needed to bring it to the point where production could begin.

Many early problems were encountered with the twin engines. They were very widely spaced, and "straight-through" from inlets to nozzles. The Klimov RD-33 was among the first Russian military turbofans and, although it has never been confirmed, it seems possible that the wide spacing was adopted to guard against disturbed airflow; a problem which had afflicted

the much earlier American TF30 of the F-111 and F-14.

What is certain is that engine problems were rife in the early days. Future Mikoyan chief test pilot Valeriy Eugenievich Menitskiy ejected from the second prototype following an engine fire in mid-1978, while Fedotov himself followed suit from the fourth prototype on 31 October 1980.

The LFI first came to the attention of the West in November 1977, when it was photographed at Ramenskoye by a U.S. satellite and given the reporting name Ram-L. The first MiG-29s were delivered to the 234th Fighter Air Regiment at Kubinka in July 1983, but state acceptance trials were not completed until the following year. Then, in July 1986, the West got its first good look at the MiG-29 when six aircraft visited Finland.

The turbofans were carried in widely spaced underslung nacelles, joined by a pancake-like rear fuselage. They had convergent-divergent nozzles at the hot end, and steeply raked variable ramp intakes at the front, to allow maximum speeds in excess of Mach 2. A previously unseen feature was the use of top-hinged perforated inlet doors which closed when the aircraft was on the ground. These were to prevent the ingestion of ice or small stones, and when in use the engines were fed via louvred doors above large wing leading edge extensions. Apart from during takeoff and landing, the doors could also be closed in flight at speeds of up to 497mph (800kph), which was handy against bird strikes. Obviously the Klimovs were not sensitive to disturbed airflow, although like all Russian military jet engines of the period they had a very short time between overhauls.

The wings were swept at the modest angle of 42deg and had, by Western standards, a relatively high aspect ratio of 3.5. Three-piece computer-controlled manoeuvre flaps occupied the leading edges, while the trailing edge carried slotted flaps inboard with ailerons outboard.

The more steeply swept tailerons were mounted on booms outboard of the engines, while the twin fins and rudders were typically Mikoyan in shape, with cropped tips. The fin leading edges carried forward onto the

Below: The MiG-29SM has more powerful turbofans and increased fuel tankage.

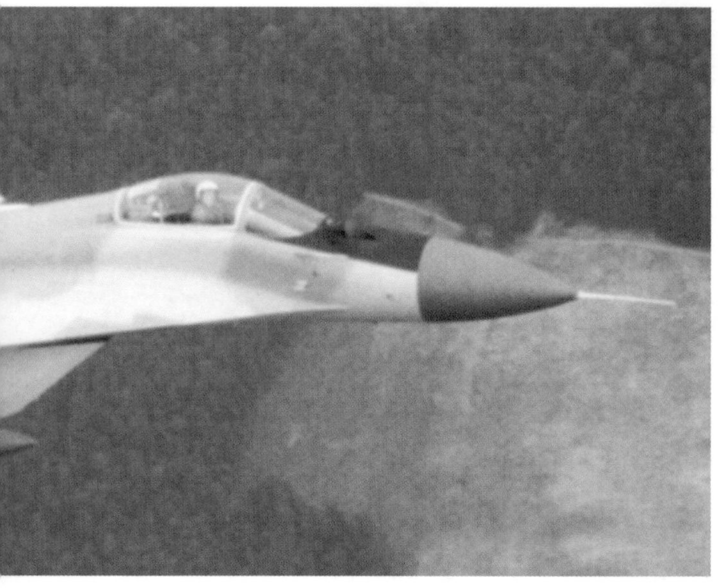

upper wing surfaces, and were used to house flare dispensers.

Construction was largely conventional – steel and aluminium/ lithium with only small areas of composites – while the flight control system wa hydraulic. The view "out of the window" was better than that of an previous MiG fighter, but still limited by Western standards, and the cockp instrumentation was "steam-gauge". The fire control system was howeve innovative. An IRST/laser rangefinder gave extremely accurate tracking, an if the target disappeared into cloud, the Phazotron N-019 Zhuk radar too over automatically. This gave exceptional accuracy to the single-barre 30mm GSh-30-1 cannon in the port wing root. In addition, a helme mounted sight allowed R-73 AAMs to be launched at high off-boresigh angles.

The time-honoured method of producing a conversion trainer was t reduce fuel capacity to make space for a second seat. As the single-seate was already short on endurance, this was not a viable option. The solutio adopted was to put the second cockpit ahead of the first, displacing th radar, although the optronics were retained. The fin extensions with flar dispensers were also omitted. The resulting MiG-29UB was not comba capable.

Also in keeping with Russian tradition, Fulcrum has been continuous

Right: A good view of the closed inlet louvres above the MiG 29 LERX.

Below: Distorted by a fish-eye lens, this shows the wide-spaced engines

upgraded. The MiG-29S had an enlarged dorsal spine to house extra fuel, two hardpoints plumbed for external tanks, five-section leading edge flaps,and the N-019M radar which was compatible with the R-77 active radar missile, and which allowed simultaneous engagement of two targets. The SE was an export variant with downgraded avionics.

First flown by Valery Menitskiy on 25 April 1986, the MiG-29M was radically different. This had an analogue fly-by-wire system, and a modified wing with a new aerofoil section. More powerful RD-33K turbofans demanded enlarged intakes, and the intake blanks were scrapped in favour of mesh guards. This made the overwing intake louvres redundant, and these gave way to increased fuel tankage. Ammunition for the cannon was reduced to 100 rounds. Other external changes were larger horizontal tails with notched leading edges, and a modified speed brake. The cockpit was raised to improve the all-round view; two multi-function displays were fitted, plus an improved radar.

Although the MiG-29M failed to enter service, it formed the basis of future types, the first of which was the MiG-29K carrier fighter. First flown by Takhtar Aubakirov on 23 June 1988, it differed in having a strengthened structure and landing gear, a larger folding wing, a tail hook, and a retractable refuelling probe. Although not selected for the Russian Navy, the MiG-29K is expected to enter service with the Indian Navy in about 2004.

Most recent variant is the MiG-29SMT, with increased internal fuel capacity and a modern "glass" cockpit. Russia is updating about 300 early models to this true multi-role configuration.

As at spring 2002, Fulcrum has seen action with three air arms. In the Gulf War of 1991, five Iraqi MiG-29s were shot down by USAF F-15s. Then in February 1999, two Eritrean MiG-29s, believed flown by Ukrainians, were shot down by Ethiopian Su-27s believed flown by Russian pilots. Shortly after, five Yugoslav MiG-29s were downed over the Balkans, one by a Netherlands F-16 and four by USAF F-15s. A victory/loss ratio of 0-12 is hardly impressive!

Right: The IRST/laser rangefinder sensor is offset to clear the HUD.

Mikoyan-Guryevich MiG-31B

Origin: Military-Industrial Group (MiG) MAPO, Russia.
Type: Two-seat, twin-engined bisonic long-range interceptor.
Engines: Two Aviadvigatel/Perm D-30F-6 twin-spool axial-flow afterburning turbofans each rated at 38,581lb (17,500kg) maximum and 20,944lb (9,500kg) military thrust.
Dimensions: Span 44ft 2in (13.46m); length 74ft 5in (22.69m); height 20ft 2in (6.15m); wing area 663sq.ft (61.60m^2).
Weights: Empty 48,104lb (21,820kg); normal takeoff 90,389lb (41,000kg); maximum 101,853kg (46,200kg).
Loadings (at normal takeoff weight)**:** Wing 136lb/sq.ft (666kg/m^2); thrust 0.85.
Performance: Maximum speed 1,864mph (3,000kph) Mach 2.83 at altitude, 932mph (1,500kph) Mach 1.23 at sea level; supersonic cruise 1,553mph (2,500kph) at altitude; sustained climb rate 7min 54sec to 32,810ft (10,000m); operational ceiling 67,589ft (20,600m); supersonic combat radius 447 miles (720km); endurance with external tanks 3hr 36min.
Armament: One 23mm GSh-23-6 six-barrel cannon with 260 rounds. Four long-range R-33, and either two R-40TD or four R-60M AAMs.
History: First flight of prototype (Ye-155MP) 16 September 1975. Production commenced 1979. Initial operational capability 1983. Low-rate production continuing at spring 2002, about 400 total.
Users: Kazakhstan, Soviet Union/Russia.

Initial design work on the MiG-31, NATO reporting name Foxhound,

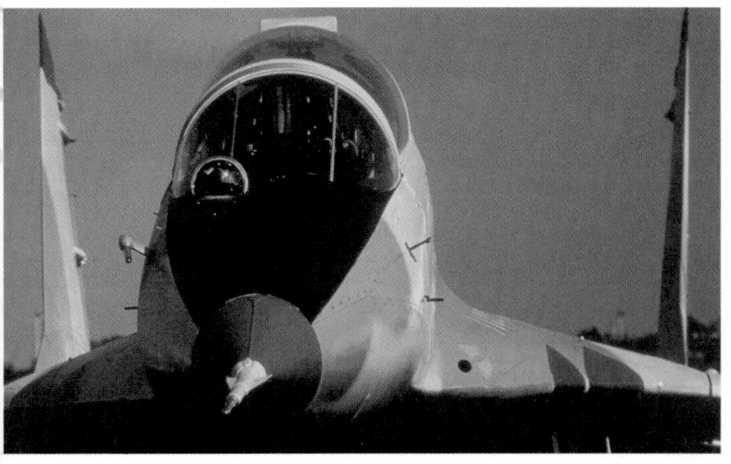

began in 1972, to counter the threat of American cruise missiles. While it was based on the MiG-25, it needed to be able to operate autonomously, to have far greater endurance with similar performance, to be supersonic at low altitudes, and to engage multiple small targets. To achieve these aims, far more economical engines and a superior weapons system were required, the latter with a specialist operator.

Surprisingly, the D-30F-6 engines were developed from a commercial turbofan adapted to use high-density T-6 fuel. The bypass ratio was reduced to 0.50, and an enormous afterburner was developed. With a turbine entry temperature limit of 1,660K, very sophisticated cooling was needed.

The fuselage was lengthened to accommodate a second seat for the

Below: Foxhound is essentially a far more capable two-seater Foxbat.

weapons systems operator, who was enclosed under a metal canopy, with only small transparencies through which to view the outside world. But, whereas Foxhound looked very much like Foxbat, under the skin it was very different.

Foxbat had consisted of 80 per cent nickel steel, 8 per cent titanium, and 11 per cent aluminium. In Foxhound these percentages became 50, 16, and 33, respectively. The weight savings that might have resulted from these changes was more than swallowed up in other areas, and Foxhound was even heavier than its predecessor.

The intakes were enlarged to accept the increased mass flow, and a third main spar was added to the wing box to strengthen it for supersonic flight at low level. Small extensions were added to the wing leading edge roots, four-piece titanium flaps occupied the entire wing leading edge, and at supersonic speeds the load limit was relaxed from 4.5g to 5g. Fuel was

Mikoyan 1.44 MFI

Origin: Military-Industrial Group (MiG) MAPO, Russia.
Type: Single-seat, twin-engined bisonic multirole fighter.
Engines: Two Lyulka AI-41F twin-spool axial-flow afterburning turbofans each rated at c39,683lb (18,000kg) maximum and (estimated) 24,250lb (11,000kg) military thrust, with variable nozzles.
Dimensions: No figures available but 1.44 is dimensionally large.
Weights (all estimated)**:** Empty 44,092lb (20,000kg); normal takeoff 61,729lb (28,000kg); maximum 77,161kg (35,000kg).
Loadings (at normal takeoff weight)**:** Wing n/a; thrust 1.29.
Performance (all estimated)**:** Maximum speed Mach 2.50 at altitude, supersonic cruise speed Mach 1.5; supersonic range 1,243 miles (2,000km).
Armament: Probably one 30mm GSh-30-1 cannon; four or six medium range R-37 and R-77 AAMs in internal bays.
History: Detail design begun 1986; taxi trials December 1994, first flight 16 February 2000 (some sources state 29 February).
Users: None.

Conceived as a counter to the American Advanced Tactical Fighter programme, the 1.44 MFI (*Mnogo Funktsionalny Istrebityel*) has been subject to unprecedented delays, and will no longer be considered for service. Like the F-22A, it was to be stealthy, agile, and able to cruise at supersonic speeds without using afterburning.

The 1.44 was delivered to Zhukovsky in 1994, and in December of that year high-speed taxi trials were carried out by Roman Taska'ev. Delays were at first attributed to technical problems, then later to lack of funding, although on several occasions it was erroneously stated to have flown. Rumours then circulated as to its reality, and it was presented in public in January 1999. Even then the first flight, by Vladimir Gorbunov, was delayed by more than a year, and little has been attempted since.

A large canard delta, the layout makes few concessions to stealth. The nose, containing a phased array radar, has just the faintest hint of chines, while no sawtooth or W-shaped edges are apparent. The variable inlets are boxy, although serpentine ducts lead to the compressor faces. The main crammed in everywhere possible, including "wet" fins, and a rather crude, semi-retractable flight refuelling probe was fitted on the port side just ahead of the cockpit.

The first prototype was actually a heavily modified Foxbat, the Ye 155MP, flown by chief test pilot Alexsandr Fedotov on 16 September 1975, but four years passed before Foxhound was ready for production. Internal fuel weight was a massive 36,035lb (16,350kg), and to keep the centre of gravity within limits in flight this had to be constantly shifted around the various tanks. Development was not without cost; on 4 April 1984, Fedotov and his backseater were killed after a systems failure.

Operational with the 786th Air Defence Fighter Regiment from 1983, Foxhound scored a notable first in the fighter world: as revealed at Le Bourget in 1991, the Phazotron S-800 Zaslon radar had a fixed phased array antenna. It can track up to ten targets, and engage four simultaneously.

---

missile armament is housed in internal bays, although external pylons are evident beneath the wings. The twin fins are canted outwards at a shallow angle, and supplemented by small moveable ventral fins beneath them, a first for a fighter. Finally, the external finish is crude, which would not help stealth.

The main stealth feature was to have been plasma shielding, using a thin layer of ionised gas to protect against hostile radar emissions. As pure speculation, it is possible that this could not be made to work, hence the interminable delays.

Below: The 1-44 was to have been the Russian answer to the F-22A Raptor.

Mitsubishi A5M4

Origin: Mitsubishi Jukogyo Kabushiki Kaisha, Japan.
Type: Single-seat, single-engined monoplane carrier fighter.
Engine: One Nakajima Kotobuki 41 nine-cylinder radial engine rated at 785hp at 9,843ft (3,000m).
Dimensions: Span 36ft 1in (11.00m); length 24ft 9.5in (7.56m); height 10ft 8.5in (3.27m); wing area 192sq.ft ($17.80m^2$).
Weights: Empty 2,784lb (1,263kg); normal takeoff 3,650lb (1,655kg); maximum 4,017lb (1,822kg).
Loadings (at normal takeoff weight)**:** Wing 19lb/sq.ft ($93kg/m^2$); power 4.65lb (2.11kg) per hp.
Performance: Maximum speed 270mph (435kph) at 9,843ft (3,000m); sustained climb rate 3in 34sec to 9,843ft (3,000m); service ceiling 31,990ft (9,750m); range 746 miles (1,200km) with drop tank; endurance 2hr 30min.
Armament: Two 7.7mm nose-mounted Type 89 synchronised machine guns.
History: First flight (as Ka-14) 4 February 1935. Accepted for service autumn 1936. Combat debut, China December 1937. Production ceased early 1941 with a total of 982 of all variants. Withdrawn from front line service mid-1942.
User: Japan (Navy).

Designed to a 1934 specification, the Ka-14 was an all-metal semi-monocoque stressed skin monoplane with a gull wing and fixed undercarriage. After the first flight, on 4 February 1935, the gull wing was omitted from the second prototype, which had split flaps. The type was selected for further development, and by the autumn of 1936 had passed its service trials. Produced as the A5M1 Type 96, and given the Western reporting name of Claude, it was the first single-seat cantilever carrier fighter to enter service.

It was followed in the late spring of 1937 by the A5M2, which differed from its predecessor mainly in having a more powerful engine. This initially had an enclosed canopy with an aft-sliding hood, but this feature was unpopular with the pilots, and it was abandoned. The A5M3 was purely experimental, with a

Hispano-Suiza liquid-cooled engine and a 20mm engine-mounted cannon. Only two were built.

The Sino-Japanese conflict broke out on 7 July 1937. On 17 August, 11 out of 12 carrier-based Japanese bombers were shot down by Chinese fighters. Fighter escort was badly needed, and Claudes arrived during the following month. They quickly achieved air superiority, even against the rather faster Russian-built but Chinese-flown Polikarpov I-16. Agility was the keynote, combined with pilot quality, which enabled the Claude to outmanoeuvre its opponents. Japanese air combat victory claims were very high considering the light armament of two rifle calibre machine guns, and the vision-restricting telescopic gunsight. In the face of serious losses, the Chinese withdrew their fighters beyond the effective operational radius of the A5M2, even though by now the latter were operating from land bases.

The final model, the A5M4, was rushed into service from early 1938. It differed from earlier variants in having a raised deck aft of the cockpit, a revised windshield and quarterlights, and the rather more powerful Kotobuki 41 engine. To improve operational radius, it was fitted with a 35 gallon (160 litre) drop tank, later supplanted by one of 46 gallons (210 litres).

The success of the A5M over China reinforced the Japanese High Command view that agility was the prime virtue of a fighter, even though bought at the expense of vulnerability, with armour protection and self-sealing tanks all omitted to save weight. That said, the Claude was a tough bird. On one occasion Petty Officer Kashimura had returned to base with more than a third of his port wing missing after colliding with a stricken victim.

Eight Japanese Navy pilots claimed double figures over China, mainly with the A5M. The leading scorer was Tetsuzo Iwamoto with 14. The A5M maintained air superiority over China through 1939, after which it was phased out in favour of the A6M Zero, and finally withdrawn from front-line service in 1942.

Below: The A5M provided fighter escort to Japanese bombers over China.

Mitsubishi A6M2 Rei-Sen

Origin: Mitsubishi Jukogyo Kabushiki Kaisha, Japan.
Type: Single-seat, single-engined monoplane carrier fighter.
Engine: One Nakajima NK1C Sakae 12 14-cylinder twin-row radial engine rated at 950hp at 13,780ft (4,200m).
Dimensions: Span 39ft 4.5in (12.00m); length 29ft 8.5in (9.06m); height 10ft 0in (3.05m); wing area 242sq.ft (22.44m^2).
Weights: Empty 3,704lb (1,680kg); normal takeoff 5,313lb (2,410kg); maximum 6,164lb (2,796kg).
Loadings (at normal takeoff weight)**:** Wing 22lb/sq.ft (107kg/m^2); power 5.59lb (2.54kg) per hp.
Performance: Maximum speed 331mph (533kph) at 14,929ft (4,550m); initial climb rate 3,101ft/min (15.75m/sec), sustained climb rate 7in 27sec to 19,686ft (6,000m); service ceiling 32,810ft (10,000m); range 1,162 miles (1,870km).
Armament: Two 20mm wing-mounted, drum-fed Type 99 cannon with 60 rounds per gun, and two 7.7mm nose-mounted Type 97 synchronised machine guns with 500 rounds per gun.
History: Design work began January 1938. First flight 1 April 1939. Accepted for production 14 September 1940. Combat debut, China August 1940. Production continued until the end of the war, with a total of 10,938 of all variants.
User: Japan (Navy).

In 1937 the Imperial Japanese Navy issued a specification for a successor to the A5M. It had to be faster, better-climbing, harder-hitting, even more manoeuvrable, and longer-ranged than any previous fighter. Only Mitsubishi attempted to meet it, with what was to become the legendary A6M Zero.

Mitsubishi designer Jiro Horikoshi produced an all-metal monocoque airframe, with a low-set, high aspect ratio wing, powered by the small diameter lightweight 780hp Mitsubishi MK2 Zuisei 13 radial. Contrary to some reports,

Below:* *The agility of the A6M2 Zero carrier fighter became legendary in WWII.

Above: ventral drop tanks increased the range of the Zero significantly.

no corners were cut structurally; the aircraft was stressed to normal fighter standards. Lacking self-sealing tanks, armour, and even a radio, weight (and therefore wing loading) was minimised. For all practical purposes the Zero was a light sports aeroplane with a high-powered engine, and this provided its adequate performance and outstanding agility. The sole concessions to modernity were a fully enclosed cockpit and a retractable undercarriage.

First flight of the prototype A6M1, by Katsuzo Shima, took place from Kasumigaura airfield on 1 April 1939. Difficulties were encountered in meeting the specified performance, but these were overcome by fitting the 925hp Nakajima NK1C Sakae 12 engine to the third prototype, which became the A6M2. In July 1940, 15 preproduction Zeros were sent to China for combat trials.

In China, the Zeros outclassed the defenders, and using drop tanks they could fly round trips of 1,150 miles (1,850km), which allowed them to escort bombers to distant targets. Their air combat debut took place near Chunking on 13 September 1940, when 27 Chinese fighters were claimed for no loss. Koshiro Yamashita was credited with five in this one mission.

Long before Pearl Harbor, Flying Tigers commander Claire Chennault had warned the USA about the capabilities of the Zero, but his words went unheeded. Consequently, the agility of the Japanese fighter came as a nasty shock to the Allies, who at first were at a loss as to how best to counter it. Not until an almost undamaged Zero was recovered and flown in the USA in mid-1942 were its weaknesses laid bare.

Speed for speed the Zero could out-turn any Allied fighter of the day, and it could sustain a high rate of climb at a steep angle, albeit at a low airspeed, that its opponents were unable to match. Its failings? Performance was poor at high altitude. Then, as speed built up above 205mph (330kph), the ailerons stiffened, reducing rate of roll, and with it the ability to change direction quickly. Heavy stick forces and excessive vibration made the Zero difficult to handle in a prolonged dive. Crucially, the lack of armour and self-sealing tanks made it vulnerable if hit. Produced throughout World War II, the Zero was continually upgraded, but it was the A6M2, flown by combat-experienced veterans of China, that gave the Zero its legendary reputation.

The A6M3, which was first operational over New Guinea in September

1942, was powered by the 1,130hp Sakae 21 engine with a two-speed supercharger. The wingspan was reduced to 36ft 1in (11.00m) by removing the folding tips. However, while diving characteristics were improved, the anticipated performance and manoeuvrability increments were marginal, and after 343 aircraft were produced, the tips were reinstated. A6M3 production ceased in mid-1943.

The high altitude optimised A6M4 failed to enter service due to problems in developing a turbo-supercharger.

By 1943, the Zero was obsolescent but a suitable replacement had not yet emerged. First flown in August 1943, the A6M5 Model 52 was powered by the Sakae 21, with the exhaust stacks modified to provide thrust. The wing was revised, with the reduced span of the cropped A6M3 but rounded rather than squared tips, and had heavier-gauge duralumin skinning. Maximum speed increased to 351mph (565kph) at 19,686ft (6,000m), while wing loading increased to 26lb/sq.ft (127kg/m^2). Handling in a steep dive was greatly improved, eroding the advantage of Allied fighters in this regime. The A6M5

was progressively improved: belt-fed cannon with 125 rounds each, 12.7mm Type 1 machine guns, bullet-proof glass, automatic fire extinguishing, and armour protection.

With water/methanol boosting to produce 1,210hp for short periods, the Sakae 31 became available late in 1944 to power the A6M6, which belatedly had self-sealing fuel tanks. The A6M7 was a fighter-bomber, production of which began in May 1945, while the extensively redesigned A6M8, powered by the MK8K Kinsei 62 radial of 1,560hp, never progressed beyond the prototype stage.

The Zero ended the war ingloriously, flown by undertrained pilots, hacked from the skies by Allied fighters, and in some cases used for *kamikaze* missions. Of the top 20 Japanese fighter aces, 13 gained most if not all of their victories with the Zero, including Hiroyoshi Nishizawa with 87. Few survived the war.

Below: The A6M5 Model 52 Zero-Sen was faster and had more protection.

Mitsubishi J2M3 Raiden

Origin: Mitsubishi Jukogyo Kabushiki Kaisha, Japan.
Type: Single-seat, single-engined monoplane land-based naval interceptor.
Engine: One Mitsubishi MK4R-A Kasei 23 Ko 14-cylinder radial with two-speed supercharging and water-methanol injection, rated at 1,800hp for takeoff.
Dimensions: Span 35ft 5in (10.80m); length 32ft 7.5in (9.94m); height 12ft 11in (3.94m); wing area 216sq.ft (20.05m^2).
Weights: Empty 5,489lb (2,490kg); normal takeoff 7,584lb (3,440kg).
Loadings (at normal takeoff weight)**:** Wing 35lb/sq.ft (172kg/m^2); power 4.21lb (1.91kg) per hp.
Performance: Maximum speed 363mph (584kph) at 17,881ft (5,450m); initial climb rate 3,839ft/min (19.50m/sec); service ceiling 39,372ft (12,000m); range 656 miles (1,055km).
Armament: Four wing-mounted 20mm Type 5 cannon with 100 rounds per gun.
History: Specification finalised April 1940. Prototype first flight 20 March 1942. Combat debut 1944. Total production 474 of all variants.
User: Japan (Navy).

Designed as a shore-based interceptor for the Imperial Japanese Navy, the Raiden, Allied reporting name Jack, was optimised for speed and climb, with agility as a secondary consideration. Unlike previous Navy fighters, it had a low (for the era) aspect ratio laminar flow wing. Initially it was powered by a 1,430hp Kasei 13 radial engine, but to minimise drag the narrow annular intake was set well forward of the engine, with a cooling fan. The three-bladed propeller was driven via an extension shaft. Also to minimise drag, the cockpit was set low in the fuselage, with a shallow curved windshield. The

prototype J2M1 Raiden was first flown on 20 March 1942.

The view from the low-set cockpit was appalling, the curved windshield caused considerable optical distortion, and handling characteristics left much to be desired. In addition, many technical difficulties were encountered. Changes resulted in the J2M2, powered by the much more potent Kasei 23 Ko, driving a four-bladed propeller via a shorter extension shaft. A larger canopy with a more orthodox windshield was introduced, and the pilot's seat was raised and moved forward. First flown on 13 October 1942, the J2M2 was accepted for production, but was overtaken by events after only 11 were built.

Whereas the J2M2 had been armed with two 20mm Type 99 cannon and two 7.7mm Type 89 machine guns, the J2M3 had four wing-mounted 20mm Type 5 (licence-built Mauser MG 151) cannon, with a much improved rate of fire and muzzle velocity. This was the first variant to enter mass production, and the first to enter service.

Service entry was far from easy. The high wing loading, coupled with the low aspect ratio, both by Japanese standards, made the Raiden difficult to handle, and with pilot standards in irretrievable decline, losses in training were appalling. In combat it was little better, even though it outclimbed the Zero with ease. Fighter ace Saburo Sakai, briefly a Raiden test pilot, commented that it was unmanoeuvrable, and flew like a truck!

With its heavy armament and armour protection, the Raiden was at first moderately effective against the huge American B-29 bomber, but when USN Hellcats or USAAF Mustangs appeared the Japanese interceptor was hacked from the skies. Only one Raiden pilot, Saadaki Akamatsu, fared well against American fighters, with eight confirmed victories.

Further Raiden variants were developed, but the J2M4 failed to enter service, and only 40 J2M5s were delivered before the end of the war.

Left: The J2M3 Raiden interceptor was a turkey in combat against fighters.

Morane-Saulnier Type N

Origin: Aeroplanes Morane-Saulnier, France.
Type: Single-seat, single-engined tractor mid-wing monoplane fighter.
Engine: One 80hp Le Rhône 9C nine-cylinder rotary.
Dimensions: Span 26ft 9in (8.15m); length 19ft 1.5in (5.83m); height 7ft 4.5in (2.25m); wing area 118sq.ft (11.00m^2).
Weights: Empty 635lb (288kg); normal takeoff 976lb (443kg).
Loadings (at normal takeoff weight)**:** Wing 8.27lb/sq.ft (40.27kg/m^2); power 12.20lb (5.53kg) per hp.
Performance: Maximum speed 89mph (144kph) at sea level; sustained climb rate 4min to 3,281ft (1,000m); service ceiling 13,124ft (4,000m); endurance 1hr 30min.
Armament: One 8mm nose-mounted Hotchkiss belt-fed machine gun with deflector plates on the propeller (France); one .303in (7.7mm) nose-mounted drum-fed Lewis or belt-fed Vickers machine gun (Britain).
History: First flown May 1914. Combat debut spring 1915 but withdrawn from front-line service late 1915 (France) and summer 1916 (Britain). Total production c80.
Users: Britain (RFC and RNAS), France, Russia.

Although not designed as a combat aircraft, the Morane-Saulnier Type N was one of the first two single-seat fighters in history, the other being the Fokker Eindecker. It was preceded by the Type L; a slab-sided parasol-wing two-seater generally armed with a swivel-mounted machine gun operated by the observer. French (and Swiss) attempts to produce a reliable synchronisation gear which would allow a fixed machine gun to be fired through the propeller disc having failed, French pilot Roland Garros fitted his Type L with steel deflectors mounted on the propeller.

Garros shot down a German Albatros on 1 April 1915, making the Type L the first ever operational tractor fighter with fixed, forward firing armament, but his success was short-lived. He fell to ground fire on 18 April.

Performance of the Type L was inadequate, and even before the war designers Léon Morane and Raymond Saulnier had produced a more refined airframe. Powered by the same engine as the Type L, it showed significant performance improvements.

This was the Type N, which first flew in May 1914. It featured a circular-section monocoque fuselage fronted by a large streamlined spinner, while the wing was set just above the mid-position. Like the Type L and also the Eindecker, lateral control was by wing-warping. The small tailplane was all-moving, anticipating the jet age by several decades.

The Type N was some 25 per cent faster than its predecessor, climbed well by the standards of the day, and was manoeuvrable. However, it was not easy to fly; the all-moving tail made it ultra-sensitive in pitch and, being a monoplane, its landing speed was on the high side. Finally, the view forward and downward from the cockpit was far from good.

It was adopted by pre-war French aerobatic pilot Eugène Gilbert as his personal mount, which he fitted with a fixed Hotchkiss machine gun and steel deflectors. Having named it *Le Vengeur*, Gilbert scored six victories in quick succession, but shortly after force-landed in Switzerland where he was interned.

The Type N was used by four squadrons of the Royal Flying Corps, up-engined with the 120hp Le Rhône rotary, but the extra weight of the more powerful engine made handling even more tricky. All in all, the Type N was not a great success, which is why so few were built.

Below: The Morane-Saulnier Type N used wing warping instead of ailerons.

Morane-Saulnier MS 406

Origin: Aeroplanes Morane-Saulnier, France.
Type: Single-seat, single-engined monoplane fighter.
Engine: One 860hp Hispano-Suiza 12Y31 liquid-cooled V-12.
Dimensions: Span 34ft 10in (10.62m); length 26ft 7.5in (8.17m); height 8ft 10.5in (2.71m); wing area 184sq.ft (17.10m²).
Weights: Empty 4,173lb (1,893kg); normal takeoff 5,348lb (2,426kg).
Loadings (at normal takeoff weight)**:** Wing 29lb/sq.ft (142kg/m²); power 6.22lb (2.82kg) per hp.
Performance: Maximum speed 302mph (486kph) at 16,405ft (5,000m); initial climb rate 2,559ft/min (13m/sec); service ceiling 32,316ft (9,850m); range 621 miles (1,000km).
Armament: One 20mm Hispano-Suiza S7 drum-fed cannon with 60 rounds firing through the propeller boss, and two wing-mounted 7.5mm MAC 1934 machine guns with 300 rounds per gun.
History: Developed from the MS 405 of 1935 vintage, with pattern aircraft for the MS 406 flown on 21 June 1938. Deliveries began late 1938. Combat debut late 1939. Production ended March 1940, with a total of 1,064 aircraft.
Users: Croatia, Finland, France (*l'Armée de l'Air* and *Vichy*), Italy, Switzerland (as D-3800), Turkey.

The MS 405, from which the MS 406 was descended, first flew on 8 August 1935. Of orthodox tubular metal construction, it was fabric-covered to the rear fuselage and tail, but to the front and wings it had a stressed skin of aluminium and plywood. Sixteen pre-series aircraft were ordered, and these were gradually modified to the point where the MS 406 designation was issued for the production aircraft.

Commencing late in 1938, production quickly built up, peaking at 11 per day

by August 1939. By the outbreak of World War II, the MS 406 was numerically the most important type in French service. It was however distinctly underpowered and lacked performance, although it was fairly agile. Even before March 1940, when French production was terminated, it was scheduled to be replaced by the Bloch MB 152, the Dewoitine D 520 and the American Curtis Hawk 75. Some of the surplus aircraft were exported, 30 to Finland between December 1939 and January 1940, and another 30 to Turkey in the following two months. A similar number were ordered by China, but were commandeered by the French in Indo-China while they were en route.

When the *blitzkrieg* commenced on 10 May 1940, of the 1,046 aircraft received by *l'Armée de l'Air*, only 278 serviceable MS 406s operated with nine of the 23 front-line *Groupes de Chasse*. Outclassed by the German Bf 109E, and with no effective system of ground control, the Morane pilots achieved little, and in fact a further six *groupes* converted onto other types during the fighting.

Following the Armistice, the MS 406s served on with the Vichy government, based in southern France. Those in Indo-China flew briefly against the Japanese during the autumn of 1940, claiming two victories. Then in January 1941, they claimed four Thai aircraft in border clashes. Then in June and July 1941, Vichy MS 406s fought against the British over Syria.

Prior to the German occupation of Vichy France in November 1942, another 43 Moranes had been exported to Finland. After the occupation, 44 went to Croatia and 52 to Italy. Meanwhile the Swiss were licence-building the type as the D 3800. These were actually MS 405s with the HS 12Y31 engine and various "tweaks". Finland was also in the modification market, fitting captured 1,100hp Klimov M-105P engines to produce the Mörkö, which first flew on 4 February 1943. In all, 41 Mörkös were produced; the type remained in service until 1948.

Left: Their homeland overrun, Polish pilots flew the MS 406 for France.

Nakajima Ki-27-Otsu

Origin: Nakajima Hikoki Kabushiki Kaisha, Japan.
Type: Single-seat, single-engined monoplane fighter.
Engine: One 780hp Nakajima Kotobuki Ha-1-Otsu 9-cylinder radial.
Dimensions: Span 37ft 1.25in (11.31m); length 24ft 8.75in (7.53m); height 10ft 9in (3.28m); wing area 200sq.ft (18.56m^2).
Weights: Empty 2,447lb (1,110kg); normal takeoff 3,411lb (1,547kg); maximum 3,946lb (1,790kg).
Loadings (at normal takeoff weight)**:** Wing 17lb/sq.ft (83kg/m^2); power 4.37lb (1.98kg) per hp.
Performance: Maximum speed 292mph (470kph) at 11,484ft (3,500m), 265mph (427kph) at 3,281ft (1,000m); sustained climb rate 2min 6sec to 6,562ft (2,000m), 5min 22sec to 2,559ft/min (13m/sec); service ceiling 30,021ft (9,150m); range 392 miles (630km).
Armament: Two nose-mounted synchronised 7.7mm Type 89 machine guns with 500 rounds per gun. Provision for four 55lb (25kg) bombs under the wing mid-section.
History: First flight of prototype 15 October 1936. Production ordered 28 December 1937. Service entry March 1938, and combat debut 10 April 1938. Remained in front-line service, in Manchuria only, until August 1945. Total production 3,396.
Users: Japan (Army), Thailand.

Designed to a specification of June 1935, the Ki-27, Allied reporting name Nate, was first flown by Kiyoshi Shinomiya on 15 October 1936. A low-wing, all-metal

Nakajima Ki-43-IIb Hayabusa

Origin: Nakajima Hikoki Kabushiki Kaisha, Japan.
Type: Single-seat, single-engined monoplane fighter.
Engine: One 1,150hp Nakajima Ha 115 14-cylinder two-row radial.
Dimensions: Span 37ft 6.5in (11.44m); length 28ft 11.5in (8.83m); height 10ft 6.5in (3.27m); wing area 237sq.ft (22.00m^2).
Weights: Empty 3,812lb (1,729kg); normal takeoff 5,320lb (2,413kg); maximum 5,873lb (2,664kg).
Loadings (at normal takeoff weight)**:** Wing 23lb/sq.ft (110kg/m^2); power 4.63lb (2.10kg) per hp.
Performance: Maximum speed 320mph (515kph) at 19,686ft (6,000m), 288mph (464kph) at sea level); initial climb rate 3,240ft/min (16.45m/sec); sustained climb rate 5min 49sec to 16,405ft (5,000m); service ceiling 36,747ft (11,200m); range 1,007 miles (1,620km).
Armament: Two nose-mounted synchronised 12.7mm Type 1 machine guns with 250 rounds per gun. Provision for two 551lb (250kg) bombs underwing.
History: First flight of prototype January 1939. Ordered into production January 1941. Service entry October 1941. Combat debut December 1941. Remained in front-line service, and in production, until August 1945. Total built 5,751.
Users: Japan (Army), Thailand (until 1949).

The requirements for the Ki-43, issued in 1938, were stringent. It had to be at least comparable to the Ki-27 in manoeuvrability and cockpit vision, with speed, rate of climb, and range all better than any known fighter under development, although armament was limited to two 7.7mm Type 89 machine guns. As a combination, it was impossible to achieve.

Right: The Nakajima Ki-27, codenamed Nate, was superbly manoeuvrable.

stressed-skin monoplane with a fixed undercarriage, it was superbly manoeuvrable, able to sustain 45deg/sec at a radius of 283ft (80.6m).

The first three production aircraft were deployed to China in 1938, where Tateo Kato claimed three Polikarpov I-15s in his first sortie on 10 April. More victories followed, until the Chinese pulled back out of range. Then in May 1939, Ki-27s clashed with Russian fighters over Khalkin Gol, where they established an ascendancy over the Polikarpov I-16. This was not done without loss; when the fighting ended in September, pilot casualties were approaching two-thirds. The top Ki-27 ace of this period was Hiromichi Shinohara, who was killed on 27 August with his score at 58.

Obsolescent at the time of Pearl Harbor, Nate still equipped all but two Japanese Army fighter units. Its agility still made it a formidable opponent, but its short range restricted its operational use. Replaced elsewhere by more modern fighters, it remained in service in Manchuria where, in the final year of the war, it unsuccessfully attempted to intercept B-29 bombers.

Above: The Hayabusa was the Japanese Army equivalent of the Navy Zero.

Powered by a 950hp Ha 25 Sakae radial, the Ki-43 Hayabusa, Allied reporting name Oscar, was an all-metal stressed-skin, low-wing monoplane with a very slim fuselage and retractable main wheels. The first of three prototypes was flown in January 1939. Service evaluation trials took place shortly after, but the reaction was unfavourable. Manoeuvrability was poor, and control response was sluggish.

Nakajima went back to the drawing board. The result was 10 pre-series Ki-43-KAI aircraft. These differed in having a slightly increased span, modified controls and, most important of all, combat flaps, which vastly improved manoeuvrability. While the controls were somewhat on the sensitive side, the Hayabusa had no vices.

With the replacement of the obsolescent Ki-27 a matter of urgency, the Hayabusa was hurried into production. The first aircraft reached the Army Air Force in June 1941, and re-equipment of operational units began in October, although at the outbreak of the Pacific War only 40 Ki-43s were available.

Although not quite as agile as the Zero, the Hayabusa posed similar problems to Allied fighters in 1942, despite the fact that its hitting power was demonstrably inadequate. At an early stage, the 7.7mm 89 weapons were

Nakajima Ki-44-II Otsu Shoki

Origin: Nakajima Hikoki Kabushiki Kaisha, Japan.
Type: Single-seat, single-engined monoplane fighter.
Engine: One 1,520hp Nakajima Ha 109 14-cylinder two-row radial with two-stage supercharging.
Dimensions: Span 31ft 0in (9.45m); length 29ft 0in (8.84m); height 10ft 8in (3.25m); wing area 161sq.ft (15.00m²).
Weights: Empty 4,643lb (2,106kg); normal takeoff 6,107lb (2,770kg); maximum 6,598lb (2,993kg).
Loadings (at normal takeoff weight)**:** Wing 38lb/sq.ft (185kg/m²); power 4.63lb (2.10kg) per hp.
Performance: Maximum speed 376mph (605kph) at 17,061ft (5,200m); initial climb rate 3,609ft/min (18.33m/sec); sustained climb rate 4min 26sec to 16,405ft (5,000m); service ceiling 36,025ft (10,980m); range 1,050 miles (1,690km) with external fuel.
Armament: Four 12.7mm Type 1 machine guns; two nose-mounted and synchronised; two wing-mounted.
History: First flight of prototype August 1940. Operational trials, China late 1941. Ordered into production September 1942. Service entry 1943. Operational debut, China, August 1944. Production ceased late 1944, with a total of 1,210 including prototypes.
Users: Japan (Army).

The Nakajima Ki-44 was a complete departure for the Japanese Army, in that it was an interceptor optimised for speed and climb at the expense of manoeuvrability. Dimensionally it was the smallest Japanese fighter to enter service, while the wing loading was nearly double that of the Hayabusa and Zero.

The three prototypes, the first of which flew in August 1940, were powered by 1,250hp Nakajima Ha 42 engines, and were armed with two 7.7mm and two 12.7mm machine guns. Seven pre-series aircraft followed, and these, with two prototypes, reached China late in 1941 for operational trials.

The leader of the trials unit was Yasuhiko

replaced on the production lines by 12.7mm guns.

The Ki-43-I was succeeded by the Ki-43-II in February 1943. The more powerful Ha 115 engine driving a three-bladed constant-speed propeller significantly improved performance; a reflector sight replaced the ring and bead; and internal fuel capacity was increased by 41 per cent. Most importantly, self-sealing fuel tanks and armour protection were introduced.

The Ki-43-IIC had the span reduced by 24in (61cm), then in December 1944 production of the IIIA began. Using the Sakae engine rated at 1,230hp, this could reach 363mph (584kph) at 19,194ft (5,850m). It was assigned to home defence, and also *kamikaze* attacks.

Most Japanese Army aces gained the majority of their victories with the Ki-43, Satoshi Anabuki leading the field with 41 of his total of 51 victories in Hayabusas.

Kuroe, who had flown the Ki-27 against the Russians over Khalkin Gol in 1939, claiming two victories. Flying the Shoki, he claimed another three victories over China before moving on to command a *Hayabusa Sentai* in Burma.

Apparently the High Command was not yet convinced, as a further pre-series batch of 40 aircraft was ordered. These differed from the originals in having four 12.7mm machine guns, a relocated oil cooler and main gear doors. The Shoki, Allied reporting name Tojo, was unusual in having a retractable tail wheel. Not until two years after first flight, in September 1942, was the type accepted and ordered into production.

Meanwhile, five prototypes and three pre-series examples of an improved

Below: The Ki-44 Shoki was designed for performance rather than agility.

variant, the Ki-44-II, were under construction. Powered by the two-stage supercharged Nakajima Ha 109 radial, these had self-sealing tanks, armour protection, and two extra 12.7mm wing-mounted guns. The weaponry was later standardised as two nose-mounted and two wing-mounted 12.7mm machine guns, and this became the Ki-44-II-Otsu, the main variant to be built. It was parallelled by the Ki-44-II-Hei, in which the wing-mounted machine guns were replaced by 20mm cannon.

A final variant was proposed; the Ki-44-III, powered by a 2,000hp Nakajima

Nakajima Ki-84-Ia Hayate

Origin: Nakajima Hikoki Kabushiki Kaisha, Japan.
Type: Single-seat, single-engined monoplane fighter.
Engine: One 1,900hp Nakajima Ha 45/11 18-cylinder two-row radial with two-stage supercharging.
Dimensions: Span 36ft 10.5in (11.24m); length 32ft 6.5in (9.92m); height 11ft 1in (3.38m); wing area 226sq.ft ($21.00m^2$).
Weights: Empty 5,864lb (2,660kg); normal takeoff 7,965lb (3,613kg); maximum 9,193lb (4,170kg).
Loadings (at normal takeoff weight)**:** Wing 35lb/sq.ft ($172kg/m^2$); power 4.19lb (1.90kg) per hp.
Performance: Maximum speed 388mph (624kph) at 21,327ft (6,500m); initial climb rate 3,790ft/min (19.25m/sec); sustained climb rate 5min 54sec to 16,405ft (5,000m), 11min 40sec to 26,248ft (8,000m); service ceiling 34,451ft (10,500m); range 1,025 miles (1,650km), or 1,128 miles (1,815km) with external fuel.
Armament: Two 12.7mm nose-mounted synchronised Type 103 machine guns with 350 rounds per gun; two 20mm wing-mounted Type 5 belt-fed

ła 145 radial, and with a wing area increased by 26.6 per cent and a larger tail. :xamples were built with differing armament: four 20mm cannon, or even two ?0mm and two 37mm cannon. The first was completed in July 1943, but the ıircraft proved unsatisfactory and was not ordered.

Although directionally stable, the Shoki was only marginally stable in ɔitch and roll, which added to its manoeuvrability, making it a formidable ɔpponent for Mustangs, Hellcats, and Corsairs. Its main failing was an ınreliable engine.

:annon with 150 rounds per gun. Maximum bomb load 1,102lb (500kg) :arried underwing.

łistory: First flight of prototype March 1943. Production began August 1943.)eliveries commenced April 1944 and continued until August 1945; total ₹,509 including prototypes.

Jsers: Japan (Army).

ʈhe specification of the Hayate, Allied reporting name Frank, was written in the ;pring of 1942, at a time when Japanese fighters were sweeping all before :hem. The requirements were the manoeuvrability of the Hayabusa coupled vith the speed and climb of the Shoki, plus adequate pilot and fuel protection, ınd heavy armament, to outfight the new generation of Allied fighters.

Powered by the 18-cylinder Ka 45 radial, initially rated at 1,850hp, the Ki-84 vas a very sleek design. As with most Japanese fighters of the period, the ving was built integrally with the central fuselage as a weight-saving measure.

Below: The Ki-84 Hayate needed an experienced pilot to get the best from it.

Construction was of all-metal stressed-skin, although the control surfaces we fabric-covered. Large hydraulically operated Fowler-type flaps occupied th inboard wing trailing edge. The cockpit floor as well as the back of the pilot seat were armoured, and the pilot was protected from the front by a 70m bullet-proof windshield. The weaponry consisted of two 12.7mm machine gur and two 20mm cannon.

The first of two prototypes flew in March 1943. Apart from problems wi the engine, the prospects were promising, and it was ordered into productic in August 1943, although due to engine problems it was April 1944 befo deliveries to the JAAF began, and the Hayate started to replace the Hayabus.

By this time, the Japanese Army fighter pilots had been bled white. As the replacements were hopelessly undertrained by Western standards, the attritic rate during conversion was horrendous. Control response was not as crisp a the Hayabusa, the rudder ineffective at low speeds, the elevators were heav and the ailerons increasingly so above 298mph (480kph). This apart, the Hayat

Nieuport Nie 11 Bébé

Origin: Societe Anonyme des Etablissements Nieuport, France.
Type: Single-sea,t single-engined tractor biplane fighter.
Engine: One 80hp Le Rhône 7-cylinder rotary.
Dimensions: Span 24ft 8in (7.52m); length 18ft 6in (5.64m); height 7ft 10.5in (2.40m); wing area 143sq.ft (13.30m^2).
Weights: Empty 705lb (320kg); normal takeoff 1,058lb (480kg).
Loadings (at normal takeoff weight)**:** Wing 7.40lb/sq.ft (36kg/m^2); power 13.23lb (6.00kg) per hp.
Performance: Maximum speed 104mph (167kph) at sea level; sustained climb rate 15min to 9,843ft (3,000m); service ceiling 15,092ft (4,600m); endurance 2hr 30min.
Armament: One .303in (7.7mm) drum-fed Hotchkiss or Lewis gun mounted on the top plane to fire over the propeller disc.
History: Developed from the two-seat Nie 10, first flight 1915. Operational from November 1915. Withdrawn from front-line service late 1917. Total production c900.
Users: Belgium, Britain (RNAS), France, Holland, Italy, Romania, Russia.

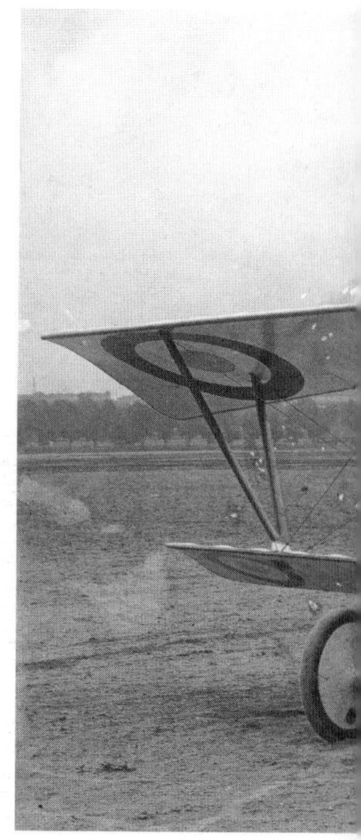

The origins of the Nie 11, christened the Bébé by its pilots due to its diminutive size, are unclear. It is believed to have evolved from a pre-World War I racing biplane designed by Gustave Delage, and developed into the Nie 10, a military two-seater, which in turn was scaled down to become the Nie 11.

The first Bébés arrived at the front in January 1916. At this time the so-called "Fokker Scourge" was at its height. The Bébé, superior in all departments, could force battle on its German opponent, or

was basically pleasant to fly, and in the hands of an experienced pilot was a dangerous opponent.

The first operational Hayate unit was the 22nd *Sentai*, operating from Hangchow from August 1944 against the U.S. 13th Air Force. Shortly after, it was moved to the Philippines where, with eight other *Hayabusa Sentais* it took part in the Leyte battles, performing well against the latest U.S. fighters.

Later variants carried four 20mm cannon, and a few were optimised as bomber destroyers with two 30mm cannon. A shortage of aluminium resulted in a change to a wooden fuselage and wingtips, at a considerable weight penalty. But, with the progressive destruction of Japanese industry, manufacturing standards fell, and performance and reliability deteriorated.

While ferrying Ki-84s to the Philippines in February 1945, JAAF top-scorer Satoshi Anabuki claimed six Hellcats, then a B-29 while on home defence in June.

---

disengage if circumstances were unfavourable. Flown by the *l'Aviation Militaire*, and aided by the Airco DH 2 of Britain's RFC, it was instrumental in defeating the Eindecker.

Often referred to as a sesquiplane, the Bébé was actually an equal-span, single-bay V-strutter biplane, with the lower plane staggered back and

Below: The horseshoe cowling identifies this aircraft as a Nie 11 Bébé.

only half the width of the top plane. The fuselage was slab-sided, with an all-moving rudder and braced tail surfaces with elevators. The rotary engine was horseshoe cowled, open at the bottom to allow fuel and oil to drain away.

The Hotchkiss or Lewis machine gun was set on the top plane, and at first could be aimed only by the pilot leaving the controls and standing on his seat, which in the unstable Bébé did nothing for marksmanship. Then it was given a fixed mounting, set at an upward angle of 15deg to clear the propeller. Replacing the ammunition drum was a two-handed task, which also involved the pilot standing on his seat. Only later was a slide invented, down which the gun could be pulled for reloading. In fact, this had two other advantages. First, the gun could be mounted higher to shoot straight ahead

Nieuport Nie 17C

Origin: Societe Anonyme des Etablissements Nieuport, France.
Type: Single-seat, single-engined tractor biplane fighter.
Engine: One 110hp Le Rhône 9Ja 9-cylinder rotary.
Dimensions: Span 26ft 9.25in (8.16m); length 19ft 0.25in (5.80m); height 7ft 10.5in (2.40m); wing area 159sq.ft (14.75m²).
Weights: Empty 827lb (375kg); normal takeoff 1,235lb (560kg).
Loadings (at normal takeoff weight)**:** Wing 7.77lb/sq.ft (38kg/m²); power 11.23lb (5.09kg) per hp.
Performance: Maximum speed 110mph (177kph) at 6,562ft (2.000m), 103mph (165kph) at sea level; sustained climb rate 11min 30sec to 9,843ft (3,000m); service ceiling 17,389ft (5,300m); range 155 miles (250km); endurance 2hr.
Armament: One .303in (7.7mm) drum-fed Lewis gun mounted on the top plane to fire over the propeller disc, or one .303in (7.7mm) synchronised belt-fed Vickers machine gun. Eight unguided Le Prieur rockets could be carried on the interplane struts for balloon busting, fired electrically.
History: Developed from the Nie 11 via the Nie 16. Operational from March 1916 until early 1918, and formed the basis for many later variants. Total production several thousand.
Users: Belgium, Britain (RFC and RNAS), Finland, France, Holland, Italy, Russia, USA.

To improve performance, the 110hp Le Rhône engine was fitted to the Nie 11 airframe to produce the Nie 16, but the combination of higher wing loading and nose heaviness adversely affected handling, and only small numbers were built. It was replaced by the Nie 17, which quickly proved to be one of the great fighters of the 1916/1917 period.

Although very similar in appearance to the Nie 16, the Nie 17 was slightly larger, with a refined airframe and a greater wing area. Externally, the main difference was a completely circular engine cowling. A few early machines were powered by 110hp or 130hp Clerget rotary engines, but most

over the propeller disc, which made aiming much easier. Second, when pulled down, the gun could be used to shoot up at an unsuspecting target directly overhead.

The Bébé was the mount of the first French double ace, Jean Navarre, who scored 11 of his 12 victories with the Bébé-equipped *N 67*. Flying a red-painted aircraft, predating the Red Baron by about a year, he was instantly recognisable to friend and foe alike. Constantly over the lines, he became known as the *Sentinal* of Verdun. By June 1916, he was badly wounded by a chance shot, and never flew operationally again.

Weakness in the lower plane caused many Nie 11s to break up in the air; on the Western Front it was soon replaced by the Nie 17, and most production took place in Italy.

---

retained the 110hp Le Rhône 9Ja, although the 130hp 9Jb was also used.

Armament varied. Many *l'Aviation Militaire* aircraft were fitted with a belt-fed synchronised Vickers, while British RFC aircraft in the main retained the Lewis gun on a Foster mounting. Some aircraft carried both, but the added weight and drag were enough to adversely affect performance. In general, the Nie 17 was used as a single-gun fighter.

By late 1916, the Nie 17 equipped almost every fighter *escadrille* in the

Below: The Nie 17 was essentially a refined and strengthened Nie 11 Bébé.

l'Aviation Militaire plus at least one naval unit, and a high proportion of RFC scout squadrons. In consequence, most of the top-scoring AM and RFC aces on the Western Front flew the Nieuport 17 at one time or another.

When the Nie 17 first entered service, it was pre-eminent in both performance and manoeuvre, but this was not to last. Aerodynamics and engine technology were developing fast, and the compromise between performance and agility could not be maintained. From the autumn of 1916 fighter design gradually diverged into two distinct paths, one of which held manoeuvre to be pre-eminent, while the other concentrated on sheer performance. The Nie 17 fell firmly into the manoeuvre category.

Nieuport-Delage Ni-D 52

Origin: Societe Anonyme des Etablissements Nieuport-Delage, France.
Type: Single-seat, single-engined tractor sesquiplane fighter.
Engine: One 500hp Hispano-Suiza 12Hb liquid-cooled V-12.
Dimensions: Span 39ft 4.5in (12.00m); length 25ft 0.75in (7.64m); height 9ft 10.5in (3.00m); wing area 299sq.ft (27.75m^2).
Weights: Empty 2,998lb (1,360kg); normal takeoff 3,968lb (1,800kg).
Loadings (at normal takeoff weight)**:** Wing 13.27lb/sq.ft (65kg/m^2); power 7.94lb (3.60kg) per hp.
Performance: Maximum speed 162mph (260kph) at 5,906ft (1,800m); sustained climb rate 13min 30sec to 16,405ft (5,000m); service ceiling c31,170ft (9,500m); range c559 miles (900km).
Armament: Two .303in (7.7mm) nose-mounted synchronised belt-fed/drum-fed Vickers machine guns.
History: A progressive development of the Ni-D 42 of 1924 vintage. First flight of prototype late 1927. Licence-production (in Spain); first deliveries 1929. Total production 135. Combat debut (Spanish Civil War) July 1936, reverted to training in December, but was restored to operational use in March 1937.
Users: Spain (Republicans and Nationalists).

Developed from the Ni-D 42, the Ni-D 52 was evolved in parallel with the Ni-D 62, which was acquired by *l'Aviation Militaire* and the *l'Aéronautique Maritime*. It was full of unusual features, many of them inherited from the Ni-D 42. The Hispano-Suiza 12Hb V-12 engine, rated at 500hp, drove a two-bladed fixed pitch propeller. It was mounted with the V upright, the two widely spaced banks of cylinders closely but separately cowled, giving a V-section to the nose profile. There was no attempt to provide exhaust stacks; stub exhaust pipes for each cylinder projected straight out, with not so much as an attempt at a bend.

The engine had six carburettors, three on each side, each serving two cylinders, which must have posed calibration problems, and each carburettor had its own intake scoop set low on the side of the nose. Twin rectangular radiators were located on the forward struts of the mainwheel legs.

Another unusual feature was the use of Y-shaped interplane struts, canted in at a steep angle and

The agility of the Nie 17 was exploited by French ace Charles Nungesser, ıose usual tactics were to plunge in headlong to cause maximum confusion, en stay and fight, gaining a reputation for hairsbreadth escapes in the ocess. Most of his 45 confirmed victories were obtained with the Nieuport. this he was just outdone by Canadian Billy Bishop, who claimed 45 of his entual 72 victories with the Nie 17.

Like the Bébé, the Nie 17 suffered from structural weakness, and was lnerable in a long steep dive. By mid-1917 its day was past, but it was cceeded by a series of Nieuport biplanes, culminating in the Nie 28, which as flown operationally by the USAS.

projecting beneath the lower plane, where they met a ventral strut which projected upwards to the fuselage, meeting it at the wing root. The wheels were mounted on N-struts, with a fairing over the axle.

Whereas the Ni-D 42 monocoque fuselage had been constructed of two tulip-wood half-shells joined horizontally, as was that of the Ni-D 62, the Ni-D 52 was of all-metal construction. The flight test programme, which commenced in December 1927, did not go smoothly. Pitchup led to inadvertent stalls, usually followed by spins. To correct this, the upper plane was redesigned to reduce both chord and area, although the span remained the same. The lower plane was also reduced in area, but the tailplane was

Below: The Ni-D 52 was flown by both sides in the Spanish Civil War.

increased in size. Another difference from the Ni-D 42 was that the wing ribs were of light alloy tube instead of wood.

L'Aviation Militaire did not order the Ni-D 52, preferring to acquire the Ni-D 62 which, having retained the tulip-wood fuselage, had greater commonality with the Ni-D 42, and was therefore cheaper. However, Spain procured a manufacturing licence, and the Ni-D 52 was built by Hispano, the only change being a single chin radiator in place of the original pair.

North American P-51D Mustang

Origin: North American Aviation Inc., USA.
Type: Single-seat, single-engined long-range monoplane fighter.
Engine: One Rolls-Royce/Packard Merlin V-1650-7 liquid-cooled V-12 with two-speed, two-stage supercharging, rated at 1,450hp for takeoff and 1,695hp war emergency.
Dimensions: Span 37ft 0in (11.28m); length 32ft 3in (9.83m); height 13ft 8in (4.17m); wing area 233sq.ft (21.65m^2).
Weights: Empty 7,635lb (3,463kg); normal takeoff 10,100lb (4,581kg); maximum 12,100lb (5,489kg).
Loadings (at normal takeoff weight/power)**:** Wing 43lb/sq.ft (212kg/m^2); power 6.97lb (3.16kg) per hp.
Performance: Maximum speed 437mph (703kph) at 25,000ft (7,620m), 395mph (636kph) at 5,000ft (1,524m); initial climb rate 3,475ft/min (17.65m/sec); service ceiling 40,000ft (12,191m); range 950 miles (1,529km), with drop tanks 1,650 miles (2,655km).
Armament: Six 0.50in (12.7mm) wing-mounted Browning MG53-2 machine guns, two with 400 and four with 270 rounds per gun. Two 1,000lb (454kg) bombs or 10 5in (127mm) HVARs carried underwing.
History: Developed for Britain's RAF. First flight 26 October 1940, although production had been ordered in August. First delivery to an operational (RAF) unit January 1942. Combat debut 10 May 1942. First flight of the Merlin engined XP-51B 30 November 1942. Combat debut of P-51B (with USAAF) 1 December 1943. Combat debut of P-51D (with USAAF) June 1944. Mustangs served in every theatre of World War II, then in Korea, the Middle East, and several other conflicts. Remained in service until 1983 with the Dominican Republic. Total production of all variants 15,675.
Users: Australia, Bolivia, Britain (RAF), Canada, Cuba, Dominican Republic, France, Guatemala, Haiti, Holland, Honduras, Indonesia, Israel, Italy, Nicaragua, New Zealand, Philippines, Salvador, Somalia, South Africa, South Korea, Sweden, Switzerland, Taiwan, Uruguay, USA (USAAF, USAF, ANG).

When in July 1936 the Spanish Civil War erupted, only about 40 Ni-D 52s remained in service, of which two thirds were in Republican hands, and the remainder with the Nationalists. In air combat it was outclassed by Heinkel He 51s and Fiat CR 32s and achieved little. Its unique record was that of a fighter which was adopted by a single country outside its country of origin, then fought on both sides in a civil war!

With war looming and with their industries at full stretch, Britain and France turned to the USA for fighters. The best American fighter of the time was the P-40, but Curtiss was heavily committed, with little spare capacity to meet export orders. California-based North American Aircraft had already begun studies for a fighter which, although using the Allison engine of the P-40, would outperform it. A contract for a prototype was issued on 23 May 1940, and piloted by Vance Breese this first flew from Mines Field on 26 October of that year. Even before this, an order had been placed for 320 aircraft, plus spares sufficient for another 80.

To outperform the similarly engined P-40, drag had to be minimised. The

Below: A late production P-51B with a Malcolm hood for improved vision.

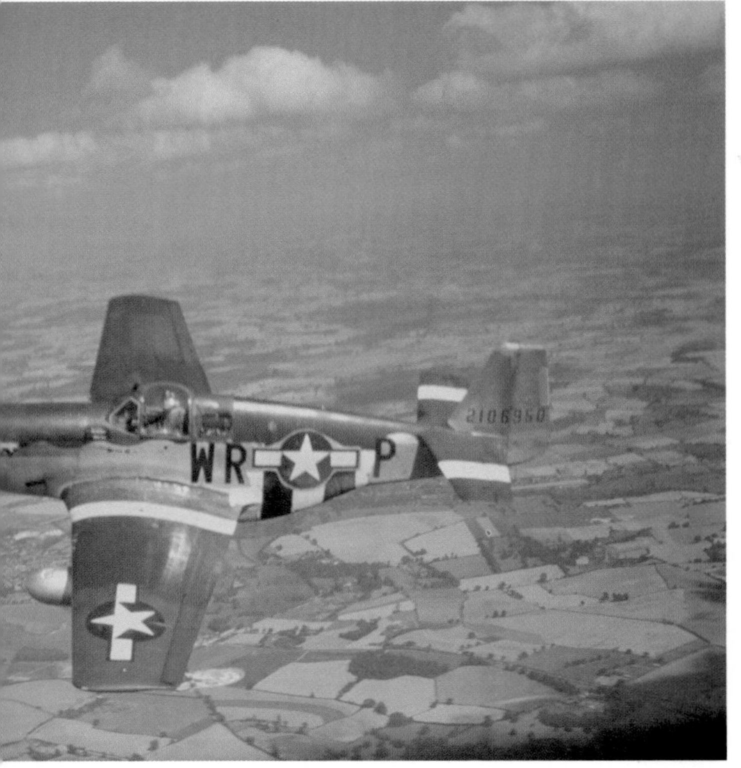

most critical feature was a laminar-flow wing, with a lower coefficient of lift being accepted in the interests of performance. Unusually, the radiator was located beneath the fuselage, aft of the cockpit. To obtain crisp handling, control rods were used instead of cables, thus eliminating the effect of stretching. The lines were sleek but angular, in the interests of ease of manufacture, while two large wing tanks gave an endurance of about four hours, more than double that of the Spitfire.

The first production Mustangs arrived in Britain by ship, and were fitted with British radios and equipment prior to evaluation. Compared to the Spitfire VB, it was faster at low and medium levels, dived better, and handled well. However, rate of climb was inferior, it was slower at altitude, and did not turn as well. Given this, the RAF used the Mustang in the low-level armed reconnaissance role; not as an air superiority fighter. Its combat debut was a

low-level sortie over Northern France on 10 May 1942, and its first air combat victory was against an FW 190 over Dieppe on 19 August.

The designation P-51 was allotted when, to overcome funding problems, the Mustang was ordered by the USAAF before being passed on to the RAF, but gradually the Americans came to realise the potential of the type. A little horse-trading resulted in the A-36 attack variant with dive brakes, underwing bomb racks, and an uprated Allison engine. Ben Chilton made the first flight in the A-36 on 21 September 1942; then on 3 February 1943 he flew the P-51A for the first time.

The greatest weakness of the early Mustang variants was the lack of high altitude capability of the Allison engine. The turning point came with the

Below: The P-51D had a bubble canopy, giving a good view all round.

installation of a Rolls-Royce Merlin 61. The change was dramatic. Flying the XP-51B, Ben Chilton reached 441mph (710kph) at 29,800ft (9,083m), and the rate of climb was almost doubled. It was immediately put into production.

Meanwhile the USAAF in Europe badly needed an effective long-range fighter. The P-47 Thunderbolt lacked range while the twin-engined P-38 Lightning was largely outclassed by the single-engined German fighters. The last few hundred P-51Bs and Cs were fitted with a large fuselage tank. With two drop tanks, the new Mustang could fly escort missions from England to Berlin. There was of course a penalty. With a full fuel load, handling was tricky, and not until the fuselage tank was nearly empty could the pilot relax.

Many problems were encountered during action from England from October 1943. The engines ran rough and overheated; sometimes the mounting bolts were faulty. These were gradually fixed. The drop tanks had to be pressurized or they might fail to feed. Then, in a turn of more than 2g, the guns often jammed. This too was eventually cured. Far more serious was structural failure. In a high-speed dive, the ammunition bay doors bulged, distorting the wing to the point where it parted company with the aircraft. An uncommanded extension of the main wheels at speed sometimes had the same effect. These faults too were finally fixed.

With everything working well, the P-51B was a formidable opponent. Trials against captured German fighters held in the spring of 1944 showed that it was

significantly faster than both the FW 190A and Bf 109G, could out-dive both, and had a similar rate of climb. In the turn it was greatly superior to the Bf 109G although only slightly better than the FW 190A.

The P-51C differed only marginally from the B. Both had a fault that stemmed from the original prototype; in the attempt to minimise drag, the cockpit had been set low and faired into the rear fuselage. While the cockpit itself was generally roomy, it was slightly cramped for a tall pilot and, as on most fighters of the era, rearward vision left much to be desired.

This was corrected in the P-51D, widely regarded as the definitive Mustang. First flown on 17 November 1943, this variant had a one-piece tear-drop sliding canopy. With the rear fuselage cut down to accommodate it, the view "out of the window" was a panoramic 360deg. To restore the always marginal directional stability, aggravated by the cut-down fuselage, a small dorsal extension was added to the fin.

The problem of gun jamming on the P-51B had still not been entirely eliminated. It was largely caused by the fact that, as fitted, the guns were canted sideways. To be unable to fire the guns during hard manoeuvres was an unacceptable handicap in combat, while the increasing use of armour protection by the Luftwaffe had shown four machine guns to be inadequate.

The answer was an extensive redesign of the wing, the chord of which was

Below: The tall fin shows this to be a postwar P-51H, the fastest Mustang.

thickened at the root. This allowed six .50in (12.7mm) Brownings to be fitted upright, the inner two with 400 rounds each, the rest with 270 rounds per gun. At the same time, the main gears were strengthened to take a greater all-up weight. Almost identical was the P-51K, which varied only in having a different propeller.

The Mustang turned the tide of the air war over Europe by virtue of its outstanding range and endurance, coupled with performance and manoeuvrability. From the end of 1944 it was also flying in the Far East and Pacific. On 7 April 1945, the P-51D flew the first of many escort missions to Japan. These were the longest and most exhausting fighter missions of the war. A return trip from their base at Iwo Jima to Japanese targets was typically 1,500 miles (2,400km), lasting between seven and eight hours. Violent tropical storms were often encountered, and one of the worst, on 1 June 1945, destroyed 27 aircraft, the heaviest Mustang loss of the war.

For its size, the Mustang airframe was heavy, and in 1943 a weight reduction programme was commenced. This gave rise to the P-51F and P-51G lightweight Mustangs which, although very fast, failed to enter service. Finally there was the P-51H, with a longer fuselage, a taller fin, and a more powerful engine. With a maximum speed of 487mph (784kph), it was the fastest propeller-driven fighter of the war.

Post-war, the Mustang began to be replaced in USAAF and USAF service by jet fighters. Its heyday was past, although it gave sterling service in Korea as a fighter-bomber, where it also flew operationally with South Korea, Australia, and South Africa. In Israeli service Mustangs gained two air combat victories for Israel in the 1948 War of Independence. The air combat swansong of the Mustang was for El Salvador, against Honduran F4U Corsairs in the "World Cup War" of 1969. A handful remained in service with the Dominican Republic until 1983.

North American F-82G Twin Mustang

Origin: North American Aviation Inc., USA.
Type: Two-seat, twin-engined, long-range night/all-weather fighter.
Engine: Two Allison V-1710 handed liquid-cooled V-12 engines with two-stage supercharging and water/alcohol injection, each rated at 1,600hp for takeoff and 1,930hp war emergency.
Dimensions: Span 51ft 7in (15.73m); length 42ft 2.5in (12.86m); height 13ft 10in (4.22m); wing area 408sq.ft (37.90m²).
Weights: Empty 15,997lb (7,256kg); normal takeoff 21,819lb (9,897kg); maximum 25,891lb (11,744kg).
Loadings (at normal takeoff weight/power)**:** Wing 53lb/sq.ft (261kg/m²); power 6.82lb (3.09kg) per hp.
Performance: Maximum speed 456mph (734kph) at 21,000ft (6,400m); initial climb rate 3,770ft/min (19.15m/sec); service ceiling 38,900ft (11,856m); combat radius 1,015 miles (1,633km).
Armament: Six 0.50in (12.7mm) fixed Browning MG53-2 machine guns in wing centre- section with 440 rounds per gun. Two 2,000lb (908kg) bombs or 20 5in (127mm) HVARs carried underwing.
History: First flight of prototype 15 April 1945. Operational from 1948 as a long-range escort fighter. Night/all-weather variant entered service 1948. Combat debut, Korea 27 June 1950. Withdrawn from service 1953. Total production all variants 272.
Users: USA (USAAF, USAF).

***Above:* The postwar era saw the red bar reinstated in the national insignia.**

***Above:* The radar scanner on the F-82G had to project beyond the propellors.**

The long range of the P-51B allowed sorties of six hours and more, most of this time over hostile territory in Europe, or over the unfriendly sea in the Pacific. This was exhausting for the pilots. As 9th Air Force ace Glen Eagleston commented, "It just knocked the raccoon pee right out of you!" Tiredness caused carelessness, and this in turn bred potentially fatal mistakes.

The obvious way of overcoming the problem was a two-man crew and North American proposed the simple and economical expedient of mating two P-51H fuselages, modified to take the latest version of the Allison V-1710, which gave adequate power at high altitude. Two prototypes were ordered on 7 January 1944, and flight testing began in April 1945.

The rear fuselages were lengthened by 57in (1.45m), and the dorsal strakes were enlarged, to improve lateral stability, They also housed the main undercarriage legs, which were redesigned to handle the increased weight. Surprisingly, the cockpits were not identical. The fully equipped command cockpit was in the port fuselage, while that on the other side was austere, with just enough instrumentation to allow basic flying or emergency operation. Two fighter pilots, each with his own cockpit, would not be a happy combination in the stress of combat. Apart from the economics, this was a reminder of precedence.

North American F-86F Sabre

Origin: North American Aviation Inc., USA.
Type: Single-seat, single-engined, swept-wing transonic fighter.
Engine: One General Electric J47-27 single-spool axial-flow turbojet rated at 5,910lb (2,681kg) thrust.
Dimensions: Span 39ft 1.5in (11.92m); length 37ft 6.5in (11.44m); height 14ft 9in (4.50m); wing area 313sq.ft (29.11m^2).
Weights: Empty 11,125lb (5,046kg); normal takeoff 15,198lb (6,894kg); maximum 20,611lb (9,349kg).
Loadings (at normal takeoff weight)**:** Wing 49lb/sq.ft (237kg/m^2); thrust 0.39.
Performance: Maximum speed 678mph (1,091kph) at sea level, 599mph at 35,000ft (10,667m); initial climb rate 8,100ft/min (41.15m/sec); service ceiling 47,000ft (14,325m); range 785 miles (1,263km), with drop tanks 926 miles (1,490km).
Armament: Six 0.50in (12.7mm) nose-mounted Browning M-3 machine guns with 300 (more usually 267) rounds per gun. Two 1,000lb (454kg) bombs or eight 5in (127mm) HVARs carried underwing.
History: First flight 1 October 1947. Supersonic in dive 26 April 1948. Service entry February 1949. Combat debut, Korea 17 December 1950. U.S. production ceased April 1956. Withdrawn from ANG service 1965. The last few Portuguese F-86s were retired on 31 July 1980. A handful remained in the Honduran inventory in the mid-1980s, status unknown. Total production of all variants including the FJ 2-4 Fury, 8,454.
Users: Argentina, Australia, Britain (RAF), Canada, Denmark, France, Greece, Holland, Honduras, Indonesia, Iraq, Italy, Japan, Malaysia, Norway, Pakistan, Peru, Philippines, Portugal, South Korea, Spain, Taiwan, Thailand, Turkey, USA (USAF, ANG, USMC, USN), Venezuela, West Germany, Yugoslavia.

At New Year 1944, the USAAF issued a request for proposals for a fighter to compete with the Lockheed P-80. North American responded with a straight-wing design, and an order for three XP-86

Joining the two fuselages was simple enough. The wing centre section housed six Browning machine guns, and also the wheel wells. A slotted flap occupied the entire trailing edge. At the rear was a horizontal tailplane with a full-span elevator.

The wings were totally redesigned to handle higher loadings, with much longer hydraulically boosted two-piece ailerons to overcome the inertia of the twin fuselages, while the problems of asymmetric flying with one engine out were minimised by "handing" the engines, the propellers of which rotated inwards.

World War II ended before the P-82, as it then was, entered service, but production continued as the F-82E escort fighter for Strategic Air Command, and phased out in 1950. However, an interim night/all weather fighter was needed to fill the gap between the obsolete Black Widow and the next generation of jets.

The Twin Mustang was an obvious choice, and with a pod housing the SCR-720C search radar slung below the wing centre-section, it became the F-82G. Flying with the 68th F(AW) Squadron from Itazuke, Japan, it claimed three victories over North Korean piston-engined aircraft on the second day of the conflict, but from then on was mainly used for night interdiction. The F-82H, a specialised cold-climate variant based in Alaska, was the final variant in service, being phased out during 1953.

---

prototypes was issued on 18 May 1944. With most company effort concentrated on improved Mustangs, progress was slow. Then, with the end of the war in Europe, heaps of German research on swept wings became available. Convinced, in September 1945, Dutch Kindelberger of NAA submitted a revised proposal, featuring 35deg swept-wings, delaying the project by about a year in the process.

Below: Two very tired F-86E-1 Sabres not bearing Korean theatre markings.

Test pilot and Pacific War ace Wheaties Welch made the first flight of the XP-86 from Muroc, later Edwards AFB, on 1 October 1947, just two weeks before Chuck Yeager became the first man to exceed Mach 1. Handling was excellent, and with the slightly more powerful Allison J35-5 installed, Welch went supersonic in a shallow dive on 26 April 1948.

The definitive engine was the General Electric J47, and with this the first production F-86A flew on 18 May 1948, and entered service with the 94th FS in February 1949. Less than two years later, the Russian MiG-15 emerged over Korea, and the 4th FIG, equipped with the F-86A, by now named Sabre, was sent to counter it. On 17 December, Sabre pilot Bruce Hinton claimed a MiG-

Above: All Japanese Self-Defense Force Sabres were F-86Fs, like this one.

15. A legend was about to be made.

Although of similar installed thrust, the Sabre was larger and heavier than its Russian adversary. At high altitude it was outperformed by its Russian adversary, which could take a perch high out of reach, then choose its moment to attack. Encounters were often fleeting; the MiG pilots, most of whom were Russian, pulled up out of reach after their attack, while the USAF pilots dived away, trying to lure the MiGs to lower altitudes where the Sabre was superior.

The greatest advantage of the Sabre lay in its handling; transient performance in pitch and roll was crisp and precise, and the stall was benign. It was also a steady gun platform, unlike the MiG-15, which snaked badly at Mach 0.86 and above. The Sabre's greatest weakness was in firepower; jets were much tougher than propeller aircraft, and six 0.50in (12.7mm) guns were inadequate.

The F-86A suffered from one major handling fault. At high Mach numbers and medium altitudes, the traditional elevators started to float, resulting in a neck-breaking 8g or more pitchup. This was cured on the F-86E by an all-moving tailplane with irreversible fully hydraulically powered controls. This had built-in artificial feel to prevent an over-enthusiastic pilot from pulling the wings off!

The best Sabre to see service in Korea was the F-86F, first flown on 19 March 1952. The J47-27 turbojet gave an extra 710lb (322kg) of thrust; wing span and area were increased, with fixed instead of slatted leading edges. These changes improved high-altitude performance and manoeuvrability at the expense of low-speed handling. Then, in an attempt to increase hitting power, a dozen Sabres were modified to take six 20mm cannon. A good idea in theory, it was less so in practice since firing more than two cannon at one time often resulted in a compressor stall.

Sabres claimed a victory/loss ratio of 7.5:1 in the skies over Korea, despite the fact that they were usually tactically disadvantaged. This can be explained by three factors: the superior transient performance of the American fighter, superior pilot quality, and finally a sortie rate of more than 2:1. There were 39 Sabre aces over Korea, 38 of them USAF plus one Marine. The list was headed by Joe McConnell with 16, and Jabby Jabara with 15.

Sabres were far from finished with combat. In September 1958 Taiwanese F-86Fs became the first fighters to use guided missiles operationally, against Chinese MiGs over the Formosa Strait. Then in 1965, and again in 1971, Pakistani Sabres fought against India, with a degree of success.

Sabre development had continued. The F-86B was never built, while the F-86C interceptor ended up as the YF-93A, only two of which were produced. The

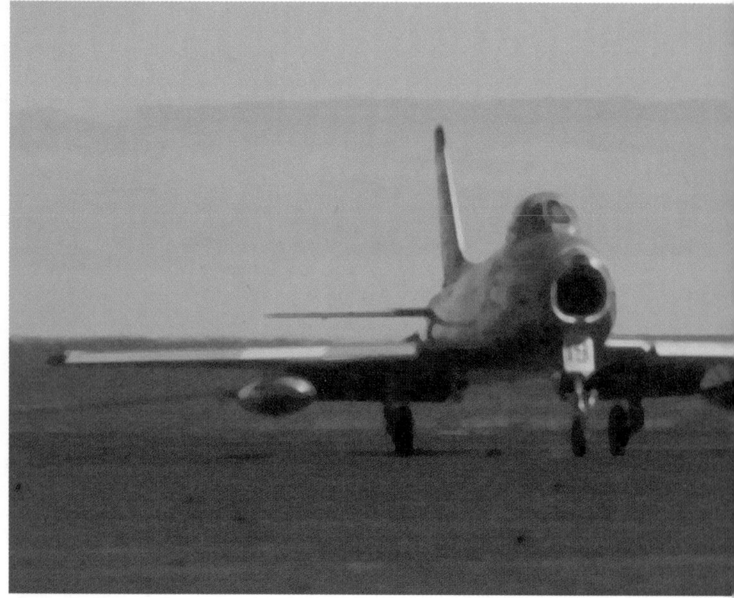

Above: This Orenda-powered Canadair CL-13 Sabre was based on the F-86F.

need for all-weather fighters then produced the F-86D, known as the Dogship Sabre. This carried the collision-course E-4 fire control system, with an APG-36 radar in the nose which necessitated a chin inlet. The sole armament consisted of 24 2.75in (70mm) Mighty Mouse FFARs in a retractable ventral box. Although the YF-86D was first flown on 22 December 1949, problems with the electronics delayed operational capability until 1954. Altogether, 2,504 Dogships were built. They were followed by the F-86G with the -33 turbojet, but this was redesignated F-86D-20.

Next in the Dogship family was the F-86K, specifically an export variant for NATO. The not very effective FFARs were deleted and replaced by four 20mm cannon set low on the sides of the nose, well away from the radar, which was retained. Two AIM-9B Sidewinder heat-seeking missiles were carried underwing.

The final all-weather variant was the F-86L. This was essentially the Dogship, but with long-span slatted wings and upgraded avionics. No new aircraft were built, but 981 F-86Ds were modified to the new standard, and served with USAF's ANG until 1965.

Meanwhile the day fighters were not neglected. The F-86H, first flown on 30 April 1953, was the final production variant for the

Left: The navalized F-86 was extensively modified to become the FJ Fury.

USAF. To improve performance, it was powered by the next-generation J73-GE-3 afterburning turbojet rated at 8,920lb (4,046kg) maximum thrust. Since this required a larger intake to provide the increased airflow, a deeper fuselage was needed, demanding extensive redesign. This in turn allowed a 29 per cent increase in internal fuel. Primarily a fighter-bomber which could at need carry a nuclear store, the first 113 aircraft retained machine gun armament, but the remaining 360 carried four 20mm cannon. Production of the F-86H ceased in April 1956.

Two nations produced their own very distinctive Sabre variants. Australia fitted the Rolls-Royce Avon RA-7 turbojet of 7,500lb thrust. As the Avon was shorter, wider, and much lighter than the J47, this involved a massive redesign, with the engine mounted further aft. Armament was also changed to two 30mm Aden cannon. First flown on 3 August 1953 as the CA-26, the first Avon Sabre was delivered to the RAAF on 1 March 1956. This formidable aircraft remained in Australian service until February 1973.

Canada also produced uprated aircraft, first the Sabre 5, based on the F-86F with the Orenda 10 turbojet of 6,355lb (2,883kg) thrust; then the Sabre 6 with the two-stage Orenda 14 rated at 7,257lb (3,300kg) thrust, and capable of 710mph (1,143kph) at sea level. As a close combat fighter, the Sabre 6 was reckoned to be the best of all, although it lacked the punch of the Australian aircraft.

The FJ-2, -3 and -4 Fury carrier fighters were close cousins of the Sabre. Navalised with wing folding, arrester hook, beefed up landing gear, catapult spools, and standard USN armament of four 20mm cannon, the J47-powered FJ-2 was not cleared for carrier operations and was assigned to the USMC.

The next Fury was the FJ-3, powered by the Wright J65-W-4 license-built Armstrong Siddeley Sapphire turbojet. The first production FJ-3 flew on 11 December 1953. In 1956, as the FJ-3M, it became the first fighter cleared to

North American F-100A Super Sabre

Origin: North American Aviation Inc., USA.
Type: Single-seat, single-engined swept-wing supersonic fighter.
Engine: One Pratt & Whitney J57-P-7 twin-spool axial-flow afterburning turbojet rated at 14,800lb (6,713kg) maximum and 9,700lb (4,400kg) military thrust.
Dimensions: Span 38ft 9.5in (11.82m); length 47ft 0.75in (14.65m); height 15ft 4in (4.67m); wing area 385sq.ft (35.77m^2).
Weights: Empty 19,270lb (8,741kg); normal takeoff 27,587lb (12,513kg).
Loadings (at normal takeoff weight)**:** Wing 72lb/sq.ft (350kg/m^2); thrust 0.54.
Performance: Maximum speed 830mph (1,336kph, Mach 1.26) at 35,000ft (10,667m), 770mph (1,239kph), Mach 1.01 at sea level; initial climb rate 13,000ft/min (66m/sec); service ceiling 48,000ft (14,630m); range 572 miles (920km), with drop tanks 926 miles (1,490km).
Armament: Four fuselage-mounted 20mm Pontiac M-39 cannon with 200 rounds per gun, plus a variety of air-to-surface stores.
History: Contract for two YF-100 prototypes and 110 production aircraft signed 1 November 1951. First flight YF-100 25 May 1953; supersonic on first flight. First production aircraft 29 October 1953. Initial operational capability 1955. Production ceased October 1959, with a total of 2,294. Air combat debut, Vietnam 4 April 1965. Phased out by USAF June 1972 (by ANG 1980).
Users: Denmark, France, Taiwan, Turkey, USA (USAF, ANG).

Above: The F-86E was the first Sabre to have an all-moving tailplane.

use the AIM-9B Sidewinder. The final FJ-4 variant was an almost totally redesigned attack aircraft. Production ceased in May 1958.

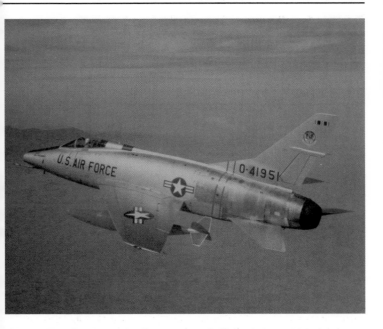

Above: The "Hun" was the first supersonic fighter to enter service.

In 1948, North American Aviation started to plan a fighter that would be supersonic in level flight. The first sketches showed something that looked like an overgrown F-86, but with all surfaces swept at 45deg. It was provisionally named Sabre 45. Wind tunnel tests caused this model to be considerably refined, although the 45deg sweep angle was retained. The critical factor was power. NAA had calculated that a minimum of 9,000lb (4,082kg) military and 12,000lb (5,443kg) maximum thrust was needed.

The selection of a suitable engine was fundamental. The choice fell on Pratt & Whitney's new J57, the design of which was finalised in 1949. This was long but slim. At more than two tonnes, it was on the heavy side, but P&W had erred on the side of reliability rather than maximum thrust/weight. It had a long single-stage afterburner, with no intermediate positions, and a variable nozzle. A two-spool turbojet, the two-stage compressor gave, for the time, a very high compression ratio of 12.5:1, which not only promised to deliver considerably more than the required thrust, but lower than average specific fuel consumption.

During 1950, the USAF decided that what they wanted was a day fighter with a secondary attack capability. With no need to house a search radar, a plain nose intake could be used. The wing was broadened to reduce the thickness/chord ratio to 6 per cent. A recurring problem of this era was that at transonic speeds movement of the ailerons often tended to merely twist the wing, sometimes to the point where aileron reversal occurred. To avoid this, large two-piece ailerons were mounted inboard to reduce the moment arm. This was all very well, but it left no room for flaps. The only high-lift devices fitted were full-span automatic leading edge slats.

Consequently stall and landing speeds were much higher than might otherwise have been the case.

On 1 November 1951, an order was placed for two YF-100 development aircraft and 110 production articles, by now called Super Sabre. As late as 1952 the shape was still being refined. The pitot-type intake was widened and flattened, the canopy was lengthened and faired into a dorsal spine, and the all-moving slab tailplane was relocated to the bottom of the rear fuselage.

On 25 May 1953, "Wheaties" Welch took the first YF-100 aloft from Edwards AFB, and at 35,000ft (10,667m) took the big fighter supersonic on its first flight. The flight test programme went well, and the "Hun", as it became familiarly called, was accepted by the USAF 0n 20 October.

The avionics fit of the F-100A was austere; little more than a radar-ranging gunsight as previously used on the F-86. Main armament consisted of four 20mm Pontiac M-39 fast-firing revolver cannon set under the cockpit.

With production well under way, the Hun was rushed into service, even though the full flight test programme had not been completed, and Air Force project pilot Pete Everest was unhappy with certain handling characteristics. Everest was overruled, and the 479th Fighter Day Wing at George AFB, was activated on 29 September 1954, making the F-100 not only the first supersonic fighter to fly, but the first to enter service.

This was not to last. On 12 October 1954, "Wheaties" Welch

Below: The Super Sabre was mainly used for the ground attack mission.

attempted the last, and most demanding, structural test, a 7.5g pull-out a maximum indicated air speed. The aircraft broke up and he was killed. A exhaustive investigation revealed inertia coupling as the cause; the F-100A had been stressed beyond its yaw design limits. On 11 November the type was grounded.

Extensive modifications were the answer. To improve directiona stability, the span was increased by 1ft 11.5in (0.60m), wing area by 9sq.f (0.84m^2), and the height of the fin by 2ft (0.61m). It was many month before the programme was back on track.

The F-100B was extensively redesigned to become the F-107, whic failed to enter service. The next variant was the F-100C, which first flew o 17 January 1955. This had a more powerful engine, increased internal fue capacity, six underwing stores stations with a maximum capacity of 6,000l (2,722kg), and a flight refuelling probe. It replaced the F-100A from 1957.

The C was followed by the F-100D, an optimised fighter-bomber, whic first flew on 24 January 1956. Rather heavier than the C, this had a slightl longer fuselage, a taller fin, and a broader wing of increased area, with kinked trailing edge with the ailerons moved outboard to make room fo broad slotted flaps.

The air combat debut of the Hun took place over Vietnam on 4 Apr 1965, with an inconclusive action against MiG-17s. But the by now elderl F-100D was inadequate as an escort fighter, and until June 1971 was largel employed for ground attack in the south. There was however a notabl exception. Two-seat F-100F operational trainer were fitted out wit electronic gear, and from November 1965 until May 1966 flew Wild Wease defence suppression missions over the north. Later they were used as fas forward air controllers. The last Super Sabre outfit in Vietnam was the Pha

Northrop P-61B Black Widow

Origin: Northrop Aircraft Inc., USA.
Type: Three-seat, twin-engined, radar-equipped night fighter.
Engine: Two Pratt & Whitney R-2800-65 Double Wasp 18-cylinder supercharged radials rated at 2,000hp for takeoff and 2,250hp war emergency.
Dimensions: Span 66ft 0.75in (20.13m); length 49ft 7in (15.11m); height 14ft 8in (4.47m); wing area 662sq.ft (61.50m^2).
Weights: Empty 21,282lb (9,653kg); normal takeoff 29,700lb (13,472kg).
Loadings (at normal takeoff weight/power)**:** Wing 45lb/sq.ft (219kg/m^2); power 7.43lb (3.37kg) per hp.
Performance: Maximum speed 362mph (582kph) at 15,000ft (4,572m), 330mph (531kph) at sea level); initial climb rate 2,550ft/min (12.95m/sec), sustained climb rate 13min to 25,000ft (7,629m); service ceiling 30,500ft (9,296m); range 940 miles (1,513km).
Armament: Four 20mm belt-fed M-2 cannon with 150 rounds per gun in bulged ventral fuselage; four .50in (12.7mm) Browning machine guns with 500 rounds per gun in remotely controlled dorsal turret.
History: First flight 21 May 1942. First delivery to operational unit late 1943. First air combat victory 7 July 1944. Equipped most USAAF night fighter units in Europe and the Far East. Total production all variants 1,068.
Users: USA (USAAF).

The Black Widow was the first bespoke night fighter to enter service, a previous attempts having failed and all successful night fighters of a nations having been conversions from existing types; even the Beaufighte (pp59-60) was a highly modified Beaufort light bomber. Optimised for th

Above: The multi-mission F-100C had six underwing stores stations.

Rang-based 35th TFW, which ceased operations on 26 June 1971, and Huns were withdrawn from front-line service a year later.

Above: The P-61B Black Widow was too large, too heavy, and too complicated.

task, the P-61 should then have been superb.

In practice the USAAC drew heavily on RAF experience when drafting the specification, and tried to please everybody. The result was a camel, defined as a horse designed by a committee. Heavy firepower, in the form of four 20mm cannon was unarguable, as was a minimum crew of pilot and radar operator. But did the P-61 really need defence to the rear or side, calling for a third crew member? Evidently it was thought so, although a nod was given to drag reduction by mounting four heavy machine guns in a remotely controlled dorsal barbette. To give the gunner a first-class view, a twin-boom layout was adopted, with a large Plexiglass bubble at the rear of the central nacelle. Given this, the Black Widow could not be other than large, complex and heavy.

Two of the most powerful engines available, driving massive four-bladed propellers with a diameter of 12ft 2in (3.71m), were selected to provide adequate performance. The aircraft was given a huge wing fitted with enormous high-lift flaps to ensure reasonable takeoff and landing, and manoeuvrability. Radar was the SCR-720.

Two XP-61 prototypes were ordered on 11 January 1941, long before the United States entered World War II. First flight took place on 21 May 1942, but

Northrop XP-79B

Origin: Northrop Aircraft Inc., California, USA.
Type: Single-seat, twin-engined, flying-wing subsonic jet fighter.
Engines: Two Westinghouse J30 single-spool axial-flow turbojets each rated at 1,365lb (619kg) thrust.
Dimensions: Span 38ft 0in (11.58m); length 14ft 0in (4.27m); height 7ft 0in (2.13m); wing area 278sq.ft (25.83m^2).
Weights: Empty 5,840lb (2,649kg); normal takeoff 8,669lb (3,932kg).
Loadings (at normal takeoff weight)**:** Wing 31lb/sq.ft (152kg/m^2); thrust 0.31.
Performance (manufacturer's estimates)**:** Maximum speed 547mph (880kph) at sea level, 508mph (817kph) at 25,000ft (7,620m); sustained climb rate 4min 18sec to 25,000ft (7,620m); service ceiling 38,000ft (11,582m); range 995 miles (1,601km).
Armament: Reinforced wing leading edges for ramming; four .50in (12.7mm) Browning machine guns as proposed secondary armament.
History: Derived from a series of Northrop flying-wing aircraft, the sole XP-79B built crashed during its maiden flight on 12 September 1945.
Users: None.

The aerodynamic advantages of the flying-wing configuration were long known, but until the advent of the Northrop B-2 Spirit bomber, the inherent stability problems had been intractable, and were not completely mastered until the era of advanced computers. Those that did fly were tail-less aircraft with a central fuselage nacelle, rather than a real flying wing. This was true of the Northrop XP-56, powered by a P&W R-2800-29 driving contra-rotating propellers, which was abandoned in mid-1944 when flight testing was deemed too hazardous.

In January 1943, Northrop was awarded a contract for three XP-79 prototypes, powered by Aerojet XCAL-200 rocket motors which ran on monoethylaniline and red fuming nitric acid. To minimise drag, a prone pilot position was adopted, but after a brief flight test programme the XP-79 was abandoned in favour of the turbojet-powered XP-79B.

This retained the prone pilot position, flanked by the two

development was slow due to the sheer complexity of the project; most systems were electrically rather than hydraulically driven. This is best illustrated by the barbette, which was not only electrically controlled, it had to have cut-outs to avoid the vast propeller discs.

Production deliveries finally began in January 1944, and the first operational unit was the 18th FG in the Pacific, in May 1944, closely followed by British-based squadrons. Black Widows scored a few victories over Europe, but were not nearly as effective as British Mosquitos. Many P-61As flew without the barbettes, but these were reinstated on the P-61B.

The P-61C was powered by turbocharged R-2800-73 engines with a war emergency rating of 2,800hp, but as all-up weight rose by a third, handling was adversely affected, and a clear takeoff run of three miles (4.62km) was recommended! Only 41 P-61Cs were completed. The P-61D was abandoned at an early stage. It is hard to avoid the conclusion that the Black Widow should have been a much simpler and smaller two-seater, with just four cannon.

---

small diameter turbojets, with twin low aspect ratio fins. Mainly constructed of magnesium, it was unique in having reinforced wing leading edges to slice through the tail surfaces of bombers. Guns were carried, but were secondary. First flown from Muroc by Harry Crosby on 12 September 1945, after 15 minutes it entered an irrecoverable spin and crashed, killing the pilot.

Below: The Northrop XP-79B was a jet flying wing with a prone pilot.

Northrop F-89D Scorpion

Origin: Northrop Aircraft Inc., California, USA.
Type: Two-seat, twin-engined, radar-equipped subsonic jet night fighter.
Engines: Two Allison J35-A-33A single-spool, axial-flow afterburning turbojets each rated at 5,600lb (2,540kg) military and 7,400lb (3,357kg) maximum thrust.
Dimensions: Span over tanks 57ft 9.5in (17.61m); length 53ft 10in (16.41m); height 17ft 5.5in (5.32m); wing area 606sq.ft (56.30m²).
Weights: Empty 27,730lb (12,578kg); maximum takeoff 38,210lb (17,332kg).
Loadings (at maximum takeoff weight)**:** Wing 63lb/sq.ft (308kg/m²); thrust 0.39.
Performance: Maximum speed 638mph (1,027kph) at 11,000ft (3,353m), 610mph (982kph) at 35,000ft (10,667m); initial climb rate 8,650ft/min (44m/sec); service ceiling 48,900ft (14,904m); combat radius 382 miles (615km).
Armament: 104 2.75in (70mm) Mighty Mouse FFARs in wingtip pods.
History: N-24 proposal accepted May 1946 and two prototypes ordered December. First flight of prototype 16 August 1948. Production approved March 1949; ceased February 1958, with a total of all variants 2,642. In service August 1951; withdrawn from USAF 1960 and ANG 1969.
Users: USA (USAF, ANG).

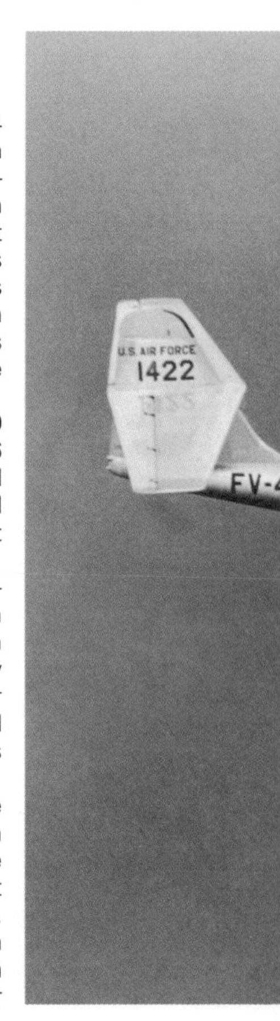

The F-89 Scorpion began as the Northrop N-24 proposal in December 1945 which was accepted in May 1946. It was a large, radar-equipped two-seater, with a projected armament of four 20mm M-24 cannon in a trainable nose to allow firing at 15deg off-boresight in every direction. This was soon dropped; not only were the aiming problems intractable, but the recoil, with a long moment arm ahead of the centre of gravity, pushed the aircraft's nose away from the target. Fixed cannon were preferred.

Fred Bretcher made the first flight of the XF-89 prototype at Muroc (later Edwards AFB) on 16 August 1948. Gradually the design was refined, and production was approved in March 1949. It entered service with Air Defense Command in August 1951.

The Scorpion was a large aircraft, with a two-man crew seated in tandem. Two Allison afterburning turbojets were located amidships on the underside of the lower fuselage, and to allow ease of access to them the broad but thin (9 per cent t/c ratio) wing was set above them. This had decelerons – split ailerons which could double as speed brakes.

To fit such a thin wing, the main wheels were narrow, of large diameter and with thin tyres, which quickly overheated on a warm day, even while taxying. The slender rear fuselage was an upswept boom, surmounted by a tall fin and a high-set tail. Armament was six 20mm cannon, coupled with a Hughes E-1 radar. Experiments were made with a trainable nose, four 30mm cannon, and even a pair of 2.75in (70mm) rocket guns, but these came to nought. Only a few F-89As were built; the main early production variant was the F-89C, powered by J35-A-33 turbojets.

This was replaced from 1953 by the F-89D. Powered by Allison J35-A-33A turbojets, this carried the Hughes E-6 collision-course fire control system, which displaced the cannon. Armament consisted of 104 2.75in (70mm) Mighty Mouse unguided rockets carried in two huge wingtip pods; they were launched automatically when the black boxes thought they had achieved an optimum firing solution, and could blanket an area of sky "as large as a football field"! The rear of the pods was occupied by yet more fuel, bringing internal capacity to an enormous 18,421lb (8,356kg).

The final variants of the Scorpion were essentially D-models with provision to carry six AIM-4 Falcon AAMs in the tip pods or, in the case of the F-89H, two unguided Genie rockets with nuclear warheads on underwing pylons. All Scorpions were pleasant to fly, although badly underpowered.

Below: The huge wingtip pods of the F-89D Scorpion contained 104 rockets.

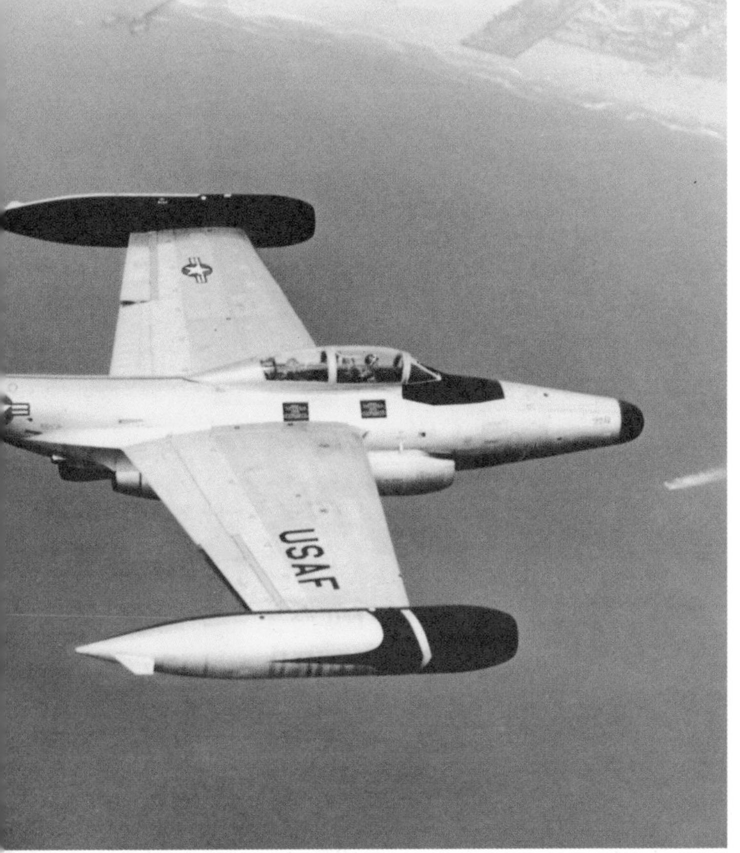

Northrop F-5E Tiger II

Origin: Northrop Corporation, California, USA.
Type: Single-seat, twin-engined supersonic light jet fighter with secondary attack capability.
Engines: Two General Electric J85-GE-21 single-spool, axial-flow afterburning turbojets each rated at 3,500lb (1,588kg) military and 5,000lb (2,268kg) maximum thrust.
Dimensions: Span 26ft 8in (8.13m); length 48ft 2.25in (14.68m); height 13ft 4.5in (4.08m); wing area 186sq.ft (17.28m²).
Weights: Empty 9,723lb (4,410kg); normal takeoff 15,745lb (7,142kg); maximum 24,675lb (11,193kg).
Loadings (at normal takeoff weight)**:** Wing 85lb/sq.ft (413kg/m²); thrust 0.64.
Performance: Maximum speed 1,082mph (1,741kph) Mach 1.63 at 36,091ft (11,000m), 753mph (1,212kph) Mach 0.99 at sea level; initial climb rate 34,500ft/min (175m/sec); combat ceiling 51,200ft (15,605m); range 553 miles (890km).
Armament: Four 20mm Pontiac M-39 revolver cannon with 280 rounds per gun, plus two AIM-9 Sidewinder AAMs.
History: First prototype N-156F (F-5A) flew 30 July 1959. Selected for MAP April 1962. Upgraded as the F-5E from 20 November 1970. First deliveries spring 1974. Production ceased 1994 with 2,626 of all variants. As at 2002, about 800 remain in service, many of which are being upgraded.
Users: F-5A/B and F-5E/F: Bahrain, Botswana, Brazil, Canada, Chile, Honduras, Ethiopia, Greece, Holland, Indonesia, Iran, Jordan, Kenya, Libya, Malaysia, Mexico, Morocco, Norway, Paraguay, Philippines, Saudi Arabia, Singapore, South Korea, Spain, Switzerland, Taiwan, Thailand, Tunisia, Turkey, USA (USAF), Venezuela, Yemen.

Design of the N-156 started in 1954. It was powered by two General Electric J85 turbojets which had been developed for the Quail decoy missile. Simple and cheap, with afterburning added, two J85s gave adequate thrust for supersonic flight while providing twin-engined safety. A moderate wing sweep ensured good low-speed handling characteristics. Gradually the airframe was refined: a cambered leading edge, low-set tailplane, and the newly discovered Area Rule. With a second seat added, this became the T-38 Talon supersonic trainer for the USAF.

With funding assured for the T-38, Northrop went ahead with the N-156F fighter as a private venture. An order for three prototypes was placed in May 1958, and the first flight, by Lew Nelson, took place on 30 July 1959. However, not until May 1962 was the N-156F, renamed F-5A Freedom Fighter, selected for supply to aligned nations under the Military Assistance Program (MAP). Production of the F-5A and the two-seat F-5B ceased in 1972.

A dozen F-5As, slightly modified as F-5Cs, were evaluated in Vietnam in 1965-66 under the codename Skoshi Tiger. This revealed several shortcomings, which were addressed by Northrop with the F-5E/F Tiger II.

J85-GE-21 engines gave 30 per cent more thrust and increased maximum speed from Mach 1.3 to Mach 1.63. A larger wing with leading edge extensions gave 38 per cent more lift. The fuselage was stretched to house 15 per cent more internal fuel, and agility was improved by automatic manoeuvre flaps. Other changes were a two-position nose leg to improve takeoff performance, an arrester hook, windshield de-icing, the Emerson APQ-153 radar, and the GE ASG-29 gyro gunsight. Armament remained the same: two M-39 cannon and two wingtip Sidewinders. Hank Chouteau first flew the F-5E from Edwards AFB on 11 August 1972.

The Tiger II was small, and with smokeless engines was difficult to see at any distance. Although sluggish in pitch, it had a very fast rate of roll. Sustained and instantaneous turn rates were very close to those of the MiG-21, while the view "out of the window" was also poor. It was therefore selected as an adversary aircraft for the USAF Aggressor and USN Top Gun programmes, for which it is probably best known. It was dropped only when it became clear that it could not simulate the MiG-29.

Many upgrades are underway, mainly with improved avionics and "glass" cockpits. The one that failed to succeed was the F-20 Tigershark, a single-engined variant with a sparkling performance first flown in 1982. It lost out to the F-16, and was terminated in October 1986.

Below: A potent if austere fighter, the F-5E remains in widespread service.

Panavia Tornado F.3

Origin: Panavia Aircraft GmbH, Britain/Germany/Italy.
Type: Two-seat, twin-engined bisonic variable-sweep long-range interceptor.
Engines: Two Turbo-Union RB 199 Mk 104 three-spool, axial-flow afterburning turbofans each rated at 9,656lb (4,380kg) military and 16,920lb (7,675kg) maximum thrust.
Dimensions: Maximum span 45ft 7in (13.89m), minimum span 28ft 2in (8.58m); length 61ft 0in (18.59m); height 19ft 8in (6.00m); wing area 286sq.ft (26.60m^2).
Weights: Empty 31,800lb (14,424kg); normal takeoff 50,200lb (22,770kg); maximum 61,700lb (28,000kg).
Loadings (at normal takeoff weight)**:** Wing 176lb/sq.ft (856kg/m^2); thrust 0.67.
Performance: Maximum speed 1,452mph (2,336kph) Mach 2.20 at altitude, 921mph (1,482kph) Mach 1.21 at sea level; initial climb rate 40,000ft/min (203m/sec); combat ceiling 50,000ft (15,239m); subsonic combat radius 1,036 miles (1,667km), supersonic combat radius 230 miles (370km); endurance 3hr at 345 miles (556km); last three with external fuel.
Armament: One 27mm Mauser BK 27 cannon with 180 rounds; four Skyflash/AIM-120 Amraam and four AIM-9 Sidewinder/Asraam AAMs.
History: First flown on 27 October 1979. First production delivery 5 November 1984. Served in the Gulf War of 1991, but no combat. Production ceased March 1993 with a total of 197.
Users: Britain (RAF), Italy, Saudi Arabia.

Competent attack aircraft have often been developed from fighters, with the F-16 as probably the classic example, but the reverse is rare. The emergence of the Tornado F.3 interceptor based on the interdictor/strike variant is, if not unique, very unusual.

Tornado IDS, the first prototype of which flew on 14 August 1974, was designed to deliver ordnance accurately at very high speed and ultra-low level. A variable-sweep wing was selected to provide a balance between the conflicting requirements of short-field performance and economic high-altitude cruising, and high speed coupled with low gust response in the final run-in to

Below: With six AAMs and two jugs, Tornado deploys its speed brakes.

Above: Tornado F.3 is a dedicated interceptor variant of the interdictor.

the target at ultra-low level. The engines were equally a compromise, designed for high performance combined with economy.

Such compromises did not bode well for a fighter variant. Variable-sweep wings are inherently lacking in area, thus wing loading is inordinately high. To a degree this can be compensated for by high-lift devices, but these are of more value in low-speed flight regimes. On the other hand, wing sweep can be optimised for air combat at a median setting, while full sweep is optimum for both acceleration and rate of roll, regardless of altitude.

The engines were less forgiving. Of a very compact three-spool configuration, they were largely designed for economy in military thrust, with the high (in fighter terms) bypass ratio of 1.02:1. For real performance, afterburner had to be used, and although this significantly increased available thrust, it markedly reduced endurance and radius of action, as can be seen in the performance section of the aircraft data.

Normally this would have ruled out Tornado as any form of fighter, but British air defence requirements were out of the ordinary. During the Cold War, the perceived threat from the Soviet Union was twofold: either long-range, missile-armed bombers sneaking round the North Cape to attack the vital supply convoys, or a more direct attack on the homeland by supersonic bombers. The area to be defended was therefore the whole of the

North Sea, and the North Atlantic from Scotland out to Iceland. Vast distances were involved, with little assistance from ground control, and with adverse weather the norm.

Given the circumstances, air combat against fighters was not a consideration. What was needed was a dedicated interceptor, able to operate with a high degree of autonomy in poor weather and in the face of intense electronic countermeasures, with very long endurance while carrying a full load of AAMs. Two American aircraft were intensively evaluated against these requirements.

The F-14 Tomcat appeared possible, but its TF30 turbofans were unreliable, and its avionics were regarded as dated. More to the point, it was unaffordable in the numbers required. The F-15 Eagle lacked the necessary range, while its one-man crew and avionics fit were judged to be inadequate for the extremely demanding conditions. At this point, a dedicated interceptor version of Tornado IDS started to look a good bet, even though this called for a major redesign.

The RB 199 turbofans were extended by 14in (36cm) aft of the flameholders to give extra burning volume. This increased maximum thrust to about 75 per cent of military, and also gave a useful drag reduction. The bucket-type thrust reversers were retained.

The main armament was to be four medium-range semi-active homing Skyflash AAMs, carried semi-submerged beneath the fuselage to minimise drag. As Tornado was quite a small aeroplane, the only way of fitting them in was to lengthen the fuselage with an extra bay astern of the cockpit, and stagger them laterally. The

space thus formed houses avionics and extra internal fuel.

Skyflash, which is largely being replaced by AIM-120 Amraam, is supplemented by four AIM-9 Sidewinders, to be replaced by Asraam, carried on pivoting underwing pylons. Only one of the two 27mm Mauser cannon carried by Tornado IDS has been retained.

A completely new nose, lengthened and reshaped, houses a GEC-Marconi AI.24 multi-mode radar, widely known as Foxhunter. AI.24 was designed to detect low-level fighter-sized targets at 115 miles (185km) and to track up to 40 targets simultaneously while displaying the 10 greatest threats. Unfortunately this has proved unreliable.

The overall fuselage lengthening improved fineness ratio but shifted the centre of gravity. To compensate for this, the sweep angle of the wing glove was increased from 60deg to 68deg. The flight control system was improved, with automatic fully variable sweep scheduled according to the flight regime, and another clever system was added to give carefree handling.

Tornado F.2 was first flown from Warton in England by Dave Eagles on 27 October 1979, and the RAF accepted the first aircraft on 5 November 1984. Tornado F.3 is the definitive type and, with a few low-observability "tweaks", flew air defence missions in the Gulf War of 1991. Since then it has operated over Bosnia. It is scheduled to be replaced by the EF 2000 Typhoon by 2008.

Below: Tornado F.3 launches an active radar homing Skyflash AAM.

Pfalz D III

Origin: Pfalz Flugzeugwerke GmbH, Germany.
Type: Single-seat, single-engined tractor biplane fighter.
Engines: One 160hp Mercedes D.III six-cylinder liquid-cooled inline.
Dimensions: Span 30ft 10in (9.40m); length 22ft 9.5in (6.95m); height 8ft 9in (2.67m); wing area 239sq.ft (22.17m^2).
Weights: Empty 1,532lb (695kg); normal takeoff 2,057lb (933kg).
Loadings (at normal takeoff weight)**:** Wing 8.61lb/sq.ft (42kg/m^2); power 12.86lb (5.83kg) per hp.
Performance: Maximum speed 102mph (165kph) at 9,843ft (3,000m), 91.4mph (147kph) at 15,093ft (4,600m); sustained climb rate 3min 15sec to 3,281ft (1,000m), 11min 45sec to 9,843ft (3,000m); service ceiling 17,061ft (5,200m); endurance 2hr 30min.
Armament: Two 7.7mm fixed, synchronised, belt-fed Spandau LMG-08/15 machine guns.
History: First flight spring 1917. In service from autumn 1917 and served until the end of the war. Total production c600.
User: Germany.

Rhineland-based Pfalz GmbH, founded in 1914, spent the early years of World War I in building aircraft based on designs by others, notably a series of monoplanes. Their only, and greatest, success was the D III biplane, which owed much to the Roland D II, built under licence by Pfalz. This successfully completed trials at Adlershof in June 1917. Ordered into production, it had reached the front by October of that year. Although outperformed by the Albatros D V, particularly in rate of climb, it was much more sturdy, and could carry out prolonged dives followed by pull-outs without shedding its lower wings.

The Pfalz D III was, if anything, even more shark-like than the Albatros. An unequal span biplane, it had a tubular fuselage of timber semi-monocoque construction, spruce longerons and ply formers, spirally wrapped from opposite directions with plywood, covered with doped fabric, closely cowled around the engine with metal.

On early production models, the twin Spandaus were mounted inside the nose, with the muzzles protruding on each side of the cylinder block. Since this arrangement made access for maintenance awkward, on later aircraft the guns were mounted on the decking ahead of the windshield.

One very unusual feature was that the tailplane had an inverted aerofoil section as an aid to rapid recovery from a dive. This also allowed the use of an unbalanced wooden-framed elevator, although the balanced rudder was of fabric-covered welded steel tube.

The Pfalz was mainly used by Bavarian *Jadgstaffeln*, although few if any were completely equipped with the type. A captured aircraft was test-flown, and was reported to have rather better control response than the Albatros D V, although roll rate was on the sluggish side. It was flown by few aces; most preferred the better-performing Albatros, despite its structural failings.

The D III was supplanted by the D IIIa from December 1917. This varied in having the 180hp Mercedes D IIIs engine, and an almost semicircular tailplane instead of the previous angular planform. About 300 Pfalz D IIIs were in service as late as August 1918.

Left: The Pfalz D III was a structurally sound workhorse of a fighter.

Phönix D I

Origin: Phönix Flugzeugwerke GmbH, Austria.
Type: Single-seat, single-engined tractor biplane fighter.
Engines: One 200hp Austro-Daimler Hiero six-cylinder liquid-cooled inline.
Dimensions: Span 32ft 2in (9.80m); length 22ft 1.75in (6.75m); height 8ft 8.5in (2.65m); wing area 269sq.ft (25.00m²).
Weights: Empty 1,578lb (716kg); normal takeoff 2,097lb (951kg).
Loadings (at normal takeoff weight)**:** Wing 7.80lb/sq.ft (38kg/m²); power 10.49lb (4.76kg) per hp.
Performance: Maximum speed 111mph (178kph) at sea level; sustained climb rate 3min 3sec to 3,281ft (1,000m); service ceiling 16,405ft (5,000m); endurance 3hr.
Armament: Two 8mm fixed, synchronised, belt-fed Schwarzlose machine guns.
History: First flight spring 1917. Accepted for production October 1917. Total production, all variants 206.
User: Austro-Hungary.

Extensively redesigned, the Phönix D I prototype was actually a heavily modified 20.16. An unequal span single-bay biplane, the D I was of wooden construction with plywood and fabric skinning. The first 11 aircraft were accepted for service in October 1917 with the comments "superb flight characteristics but only average performance".

D I production totalled a mere 120 aircraft. It was followed by the slightly lighter D II, which had no dihedral on the wings, a higher aspect ratio, balanced ailerons, and a smaller area tailplane. Powered by the 230hp Hiero engine, 96 of the slightly faster and better-climbing D IIs entered service. The D IIa had ailerons on all four planes.

Polikarpov I-153

Origin: Polikarpov OKB, Soviet Union.
Type: Single-seat, single-engined sesquiplane fighter.
Engines: One 1,000hp Shvetsov M-62 nine-cylinder radial.
Dimensions: Span 32ft 9.5in (10.0m); length 20ft 3in (6.17m); height 9ft 2.25in (2.80m); wing area 238sq.ft (22.14m²).
Weights: Empty 3,201lb (1,452kg); normal takeoff 4,101lb (1,860kg); maximum 4,431lb (2,010kg).
Loadings (at normal takeoff weight)**:** Wing 17.23lb/sq.ft (84kg/m²); power 4.10lb (1.86kg) per hp.
Performance: Maximum speed 276mph (444kph) at 15,093ft (4,600m); sustained climb rate 3min to 9,843ft (3,000m); service ceiling 35,107ft (10,700m); range 298 miles (480km).
Armament: Four 7.62mm fixed, synchronised, belt-fed ShKAS machine guns with 650 rounds per gun; 220lb (100kg) bomb load.
History: First flight I-15 prototype October 1933 by Valery Chkalov. Entered production early 1934. Combat debut Spanish Civil War 4 November 1936. I-15bis delivered during 1937. I-153 in service from May 1939. Production ceased late 1940 with a total of all variants 6,578. Used mainly in the attack role in the Great Patriotic War. Withdrawn from front-line service 1943.
Users: China, Finland, Soviet Union, Spain (Republican).

Nikolai Polikarpov commenced design work on the TsKB-3, later the I-15, in February 1932. An unequal span biplane with single streamlined I struts, it was of composite construction with wooden wings and a tubular steel fuselage. At first lacking a suitable indigenous engine, it was powered by a 715hp Wright

Above: The Phönix D I, like several Austrian fighters, used the star struts.

Evaluated by aces Frank Linke-Crawford (30 victories) and Benno von Fiala (29 victories), the D IIa was preferred. Work immediately began on the upgraded Phönix D III, but none entered service before the end of the war. Postwar, a handful were built for Sweden. These were relegated to training in 1928, and finally withdrawn from service in 1933.

Above: A retractable undercarriage was an unusual feature in a biplane.

Cyclone radial. An unusual feature was the upper plane centre section, which could be pulled down to improve forward view, although in production this was amended to a gull-wing section.

First flight, by Valery Chkalov, took place in October 1933, and the test programme was completed in a month. Production was initiated at the beginning of 1934, although with the non-availability of the Cyclone the first batch was fitted with the 480hp M-22 radial. The Cyclone, licence-built as the Shvetsov M-25, arrived in time to power the final 270 I-15s. M-22-powered aircraft were armed with two 7.7mm PV-1 machine guns with 750 rounds each, while M-25 aircraft had four of these weapons and an armoured seat for the pilot.

Altitude performance was outstanding, and on 21 November 1935 Vladimir Kokkinaki reached 47,821ft (14,575m) in a stripped aircraft, although this could not be ratified by the FAI. A year later, the first I-15s reached Spain.

While the gull-winged upper plane improved the view upwards, it seriously obstructed the view to the sides, and was a positive impediment to landing. In consequence, an extensive redesign took place in 1936, resulting in the I-152,

Polikarpov I-16 ISHAK Tip 24

Origin: Polikarpov OKB, Soviet Union.
Type: Single-seat, single-engined low-wing monoplane fighter.
Engines: One 1,000hp Shvetsov M-62 (R) nine-cylinder radial.
Dimensions: Span 29ft 1.5in (8.88m); length 20ft 1.5in (6.13m); height 7ft 11in (2.41m); wing area 160sq.ft (14.87m^2).
Weights: Empty 3,252lb (1,475kg); normal takeoff 4,215lb (1,912kg); maximum 4,546lb (2,062kg).
Loadings (at normal takeoff weight)**:** Wing 26lb/sq.ft (129kg/m^2); power 4.55lb (2.06kg) per hp.
Performance: Maximum speed 326mph (525kph) at sea level, 304mph (489kph) at 15,749ft (4,800m); sustained climb rate 5min 48sec to 16,405ft (5,000m); service ceiling 29,530ft (9,000m); range 248 miles (400km).
Armament: Two 7.62mm nose-mounted, synchronised, belt-fed ShKAS machine guns with 450 rounds per gun and two wing-mounted 20mm ShVAK cannon with 90 rounds per gun. Possibly six RS-82 unguided rockts underwing.
History: First flight I-16 prototype 31 December 1933. Entered production early 1934, and squadron service late that year. Combat debut, Spanish Civil War 5 November 1936. Production terminated in spring 1940, but resumed in the following year. Total production 7,005, plus 1,639 two-seat trainers. Withdrawn from Soviet front-line units mid-1943. Used as a trainer by Spain until July 1952.
Users: China, Soviet Union, Spain (Republican during the civil war; Spanish Air Force afterwards).

First flown by Valery Chkalov on the last day of 1933, the I-16 was a cantilever monoplane with retractable main gears and a fully enclosed cockpit with a wrap-around windshield. This effectively made it the forerunner of a new fighter generation which reached its peak during World War II, predating the Bf 109, the Spitfire and the Curtiss P-36. As if that was not enough, by 1939 it had, by a considerable margin, become the most heavily armed fighter in service anywhere in the world.

ater designated I-15bis. An orthodox upper plane with a new aerofoil section, greater span and area was carried on cabane struts above the fuselage. The 775hp Shvetsov M-25V radial, enclosed in a long-chord cowling, was adopted. This, plus greater fuel capacity, resulted in a 4in (10cm) increase in length. Flight testing began early in 1937, followed by production, with deliveries from mid-summer. At some point in production, the PV-1 machine guns were replaced by 7.62mm ShKAS machine guns which had a much higher rate of fire and muzzle velocity. The I-15bis was used operationally in both Spain and in China (against the Japanese).

The final aircraft in the series was the I-153, which reverted to the gull-wing configuration. The 1,000hp Shvetsov M-62 radial was standardised at an early stage of production, and the other main change was a retractable undercarriage. Not only did this improve performance, but left unretracted it was a deception measure. Over Khalkin Gol in 1939, Japanese fighters attacked what they thought were inferior I-15s, only to find they were up against a far superior aircraft.

Intent on minimising weight, Nikolai Polikarpov designed a dimensionally small fighter. A span of just nine metres allied to a broad chord gave a relatively low aspect ratio wing, of which two notable features were extremely long-span ailerons and a large fillet at the trailing edge root. Initially the engine was the Shvetsov M-22 radial, supplanted by the more potent M-25 (licence-built Wright Cyclone) when this became available in quantity. This caused problems. Unusually, the engine projected only a little ahead of the wing leading edge, making it much too close to the centre of lift. The cockpit was located about level with the wing trailing edge. Coupled with a very short and stubby fuselage, this resulted in inadequate longitudinal stability. In fact, inertia

Below: In 1934, the I-16 was the most modern fighter concept in the world.

moments about all three axes were small; control response was oversensitive, although to an experienced pilot in combat this could be turned to his advantage.

Instability in pitch was aggravated by the undercarriage retraction mechanism, a hand crank which needed 44 turns, getting progressively stiffer, before the wheels were fully up. This was carried out by the right hand while the control column was held in the left, and an undulating climbout was the norm. Another idiosyncracy was a tendency for the undercarriage to jam in a partially retracted position. The solution to this was a cable cutter in the cockpit; in extremis the pilot could sever the cables, allwong the wheels to drop. Landing was only slightly better. The suspension was harsh, giving a tendency to bounce on touchdown, and nosing over occurred occasionally.

The cockpit canopy was unusual, being made to slide forward in a single piece which included the windshield. This brought the glazing unpleasantly close to the pilot's face, and it was generally unpopular; most preferred to fly with it in the open, fully forward position. Many later variants had an open cockpit with just a fixed front section.

A few early production models were built with the inadequate M-22 engine, and deliveries to front line units began in late 1934. The first M-25-powered aircraft was the Tip 4, which carried the twin ShKAS machine gun armament of

the first production model. It was succeeded by the Tip 5, which varied mainly in having 9mm seat armour, and the Tip 6 with the M-25A engine. This was the first I-16 used in combat, during the Spanish Civil War. For winter use in northern Russia, it was fitted with fixed skis for operations from snowbound airfields, although these reduced maximum speed to 239mph (385kph).

The Tip 10, delivered from 1937, had the more powerful M-25V engine, and two extra ShKAS machine guns under the nose decking. It also had a modified wider canopy, increasing the distance from the pilot's head, but most pilots still preferred to fly with it open. This variant could also be fitted with retractable skis.

Development continued apace, and the Tip 17 appeared in 1938. While it retained the nose-mounted machine guns, 20mm ShVAK belt-fed cannon were mounted in the wings. The rate of fire of the ShVAK was 800 rounds per minute, and its muzzle velocity 2,600ft (792m) per second. This combination gave the I-16 a weight of fire far heavier than any of its contemporaries, and this would not be exceeded by a single engined fighter until 1941.

There was, however, a price to be paid; galloping weight growth reduced both performance and manoeuvrability. The definitive I-16, the Tip 24, which

Below: The squat fuselage gave the I-16 short moment arms about the center of gravity.

was built in greater numbers than any other variant, had a structurally strengthened wing, and the Shvetsov M-63 engine, which went some way to restoring performance. Provision was also made for flush-fitting underwing drop tanks. The final production models were the Tip 27 and Tip 29, which varied little from the Tip 24.

Several Soviet I-16 pilots became aces during the Spanish Civil War, with Anatoliy Serov (16 victories) and Pavel Rychagov (15) leading the way, but this was only after they had learned to fight in the vertical, using dive and zoom tactics, against the agile Fiat CR 32s. Against the Bf 109 the Mosca, as the I-16 was called in Spain, was fairly equal.

In the Great Patriotic War, the I-16 could spin through 180deg quickly enough to convert an enemy attack from astern into a head-on pass, the heavier armament of the Soviet fighter giving it the edge. Top scorer on the I-16 was Mikhail Vasiliev with 22 victories before his death in action on 5 May 1942. Mention should also be made of 28-victory ace Boris Kobzan, who downed four German aircraft by ramming them while flying I-16s.

When first flown, the I-16 was ahead of its time. It fought over Spain, China, and Finland, but when the time came for it to defend its homeland it was obsolete.

***Right:* The early I-16 with the sliding canopy and telescopic sight.**

PZL P-11c

Origin: Panstwowe Zaklady Lotnicze, Poland.
Type: Single-seat, single-engined high-wing monoplane fighter.
Engines: One 645hp Bristol Mercury VI S2 nine-cylinder radial.
Dimensions: Span 35ft 2in (10.72m); length 24ft 9.25in (7.55m); height 9ft 4.25in (2.85m); wing area 193sq.ft (17.90m²).
Weights: Empty 2,529lb (1,147kg); normal takeoff 3,968lb (1,800kg).
Loadings (at normal takeoff weight)**:** Wing 21lb/sq.ft (101kg/m²); power 6.15lb (2.79kg) per hp.
Performance: Maximum speed 242mph (390kph) at 18,046ft (5,500m); initial climb rate 2,440ft/min (12.40m/sec); service ceiling c26,248ft (8,000m); range 435 miles (700km).
Armament: Two 7.7mm nose-mounted, synchronised, belt-fed KM Wz.33 machine guns; some aircraft carried two more in the wings.
History: First flight P11/I prototype August 1931. P.11c first flown late 1933. Entered service 1934. Combat debut against Germany 1 September 1939. Total production c325.
Users: Poland, Romania.

In the 10 years from 1929, the Polish National Aviation Establishment PZL produced a series of all-metal monoplane fighters. All had braced parasol-wings with a gull centre section, and fixed undercarriages, and were essentially a series of progressive developments. First flown on 25 September 1929, the P.1 was powered by a 630hp liquid-cooled Hispano-Suiza V-12, and was armed with two 7.7mm Vickers machine guns. Since the Polish air arm was biased against liquid-cooled power plants, the P.1 was discontinued in 1930 in favour of a radial-engined variant.

Two fighters, the radial-engined P.6 and P.7, were developed in parallel from 1930; the P.6 was first flown in August 1930, the P.7 two months later. Powered by a supercharged Bristol Jupiter VIIF radial, the P.7 demonstrated

Above: The PZL P.11c was the most advanced Polish fighter in 1939.

the better performance of the two. Selected for production from June 1931, it began to enter service at the end of 1932.

In 1931 it was decided to improve performance by fitting the P.7 with the Bristol Mercury. First flight of what became the P.11a took place in August 1931, and an order was placed for 30, which were very similar in appearance to the P.7. Romania purchased 50 aircraft as the P.11b, fitted with 670hp Gnome-Rhône 9Krsd Mistral radials.

The first P.11c, which took to the air late in 1933, was extensively modified with a lower thrust line for the 600hp Mercury V S2, and later the 645hp VI S2. Dimensionally it was a few inches larger overall, although official wing area remained constant, despite an increase in span of 6in (15cm). The wing centre section was modified slightly, the cockpit located aft, and the fin and rudder assembly was redesigned to be taller and less steeply raked. The two 7.92mm machine guns were retained, and provision was made for two more in the wings. Eventually the installation of these was started, but only about 40 were

Reggiane Re 2000

Origin: Officine Meccaniche Italiane Reggiane, Italy.
Type: Single-seat, single-engined monoplane fighter.
Engine: One Piaggio P.XI RC 40D 14-cylinder two-row radial rated at 1,040hp at 13,124ft (4,000m) driving a three-bladed constant-speed metal propeller.
Dimensions: Span 36ft 1in (11.00m); length 26ft 2.75in (7.99m); height 10ft 6in (3.20m); wing area 220sq.ft ($20.40m^2$).
Weights: Empty 4,564lb (2,070kg); normal takeoff 6,349lb (2,880kg).
Loadings (at normal takeoff weight)**:** Wing 29lb/sq.ft ($141kg/m^2$); power 6.10lb (2.77kg) per hp.
Performance: Maximum speed 329mph (530kph) at 16,405ft (5,000m), 255mph (410kph) at sea level; sustained climb rate 4min 42sec to 13,124ft (4,000m); service ceiling 36,747ft (11,200m); range 339 miles (545km), endurance 1.25hr.
Armament: Two nose-mounted, synchronised, belt-fed 12.7mm Breda-SAFAT machine guns with 300 rounds per gun.
History: First flight of prototype 24 May 1939. Pre-series production ordered September 1939, but cancelled April 1940. First export contract signed December 1939. Accepted for Italian service from spring 1941. Combat debut September 1941. Production ceased 1 August 1944 with a total of 358. Withdrawn from service (Sweden) 1946.
Users: Italy (*Regia Aeronautica/Regia Marina*), Hungary, Sweden.

Early in 1938, designer Roberto Longhi was lured back to Italy from the USA, where he had gained experience of the latest manufacturing techniques, to design a new fighter for the *Regia Aeronautica*. This was a tall order; the Fiat G.50 and Macchi C.200 had already flown; to compete, the new Reggiane had to be really outstanding.

The prototype was rolled out at Reggio Emilia in May 1939. The large Piaggio P.XI radial engine was closely cowled, leading back to a circular section monocoque fuselage. Unlike the G.50 and C.200, the high seating position was not adopted, and the fairing behind the canopy was tapered back into the fuselage, with glazed panels to improve rearward vision. The five-spar semi-elliptical wings had Frise-type ailerons and manually operated split flaps occupying the entire trailing edge. Most unusually for the time, it had integral fuel tanks. The construction of the Reggiane 2000 was

›o armed at the outbreak of war. Romania licence-built the P.11c.

The P.24 was an up-engined export version, with two 20mm Oerlikon ›annon and two machine guns. It was operated by Bulgaria, Greece, Romania, ›nd Turkey.

When Germany invaded Poland in September 1939, the P.7 and P.11 were ›uickly in action, but were generally outclassed by the German fighters. The ›nly P.11 ace was Stanislaw Skalski, who claimed three observation aircraft and ›hree bombers.

›lmost entirely of aluminium alloy and stressed skin, with only the rudder and ›levators fabric-covered.

First flight, by 1926 Schneider Trophy winner Mario de Bernardi, took place ›n 24 May. No major problems arose. Handling and manoeuvrability were good, ›part from slight nose-heaviness on the landing approach. Trials showed it to be ›uperior to the Bf 109E in close combat, although it was unable to match the ›erman fighter in a dive. In September a batch of 12 pre-series aircraft was ›rdered.

By the end of 1939 many other nations were showing interest, notably ›ritain, with a potential order for 300, although this fell through when Italy

›elow: In many ways the Reggiane Re 2000 was superior to the Bf 109E.

entered World War II six months later. Hungary and Sweden both place substantial orders. Fazed by the idea of integral wing tanks, however, Ita cancelled the pre-series aircraft.

The obvious weakness of the Re 2000 was the armament; the 12.7m Breda-SAFAT was not the best heavy machine gun around, and with only tw of them the Re 2000 lacked hitting power. The less obvious weakness was th Piaggio engine, which in service proved unreliable and difficult to maintai

Republic P-47D Thunderbolt

Origin: The Republic Aviation Corporation, USA.
Type: Single-seat, single-engined monoplane fighter.
Engine: One Pratt & Whitney R-2800-59 Double Wasp 18-cylinder two-row radial developing 2,000hp for takeoff and 2,300hp at 31,000ft (9,448m) with turbo-supercharging.
Dimensions: Span 40ft 9in (12.42m); length 36ft 1in (11.00m); height 14ft 2in (4.32m); wing area 300sq.ft (27.87m^2).
Weights: Empty 10,700lb (4,853kg); normal takeoff 14,600lb (6,623kg); maximum 17,500lb (7,938kg).
Loadings (at normal takeoff weight and power)**:** Wing 49lb/sq.ft (238kg/m^2); power 7.30lb (3.31kg) per hp.
Performance: Maximum speed 426mph (685kph) at 30,000ft (9,144m), 350mph (563kph) at sea level; initial climb rate 3,120ft/min (15.85m/sec); service ceiling 40,000ft (12,191m); range 950 miles (1,529km).
Armament: Eight wing-mounted belt-fed 0.50in (12.7mm) Browning machine guns with 425 rounds per gun. Provision for 2,000lb (907kg) bombload or 10 5in (127mm) high velocity rockets.
History: Prototype ordered 6 September 1940; first flight 6 May 1941. Production commenced spring 1942; P-47Bs to squadrons from November 1942. Combat debut, Europe 8 April 1943. Production ceased December 1945 with a total of 15,660 of all variants. Combat swansong Salvador versus Honduras 1969.
Users: Bolivia, Brazil, Britain (RAF), Chile, China (Nationalist), Colombia, Dominican Republic, Ecuador, El Salvador, France, Honduras, Iran, Italy, Mexico, Nicaragua, Peru, Portugal, Soviet Union, Turkey, USA (USAAF), Venezuela, Yugoslavia.

Faced with a demand for a fighter with unprecedented high altituc performance, Republic chief designer Alexander Kartveli started with th most powerful engine available, the 2,000hp Pratt & Whitney Double Wasp To obtain the required high altitude performance, turbo-supercharging, a used by the Lockheed P-38 was needed. The idea of using engine exhaus gases to power the supercharger turbine was superficially attractive, as gave the impression of something for nothing.

This was however far from the case, and the constraints of turbo supercharging had resulted in the twin-boom configuration of the P-38. Th problems of installing it in a single-engined fighter were extreme. Havin assessed his priorities, Kartveli reversed the usual procedure of designing th fighter and then trying to shoehorn the turbo-supercharger into it. Instead, h decided to sort out the system first, then design the fighter around it.

The turbo-supercharger could realistically be located only in the fuselag aft of the cockpit. Air to feed the engine had to be gathered at the nose then ducted aft to the turbine of the first stage supercharger where it wa compressed, a distance of roughly 19.7ft (6m). From there it was fed bac to the second-stage supercharger at the rear of the engine. This demande cence-built in Hungary as the Héjja II, the Re 2000 was powered by the naller and lighter Gnome-Rhône 14Kfs.

When the Re 2000 was finally adopted by Italy, two modified variants were 'oduced. These were the Re 2000GA; 16 were built with a fuselage tank to crease range, and eight were fitted with catapult attachments for use from attleships. The Re 2000 was mainly used for close air support, like its Re 2001 nd Re 2002 successors, and saw little air combat.

Above: The P-47 Thunderbolt was the largest single engined fighter of WWII.

special high-pressure ducting. Having been burnt in the fuel/air mix as it passed through the engine, the air emerged as hot exhaust gas. This was led back to the turbine in ducts which needed sliding joints if they were not to buckle from the heat. Only when the exhaust gases had driven the turbine could they be vented overboard. As the turbine ran at about 22,000rpm and a temperature of between 600-800deg Celsius, intercoolers and ventilation were essential.

Other design considerations were the location of the main fuel tank and the cockpit. The former, holding 170 Imperial gallons (776 litres), had to be positioned close to the centre of gravity to minimise effects on handling as the fuel was burned off. Aft of the engine was the only possible place, and aft of this was the best place for the cockpit. This left behind the cockpit as the only possible position for the turbo-supercharger, with the ducting running beneath it. Given these considerations, the P-47 could hardly be other than large.

To utilise the engine output, a huge 12ft (3.66m) diameter four-bladed propeller was needed. To provide sufficient ground clearance, the main gear legs, mounted in the wings to retract inwards, had to be long. Too long in fact, to allow the wing installation of four .50in (12.7mm) Browning machine guns per side the main gear legs were made telescopic, shortening by 9in (23cm) when retracted.

The wings were of semi-elliptical planform, with large ailerons outboard and flaps inboard. At 300sq.ft (27.87m^2), wing loading was unavoidably on the high side, but this was to a degree compensated by an extremely fast

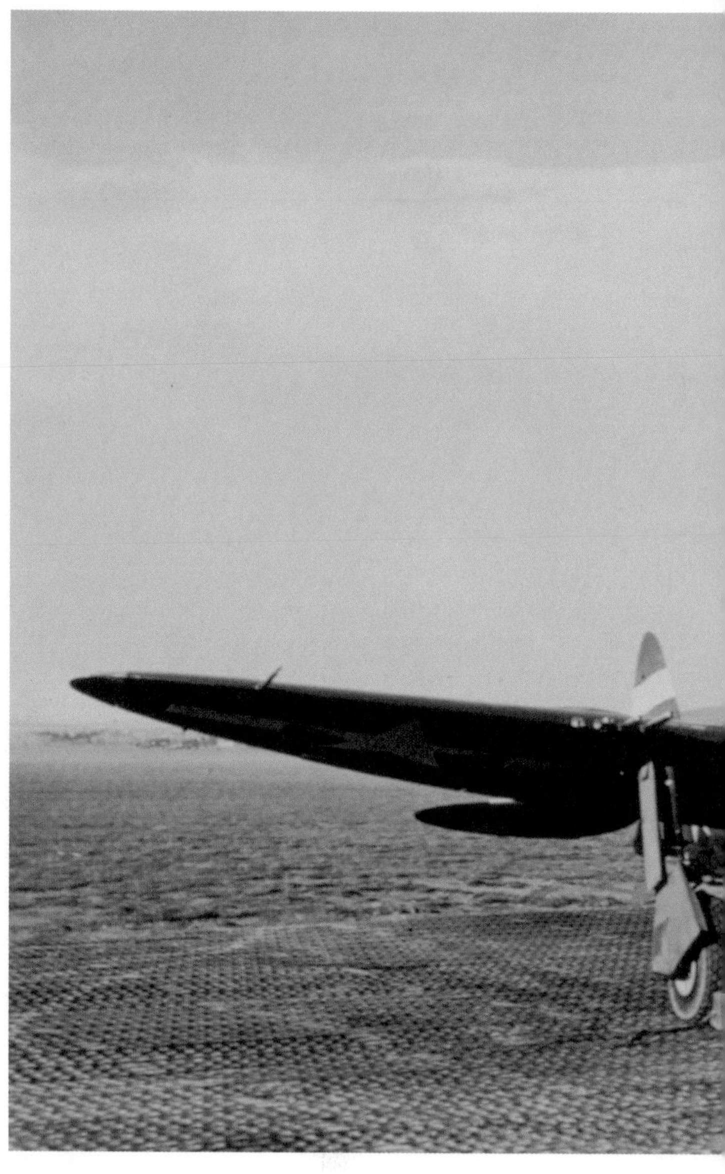

rate of roll. Mounted outboard, the guns were staggered to give clear belt-feed access to the breeches. The muzzles, projecting from the leading edge, show exactly how much.

First flight took place from Farmingdale on 6 May 1941, but many bugs remained to be ironed out. At high altitudes, ailerons snatched and froze, and control forces became excessive. These faults were eventually cured, and production commenced in spring 1942, with the first P-47Bs joining the squadrons in November.

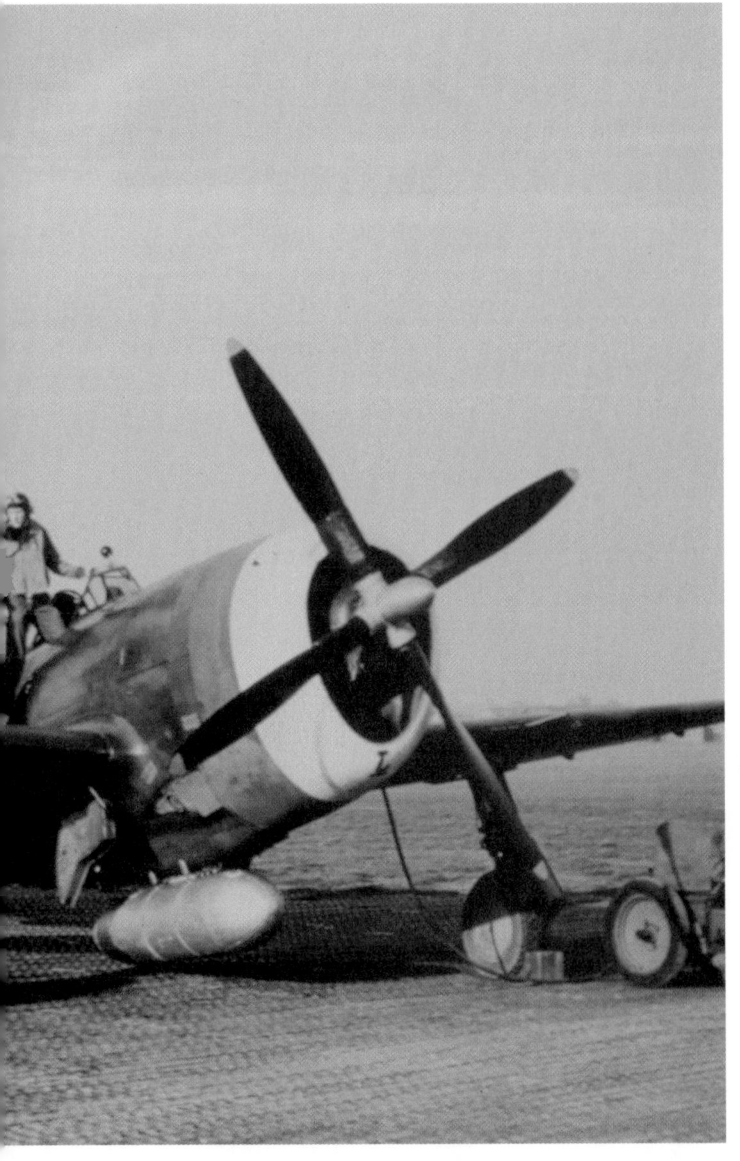

Above: A P-47D operating in the ground attack role from a temporary strip.

In January 1943 the 56th and 78th Fighter Groups arrived in England, although not until 8 April did the Thunderbolt enter combat. There its shortcomings quickly became evident. It was easily out-turned by the agile German single-seaters, although its sparkling rate of roll compensated for this to a degree, and at low and medium altitudes it was easily outclimbed by them.

Its huge size led to it being christened the Juggernaut, quickly shortened to Jug, and its lack of turning capability led Spitfire pilots, American (Eagle Squadron) as well as British, to jibe that the only way to take evasive action was to undo the straps and run around the cockpit! However, the Thunderbolt had qualities of its own. Roll rate has already been mentioned; its hitting power was enormous, doubts about its ability to sustain battle damage, notably in the turbo-supercharger ducting, were quickly laid to rest, and in a sustained dive nothing could stay with it. There was however a price to be paid: compressibility effects at Mach 0.7, buffeting, and a nose-down trim change if the engine was throttled back. Small dive recovery flaps were added on later variants.

RAF Spitfire ace Johnnie Johnson once complimented Don Blakeslee, a former Spitfire pilot with the Eagle squadrons, on the diving capability of his new mount, only to draw the retort: "It ought to; it certainly won't climb!"

The next Jug to see action was the P-47C. Some 13in (33cm) longer, this variant carried a ventral drop tank which enabled it to escort bombers to the German border from July 1943.

The main variant was the P-47D, with water injection, which increased the time that emergency power was available, and which had increased armour protection. A weak point had emerged in combat: rearward vision was inadequate. This was solved by cutting down the rear fuselage and fitting a bubble canopy. Since this reduced lateral stability, a dorsal fin was added to restore keel area. A paddle-bladed propeller was used to increase rate of climb, at the expense of level speed.

The two top P-47D aces, both in Europe, were Francis "Gabby" Gabreski and Bob Johnson, with 28 victories apiece. Johnson in particular used the superb roll capability of his Jug to negate the better-turning of the German fighters.

As the P-51 Mustang entered service in Europe, it progressively supplanted the Jug, which was largely switched to close air support, where its high altitude capabilities were not needed. Oddly enough, all that ducting

Below: The Jug was a rugged bird, and could absorb much battle damage.

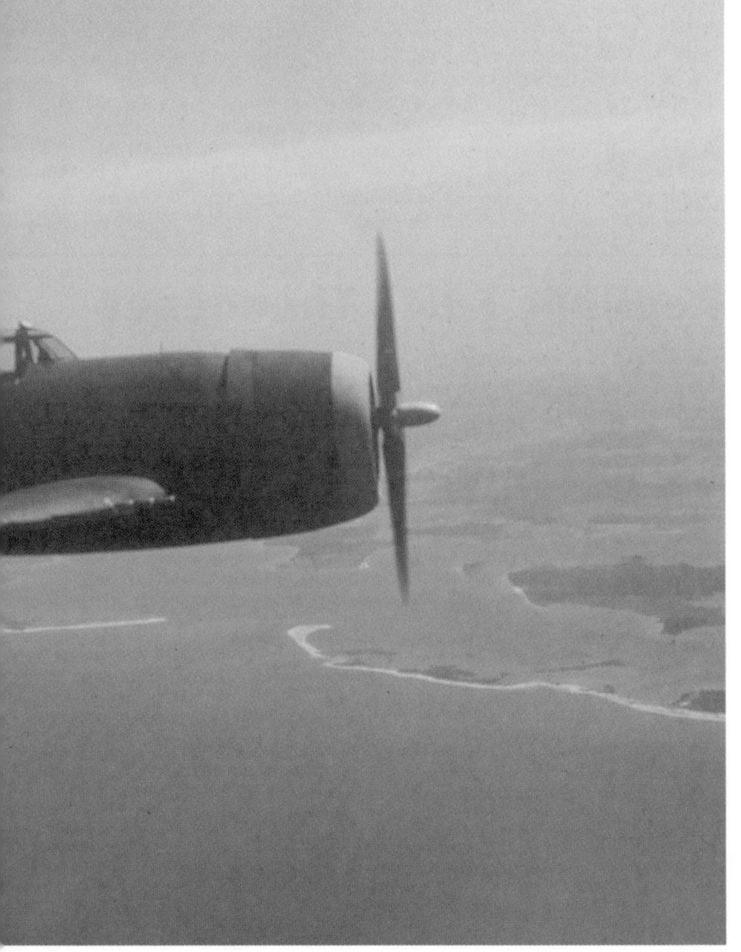

still served a useful purpose. Hit by ground fire at low level and forced to belly in, Jug pilots were protected by all that space and metal beneath their seats, which absorbed the impact.

When in 1944 German jet- and rocket-powered aircraft appeared, the P-47M "sprint" variant, capable of 470mph (756kph), was rushed into service. Only 130 were built. Delivered from December 1944, these saw little action.

Several "one-off" Jugs were built; such as the XP-47E with a pressurised cockpit, the XP-47F with a laminar flow wing, the XP-47H with a 2,500hp liquid-cooled V-16 Chrysler engine, and, fastest of all, the XP-47J, which in August 1944 reached 504mph (811kph).

The Jug was also used in the Far East and Pacific. To cover the vast distances involved, a larger wing with internal fuel tanks and a stronger undercarriage resulted in the P-47N. Produced from December 1944, when based on Saipan it could rendezvous with B-29 bombers and escort them over mainland Japan.

The leading Jug protagonist in the Pacific was Neel Kearby of 5th Air Force with 22 victories. He was killed in action on 5 March 1944. Kearby was followed by William Dunham, who survived the war with 16 victories.

With the advent of jet fighters, the P-47 was rapidly phased out of USAAF service, and many hundreds were sent to aligned nations, with some of whom it remained in service into the 1970s.

Right: Lack of range and manoeuvrability caused the P-47 to be dropped from the escort fighter role.

Republic F-84E Thunderjet

Origin: The Republic Aviation Corporation, USA.
Type: Single-seat, single-engined, straight-winged subsonic jet fighter.
Engine: One Allison J35-A-17D single-spool axial-flow turbojet rated at 5,000lb (2,268kg) military thrust.
Dimensions: Span 36ft 5in (11.10m); length 38ft 6in (11.73m); height 12ft 10in (3.91m); wing area 260sq.ft (24.15m²).
Weights: Empty 10,995lb (4,987kg); normal takeoff 16,685lb (7,568kg); maximum 22,463lb (10,189kg).
Loadings (at normal takeoff weight)**:** Wing 64lb/sq.ft (313kg/m²); thrust 0.30.
Performance: Maximum speed 587mph (945kph) at 4,000ft (1,219m); initial climb rate 4,060ft/min (20.62m/sec); service ceiling 40,750ft (12,420m); range 1,198 miles (1,928km) with tip tanks.
Armament: Six belt-fed 0.50in (12.7mm) Colt-Browning M-3 machine guns, four in the nose and two in the wing roots, all with 300 rounds per gun. Provision for 2,000lb (907kg) external ordnance.
History: Design begun October 1944. First flight 28 February 1946. Production deliveries commenced August 1947. Combat debut, Korea 6 December 1950. Production ended July 1953 with a total of 4,542 straight-winged variants. Used operationally by France over Suez 1956. Retired by ANG 1957, but remained in service until 1976 with Portugal.
Users: Belgium, Denmark, France, Holland, Iran, Italy, Norway, Portugal, Taiwan, Thailand, Turkey, USA (USAF/ANG), Yugoslavia.

Design of the F-84 Thunderjet began in October 1944. The Allison J35 axial-flow turbojet was located just astern of the cockpit and secured to the rear spar,

Above: The F-84E Thunderjet served as an escort fighter in Korea.

allowing the entire rear end to be disconnected and pulled back for access. The J35 was fed by a pitot nose inlet, with a bifurcated duct passing on each side of the cockpit. This configuration allowed a fuselage with a good fineness ratio, the only disadvantage being that with no spare volume, all internal fuel had to be housed in the wings. The mid-set wings were straight, with only a slight taper, giving rise to the appellation "plank-wing". Of laminar flow section, they had a constant thickness/chord ratio of 12 per cent.

The inward-retracting main gear legs were located towards the rear of the wings, leaving maximum space available for fuel. The nose gear leg was hinged at the extreme front, and the rear fuselage carried a tail bumper to guard against misjudgements during takeoff and landing.

The XP-84 was first flown from Muroc on 28 February 1946 with an engine rated at only 3,750lb (1,701kg) thrust. The first production variant was the F-84B, deliveries of which commenced in August 1948. It varied from pre-series aircraft in having faster-firing M-3 machine guns, an ejection seat, and tip tanks. Some B-models had retractable underwing rocket mounts.

The F-84B, with its high wing loading and pathetic thrust loading of 0.25, was unmanoeuvrable at high altitudes, while on hot days it was reluctant to leave the runway. It was quickly dubbed Groundhog. The A-13 engined F-84C was little better.

Republic F-84F Thunderstreak

Origin: The Republic Aviation Corporation, USA.
Type: Single-seat, single-engined, swept-winged subsonic jet fighter.
Engine: One Wright J65-W-7 twin-spool, axial-flow turbojet rated at 7,800lb (3,538kg) military thrust.
Dimensions: Span 33ft 7.25in (10.24m); length 43ft 4.75in (13.22m); height 15ft 0in (4.57m); wing area 325sq.ft (30.19m^2).
Weights: Empty 13,645lb (6,189kg); normal takeoff 19,335lb (8,770kg); maximum 27,000lb (12,247kg).
Loadings (at normal takeoff weight)**:** Wing 59lb/sq.ft (290kg/m^2); thrust 0.40.
Performance: Maximum speed 695mph (1,118kph) Mach 0.91 at sea level, 658mph (1,059kph) Mach 0.94 at 20,000ft (6,096m), 612mph (985kph) Mach 0.92 at 35,000ft (10,667m); initial climb rate 7,400ft/min (37.59m/sec); service ceiling 46,500ft (14,173m); range 860 miles (1,384km).
Armament: Six belt-fed 0.50in (12.7mm) Colt-Browning M-3 machine guns, four in the nose and two in the wing roots, all with 300 rounds per gun. Up to 6,000lb (2,722kg) external ordnance.
History: Design begun 1949. First flight (as YF-96A) on 3 June 1950. Production deliveries commenced 3 December 1952, but operational deployment delayed until January 1954. Production ended August 1957 with a total of 2,348. Phased out by USAF in July 1964 and the ANG in November 1971. Served with Greece and Turkey until 1976.
Users: Belgium, Denmark, France, Greece, Holland, Italy, Norway, Turkey, USA (USAF/ANG), West Germany.

The original concept was to improve the performance of the plank-wing F-84 by fitting swept flying surfaces to the fuselage of an F-84E. This duly emerged as the YF-96A, which was first flown by O. P. Hass from Farmingdale on 3 June 1950. However, with the outbreak of war in Korea, policy changes meant that there was more funding available to develop existing combat aircraft than to produce new types. With this in mind, the USAF

The J35-A-17D, rated at 5,000lb (2,268kg) thrust, offered some improvement, and was used in the F-84D. This variant had thicker wing skinning, and general structural strengthening. It was however quickly replaced in production by the F-84E. This had a 12in (30.5cm) fuselage stretch, a radar-ranging gunsight, and provision for two JATO rockets.

Deployed to Korea, F-84Es of the 27th Fighter Escort Group flew their first combat mission on 6 December 1950, but were generally outclassed by the communist MiG-15s. There were no Thunderjet aces; the leading scorer on type was Jacob Kratt with three victories. Ineffective as an escort fighter, the Thunderjet was switched to ground attack, in which role it performed with distinction.

The final "plank-wing" variant was the F-84G, of which 3,024 were built, most of which were exported. The G had the 5,600lb (2,540kg) thrust -29 turbojet, air refuelling and a multi-paned canopy.

---

quickly reverted to the designation F-84F, renaming it Thunderstreak.

The leading edge sweep adopted was 40deg; thickness/chord ratio was reduced to 9 per cent, although the actual thickness remained pretty much the same. Ailerons were supplemented by spoilers, while a 25 per cent increase in wing area brought wing loading down to more manageable levels. The problem of inadequate thrust loading remained.

At this point, Wright Aeronautical negotiated a licence agreement to build the Armstrong Siddeley Sapphire as the J65, with Buick as a sub-licensee. With about 8,000lb (3,629kg) promised, this looked to be an answer, the only problem being that a mass flow nearly 50 per cent greater called for a complete

Below: The F-84F Thunderstreak had little in common with the Thunderjet.

redesign of the fuselage. Effectively, the F-84F had become an entirely new aircraft, with hardly any commonality with the E.

The second YF-84F flew on 14 February 1951, powered by a J65 constructed mainly of British-made components, and giving 7,200lb (3,266kg) of thrust. But Wright then shot themselves in the foot. Committed to the Americanisation of the Sapphire, they ran into all sorts of technical problems. Production deliveries began in December 1952, but lack of developed engines meant that at one point more than 200 F-84F airframes sat around Farmingdale. More than a year passed before the first operational deployment.

Even then, problems remained. For a long while J65 turbojets remained

Royal Aircraft Factory F.E.2b

Origin: Royal Aircraft Factory, England.
Type: Two-seat, single-engined pusher biplane fighter.
Engine: One 160hp Beardmore 6-cylinder liquid-cooled inline mounted behind the cockpit.
Dimensions: Span 47ft 9in (14.55m); length 32ft 3in (9.83m); height 12ft 7.5in (3.85m); wing area 494sq.ft (45.89m²).
Weights: Empty 2,061lb (935kg); normal takeoff 3,037lb (1,378kg).
Loadings (at normal takeoff weight)**:** Wing 6.15lb/sq.ft (30kg/m²); power 19lb (8.61kg) per hp.
Performance: Maximum speed 91.5mph (147kph) at sea level, 76mph (122kph) at 10,000ft (3,048m); sustained climb rate 9min 51sec to 4,000ft (1,219m); service ceiling 11,000ft (3,353m); range 248 miles (399km); endurance 3.5hr.
Armament: Two swivel-mounted, drum-fed .303in (7.7mm) Lewis guns, one firing forward, the other rearward over the top plane.
History: First flown (F.E.2a) 26 January 1915. In service (F.E.2b) late 1915. Combat debut January 1916. Relegated to bombing, night operations, and home defence from 1917. Total production all variants 1,939. Withdrawn from service late 1918.
Users: Britain (RFC and RAF).

From 1912, the Royal Aircraft Factory at Farnborough produced a series of pusher biplanes in the Farman Experimental (FE) series, of which the F.E.2 was the most successful and the most widely used. The aerodynamically inefficient two-seater pusher configuration was adopted prior to the invention of a workable synchronisation gear, to give a clear field of fire in the forward hemisphere, with assorted gun mountings ahead and to the sides of the front cockpit. The pilot was seated behind and rather higher than the gunner to give him good all-round vision.

The F.E.2a prototype, first flown on 26 January 1915, was powered by a 100hp Green liquid-cooled inline engine. This proved to be underpowered, and was replaced by the 120hp Beardmore, actually a licence-built Austro-Daimler.

A two-bay, equal-span biplane, the F.E.2a had a

unreliable, which was hardly helped when small turbine starters broke up when the clutch to the J65 failed to disengage. The tailplane had old-style elevators, with a disastrous effect on control response in the higher speed range. Early F-84Fs were quickly christened "Superhogs"! Only when at a late stage an all-flying tail was introduced did the Thunderstreak start performing as advertised. Pilots also took a while to acclimatise to landing at 190mph (306kph) or more, although practice eventually made perfect. In addition, the canopy design made ejection a risky business. In the air superiority role, the Thunderstreak lacked manoeuvrability, and it was mainly used as a fighter-bomber.

---

nosewheel under the front of the nacelle braced to the main gear. This was a necessary precaution. If the aircraft nosed over hard enough on landing to break the engine mounts, the pilot was in danger of being crushed if it moved forward.

The whole of the upper plane centre section was hinged for use as a flap/speed brake. The tail surfaces, carried on four braced booms, consisted of a high-set tailplane and elevators, a small triangular fin above the tailplane, and a large kidney-shaped rudder between the upper and lower booms. Only a

Below: Large and heavy, the FE 2b helped defeat the Fokker Eindecker.

dozen models of the F.E.2a were built, although these found their way to the front in 1915, where they were flown by No 6 Squadron, mainly on reconnaissance and artillery spotting missions.

Simplified for ease of production, the F.E.2b, which mainly differed in lacking the flap, and having an extra Lewis gun for rear defence, arrived at the front in January 1916. For the gunner, the extra Lewis was a mixed blessing, since to use it he was forced to stand on his seat with the cockpit coaming at ankle level; not a good position if his pilot took evasive action.

The Fee, as it was known, was very stable, and needed a lot of muscle to manoeuvre. Against agile single-seaters it was outclassed in all departments, but it had its successes, shooting down German aces Max Immelmann, Karl Schaefer and, in July 1917, Richthofen himself, although the Red Baron survived a head wound.

At an early stage, the F.E.2b was fitted with a 160hp Beardmore, then from mid-1916 the 250hp Rolls-Royce Eagle V-12, to become the F.E.2d. The Eagle added little to maximum speed, but rate of climb and ceiling improved considerably. Still outclassed, it was rarely used as a fighter after autumn 1917.

Right: A night fighter FE 2b, a mission for which the type was well suited.

Royal Aircraft Factory S.E.5a

Origin: Royal Aircraft Factory, England.
Type: Single-seat, single-engined tractor biplane fighter.
Engine: Typically one 200hp Hispano-Suiza 8B liquid-cooled V-8 driving a four-bladed propeller.
Dimensions: Span 26ft 7.5in (8.11m); length 20ft 11in (6.38m); height 9ft 6in (2.90m); wing area 246sq.ft (22.85m^2).
Weights: Empty 1,531lb (694kg); normal takeoff 1,940lb (880kg).
Loadings (at normal takeoff weight)**:** Wing 7.89lb/sq.ft (39kg/m^2); power 9.70lb (4.40kg) per hp.
Performance: Maximum speed 138mph (222kph) at sea level, 126mph (203kph) at 10,000ft (3,048m), 116mph (187kph) at 15,000ft (4,572m); sustained climb rate 13min 15sec to 10,000ft (3,048m); service ceiling 17,000ft (6,096m); range 345 miles (555km); endurance 2.25hr.
Armament: One fixed, drum-fed .303in (7.7mm) Lewis gun on a Foster mount above the top wing with four 97 round drums; and one fixed synchronised belt-fed .303in (7.7mm) Vickers machine gun mounted above the nose, with 400 rounds.
History: Designed around the 200hp Hispano-Suiza engine which became available in 1916. First flight of prototype S.E.5 on 22 November 1916, but with 150hp Hispano. In service with No 56 Squadron March 1917. Combat debut 22 April 1917. Quickly superseded by the S.E.5a. Total production all types 5,205.
Users: Australia, Britain (RFC and RAF), Canada, Poland, South Africa, USA.

The finest product of the Royal Aircraft Factory, the S.E. (Scouting

Above: The SE 5a was the best RFC/RAF performance fighter of the Great War.

Experimental) 5a was designed for performance rather than manoeuvrability around the 200hp Hispano-Suiza V-8 engine which was just becoming available, and the intended armament was a single Lewis gun firing through a hollow propeller shaft. As the 200hp engine was not initially available, the prototype S.E.5 first flew on 22 November 1916.

A single-bay, equal-span biplane with raked wingtips, it had a tailplane that was similarly raked. Construction was conventional, fabric-covered timber. At this point the twin gun armament was adopted, with an Aldis telescopic sight. An early innovation was a rather cumbersome "greenhouse" type windshield which, while it offered exceptional weather protection for the pilot, was not popular since it was considered to be a hazard in a crash (and in those days crash-landings were an everyday occurrence). Be that as it may, the greenhouse was soon dumped for something simpler.

The greatest exponent of the S.E.5 was the redoubtable Albert Ball. This was in a way surprising since at first he genuinely disliked the type for its, to his mind, too great stability. Always mechanically minded, he made several modifications to his personal aircraft, one of which was to strip out the Vickers and use the space for extra fuel. He scored 10 victories with the S.E.5 before falling himself on 7 May, untouched by enemy fire.

As it happened, few S.E.5s were built before production changed to the 200hp-engined S.E.5a. So far as stability went, little could be done in pitch; the long moment arm between the engine and the cockpit prevented it. Laterally though, things were improved. The wingtips were shortened for greater strength, giving a reduction in span of 15.5in (39.4cm) and wing area of 4sq.ft (0.37m^2); aileron responsiveness was improved by shortening the levers; while at a later stage, narrow-chord ailerons were fitted. The result was better roll performance.

The S.E.5a represented the peak of the performance fighter in World War

I. It was very fast, it climbed well, and it could be dived at any angle without pulling the wings off. In effect this allowed it to force combat on an opponent, while allowing it to disengage if circumstances were unfavourable. Even at the highest speeds attainable in a dive, and on at least one occasion an indicated speed of 200mph (322kph) was recorded, the S.E.5a remained a stable gun platform. In addition, handling was docile, and the stall innocuous, making it suitable for the undertrained pilots of the time.

Rate of turn was unexceptional, but was good enough to allow survival in a confused multi-bogey fight. Sholto Douglas, commanding No 84 Squadron, laid down tactical principles for its use. The flight attacked as a unit and disengaged as a unit, never breaking formation unless it was absolutely unavoidable. Of course, not all squadrons flew like this. The S.E.5a also had an unexpected attribute, which was much appreciated by its pilots. It was a warm aeroplane, even at high altitudes.

While S.E.5a pilots were credited with fewer victories than those flying the Sopwith Camel, most of the high-scoring British and Commonwealth aces gained many, if not the majority, of their victories with the S.E. The list includes Beauchamp-Proctor, Bishop, Mannock, McCudden, McElroy, to name but a few. Mannock in particular could lay claim to being the finest patrol leader of the entire war, while his pupil, 40-victory ace Ira Jones, flew nothing else.

Below: This SE 5a was carefully restored to flying condition in 1972.

Apart from rigging an aircraft to suit their own personal taste, pilots were given a fairly free hand in "customising" their personal machines. Ball has already been mentioned in this connection. James McCudden, whose speciality was stalking high-altitude reconnaissance machines, had fine-tuned and modified his S.E.5a so that it would reach 20,000ft (6,096m), well above the normal ceiling of the type. The modifications included high-compression pistons, and a spinner "liberated" from a captured LVG, which added 3mph (5kph) to the maximum speed. Bill Lambert, an American whose entire operational career was spent with No 24 Squadron of the newly formed RAF, was equally enterprising. Having trimmed his S.E.5a to fly hands-off, he reduced the wing dihedral by about half to reduce stability and improve control response. He survived the war with 22 victories.

Although there were no official subtypes of the S.E.5a, it was powered by a variety of different engines. Problems were at first experienced with the 200hp geared Hispano, and many were produced with the direct drive Wolseley W.4A Viper V-8, also of 200hp, but with a two-bladed propeller. Other engines fitted were Hispanos of 220 or 240hp, and, on at least six aircraft, the 200hp Sunbeam Arab in both geared and direct drive versions.

The S.E.5a was phased out shortly after the end of the war, having served with 22 RAF and one USAS squadrons.

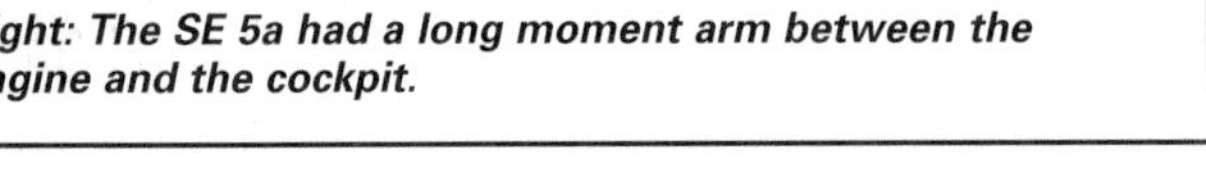

Right: The SE 5a had a long moment arm between the engine and the cockpit.

Ryan FRS-1 Fireball

Origin: Ryan Aeronautical Corporation, USA.
Type: Single-seat, twin-engined, mixed power monoplane carrier fighter.
Engines: One 1,350hp Wright R-1820-72W Cyclone 9-cylinder radial in the nose, supplemented by one General Electric J31 single-spool axial flow turbojet in the fuselage, rated at 1,600lb (726kg) thrust.
Dimensions: Span 40ft 0in (12.19m); length 32ft 4in (9.85m); height 13ft 11in (4.24m); wing area 275sq.ft (25.54m^2).
Weights: Empty 7,689lb (3,488kg); normal takeoff c10,600lb (4,808kg); maximum 11,652lb (5,285kg).
Loadings (at normal takeoff weight)**:** Wing 39lb/sq.ft (188kg/m^2); power (Cyclone) 7.85lb (3.56kg) per hp; thrust (J31) 0.15.
Performance (with both engines)**:** Maximum speed 426mph (686kph) at 18,100ft (5,517m), 399mph (642kph) at sea level; initial climb rate 4,800ft/min (24.38m/sec); sustained climb rate 5min 36sec to 20,000ft (6,096m); service ceiling 43,100ft (13,136m); range 1,030 miles (1,657km).
Armament: Four wing-mounted, belt-fed 0.50in (12.7mm) Browning machine guns. Provision for one 1,000lb (454kg) bomb underwing.
History: Order for prototypes placed 11 February 1943. Production order placed 2 December 1943. First flight of XFR-1 25 June 1944. Production deliveries January to November 1945, total 66 plus three prototypes. In USN service March 1945 to summer 1947.
User: USA (USN).

In 1942, with no end to the war in sight, the U.S. Navy decided to explore the potential of turbojets. Slow throttle response, poor acceleration, and high fuel

Above: The Ryan FRS-1 Fireball had both piston and turbojet engines.

consumption of the early engines made them unsuitable for carrier operations, but it was thought that they might be used to increase the performance of a conventional fighter.

Of nine manufacturers approached, Ryan Aeronautical of San Diego showed the greatest appreciation of the problems and, despite never having produced a combat aircraft of any sort, on 11 February 1943 were awarded a contract for three prototypes. Preflight development looked promising, and on 2 December 1943 a production contract for 100 FR-1 Fireball aircraft was placed, nearly seven months before first flight.

The first XFR-1 took to the air on 25 June 1944, powered by the Cyclone only, although the J31 turbojet, then known as the I-16, was fitted and flown within days. It was of conventional low wing configuration, with the cockpit set further forward than was then usual. A laminar-flow wing section was used, a first for a Navy fighter, as were flush riveted skins, metal-covered control surfaces, and a tricycle undercarriage. A triangular fin and rudder, with a high-set tailplane, overhung the jet exhaust in the rear fuselage. The J31 turbojet, mounted aft of the cockpit, was fed by shallow intakes in the wing centre section. Each intake was flanked by two 12.7mm machine guns, outboard of which was the break for hydraulic wing folding.

Serious problems during the initial flight testing, notably in pitch control and longitudinal stability, resulted in a major redesign of the tail surfaces. The fin and rudder assembly was made taller, while the horizontal tail was lowered, and

SAAB J 21R

Origin: Svenska Aeroplan AB (SAAB), Sweden.
Type: Single-seat, single-engined subsonic jet fighter.
Engine: One de Havilland Goblin centrifugal flow turbojet rated at 3,000lb (1,361kg) thrust.
Dimensions: Span 37ft 3.75in (11.37m); length 34ft 7.75in (10.56m); height 9ft 6.25in (2.90m); wing area 240sq.ft (22.30m^2).
Weights: Empty 6,861lb (3,112kg); normal takeoff c9,480lb (4,300kg); maximum 11,096lb (5,033kg).
Loadings (at normal takeoff weight)**:** Wing 40lb/sq.ft (193kg/m^2); thrust 0.32.
Performance: Maximum speed 497mph (800kph) at sea level; initial climb rate 3,346ft/min (17m/sec); service ceiling 34,451ft (10,500m); range c298 miles (480km); endurance 40min.
Armament: One 20mm Hispano cannon and four 13.2mm M/39A machine guns, all nose-mounted. Provision for a variety of stores underwing.
History: Developed from the piston-engined J 21A of 1943 vintage which was adapted to take a jet engine from late 1945. First flight of converted J 21A as J 21R 10 March 1947. Service entry early 1950. Withdrawn from service mid-1954. Total production 60.
User: Sweden.

During World War II, Sweden, pursuing a policy of neutrality, commenced an unbroken series of "homebrew" SAAB fighters notable for their disregard of convention, which has persisted into the 21st century culminating in the JAS 39 Gripen. SAAB's first attempt at fighter design was the J 21A, which was powered by the Daimler-Benz DB 605 engine, rated at 1,475hp.

Untrammelled by preconceptions, SAAB adopted a pusher layout, with the tail surfaces carried on twin booms. The advantages of this were that it allowed the cockpit to be set well forward, giving the pilot an excellent view to the front hemisphere, with the guns rigidly mounted in the nose about the centreline. It also allowed a tricycle undercarriage to be used, making taxying much easier than with a tail-dragger.

However, this configuration had serious

made very much larger in span and area, with pronounced trim tabs.

A further 600 Fireballs were ordered on 31 January 1945, only days after the first production aircraft was delivered. In March it reached VF-66, an evaluation squadron formed for the task, and carrier qualification trials were successfully completed aboard USS *Ranger* on 1 May. Further production was cancelled when hostilities ceased in August, and VF-66 was decommissioned on 18 October; its aircraft and personnel were transferred to VF-41. The 66th and last production Fireball was delivered in the following month.

VF-41 (later VF-1E) made four carrier deployments between November 1945 and June 1947, but these were training and evaluation rather than operational cruises. Overtaken by events, the Fireball was withdrawn from service in the summer of 1947.

---

disadvantages. Rearward view was virtually nil, an appalling handicap in combat, while if the pilot was forced to abandon the aircraft he stood a good chance of being minced by the propeller. Little could be done about the first problem; the second was overcome by using a primitive ejection seat. The first operational aircraft thus fitted was the Heinkel He 219; the J 21A was destined to become the second!

First flown on 30 July 1943, the J 21A entered service in July 1945, but was

Below: The J 21R was the first of a series of unorthodox Swedish fighters.

compromised in the fighter role by heavy control forces and engine overheating. But by virtue of its layout, it was a prime candidate for jet propulsion. Fitted with the rotund centrifugal flow DH Goblin, it became the J 21R; one of only two fighters (the other was the Yak-15) to successfully transition from piston to turbojet power. Its altogether lighter powerplant, fed by side inlets, was installed further aft to maintain the existing centre of gravity. The only other major change needed was to reshape the fin/rudder assembly, with a high-set tailplane to clear the jet efflux.

SAAB J 29F Tunnan

Origin: Svenska Aeroplan AB (SAAB), Sweden.
Type: Single-seat, single-engined subsonic swept-wing jet day fighter.
Engine: One Svenska Flygmotor RM2B (DH Ghost 50) centrifugal-flow afterburning turbojet rated at 6,173lb (2,800kg) maximum and 4,750lb (2,155kg) military thrust.
Dimensions: Span 36ft 11in (11.00m); length 33ft 7in (10.23m); height 12ft 3in (3.75m); wing area 271sq.ft (25.18m^2).
Weights: Empty 10,681lb (4,845kg); normal takeoff c14,991lb (6,800kg); maximum 18,464lb (8,375kg).
Loadings (at normal takeoff weight)**:** Wing 55lb/sq.ft (270kg/m^2); thrust 0.41.
Performance: Maximum speed 659mph (1,060kph) at low level, 625mph (1,006kph) at 34,451ft (10,500m); initial climb rate 11,812ft/min (60m/sec); sustained climb rate 5min 12 sec to 32,810ft (10,000m); service ceiling 50,856ft (15,500m); range 684 miles (1,100km).
Armament: Four nose-mounted 20mm Hispano V cannon and two Rb 24 (AIM-9 Sidewinder) AAMs on underwing pylons.

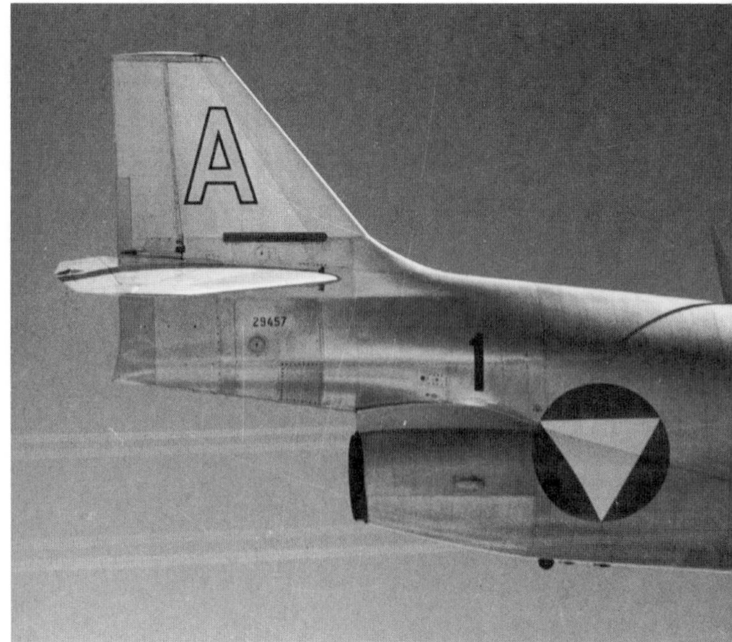

Four J 21As were converted to take the Goblin; first flight was on 10 May 1947. The J 21R, as the type had become, was not a great success; performance in no way matched that of the similarly configured and powered DH Vampire, a variant of which entered Swedish service as the FB 50, while endurance, at 40 minutes, was far too short. Production was limited to 60 aircraft. Entering service in early 1950, it was relegated to the attack mission in that same year, and withdrawn in mid-1954. What it really did was to establish Sweden as a jet fighter manufacturer.

History: Design begun October 1945. First flight of prototype 1 September 1948. First production deliveries 10 May 1951. Production terminated April 1956, although upgrading continued after this time. Total built 661. Operational debut, Congo (with UN) 1961. Withdrawn from service 29 August 1976.
Users: Austria, Sweden.

The design of Projekt R 1001, soon to become the J 29, was frozen in spring 1946. The engine was the de Havilland Ghost; licence-built as the RM2. Much more powerful but fatter than the Goblin used in the J 21R, it was located beneath the mid-set wing, with a short nose inlet leading straight to the eye of the impeller. The cockpit was set high above the inlet duct, resulting an exceptionally deep fuselage which was responsible for the affectionate soubriquet of Tunnan (Barrel), by which the J 29 was universally, but never officially, known.

Below: AUstria was the only export customer for the capable J 29F Tunnan.

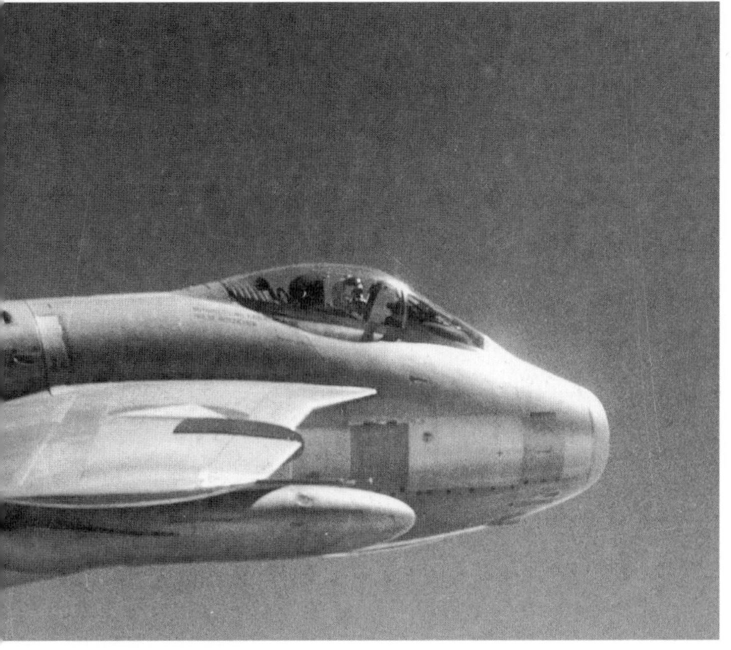

The RM2 exhausted through a short tailpipe, above which the tail surfaces were carried on what almost amounted to a boom, a configuration widely used by American fighters of the period. The horizontal tail had electric trimming through +1 to -6deg.

In a policy of small benefits at minimum risk, the wings were swept at the unadventurous angle of 25deg. They had outboard slats, which automatically locked closed at high speeds; while the trailing edges had hydraulically powered separate inboard and outboard control surfaces, all of which moved differentially as ailerons and in unison as flaps. The main undercarriage retracted into the fuselage. Since this gave a very narrow track, problems were anticipated, but in the event none arose.

First flight took place from Linköping on 1 September 1948. Surprisingly the pilot was English: Bob Moore, who in all made 94 sorties during the flight test programme. Few problems were encountered; a slight tendency to

SAAB J 35F Draken

Origin: SAAB Aktiebolag, Sweden.
Type: Single-seat, single-engined bisonic tail-less delta all-weather jet interceptor.
Engine: One Volvo Flygmotor RM6C (Rolls-Royce Avon 60) two-spool, axial-flow afterburning turbojet rated at 17,737lb (8,000kg) maximum and 12,787lb (5,800kg) military thrust.
Dimensions: Span 30ft 10in (9.40m); length 50ft 4in (15.35m); height 12ft 9in (3.89m); wing area 530sq.ft (49.20m^2).
Weights: Empty 17,339lb (7,865kg); normal takeoff 25,132lb (11,400kg); maximum 35,274lb (16,000kg).
Loadings (at normal takeoff weight)**:** Wing 47lb/sq.ft (232kg/m^2); thrust 0.71.
Performance: Maximum speed 1,321mph (2,126kph) Mach 2 at 36,091ft (11,000ft); initial climb rate 34,450ft/min (175m/sec); sustained climb rate 2min 36 sec to 36,091ft (11,000m), 5min to 49,215ft (15,000m); service ceiling 54,957ft (16,750m); combat radius 395 miles (635km).
Armament: One 30mm Aden M/55 cannon with 100 rounds; two radar-homing Rb 27 and two heat-homing Rb 28 AAMs (AIM-4 Falcons) on ventral pylons. External ordnance capacity 8,818lb (4,000kg).
History: Specification issued 1949. Small-scale proof of concept aircraft flown 21 January 1952. Design finalised March, and prototypes ordered August 1953. First flight of prototype 25 October 1955. Service entry from 8 March 1960. Production ceased 1978. Withdrawn from Swedish service from early 1990s, from Finland in August 2000, but remains in service with Austria.
Users: Austria, Denmark, Finland, Sweden.

By 1949, Sweden had determined to defend its neutrality against the future threat of the fast and high jet bomber. Like NATO, Sweden needed a supersonic all-weather interceptor with a very high rate of climb. Erik Bratt's SAAB design team set to work.

The accepted way to achieve outstanding performance is to wrap the smallest possible airframe around the most powerful available engine. A single-engined configuration

buffeting was overcome by a minor change to the fin shape.

For its day, the J 29 was fast, with a limiting Mach number of 0.86, although it could be dived at Mach 0.95, and there were no gun firing restrictions. It was the first European swept-wing fighter to enter production, and the first to become operational, with F13 Wing at Norrköping in 1951.

The J 29D was fitted with a Swedish-designed afterburner. Given the unchanged limiting Mach number, this made little difference to maximum speed, but it increased rate of climb by nearly two-thirds as much again. It was followed by the J 29E, with a revised wing. The slats were replaced by a fixed leading edge with a discontinuity and wing fence, outboard of which the thickness/chord ratio and upper surface camber were reduced.

The final, and definitive Tunnan was the J 29F, all of which were converted from earlier variants, with afterburning, the new wing, and modified to carry two heat-seeking AAMs. A much under-rated fighter, it remained in service for 25 years.

---

was preferred, minimising structural weight and complexity while maximising affordability. Instead of sketching out the airframe best able to deliver the specified performance, then trying to cram all the important bits into it somewhere, Bratt's team did the opposite.

The first part was relatively easy. Radar, cockpit, and engine were unavoidably in a straight line from front to rear. It then became a matter of

Below: The J 35A Draken was the first Swedish supersonic fighter.

packaging the other essential bits – landing gear, avionics, systems, fuel weaponry etc. – in a manner most economical of space. Of these, fuel was probably the least difficult: provided sufficient volume could be found, the tanks could be shaped to suit.

One of the few airframe constraints was that for supersonic flight; the wing thickness/chord ratio had to be held down, with 5 per cent regarded as optimum. Lockheed had dealt with this on the closely contemporary F-104 Starfighter by shoehorning everything into a very long and streamlined fuselage, with wings that were little more than running boards and a more or less conventional tail. SAAB briefly nodded in the same direction before taking an altogether different approach.

Low thickness/chord was not an absolute; it was a ratio. Given sufficient distance between the front and back of the wing (i.e. the chord), a low t/c ratio could be obtained in a wing that was still thick enough to give useable volume. For SAAB this was a solution which would allow both main gears and fuel to be accommodated with ease. The initial layout sketch showed a pure delta, with the astonishing sweep angle of 70deg, and a nose inlet. This was well ahead of its time and, since handling problems were foreseen, it was modified to a cranked delta shape, with an inboard sweep of 76deg, reducing to 57deg outboard.

As it was such a radical layout, SAAB built a half-scale research aircraft, the

Below: The double delta planform of the J 35F Draken is unique.

SAAB 210, to explore low-speed handling. First flown by Bengt Olow on 21 January 1952, this flew many sorties, revealing no undue problems, even though the controls were manual. In all, two changes emerged. The forward portion of the wing was cut back, giving a "proper" radar-type nose, and wing root inlets were included. The need for control autostabilisation on the full-scale machine also became obvious.

The layout was frozen in March 1953, and after a certain amount of hesitation an order was placed for three prototypes, three pre-production aircraft, and the front end of a two-seat conversion trainer. With Bengt Olow at the controls, the maiden flight took place on 25 October 1955.

With the aircraft ordered into production in August 1956, deliveries began on 8 March 1960. The RM6B turbojet, essentially a Rolls-Royce Avon with a Swedish afterburner and tailpipe, fed by plain oval inlets in the wing roots, gave it outstanding performance, with a maximum level speed of Mach 1.8 at altitude. The trailing edge, which reached almost to the tailpipe, was swept forward inboard but straight outboard, making the wing planform totally unique. The vertical tail was also quite spectacular; steeply raked and of very low aspect ratio, mounted on a dorsal spine which ran from behind the cockpit. At the sharp end was the Ericsson radar, based on an early French Cyrano. Armament consisted of two 30mm Aden cannon mounted in the inboard wing section.

The Draken was undoubtedly a hot ship. Over-sensitivity on the controls made it unforgiving of ham-fisted pilots. On the other hand, attrition remained within acceptable limits despite the fact that to guard against a surprise attack the Royal Swedish Air Force operated for years from selected stretches of road. Taking off presented no problems, although landing and pulling up in a short distance did. A brake parachute was added, and since nose-high aerodynamic braking was also used, twin retractable tailwheels replaced the tailskid,

SAAB JAS 37 Viggen

Origin: SAAB-Scania Aktiebolag, Sweden.
Type: Single-seat, single-engined bisonic canard delta multi-role fighter.
Engine: One Volvo Flygmotor RM8B (based on Pratt & Whitney JT8D) two-spool axial-flow afterburning turbofan rated at 28,110lb (12,750kg) maximum and 16,208lb (7,352kg) military thrust.
Dimensions: Span 34ft 9.25in (10.60m); length 53ft 9.75in (16.40m); height 19ft 4.25in (5.90m); wing area (not incl. canards) 495sq.ft (46.00m^2).
Weights: Empty 23,655lb (10,730kg); normal takeoff 37,478lb (17,000kg); maximum 44,092lb (20,000kg).
Loadings (at normal takeoff weight)**:** Wing 76lb/sq.ft (370kg/m^2); thrust 0.75.
Performance: Maximum speed 1,364mph (2,195kph) Mach 2.1 at 36,091ft (11,000ft), 839mph (1,350kph) at 1,000ft (305m); initial climb rate 39,963ft/min (203m/sec); sustained climb rate 1min 24sec to 36,091ft (11,000m); service ceiling 60,042ft (18,300m); tactical radius 621 miles (1,000km); endurance 2hr.
Armament: One 30mm Oerlikon KCA cannon with 150 rounds; two RB74 Sidewinders and either two Rb71 Skyflash or four Rb99 Amraam AAMs.
History: Specification issued autumn 1961. First flight of prototype 8 February 1967. Production order 5 April 1968. First flight of interceptor variant 15 December 1979, and in service from 1980. Production ceased June 1990, with a total of 329 of all variants. Replacement by Gripen commenced October 1995, but a few upgraded Viggens will remain in service until 2007.
User: Sweden.

The Draken had been an optimised air superiority fighter and interceptor. While it could be, and was, fitted with air-to-surface ordnance, the existence of the A

***Above:* Falcon AAMs and the undernose IR sensor identify this as a J 35F.**

preventing damage if the pilot got too enthusiastic.

Draken development was an ongoing process. From October 1960, a new afterburner involved a lengthened fuselage, and a year later Sidewinders were carried. Then came the J 35B, with data links to ground control and unguided rockets for collision course interception. The J 35D was the first variant to have the RM6C engine, which pushed maximum speed up to Mach 2. With a new radar and fire control system, it entered service from 1963. The final variant (apart from export machines) was the J 35F. Operational from the mid-1960s, it had improved avionics, some displacing the port cannon, and Swedish versions of the Hughes AIM-4 Falcon, typically two SARH Rb27s beneath the fuselage and two heat-homing Rb28s under the wings, the latter coupled with a Hughes IR sensor beneath the nose. Carriage of four AAMs limited maximum speed to Mach 1.4.

***Above:* The cranked delta wing of Viggen had its minimum sweep inboard.**

32 Lansen fighter-bomber made this a low priority. But looking to the future, costs were rising and force sizes were shrinking. Sooner or later, both types would need replacing, and the most economic way of doing this was to produce a new aircraft with specialised variants for each role, thus amortising the development costs over a larger number of aircraft. Four basic variants were needed, for air superiority and interception, attack, reconnaissance, and training. All needed to operate from offsite bases at need. SAAB set to work.

Cost considerations demanded a single-engined single-seater, but engine choice was affected by the fact that in its attack incarnation the aircraft would have to lift a heavy ordnance load out of short strips. Pratt & Whitney's JT8D turbofan was a surprising choice, since it was essentially an airliner engine, but militarised with a reduced bypass ratio and augmentation, it would serve.

Gradually the Viggen took on its outlandish shape. The wing was a cranked delta, but almost perversely the sweep angle was shallower inboard than it was outboard. Ahead of the wing, mounted on the air intakes, were large fixed canards with moving control surfaces on their trailing edges. These had a dual function. They provided extra lift for short field performance, and produced vortices across the main wing surfaces at high angles of attack. Unlike modern all-moving canards, they do little for rate of turn, which is a mere 6.3deg/sec at 20,014ft (6,100m). The other concession to off-site basing is thrust reversing, which enables Viggen to pull up quickly even on icy surfaces.

Erik Dahlström made the first Viggen flight on 8 February 1967. Progress was rapid, and production was ordered on 5 April 1968. The immediate priority was to replace the Lansen, and the first Viggen to enter service was the AJ 37 attack variant, in 1971. Trainers and reconnaissance aircraft followed, and it was another eight years before the first fighter JA 37 flew.

The JA 37 differs from earlier Viggens in having the more fighter-friendly RM8B turbofan, a gas-operated 30mm Oerlikon KCA cannon, and the Ericsson PS-46/A pulse-Doppler radar. Other weaponry consists of the SARH Skyflash and IR Sidewinder AAMs, and, most recently, the Amraam fire and forget missile. Production ended in June 1990, but upgrades will keep a few JA 37s in service until 2007.

Right: The canard surfaces of Viggen are fixed, unlike those of Gripen.

Saunders-Roe SR.A/1

Origin: Saunders-Roe Ltd., England.
Type: Single-seat, twin-engined subsonic jet flying boat fighter.
Engines: Two Metropolitan-Vickers F2/4 Beryl single-spool axial-flow turbojets each rated at 3,850lb (1,746kg) thrust.
Dimensions: Span 46ft 0in (14.02m); length 50ft 0in (15.24m); height 16ft 9in (5.11m); wing area 415sq.ft (38.60m^2).
Weights: Empty 11,262lb (5,108kg); maximum takeoff 19,033lb (8,768kg).
Loadings (at maximum takeoff weight)**:** Wing 46lb/sq.ft (227kg/m^2); thrust 0.40.
Performance: Maximum speed 512mph (824kph) at sea level; initial climb rate 5,800ft/min (29.46m/sec); service ceiling n/a; endurance 2hr 24min.
Armament: Four 20mm Hispano-Suiza cannon mounted above the intake.
History: Proposed 1943. Contract for three prototypes issued May 1944. First flight 16 July 1947. Project terminated June 1951.
Users: None.

In 1943, a jet flying boat, operating from sheltered lagoons among the Pacific islands, seemed like a good idea. Floatplane fighters were widely used, although the lack of conspicuous success was not yet evident. Be that as it may, Saunders-Roe proposed a jet flying boat, and a contract for three prototypes was placed in May 1944, by which time urgency was lacking. Not until 16 July 1947 did the SR.A/1 take to the air, piloted by Geoffrey Tyson, later to gain brief fame as test pilot for the huge 12-turboprop Princess flying boat.

The two Metrovick Beryl turbojets were fed from a high-set nose intake, and exhausted outward at a 5deg angle high on the mid-fuselage. The straight

Above: The unsuccessful SR A/1 was the only jet flying boat fighter.

shoulder-mounted wing had stabilising floats which retracted inwards to form a clean bulge, and provision was made for auxiliary underwing fuel tanks.

The SR.A/1 handled pleasantly enough, and given its bulk was surprisingly manoeuvrable, but it was soon clear that in combat its performance would be inadequate if pitted against land-based fighters. The beginning of the Korean War saw a brief resurgence of interest, but in June 1951 the flying boat fighter project was laid back in the closet.

Saunders-Roe SR.53

Origin: Saunders-Roe Ltd., England.
Type: Single-seat, twin-engined mixed-power bisonic jet interceptor.
Engines: One 1,640lb (744kg) thrust Armstrong-Siddeley Viper single-spool, axial-flow turbojet cruise engine and one 8,000lb (3,629kg) de Havilland Spectre 3A liquid-fuelled rocket.
Dimensions: Span 25ft 1.25in (7.65m); length 45ft 0in (13.72m); height 10ft 10in (3.30m); wing area 274sq.ft ($25.46m^2$).
Weights: Empty 7,400lb (1,631kg); normal takeoff 18,400lb (8,346kg).
Loadings (at normal takeoff weight)**:** Wing 67lb/sq.ft ($328kg/m^2$); thrust (both engines operating) 0.52.
Performance: Maximum speed 1,321mph (2,126kph) Mach 2 at 36,091ft (11,000ft); initial climb rate 46,500ft/min (236m/sec); sustained climb 2min 12sec to 50,000ft (15,239m); service ceiling 78,000ft (23,773m); typical endurance about 1hr.
Armament: Two de Havilland Blue Jay (Firestreak) IR-homing AAMs on wingtip rails.
History: Studies commenced 1950; order for three prototypes October 1952. First flight 16 May 1957, but project terminated soon after, and SR.53

elegated to research. Prototype crashed on takeoff 5 June 1958, and all lying ceased.
Jsers: None.

'he first operational rocket fighter was the German Me 163 Komet. This had an overwhelming rate of climb, but its endurance under power was less than 500 seconds. In 1950, faced with a projected threat 10 years hence of bombers lying at nearly four times the speed and two and a half times the altitude of the World War II B-17, the RAF looked long and hard at rocket-powered point defence interceptors.

Whereas the thrust of a turbojet decreases as altitude increases (and a urbofan is even worse), reducing air density actually increases rocket thrust, making it optimum for high-altitude work. The problem of short endurance could be overcome by adding a small turbojet "get you home" cruise engine.

This was the solution adopted by Maurice Brennan of Saunders-Roe. For he main propulsion engine, he settled on the de Havilland Spectre, which used he very expensive high test (85 per cent solution) hydrogen peroxide (HTP) as an oxidant, rather than the much cheaper, far more dangerous, and operationally difficult to handle liquid oxygen (LOX). Supplementary power was provided by the Viper turbojet, installed above the Spectre, with a mere 500lb (227kg) of fuel, just enough to allow a 30 minute return to base.

The SR.53 was first flown by John Booth on 16 May 1957. It had a deep fuselage to accommodate the two engines one above the other; a simple 6 per cent delta wing with a drooped leading edge, slotted flaps inboard and powered ailerons outboard, and cropped tips to hold launch rails for Blue Jay missiles. The low aspect ratio fin and rudder were surmounted by a triangular all-moving tailplane, which had an elevator to increase camber rather than for control.

Meanwhile, Brennan had realised that an effective radar was needed. As this could not be crammed into the SR.53, he set to work on an improved aircraft, the SR.177. Powered by a Spectre rated at 10,000lb (4,536kg) thrust at sea level, and 11,700lb (5,307kg) thrust at 35,000ft (10,667m), with the de Havilland Gyron Junior cruise engine with an afterburning thrust of 14,000lb (6,350kg), the SR.177 was expected to attain Mach 2.5, an initial climb rate of 55,000ft/min (279m/sec), and a ceiling of 85,000ft (25,907m).

Political considerations intervened. The SR.177 project was terminated in the summer of 1957, despite the fact that the Royal Navy and Germany were very interested. The SR.53 made ony 42 flights before crashing on takeoff, killing John Booth.

Left: The SR 53 potentially outperformed all other fighters of its day.

Shenyang J-8 IIM

Origin: Shenyang Aircraft Corporation, China.
Type: Single-seat, twin-engined bisonic jet interceptor.
Engines: Two Liyang WP-13B two-spool, axial-flow afterburning turbojets each rated at 15,432lb (7,000kg) maximum and 10,597lb (4,807kg) military thrust.
Dimensions: Span 30ft 8in (9.34m); length 70ft 2in (21.39m); height 17ft 9in (5.41m); wing area 454sq.ft (42.20m²).
Weights: Empty 22,864lb (10,371kg); normal takeoff 33,704lb (15,288kg).
Loadings (at normal takeoff weight)**:** Wing 74lb/sq.ft (362kg/m²); thrust 0.92.
Performance: Maximum speed 1,453mph (2,338kph) Mach 2.20 at 36,091ft (11,000ft), 807mph (1,300kph) Mach 1.06 at sea level; initial climb rate 44,097ft/min (224m/sec); operational ceiling 59,058ft (18,000m); range with external fuel 1,367 miles (2,200km).
Armament: One 23mm 23-3 twin-barrel cannon with 200 rounds; two PL-2B IR and four PL-7A SARH AAMs.
History: Development work on the J-8 from 1964; first flight of prototype 5 July 1969. First pre-production aircraft flown 24 April 1981. Redesigned as J-8 II and first flown 12 June 1984. Pre-series aircraft delivered in 1988. Scheduled to receive U.S. avionics from 1989, but this was cancelled after Tiananmen Square massacre. Maiden flight of J-8 IIM 1996. Remains in service 2002, with production exceeding 400 of all variants.
User: People's Republic of China.

Rumours to the effect that the J-8, NATO reporting name Finback, is based on the Mikoyan Ye-152, are probably unfounded, although it does use a similar, but not identical, configuration. Finback appears to be a larger, twin-engined variant of the MiG-21, with a slightly steeper wing sweep. First flight of the prototype J-8 I took place on 5 July 1969, but various problems meant that the first pre-production aircraft did not fly for nearly 11 years, and few production aircraft entered service.

It was soon obvious that Finback needed a capable radar, and it was rehashed to suit, with a "solid" nose and side inlets replacing the original pitot inlet, to become the J-8 II, the first prototype of which flew on 12 June 1984. This is remarkable in that the radar nose has a greater diameter than the cockpit. This results in the forward fuselage tapering sharply in to the cockpit, with variable side inlets, enlarged to accommodate the greater airflow needed by more powerful engines, flaring dramatically outwards.

Finback's only appearance in the West was at Le Bourget in 1989, when the writer was privileged to sit in the cockpit. The cockpit layout was old-fashioned "steam gauge", with a hooded radar screen and forward vision restricted by a heavy canopy bow. Rear visibility was also poor. The delta wing was thin, with conical camber outboard, and small wing fences. The most remarkable thing was the ratio of length to span, which was reminiscent of U.S. fighters of the late 1950s, notably the F-101.

In 1989, moves were afoot to equip Finback with U.S. radar and avionics under the Peace Pearl programme, but this was cancelled in the wake of the Tiananmen Square massacre in the same year. By default, the Russians moved in, and the latest variant, the F-8IIM, which first flew in 1996, is fitted with the Phazotron Zhuk-8 multi-mode pulse-Doppler radar. Cockpit instrumentation is still largely "steam gauge", but is now supplemented by two multi-function displays, and a move towards HOTAS.

Finback is far from the most manoeuvrable fighter around. At Mach 0.9 at 3,281ft (1,000m), it has a sustained turn rate of 6.9g, which frankly is nothing special. At 16,405ft (5,000m), it can accelerate from Mach 0.6 to Mach 1.25 in 55 seconds, but is reported to be sluggish in pitch, although roll rate is rapid.

Finback's sole exploit of note has been forcing down a USN reconnaissance aircraft following a collision in 2001, during which the Chinese pilot, noted for dangerous flying, was lost.

Below: The J-8 IIM is the latest variant of a design nearly 40 years old.

Sopwith Scout (Pup)

Origin: Sopwith Aviation Co Ltd., England.
Type: Single-seat, single-engined tractor biplane fighter.
Engine: One 80hp 9-cylinder Le Rhône 9C rotary.
Dimensions: Span 26ft 6in (8.08m); length 19ft 4in (5.89m); height 9ft 5in (2.87m); wing area 254sq.ft (23.59m^2).
Weights: Empty 787lb (357kg); normal takeoff 1,099lb (498kg).
Loadings (at normal takeoff weight)**:** Wing 4.33lb/sq.ft (21.11kg/m^2); power 13.74lb (6.23kg) per hp.
Performance: Maximum speed 111.5mph (179kph) at sea level, 94mph at 15,000ft (4,572m); sustained climb rate 5min 10sec to 5,000ft (1,524m), 13min 10sec to 10,000ft (3,048m); service ceiling 17,500ft (5,334m); endurance 4hr.
Armament: One .303in (7.7mm) belt-fed, nose-mounted synchronised Vickers machine gun with 400 rounds, or one .303in (7.7mm) drum-fed Lewis gun with 291 rounds mounted on the top plane. A few carried eight Le Prieur unguided rockets on interplane struts.
History: First flown February 1916; in service from August 1916 and combat debut October. Also used as a carrier fighter from early 1917. Withdrawn from front-line service late 1917, although production continued (as a trainer) until November 1918. About 1,770 built.
Users: Britain (RNAS and RFC).

First ordered by the Admiralty as a land-based navy fighter, the Sopwith Scout, as it was officially named, was also adopted by the Royal Flying Corps. A tiny, rotary-engined biplane, it was very similar in appearance to the rather earlier and much larger Sopwith 1½-Strutter, a two-seater primarily used for reconnaissance and bombing. This resemblance led to the quip that the 11/2-Strutter had pupped, and the unofficial name Pup was universally used for the new fighter.

A single-bay equal span biplane of mainly fabric-covered wooden construction, the Pup could lay claim to being one of the best-handling fighters ever built. When it first entered service it could outfight the early German opposition, but its position of superiority was lost within a few months as better-performing opponents arrived at the front.

Rotary engines tended to lose power with increased altitude rather more than did inline engines, and the Le Rhône rotary of the Pup had only between three quarters and half the output of the newer German engines then entering service. In theory the Pup was overmatched from March 1917, but in practice its incredibly light weight proved its saving grace. Underpowered as it was, it was not too far adrift in terms of power/weight ratio, and it was supreme in low wing loading.

High-scoring ace James McCudden flew Pups in 1917 for a short while. He recorded that at higher altitudes, typically 16,000ft (4,877m) or more, the Albatros DV was unable to turn hard without losing height. By contrast, the Pup could still make hard level turns near its ceiling. McCudden recorded two complete circles to one by the Albatros, with the result that in a manoeuvring combat the Pup would quickly gain a height and positional advantage. Lower down it was a different story; the DV was faster, and outclimbed the tiny Sopwith with ease. Some idea of the agility of the Pup can be gained by the fact that it could be looped directly after takeoff, and could continue to gain height in a series of loops!

The RNAS squadrons in France phased out the Pup quite early in 1917 in favour of the Sopwith Triplane, but the RFC soldiered on with it until the end of that year. However, the Pup was used by the RNAS in carrier trials, and on 2 August 1917 E. H.Dunning made the first ever landing on a carrier under way in a Pup. Pups with skid landing gear later served on the carriers *Campania*, *Furious*, and *Manxman*.

Left: August 1917, a Pup lands on HMS* Furious *while the ship is underway.

Sopwith Triplane

Origin: Sopwith Aviation Co Ltd., England.
Type: Single-seat, single-engined tractor triplane fighter.
Engine: One 130hp 9-cylinder Clergét 9B rotary.
Dimensions: Span 26ft 6in (8.08m); length 19ft 6in (5.94m); height 10ft 6in (3.20m); wing area 231sq.ft (21.46m^2).
Weights: Empty 993lb (450kg); normal takeoff 1,415lb (642kg).
Loadings (at normal takeoff weight)**:** Wing 6.13lb/sq.ft (30kg/m^2); power 10.88lb (4.94kg) per hp.
Performance: Maximum speed 116mph (179kph) at 6,500ft (1,981m); sustained climb rate 6min 20sec to 6,500ft (1,981m), 10min 30sec to 10,000ft (3,048m); service ceiling 20,500ft (6,248m); endurance 2hr 45min.
Armament: One .303in (7.7mm) belt-fed, nose-mounted, synchronised Vickers machine gun with 400 rounds.
History: First flown 28 May 1916. In service late 1916, combat debut February 1917. Replaced in front-line service by the Sopwith Camel between June and November 1917. Total production about 140.
Users: Britain (RNAS).

The Triplane, affectionately known to its users as the "Tripehound", was an attempt to improve the performance of the Pup while retaining its manoeuvrability. In this it succeeded admirably, although its operational career was brief, due to the availability of the even better Camel.

The fuselage and tail were essentially similar to those of the Pup, although constructionally they differed in detail. The main difference was the use of three

Sopwith F.1 Camel

Origin: Sopwith Aviation Co Ltd., England.
Type: Single-seat, single-engined tractor biplane fighter.
Engine: One 130hp 9-cylinder Clergét 9B rotary.
Dimensions: Span 28ft 0in (8.53m); length 18ft 9in (5.71m); height 8ft 6in (2.59m); wing area 231sq.ft (21.46m^2).
Weights: Empty 929lb (421kg); normal takeoff 1,453lb (659kg).
Loadings (at normal takeoff weight)**:** Wing 6.29lb/sq.ft (30.71kg/m^2); power 11.18lb (5.07kg) per hp.
Performance: Maximum speed 115mph (179kph) at 6,500ft (1,981m), 113mph (182kph) at 10,000ft (3,048m); sustained climb rate 6min to 6,500ft (1,981m); service ceiling 19,000ft (5,791m); endurance 2hr 30min.
Armament: Two .303in (7.7mm) belt-fed, nose-mounted, synchronised Vickers machine guns each with 250 rounds.
History: F.1 prototype first flown late December 1916; 2F.1 prototype in March 1917. In service June 1917 and combat debut the following month. Production cancelled at the Armistice, and F.1 largely withdrawn from British service shortly after. The ship-borne 2F.1 variant remained in service until the mid-1920s. Total production 5,490.
Users: Belgium, Britain (RFC, RAF, RNAS), Canada, Greece, Latvia, Estonia, and the Allied Expeditionary Force in Russia.

A hump over the twin Vickers machine guns caused the Sopwith Scout F.1 to be dubbed Camel, a name which was later officially adopted. Always controversial, it was hailed by some as the greatest fighter of the war. In the final 16 months of the conflict, British Camels were credited with 1,294 air

***Above:* Ailerons on all three planes were a mark of the Sopwith Triplane.**

narrow chord wings, of the same span but less area than the Pup; with ailerons on all three, separated by single broad interplane struts, and the upper plane set very high by the standards of the day. This configuration gave an extremely rapid rate of roll, and a high rate of climb was achieved at a very steep angle, so much so that a Triplane pilot could often disengage by climbing away.

Used only by the RNAS, the Triplane not only earned an enviable reputation, but spawned a host of imitators, the most notable of which was the Fokker Dr 1, which was flown by many of the top German aces, including the Red Baron, Manfred von Richthofen.

***Above:* The Sopwith F.1 Camel was very manoeuvrable, but also unstable.**

combat victories, of which 386 fell to RNAS squadrons. This was far more than any other type in the conflict. For others, it was far too dangerous to its own pilots, many of whom failed to master its foibles and paid the supreme price.

In appearance it was a shorter and chunkier Pup, only a little heavier, but with nearly two-thirds more power, a slightly increased span, but 10 per cent less wing area. The lower plane had a pronounced dihedral.

Performance was nothing special, but manoeuvrability was something else again. All heavy weights – engine, pilot, fuel and ammunition – were crammed together, giving a very short moment arm, and unlike the Pup the Camel was totally unstable. Tail-heavy, it could not be flown hands-off. Post-World War II test pilot Tom Neil commented that if anyone was silly enough to try it, it would whip into a fast climbing turn to the right, before ending in an inverted spin. The climb was due to tail-heaviness, and the fast turn to the right was largely the result of torque from the engine. While these features made it tricky to fly, an experienced pilot could turn them to advantage in combat. Tail-heaviness made the Camel responsive in pitch, while torque, aided by ailerons on both upper and lower planes, could be used to make an astonishingly fast right turn.

For the inexperienced, the Camel was a potential killer, and attrition during training was high. Bill Lambert, a future S.E.5a ace, flew the Camel for 10 hours during training. He commented: "...that was 10 hours too much. To me that was a dangerous airplane. You had to give it your personal attention with your eyes and your hands all the time." A saying of the time was that the average German never much liked tackling a Camel because he never knew what it was likely to do, which was not at all surprising since the pilot flying it was very often in doubt!

Experienced pilots had fewer problems. As 1917 drew to a close, squadrons still flying the badly outclassed Pup were increasingly taking a beating, and their pilots were only too pleased to receive Camels which, whatever their shortcomings, redressed the balance. No 46 Squadron converted to Camels from Pups in November 1917, and veteran Arthur Gould Lee recorded only the razor-sharp control reactions, and the tendency to swing to the left on takeoff, which demanded full right rudder. The top-scoring Camel ace was also from No 46 Squadron: Canadian Donald McLaren with 54 victories.

The Camel was widely considered impossible to fly at night, but on 3 September 1917 Gilbert Murlis-Green and two others took off to intercept German bombers raiding London. While they failed to intercept, they all landed safely. By the end of the year, a few Camels had been specially adapted for night fighting. The guns, fitted with flash eliminators, were located on the top plane where they were less likely to dazzle the pilot. Angled upwards, they were aimed with an illuminated sight. The fabric to the wing centre-section was removed to improve the view, and the cockpit was moved one bay further back.

Although the difficulties of interception remained extreme, a few victories were scored, including one by Quintin Brand, who got so close that his moustache was singed by flames from the bomber. No 151 Squadron, a Camel night fighter unit commanded by Murlis-Green, who ended the war with 20 victories, served in France from June 1918 on both defensive and offensive operations. The squadron recorded 26 victories in five months.

The Camel 2F.1 differed quite considerably from the F.1. A shipboard variant, its wing span and area were roughly 5 per cent less, the rear fuselage was detachable to facilitate on-board stowage, it had tubular steel cabane struts in lieu of wood, and the 150hp Bentley BR 1 rotary engine. Armament also differed: a single Vickers above the cowling supplemented by a Foster-mounted Lewis gun on the top plane.

Only 200 2F.1s were produced, their main function being to provide air

Right: Camels scored more air victories than any other type in WWI.

cover for the fleet over the North Sea. Heavier, but slightly faster than the F.1, they were carried on flying platforms mounted above gun turrets on capital ships, on the early carriers, and even from towed lighters.

The first air combat success of a carrier-borne fighter came on 18 June 1918, when Camels from HMS *Furious* shot down a German seaplane over the Skaggerak. This was followed exactly two months later by the destruction of Zeppelin L.53, by a Camel flown off a lighter. In 1919, Camels took part in arrested deck landings aboard HMS *Argus*.

Right: A Lewis gun on the top plane marks this as a 2F.1 Camel of the RNAS.

SPAD S VII

Origin: Société Anonyme Pour l'Aviation et ses Dérivés, France.
Type: Single-seat, single-engined tractor biplane fighter.
Engine: One 150hp Hispano-Suiza HS 8Aa liquid-cooled V-8.
Dimensions: Span 25ft 8in (7.82m); length 19ft 11in (6.08m); height 7ft 2.75in (2.20m); wing area 192sq.ft (17.85m^2).
Weights: Empty 1,102lb (500kg); normal takeoff 1,552lb (704kg).
Loadings (at normal takeoff weight): Wing 8.08lb/sq.ft (39kg/m^2); power 10.35lb (4.69kg) per hp.
Performance: Maximum speed 119mph (191kph) at 6,562ft (2,000m); sustained climb rate 6min 30sec to 6,562ft (2,000m); service ceiling 18,046ft (5,500m); endurance 2hr 15min.
Armament: One .303in (7.7mm) belt-fed synchronized nose-mounted Vickers machine gun with 400 rounds.
History: First flown (as the SH 1) April 1916, and production ordered 10 May as the Spa VII C1. First deliveries September 1916, and combat debut later that year. Superseded in front line French service by the SPAD S XIII from early summer 1917 but remained in service until the end of the war. Total production more than 5,800.
Users: Belgium, Brazil, Britain, Czechoslovakia, Estonia, Finland, France, Greece, Italy, Peru, Poland, Portugal, Romania, Russia, Thailand, USA, Yugoslavia.

From 1915 onwards, French fighter design was dominated by Nieuports, agile but slightly delicate rotary-engined biplanes (pp337-340). In an attempt to combine the advantages of the tractor and pusher layouts, SPAD produced four

Above: Not very agile, the SPAD S VII was fast and structurally strong.

two-seater designs of "pulpit" configuration, in which the gunner was seated in a small nacelle mounted ahead of the engine, supported by a ball-race on the end of the propellor shaft, and braced to the wheel struts. These were both unsuccessful and unpopular, as in the event of a crash landing, the gunner was either minced by the propellor, or crushed by the engine. Few saw service with *l'Aviation Militaire*.

In 1916 SPAD designer Louis Béchereau reverted to the orthodox, resulting in the SH.1 prototype. First flown at Villacoublay in April 1916, It was a rather brutal-looking two-bay unstaggered biplane, powered by a 140hp Hispano-Suiza V-8, fronted by a circular radiator and a large spinner. While it lacked the manoeuvrability of the dainty Nieuport 17, it more than compensated by sheer strength and performance. Ordered into production on 10 May as the Spa VIIC1, it was to achieve lasting fame as the S VII.

The production aircraft differed in detail from the SH.1 in that the spinner was deleted, and the wing area was increased by nearly 20sq.ft (1.85m²). It was powered by the 150hp Hispano-Suiza 8Aa. A single bay braced biplane, it had two sets of interplane struts, wjich gave the appearance of a twin-bay type. Two of its more notable recognition features were the steeply raked low aspect ratio fin/rudder, and the fact that all trailing edges were braced with steel wire, giving a scalloped appearance.

The first fighter units to equip with the SPAD were the elite *Cicognes*, which from September 1916 traded in their Nie 17s and proudly painted the Stork insigne on the fuselages of thie new aircraft. The very first unit to convert was *N 3*, which then became *Spa 3*. Among its pilots was rising French ace Georges Guynemer, then with 11 victories, who transferred the name *Le Vieux Charles* from his Nieuport to his new SPAD.

Despite reports to the contrary, the SPAD VII was not easy to fly, although

contemporary accounts state that it was rather more manoeuvrable than the later SE 5a, and was its equal in a dive. However it was reported to "hunt" in a hard level turn; low-speed handling was poor, and with power off, it glided like a tired brick. To land, it had to be flown into the ground with power on, which was not easy. Fortunately it was very strong, and could take a considerable amount of mishandling.

Guynemer quickly mastered his new mount, taking full advantage of its speed and diving ability. On 23 September he accounted for three Fokker biplanes in the space of five minutes, and by January 1917 his score had risen to 30.

In air warfare, nothing stands still, and by early 1917 a new generation of German two-gun fighters had started to out-perform and out-shoot the single-gunned S VII. In the spring of that year, the 180hp Hispano-Suiza HS 8Ab-powered S VII started to enter service, which redressed the balance a little.

Aware from personal experience that aircraft could sustain dozens of non-lethal hits, Guynemer, with Béchereau's backing, sought greater weaponry effectiveness. He found it in the form of the 37mm Puteaux cannon, a single hit from which would knock an opponent out of the sky. The problem of the recoil of this weapon then had to be overcome; in any normal gun mounting position it would cause structural failure.

Below: Checking the alignment of a rather tired SPAD S VII of the RFC.

The solution adopted was to mount it on the engine, firing through a hollow propellor shaft. This could be done by using the 220hp Hispano-Suiza 8Cb engine with spur reduction gear. Much redesign was needed, and the S XII, as it became, was larger overall, with staggered mainplanes, and revised flying controls. In level flight it was slightly faster than the standard S VII, but in all other respects performance was inferior.

Operationally the problems were almost insurmountable. As the cannon was a single-shot weapon, the 7.7mm Vickers had to be retained for sighting purposes. Only when the aim was true could the cannon be fired, when it filled the cockpit with smoke, almost asphyxiating the pilot, who then had to reload. Guynemer first flew the S XII operationally on 5 July 1917, but only a handful ever entered service.

The SPAD S VII was used by almost every French escadrille de chasse, and a high proportion of top-scoring aces, including René Fonck and Charles Nungesser, the aircraft of the latter carrying the unwarlike name of Le Verdier (Greenfinch). The S VII was also operated by two RFC squadrons, and on almost every front; Imperial Russian aircraft carrying Le Prieur rockets. It remained in service until 1923.

Right: Most high-scoring French aces flew the S VII at one time or another.

SPAD S XIII

Origin: Société Anonyme Pour l'Aviation et ses Dérivés, France.
Type: Single-seat, single-engined tractor biplane fighter.
Engine: One 220hp Hispano-Suiza HS 8BEa liquid-cooled V-8.
Dimensions: Span 26ft 6in (8.08m); length 20ft 6in (6.65m); height 8ft 6.5in (2.60m); wing area 217sq.ft (20.20m²).
Weights: Empty 1,325lb (601kg); normal takeoff 1,887lb (856kg).
Loadings (at normal takeoff weight): Wing 8.70lb/sq.ft (42kg/m²); power 8.58lb (3.89kg) per hp.
Performance: Maximum speed 132mph (213kph) at 6,562ft (2,000m), 127mph (205kph) at 13,124ft (4,000m); sustained climb rate 5min 10sec to 6,562ft (2,000m), 8min 20sec to 9,843ft (3,000m); service ceiling 22,311ft (6,800m); endurance 1hr 51min.
Armament: Two .303in (7.7mm) belt-fed synchronised nose-mounted Vickers machine guns with 400 rounds per gun.
History: Prototype first flown 4 April 1917. In service and combat debut from late May. Remained in French front line until the end of the war. Production terminated 1919 with a total of c7,300. In service with France until 1923; Turkey until 1930.
Users: Belgium, Britain, Czechoslovakia, France, Italy, Japan, Poland, Turkey, USA.

Externally there was little to distinguish the SPAD S XIII from the S VII; two Vickers machine guns instead of one, and a slightly different arrangement of the cabane struts with a V at the front. It was powered by a 220hp geared Hispano-Suiza HS BEa liquid-cooled V-8 engine, and the circular radiator, with the vertical blind-type shutters which regulated cooling, remained the same as

Above: Very similar to the S VII, the S XIII was also flown by the USAS.

on the S VII. The intermediate interplane struts within the single bay brace wing of the earlier aircraft were also retained.

Although very similar to the S VII in external appearance, the S XIII wa structurally rather different; if anything even stronger than its doughty predecessor, dimensionally larger, and some 20 percent heavier. A few mino aerodynamic "tweaks" improved manoeuvrability, although in a dogfight it wa no more than adequate. Compared to the S VII, it was faster, climbed bette and had a higher ceiling, but retained all the original handling faults, includin tail-heaviness, although this made it very responsive in pitch. At high speeds i was, like the S VII, a very stable gun platform.

The prototype S XIII first flew on 4 April 1917, and by May of that year th first production aircraft had begun to reach the *escadrilles*, although due t engine problems it was not until August that it was in widespread use. In all i equipped 81 French *escadrilles*, 16 squadrons of the Allied Expeditionary Force 11 Italian and one Belgian squadron.

Given its ubiquity, it is hardly surprising that many French aces flew the S XIII. Guynemer was shot down and killed while flying a war-weary spare rathe

Sud-Ouest SO 9050 Trident II

Origin: Sud-Ouest Aviation, France.
Type: Single-seat, three-engined mixed power supersonic interceptor.
Engine: One SEPR 631 liquid-fuelled two chamber rocket rated at 2,756lb (1,250kg) thrust per chamber, and two wingtip-mounted Turboméca Gabizo single-spool turbojets each rated at 2,425lb (1,100kg) thrust.
Dimensions: Span 22ft 5.75in (6.95m); length 43ft 6in (13.26m); height 12ft 1.5in (3.69m); wing area 156sq.ft (14.50m^2).
Weights: Empty 6,415lb (2,910kg); normal takeoff 13,007lb (5,900kg).
Loadings (at normal takeoff weight): Wing 83lb/sq.ft (407kg/m^2); thrust 0.57.
Performance: Maximum speed 1,254mph (2,018kph) at 63,980ft (19,500m) Mach 1.9; sustained climb rate 2min 30sec to 49,215ft

han his regular aircraft. A few of Nungesser's 45 victims were gained with the SPAD, although most were with Nieuports.

The greatest exponent of the SPAD as René Fonck, who flew the type exclusively for 73 of his 75 confirmed victories. His secret was superb marksmanship, aided by the excellent stability of the SPAD as a gun platform. Not the most modest of men, he once stated; "I place my bullets in the target as if by hand!"

Fonck joined *SPA 103, Groupe de Chasse No 12,* the Cicognes, on 15 April 1917, and his first confirmed victory with the unit came on 5 May. Further progress was slow as Fonck learned his trade, and over the next nine months, he claimed only about one victory a fortnight. The tide now turned.

On 9 May 1918, Fonck scored three victories within 45 seconds; followed by another triple victory that evening. On 14 August he shot down three German aircraft in a single head-on pass in just ten seconds; His victims falling within 100m of each other. He shot down six on 26 September, and his 75th confirmed victory came on 1 November. His unconfirmed victories totalled 52. He was the unrivalled exponent of the SPAD.

15,000m); ceiling more than 85,306ft (26,000m); endurance, "short".
Armament: One Matra R 510 or Nord 5103 AAM.
History: Studies began October 1948. Prototype (SO 5000) first flown 2 March 1953. Preseries aicraft ordered 11 June 1956. Programme cancelled 26 April 1957. In service with France until 1923; Turkey until 1930.
Users: None.

Initially conceived as a point defence interceptor, Trident was primarily rocket-powered, using the highly dangerous red fuming nitric acid and

Below: The Trident II was a mixed power point defence interceptor.

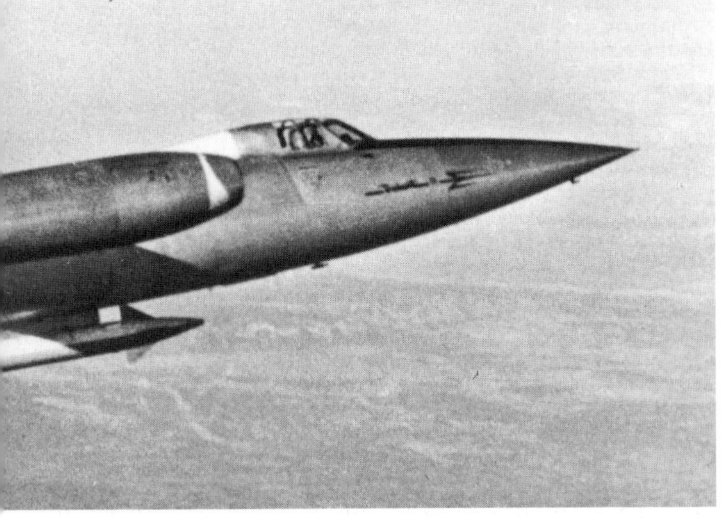

furaline. This vicious mixture needed stainless steel engine interiors with special coatings. For the record, nearly four decades later, the waste disposal process of the McCain frozen food plant at Whittlesey played havoc with stainless steel fittings, and that was just the leftovers from frozen vegetables so the problems of dealing with RFNA can be imagined! To extend range enough to allow a safe return to base, two small Turboméca Marboré turbojets each of 882lb (400kg) thrust, were located on the wingtips.

First flight, at Istres, took place on March 1953, when test pilot Jacques Guignard staggered into the air on the power of the turbojets only. The SO 5000 consisted of a sleek fuselage, broken only by the cockpit canopy, with thin straight wings. Ailerons on these were supplemented by all-moving tailerons, low set with a steep anhedral. Not until September 1954 was the SEPR 481 rocket motor finally ready and flown.

By this time the SO 9000 had been overtaken by events in the shape of the advanced SO 9050, and the test programme was terminated on 10 December 1956. The SO 9050 had a smaller and thinner wing, more

Sukhoi Su-9 II Fishpot B

Origin: Sukhoi OKB, Moscow, USSR.
Type: Single-seat, single-engined supersonic tailed delta all-weather interceptor fighter.
Engine: One Ly'ulka AL-7F single-spool afterburning turbojet rated at about 15,432lb (7,000kg) military and 19,841lb (9,000kg) maximum thrust.
Dimensions: Span 31ft 0.50in (9.45m); length 56ft 9in (17.30m); height 16ft 0in (4.88m); wing area 283sq.ft (26.25m^2).
Weights: Empty 19,996lb (9,070kg); normal takeoff 29,983lb (13,600kg).
Loadings (at normal takeoff weight): Wing 106lb/sq.ft (518kg/m^2); thrust 0.66.
Performance: Maximum speed 1,190mph (1,915kph) Mach 1.80 at 39,372ft (12,000m), 721mph (1,160kph) Mach 0.95 at sea level; initial climb rate 26,970ft/min (137m/sec); sustained climb rate 4min 30sec to 39,372ft (12,000m); service ceiling 44,622ft (13,600m); range 699 miles (1,125km).
Armament: Four beam-riding RS-2U AAMs.
History: First flight of prototype 26 May 1956. Production ordered 1959, in service from 1961 to 1982. Total built c1,000.
User: Soviet Union.

Although the Sukhoi OKB had been formed in 1938, it was for many years overshadowed by Ilyushin, Lavochkin and Yakovlev, and later by Mikoyan and Guryevich, then closed down in 1949 when a prototype broke up in the air. Reinstated after the death of Stalin in 1953, Pavel Sukhoi began designing supersonic interceptors.

The first aircraft of the reformed OKB to fly, on 8 September 1955, was the Su-7. The first Soviet aircraft to have an all-moving slab tail and a translating shock-cone in its nose inlet, it was the forerunner of a series of fighter-bombers. The second, flown by V. Makhalin on 26 May 1956, was the Su-9, an interceptor destined to become the backbone of Soviet air defence for nearly two decades.

The Su-9 was a tailed delta, similar in appearance to the MiG-21, but dimensionally larger and very much heavier. Like the Su-7, it had a slab tail and translating shock-cone. Leading edge sweep

powerful turbojets to allow it to take off at maximum weight without rocket power, and a longer undercarriage.

The first SO 9050 prototype was flown on turbojet power on 19 July 1955, and with rocket power on 21 December. The power balance had been altered, mainly due to a full-power rocket endurance of just 4min 30sec, which was judged to be inadequate. The turbojets gave greater thrust, the rocket rather less. A second SO 9050 prototype was lost during its second test flight, but a third was on order, followed on 11 June 1956 by an order for six pre-series aircraft.

These had provision for Gabizo turbojets rather than the previous Dassault MD 30s; a radar mounted in the nose, and provision for a single under-fuselage Matra R 510 air to air missile, a dummy of which was carried on the first flight with the SEPR 631 installed, on 21 December 1955.

The programme was cancelled on 26 April 1957, after speeds exceeding Mach 1.8 had been routinely reached, and an altitude in excess of 85,306ft (26,000m).

---

was 53deg, with outboard ailerons and large inboard flaps on the trailing edge. The tail surfaces were identical with those of the Su-7. First seen in public at Tushino on Aviation Day, 24 June 1956, after a great deal of confusion as to its identity, not least because it was the second type to be called Su-9, it was given the NATO reporting name of Fishpot.

A limited all-weather interceptor, the Su-9 carried the R1L radar, NATO reporting

Below: The Su-9 II Fishpot B was a tailed delta larger than the MiG-21.

name Spin Scan, in the nose cone. This provided tracking for four RS-2U beam-riding AAMs; NATO reporting name AA-1 Alkali, carried on underwing pylons.

Wing loading was very high, but altitude performance was more important than manoeuvre. Suitably "tweaked", the T-431 prototype set three world records. On 4 July 1959, Vladimir Ilyushin reached an absolute altitude of 94,663ft (28,852m). Then on 4 September 1962 the same pilot hit 1,305mph (2,100kph) Mach 1.977 at a sustained altitude of 69,455ft (21,169m). Finally, on

Sukhoi Su-15TM Flagon

Origin: Sukhoi OKB, Moscow, USSR.
Type: Single-seat, twin-engined bisonic tailed delta all-weather interceptor fighter.
Engines: Two Tumansky R-13F2-300 twin-spool afterburning turbojets each rated at 11,243lb (5,100kg) military and 15,873lb (7,200kg) maximum thrust.
Dimensions: Span 30ft 0in (9.15m); length 64ft 11.5in (19.80m); height 16ft 6in (5.00m); wing area 385sq.ft ($35.77m^2$).
Weights: Empty 24,251lb (11,000kg); maximum takeoff 39,683lb (18,000kg).
Loadings (at maximum takeoff weight): Wing 103lb/sq.ft ($503kg/m^2$); thrust 0.80.
Performance: Maximum speed 1,386mph (2,230kph) Mach 2.10 at 39,372ft (12,000m), 837mph (1,347kph) Mach 1.10 at sea level; initial climb rate 35,041ft/min (178m/sec); sustained climb rate 2min 30sec to 36,091ft (11,000m); service ceiling 65,620ft (20,000m); combat radius 451 miles (725km) on internal fuel.
Armament: Two SARH R-23RE and two IR R-23TE AAMs. Gun pods with 23mm twin-barrel GSh-23 cannon can be carried, each with 200 rounds.
History: First flight of prototype T-58 on 30 May 1962. In production from

25 September 1962, Anatoliy Kozlov stormed around a 500km (311 mile) closed circuit at 1,452mph (2,337kph) Mach 2.20. Although impressive, these figures were in no way representative of the production aircraft.

In the mid-1960s, the Su-9 was given the Uragan 5B radar with a redesigned nose to suit; four R-60 AAMs; two SARH and two IR homing; and the AL-7F-1 turbojet rated at 22,046lb (10,000kg) maximum thrust. In this guise it became the Su-11.

1969 to 1978, and service from 1972 to 1993. Total production c1,500.
User: Soviet Union.

The greatest shortcomings of the Su-9/Su-11 were an inadequate operational ceiling; poor radar capability, and a combat radius which limited it to the point defence mission. In the late 1950s, the Sukhoi OKB set out to correct these faults with what was to become the Su-15.

It had soon become obvious that the required performance could only be attained with two engines. Two Ly'ulka AL-7F turbojets were probably considered, and while they would have resulted in a thrust/weight ratio approaching, or even exceeding unity, giving outstanding performance, their sheer size and excessive fuel consumption would have increased weight and drag, and reduced range.

In a departure from what had become a Sukhoi custom, two slimmer Tumansky R-13F turbojets were selected. These provided a more than adequate thrust/weight ratio while allowing the fuselage width to be held down

Below: The Su-15TM carried four large R-23 AAMs in the air defence role.

to within acceptable limits. They were fed by laterally raked side inlets with variable ramps, optimised for speeds in excess of Mach 2. Side inlets allowed a conical radome, housing a large diameter scanner, thus improving detection range, even with the old hat R1L radar. The overall result was a very sleek fuselage with an excellent fineness ratio, broken only by the canopy. Like all Soviet fighters of the era, the pilot sat low, with almost non-existent rearward, and poor sideways and downwards vision.

Rather surprisingly, the wing of the Fishpot was retained, with one major difference; the distance between the root and the tip was shorter, resulting in the main wheels being partially retracted into the fuselage.

The prototype T-58 first flew on 30 May 1962, but it was not seen in public until

Sukhoi Su-27 Flanker B

Origin: Sukhoi OKB, Moscow, USSR.
Type: Single-seat, twin-engined bisonic all-weather air superiority fighter.
Engines: Two Ly'ulka Saturn AL-31F twin-spool afterburning turbofans each rated at 16,755lb (7,600kg) military and 27,558lb (12,500kg) maximum thrust.
Dimensions: Span 48ft 3in (14.70m); length 71ft 11in (21.94m); height 19ft 6in (5.93m); wing area 668sq.ft (62.04m^2).
Weights: Empty 36,112lb (16,380kg); normal takeoff 51,015lb (23,140kg); maximum takeoff 62,391lb (28,300kg).
Loadings (at normal takeoff weight): Wing 76lb/sq.ft (373kg/m^2); thrust 1.08.
Performance: Maximum speed 1,553mph (2,500kph) Mach 2.35 at 39,372ft (12,000m), 870mph (1,400kph) Mach 1.14 at sea level; initial climb rate c60,041ft/min (305m/sec); service ceiling 60,699ft (18,500m); combat radius 677 miles (1,090km) on internal fuel with 10 AAMs.
Armament: One 30mm single barrel GSh-301 cannon with 150 rounds; up to ten AAMs in a combination of R-27ER/ETs, R-27R/Ts, R-73s and R-77s.
History: First flight of prototype T-10-1 on 27 May 1977, followed by the revised T-10-7 on 20 April 1981. Production commenced 1982, and continues in 2002, with a total c1,200 of all variants incl. licence-building. Operational from 1986. Combat debut (for Ethiopia) 25 February 1999.
Users: Belarus, China, Ethiopia, India, Kazakhstan, Russia, Syria, Ukraine, Uzbekistan, Vietnam.

In 1969, the USAF FX competition for an air superiority fighter was in its final stages, with the McDonnell Douglas F-15 Eagle as front runner. At this point, the standard Soviet tactical fighter was the MiG-23 Flogger, which would be totally outclassed by the F-15. To match it, the Soviet Union urgently needed an agile high performance fighter with outstanding combat persistence in terms of both endurance and the number of AAMs carried.

Sukhoi offered the T-10 heavy fighter, which was accepted in 1971, and detail design commenced. It used a TsAGI-recommended configuration: twin widely-spaced engines and a wing of moderate sweep, and high (for a 1980s fighter) aspect ratio.

Vladimir Ilyushin first flew the T-10-1 prototype on 27 May 1977, by which time the F-15 had been operational for nearly two years. The moderately swept wing had leading edge root extensions and curved tips. The horizontal all-moving tails were low-set, and twin fins were set forward atop widely spaced engine nacelles housing Ly'ulka AL-23F3 turbofans. With neutral rather than relaxed stability, the flight control system was triplex analogue FBW, with mechanical backup.

Right: This Flanker B carries four R-27 AAMs, NATO code AA-10 Alamo.

July 1967, when 10 Su-15s appeared at Domodedovo, led by Vladimir Ilyushin in a dramatic all-black machine. It was given the NATO reporting name of Flagon.

The Su-15T appeared in 1969. It had a cranked wing leading edge, with sweep reduced to 47deg outboard, but only ten were built. The major production variant was the Su-15TM, often wrongly identified as the Su-21, which appeared in 1972 and became operational late in 1973, the cranked wing of which had a span increase of 1ft 11.5in (.60m). It also had the Taifun-M radar, and carried four AAMs instead of two. Finally, in 1975, the conical radome gave way to an ogival shape.

Flagon became notorious for shooting down two Korean airliners; one near Murmansk on 20 April 1978; the second off Sakhalin on 1 September 1983.

Problems were encountered from the outset. Directional stability at bisonic speeds was marginal; fuel consumption and drag were higher than predicted; while flutter and aileron reversal degraded handling. There were also problems with the FBW system which caused the second prototype to crash, killing Eugeny Soloviev. Then, if this was not enough, computer studies indicated that the T-10, by now given the NATO reporting name of Flanker A, was greatly inferior to the F-15.

At this point Flanker might conceivably have been cancelled, but there was no realistic alternative. The MiG-31 lacked agility; the MiG-29 lacked endurance; and a completely new fighter might take an unacceptable 10 years to develop from scratch. Sukhoi tried again.

Among the many changes were a larger area wing with reduced sweep and squared tips with missile rails, and full-span leading edge slats which could also operate as manoeuvre flaps. The tailplane was enlarged and its tips were cropped. The vertical fins, which had been located on top of the engines, were now carried outboard on booms and increased in height. The spine aft of the cockpit was extended, ending in a long "sting", which replaced the original "beaver tail" between the engine exhausts. A large dorsal speed brake, similar

to that of the F-15, was fitted, while the forward-retracting nosewheel was set further aft to improve ground handling.

Further changes were under the skin; a quadruplex analogue flight control system, and in the cockpit the first Russian attempt at HOTAS, although the instrumentation was still "steam-gauge". The pilot sat high under a two piece bubble canopy, with view through 360deg as good as anything the West had to offer.

An impressive internal fuel capacity gave more than adequate range in overload condition, although manoeuvre capability was restricted until the excess had been burned off. This had one tremendous advantage; it eliminated the need for external tanks, leaving all 10 (later 12) hardpoints free for weaponry. On the other hand, a computerized fuel control system was needed to keep the centre of gravity within limits.

A 30mm GSh-301 cannon was located in the starboard wing root. For accurate aiming under all conditions, a combination of radar, IRST and laser ranger was used as described for the MiG-29. Main armament consisted of AAMs, a combination of R-27ER/ETs, R-27R/Ts, R-73s and R-77s, the latter the Russian equivalent of Amraam, and up to 10 in all. Under the massive radome was a huge and very capable NIIP-001 multi-mode pulse-Doppler radar.

This was not done at all once, but many of the improvements were featured on the T-10-7, powered by Ly'ulka AL-31F turbofans and first flown by Vladimir Ilyushin on 20 April 1981. But Sukhoi was not yet out of the wood. He was forced to eject following a fuel system failure on 3 September 1981. Then on 23 December, Aleksandr Komarov was killed when his aircraft broke up when the leading edge flaps failed. The cause was discovered after Nikolai Sadovnikov duplicated Komarov's flight and lost most of one wing.

Production commenced in 1982, but problems with the flight control software, the fuel system and the radar, delayed service entry until 1986; nine years after the first flight. It was then dubbed Flanker B by NATO.

Since then, Flanker has spawned many offshoots: the Su-27UB combat-capable trainer, the export Su-27SK and the Su-27K carrier fighter among them, and several attack and interdiction variants. Its only air combat to date was for Ethiopia in February 1999; ironically its two victims were MiG-29s.

Below: Flanker's IRST sensor is central, unlike that of the MiG-29.

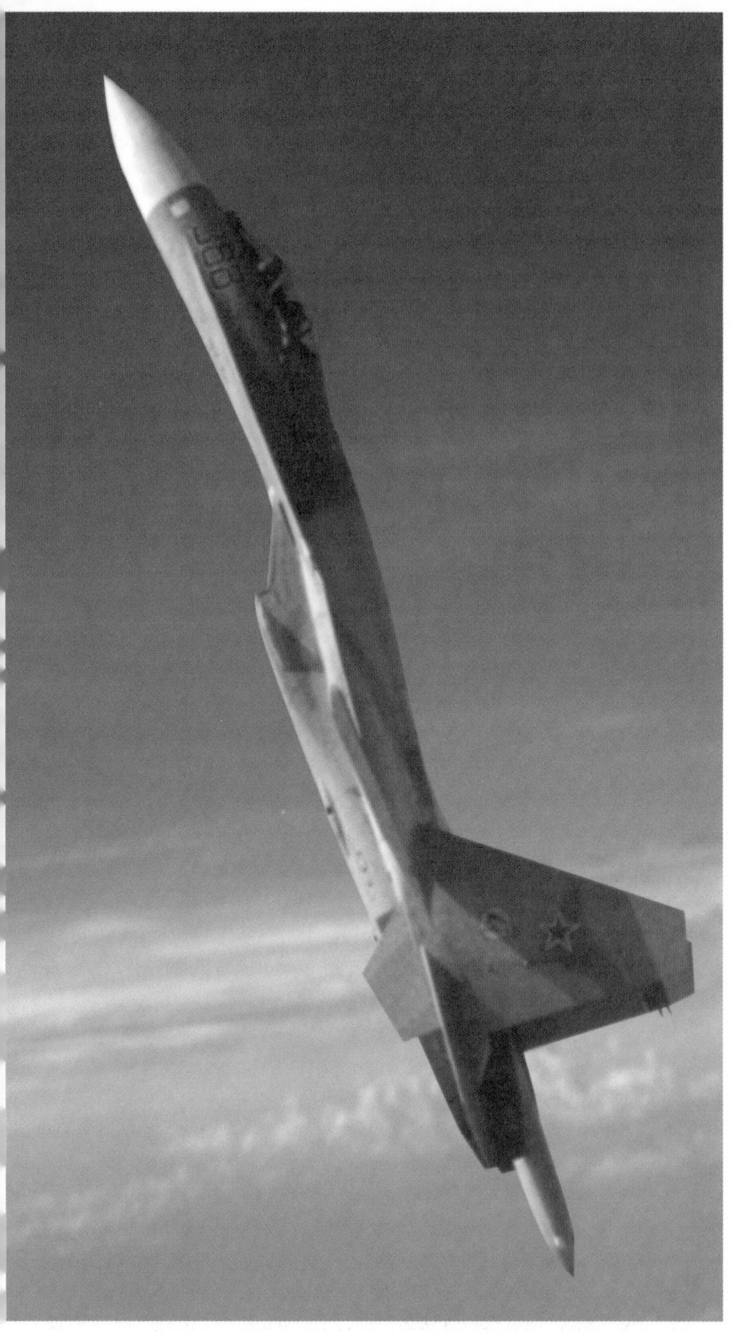

Above: Flanker B was the Russian answer to the American F-15 Eagle.

Sukhoi Su-35 Super Flanker

Origin: Sukhoi OKB, Moscow, USSR.
Type: Single-seat, twin-engined bisonic all-weather air superiority fighter.
Engines: Two Ly'ulka Saturn AL-31FM twin-spool afterburning turbofans each rated at 17,637lb (8,000kg) military and 30,865lb (14,000kg) maximum thrust.
Dimensions: Span 48ft 3in (14.70m); length 72ft 6in (22.10m); height 20ft 9in (6.32m); wing area 668sq.ft (62.04m^2).
Weights: Empty 40,565lb (18,400kg); normal takeoff 56,568lb (25,700kg);

maximum takeoff 74,956lb (34,000kg).
Loadings (at normal takeoff weight): Wing 85lb/sq.ft (414kg/m^2); thrust 1.09.
Performance: Maximum speed 1,553mph (2,500kph) Mach 2.35 at 39,372ft (12,000m), 870mph (1,400kph) Mach 1.14 at sea level; initial climb rate 60,041ft/min (305m/sec); service ceiling 59,058ft (18,000m); range 2,051

Below: Moving canard foreplanes distinguish the Su-35 from the Su-27.

miles (3,300km) on maximum internal fuel.
Armament: One 30mm single barrel GSh-301 cannon with 150 rounds; up to ten AAMs in a combination of R-27ER/ETs, R-27R/Ts, R-73s and R-77s.
History: First flight of prototype T-10-M1 28 June 1988. Vectored thrust trials (T-10M-11) began 31 March 1989. Su-37 first flown 2 April 1996. International debut September 1996. So far as is known, no production as at 2002.
Users: Probably Russia.

Since it first appeared in the West at Le Bourget in 1989, Flanker has been a byword for pointability ever since Viktor Pugachev demonstrated the Cobra manoeuvre. Starting in level flight at quite a moderate speed, he suddenly thrust the nose up past the vertical, to about 100deg, before letting it drop back into level flight with little apparent altitude loss.

Many Western commentators seized upon this as a valid combat manoeuvre; the ability to yank the nose through more than 90deg to get a missile away. In fact it was nothing of the sort. As Sukhoi chief test pilot Eugeny Frolov confirmed to the writer, it was just an aerodynamic trick, for which the alpha limiter, normally set at 26deg, had to be switched off. Only when Western reactions were known did the Russians even start to consider the combat implications, only to conclude that there were none.

Sukhoi set out to improve manoeuvrability. The result was the Su-35 Super Flanker, in which neutral stability was replaced by relaxed stability to improve control responsiveness, the alpha limit was increased to 30deg, and all-moving canard surfaces were added, producing what the brochure called "a triplane aerodynamic configuration fighter". Less obvious changes were more powerful turbofans, a glass cockpit, and the extensive use of aluminium lithium and advanced composites to keep weight down. An enlarged radome housed the N-011 multi-mode radar able to track 24 targets and simultaneously engage eight. A rear-facing radar in the sting could provide guidance for a rear-firing AAM. Internal fuel capacity was increased by using "wet" fins; the wingtips were occupied by ECM pods, and weaponry hardpoints increased to 14.

The first Flanker to carry canards had been the Su-27K naval fighter, used to improve low-speed control for carrier operations rather than overall manoeuvrability. It was however the Super Flanker that introduced another manoeuvre to the air show repertoire, the hook; which in essence was a horizontal cobra.

The next developmental step was thrust vectoring. Vectored thrust trials were commenced by Oleg Tsoi flying T-10M-11 on 31 March 1989. This was followed by the Su-37, powered by two AL-37FU turbofans with pitch-vectoring nozzles, each rated at 18,739lb (8,500kg) military and 32,000lb (14,515kg) maximum thrust. Flying this aircraft, Eugeny Frolov introduced two more air show manoeuvres at Farnborough '96; the Super Cobra and the Kulbit (somersault). While these appeared to have combat potential, it must be doubted whether the average squadron pilot could hack the course. Super Flanker is expected to enter Russian service before 2004, but whether it will remains to be seen.

Right: The Su-37 performs unorthodox manoeuvres using thrust vectoring.

Above: The enlarged radome of the Su-35 houses the N-011 multi-mode set.

Sukhoi S-37 Berkut

Origin: Sukhoi OKB, Moscow, USSR.
Type: Single-seat, twin-engined supersonic air superiority fighter FSW demonstrator.
Engines: Two Perm D30-F6 twin-spool afterburning turbofans each rated at 16,755lb (7,600kg) military and 27,558lb (12,500kg) maximum thrust (but see notes below)..
Dimensions: Not released.
Weights: Empty c43,692lb (19,819kg); normal takeoff 52,910lb (24,000kg).
Loadings (at normal takeoff weight): Wing n/a ; thrust 1.04.
Performance: Maximum speed 1,056mph (1,700kph) Mach 1.60 at altitude, although Mach 2 has been claimed.
Armament: None.
History: First flight of prototype 25 September 1997. Will almost certainly not enter production.
User: None.

In the early 1990s, it was rumoured that Sukhoi were working on a forward-swept wing fighter provisionally designated S-32. FSW is not a new idea; it was explored by the Grumman X-29A technology demonstrator between 1984 and 1991, but for various reasons it was not pursued in the USA.

In theory, a forward-swept wing offers many advantages. These are higher usable lift, lower supersonic drag, improved low-speed handling, reduced wing bending, and better area and volume distribution. The result is a smaller aeroplane for the same performance, or improved performance for a larger aeroplane.

Whereas conventional aft sweep allows the leading edge to twist downwards

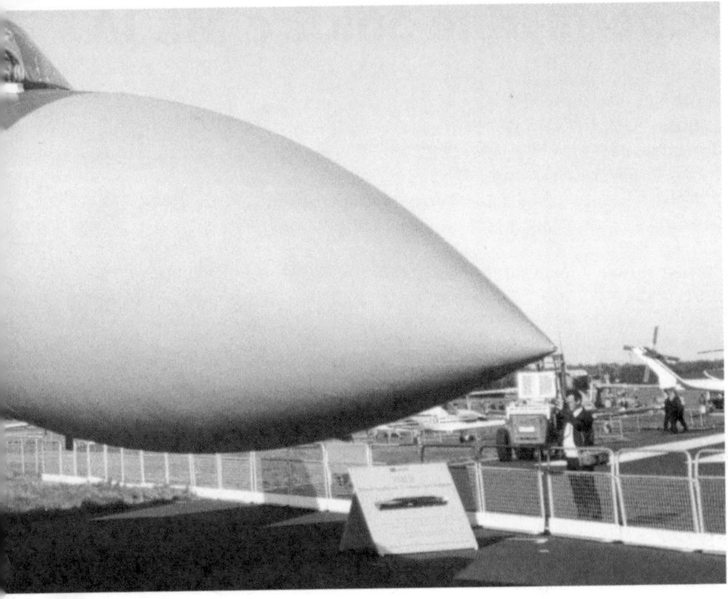

Above: Forward-swept wings were investigated by the S-37 Berkut.

under high g-loads, forward sweep tends to twist it upwards. With conventional construction, this is asking for catastrophic failure, but aero-elastic tailoring of advanced composite materials can resist this.

Berkut, which is obviously based on Flanker, was first flown by Igor Votintsev on 25 September 1997. A strange anomaly is that while one would expect Su-27 engines to be used, the engines are described as Perm D30-F6s as used by Foxhound, although the ratings released match those of the AL-31Fs used by Flanker B.

A comprehensive flight test programme has been flown, and while results are reported as satisfactory, the S-37 is unlikely to be developed further.

Supermarine Spitfire Mk IA

Origin: Supermarine Aircraft Company, England.
Type: Single-seat, single-engined monoplane fighter.
Engine: One 1,030hp Rolls-Royce Merlin II supercharged liquid-cooled V-12.
Dimensions: Span 36ft 10in (11.23m); length 29ft 11in (9.12m); height 12ft 7.75in (3.85m); wing area 242sq.ft (22.48m²).
Weights: Empty 4,517lb (2,049kg); normal takeoff 5,844lb (2,651kg).
Loadings (at normal takeoff weight): Wing 24lb/sq.ft (118kg/m²); power 5.67lb (2.57kg) per hp.
Performance: Maximum speed 346mph (557kph) at 15,000ft (4,572m); sustained climb rate 6min 51sec to 15,000ft (4,572m); service ceiling 30,500ft (9,296m); range 415 miles (668km); endurance typically 1.50 hr.
Armament: Eight wing-mounted .303in (7.7mm) belt-fed Browning Mk 2 machine guns with 300 rounds per gun.
History: Prototype first flight 6 March 1936. Ordered into production 3 June 1936. Service entry August 1939. Combat debut 16 October 1939. Continually developed throughout World War II in a dozen different Merlin-engined variants for the RAF, and three carrier-compatible Seafire variants for the FAA. Used in every theatre of war, and in action postwar by Egypt and Israel. Total production 19,833. Phased out of RAF service 1947-48.
Users: Australia, Belgium, Britain (RAF and FAA); Burma, Canada, Czechoslovakia, Denmark, Egypt, Eire, France, Greece, Holland, India, Italy, Israel, New Zealand, Norway, Portugal, Southern Rhodesia, Soviet Union, Thailand, Turkey, USA, Yugoslavia.

Supermarine chief designer Reginald Mitchell had learned much about high speed flight from his series of successful racing floatplanes, but his first attempt at producing a fighter, the Type 224, which first flew in February 1934, was slow and climbed poorly. His next attempt was the Type 300, work on which began in the summer of 1934. A development contract for a prototype was issued on 1 December of that year.

The engine selected was the new Roll-Royce PV XII engine, which promised about 1,000hp when fully developed. Later named Merlin, this was a major factor in the success of what became the Spitfire. Even more important

Below: Spitfire 1As of No 610 squadron in standard 1940 camouflage.

Above: The Spitfire prototype, K5054, seen during prewar trials.

was the wing design. The elliptical planform chosen had the lowest lift/drag ratio of any shape, and for its day was astonishingly thin, with a thickness/chord ratio of 13 percent at the root and six percent at the tip. This gave the Spitfire a higher critical Mach number than any other wartime fighter; even the jets of 1944/45. The other effect of the thin wing was that when the specification was changed from four guns for eight, keeping the ammunition feeds out of each other's way meant that the guns had to be widely spaced, and the outboard guns needed just a hint of a bulge to accommodate them.

The Spitfire was tightly packaged, and this led to its greatest failing. The more chunky Hurricane had the main gear legs set outboard, with the wheels retracting partly into the fuselage underside. By contrast, the main gear legs of the Spitfire were located in the wing roots, with the wheels retracting outboard

into the wings. This resulted in a narrow track undercarriage, which was less than ideal for operating from rough strips, or in a cross-wind.

Piloted by "Mutt" Summers, the prototype first flew at Eastleigh, Hampshire, on 6 March 1936. From the outset it handled well, and few modifications were needed. The tail skid was replaced by a wheel; the canopy was bulged to accommodate a taller pilot, and the fixed pitch two-bladed wooden propeller replaced by a two-pitch metal one. This in turn was soon superseded by a three-bladed propeller. One problem that took longer to fix was the freezing of the guns at high altitude.

The Spitfire was ordered into production in November 1936, and the first series aircraft flew on 14 May 1938. Tragically, Reginald Mitchell did not live to see it. Deliveries commenced in August of that year, to Nos 19 and 66 Squadrons at Duxford.

On 16 October 1939, Spitfires intercepted Ju 88s attacking naval units in the Firth of Forth, shooting down two and damaging a third, but not until 21 May 1940 did they encounter the Bf 109E over Dunkirk. Heavy fighting here was followed by the Battle of Britain, which lasted through the summer of 1940. Designed as an air defence fighter, the manoeuvrability of the Spitfire

stood it in good stead against the '109s, which often had a positional advantage.

Further development had already started. The Mark II, which entered service in August 1940, mounted the Merlin XII, rated at 1,175hp. However, most of performance improvements were swallowed up by the weight of extra armour protection for the pilot, the coolant header tank, and the upper fuel tank. Almost one fifth of these were Mk IIBs, with two 20mm Hispano drum-fed cannon each with 120 rounds, displacing the four inner machine guns.

In January 1941, the Bf 109F entered service. To counter it, the Spitfire V was rushed into service. Bypassing the III and IV, which never entered production, the Mk V had the more powerful Merlin 45 in a strengthened Mk I airframe, and a larger radiator.

The most numerous Spitfire variant, the Mk V was produced in many subtypes. For North Africa, a Vokes filter to guard against engine wear caused by sand ingestion spoiled the clean lines of the nose. Many VCs carried four 20mm Hispano cannon, although in practice two of these were routinely

Below: Spitfire VC with dust filter and cannon, seen on Malta in 1942.

removed. Then there was the low altitude LF V, "clipped, cropped and clapped". The wingtips were clipped to improve roll rate, at the expense of turn radius. The supercharger diameter was reduced "cropped" to give maximum boost at low level. This reduced engine life, hence "clapped".

To intercept high altitude intruders, the HF VI and HF VII were introduced. These had an extended span wing with pointed tips and a pressurized cockpit. The HF VI had a Merlin 47, driving a four-bladed propeller, while the HF VII, powered by a Merlin 61, had a larger rudder. Its service ceiling was 42,500ft (12,962m), and maximum speed 408mph (656kph).

Development continued with the Spitfire VIII, arguably the most advanced of the Merlin-engined fighters. Powered by a Merlin 61 with two-speed, two-stage supercharging, this was built in F, HF and LF variants, later models of which had a raised pointed fin. Entering service in August 1943, it was used in Italy, briefly in Russia, and in the Far East, but never in the West.

Once again the Spitfire had been overtaken by events. The Focke-Wulf FW 190A which entered service late in 1941, outclassed the Spitfire V in all departments except for turn radius. As the Mk VIII could not be available in time, Merlin 60 series engines were fitted to a VC airframe.

This hybrid produced the Spitfire IX; the second most numerous subtype built. Entering service with No 64 Squadron in July 1942, it quickly proved a match for the FW 190A. Externally it was virtually identical to the Mk V, which made life very difficult for the *Jagdflieger*, as until combat was joined they could not be sure which they were taking on. The Spitfire IX was built in F, HF and LF subtypes, and remained in service until the end of the war. A few had the two outboard Brownings replaced by a single 0.50in (12.7mm) Browning machine gun to become the IXE.

The next few Merlin-Spitfires were photo-reconnaissance types, and the only other major variant was the Mk XVI. This varied primarily in having a Packard-built Merlin, which was not interchangeable with the Rolls-Royce article.

Most RAF and Commonwealth aces, and not a few Americans, flew Spitfires at some time or other. The Battle of Britain top-scorer was Spitfire pilot Eric "Sawn-off" Lock with 21 victories, of which 13 were Bf 109s, while all 15 of Brian Carbury's victims were Bf 109s. Over

Malta, Canadian George "Screwball" Beurling scored 26 victories, 23 of them fighters, in 27 flying days, the majority Bf 109s. Top RAF ace Johnnie Johnson scored all his 34 destroyed and seven shared with Spitfires; two with a Spitfire IIA, five with a Spitfire VB, and the remainder with a Spitfire IX. All his victims were fighters; 22 of them FW 190As. French-Canadian Dick Audet was the only Spitfire "ace in a day", with five victims in a single sortie on 29 December 1944.

The Spitfire was adapted for carrier operations with the addition of a tailhook, lifting points, and the ASI calibrated in knots rather than mph, to become the Seafire. The first was the Seafire IB, a converted VB, which entered service in June 1942. It was followed by the IIC, then the low-altitude LF IIC, powered by a Merlin 32 with a four-bladed propellor. Late model IICs were fitted with spools for catapult launching.

The final Merlin-engined Seafire was the Mk III, which was the first to have wing-folding. However, the narrow-track main gear was far too ladylike for the rough and tumble of carrier operations, while endurance was too short. As a carrier fighter, the Seafire was not a success. The top-scoring Seafire pilot of the war was Richard Reynolds, with two confirmed and three shared victories.

Below: A Seafire III. The landing gear was too delicate for carrier work.

Supermarine Spitfire Mk XIVE

Origin: Supermarine Aircraft Company, England.
Type: Single-seat, single-engined monoplane fighter.
Engine: One 2,050hp Rolls-Royce Griffon 65 supercharged liquid-cooled V-12.
Dimensions: Span 36ft 10in (11.23m); length 32ft 8in (9.96m); height 12ft 7.75in (3.85m); wing area 242sq.ft (22.48m²).
Weights: Empty 6,600lb (2,994kg); normal takeoff 8,490lb (3,851kg).
Loadings (at normal takeoff weight): Wing 35lb/sq.ft (171kg/m²); power 4.14lb (1.88kg) per hp.
Performance: Maximum speed 448mph (721kph) at 26,000ft (7,924m); sustained climb rate 7min to 20,000ft (6,096m); service ceiling 44,500ft (13,411m); range 460 miles (740km); endurance typically 1.50 hr.
Armament: Two wing-mounted 20mm Hispano cannon with 125 rounds per gun; two wing-mounted 0.50in (12.7mm) Browning machine guns with 250 rounds per gun.
History: Prototype (Mk XII) first flight 24 August 1942. Service entry January 1944. Combat debut October 1944. Production ceased March 1948 with a total of 2,028 Griffon-engined Spitfires/ Seafires built. Phased out of RAF service June 1957.
Users: Belgium, Britain (RAF, RAuxAF, and FAA), Canada, Egypt, India, Southern Rhodesia, Syria.

Even before the war, Rolls-Royce were working on a larger successor to the Merlin, with a cubic capacity 36 per cent greater. A requirement was that its size should be held down so that it could replace the Merlin in existing aircraft with a minimum of structural alteration. The new engine duly emerged as the Griffon; barely 3in (76mm) longer than the Merlin, while its frontal area was only six per cent greater. It was of course about 350lb (159kg) heavier, and oddly enough, it ran rather slower; maximum rating was achieved at 2,750rpm rather than the 3,000rpm of the Merlin.

The Spitfire IV was the first planned to have the Griffon engine. The engine mounting was modified, and the cowling redesigned. Fuel capacity was increased with integral wing tanks, the landing gear was strengthened, and the proposed armament was six 20mm Hispano cannon. Slotted flaps were considered, but the original plain type were found to be quite adequate. First flown on 27 November 1941, it did not enter production. In early 1942 it was redesignated Mk XX to avoid confusion with the PR IV.

The Mk XX became the prototype Spitfire XII, which first flew on 24 August 1942 and entered service in the following year. A dedicated low altitude fighter, it had clipped wings, a broad-chord rudder, and a retractable tailwheel. Used by only two squadrons, at its best fighting altitude of 12,000ft (3,657m) it was far superior to the contemporary FW 190A.

The major Griffon-engined Spitfire variant to see action in World War II was the Mk XIV. Like the very successful Mk IX, this was a lash-up, with the Spitfire VIII airframe strengthened and modified to take the Griffon 65 and its five-bladed propellor. The fin area was increased, and the final production machines had a cut-down rear fuselage with a tear-drop canopy. Initially the armament was two 20mm cannon and four .303in (7.7mm) machine guns, but later the light machine guns were replaced by two 0.50in (12.7mm) Brownings.

Although tremendously fast, and possessed of an outstanding rate of climb, the increased weight took its toll on handling, and it was not nearly as nice as the Merlin-engined Spitfires. Terminal velocity was restricted to 470mph (756kph) by aileron "float"; a fault that was never entirely cured. Controls were always on the heavy side, although moving the ailerons inboard a tad improved lateral control.

Above: Griffon-engined spitfires used Koffman cartridge starting.

Above: The Spitfire XIVE had a five-bladed Rotol propeller as standard.

Below: The Seafire 46 was the navalized variant of the Spitfire 22.

The first unit to receive the Spitfire XIV was No 610 Squadron, at Exeter o
1 January 1944. The top-scoring Spitfire XIV pilot of the war was Harr
Walmsley, with nine out of his war total of 11, flying with Nos 130 and 35
Squadrons. On 5 October 1944, a Mk XIV of No 401 Squadron was als
responsible for downing the first Me 262 jet of the war. Prior to this the typ
had been successful against the V-1 flying bomb offensive, Dutch pilot R.
Burgwal of No 322 Squadron claiming 21.

The Spitfire FR XIVE carried a camera in the fuselage, but was otherwis
fully armed. Wingtips clipped for low altitude work, this was the first Spitfir
variant to carry the new gyro gunsight.

Just too late to participate in the war, although it saw action in Malaya an
the Middle East, the Spitfire XVIII was the final development of the origin
airframe. It differed from the Mk XIV in having increased fuel capacity
strengthened wings, teardrop canopy as standard, and beefed up landing gea

The Griffon engine in the developed original airframe had resulted in a
imbalance. It was early recognized that to gain the utmost from the Griffon, a
airframe redesign was urgently needed. The Spitfire 21 was born.

The wing was redesigned to give greater stiffness, and with large
ailerons to improve rate of roll. This resulted in a one inch (25mm) increas
in span, and 2sq.ft ($0.19m^2$) more area. Four 20mm Hispano cannon wer

carried. The main gear track was widened to improve ground handling, and the legs lengthened to allow the use of a huge 11ft (3.35m) diameter five-bladed propeller.

First flown in July 1944, the controls were oversensitive and the aircraft was laterally unstable. While these faults were eventually cured, it was too late for the war, and only 120 were built. The Mk 21 was followed by the Mk 22, with a bubble canopy and enlarged tail surfaces. This was mainly used by Auxiliary squadrons. The final variant was the Mk 24, with extra fuel and underwing rockets. It was used by only one squadron.

A few Seafires were also Griffon-engined. The Seafire XV was basically a navalized Spitfire XIV, with wing folding and a tail hook. It was just too late to see action in the Pacific. Next was the Seafire XVII with a cut-down rear fuselage and teardrop canopy, and longer-stroke oleos. The Spitfire 21 was navalized as the Seafire 45; the Spitfire 22 as the Seafire 46; and the Spitfire 24 as the Seafire 47. Unlike the 45 and 46, the 47 had folding wings, and a six-bladed contra-rotating propeller, which made carrier operations easier. The Seafire 47 entered service in February 1948, flew against insurgents in Malaysia, then until 1951 took an active part in the Korean War.

Below: The bulged cowling and pointed fin show this to be a Seafire XV.

Supermarine Attacker F 1

Origin: Supermarine Aircraft Company, England.
Type: Single-seat, single-engined subsonic jet carrier fighter.
Engine: One Rolls-Royce Nene 3 centrifugal flow turbojet rated at 5,100lb (2,313kg) thrust.
Dimensions: Span 36ft 11in (11.25m); length 37ft 6in (11.43m); height 9ft 11in (3.02m); wing area 226sq.ft (21.00m^2).
Weights: Empty 8,434lb (3,826kg); normal takeoff 11,500lb (5,216kg).
Loadings (at normal takeoff weight): Wing 51lb/sq.ft (248kg/m^2); thrust 0.44.
Performance: Maximum speed 590mph (949kph) at sea level, 538mph (866kph) at 30,000ft (9,144m); initial climb rate 6,350ft/min (32.25m/sec); sustained climb rate 6min 40sec to 30,000ft (9,144m); service ceiling 45,000ft (13,715m); range 590 miles (949km), or 1,190 miles (1,915km) with conformal ventral tank.
Armament: Four wing-mounted 20mm Hispano cannon with 125 rounds per gun.
History: Prototype first flight 27 July 1946. Production order November 1949. Service entry August 1951. Total production 183. Phased out of front line FAA service 1954, and RNVR in 1957.
Users: Britain (FAA/RNVR), Pakistan.

Late war attempts to improve the Spitfire/Seafire by fitting a laminar-flow wing had resulted in the Spiteful and Seafang. To Supermarine chief designer Joseph Smith, the same wing looked a good bet for a jet fighter, as did the new Rolls-Royce Nene turbojet, on which work had only recently begun, but which appeared to promise a thrust of 4,000lb (1,814kg) plus, much more than the Welland and Derwent.

His proposal was quickly accepted, and an order for three prototypes with the Spiteful laminar flow wing, lacking only the radiators, followed on 5 August

Below: A laden Attacker needed rocket assistance for deck launches.

Above: In 1951 the Attacker became the first British jet carrier fighter.

1944. Further approval followed for 24 Jet Spitefuls (as it was then called) in July 1945, but aerodynamic problems were than encountered with the wing.

The prototype 392 was first flown from Boscombe Down by Jeffrey Quill on 27 July 1946. A pleasantly sleek machine, with the mid-mounted Nene fed by side inlets, it was however very basic; the only truly unusual feature being the retractable twin tailwheel. With little RAF interest evident, the next prototype was navalized; first flown by Mike Lithgow on 17 June 1947, it had plain rather than split flaps, an A-frame arrester hook, catapult points, tie-down points, provision for rocket-assisted takeoff, long-stroke oleos, and an ejection seat. Carrier trials were completed aboard HMS *Illustrious* (the previous one!) in October 1947.

Meanwhile the Navy had been playing around belly-landing Sea Vampires on rubber decks. Not until November 1949 did they wake up and place an order for what was now called the Attacker. The ailerons were modified and spoilers added; the wings were moved further aft and the intakes revised slightly. A dorsal strake was introduced ahead of the fin. A low-drag conformal ventral fuel tank was fitted to extend range. Although detachable, this was not a drop tank. It had other uses, notably as a cushion when belly-landing.

The Attacker F 1 entered service with No 800 Squadron in August 1951. It was trouble-free; there was little to go wrong. At medium and low altitudes it performed well, but was poor up high, and suffered from severe pitch-down at Mach 0.82. The F 1 and the subsequent FB 1 served briefly with the FAA before they were replaced by the superb Sea Hawk.

The only overseas customer was Pakistan, which bought 36 denavalised F 1s, reportedly for £41,000 each. Able to carry two 1,000lb (454kg) bombs or 16 unguided rockets, these were flown to Karachi from June 1951.

Tupolev Tu-28P Fiddler

Origin: Tupolev OKB, Soviet Union.
Type: Two-seat, twin-engined supersonic long range all-weather interceptor.
Engine: Two Ly'ulka AL-7F-2 two spool axial flow afterburning turbojets each rated at 16,369lb (7,425kg) military and 22,046lb (10,000kg) maximum thrust.
Dimensions: Span 57ft 5in (15.50m); length 98ft 5in (30.00m); height 22ft 11.5in (7.00m); wing area 807sq.ft (75.00m²).
Weights: Empty 57,231lb (25,960kg); normal takeoff 94,798lb (43,000kg).
Loadings (at normal takeoff weight): Wing 117lb/sq.ft (573kg/m²); thrust 0.47.
Performance: Maximum speed 1,036mph (1,667kph) Mach 1.57 at 39,372ft (12,000m); initial climb rate (est) 17,127ft/min (87m/sec); service ceiling 52,496ft (16,000m); range 1,594 miles (2,565km); endurance 3hr 30min.
Armament: Four Bisnovat R-4 AAMs on underwing pylons; two SARH; two IR homing.
History: Prototype first flight 18 March 1961. In production from 1966 to 1969; total about 200. In service from 1967; finally withdrawn 1990.
User: Soviet Union.

Believed to have first flown in 1956, the Tu-98 supersonic bomber, NATO reporting name Backfin, failed to enter service. It did however form the basis of the dimensionally slightly smaller Tu-28P, NATO reporting name Fiddler, the largest and heaviest fighter ever to enter service.

Although capable of supersonic dash speed, the greatest strengths of the Tu-28P (confusingly given the designation Tu-128 by the US Department of Defense) was its endurance, which enabled it to remain on station long after the standard interceptors had gone home, and the huge long range "Big Nose" radar, about which little is known. Unconfirmed reports suggest a detection

range of 124 miles (200km), with lock on to a fighter-sized target (5m^2 RCS) at 50 miles (80km). Coupled with two huge SARH medium range; about 34 miles (55km) R-4 AAMs and two visual; about 12 miles (20km) range IRH AAMs, NATO reporting name for both AA-5 Ash. These were similar in configuration to the Hughes AIM-4 Falcon but much larger; about 12in (305mm) diameter and more than 17ft (5.18m) long. The Tu-28P was potentially very effective.

First flight of the prototype took place on 18 March 1961. The sharply swept wing had track-mounted slotted flaps on each side of pods which held the main gear, and fences at about midspan. The all-moving tailplanes had what appeared to be elevators, but these were used only for trimming. High-set semi-circular inlets with moveable shock half-cones fed the rear-mounted engines, involving very long inlet ducts.

This configuration allowed an enormous internal fuel capacity, estimated at more than 30,000lb (13,608kg), to be carried internally; to a degree displacing the weapons bay of the bomber. The pilot and radar operator were seated in tandem under clamshell canopies, the former with a V-shaped windshield. A feature of the the Tu-102 prototype which was not repeated on production aircraft was a large ventral radome, presumably housing a search radar. Had Fiddler entered service in this format, it would have combined the dual functions of AWACS and interceptor.

Ordered into production in 1966, Fiddler started to enter service from 1967. Superseded by the MiG-31 Foxhound, it was progressively withdrawn from the early 1980s, although the process was not complete until 1990. More than a decade later, information remains sparse.

Below: The huge Tu-28P all-weather interceptor had exceptional endurance.

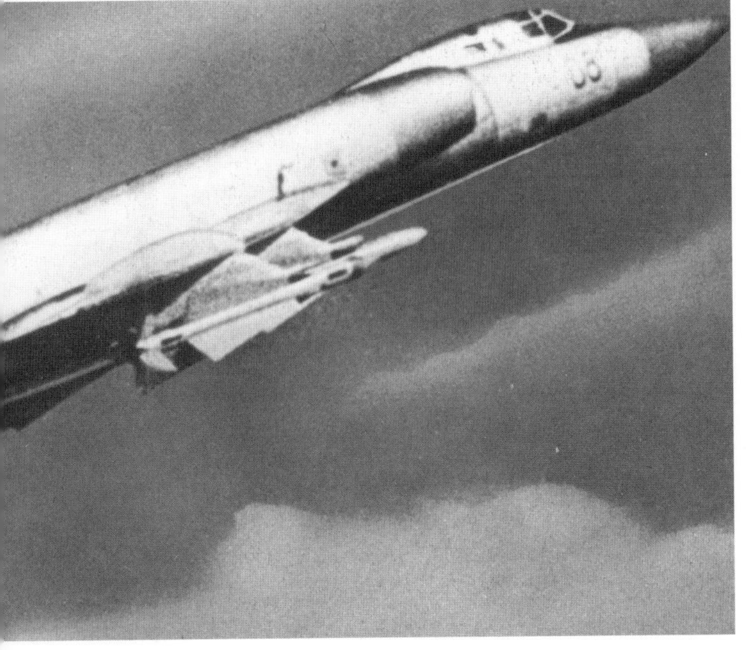

Vickers FB 5 Gunbus

Origin: Vickers Ltd., England.
Type: Two-seat, single-engined pusher biplane fighter.
Engine: One 100hp Gnome Monosoupape 9-cylinder rotary.
Dimensions: Span 36ft 6in (11.12m); length 27ft 2in (8.28m); height 11ft 1in (3.38m); wing area 382sq.ft (35.49m^2).
Weights: Empty 1,220lb (553kg); normal takeoff 2,050lb (930kg).
Loadings (at normal takeoff weight): Wing 5.37lb/sq.ft (26kg/m^2); power 20.5lb (9.29kg) per hp.
Performance: Maximum speed 70mph (113kph) at 5,000ft (1,524m); sustained climb rate 16min to 5,000ft (1,524m); service ceiling 9,000ft (2,743m); endurance 4hr 30min.
Armament: One flexibly mounted .303in (7.7mm) drum-fed Lewis gun.
History: First flight 17 July 1914. Production order placed 14 August; total 352. In service and combat debut February 1915. Withdrawn from front line service autumn 1916.
Users: Britain (RFC and RNAS), Denmark.

On 19 November 1912, Vickers received an order from the Admiralty for an experimental fighting biplane (EFB). After three rather hesitant attempts, this emerged as the Gunbus, which first flew at Joyce Green on 17 July 1914. Of pusher configuration more or less by default, as this was the only way to obtain a field of fire ahead, it was ordered into production on 14 August. A two-bay equal-span biplane, the tail surfaces were carried on four braced booms, with a high-set tailplane and an all-moving rudder. The first production aircraft was

Vought F4U-1 Corsair

Origin: Chance Vought Aircraft Division, United Aircraft Corporation, USA.
Type: Single-seat, single-engined monoplane carrier fighter.
Engine: One 2,000hp Pratt & Whitney R-2800-8 Double Wasp two-row 18-cylinder radial.
Dimensions: Span 40ft 11.75in (12.49m); length 32ft 9.5in (9.99m); height 15ft 0.25in (4.58m); wing area 314sq.ft (29.17m^2).
Weights: Empty 8,873lb (4.025kg); normal takeoff 11,878lb (5,388kg); maximum 13,846lb (6,280kg).
Loadings (at normal takeoff weight): Wing 38lb/sq.ft (185kg/m^2); power 5.94lb (2.69kg) per hp.
Performance: Maximum speed 417mph (671kph) at 19,900ft (6,065m), 320mph (515kph) at sea level; initial climb rate 2,890ft/min (14.68m/sec); sustained climb rate 5min 6sec to 10,000ft (3,048m); service ceiling 37,100ft (11,308m); range 1,070 miles (1,722km).
Armament: Six 0.50in (12.7mm) wing mounted Colt-Browning M.2 machine guns, four with 400 rounds per gun, two with 375 rounds per gun.
History: First flight of prototype 29 May 1940. Production order placed 30 June 1941. First flight of production aircraft 25 June 1942. Operational from 28 December 1942. Combat debut 14 February 1943. Production ceased 31 January 1953, with a total of 12,571. Postwar used in action in French Indo-China and Korea. Withdrawn from first line USMC service early 1960s. Combat swansong 1969, for Honduras versus El Salvador.
Users: Britain, France, Honduras, New Zealand, Uruguay, USA (USN and USMC).

Faced in February 1938 with a US Navy requirement for a high performance

Above: The Vickers FB 5 lacked the performance to be really effective.

delivered in October, and its combat debut in France was in February 1915.

Performance was marginal; it could neither force combat on an opponent, nor disengage at will. Matters were not helped by the unreliability of its Gnome Monosoupape engine. Its greatest claim to fame was that it constituted the first fighter squadron (No 11 RFC) to be equipped with a single type.

Further development was undertaken, culminating in the FB 9, which emerged at the end of 1915. This showed fairly marginal performance improvements, and a handful were used during the Battle of the Somme in July 1916, but shortly after the type was relegated to training.

Above: The Corsair trademark was its inverted gull wing, seen here.

carrier fighter, designer Rex Beisel settled on the the Pratt & Whitney Double Wasp radial. Although still in the early development stage, at 2,000hp it was the most powerful engine available in the immediate future. A contract for the prototype XF4U-1 was issued on 11 June 1938.

A very large diameter propeller was needed to make full use of the available power. The ground clearance needed for this would normally have resulted in unacceptably long (for a carrier aircraft) main gear legs, but the problem was solved by cranking the inner wing downward to form an inverted gull shape. The legs were located at the crank, and retracted aft, just clearing the wing fold joint.

Piloted by Lyman Bullard Jr, the prototype first flew from Stratford, Connecticut, on 29 May 1940. Designed with ease of production in mind, it was not a pretty aeroplane. In fact, FAA pilot Norman Hanson of No 1833 Squadron, who first set eyes on the bird three years later, was not impressed. He commented; "... of all the aircraft I had seen, these were the most wicked-looking bastards." From the outset, performance was outstanding, and on 1 October of that year it became the first US aircraft to exceed 400mph (644kph) in level flight. There were however problems. Lateral stability was poor, and spin recovery far from satisfactory. This last was never completely cured.

The original armament of the Corsair, as it was named, was demonstrably inadequate, and was changed to six 0.50in (12.7mm) wing-mounted Brownings with increased ammunition. These displaced integral fuel tanks in the wings, and a large fuselage tank was substituted on the centre of gravity, to

Right: Although a carrier fighter, the Corsair flew mainly from land bases.

accommodate which the cockpit was moved three feet (0.91m) further aft. The fuselage was lengthened by 17in (43cm), aileron span was increased to improve rate of roll; armour protection was added, and two small leading edge fuel tanks were added outboard of the guns.

The first production contract was placed on 30 June 1941, and the first production aircraft flew on 25 June 1942. But by now the US Navy was unhappy with the Corsair. Carrier trials on 25 September were curtailed when severe problems were encountered during deck landings. The aft-set cockpit badly restricted the view during the final stages, and the oleo main gear legs had a built-in bounce. This last, coupled with a tendency to swing violently on touchdown, made a safe arrival problematical.

Raising the cabin 7in (18cm) improved forward view a mite; a spoiler on the starboard wing and a lengthened tailwheel leg offset the tendency to swing, while the bounce was eventually cured. But all this took time; the US Navy considered the Corsair too dangerous for carrier work, and at first it was assigned to land-based units, mainly with the US Marines.

Its combat debut occurred on 14 February 1943, with VMF-124. Once familiar with the Corsair, the Marines cut a deadly swathe through the opposition. Top scorer was "Butcher Bob" Hanson with 25 victories; 20 of which came in sixteen days in January 1944. He was followed by former Flying Tiger ace "Pappy" Boyington with 22, and Donald Aldrich with 20. For the US Navy, Ira Kepford of VF-17 led the field with 17.

Lacking a suitable indigenous carrier fighter, the Fleet Air Arm became by default the first to take the Corsair to sea. To fit below deck on the smaller British carriers, 8in (20cm) was clipped off each wingtip, with a corresponding reduction in area. Oddly enough, this improved deck-landing characteristics. The first squadron started to equip on 1 June 1943, and the first British Corsair operations were flown on 3 April 1944, over Norway. The type was later flown extensively by the FAA against the Japanese, but lack of opportunity resulted in no British Corsair aces. Top scorer was Marine Ronnie Hay, with two confirmed and two shared victories; all fighters.

The raised-cockpit Corsair was the F4U-1A; this was later given water injection which raised power to 2,250hp to become the F4U-1D. Meanwhile, as USMC Corsair squadrons were land-based, Goodyear built a variant without wing-folding and other carrier features as the FG-1. The F4U-1C was armed with four 20mm Hispano cannon, although only about 200 were built. Rather more exotic was the F4F-2N, a night fighter with a radar pod on the starboard wing. The XF4U-3 was a prototype high-altitude fighter which failed to enter production. The final wartime variant was the F4U-4 which used water-methanol injection to boost output to 2,450hp, maximum speed to 446mph (718kph) at 26,200ft (7,985m), and initial climb rate to 3,870ft/min (19.65m/sec).

The Corsair was finally accepted for shipboard use by the US Navy from early 1945, but less than 15 per cent of its sorties were flown from carriers. Production continued until 31 January 1953. The F4U-5N night fighter served in Korea from land bases and from carriers, scoring a handful of victories. The Corsair remained in front-line US service into the early 1960s.

Right: The F4U Corsair was one of the fastest fighters of WWII.

Vought F7U-3 Cutlass

Origin: Chance Vought Aircraft Division, United Aircraft Corporation, USA.
Type: Single-seat, twin-engined transonic jet carrier fighter.
Engines: Two Westinghouse J46-WE-8B single spool axial flow afterburning turbojets each rated at 4,600lb (2,087kg) military and 6,100lb (2,767kg) maximum thrust.
Dimensions: Span 39ft 8in (12.09m); length 43ft 1in (13.13m); height 14ft 4in (4.36m); wing area 496sq.ft (46.08m^2).
Weights: Empty 18,210lb (8,260kg); normal takeoff 28,140lb (12,764kg); maximum 31,642lb (14,353kg).
Loadings (at normal takeoff weight): Wing 57lb/sq.ft (277kg/m^2); thrust 0.43.
Performance: Maximum speed 696mph (1,120kph) Mach 0.91 at sea level, 680mph (1,094kph) Mach 0.93 at 10,000ft (3,048m); initial climb rate 11,150ft/min (56.64m/sec); service ceiling 40,000ft (12,191m); range 696 miles (1,120km).
Armament: Four fuselage mounted 20mm Colt-Browning M3 cannon with 180 rounds per gun. Later models could carry 32 Mighty Mouse FFARs, or four Sperry Sparrow 1 beam-riding AAMs.
History: Three prototypes ordered 25 June 1946; first flight 29 September 1948. 14 pre-series F7U-1s ordered 28 July 1948. Production order for F7U-3 placed 21 August 1950. Service entry spring 1954. Production ceased August 1955, after 307 of all variants. Finally withdrawn from service 2 March 1959.
User: USA (USN).

On 1 June 1945, the US Navy launched a competition for a single seat carrier fighter capable of 600mph (965kph) at 40,000ft (12,191m). Vought's totally

Above: The unorthodox F7U-3 cutlass had the worst accident rate in the USN.

unconventional V-346 was adjudged the winner, and three prototype XF7U-1s were ordered on 25 June 1946.

Two Westinghouse J34 afterburning turbojets, fed by fixed cheek inlets just ahead of the wing leading edge, were widely spaced in a broad fuselage which, although the term was not current at the time, acted as a lifting body. More surprisingly, horizontal tail surfaces were omitted in favour of a broad-chord 38deg swept wing, with huge hydraulically powered elevons outboard for roll and pitch control. In what was inevitably a large fighter, this gave a compact layout suitable, with hydraulic wing folding at about one third span, for carrie stowage. Inboard of the wing fold were split speed brakes, opening above anc below the wing. This configuration gave a large wing area, and plenty of wing volume for integral fuel tanks.

To keep carrier landing speeds down, the entire leading edge was occupiec by two-piece slats, with a broader chord on the outboard section than the inboard. Twin fins and rudders were located just inboard of the wing fold extending well below the wing. This ventral section had a triple purpose; addec stability at high angles of attack; reinforced as a bumper in the event of an over enthusiastic angle of attack on takeoff and landing, and as a housing for the aft retracting main wheels. Other features were a primitive Vought ejection seat and a pressurized cockpit.

The first XF7U-1 prototype was flown by Robert Baker at NAS Patuxen River on 29 September 1948. It soon proved to be a "hot ship"; two of the three prototypes were lost within weeks, and the third on 7 July 1950. Only 14 pre series F7U-1s were built; the proposed F7U-2 powered by J34s was cancelled and the definitive model was the F7U-3, powered by afterburning J46s, the firs of which flew on 20 December 1951. Extensively redesigned, with a deepe fuselage, the cockpit set higher, and a nosewheel leg that gave a "sit" angle o 20deg, this entered service in April 1954.

The Cutlass was agile, partly by virtue of its low aspect ratio (3.0), bu low-speed handling left much to be desired. The final variant was the F7U 3M, armed with Sparrow beam-riding AAMs. However, the accident rate o more than 25 percent remained horrendous, with a high proportion o fatalities, and the Cutlass was withdrawn from service between 1957 anc 1959. Unlike most other fighters of the period, it was not issued to the Reserve.

Vought F-8D Crusader

Origin: Chance Vought Corporation, USA.
Type: Single-seat, single-engined supersonic limited all-weather carrier fighter.
Engines: One Pratt & Whitney J57-P-20 twin spool axial flow afterburning turbojet rated at 10,700lb (4,853kg) military and 18,000lb (8,165kg) maximum thrust.
Dimensions: Span 35ft 8in (10.87m); length 54ft 3in (16.53m); height 15ft 9in (4.80m); wing area 375sq.ft (34.84m^2).
Weights: Empty 17,541lb (7,957kg); normal takeoff 27,550lb (12,497kg); maximum 34,000lb (15,422kg).
Loadings (at normal takeoff weight): Wing 73lb/sq.ft (359kg/m^2); thrust 0.65.
Performance: Maximum speed 1,228mph (1,976kph) Mach 1.86 at 36,000ft (10,972m), 762mph (1,226kph) Mach 1.00 at sea level; initial climb rate 31,950ft/min (162m/sec); sustained climb rate 5min to 40,000ft (12,191m); service ceiling 42,900ft (13,075m); combat radius 455 miles (732km).
Armament: Four fuselage-mounted 20mm Colt-Browning Mk 12 cannon with 125 rounds per gun; four cheek-mounted AIM-9 Sidewinders.
History: Two prototypes ordered 29 June 1953; first flight 25 March 1955. Production order placed November 1956. Service entry from March 1957; operational later that year. Production ceased June 1965, with 1,261 of all variants. Many were extensively upgraded after this time. Combat debut 2 March 1965. Withdrawn from USN service 1976, from Aeronavale mid-2000.
User: France, Phillippines, USA (USN and USMC).

Right: An F-8D with the unique, cheek-located twin Sidewinder launch rails.

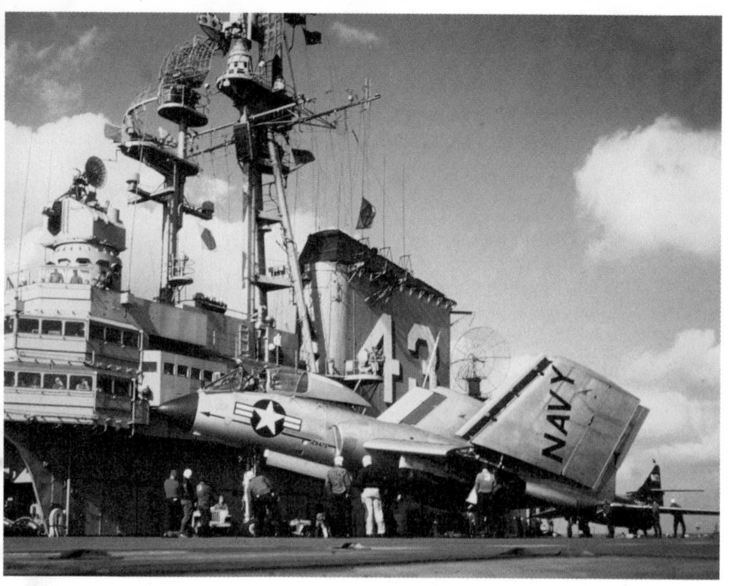

Above: A long nosewheel leg gave the Cutlass an angle of attack of 20deg.

When in 1952 Vought responded to a US Navy requirement for a supersonic carrier fighter, the lessons of the F7U Cutlass were being hard-learned, even though that aircraft had not yet entered service. The main problem was that swept wings demanded a much higher angle of attack at low speeds than straight wings. With a ground sit angle of 20deg, the Cutlass was extreme, and

its attrition rate horrendous. Vought concentrated on designing a truly carrier compatible fighter.

Three critical decisions were taken at the outset; a conventional tailed configuration; a single Pratt & Whitney J57 afterburning turbojet, and the best possible view for the pilot during the critical carrier landing phase.

The solution adopted, never previously used by an operational fighter, was a variable-incidence wing. Hinged at the rear, and hydraulically operated, this could be tilted upwards to an angle of seven degrees for takeoff and landing, thus keeping the fuselage as near horizontal as possible. A side effect was that little ground clearance was needed, although there was a penalty to be paid in weight and complexity.

In practice the weight penalty was largely offset. The single-piece wing had to be mounted level with the top of the fuselage, which virtually ruled it out as a location for the main gear. Retracting the undercarriage into the fuselage allowed very short legs to be used; a factor that was helped by the low ground clearance. While this gave a narrow track, sturdy construction ensured that it was adequate for carrier operations. This arrangement cancelled out the weight of the wing incidence mechanism, although not of course the complexity.

Having solved the angle of attack problem, Vought then placed the cockpit as far forward as it was possible to get; near the crash, as one wag put it. Forward and sideways visibility was excellent, but in the quest for performance, the canopy was faired into the fuselage, giving virtually no rearward vision.

Designed for supersonic flight, the quarter-chord sweep angle of the wing

was 35deg, and the thickness/chord ratio was five percent. Unencumbered by the need to house the main gears, this was enough to allow a significant volume for fuel. The two-piece leading edge slats had a greater chord outboard than inboard, and when drooped formed a dogstooth discontinuity. On the trailing edge, the ailerons were set centrally, like those of the F-100 , as a measure against aileron reversal. Flaps were located inboard of the ailerons. Low deck clearance combined with five degrees of wing anhedral, eased the task of loading underwing stores.

The engine was fed by a plain chin inlet, with a small radar nose above it. The pilot was seated high above the intake duct, which made for a rather deep and slab-sided fuselage. Initially the main armament comprised four 20mm cannon, their muzzles emerging from the fuselage on each side of the cockpit. At a later date a unique double pylon for Sidewinder AAMs was also attached to the fuselage sides. A flight refuelling probe was included from the outset, just aft of the cockpit on the port side. Bladder tanks amidships added to the fuel capacity.

The rear end was conventional; a sharply swept fin and rudder; all-moving low-set tail surfaces, and small ventral strakes. The only unusual feature was the extensive use of titanium, then a difficult material to work, at the hot end.

First flight was made at Edwards AFB on 25 March 1955, when John Konrad went supersonic; something now unthinkable, but then fashionable for

Below: Variable incidence wing raised, a French Crusader is ready to launch.

publicity purposes. During the flight test programme, the F8U (later F-8) Crusader demonstrated a better performance across the board than the slightly earlier F-100.

The F-8A entered service with VF-32 in March 1957, and many other squadrons followed. Nor did the aircraft itself stand still; more powerful engines, changes in armament, radar and avionics followed in quick succession. The F-8A had a retractable belly pack of 78 Mighty Mouse FFARs in addition to its cannon. Later these were deleted and two Sidewinders were substituted. The F-8B was given limited all-weather capability via the APS-67 radar. The F-8C had the uprated -16 turbojet; this had ventral fins; added for yaw stability at high altitude, and provision for four Sidewinders. The F-8D had even more power, increased internal fuel, and improved avionics. The final new production variant was the F-8E, with the APQ-94 radar and increased air to surface weaponry. Many were later rebuilt and upgraded.

Widely used in Vietnam, the Crusader was called the last of the gunfighters by its pilots. While it achieved a favourable kill/loss ratio against the opposing MiGs, most of its 20 confirmed victories were scored with Sidewinders. The guns proved mechanically unreliable, and the gunsight was inadequate. It was phased out of first line US Navy service from 1972, but a much modified variant, the F-8E(FN) soldiered on with *l'Aeronavale* until mid-2000.

Right: **L'Aeronavale** ***was the last Crusader user, with the F-8E(FN).***

Westland Pterodactyl V

Origin: Westland Aircraft Ltd., Yeovil, England.
Type: Two-seat, single-engined tail-less sesquiplane turret fighter.
Engines: One 600hp Rolls-Royce Goshawk I supercharged liquid-cooled V-12.
Dimensions: Span 46ft 8in (14.22m); length 20ft 6in (6.25m); height 11ft 8in (3.56m); wing area 396sq.ft (36.79m^2).
Weights: Empty 3,534lb (1,603kg); normal takeoff 5,100lb (2,313kg).
Loadings (at normal takeoff weight): Wing 12.87lb/sq.ft (63kg/m^2); power 8.50lb (3.86kg) per hp.
Performance: Maximum speed 165mph (266kph) at 15,000ft (4,572m); sustained climb rate 12min 45sec to 15,000ft (4,572m); service ceiling 30,000ft (9,144m).
Armament: Two fixed synchronised nose-mounted .303in (7.7mm) belt-fed Vickers machine guns; one ring or turret-mounted .303in (7.7mm) Lewis machine gun.
History: Proposal submitted 1931; specification issued 1932. First flight May 1934. Development abandoned late 1935. Sole prototype scrapped July 1937.
User: None.

Geoffrey Hill of Westland first became interested in tail-less aircraft in 1924. As J.W.Dunne had shown with his swept-wing D.8 biplane in 1913, there was no difficulty in producing an ultra-stable aircraft with this configuration. The problems came when trying to build a fighter. The experimental Pterodactyl I, first flown in June 1928, was bedevilled by pitch oscillations, and the proposed fighter variants, the Pterodactyl II and III, were never built. Development ceased in 1930.

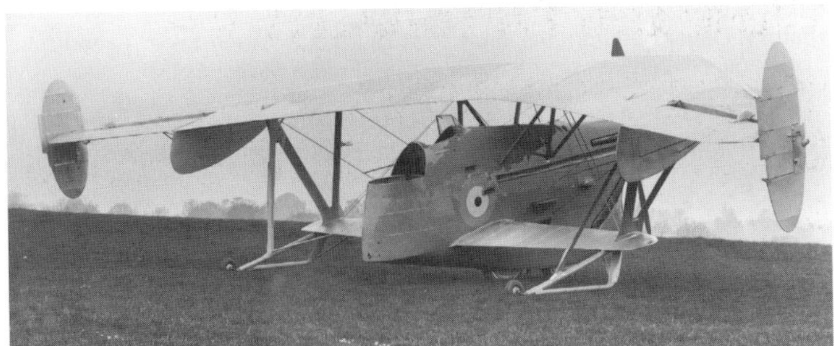

Above: The Pterodactyl V was an extraordinary turret fighter concept.

The next step was the Pterodactyl IV, a three-seat cabin monoplane with a high set wing and a pusher engine. Remarkable for having variable sweep, although only through 4.75deg, it was flown for two years from June 1930. Laterally heavy and sensitive in pitch, performance was disappointing, and it was abandoned.

The Pterodactyl V was designed from the outset as a fighter. The engine selected was the Rolls-Royce Goshawk, the evaporative cooling system of which was never made to work satisfactorily. It was tractor-mounted, allowing a rear crew position with a completely free field of fire astern. The wing was a hybrid. The leading edge of a large centre section was straight, with outer panels swept back at 47deg, with short spoilers outboard, linked to Handley-Page automatic slats. By contrast, the entire trailing edge was swept, with large elevons at the extremities. Small oval fins and rudders were mounted on the wingtips; these were also able to double as speedbrakes.

To obtain the extra strength needed for a fully aerobatic machine, straight narrow chord stub wings were fitted low on the fuselage with V interplane struts to the upper wing. These managed to fulfil a secondary purpose. The short and stumpy fuselage housed a bicycle-type undercarriage; small trailing outriggers were mounted on the stub wings.

Fuselage construction was of box-section duralumin, metal-clad, with box-section steel engine bearers. The wings were also of metal construction but fabric-covered. The pilot's position was open, but that for the gunner was

Yakovlev Yak-9D

Origin: Yakovlev OKB, Soviet Union.
Type: Single-seat, single-engined low-wing monoplane day fighter.
Engines: One 1,360hp Klimov M-105PF-3 supercharged liquid-cooled V-12.
Dimensions: Span 31ft 11.5in (9.74m); length 28ft 0.75in (8.55m); height 9ft 10in (3.00m); wing area 185sq.ft (17.15m^2).
Weights: Empty 6,107lb (2,770kg); normal takeoff 6,867lb (3,115kg); maximum 7,055lb (3,200kg).
Loadings (at normal takeoff weight): Wing 37lb/sq.ft (182kg/m^2); power 5.05lb (2.29kg) per hp.
Performance: Maximum speed 374mph (602kph) at 10,171ft (3,100m); 332mph (534kph) at sea level; sustained climb rate 6min to 16,405ft (5,000m); service ceiling 32,318ft (9,850m); combat range 447 miles (720km).
Armament: One 20mm ShVAK cannon with 120 rounds firing through the propeller shaft, and one nose-mounted synchronised 12.7mm Beresin UBS machine gun with 180-220 rounds.
History: Developed from the Yak-1 of 1939 vintage via the Yak-7. Tested July 1942, and ordered into production. First production deliveries December 1942; combat debut Stalingrad early 1943. Production continued until 1947, with a total of 16,769. In service with Hungary until 1956.
Users: Bulgaria, China, Hungary, North Korea, Poland, Yugoslavia, Soviet Union.

Prewar, the aircraft designer Aleksandr Yakovlev travelled abroad to study fighter developments in the West. In Britain he inspected the Spitfire; in Germany the Bf 109 and He 100. These influenced his thinking; a high-performance fighter should be light, agile, aerodynamically clean, and easy to build and repair. Although with little previous experience of military aircraft, in 1939 Yakovlev set his OKB to work to meet these requirements. The result was an excellent low and medium altitude fighter which became the basis of an outstanding series of Russian fighters, culminating in the Yak-9, which with the SAAB J 21 was the only fighter to make the transition from the reciprocating engine to the turbojet.

The Yak-1 was the first of the breed, flown on 13 January 1940 by Ye Piontkovsky. Pleasant to look at, it had a welded steel tube fuselage framing clad with canvas-covered Shpon ply aft and metal panels forward. The wings, which tapered evenly out to rounded tips, were all-wood, with ply skinning. At first overweight, it was pruned, then re-engined. It started to enter service in spring 1941, but it was spring 1942 before it was available in any quantity.

Next came the Yak-1M (modified). The engine was the uprated M-105PF, although as the second stage of the supercharger cut in at a lower altitude, it was handicapped higher up. The 20mm cannon was retained, but the two nose-mounted 7.62mm machine guns of the original were replaced by a single 12.7mm Beresin UBS. Other changes, which were introduced gradually, were

intended to have a purpose-designed turret, although for a single Lewis gun, this seems excessive. Main armament was two Vickers guns, one on each side of the fuselage.

Taxi trials in autumn 1932 revealed structural weaknesses and engine overheating problems. It was May 1934 before trials were resumed, and Harald Penrose took the Pterodactyl V aloft from RAF Andover. Other faults were found. In a dive the wings lacked torsional stiffness, and more redesign work was needed. Then on 20 February 1936, the Air Ministry cancelled further flight testing. This hardly surprising; the Hurricane had already flown and the Spitfire was about to fly. Like its saurian namesake, the Pterodactyl's time was past.

Above: The Yak-3s seen here were almost indistinguishable from the Yak-9.

slightly reduced wing span and area, and from January 1943, a cut-down rear fuselage with a bubble canopy and a retractable tailwheel.

With experience of the Polikarpov I-16 (pp377-380) in mind, a two-seat conversion trainer was flown on 4 July 1940 and put into limited production. While this was useful, the desperate need was for fighters, and a single-seater was developed as the Yak-7. A fuel tank replaced the second seat; at need this could be removed to allow the carriage of a ground crewman; a valuable asset given the fluidity of the Eastern Front. Modifications from early 1942 were a jettisonable canopy, a redesigned main gear, and provision for RS-82 rockets or bombs underwing. Refined still further, this became the Yak-9.

The Yak-9 differed from its predecessor in minor detail: a deeper radiator bath, a sleeker oil cooler; larger flaps. Optimised for low-level operations, it made its combat debut over Stalingrad in January 1943.

The most used *Jagdflieger* tactic of the war, and not just on the Eastern Front, was the surprise bounce from a high perch. As the German Bf 109G had a far better altitude performance than the Russian fighters, there was little to be gained by trying to climb up to them; in any case the priority was protect the Il-2 Sturmovik ground attack aircraft, and to a lesser degree, to interdict the *Luftwaffe* bombers and Stukas. In consequence, the '109s usually had height, position, and initiative.

To offset this, the Russian fighters took to flying at full throttle (but not emergency power) all the time. The idea was that this would not only increase the difficulty of interception, but give an extra few seconds in which the attackers could

be spotted. This did nothing for engine life, but as a Russian fighter lasted an average of barely 80 hours, it hardly mattered. What was important was that it used fuel at a high rate, restricting combat radius and endurance.

To offset this, the Yak-9D (*dal'ny* = long range) was introduced from May 1943. This had additional fuel tanks in the outer wing panels, and an optional auxiliary tank beneath the cockpit. It was followed into service by the Yak-9DD, which had almost double the fuel capacity of the original Yak-9, giving a still air range (a theoretical calculation) of 1,367 miles (2,200km).

An interesting innovation on the Yak-9B fighter bomber was its method of carry air to surface ordnance. Whereas the standard method was to hang bombs under the wings, the Yak-9B carried four 220lb (100kg) bombs in the fuselage just behind the cockpit. Stowed nose-up at an angle, this allowed a greater load than could be carried underwing, without the excess drag. Accuracy was of course another matter! Other variants were the Yak-9T, fitted with heavy cannon for anti-shipping operations, the Yak-9U, which served during the closing months of the war, and the Yak-9P.

Perhaps the best air combat fighter of all was the Yak-3, a small, light, and agile fighter, but still unmistakeably a Yak, which many of those who flew both preferred to the Spitfire. This entered large-scale service from June 1944.

What of the Yak pilots? Top scoring French ace Marcel Albert of the

Below: Yak-9Ds of a Guards Fighter Regiment over the Crimea in summer 1943.

Normandie-Nieman Regiment scored all his 22 victories with Yaks, as did top-scoring woman pilot Lilya Litvak (13). Olga Yamshchikova of the 586th Fighter Air Regiment scored the first ever night victory by a woman on 24 September 1942, while A.K.Gorovetz claimed nine Ju 87s shot down in a single sortie over Kursk. The final air victory over Europe was scored by 39-victory ace Viktor Golubev on 9 May 1945.

Right: The Yak-3 was the preferred mount of the Normandie Niemen Regiment.

Yakovlev Yak-28PM Firebar

Origin: Yakovlev OKB, Soviet Union.
Type: Two-seat, twin-engined supersonic all-weather interceptor.
Engines: Two Tumansky R-11AF-2-300 twin spool afterburning turbojets each rated at 8,708lb (3,950kg) military and 13,492lb (6,120kg) maximum thrust.
Dimensions (all est): Span 38ft 2.5in (11.64m); length 67ft 10.5in (20.69m); height 14ft 1.25in (4.30m); wing area 404sq.ft (37.50m^2).
Weights: Empty c23,148lb (10,500kg); normal takeoff 37,478lb (17,000kg); maximum 40,785lb (18,500kg).
Loadings (at normal takeoff weight): Wing 93lb/sq.ft (453kg/m^2); thrust 0.72.
Performance: Maximum speed 1,175mph (1,890kph) Mach 1.78 at 39,372ft (12,000m) clean, reducing to Mach 1.48 with four AAMs; initial climb rate c19,686ft/min (100m/sec); service ceiling 52,496ft (16,000m); range 1,212 miles (1,950km).
Armament: Two R-30 AAMs with both SARH and IR homing, and two R-3 short-range IR AAMs, all on underwing pylons.
History: Developed from the Yak-28 Brewer multi-role aircraft which first flew on 5 March 1958. All-weather interceptor variant flew in 1960. Production commenced 1963 and terminated in 1967, with a total of 437 interceptors. Withdrawn from service from 1983.
User: Soviet Union only.

Although of similar configuration to the Yak-25 Flashlight, with underslung turbojets at about one third span on swept wings, a two-man crew seated in tandem, a double twin-wheel bicycle main gear with outriggers on the wingtips, and a high-set tailplane, the Yak-28 Firebar differed significantly in detail from its predecessor.

The wing was shoulder, as opposed to mid-mounted, with a cranked leading edge swept at 63deg inboard of the engine nacelles and 44deg outboard, the latter featuring a dogtooth discontinuity, while anhedral was increased to minimise the length of the outriggers. The engine nacelles were increased in length, projecting well ahead of the wing, while the blunt radome was replaced by a less draggy pointed nose housing the Orel-D pulse radar. Avionics apart, the other main change was increased

spacing between the twin legs of the bicycle undercarriage.

Firebar entered service in about 1964, and surprisingly, given that it was an interim type pending the service entry of the Su-15, remained in the front line for some 20 years. Its greatest failing arose from the combination of widely spaced engines and sharply swept wings. With one engine out, its asymmetric handling was truly horrible.

Below: The bicycle main gear with outriggers was a feature of the Yak-28PM.

Yakovlev Yak-38M Forger A

Origin: Yakovlev OKB, Soviet Union.
Type: Single-seat, three-engined (one vectored thrust propulsion, two lift) transonic STOVL carrier fighter.
Engines: One Tumansky R27V-300 twin spool unaugmented turbojet with twin vectoring nozzles, rated at 14,991lb (6,800kg) military thrust and two Koliesov RD-36-35 lift jets each rated at 7,881lb (3,575kg) thrust.
Dimensions: Span 24ft 0in (7.32m); length 50ft 10.25in (15.50m); height 14ft 4in (4.37m); wing area 199sq.ft (18.50m²).
Weights: Empty 16,975lb (7,700kg); short takeoff 24,030lb (10,900kg); maximum 25,794lb (11,700kg).
Loadings (at short takeoff weight): Wing 121lb/sq.ft (588kg/m²); thrust (propulsion engine only) 0.62.
Performance: Maximum speed 628mph (1,010kph) Mach 0.94 at 36,091ft (11,000m), 608mph (978kph) at sea level; initial climb rate 14,961ft/min (76m/sec); service ceiling 39,372ft (12,000m); combat radius with external fue and 1hr 15min on station, 115 miles (185km).
Armament: Two R-60 IR AAMs with provision for two 23mm GSh-23 twin-barrel gun pods. A variety of air to surface stores can also be carried.
History: Prototype first flown 15 January 1971. Carrier trials 1972, pre-series order placed 1973. Production commenced 1975; service entry 1978. Combat evaluation (Afghanistan) 1980. Production completed 1987 with a total of 231 Withdrawn from service 1993.
User: Soviet Union/Russia (Navy) only.

Yakovlev Yak-141 Freestyle

Origin: Yakovlev OKB, Soviet Union.
Type: Single-seat, three-engined (one vectored thrust propulsion, two lift) supersonic STOVL carrier fighter.
Engines: One Soyuz R-79V-300 twin spool afterburning turbofan with vectoring nozzle, rated at 23,148lb (10,500kg) military and 34,171lb (15,500kg) maximum thrust, plus two Rybinsk RD-41 turbofan lift engines each rated at 9,039lb (4,100kg) thrust.
Dimensions: Span 33ft 1.5in (10.10m); length 60ft 0.5in (18.30m); height 16ft 5in (5.00m); wing area 341sq.ft (31.70m²).
Weights: Empty 25,684lb (11,650kg); vertical takeoff 34,833lb (15,800kg); maximum 42,990lb (19,500kg).
Loadings (at vertical takeoff weight): Wing 102lb/sq.ft (498kg/m²); thrust (propulsion engine only) 0.98.
Performance: Maximum speed 1,119mph (1,800kph) Mach 1.69 at 36,091ft (11,000m), 777mph (1,250kph) Mach 1.02 at sea level; initial climb rate 49,215ft/min (250m/sec); service ceiling 49,215ft (15,000m); range 870 miles (1,400km).
Armament: One 30mm GSh-301 cannon with 120 rounds; four R-27 SARH, R-77 IR, or R-73 IR AAMs, or air to surface ordnance.
History: Prototype first flown 9 March 1989. Twelve class records set April 1991. The second prototype crashed 5 October 1991. Publicly demonstrated Farnborough 1992. Programme abandoned by Russia 1993, but remained current for two more years in the hope of attracting overseas interest and funding. Four prototypes built, two for static testing. The two flown amassed slightly more thar 250 sorties.
User: None.

ight: The Yak-38 orger was the only oviet STOVL fighter in ervice.

ver the years, the Soviet nion made many VSTOL xperiments using lift ngines coupled to ectored thrust. The Yak-8, NATO reporting name orger, was the only one o enter service, as perations from a carrier eck did not involve the round erosion problems encountered by land-based aircraft.

Forger was just supersonic in a dive; rate of climb was poor, avionics were asic, and it lacked the versatility of the Sea Harrier. However, it marked the tart of Soviet carrier operations.

In hovering flight, the three engines of Forger posed a considerable risk, as oss of power on any one of them would put the aircraft into an irrecoverable ituation. Yakovlev addressed this with Eskem, an automatic system which, if ny pitch, roll and yaw limits were exceeded in thrust-borne flight, promptly jected the pilot. This was important; more than 40 ejections were made during orger's service life; more than 17 percent of the entire fleet. When it was ound possible to operate Su-27s and MiG-29s from carriers, its days were umbered.

Above: The Yak-141 Freestyle was a supersonic STOVL carrier fighter.

The origins of the Yak-141 lay in a specification for a supersonic STOVL carrier fighter issued in 1975. State of the art technology was required: digital triplex fly-by-wire; integrated engine controls for balance during thrust-borne flight; a vectoring afterburning nozzle; and some means of minimising the problems that had dogged all previous STOVL jets – hot gas re-ingestion and ground erosion.

For hovering flight, the vectored thrust of the main engine has to balance that of the two lift engines, the total acting around the centre of gravity. This being the case, the nozzle of the main engine could not exhaust too far aft. The Yak-38 had twin vectoring nozzles exhausting on each side of the rear fuselage, which in wingborne flight involved thrust losses. The solution for the Yak-141 was far more ingenious. A large "bite" was taken out of the rear fuselage; leaving a single afterburning nozzle in the correct location, bypassed on either side by deep booms which carried the stabilizers and twin fin and rudder assemblies. On either side of the "bite", what remains of the fuselage tapers away, shielding the inside of the booms from the hot efflux. In conventional flight the "straight-through" nozzle minimised thrust losses, while for wholly or partial thrust-borne flight the large three segment lobsterback tailpipe articulated downwards. The engine controls were carefully integrated to match the available thrust between the two lift engines and the main engine which, when the nozzle was vectored, was limited to 27,337lb (12,400kg); 80 per cent of the normal maximum thrust.

Analysis showed that some 95 per cent of all sorties by STOVL aircraft used a short rolling takeoff. This reduced ground erosion, as the exposure time to the effluxes was shortened; the forward movement minimised hot gas ingestion; while payload/range was increased by the addition of a wing-lift component.

Yakovlev took advantage of this. The two lift turbofans located in tandem just behind the cockpit, were normally inclined aft at 15deg to give a small forward thrust component. They could however be rotated 24deg aft to assist a rolling takeoff. Coming the other way, they could also be inclined 2deg forward for thrust braking when coming to the hover.

The propulsion engine was fed via plain rectangular section wedge-shaped side inlets, located just aft of the cockpit. The fuselage was slab-sided, running back to the booms, almost mini-fuselages, which carried the tail surfaces. Roll control in the hover was provided by wingtip puffers. For yaw control, the first prototype used air-bleed ejectors at the very end of the booms, but this evidently proved unsatisfactory, as the second was fitted with a two-way nose-mounted puffer.

Development was slow, and the first flight, at Zhukovsky, piloted by Andrei Sinitsin, took place on 9 March 1989, although the first full hovering flights were not until 29 December. In April 1991 Sinitsin set 12 new world records for STOVL aircraft, most of them time to altitude with various payloads. Carrier trials aboard the Admiral of the Fleet Gorshkov began on 21 September 1991, but in the following month Sinitsin "dropped it", when landing on, although he ejected safely.

Like Forger, Freestyle has an automatic ejection system which operates instantly when preset limits are exceeded. Unlike the earlier aircraft, in which the system had to be armed manually, on Freestyle it automatically activates when the main nozzle passes a 30deg angle.

Demonstrated at Farnborough '92 by Vladimir Yakimov, conventional takeoffs and landings were made, in deference to the runway surface. In a high hover, it appeared to be rock-steady, but while Yakovlev have stated that the Yak-141 is almost as agile as the MiG-29M, there was little sign of this; hardly surprising given the wing loading.

The cockpit layout of the Farnborough aircraft was old-hat "steam-gauge", albeit with a move towards HOTAS. The projected radar was the Phazotron NO-193 multi-mode pulse-Doppler, and the single 30mm cannon was semi-embedded in the lower fuselage. But as the problems of ground erosion and hot gas ingestion were never satisfactorily overcome, the project was quietly abandoned.

Below: The Yak-141 failed to win orders either at home or abroad.